Glencoe

Applying
Life Skills

Mc
Graw
Hill
Education

COVER: PeopleImages.com/Getty Images

mheducation.com/prek-12

Send all inquiries to:
McGraw-Hill Education
8787 Orion Place
Columbus, OH 43240

ISBN: 978-0-02-140252-6
MHID: 0-02-140252-3

Printed in the United States of America.

5 6 7 8 9 10 QVS 22 21 20 19 18

Reviewers

Reviewers

Suzi Beck
Family and Consumer Sciences
Teacher
Trenton Middle School
Trenton, Missouri

Dana Bertrand
Family and Consumer Sciences
Teacher
Lake Arthur High School
Lake Arthur, Louisiana

Kay Brown
Family and Consumer Sciences
Teacher
Franklin Central High School
Indianapolis, Indiana

Linda D. Brown
Early Childhood Education
Coordinator
Sanderson High School
Raleigh, North Carolina

Felicia Drake
Family and Consumer Sciences
Teacher
Chapman Middle School
Huntsville, Alabama

Ann Harbertson
Family and Consumer Sciences
Teacher
Viewmont High School
Bountiful, Utah

Vikki Jackson
Family and Consumer Sciences
Teacher
Kathleen Middle School
Lakeland, Florida

Lisa Kelley
Family and Consumer Sciences
Teacher
Monticello High School
Monticello, Arkansas

Sally A. Lessen
Family and Consumer Sciences
Teacher
Delavan High School
Delavan, Illinois

Dawn Lewis
Family and Consumer Sciences
Teacher
Coffee High Freshman Campus
Douglas, Georgia

Sharon Mang
Family and Consumer Sciences
Teacher
Greensburg Community High
School
Greensburg, Indiana

Kimberley Myers, MEd, NBPTS
Family and Consumer Sciences
Teacher
Aynor High School
Aynor, South Carolina

Pamela S. Pruett
Family and Consumer Sciences
Teacher
Blytheville High School
Blytheville, Arkansas

Nicole Ruge
Family and Consumer Sciences
Teacher
Lakeside Middle School
Evans, Georgia

Annette R. White
Family and Consumer Sciences
Teacher
Captain Shreve High School
Shreveport, Louisiana

Rhonda Wills
Family and Consumer Sciences
Teacher
Springfield Public Schools
Springfield, Missouri

Technical Reviewers

Angie Lustrick, C.N., C.P.T.
Nutritionist and Certified
Personal Trainer
Angie's World
Riverside, California

Bill Dueease
Life Coach
Fort Myers, Florida

Gina Marie Montefusco, BSN
Pediatrics Nurse
Children's Hospital Los Angeles
Los Angeles, California

Scavenger Hunt

Applying Life Skills contains a wealth of information. The trick is to know where to look to access all of the information in the book. Use this Scavenger Hunt to preview the text and help you get the most out of this book.

1 How many chapters are in the book? How many units?

2 Where can you find tips for reading strategies that you can use to better comprehend this book?

3 Where can you find a preview of a unit's Life Skills project?

4 Where can you find tips on health and wellness?

5 Where can you learn the definitions of *entrepreneur* and *hybrid*?

6 What does Figure 2.1 in Chapter 2 show?

7 Where can you find out how to make decisions and solve problems?

8 Where can you find the summary of each chapter?

9 Which feature shows you how to calculate your take-home pay?

10 Where can you find math help to assist you in completing chapter features such as Math You Can Use and Financial Literacy?

Table of Contents

UNIT 1 **You and Your World** 2

CHAPTER 1 Learning About Yourself 4
Section 1.1 Growing and Changing 6
Section 1.2 The Balancing Act 20
➤ *CHAPTER 1 Review and Applications* 31

CHAPTER 2 Character Development 34
Section 2.1 Building Character. 36
Section 2.2 Taking Responsible Action 44
➤ *CHAPTER 2 Review and Applications* 53

UNIT 1 **Life Skills Project** Create a Goal Checklist. 56

FOCUS ON Reading Strategies
Look for these reading strategies in each chapter:

- Before You Read
- Graphic Organizer
- Reading Check
- After You Read

Creatas/Jupiter Images

Table of Contents

UNIT 2 / **Exploring Careers** 58

CHAPTER 3 **Pathways to Careers** 60

Section 3.1 Work and You 62
Section 3.2 Investigating Careers 69
➤ *CHAPTER 3 Review and Applications* 81

CHAPTER 4 **Workplace Skills** 84

Section 4.1 Employability Skills 86
Section 4.2 Navigating the Workplace 95
➤ *CHAPTER 4 Review and Applications* 103

CHAPTER 5 **Entering the World of Work** 106

Section 5.1 The Job Application Process 108
Section 5.2 Your New Job. .121
➤ *CHAPTER 5 Review and Applications* 127

UNIT 2 / **Life Skills Project** Career Map and Ladder 130

FOCUS ON

Academic Success
To help you succeed in your classes and on tests, look for these academic skills:

• Reading Guides
• Writing Tips
• Math You Can Use
• Science You Can Use
• Financial Literacy

Table of Contents

UNIT 3 / Building Relationship Skills 132

CHAPTER 6 Communication with Others 134
Section 6.1 Speaking, Writing, and Listening Skills 136
Section 6.2 Communicating Respect 143
➤ CHAPTER 6 Review and Applications 149

CHAPTER 7 Conflict Resolution 152
Section 7.1 Preventing Conflict 154
Section 7.2 Working Through Conflict 162
➤ CHAPTER 7 Review and Applications 169

CHAPTER 8 You and Your Peers 172
Section 8.1 Dealing with Peer Pressure 174
Section 8.2 Enjoying Friendships 182
➤ CHAPTER 8 Review and Applications 195

UNIT 3 Life Skills Project Healthy Relationships 198

UNIT 4 / Relating to Family and Children 200

CHAPTER 9 Building Strong Families 202
Section 9.1 The Anatomy of a Family 204
Section 9.2 Family Dynamics 211
➤ CHAPTER 9 Review and Applications 221

CHAPTER 10 Family Challenges 224
Section 10.1 Changes in the Family 226
Section 10.2 Abuse and Addiction in the Family 237
➤ CHAPTER 10 Review and Applications 245

CHAPTER 11 Child Development and Care 248
Section 11.1 How Children Grow 250
Section 11.2 Caring for Children 261
➤ CHAPTER 11 Review and Applications 273

CHAPTER 12 Understanding Parenting 276
Section 12.1 Considering Parenthood 278
Section 12.2 Caring for Children 284
➤ CHAPTER 12 Review and Applications 291

UNIT 4 Life Skills Project Learn Parenting Skills 294

Table of Contents

UNIT 5 / Managing Your Life 296

CHAPTER 13 Be a Responsible Consumer 298
Section 13.1 Making Consumer Choices 300
Section 13.2 Living with Technology 313
➤ CHAPTER 13 *Review and Applications* 325

CHAPTER 14 Your Health 328
Section 14.1 Staying Healthy and Fit 330
Section 14.2 Health Risks. 344
➤ CHAPTER 14 *Review and Applications* 357

UNIT 5 / Life Skills Project Manage Yourself 360

UNIT 6 / Food and Nutrition 362

CHAPTER 15 How Nutrients Work 364
Section 15.1 Nutrients at Work 364
Section 15.2 The Process of Digestion 376
➤ CHAPTER 15 *Review and Applications* 383

CHAPTER 16 Guidelines for Healthy Eating 386
Section 16.1 Dietary Guidelines for Americans
and MyPyramid. 388
Section 16.2 The Dietary Guidelines and Your Lifestyle . . .400
➤ CHAPTER 16 *Review and Applications* 409

CHAPTER 17 Meal Planning 412
Section 17.1 Planning Meals and Snacks. 414
Section 17.2 Preparing Meals and Snacks 424
➤ CHAPTER 17 *Review and Applications* 431

UNIT 6 / Life Skills Project Research Food Choices. 434

FOCUS ON Visuals
Images help you comprehend key ideas. Answer the questions for all:

- Unit and Chapter Openers
- Photos and Captions
- Figures and Tables

Table of Contents

UNIT 7 — Working in the Kitchen 436

CHAPTER 18 Food Shopping, Storage, and Sanitation 438
Section 18.1 Shopping for Food 440
Section 18.2 Food Safety and Sanitation 450
➤ CHAPTER 18 Review and Applications 459

CHAPTER 19 Kitchen Equipment Selection and Safety 462
Section 19.1 Selecting Utensils and Cookware 464
Section 19.2 Appliance Selection and Safety 472
➤ CHAPTER 19 Review and Applications 483

CHAPTER 20 Recipes and Measuring 486
Section 20.1 Reading Recipes and Measuring Ingredients . .488
Section 20.2 Altering Recipes 499
➤ CHAPTER 20 Review and Applications 505

UNIT 7 Life Skills Project Design Your Dream Kitchen .508

UNIT 8 — From Kitchen to Table 510

CHAPTER 21 Basic Cooking Techniques 512
Section 21.1 Choosing Cooking Techniques 514
Section 21.2 Healthy Cooking Methods 523
➤ CHAPTER 21 Review and Applications 529

CHAPTER 22 Preparing Grains, Fruits, and Vegetables 532
Section 22.1 Grains in Your Diet 534
Section 22.2 Fruits and Vegetables in Your Diet 541
➤ CHAPTER 22 Review and Applications 549

CHAPTER 23 Preparing Protein Foods 552
Section 23.1 Meat, Poultry, and Fish . 554
Section 23.2 Eggs, Legumes, Milk, and
Milk Products 561
➤ CHAPTER 23 Review and Applications 571

CHAPTER 24 Eating Together 574
Section 24.1 Enjoying Family Meals . 576
Section 24.2 Special Occasions 583
➤ CHAPTER 24 Review and Applications 589

UNIT 8 Life Skills Project
Plan a Meal 592

FOCUS ON Project-Based Learning

Projects throughout this book can help you use your skills in real-life situations:
• Real-world scenarios
• Step-by-step instructions
• Team or individual based learning

Table of Contents

UNIT 9 | Clothing 594

CHAPTER 25 Clothing That Suits You 596
Section 25.1 Your Clothing Style 598
Section 25.2 Your Working Wardrobe 609
➤ CHAPTER 25 Review and Applications 615

CHAPTER 26 Selection and Care of Fibers and Fabrics 618
Section 26.1 Fibers and Fabrics 620
Section 26.2 Caring for Clothing. 630
➤ CHAPTER 26 Review and Applications 643

CHAPTER 27 Preparing to Sew 646
Section 27.1 Sewing Equipment. 648
Section 27.2 Patterns, Notions, and Fabric Equipment . . .659
➤ CHAPTER 27 Review and Applications 671

CHAPTER 28 Sewing Basics 674
Section 28.1 Basic Sewing Techniques 676
Section 28.2 Hems, Simple Alterations, and
                     Special Touches. 687
➤ CHAPTER 28 Review and Applications 695

UNIT 9 Life Skills Project Your Personal Style 698

Vico Collective/Alamy

FOCUS ON Assessment
Look for review questions and activities to help you remember important topics.

• Reading Checks
• Section and Chapter Reviews
• Unit Thematic Projects

UNIT 10 Housing and the Environment   **700**

CHAPTER 29 Your Home   **702**

Section 29.1 Housing and Human Needs. 704
Section 29.2 Decorating Living Space. 715
➤ *CHAPTER 29 Review and Applications* 725

CHAPTER 30 Clean and Safe Environments   **728**

Section 30.1 Establishing a Safe and
Clean Home Environment 730
Section 30.2 The Earth—Your Home 741
➤ *CHAPTER 30 Review and Applications* 749

UNIT 10 Life Skills Project Design Your Ideal Room 752

Math Skills Handbook 754
Career Skills Appendix 760
Glossary 775
Index 784

Features Table of Contents

Academic Skills for Life!

How much will you pay in interest on a credit card? Do you know how to compare products to get the best value for your money? Use these academic features to succeed in school, on tests, and with life!

Math You Can Use

Saving Your Money 14
Take-Home Pay 114
Calculate Gross Profit 147
Calculate Interest 208
Unit Conversion 265
Finding a Healthy Weight Range 346
Sources of Calories 379
Change Yield........................503
Cooking Time 525
Choose the Right Table 578
Price vs. Cost........................604

Science You Can Use

Workplace Ergonomics 88
The Science of Emotions 192
Invent New Vaccines 286
Design Communications Technology ...315
The Science of Allergies................403
Brand Names Vs. Generic Names........444
Effects of Yeast.......................538
Get Technical 622
Now You See It, Now You Don't 664
Fire Safety 712
Water Safety 733

Financial Literacy

Calculate Percent Discount 39
Summer Business 65
Bike Repair Conflict 160
Credit Card Finance Charges 230
Child Care Costs 281
A Food Budget.......................417
Cost of Appliances....................475
Food Budget.........................558
Calculate Bonuses....................678

Tips for Success Throughout Your School Years

How can you study effectively? Why is it important to get a good night's sleep? Look for the Succeed in School tips in every chapter to help you in every class you take.

SUCCEED IN SCHOOL

Avoid Comparisons 11
Define Success 24
Reading Time 42
Plan Ahead 51
Communicate for Success 64
School Library 73
Family Support 88
Making Mistakes 98
After-School Programs 112
Get Plenty of Sleep 125
Create a Study Buddy List 139
Media Tour 146
Fun Is Important 158, 266
Prepare a Speech 166
Attendance 179
Take a Break 190
Family and Friends 208
Sibling Rivalry 214
Guidance Counselors 232
Skimming Skills 242
Discover Learning Styles 252
Do Your Part 282
Determine Progress 289
Public Speaking Anxiety 310
Make Connections 316
Manage Stress 341
Take a Break 354
Give Full Attention 370
Sleep On It 378

Two-Column Notes 389
Making Connections 407
Ask for Help 418
Organize Your Schedule 429
Ask for Explanations 445
Avoid Distractions 455
Study Time 467
Three-Ring Binder 476
Ask Your Teacher 494
Your Expectations 502
Understand Criticism 516
Your Teacher 527
Reach Out 539
Get Ahead 547
Time for Tasks 560
Update Your Daily Schedule 566
Online Research 578
Reading Assignments 581
Ask Questions 604, 666
Achieve Your Goals 610
Look to Friends 624
Follow Up 639
Learn from Mistakes 652
Act the Part 681
All Work and No Play 693
Find Space 713
Avoid Distraction 721
Study Location 733
Presentation Preparation 743

Features Table of Contents

Life Skills for Every Day

Do you know how to set a goal? How do you make time for friends, family, and school? These activities and ideas show you how to apply new skills to everyday life.

➤ TAKE CHARGE!

Explore Your Heritage 10
Take Good Notes 23
Promote Diversity 40
Attend a Job Fair 74
Solve Problems 100
Achieve Workplace Harmony...........123
Make Effective Presentations 138
Forgive and Forget 166
Stand Up for Yourself 179
Be Responsible 189
Strengthen Your Relationship with
    a Stepparent 207
Make New Friends 228
How to Help Someone Who Abuses
    Alcohol 238
Become an Expert Childcare Provider 267
Build Interest in Reading 287

Buyer Beware 303
Put Your Technology Skills to Work 314
Saying No 349
Tame Your Sweet Tooth 368
Create a Nutrition Plan 395
Get a Good Start 416
Prevent Poisoning......................453
Try Herbs and Spices 494
Use a Convection Oven 517
Prepare Appealing Produce 543
Cut the Fat.............................557
Shop Responsibly 612
Sort Your Laundry 636
Care for Your Sewing Machine...........654
Keep Your Family Strong 706
Clean Outdoors 732

HOW TO...

Set Goals 16
Manage Your Time 24
Make Sound Decisions 48
Work Ethic.................. 66
Try Out Careers 76
Be a Team Player 92
Deal with Bullies 164
Make New Friends 186
Make Time for One Another .. 216
Break the Silence of Abuse ... 240

Handle Tantrums........... 256
Be a Positive Example 288
Protect Your Identity 318
Protect Your Skin 334
Maintain a Healthy Weight... 378
Lower the Fat 392
Help with Family Meals 420
Store Food Safely........... 454
Grill Healthy Food 478
Make Salsa 500

Buy Great Grains 536
Plan a Celebration........... 586
Select Quality Clothing 610
Pack a Bag................. 632
Select Notions 662
Serge Seams................ 682
Meet Special Family Needs... 708
Clean As You Go............. 734

Learn to Be Healthy and Safe

To be a healthy person you must take care of yourself both mentally and physically. Find tips to keep yourself safe and healthy throughout your lifetime. Learn to cook with ingredients that are nutritious, and learn how to keep yourself physically fit.

Light and Healthy Recipe

Marinated Vegetables 380
Chicken Salad Extraordinaire 419
Green Bean Salad 404
Banana Cream Trifle 456
Asian Pasta Salad 480

Tuna Melt Stuffed Tomatoes................526
Crunchy Melon Bowl.......................545
Mediterranean Hummus and
    Vegetable Dip 568
Potato-Tomato Soup in a Bread Bowl 582

Safety Check

Adjusting to Change..........8
Workplace Dangers........ 123
Use Cell Phone Safely...... 144
Prevent Road Rage 156
Know When to Leave 180
Make an Escape Plan 205
Dangers of Running Away . 243
Plant Safety............... 268
Shaken Baby Syndrome.... 290
Shopping Safely........... 302
ATM Safety 317
Dangers of Food Allergies.. 402
Purchase Safe Foods....... 449
Kitchen Fire Safety 476
Avoid Scalds 521
Food Allergies 564
Grilling Fire Hazard........ 588
Avoid Injury 637
Serger Safety 657
Sewing Equipment 680
Light the Way 722

Health & Wellness TIPS

Control Anxiety 28
Emotional Health 47
Prioritize Health 67
Positive Attitude 96
Eat Breakfast 118
Avoid Office Injuries 124
Reduce Stress 140
Work Off Stress 159
Healthy Friendships 193
Family Exercise 213
Take Care of Yourself 231
Self-Worth 242
Limit TV Time 255
Encourage Exercise 286
Social Interaction 320
Healthy Teeth 335
Safe Weight Loss 339
Prevent Dehydration 374
Prevent Anemia 381
Avoid Fad Diets 391
Functional Foods........ 407

Dining Out 418
Soda 428
Saving Leftovers 446
Personal Hygiene 453
Nutrition Appeal 465
Keep Your Refrigerator
    Healthy 475
Healthful Substitutions ... 504
Avoid Added Fat 519
Fiber and Oats 538
Tasty Tomatoes 543
Frozen for Convenience... 546
Nutrition Challenges 567
Grill with Safety.......... 587
Use Your Colors 601
Fabric Allergies 634
Back Basics 650
Healthy Identity.......... 689
Health and Saftey in
    the Home 721
Mood and Natural Light .. 745

Features Table of Contents

Connect to Your Community

Are you prepared for life outside of school? As you prepare to enter the world of work learn how to share your talents with others. These features will help you learn about how you can contribute to your community.

Community Connections

Community Resources 46

Volunteer 75

Work Well with Others 99

Global Interaction..................148

Cultural Knowledge 157

Community Pride 176

Give Back 184

Share Your Culture 210

Promote School Safety 241

Health Fair 270

Recycled Treasures 309

Anti-Smoking Campaign 348

Food Banks 369

Hometown Foods 402

International Flavor 416

Surplus Food.......................442

Kitchen Stores 478

Convert Measurements 491

Environmentally-Friendly Cooking......517

Preferred Pasta.....................537

Farmers' Market....................563

Serving Your Community 580

Shades of Uniformity 609

Consumer Research 638

On the Job.........................662

Sewing for a Cause 679

Housing in Your Community 712

A World-Wide Concern...............742

Exploring Careers

Life Coach 30

Landscape Architect 80

Retail Buyer 102

Correctional Officer 168

Computer Programmer 220

Early Childhood Teacher 272

Investment Advisor 324

EMT/Paramedic 382

Legislator 430

Bookkeeping Clerk 458

Power Plant Dispatcher 482

Dietitian...........................528

Environmental Scientist 570

Information Designer.................614

Pilot...............................670

Veterinarian 724

Learn to Solve Problems

Learn to look at problems in a positive manner. These features will allow you to give your opinion about issues that today's teens face.

How I See It

Potential 13
Caring 46
Work Ethic 66
Skills for Life 90
Truthfulness 118
Peer Pressure 140
Peaceful Solutions. 158
True Friends 177
Sibling Rivalry 215
Stepparents 233
Gift Giving 263
Teen Pregnancy 282
E-Manners........................... 321
Nutrition and Exercise 337
Healthy Weight Gain 405
Grocery Shopping Techniques.........443
Healthy Cooking 520
Produce and Grains. 546
Family and Friends 580
Shopping Buddies. 601
Well-Suited for the Occasion 625
Handle with Care.................... 665
Living Spaces 711

Building Character

Commitment 18
Collaboration 26
Caring 41
Good Citizenship 51
Respect 73
Politeness 90
Trustworthiness 97
Speak Up 117
Tact 138
Proactive Support 157
Loyalty 185
Dependability 213
Empathy 234
Support 239
Gratitude 252
Handle Tantrums 254
Self-Control 270
Fairness 280
Honesty 305, 626
Kindness Counts 338
Willpower 371
Courtesy 422
Withhold Judgement 447
Responsibility....................... 477
Open-Mindedness................... 490
Self-Sufficiency 519
Resourcefulness..................... 544
Tolerance........................... 556
Ethical Behavior..................... 586
Sensitivity 600
Consideration....................... 667
Generosity.......................... 690
Compromise 710
Positive Attitude 737

UNIT 1

You and Your World

Chapter 1 Learning About Yourself
Chapter 2 Character Development

Unit Life Skills Project Preview

Create a Goal Checklist

In this unit you will learn about yourself and your world. In your life skills project you will create a plan to achieve one of your goals.

 My Journal

Dream Big Write a journal entry about one of the topics below. Be descriptive. This will help you prepare for the unit project at the end of the unit.
- Describe a long-term goal that you have, or think of a new goal if you do not have one already.
- Imagine your life after you have achieved your goal, and how it would be different than if you had not achieved it.
- Explain why your goal is important to you.

Explore the Photo

Everyone has their own dreams and goals for the future. *What are some ways you can use goals to make your dream a reality?*

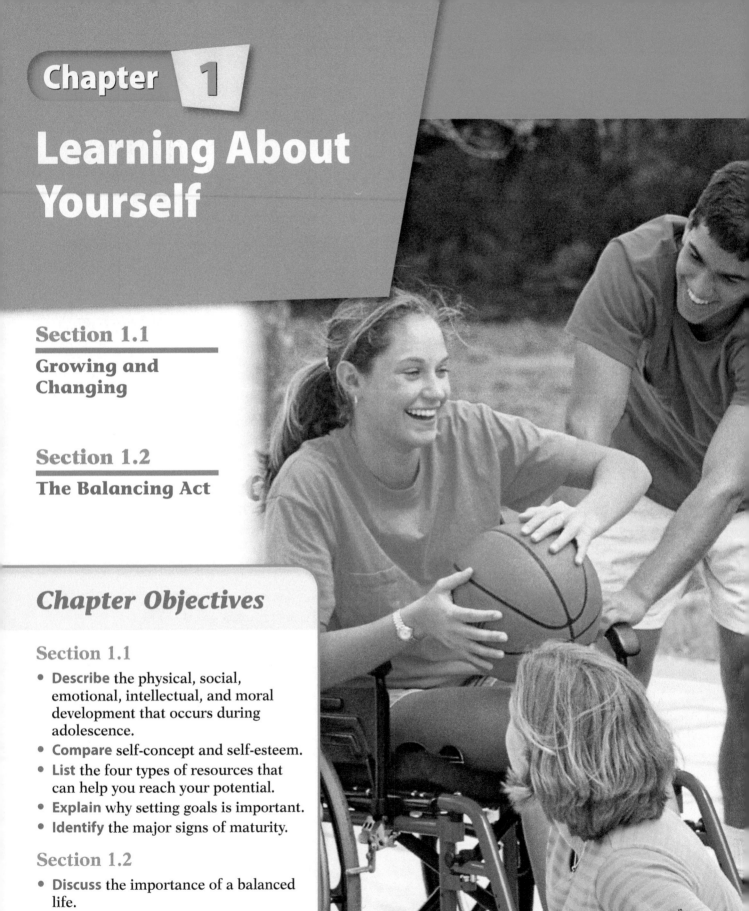

Chapter 1

Learning About Yourself

Section 1.1
Growing and Changing

Section 1.2
The Balancing Act

Chapter Objectives

Section 1.1
- **Describe** the physical, social, emotional, intellectual, and moral development that occurs during adolescence.
- **Compare** self-concept and self-esteem.
- **List** the four types of resources that can help you reach your potential.
- **Explain** why setting goals is important.
- **Identify** the major signs of maturity.

Section 1.2
- **Discuss** the importance of a balanced life.
- **Summarize** the strategies that help save time and energy.

Creatas/Jupiter Images

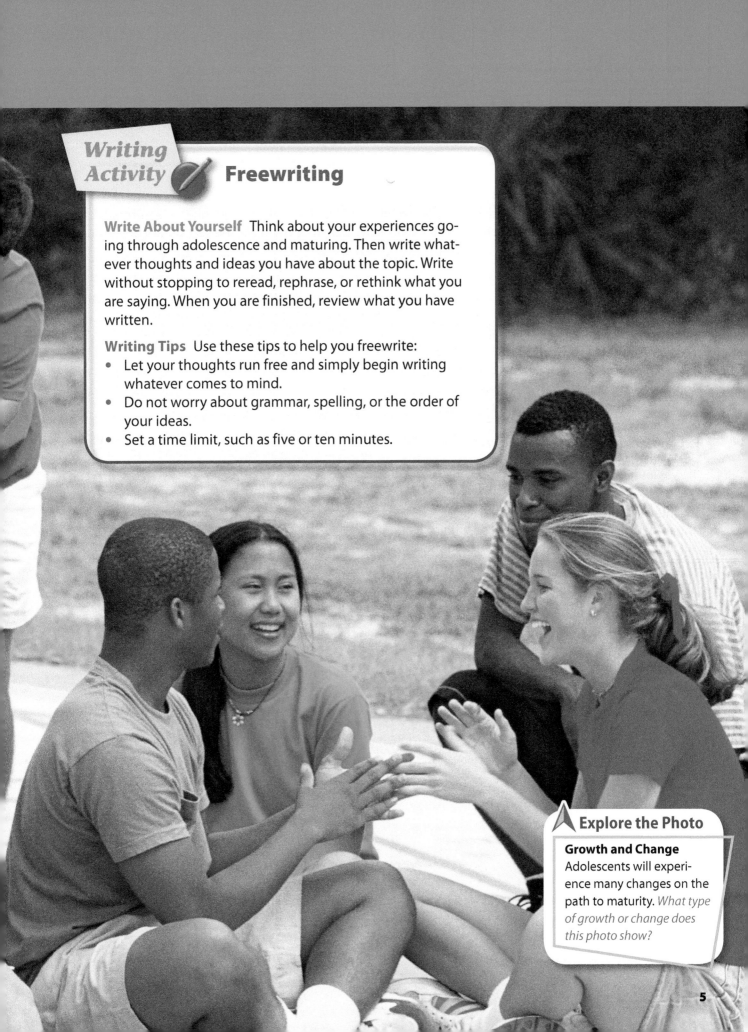

Writing Activity

Freewriting

Write About Yourself Think about your experiences going through adolescence and maturing. Then write whatever thoughts and ideas you have about the topic. Write without stopping to reread, rephrase, or rethink what you are saying. When you are finished, review what you have written.

Writing Tips Use these tips to help you freewrite:
- Let your thoughts run free and simply begin writing whatever comes to mind.
- Do not worry about grammar, spelling, or the order of your ideas.
- Set a time limit, such as five or ten minutes.

Explore the Photo

Growth and Change Adolescents will experience many changes on the path to maturity. *What type of growth or change does this photo show?*

Section 1.1

Growing and Changing

Before You Read

Preview Take a few minutes to examine the images and the features in this section. Discuss with a partner what you think the section will be about.

Read to Learn

Key Concepts

- **Describe** the physical, social, emotional, intellectual, and moral development that occurs during adolescence.
- **Compare** self-concept and self-esteem.
- **List** the four types of resources that can help you reach your potential.
- **Explain** why setting goals is important.
- **Identify** the major signs of maturity.

Main Idea

Many intellectual, physical, and emotional changes take place during adolescence. Learning to set and meet goals is an important step on the road to maturity.

Content Vocabulary

- ◇ adolescence
- ◇ puberty
- ◇ hormone
- ◇ personality
- ◇ heredity
- ◇ environment
- ◇ self-esteem
- ◇ potential
- ◇ priority
- ◇ resource
- ◇ goal

Academic Vocabulary

You will find these words in your reading and on your tests. Use the glossary to look up their definitions if necessary.

- ▢ enhance
- ▢ insight

Graphic Organizer

As you read, list details about the types of changes that occur during adolescence. Use a chart like the one below.

Changes that Occur During Adolescence

Physical	Social and Emotional	Intellectual	Moral

 Graphic Organizer Go to **connectED.mcgraw-hill.com** to download this graphic organizer.

Understand Changes in Your Life

At the beginning of this school year, did you notice that some of your classmates had grown much taller over the summer, while others looked the same? You may be aware of some changes in yourself as well. **Adolescence**, the stage of growth between childhood and adulthood, is a time of amazing changes. During adolescence, you will change more in a shorter time frame than you ever will again.

Physical Changes

Your body's rapid changes during adolescence affect the way you think and feel about yourself and your relationships with others. Adolescence begins with **puberty**, the time when teens start to develop the physical characteristics of men and women. Both girls and boys usually experience a growth spurt, or rapid increase in height. Girls may also notice body shape changes. For girls, the start of menstruation, a monthly discharge of blood from the uterus, is an early sign that puberty has begun. Boys' reproductive systems begin to produce sperm. Boys also begin to grow facial hair, and their voices deepen.

During puberty, your hormones reach a very high level. A **hormone** is a chemical substance in the body that helps stimulate body changes and the development of the reproductive system. Puberty, which lasts an average of three years, starts at different ages for teens. Changes for both boys and girls usually start between the ages of 10 and 15. The changes end between the ages of 16 and 20.

Many teens worry that they are changing too slowly or too quickly during puberty. Girls often undergo physical changes earlier than boys. Some teens look older than most of their peers; others look much younger. It is completely normal for teens to develop at different rates.

As You Read

Connect Think about the changes adolescence brings. What physical and emotional changes have you noticed in yourself over the past year?

Vocabulary

You can find definitions in the glossary at the back of your book.

rubberball/GettyImages

Physical Changes

As you move through adolescence, it is important to remember that everyone—not only you—experiences many physical changes. *Based on what you have learned about puberty, can you determine whether these boys are the same age?*

Safety Check

Adjusting to Change

During puberty, both girls and boys experience growth spurts. During these periods of rapid growth, teens tend to be more accident prone. Why do you think this is?

Write About It

Research the effect growth spurts have on coordination. What specifically causes the clumsiness associated with growth spurts? Share your findings with the rest of the class.

Social and Emotional Changes

Changing hormones in the body can make you feel like you are on an emotional roller coaster. Take positive actions to deal with your changing emotions and energy during adolescence:

- **Exercise.** Play a sport, or go for a walk or run. As you exercise, your brain releases chemicals called endorphins, which reduce feelings of anxiety and enhance, or improve, your mood.
- **Eat right.** Make sure to get plenty of protein, dairy, and whole grains fortified with vitamin B12. Studies show this vitamin can reduce depression and increase energy. Avoid sugar and caffeine. These ingredients cause mood and energy swings.
- **Make friends.** Rather than spending long hours in your room, take advantage of opportunities to make new friends. Positive friendships can help you feel better about yourself and help you develop important social skills.
- **Volunteer.** Volunteer in your community. Helping others can make you feel better and worry less about yourself.

Intellectual Changes

During adolescence you also change intellectually. With increased experience and knowledge, you learn to solve more complex problems and to make more mature decisions. Your education provides you with new insight, or the power to understand the inner nature of things.

Moral Development

Suppose your friend is afraid of failing a class and asks you if he can copy your homework. Looking out for your friends is important to you, but cheating goes against your personal values. How should you handle the situation?

As a teen, you start to make more and more decisions that deal with issues of right and wrong behavior. Although you want to do what's right, sometimes it is not clear how you should act. Your choices may also be more difficult if you feel pressure from your friends.

The challenge is to base moral decisions on a set of generally accepted guidelines for right and wrong behavior. From the time you were born until now, your parents and other adults in your life have set the standards for right and wrong behavior. As you move through adolescence, it is up to you to apply these standards in the choices you make. For example, telling the truth and treating people fairly are commonly accepted standards of moral behavior. Lying and cheating are not. Having a strong sense of right and wrong can guide you through tough times. Parents, teachers, coaches, religious leaders, and counselors can also help you determine the right course of action in difficult situations.

✓ **Reading Check** **Explain** How would you describe the state of growth between childhood and adulthood?

Appreciate Who You Are

This time of your life is one of many changes, physical and emotional. When you were younger, you likely spent most of your time discovering and thinking about the world around you. During adolescence you may find yourself becoming more introspective, trying to make sense of your new likes, dislikes, and changing personality. During this period, it is perfectly natural to wonder about who you really are, how others see you, and what sort of person you will become. With discovery comes appreciation for who you are.

Your Personality

Your **personality** is the combination of feelings, traits, attitudes, and habits that you show others. This combination of characteristics makes you unique, or one of a kind. Whether you are shy or outgoing, creative or strictly logical depends upon your personality. How strongly you experience certain emotions, and how often, is also part of your personality. Personality grows and changes as a person does.

Heredity

The stage was set for your personality before you were born. You received genes from each of your parents. These genes determined physical traits, such as your height, eye color, and hair color. **Heredity**, the characteristics passed from parents to children, also influences your personality.

It is often easy to see how your immediate family shapes who you are. You may have red hair like your mother and a love of baseball like your father. However, the unique combination of characteristics that you inherited from your ancestors also plays a major role in who you are. Getting to know and appreciate your relatives is an effective way to get to know and appreciate yourself.

Seeking Advice

Adults can help guide you in making good choices. *Which trusted adults can you turn to for advice?*

Environment

Your personality may have begun with your heredity, but it is shaped even further by your environment. Your **environment** is everything around you, including people, places, things, and events. Everything you experience influences your personality, for better or worse. Your family and your culture are usually your most important environmental influences. Children raised in an environment filled with love and emotional support are more likely to appreciate their worth and develop healthy personalities.

Design Pics/Don Hammond

TAKE CHARGE!

Explore Your Heritage

Heritage ('her-ə-tij) is traditions inherited from one generation to another. Discovering and appreciating your heritage can be fun and interesting detective work. Families celebrate their heritage in different ways. Some pass on stories that are told and retold by their children, and some pass on photographs, recipes, or keepsakes from one generation to the next. Here are some ways you can explore and appreciate your family heritage:

- **Interview Family Members** Find out what your living relatives know about your family heritage. Keep a journal of what you learn.
- **Create a Family Scrapbook** Gather photographs, stories, and other keepsakes to document your family's history.
- **Research Your Ethnic Background and Culture** Use online sources to research your genealogy (ˌjē-nē-ˈä-lə-jē), or family history.
- **Establish Relationships with Distant Relatives** Share family stories and photographs with distant relatives by e-mail or letters.

Real-World Skills

Share Your Heritage After you have researched your heritage, give a short presentation to your classmates discussing how your heritage impacts your daily life. Which of your daily activities reflect your heritage? What interests do you have that are not related to your heritage?

Your Self-Concept

The mental picture you have of who you are, and the way you think others see you, is your self-concept, or self-image. Your self-concept is shaped and influenced by comments about you from family, friends, other people in your life, and even yourself. Since infancy, you have heard these messages, and they have affected your view of yourself. Positive messages are more likely to lead to a positive self-concept. Hearing and believing negative messages, both from yourself and from others, can lead to a negative self-concept.

A positive self-concept is related to high **self-esteem**, or the confidence you feel about yourself. Your self-esteem affects many aspects of your life. For example, when you have high self-esteem, you feel good about yourself, believe you can be successful, and have the confidence to try new things. This might mean you take an art class or join the swim team instead of spending another summer at home in front of the television.

There are ways to boost your own self-esteem. One of these ways is to maintain a positive and realistic outlook. There are qualities about you that are special that allow you to be the best you can be. Identify these talents and work to become the best that you can be.

Build Confidence

Your self-esteem can be lower at some times than at others. Your thoughts, mistakes, and the way some people treat you can cause you to feel down about yourself.

To strengthen your self-esteem, you can do the following:

- **Talk positively to yourself.** Analyze the messages you send to yourself. Never put yourself down. Instead, send yourself positive messages such as "I can do this" and "I am doing better today than yesterday."
- **Focus on your strengths.** Concentrate on what you do well. Keep a record of past and present successes. Review your achievements often, and remind yourself that you are capable of even more success in the future.
- **Seek support.** Spend time with positive, supportive people. It is important to be around family and friends who believe in you. Their positive messages will help build your confidence.
- **Address weaknesses.** Do not be afraid of failure! Instead of dwelling on past mistakes or perceived weaknesses, view them as learning experiences. Take time to determine what you can do to improve. Constant improvement will help you meet future challenges, which in turn will help you feel better about yourself.

✓ Reading Check **Discuss** What is personality, and how does it make you unique?

SUCCEED IN SCHOOL

Avoid Comparisons

Recognize that comparing yourself to others does not help you succeed in school. Each student has unique strengths. Concentrate on doing your best without comparing yourself to your friends, siblings, or other students in your classes.

Self-Esteem

When you feel good about yourself, you feel more confident and in control of your life. *When do you feel most confident about yourself?*

Discover Your Potential

Hopefully, many of the experiences you have had since you were a young child were positive as you learned to walk, talk, and understand more of your world. Although what you want to achieve today is different, every past success helps you understand what you are capable of achieving if you put your mind to it.

Everyone has different dreams that they want to achieve in their lives. Some of these dreams require extra effort to achieve. Whatever your dreams are, it is important to find one that will help you feel confident and happy with what you have added to your community.

Jason has won several science awards and hopes to be a doctor someday. He has a friend who enjoys building things and wants to build homes someday. Like everyone, Jason and his friend have **potential**, or the possibility of becoming more than they are right now. Reaching your potential means becoming all you can be. This applies to how you treat others as much as it applies to doing your part in the community. Success is not always a measure of money or title.

Plush Studios/Blend Images LLC

You may have heard the saying, "Anything worth having doesn't come easily."

What does this saying mean?

UpperCut Images/Glowimages

Reach Your Potential

What does it take to achieve a dream? How do you know where to start? A good place to begin is in your mind. Think about something you want to do and picture it as clearly as you can. Maybe you want to learn to play the guitar, fly a plane, or be senior class president. Though these dreams may seem far-fetched or a long way away, the things you do to prepare yourself now can increase the likelihood that your dreams can be realized in the future. Even if you only have a general idea in mind, each day can bring you closer to achieving your dream.

To maximize your potential so that you are prepared for the future you want, try these suggestions:

- **Set priorities.** It is important to set priorities. A **priority** is something that is important to you. Priorities are ranked in order of importance. Once you decide what you want to accomplish, stay focused and avoid distractions.
- **Consider interests and activities.** Make a list of each one. Next, compare your interests and activities to your priorities. Suppose you enjoy working on engines and want to work as an airline mechanic or own your own auto repair shop someday. You might choose to spend more time fixing cars at your uncle's shop than playing soccer.
- **Develop supportive friendships.** To be your best, surround yourself with friends who have positive attitudes and who encourage you to achieve your dreams.
- **Be health-smart.** You are much more likely to do your best if you are healthy and full of energy. Eat a variety of healthful food. Get enough sleep, and take time to exercise. Avoid substances that can harm your health.

Make the Most of Your Resources

Resources affect your potential. Anything you use to help accomplish something is a **resource**. The more resources that are available to you, the greater your chance of achieving whatever you decide to do. There are many types of resources, often categorized into four groups:

- **Material Resources** Material resources include money, supplies, and property.
- **Community Resources** Resources that are available to all members of a community include libraries, schools, places of worship, hospitals, and parks.
- **Natural Resources** Natural resources include everything in the natural environment, such as air, water, and trees.
- **Human Resources** Perhaps the most important resources of all, human resources include people, time, energy, knowledge, and skills. You also have your own personal set of human resources. They include your health, interests, skills, knowledge, abilities, and attitudes.

Identify the resources that are available to you and put them to work. Whether plentiful or limited, you can make the most of the resources you have by following these suggestions:

- **Expand your resources.** Get to know a variety of people. Individuals you meet may be able to help you learn a skill or find a job. Read newspapers, bulletin boards, and pamphlets available in your community to get a sense of the opportunities available to you. Develop your own knowledge and abilities. When you train and sharpen your skills in a subject that interests you, you start down a path that can lead to a successful adult career.

How I See It

POTENTIAL

Tyrone, 15

Friends and teachers often come to me with their computer questions because I know a lot about technology. Most people think my knowledge comes naturally. They don't know that I have worked really hard to improve my computer skills. My dream is to become a software designer. I want to create computer programs that will help doctors find cures for diseases. I already know a lot about computers, but I need to keep working hard to make sure I fulfill my potential and make my dream a reality.

Critical Thinking
Tyrone suggests that living up to one's potential is dependent on hard work. He says it is not just about natural talent. Do you agree or disagree? Explain.

Reach Your Potential

Healthy practices, such as eating healthful food and exercising regularly, can help you reach your potential. *How are you striving to meet your potential?*

- **Conserve your resources.** Spending all your money on video games may be fun at the moment, but it wastes a valuable resource. Putting some of your cash in a savings account rewards you with more money in the long run. You can also save money, time, and energy by taking care of your possessions. They will last longer, so you will not have to replace them often.
- **Substitute resources.** What if you are short on cash, and your best friend's birthday is approaching? Substitute time and energy for money and make a birthday gift. If you enjoy books and tapes, save money by borrowing them from the library instead of buying them. You also can save money by renting a video and having friends over, rather than going to the movies.
- **Share resources.** You can share resources and increase your brainpower at the same time by working with a study group on a difficult class assignment. You also share resources when you trade books, CDs, or sports equipment with friends. Often, sharing can be beneficial for everyone involved.

Resources are everywhere. Look for them, and learn how to use them effectively and ethically. By doing so, you will enhance your problem-solving capabilities and increase your potential.

Saving Your Money

You have made saving money for college a priority. You make $8.50 an hour at your part-time job. You want to save $1,000. If you save half of your money, about how many hours will you have to work to meet your goal of saving $1,000?

Math Concept **Division** Before dividing numbers, remember to note where the decimal point is located. When you complete the division, you will need to move it back the same number of places.

Starting Hint First, divide your hourly rate by 2 because you can only save half of your earnings. Then, divide the amount you want to save by that new hourly rate.

 For math help, go to the Math Appendix at the back of the book.

✓ **Reading Check** **Explain** What is potential, and how can you develop your own?

©Digital Vision/Alamy

The Importance of Goals

Nearly everyone has goals in life, but not everyone is able to achieve them. A **goal** is something that you want to achieve. It is ultimately what you are willing to work for. Goals should be positive and something you really want. Your goals should also be realistic, or possible to reach. Chris set a goal to start a pet-sitting business. After thinking about her goal, she realized it was not realistic because she is allergic to animal hair!

Like road signs, goals give you direction, keeping you focused on where you want to go. Goals can also help you see what you achieved—and did not achieve. People who set goals and work to achieve them are much more likely to gain success and satisfaction in life. Without goals, it is easy just to drift along, letting circumstances control your future.

Personal Goals

Some goals, like trying out for the school play or applying for a part-time job, are short-term goals or goals that can be accomplished in the near future. Finishing high school, going to college, starting your own business, and getting married are examples of long-term goals. Long-term goals are more far-reaching and take longer to achieve.

Both short- and long-term goals are important. Short-term goals, such as reading a book, cleaning your room, or writing a letter, are easier to complete than long-term goals. By setting and reaching short-term goals, you gain a sense of accomplishment. Short-term goals can also serve as stepping stones to long-term goals. As a Chinese proverb says, "The journey of a thousand miles begins with a single step."

Share Resources

These friends are sharing a music player. People can also share time and friendship. *What other resources can friends share?*

There are also flexible and fixed goals. Both flexible and fixed goals can be either short- or long-term. A flexible goal is one that has an outcome, but no time limit. Saving money would be an example of a flexible goal. When you are in the habit of saving your money for the future, you may or may not have a specific way you want to spend it. A fixed goal means that the outcome has a specific date or time, such as saving a specific amount of money for your best friend's birthday gift. Understanding the ways that you may need or want to spend your money will help you decide how to use it when the time comes. Deciding ahead if something is flexible or fixed helps you manage your time and meet your goal.

It is important to recognize the goals that you want to achieve and the path you need to follow to achieve them. Some goals require more preparation than others. Almost all goals have more than one step before you can achieve them. When you work toward a large goal, it may be useful to have several smaller goals that you can achieve gradually on the way to the larger goal. Stay positive and celebrate your accomplishments with something that will keep you motivated.

HOW TO . . . Set Goals

As a child, you may have set remarkable goals for yourself. Now that you are a young adult, you may see those goals as fantasies. However, with a better sense of reality, you can set more realistic goals. That does not mean they have to be boring! They can be just as exciting as your childhood goals if you know how to make them achievable. These tips can help:

Be Specific Giving yourself a clear target has several advantages. First, it is easier to chart your course and mark your progress when you know exactly what you are aiming for. Also, achieving precisely what you set out to do gives you a greater sense of satisfaction and confidence.

Look at the Big Picture Consider how a proposed goal could affect other commitments, other people, and even other goals. Deciding in advance what is most important can help if conflicts arise later.

McGraw-Hill Education

Group Goals

People often work with members of a group to achieve common goals. Families may have common goals, such as planning a holiday dinner or planting a garden. As a group, the family maps out steps to take and works together to meet its goals. Working together to reach a goal can be fun. It can also strengthen your relationships with other family members and make you appreciate each other more. The process of working toward a goal can be as rewarding as the end result.

Groups outside the family often share organizational goals. A community or religious youth group may decide to help less fortunate families. They meet their goal by holding a car wash, cookout, or sports event to raise money. When people pull together for common goals, they can accomplish great things.

✓ **Reading Check** **Compare** What is the difference between short- and long-term goals?

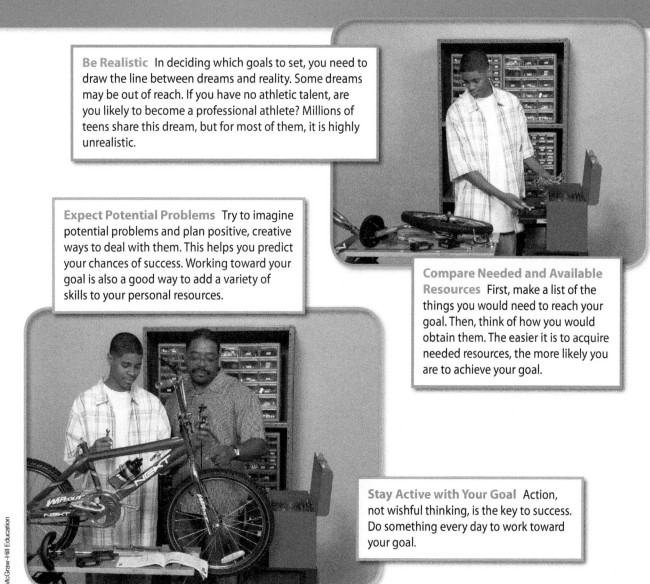

Be Realistic In deciding which goals to set, you need to draw the line between dreams and reality. Some dreams may be out of reach. If you have no athletic talent, are you likely to become a professional athlete? Millions of teens share this dream, but for most of them, it is highly unrealistic.

Expect Potential Problems Try to imagine potential problems and plan positive, creative ways to deal with them. This helps you predict your chances of success. Working toward your goal is also a good way to add a variety of skills to your personal resources.

Compare Needed and Available Resources First, make a list of the things you would need to reach your goal. Then, think of how you would obtain them. The easier it is to acquire needed resources, the more likely you are to achieve your goal.

Stay Active with Your Goal Action, not wishful thinking, is the key to success. Do something every day to work toward your goal.

McGraw-Hill Education

Building Character ?!

Commitment Marjan's father needs her help tomorrow night to create an important electronic presentation for his work. He tells Marjan that it would mean a lot to him if she helped. She agrees, but then her friend calls with tickets to a professional basketball game on the same night. Marjan's favorite team is playing. What should she do?

You Make the Call

Marjan told her father she would help him before she found out about the game. Should she go to the game, or stay and help her father? Explain your answer.

Move Toward Maturity

The desire to become an adult is not just normal, it is important. That is what gives you the incentive to learn about your own life and the workings of the world as you move toward adulthood and independence.

Reaching adulthood is not the real goal, however. Becoming mature is. Maturity means reaching full development—physically, emotionally, socially, intellectually, and morally.

Signs of Maturity

Some people seem to be older than their actual age, possessing attributes that can come from a variety of factors. These factors can include personality, environment, heredity, past experiences, and parental modeling.

One of the most common signs of maturity is age. Some laws require you to be a certain age before you can obtain a driver's license or vote. However, just because you are no longer a young child does not mean you are mature in all ways.

As you age, you change. You may look older, your verbal responses may sound more adult, but you may feel awkward in social situations and confused about the direction your life is taking. Someone else may look young but have it all together when it comes to making good decisions.

People do not mature at the same rate. Some people mature faster than others, and some people mature rapidly in one area but lag behind in others. For most people, personal development continues throughout life. Some signs of maturity include the following:

- **Independence** Think about what you need to know before being on your own. You need to understand how to make good decisions, how to manage money, and how to take care of housing and health needs, for example.
- **Emotional Control** Mature people are in charge of their emotions and do not allow their emotions to overwhelm them. They use logic, not gut reactions to make rational decisions.

◄ **Help Others**

Teens can make a difference in the world by helping others succeed. *In what ways do you help others succeed?*

Realistic Reflections

- **Dependability** Being dependable means you can be counted on. You go to school or work every day, show up on time for appointments, and keep your promises.
- **Willingness to Work Hard** Little is accomplished without hard work. Good grades come with effort. Winning teams develop with practice. Successful employees are rewarded for working hard.

Help Others Succeed

Think about times when someone encouraged you to succeed. Did encouragement make you feel more capable and worthwhile? Remember this, and give the same encouragement to people in your life. Positive comments such as "I know you can do it," "I am proud of you," and "I'm glad you're my friend" go a long way toward motivating others to do their best.

It is easy to get caught up in your life and forget about others. But your life is closely intertwined with many people. The positive way you treat others comes back to you when others treat you positively. You truly can make a difference in the world by helping others succeed.

Section 1.1

After You Read

Review Key Concepts

1. **List** four actions you can take to cope with changing emotions and energy during adolescence.
2. **Explain** how a high self-esteem might affect a person's life.
3. **Explain** how to set priorities, and why setting priorities is important.
4. **Identify** the six keys to setting achievable goals.
5. **Describe** what it means to become mature.

 **Check Your Answers** Go to connectED. mcgraw-hill.com to check your answers.

Practice Academic Skills

 **English Language Arts**

6. With a partner, think of goals your school may have. They can be short-term goals, such as starting a recycling program, or long-term goals, such as preparing students for life after school. Write a paragraph about how achieving these goals would benefit students.

 **Social Studies**

7. Think about your personality. What traits do you share with other members of your family? What traits do you have that other members of your family do not? Where do you think these traits came from? Write a paragraph describing your favorite personality trait and its influence.

The Balancing Act

Before You Read

Preview Take a few minutes to scan the headings in the section. Then, write a brief paragraph describing what you think the section will be about.

Read to Learn

Key Concepts
- **Discuss** the importance of a balanced life.
- **Summarize** the strategies that help save time and energy.

Main Idea

Maintaining a balanced life means carefully planning how to use your time and energy. Learning to manage stress will help keep your life in balance.

Content Vocabulary
◇ obligation
◇ work simplification
◇ stress

Academic Vocabulary

You will find these words in your reading and on your tests. Use the glossary to look up their definitions if necessary.
☐ designate
☐ immerse

Graphic Organizer

As you read, identify the four areas you need to manage for a balanced life. Use a graphic organizer like the one below to organize the information.

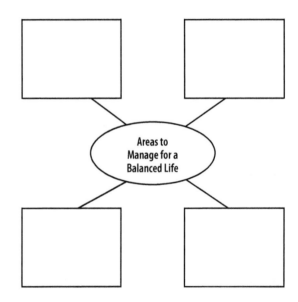

 Graphic Organizer Go to **connectED.mcgraw-hill.com** to download this graphic organizer.

Balancing Your Life

"Everything was going along just fine," said Rob. "I was passing all my courses, and I had just been selected for the soccer team. Then, all of a sudden, everything crashed in on me. Mom got really sick, and now she needs me to do more around the house and help with my little brother. I'm sleeping less, and I can't concentrate in school. I need to keep my grades up, but I can't seem to find time to study." Have you ever been in a situation like this?

The Importance of Balance

A balanced life is important, but difficult to achieve. Balance involves making wise use of your time and energy. When you achieve balance, your values and actions work in harmony. Balance gives you strength and confidence to meet life's demands.

When things shift out of balance, as in Rob's situation, you may feel like your life is spinning out of control, with too many problems to solve, too many things to do, or too many decisions to make. A hectic schedule, too many commitments, and unrealistic expectations are just a few factors that can tip a life out of balance. Besides negative feelings, a loss of balance can cause fatigue, loss of appetite or overeating, disturbed sleep patterns, and difficulty concentrating.

As You Read

Connect As you read this section, think about a time when you felt overwhelmed by the obligations in your life. How did you deal with the situation?

Time Management

Effective time management is key to meeting your goals. *What time management skills do you currently use?*

©Ingram Publishing/AGE Fotostock

Create a Management Plan

Regaining balance in your life is not easy, but it is possible. A management plan can help you reach your goals. Think of your management plan as a road map. It can help you find the most effective ways to use your resources in order to achieve your goals. People who manage their resources, such as time and energy, accomplish more. The following steps can help you manage your life:

- **Identify what is important.** Write down what you would like to accomplish. Perhaps you need to do laundry, write an essay for school, and call one of your friends.
- **Prioritize your tasks.** Look at your list. Which are your top priorities? Number the tasks, starting with "1" for the most important task. For example, if writing the essay is most important, label it "1." Your last priority should have the highest number.
- **Make a plan.** Decide how you are going to accomplish your tasks. Use tools, such as a day planner or calendar, to help you organize your plan. Set a reasonable time limit for each task. Also, list any resources you need, such as books for researching your essay.
- **Put the plan into action.** Begin working on your tasks, starting with your highest priority (number one on the list). Refrain from thinking about anything but the task at hand.
- **Evaluate the results.** Did you accomplish everything on your list? If not, what would you do differently next time?

These steps can help you get started on the road to regaining balance. Also keep in mind that good management involves a variety of skills that you can learn through observation and through personal experience. Those skills include decision making, problem solving, communication, leadership, organization, critical thinking, and creative thinking. Once you begin to see positive results, the negative feelings will lessen, and your confidence will return. To maintain balance, consistently keep your priorities and stay focused. Staying focused will help you make the most of your resources.

Study Plan

A management plan can help you organize your study time to finish schoolwork on time.

In what other areas of life can a management plan be helpful?

✓ **Reading Check** **List** What are five steps that can help you manage your life?

Manage Your Resources to Maintain Balance

Everything you do takes time and energy. Do you sometimes commit to activities, then wonder how you will ever find the time or energy to do them? Finding enough time and energy for all you need and want to do is not easy, but it is possible.

Manage Your Time

You most likely have obligations. An **obligation** is something you must do, such as a homework assignment, household chore or after-school activity. Obligations often require most of your time. After you finish these obligations, you can spend what time you have left on other activities of your choice, such as your hobbies or favorite sports. By making the most of your time, you can accomplish most tasks yet still maintain a balanced life.

Time for Learning

You spend at least half of your waking hours at school or doing homework. Education is vital at this point in your life and for your future. To get the most out of your school-related hours, follow these suggestions:

- **Focus on learning.** This means paying attention and listening closely to your teacher and to class discussions. You have a better chance of understanding what is going on if you stay focused, especially if the subject matter is difficult.

> ◆ **Vocabulary**
>
> You can find definitions in the glossary at the back of this book.

TAKE CHARGE!

Take Good Notes

The same skills that help you balance your life will also help you take good notes in school. Good notes help streamline your studying. Try these tips for taking notes in class:

- **Get Organized** Use a three-ring binder to store and rearrange your notes. Date and label all of them. Use double or triple spacing.
- **Listen** Be on the lookout for cues that indicate important points. If your teacher repeats something or writes it on the board, it is probably worth writing in your notes.
- **Rewrite the Main Ideas** Use your own words to explain important concepts. Emphasize important ideas by developing a system of shorthand.
- **Create Graphics** Diagrams, pictures, tables, and charts can create "snapshots" that help fix the information in your mind.

Real-World Skills

Notes in Action With a partner, practice your note-taking skills while watching a news program or reading a magazine article. Compare notes. Did your partner include points that you left out? What was his or her reasoning for doing so? Did your partner use a different method of organization? Write a paragraph to compare and contrast your and your partner's note-taking techniques.

Define Success

Realize that your definition of success may be different from that of your friends. Speak with an adult or guidance counselor to explore different types of success.

- **Take notes.** Good notes help refresh your memory when you study. Write down important points that are presented and discussed in class. Also write down assignments, instructions for doing them, and the dates they are due. If you are unclear about any information, ask questions.
- **Stay on top of homework.** You will get more out of class time if you do your homework as soon as you can each day. Also, start projects soon after they are assigned. A little work on a report every week until it is due will give you ample time to complete it and add quality to your work.

Time for Family, Friends, and Activities

Suppose you want to join the jazz band, but you work in the library after school, which does not leave you time to practice. Like many people, you realize it is not possible to find the time to do all of the activities you would like, so you are forced make a choice.

Almost everything you want and need to do requires time. It takes time to be a good family member or friend. Personal interests, such as hobbies, sports, exercise, and even relaxation require time. A little planning can help you do more of the things you need and want to do, without overscheduling your time. Before you decide which activities to pursue, remember that the time you spend at school or at home studying is very important.

HOW TO ... Manage Your Time

You have the same amount of time each day—24 hours. In these hours, you need to squeeze in time to eat, sleep, go to school, do homework and household chores, work on hobbies, and spend time with your family and friends. These tips can help you manage your time and accomplish everything you need to do:

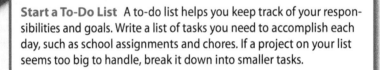

Start a To-Do List A to-do list helps you keep track of your responsibilities and goals. Write a list of tasks you need to accomplish each day, such as school assignments and chores. If a project on your list seems too big to handle, break it down into smaller tasks.

Determine Your Priorities Prioritize your to-do list. Put a "1" next to tasks that must be done, such as homework. Put a "2" next to tasks that should be done, such as making your bed. Put a "3" next to tasks you hope to do, such as playing flying disc golf with a friend.

Planning your time means you have to make choices based on what you value. To decide whether being a library assistant is more important than being in jazz band, for example, think about what you value more: making money and building transferable job skills for the future, or releasing stress and developing skills that will support a future in a music-related industry. If you value time with your brother, plan an activity you both enjoy or just sit and talk. If you and a friend share an interest in sports, make plans to go to a game. Remember to make time for yourself, too. Creating time for yourself each day to read, listen to music, write in a journal, or exercise is important to help regain your sense of balance. Making time for yourself also helps you learn more about who you are and what is truly important to you.

Manage Your Energy

Jenna is an early riser. She is at her best in the morning and early afternoon. Maybe you are just the opposite. You may start slowly but pick up steam later at night. Like everyone else, you have a regular energy cycle. Try to schedule tasks that require alertness and energy when you are at your peak. You can increase your energy level in general by improving your health habits. Eat healthful foods, exercise regularly, and get enough rest. Check out Chapters 14, 15, and 16 for more information about health, nutrition, and fitness.

Health & Wellness TIPS

Cell Phone Boundaries

Is it hard to focus on schoolwork when your cell phone keeps ringing with new text messages, social media updates, and other notifications? Use the following tips to set limits on cell phone use:

- ▶ Put your phone on silent.
- ▶ Turn off notifications from e-mail, social networking sites, and other apps.
- ▶ If you are busy with a task, make the area you are working in a cell phone-free zone.

Plan Your Schedule Record tasks that must be accomplished at a certain time on a calendar, a mobile device, or in a day planner. Be sure to give yourself enough time to accomplish each task. Check for any scheduling conflicts and resolve them immediately. Also, think of ways to overlap activities, such as reading on the bus or car ride home.

Get Things Done As you finish a task, check the item off on your to-do list. Avoid procrastinating, or putting off what you need to do. Also, be flexible. Anticipate problems and have backup plans. For instance, if your computer network goes down for several hours, finish your reading assignment while you wait for the computer to come back online.

Keep the Right Attitude Be fair to yourself. Set realistic goals about what you can accomplish. If you have unrealistic goals, you set yourself up for failure. A good attitude begins with good health. Eat a nutritious diet and get plenty of sleep. When you are tired, even the easiest tasks can cause frustration. Good health will give you the energy to be successful.

Blend Images/Alamy

Manage Your Possessions

When you donate used items, you help others and yourself at the same time. *What items could you donate to reduce your clutter?*

Another important aspect of energy management is **work simplification**, finding the easiest and quickest way to do a job well. By simplifying tasks, you save energy. Follow these guidelines to help conserve your energy as you work at home, at school, or in the workplace:

- **Analyze each job.** What are the steps you need to take to do a project? Can any steps in the process be omitted or combined?
- **Use the most appropriate tools for the job.** The right tools can save you time and frustration. A toothbrush might clean a floor, but it will not finish the job quickly. This same principle applies to almost any job.
- **Organize your workspace.** Place items you use frequently where you can easily reach them. Use free or inexpensive containers to separate items in drawers and on shelves.

Manage Your Possessions

Jared looked around his room. The closets and drawers were bulging with clothes, and the shelves were stuffed with papers and books. The computer equipment he bought last week was stacked in boxes on the floor, with CDs scattered around them. Jared let out a defeated sigh. "It will take me a year to find my brother's MP3 player in this mess."

Many people have experienced Jared's problem. They spend much time searching for items in cluttered and disorganized spaces. Locating items in sloppy spaces can also cause frustration. Taking charge and organizing what you own can ultimately help you save time, leaving you more time and energy for other activities.

To begin, take a mental tour of your room, noting places where you might eliminate some unused items. Assess clutter realistically. What items do you need? Set any needed items aside. If an item is not necessary, decide whether or not you need to keep it. If you think you will want the item a year from now, keep it. Sentimental items, such as photos, and collectable items are usually worth keeping. Put all remaining items in a pile to be recycled, donated, sold, or discarded.

Building Character ?!

Collaboration Stephanie is working on a class project with three classmates. One of the group members, Mark, has divided the project up and given each member a time limit for completing his or her part. Stephanie does not agree with how he divided the project. How should Stephanie handle this situation?

You Make the Call

Should Stephanie go along with the plan, even though she does not agree with it? Or, should Stephanie share her ideas with the group? Explain your answer.

JUPITERIMAGES/Brand X/Alamy

After reducing clutter, create or purchase an efficient storage system. Proper storage will help you feel more organized and will save you time. It can also reduce frustration and **stress**, or the pressure people feel as the result of their ability or inability to meet the expectations of others or themselves. Check out how some teens used storage to manage their belongings:

- **Frequently Used Items** Make sure items you use often are in view and easy to reach. Designate, or select, a specific place for these items. This way you will not waste time searching for wanted items. Greg keeps his workout gear in a duffle bag in the mudroom. This way he can grab it on his way out the door. If he knows it is always in this spot, he can direct someone else to bring it to him if he is elsewhere.

- **Seldom-Used Items** Store items you use less frequently in out-of-the-way places. Shannon's family camps out only once a year. Instead of storing camping gear in a closet, they keep the camping gear in the attic where it is out of the way.

- **Similar Items** Keep similar belongings, such as school supplies, craft items, hair care products, or sports equipment, in one place. Marla stores her gift-wrapping supplies in a labeled container under her bed. When she needs to wrap a friend's birthday gift, she is all set.

- **Papers and Photos** Develop a simple filing system for important papers and treasured photos. Emma uses an alphabetical system to file her papers, and Karen has begun making scrapbooks to keep her photos organized.

Manage Your Stress

Disorganization and unmanaged time and energy can lead to stress. The level of pressure varies with each situation. Participating in a hockey match might cause enough stress to motivate you to perform your best. Some situations, however, can cause overwhelming, negative stress. A family illness and intense academic pressure are just two causes of negative stress. This negative stress can cause you to feel pressured, frustrated, hopeless, jittery, or out of control. When negative stress begins to affect your health, schoolwork, and relationships, your life can quickly slip out of balance. If this happens to you, it is important to remember that you can manage your stress and regain balance.

⌄ Achieve Balance

Balancing your life will help you manage stress. *What can you do to gain more balance in your life?*

Masterfile

Manage Stress

Do not be afraid to ask for support when you need it. *Who can you go to when you need support? Explain.*

Control Anxiety

Have you ever been so anxious that you cannot fall asleep? Use the following tips to rid yourself of anxiety so that you can get the rest you need:

▶ Completely relax the muscles in your face.

▶ Breathe slowly and deeply.

▶ Listen to your breathing. Push all other thoughts out of your mind.

Identify the cause. To successfully manage stress, first identify the cause. Some sources of stress are easy to identify, such as a major exam or a piano recital. Others may be less obvious. For example, you may feel uncomfortable talking to classmates who frequently pressure you to give them answers on unfinished homework. That uncomfortable feeling causes you constant stress.

Take action. The next step in a stress management plan is to take action. If the stress is caused by an event, such as an exam, prepare yourself. Not only will the preparation help you do your best, but it will keep your mind busy, so that you do not become occupied with worry and anxiety. After the event ends, the stress will probably go away.

Remove yourself from the situation. If you can avoid the situation or person, do so as much as possible. Removing yourself from the situation can help decrease stress. If the stress is caused by something other than a specific event, such as pressure from a friend or a difficult class, the stress might not go away completely. However, you can keep it to a low level.

Change your perspective. You can also try to change the way you perceive or react to the stress. Rethinking, or gaining a new perspective on, a stressful situation can help you make it a learning opportunity rather than a threat. For example, instead of thinking of math as too difficult to learn, think of it as an interesting puzzle to figure out.

OJO Images/SuperStock

- **Find a healthy distraction.** Sometimes obsessing over a stressful situation can make you feel as though your head will explode. To get your mind off of whatever it is that is causing you stress, you can immerse yourself, or completely engage yourself, in a good book, movie, or game. Other effective ways to manage stress include exercising, getting plenty of rest, and spending time with family and friends.
- **Get support.** Sometimes when life gets out of balance, people become overwhelmed and feel unable to cope. If this happens to you, reach out to people who care about you. Talk to a family member, close friend, favorite teacher, counselor, coach, or religious leader. Share your concerns and ask for help when you need it.

Keeping a sense of balance in your life will require effort. Remembering your values and priorities; managing your time, energy, and stress; and getting support from others who care about you can help you maintain a balanced life.

It is also important to remember that stress from classes at school can be minimized. If you feel that a class is too hard, or you do not understand the material, talk to a teacher or a school counselor. They will have some helpful ideas about your situation, and ways to help you get the assistance you need.

Section 1.2

After You Read

Review Key Concepts

1. **Explain** why is it important to manage your time.
2. **Define** stress and describe how it affects your life.

Practice Academic Skills

 **English Language Arts**

3. You may have used time management skills and strategies without realizing it. Now that you know about these skills, conduct research to find two time management skills that you use or have used in the past. What information can you find to improve the skills you already use? What strategies can you use that you never tried before? Share your information in a brief report for the class, and explain how you think these strategies can balance your life.

 **Social Studies**

4. Interview a person about how he or she handles stress. You might interview a teacher, classmate, family member, or friend. Ask the person to suggest tips for coping with stress. Share the tips with the class.

 **Check Your Answers** Go to connectED. mcgraw-hill.com to check your answers.

What Does a Life Coach Do?

A life coach helps others set and achieve personal and professional goals. Life coaches serve as sounding boards and motivators. They help people assess their needs and values and then change their behavior to meet their new goals and create more fulfilling lives.

Lisa F. Young/Alamy

Skills To be a successful life coach, you should have a strong desire to help others. You also need effective communication skills, a sense of responsibility, and the ability to set goals and manage time. Patience and understanding are also valuable skills.

Education and Training You can study human services or social or behavioral sciences at a two-year college. You can also get skills you need through executive coaching, management consulting, or leadership training programs. Private certification and credentialing programs are available.

Job Outlook Most life coaches are self-employed. The number of jobs is expected to grow as the population increases and more people turn to life coaches for help.

Critical Thinking Find articles about life coaches and the people they have helped. Then, write a paragraph describing the job. Do you think a life coach would be useful to you? Explain your answer.

Career Cluster

Human Services

Life coaches work in the Human Services career cluster. Here are some of the other jobs in this career cluster:

- Social Worker
- Clergy
- Counselor
- Psychologist
- Child Care Worker
- Occupational Therapist Assistant
- Physical Therapist Assistant
- Nursing Aide
- Home Health Aide
- Psychiatric Health Aide
- Mental Health Aide
- Community Outreach Worker
- Gerontology Aide
- Human Service Worker
- Case Management Aide
- Education Administrator
- Public Relations Specialist

Explore Further Research this career cluster. Choose a career in this cluster that appeals to you and write a career profile.

CHAPTER SUMMARY

Section 1.1
Growing and Changing

Adolescence is a time of many changes that affect the way you think and feel about yourself. Your experiences in life shape your self-concept and self-esteem. Your heredity and environment help create your personality. Your potential and resources can help you achieve your dreams. Goals help you focus on what you want and the steps needed to reach your dream. People grow and mature at different rates over a lifetime.

Section 1.2
The Balancing Act

Balance involves making wise use of your time and energy. By making the most of your time, you can accomplish most tasks yet maintain a balanced life. Work simplification is a very important part of energy management. People who manage their belongings effectively have more time and energy to concentrate on other activities. Stress varies with each situation. Some stress goes away after an event ends. Other stress is continuous and must be managed.

Vocabulary Review

1. Create a multiple-choice test question for each content and academic vocabulary term.

Content Vocabulary
- adolescence (p. 7)
- puberty (p. 7)
- hormone (p. 7)
- personality (p. 9)
- heredity (p. 9)
- environment (p. 9)
- self-esteem (p. 10)

- potential (p. 11)
- priority (p. 12)
- resource (p. 13)
- goal (p. 15)
- obligation (p. 23)
- work simplification (p. 26)
- stress (p. 27)

Academic Vocabulary
- enhance (p. 8)
- insight (p. 8)
- designate (p. 27)
- immerse (p. 29)

Review Key Concepts

2. Describe the physical, social, emotional, intellectual, and moral development that occurs during adolescence.

3. Compare self-concept and self-esteem.

4. List the four types of resources that can help you reach your potential.

5. Explain why setting goals is important.

6. Identify the major signs of maturity.

7. Discuss the importance of a balanced life.

8. Summarize the strategies that help save time and energy.

Critical Thinking

9. Choose In your opinion, which is more important, managing time or managing stress? Explain your answer.

10. Examine Do you know of someone who is reaching his or her potential? Write the reasons you believe this individual is successful in achieving his or her goals.

11. Create Design a plan for how you might improve your study habits at school to make the most of your education and prepare for your future.

ACTIVE LEARNING

12. Set Goals You are more likely to be happy with your career choices if you consider your interests and abilities when setting your goals. List three careers you are interested in at the top of a sheet of paper. Divide the bottom of the paper into two columns. Write "Interests" in the left column and "Abilities" in the right column. Fill in the columns with your main interests and abilities. Then, compare them against the careers you listed. How closely do your goals match your interests and abilities? Do any of your career goals match your interests but not your abilities? If so, brainstorm ways that you can cultivate abilities necessary to meet those career goals.

Family & Community Connections

13. Accomplish Your Goals Think about your own personal development. What are your long-term goals? After finishing high school, you may plan to enter the workforce, attend a trade school, or enroll in college. What roadblocks or challenges do you face on your path to accomplishing your long-term goals? How can you conquer those challenges? What short-term goals can you set to help you reach your ultimate goal? Discuss these questions with a family member, friend, or neighbor. He or she will be able to look objectively at your situation and point out hidden obstacles and show you the smartest approach to your goal. Make a chart with your long-term goal at the top. Below that, place short-term goals that you will need to accomplish in order to eventually reach your long-term goal. Discuss your chart with a classmate.

Real-World Skills and Applications

Leadership Skills	**14. Improve Resources** Think of a community resource available to you that could be improved. In one paragraph, describe a plan to help improve the resource. For example, your public library might be improved by acquiring more books for its collection. You may suggest a bake sale to raise money for the library. When creating your plan, be as detailed as possible.
Financial Literacy	**15. Evaluate Costs** You are considering buying three books. Book A costs $9.95, Book B costs $12.00, and Book C costs $6.99. Book C is a reference guide and you want to be able to keep it accessible at all times. How much money could you save by borrowing books A and B at the library instead of buying them? How much money could you save by borrowing all three books?
Cooperative Learning	**16. Overcome Distractions** What distractions do you face most while working to accomplish your goals? Follow your teacher's instructions to form groups. Discuss this question with your group, and look for distractions common to people your age. How can you overcome these distractions in order to pursue your goals? Work with your group to come up with five distractions, and list three ways you can deal with each of these distractions.

Creatas/Jupiter Images

Academic Skills

English Language Arts

17. Self-Esteem and Success Read a newspaper or magazine biographical article about a successful person such as a politician, an activist, or a celebrity. Write a paragraph describing the obstacles this person faced. How can you use your knowledge of the person's experiences to help you overcome similar obstacles?

Science

18. Survey and Chart Goals Survey at least 12 people about long-term goals in their life. These can be friends, relatives, or others that you know.

Procedure Survey to ask the question, "On a scale of 1 to 5, with 5 being most important, how would you rank the importance of setting short-term goals to achieve a long-term goal?"

Analysis Record the responses. Create a graph showing the frequency of each rank, 1, 2, 3, 4, and 5. Summarize your findings in a sentence below the graph.

Mathematics

19. Manage Your Time There are 24 hours in a day. Suppose that you sleep for 8 hours a day and are at school for 7.5 hours a day. Eating breakfast and dinner with your family takes 1 hour each day. You need 2 hours to study and complete your homework, and you spend another 30 minutes getting to and from school. It also takes you 45 minutes to get ready in the morning. On any given school day, how much free time do you have to do other things?

Math Concept **Addition and Subtraction** A sum is the result when two values are added together, while a difference is the result when one value is subtracted from another.

Starting Hint First, add together all the hours that you are busy in a day. Then, subtract that sum from the number of overall hours in a day.

 For math help, go to the Math Appendix at the back of the book.

Standardized Test Practice

SCIENCE WORD PROBLEMS
Directions Read the word problem, then choose the correct answer.

Test-Taking Tip It is not always clear what is being asked in a word problem. After identifying the question, consider the information you need to answer that question. Then, find the necessary information and form equations to help you find the answer.

20. In order to maintain your weight, you must consume as many calories daily as you use. Suppose that you burn approximately 500 calories while sleeping. You burn 1,000 calories through your daily activities. You also go for a daily run that burns an additional 450 calories. How many calories do you need to consume in order to maintain your weight?

a. 1,450 calories   **b.** 950 calories
c. 1,950 calories   **d.** 450 calories

Chapter 2

Character Development

Section 2.1
Building Character

Section 2.2
Taking Responsible Action

Chapter Objectives

Section 2.1
- **Explain** why character and values are important.
- **Describe** the importance of personal responsibility.

Section 2.2
- **Identify** the factors that influence decisions.
- **List** the six steps of the decision-making process.
- **Describe** the qualities of responsible leaders.

Getty Images/Hero Images

Explore the Photo

Volunteering in the community is one way teens can build character and develop leadership skills. *What qualities are these teenagers displaying by working in a community garden?*

Writing Activity

Outlining

Building Character Outlines consist of the main ideas you want to cover and the subtopics and details that support each main idea. Write an outline detailing an event that helped build your character. Be sure to list main ideas, subtopics, and details in a logical order.

Writing Tips Use these tips to write an outline.

1. List the main topics you want to write about in a logical order.
2. Under each main topic, list at least two subtopics that support the main topic.
3. Under each subtopic, list supporting information or details you want to include in your assignment.

Section 2.1

Building Character

Before You Read

Preview Read the key concepts and vocabulary terms on this page. Write one or two sentences predicting what you think the section will be about.

Read to Learn

Key Concepts

- **Explain** why character and values are important.
- **Describe** the importance of personal responsibility.

Main Idea

Developing strong character traits and personal responsibility makes a positive difference in your life and in the lives of others.

Content Vocabulary

◇ character
◇ ethical principle
◇ role model
◇ value
◇ universal values
◇ responsibility
◇ citizen
◇ citizenship

Academic Vocabulary

You will find these words in your reading and on your tests. Use the glossary to look up their definitions if necessary.

☐ reinforce
☐ thrive

Graphic Organizer

As you read, note the values that are generally accepted and shared by people worldwide. Use a chart like the one below to organize your information.

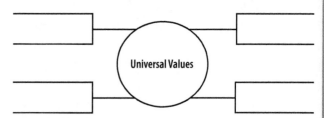

Universal Values

 Graphic Organizer Go to **connected.mcgraw-hill.com** to download this graphic organizer.

Recognizing Character

Think of people in your community whom you admire. Perhaps they are friends, family members, teachers, or religious leaders. What makes them stand out? Chances are, they are people of character.

Calling someone a person of character may be the biggest compliment you can pay that individual. **Character** is a combination of traits that show strong ethical principles and maturity. An **ethical principle** is a standard for right and wrong behavior. A person's character shows in his public behavior and his private behavior. Character gives a person the strength and courage to do the right thing every day, no matter what.

An individual that lives according to his or her ethical principles is not just a person of character. He or she is also a positive **role model**, or a person who sets a positive example for others. You may be a role model for younger children. Perhaps they see you as someone they want to be like when they are older. They watch you closely and follow your example, in behavior, language, and even the way you dress. Picture yourself as a role model for young children. Does your behavior show your true character?

Values and Character

Values and character go hand in hand. A **value** is a belief or idea about what is important. Your character is based on a set of values you have learned since childhood. You use your values to guide the choices you make every day. For example, bringing an extra sandwich to give to a classmate who cannot afford to buy lunch shows your value of compassion. You show the value of honesty when you refuse to shoplift, even though your peers may be pressuring you to steal.

Values also show in what you say and how you say it. For example, you display the value of courtesy when you speak kindly and respectfully to others. Your values also can be seen in how you spend money. Buying a gift for someone who has been ill shows the value of caring.

As You Read

Connect Think about someone you admire. What qualities does he or she have that you respect the most?

Vocabulary

You can find definitions in the glossary at the back of this book.

> **Character in Action**

Role models are chosen for their character and integrity.

How are you a role model for others?

PhotoAlto/Laurence Mouton/Getty Images

Finally, your values show in what you are willing to stand up for. A person who risks criticism from others to stand up for a principle sends a clear message about moral strength, or integrity. How have your values influenced your behavior in a positive way?

Learned Values

You learn values from your family and others in your life directly through what they teach you, and indirectly through the examples they set. For instance, Kevin's mom donates time on weekends to a neighborhood cleanup project. She shows Kevin that concern and a sense of responsibility for the community are important values.

Throughout life you may also learn values from other sources. Schools and places of worship teach values, as do friends, books, and community organizations. Some of these sources reinforce, or strengthen, the values you learned earlier in your life, but others may teach you new ones. Some books, Internet sites, and television programs may show people who display unacceptable values. What negative values might a person learn from each of these sources?

Set an Example

You set an example for others when you exhibit caring and respect. *What other values can you learn from these teammates?*

Shared Values

Think about your family's values and the values of other families you know. Are they the same? Which values do all families share? Look around and you will see that people's values often vary. However, people of all cultures share some common values.

Values that are generally accepted and shared worldwide are sometimes called **universal values**. They are the qualities that make positive and peaceful interaction among people possible. The following values are examples of universal values:

* **Caring,** or compassion, is how you actively show concern about the well-being of another living being. You can show caring about a person or an animal or even the environment.
* **Fairness** means being open-minded and willing to consider all sides of an issue. People who demonstrate fairness accept other people. They do not make judgments until they understand all the facts.
* **Honesty** means you are truthful and act real, not fake. Honest people do not try to be something they are not. They do not cheat or take things that do not belong to them.
* **Integrity** is when you always act according to your values. Integrity gives you the strength to make wise choices when you are pressured to go against your values.

Masterfile

The universal value of respect is shown in various ways, even by opponents. *How can you show respect when you compete with someone?*

- **Respect** means treating others as you would like to be treated. People who show respect are not hateful or cruel.
- **Responsibility** means you are accountable for choices you make and things you do. It involves making a decision and accepting the consequences of your choices and behaviors.
- **Self-discipline** is when you have control over your behavior. You can control your temper, your actions, and any tendency to put off tasks at work, school, or home.
- **Trustworthiness** means people can trust what you say and do. When people are trustworthy, you can take them at their word.

Although these values are held around the world, people place different levels of importance on them. Even among your own friends, you may share similar values but express them differently. For example, Tanya believes respect is very important. She believes the best way to show respect is to be open to other people's views, and careful with their feelings. Her friends often confide in her because they know she will listen and show respect without judging them. Tanya's best friend also believes respect is important. She believes complete honesty is the best way to show respect, even when sharing her opinions leads to debates and disagreements with others. What values are the most important to you? How do you show them?

✓ **Reading Check** **Contrast** What is the difference between learned values and shared values?

Financial *Literacy*

Calculate Percent Discount

You want to buy a shirt to donate to a clothing drive. You have $18.00. You find a shirt that is priced at $31.74 and is 20% off with an additional 35% discount. You find the same shirt in another store. It is marked $38.57 and is 50% off. Which shirt would you choose to buy?

Math Concept **Percents** Divide the percent by 100 to get the decimal number. For example, 47% would become .47. Then, multiply the decimal number by the original price to find out the discount.

Starting Hint Multiple percent discounts have to be calculated separately. First, figure out the 20% discount. Then, use that figure to calculate the price of the shirt after the 35% discount.

 Math For math help, go to the Math Appendix at the back of the book.

Corbis RF/Alamy

Character as Your Guide

When she was younger, Stacy quickly became angry when things did not go her way. She would throw things and mock others in a nasty tone of voice. Stacy upset a lot of her good friends this way. Even her best friend, Alisha, started saying she was too busy to hang out.

With her parents' help, Stacy saw how her behavior hurt the people she cared about. She realized that to be a good friend, the kind of friend she would like to have, she would need to be more cooperative, patient, and kind. Stacy began to plan activities with her friends instead of bossing them around, and she began to behave more maturely when angry. Stacy's choices improved her character and her friendships.

Personal character develops over time. It comes from thinking about, and consciously living by, your values. In time, putting your values into action becomes automatic. Good habits are hard to break. What values have become habits in your life?

Personal Responsibility

It is easy to identify people who accept responsibility. It shows in their words and in their actions. Responsible people say things like, "Let me help," "I'll do it," or "I made a mistake, and I'll correct it if I can." Responsible people do not need to be reminded or pressured to do a job. They simply work to accomplish things that need to be done. They keep their own and others' best interests in mind.

➤ TAKE CHARGE!

Promote Diversity

There are several steps you can take to understand and appreciate cultural diversity. The following tips will help you promote diversity, which is a key part of being a great leader.

- **Speak Up** Ask that your school library and classrooms contain materials that reflect various cultures and backgrounds.
- **Reach Out** Include people of different ages and backgrounds in school and community groups.
- **Work with Others** Create an inclusive environment free of discrimination or harassment. Encourage people to share their talents and experiences.
- **Respect Others' Values** Avoid forcing your own values on others. They may be different from the values of others.
- **Set an Example** Treat everyone as equals. Reach out to those from different backgrounds.

Real-World Skills

Try Something New Make friends with a classmate who is from a different culture or background. Get to know the person by learning about his or her heritage and customs. Create a journal describing what you have learned and how you might help your new friend get to know others.

Citizenship

Small actions can make a big difference to others. *What small act of caring and compassion can you do today to make a difference in your community?*

Think about ways those in your family show responsibility. Maria's grandmother asked her to help make tamales for their community center's fundraiser. Maria's grandmother has arthritis, which makes it hard for her to tie the corn husks as tightly as they need to be. Maria respects her grandmother and enjoys listening to stories of her childhood. Maria could have gone to a movie with her friends, but she decided to help her grandmother instead. How does your family responsibility influence your decisions?

Every day you have dozens of ways to show whether you are responsible. Do you keep promises and avoid gossip? Do you refuse to be pressured into negative behavior and activities? Do you try to get the most out of school? How do you choose friends and activities that reflect your personal values?

Become a Responsible Citizen

Each year Kelsey wins an award for good citizenship in school. What do you think the award stands for? A **citizen** is a member of a community, such as a school, city or town, or country. Unfortunately, just being a citizen does not automatically mean you are a good one. The way that you handle your responsibilities as a citizen is known as **citizenship**.

As community members, citizens have certain rights and privileges. For example, community members have the right to vote for city officials and the privilege of fire protection. In return, citizens owe certain responsibilities to the community, such as following its laws. This allows the community to run smoothly and serve the needs of its citizens. To thrive, or do well, a community requires responsible citizens. Kelsey follows the rules of her school, respects her fellow school citizens, and behaves responsibly. Her good citizenship not only earns her an award each year, but also earns her the respect of her peers and teachers.

Don Bayley/Getty Images

Building Character ?!

Caring Your friend Michael says that he has been leaving notes in Sheila's locker that make fun of her. Michael says he is just teasing. You are not friends with Sheila, but you think Michael is being insensitive to other people's feelings. Later, you overhear Sheila crying and telling her friends about the hurtful notes. What should you do?

You Make the Call

Should you talk to Michael about his behavior? Or, should you not get involved? Write a paragraph explaining what you would do in this situation and why.

Figure 2.1

Volunteer Opportunities for Teens

Volunteer Most communities have nonprofit service organizations that offer volunteer opportunities. Contact a local organization that interests you to begin volunteering in your community. *Which volunteer opportunity in this list most interests you, and why?*

Tutor younger children.	Help build homes for Habitat for Humanity.
Volunteer at the hospital.	Visit and help residents at nursing homes.
Deliver meals to people confined to their homes.	Read to the visually impaired.
Collect recyclable materials.	Lead a youth group.
Become a camp counselor.	Participate in a park or beach clean-up event.
Participate in food, clothing, and toy drives for people in need.	Create a Web site for a small charity.
Coach a youth team or Special Olympian.	Become a museum tour guide.
Volunteer at an animal shelter or veterinary office.	Volunteer at a zoo or aquarium.
Volunteer at the public library.	Serve food at a soup kitchen.
Become a Big Brother or Big Sister to a child in need.	Help at a charity race or event that benefits a cause you believe in.

Get Involved

You first learn and practice good citizenship in your home and school, where you have a chance to exercise your personal values. The two most important qualities of citizenship are caring for the greater good of individuals and the community and acting on your concerns.

Dan shows concern for, and commitment to, his community by coaching a Little League baseball team. Kayla is elected to a class office because she cares about her peers, and treats classmates equally, with honesty and respect. Kayla's brother volunteers at the animal shelter. Some teens incorrectly believe they have to reach adulthood before they can make a contribution to their community. The good news is you can become a valuable member of your community now.

Regularly read newspapers, listen to radio and television news programs, and follow news organizations' social media sites. This will help you keep up with what is happening in your local community and throughout the world. When you learn about current issues and the needs of those around you, you will be more likely to make a positive difference in your community. Eventually, as a voter, you will help choose public officials that have wider-reaching influence. The more you know about your community and beyond, the more sound your decisions will be.

Participating in volunteer work is a great way to demonstrate leadership, commitment, and character. Volunteer for the benefit of others, but do it for yourself, too. Helping others can increase your self-esteem when you know that you are doing something worthwhile. It can also help when you apply to college and look for paying jobs. Schools and employers appreciate people who make a difference in their communities.

SUCCEED IN SCHOOL

Reading Time

Set aside a specific time every day to read a book, magazine, or newspaper of your choice. This daily habit will improve your reading speed and comprehension without feeling like a chore.

Finding Volunteer Opportunities

Many teens would like to volunteer for a good cause or an organization they have heard about, but they do not know where to find volunteer opportunities. Opportunities exist in most communities for volunteer service.

Before jumping in to help local groups or organizations, spend a moment thinking about your own skills and interests. What causes are you interested in? Perhaps you would like to help older people. You might find volunteer work at an adult care facility, visiting and reading to the residents. What skills can you lend to an organization? Perhaps you like and are good with animals. Your local animal shelter might be able to put you to work feeding and walking dogs. **Figure 2.1** lists some volunteer opportunities for teens. You can use ideas from the list or contact local service organizations to find out about other opportunities in your community.

Making a Difference

Learning to develop and display positive qualities of character and values takes time and effort, but the rewards are great. People in your family and community will respect you for who you are. They will observe your commitment and willingness to help achieve family goals and be a part of your community.

As you grow older and become more involved in your community, people may begin to see you as a leader. Whether you choose to be a leader or not, being a responsible person and citizen makes it possible for you to make a difference in your life and in the lives of others.

Section 2.1

After You Read

Review Key Concepts

1. **Describe** the characteristics of a role model.
2. **Explain** how a person develops character.

Practice Academic Skills

English Language Arts

3. Think about a citizen in your community who has served as a role model to you or others. Write a letter expressing thanks for the person's efforts. Remember to include a heading, greeting, body, closing, and signature.

Social Studies

4. Read a story about a teen in a different country or culture. Write two paragraphs about the values of the culture, how the teen's behavior demonstrates these values, and how the values compare to your own.

 Check Your Answers Go to connected. mcgraw-hill.com to check your answers.

Section 2.2

Taking Responsible Action

Reading Guide

Before You Read

Preview Skim through this section, scanning the main headings as you go. Write one or two sentences predicting what you think the section will be about.

Read to Learn
Key Concepts
- **Identify** the factors that influence decisions.
- **List** the six steps of the decision-making process.
- **Describe** the qualities of responsible leaders.

Main Idea
Make good decisions, put problem-solving skills to work, and understand leadership to help you take responsible action and become more independent.

Content Vocabulary
◇ decision making
◇ need
◇ want
◇ leader
◇ leadership

Academic Vocabulary
You will find these words in your reading and on your tests. Use the glossary to look up their definitions if necessary.
▢ consideration
▢ demographics

Graphic Organizer
As you read, list the four types of skills needed by leaders. Use a chart like the one below to organize your information.

 Graphic Organizer Go to connected.mcgraw-hill.com to download this graphic organizer.

Sound Decision Making

"Should I help the Outreach Club put up banners for the Martin Luther King, Jr. Day parade, or study for tomorrow's math test?" You make decisions every day. Many decisions you make are almost automatic. You choose to brush your teeth, comb your hair, or pick out a shirt to wear to school.

Other decisions are more complicated. Should you continue a friendship that is troubled? Should you become involved in a school activity? These decisions take time and **consideration**, or continued and careful thought. They affect not only you but also your family and friends. Some of your decisions even affect the community you live in and future generations.

Decision making is the act of making a choice. Making responsible decisions helps you achieve personal goals. Each year, you will make a number of major decisions about school, health, work, and how you can contribute to society. Your decisions determine your behavior. At times, you may choose to do nothing about a situation, or you may let someone else decide for you. That is a decision, too.

What Influences Your Decisions?

Think about a recent decision you made. Did you make the decision yourself? Did you get help from a family member or teacher? A variety of influences shape your decisions. Some influences are external, like family, friends, and society. Others are internal and come from your own knowledge and attitudes. Which of the following influences have played a major part in your decisions?

As You Read

Connect Think about someone who helps you make difficult decisions. What qualities of character does that person have?

Vocabulary

You can find definitions in the glossary at the back of this book.

Creatas/PhotoLibrary

Family Influence

Caring family members influence you to make good decisions. *Why are family members good resources when you need to make a decision?*

Family

Family members can strongly influence your decisions. Sometimes parents or guardians make a decision for you, especially if they feel you are not ready or able to make the decision on your own. They know that you learn from mistakes, but they choose to make the decision because it is their responsibility to protect and teach you.

Culture

Your family's beliefs and customs directly affect your decisions. For example, Miranda had to choose between attending her sister's Quinceañera (ˌkēn-(t)sin-ˈyer-ə) and going on a class trip. A Quinceañera is a celebration in many Hispanic families of a girl's transition to adulthood at age 15. It emphasizes family values and social responsibility.

Friends

As you grow older, it is natural to turn to friends for help with decisions. Some friends will have a positive influence on your decisions. Others will have a negative influence. Your friends often have no more experience or knowledge than you do and might give you poor advice. Some may want to influence you to do things that are not in your best interest. You can always listen and learn from others, but you must make your own decisions in the end.

Values

Many decisions you make are based on your values. As a result, your decisions are a clear expression of your values. Choosing to complete your homework instead of going to the movies shows that you know the value of responsibility.

How I See It

CARING

Tracy, 17

Sometimes when I am upset, I feel like I am totally alone. But I always remind myself that there are people in my life who truly care for me. Even if they cannot completely relate to a particular situation in my life, they are always willing to listen to my problems and help me find positive solutions. The kindness my friends and family members show me inspires me to be kind to others. Their support has taught me that being a caring person can be as simple as just listening without judging.

Critical Thinking Think about a time when you helped a friend or family member through a difficult time. How did your actions show caring?

Resources

Your decisions are also affected by your resources, such as people, time, money, energy, knowledge, skills, and technology. If you are low on money, do you go to the game or go cycling in the park? If you just got paid from an after-school job, do you use your earnings to buy a new bike or use your skills to repair the bike you already have?

Demographics

Changes in the characteristics of the population, or demographics, affect everyone. Our society has more older adults than ever before. How might that affect your career choice? What other demographic changes can you name? What effects do they have on your behavior?

Needs

People's needs exert a strong influence on their decisions. A **need** is one of those things essential to your survival and well-being. Food, clothing, and shelter are physical needs, and affection, security and safety, belonging, and achievement are emotional needs. Your desire to learn is an intellectual need, and maintaining positive relationships with other people is a social need.

Wants

Something you desire, even though it is not essential, is a **want**. A new DVD, makeup, and video games are wants, not needs, because those items are not essential to your survival or well-being. It is easy to convince yourself that certain wants are needs. For example, you may need transportation to get to work, but an expensive sports car is a want that you can live without. Wants can have a powerful influence on your decisions.

Media

Newspapers, magazines, radio, television, movies, Web sites and social media all present facts, fiction, and opinions. Much of the information is designed to influence your thinking and choices.

Society

Society refers to a group you belong to, such as your school, community, or country. Your decisions and behavior are influenced by the society in which you live. For example, Jamail's neighborhood takes pride in keeping the area safe. Jamail and his friends decided to attend next weekend's neighborhood watch meeting to find out how they can contribute to neighborhood safety. What are some of the ways society can influence your decisions?

Wants

Many items, and their advertisements, are designed to have a powerful influence on your decisions. *How have you been influenced by advertisements or the way an item is displayed?*

Health & Wellness

TIPS

Emotional Health

Counselors from a community counseling agency or school can help you make decisions related to your emotional health and well-being. Use these tips to maintain your emotional health:

▶ Focus on the positive.
▶ Recognize that life is what you make of it.
▶ Learn from your successes and mistakes.

Picturenet/Getty Images

Building Character ?!

Balance Asher and Sasha are two of the top sprinters on the track team. They were both invited to play an online video game with a few teammates last night. Sasha wanted to, but since it was a school night, she refused. Today at practice, Sasha noticed Asher's times on the track were a lot slower than normal. There is an important track meet tomorrow and there's another video game meet-up scheduled for tonight. Asher says he will take a nap before the track meet, but Sasha isn't so sure. How should Sasha respond?

You Make the Call

Sasha is torn because she likes Asher and the other teammates. She also likes to play video games. But she cares about the results of her track team, too. Explain how Sasha may be able to help Asher balance his hobbies with his commitments.

Consider the Consequences

The consequences of some decisions you make affect only you. Some consequences may be minor, and some may be very serious. Many decisions affect other people, too. That is why it is important to think about the impact of your decisions on your family, your friends, and, ultimately, your community. When you care about other people and want their respect, you will make decisions carefully. Even minor decisions, such as deciding not to wear a safety belt when riding in a car, can have far-reaching consequences.

Remember that the personal decisions you make may alter the direction of your life. Think about what and who have influenced those decisions. For example, what do you think would happen if you decided to drop out of school? What effect would such a decision have on your life? What effect would it have on your family? Choosing to stay in school and graduate is a responsible decision that will set you on a winning course in life.

HOW TO ... Make Sound Decisions

Until now, the major decisions in your life have been made by adults. As you mature, you will make more decisions on your own. Now is the time to learn how to make decisions wisely. These steps will help you better understand the decision-making process. The process is not like a math formula, which always leads to the correct answer if applied exactly. Rather, it is a flexible outline that can be changed if needed. Using it successfully takes judgment and honesty.

©Wave Royalty Free/Alamy

Identify the Decision State or write the decision to be made as specifically as you can. Having a clear image from the start will help reveal the best course of action.

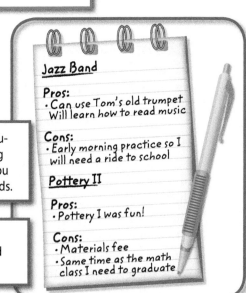

Consider Your Options Available resources strongly influence your options. Suppose you are trying to choose among several after-school activities. You need to know whether you have, or can acquire, the skills and time each option demands.

Analyze Your Options Once you have settled on some promising options, think about the possible outcomes of each one. Be realistic, and include both pros and cons.

Learn from Your Decisions

Good decisions are choices you can be proud of. Think through your decisions carefully. Are they realistic, responsible, and respectful for everyone involved? Making choices you feel good about can result in the following:

- Improved self-esteem
- Increased respect from family and friends
- More independence as you become responsible for yourself and your actions

Every decision does not always work out the way you might expect it to. When you make a mistake, do not blame others. Take responsibility for it, and learn as much as you can about the experience. Sometimes you have to live with the consequences of a wrong decision and say, "I will make a better choice next time."

✓ **Reading Check** **Identify** Why is it important to consider the consequences of a decision before acting?

Choose the Best Option For some people, this step is the hardest. If no option seems right, you may need to go back a step or two. Perhaps you sense that you are ignoring a possible, unpleasant outcome. On the other hand, it could be that several options look equally good. Let your goals and values guide you.

Act on Your Decision Give it your best effort, with the confidence that you have made the best decision possible. Make sure that your actions reflect your decision as you are doing them.

Evaluate the Results Are you happy with your decision? If so, congratulations! If not, try to pinpoint the cause of the problem. Maybe you overlooked a resource or something unexpected happened. Remember, working through each step carefully does not guarantee success. Either way, remember the experience, and refer to it the next time you make an important decision.

Putting Problem-Solving Skills to Work

Michelle has to make a decision. Her best friend is using drugs, and she needs to decide whether to continue the friendship or back away. Making decisions is part of solving complex problems. Practical problems are problems that involve morals and values. Problem solving helps break problems into pieces you can handle better and keeps you from becoming overwhelmed. This, in turn, helps you make better decisions.

When solving a problem, consider the available resources and possible options. What are the short- and long-term consequences of each option? What results do you want to achieve? Keep in mind that few solutions are perfect. Michelle might choose to keep her friend and risk her parents' disapproval, or she might choose to end the friendship, which means losing her best friend.

Problem solving is a continuous process, and an opportunity to grow. Apply what you learn to new situations. Using what you have learned in previous situations can help keep problems from becoming bigger issues. Michelle's decision to continue or end her friendship will take some time and careful thought, but the experience will help her use the decision-making process.

✓ Reading Check **Explain** What do problem-solving skills allow a person to do?

▼ Leadership Opportunities

Not all leaders are born leaders. Many people learn effective leadership skills from everyday activities. *What opportunities for leadership do you have in your daily life?*

Responsible Leadership

Do you see yourself as someone who leads or someone who prefers to follow? A **leader** is a person who has influence over and guides a group. It takes a leader to motivate others to action, and it takes followers, as well as leaders, to get things done.

Leadership is the ability to lead, not just hold an office, such as student body president. When Danielle organizes her friends to go bowling, she acts as a leader. Leaders have two main functions: to get a job done and to keep the group members together. The "job" is whatever the team is organized to do. The job might be to play a game, win a contest, or make a committee decision.

Corbis Super RF/Alamy

Leadership Skills

To lead others, you must learn certain skills. Sometimes being a follower first can teach you how to be a good leader later. As a follower, you can observe leadership skills in action and practice them at home, at school, and with your friends. The following are some of the skills you need as a leader:

- **Management Skills** Effective leaders can manage time, money, and other team resources. They know what must be done and what resources their team needs to meet its goals. They manage human resources by using the skills and talents of everyone in the group.
- **Motivational Skills** Effective leaders are skilled at motivating others to take action. As leader of the school's debate team, Mike uses praise and encouragement to motivate his team to work hard. Mike's motivational skills helped his team earn first place at the state competition.
- **Communication Skills** Leaders are able to explain the goals of the team and each team member's specific job. Leaders not only talk to but also listen to team members and respond to their suggestions, problems, concerns, and feelings.
- **Problem-Solving Skills** The problem-solving skills of leaders help them solve the varied problems they encounter. They use decision-making skills and are willing to look for new ways to achieve goals. For example, a good leader can solve problems among team members that might divide the group. The leader's solution helps the team move forward toward its goals.

The leadership skills that you develop now will help you prepare for your future roles at home and in the workplace.

Leadership Opportunities

Where can you find opportunities to lead? Opportunities for leadership are all around you. In a group of friends, someone leads and directs others in deciding where to go and what to do. In class, student leaders spark discussions and influence others by what they say.

You can also find leadership opportunities in student organizations, such as Family, Career and Community Leaders of America (FCCLA). FCCLA is a dynamic and effective national student organization. Students in middle and high schools who are currently or previously enrolled in a family and consumer sciences class can join FCCLA. FCCLA teaches students personal growth and leadership development. It helps teens focus on their multiple roles as family member, wage earner, and community leader through fun and challenging activities and competitions.

Opportunities for leadership in FCCLA are limitless. In your local FCCLA chapter, or group, you can lead a committee or become a chapter officer. In these roles, you coordinate projects and manage people. For example, you might create a program that teaches young children how to deal with bullies, or you might coordinate a canned food drive for a local food bank.

Building Character ?!

Good Citizenship Sometimes Ebony and Lindsay eat lunch together in the park. The closest trashcan is on the other side of the baseball diamond. Lindsay often throws her trash on the ground. She points out that there is already litter everywhere and it is not her job to pick it up. How should Ebony respond?

You Make the Call

Ebony knows that it is not right to litter, but she does not want to argue with her friend. Write a paragraph explaining what she should do, and why.

SUCCEED IN SCHOOL

Plan Ahead

If you know that you are going to be absent from school, talk to your teachers. They can set aside any important handouts for you, or post them on a class website, and can inform you about anything you might miss in class.

FCCLA also offers leadership positions at the district, regional, state, and national levels. Teens nominated and elected to these positions work in groups to raise awareness of teen issues and create positive changes. As a state or national officer, you might meet with legislators to address problems such as teen substance abuse, teen pregnancy, or workplace safety for teens.

Some people know that they would like to be a leader but do not know where to start. If you are interested in leading but unsure of your leadership skills, FCCLA can help. Among other programs, FCCLA offers the Dynamic Leadership program, which helps teens model good character, solve problems, foster relationships, manage conflict, and build teams.

In families, older brothers or sisters show leadership when they model positive behavior for younger family members. Just as you may look to someone for guidance and behavior worth imitating, young people may do the same with you as their role model.

In sports, a junior on the track team can show a freshman what it means to win or lose with a positive attitude. Leadership is not only for sports and family. At work, a long-time employee at a fast-food restaurant can show someone new on the job how to work well as a team member. Making the effort to practice leadership today can prepare you for bigger opportunities. Leadership skills will help you in your future workplace, or in social settings with your friends and family.

Section 2.2

After You Read

Review Key Concepts
1. **Describe** why it is important to learn from good and bad decisions.
2. **Define** leadership.
3. **Explain** the importance of learning leadership skills.

Check Your Answers Go to connected.mcgraw-hill.com to check your answers.

Practice Academic Skills

English Language Arts
4. Think of a story you have read in which a character makes a tough decision. Evaluate the decision, and state whether you think the character chooses wisely. Support your conclusion by citing benefits and drawbacks of the character's choice.

Social Studies
5. Describe a practical problem faced by some of your classmates. Remember that even practical problems involve morals and values. What are some of the decisions related to the problem? What might cause your classmates to make different decisions than you would?

CHAPTER SUMMARY

Section 2.1
Building Character

Values you learn from your family, people you respect, your school, places of worship, friends, books, the community, and youth organizations are learned values. Values you share with others worldwide are universal values. Character comes from putting your values into practice in a positive way. Citizens have certain rights and privileges but also have responsibilities to their communities.

Section 2.2
Taking Responsible Action

Family, friends, personal values, resources, needs, wants, culture, society, and demographics all contribute to the decisions you make. The decision-making process can help you make effective decisions. Decisions have positive and negative consequences. Leadership skills you develop now will help you as an adult. Leaders have certain qualities and skills that can be learned and practiced.

Vocabulary Review

1. Write your own definition for each content and academic vocabulary term.

Content Vocabulary
- ◇ character (p. 37)
- ◇ ethical principle (p. 37)
- ◇ role model (p. 37)
- ◇ value (p. 37)
- ◇ universal values (p. 38)
- ◇ responsibility (p. 39)
- ◇ citizen (p. 41)
- ◇ citizenship (p. 41)
- ◇ decision making (p. 45)
- ◇ need (p. 47)
- ◇ want (p. 47)
- ◇ leader (p. 50)
- ◇ leadership (p. 50)

Academic Vocabulary
- ▪ reinforce (p. 38)
- ▪ thrive (p. 41)
- ▪ consideration (p. 45)
- ▪ demographics (p. 47)

Review Key Concepts

2. Explain why character and values are important.
3. Describe the importance of personal responsibility.
4. Identify the factors that influence decisions.
5. List the six steps of the decision-making process.
6. Describe the qualities of responsible leaders.

Critical Thinking

7. Apply Consider the ethical principles in this situation: You are the only person to see someone unknowingly drop a $20 bill. What do you do?
8. Hypothesize Describe a situation where you could serve as a role model at home, at school, at work, or in the community.
9. Devise Generate a plan for how you might help an English learner who is new to your school. What actions could you take to help?
10. Summarize Describe what makes a responsible citizen. Then, share ways that you can demonstrate good citizenship within your school or community.
11. Analyze Think about the results of a good decision you have made. What might have been the results if you had made a different choice? Explain.

 ACTIVE LEARNING

 Family & Community Connections

12. Personal Choices Follow your teacher's directions to form groups. With your group, develop and present a short skit about a teen struggling to make an important decision. The teen should weigh the possible consequences of his or her choice. For example, the teen might have to choose between two after-school activities with the same meeting time. The teen should consider the benefits of each activity, as well as the drawbacks of participating in one rather than the other. The teen should then make a choice and explain his or her reasoning for doing so. Afterward, ask the class to evaluate the decision. Were there possible consequences that the teen did not consider?

13. Leadership Skills in Action Seeing strong leaders in action can help you learn how to become an effective leader yourself. Observe someone with an official or unofficial leadership role whom you respect. You can choose a friend, teammate, parent, co-worker, or community leader. What is it about this person that commands attention? How does this person talk to others? What sort of problem-solving skills does he or she exhibit? What does this person do or say to motivate and inspire others? Based on your observations and the reactions of other people to this person, what leadership skills do you feel are most valuable to have? What leadership skills would make this person even more influential? Present your findings to the class. As you share your opinions, try to apply what you have learned in your own presentation.

Real-World Skills and Applications

Leadership Skills

14. Community Search Write a brief help-wanted ad seeking a teen leader for an after-school community service club. Describe the needs of the club, the skills required to meet those needs, and why those skills would be very useful for a leader of the club to have. If you have trouble thinking of the club's needs, consider its purpose and the activities it usually performs.

Financial Literacy

15. Traveling Costs You are planning to volunteer at a zoo that is 60 miles from your home. You can either take Stephanie's car, which gets 20 miles to the gallon, or Manuel's car, which gets 30 miles to the gallon. Gas costs $3.99 per gallon. How much will the gas cost for each car to drive roundtrip?

Technology Skills

16. Volunteer Call Find out about several places that use volunteers. Create a public service announcement that motivates people to volunteer at places such as these. The announcement should last between thirty and sixty seconds. It should also describe the benefits of volunteering. You can plan a public service announcement to perform in front of the class. Or, you can videotape your public service announcement beforehand.

Getty Images/Hero Images

Academic Skills

English Language Arts

17. Create a Pamphlet Sometimes lack of information is all that prevents a person from volunteering. Choose a volunteering opportunity that appeals to you. Create a pamphlet about this opportunity that will appeal to your peers. The pamphlet should describe the opportunity in detail, explain who it helps, and provide contact information for places that offer this volunteering opportunity. Share the pamphlet with your class.

Social Studies

18. Compare Values Compare your values with those that are reflected in the words and actions of your classmates. Which of your classmates' values do you believe you share? Do you express these shared values in the same way? If not, describe the ways your expressions differ. Which of your classmates' values inspire you? Why is it important to respect your classmates' values?

Mathematics

19. Measure Ingredients Juan is baking three cakes for his school's bake sale. The first cake calls for ¼ cup of flour. The second cake calls for ⅛ cup of flour. The third cake calls for ½ cup of flour. How many cups of flour does Juan need in all to bake his cakes?

 Add Fractions Fractions need to have common denominators in order to be added. When fractions contain common denominators, their numerators can be added to find their sum.

Starting Hint First, find the least common denominator. Because 8 is evenly divisible by both 4 and 2, it is the least common denominator. Eight divided by 4 is 2. Thus, multiply ¼ by 2 to get ⅜. Eight divided by 2 is 4. Thus, multiply ½ by 4 to get ⅘. With all fractions containing a denominator of 8, their numerators can be added together to find their sum.

 For math help, go to the Math Appendix at the back of the book.

Standardized Test Practice

MATH WORD PROBLEMS
Directions Read the problem and answer the question.

Test-Taking Tip Simplify a word problem by identifying necessary information and unnecessary information. Once you have isolated the necessary information, form equations from that information to find the correct answer.

20. There are three candidates in your local election for mayor. Antoinette Hernandez is 38 years old and originally from Iowa City. Joseph Billings is a 47-year-old former senator. The current mayor, Kathleen Johnson, is 67 years old. What is the average age of the candidates? Round your answer to the nearest year.

Life Skills Project

Create a Goal Checklist

In this project you will set a long-term goal for yourself, and identify the steps you need to take to accomplish it. You will also interview an adult about a goal that he or she has achieved.

 ## My Journal

If you completed the journal entry from page 2, refer to it to see if your thoughts have changed after reading the unit.

Project Assignment

In this project you will:
- Identify a long-term goal for yourself.
- Research the resources you will need to achieve this goal.
- Interview an adult in your community who has accomplished an important goal.
- Prepare a goal checklist to share with your class.

STEP 1 Set a Long-Term Goal

Think about something you have always wanted to accomplish, or research activities that interest you in order to set a long-term goal. Why is this goal important to you? Write an essay to:

The Skills Behind the Project

Life Skills

Key personal and relationship skills you will use in this project include:
- Planning ahead
- Analyzing skills
- Asking for advice

- Identify the goal you want to achieve and why it means something to you.
- Describe the ways achieving this goal will affect your future.
- Imagine how your life will improve after you achieve this goal.
- Predict how long it will take you to achieve your goal.

Analytical Skills
- Organize your essay in logical order.
- Use facts to back up your views.
- Summarize your opinions concisely.

STEP 2 Plan Your Interview

Use the results of your research to write a list of interview questions to ask an adult in your community about a time when he or she achieved an important goal. Your questions might include:
- Why was this goal so important to you?
- What steps did you take to achieve your goal?
- What do you think was the most important thing you did in order to achieve your goal?
- How has your life changed since you achieved your goal?

Life Skills Project Checklist

Plan	☑ Use independent reflection and research to identify a long-term goal.
	☑ Write a goal checklist of things you can do to achieve your long-term goal.
	☑ Plan and write your interview questions.
	☑ Interview an adult in your community and write a summary of what you learned.
Present	☑ Make a presentation to your class to describe your goal and explain the steps you would need to take to reach your goal. Also tell what you learned from your interview.
	☑ Invite the students in your class to ask you any questions they may have. Answer these questions.
	☑ When students ask you questions, demonstrate in your answers that you respect their perspectives.
	☑ Turn in the essay about your goal, your goal checklist, and the notes from your interview to your teacher.
Academic Skills	☑ Communicate effectively.
	☑ Speak clearly and concisely.
	☑ Adapt and modify language to suit different purposes.
	☑ Thoughtfully express your ideas.

STEP 3 Connect to Your Community

Interview an adult in your community who has achieved a long-term goal that was important to him or her. Conduct your interview using the questions you prepared in Step 2. Take notes and write a summary of the interview.

Listening Skills
- Make eye contact and respond appropriately and with interest to stories.
- Ask questions if you do not understand.
- Encourage the speaker to share with positive body language, such as nodding and smiling. Open-ended questions also encourage conversation.

STEP 4 Share What You Have Learned

Use the Life Skills Project Checklist above to plan and create your goal checklist to share what you have learned with your classmates.

STEP 5 Evaluate Your Life Skills and Academic Skills

Your project will be evaluated based on:
- Organization of your checklist.
- Content of your essay.
- Clarity of your presentation.
- Speaking and listening skills.

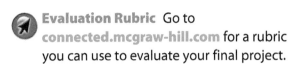

Evaluation Rubric Go to connected.mcgraw-hill.com for a rubric you can use to evaluate your final project.

Exploring Careers

Chapter 3 Pathways to Careers

Chapter 4 Workplace Skills

Chapter 5 Entering the World of Work

Unit Life Skills Project Preview

Career Map and Ladder

In this unit you will learn about the world of work. In your unit thematic project you will create a plan for achieving a career that interests you. You will also create a career ladder. A career ladder is a planned sequence of jobs through which a person progresses to achieve his or her career goals.

 My Journal

Explore your Interests Write a journal entry about one of the topics below. This will help you prepare for the unit project at the end of the unit.

- List ten subjects that interest you and explain why each interests you. These interests can vary widely and may or may not be a part of your current daily life.
- Identify and describe a career that can grow from one of your interests.

Explore the Photo

Often, part-time or summer jobs can open the door to future career opportunities. *Why is it important to maintain a good relationship with your contacts even after you move on?*

Chapter 3

Pathways to Careers

Section 3.1
Work and You

Section 3.2
Investigating Careers

Chapter Objectives

Section 3.1

- **Identify** the four major reasons people work.
- **Describe** the connection between school and work.

Section 3.2

- **Summarize** why it is important to consider skills, interests and lifestyle before choosing a career.
- **Identify** five different strategies for researching career options.
- **Describe** the benefits of experiencing a career firsthand.
- **Explain** why some occupations will no longer exist in the future.

Career Interests The more you know about a career, the better you will be able to decide whether you should pursue it or not. Many magazines, newspapers and Websites have articles about employees in different industries. Read a profile on someone who has a job in an industry you are interested in, and write a paragraph summarizing what you learn about his or her job. Summarizing the key responsibilities and required skill sets can help you see if a job is truly right for you.

Writing Tips Use these tips to write a summary:
1. A summary should present what you read in your own words and in a more condensed form.
2. Keep your summary short and to the point.
3. Summaries should cover only the most important points and major supporting details.

Explore the Photo

Career Path Your unique set of interests, skills, and talents can lead to a future career. *What factors might influence you to choose a particular career path?*

Work and You

Reading Guide

Before You Read

Predict Before you read this section, browse the content by reading the headings, bold terms, and photo captions. Then make a short list predicting what you think the section will be about.

Read to Learn
Key Concepts
- **Identify** the four major reasons people work.
- **Describe** the connection between school and work.

Main Idea
You can prepare for a career by learning about different businesses and employment options, setting goals, and gaining skills and experiences.

Content Vocabulary
◇ job
◇ occupation
◇ career
◇ entrepreneur
◇ lifelong learning

Academic Vocabulary
You will find these words in your reading and on your tests. Use the glossary to look up their definitions if necessary.
▢ philanthropy
▢ current

Graphic Organizer
List the main business types in the United States and their characteristics in a chart like the one below.

Business Types			
Characteristics			

 Graphic Organizer Go to **connected.mcgraw-hill.com** to download this graphic organizer.

What Is Work?

Imagine your life after high school. Will you go to a trade school or college? Will you find a job? What kind of work will you do? You may not have answers for these questions yet, but it is important to start thinking about your options so that you can prepare for them. Some day, work will be a big part of your life.

What is work? Work refers to any useful activity. Work is doing something productive with your time, whether it is cleaning your room or managing a small business. You may or may not be paid for it. Work that you do for pay is called a **job**. A job consists of certain tasks, and is a specific position with a company. Similar jobs are grouped to form occupations. An **occupation** is the type of work you do. You can change jobs and still have the same occupation. Say your occupation is graphic design, for example. Your job title could be Production Artist at one company, and you could take a new job as a Web Designer for another company, but either way, you are still a graphic designer. A **career** is a series of related jobs or occupations in a particular field over a lifetime.

Work takes up a lot of time. With a full-time job, you could spend more than 2,000 hours a year at work. That is why it is important to find a job that you enjoy. To choose an occupation or career that is right for you, you need to identify your skills and interests, as well as available opportunities. There are tens of thousands of occupational titles in the United States alone!

Why People Work

All over the world, people spend their days learning, making things, providing services, solving problems, and traveling. They perform a variety of jobs that provide goods and services. It is not possible for one person to make all of the goods and provide all of the services he or she needs in life. Can you imagine what life would be like if you had to grow your own food and make all of your own clothes, shoes, electronics, and sports equipment?

As You Read

Connect Think about the different types of jobs you observe people performing throughout your day. What jobs can you identify? Which do you find interesting?

◇ Vocabulary

You can find definitions in the glossary at the back of this book.

Ingram Publishing/SuperStock

> **Skills for Success**
>
> Many people learn new skills on the job. *What are some other benefits of work?*

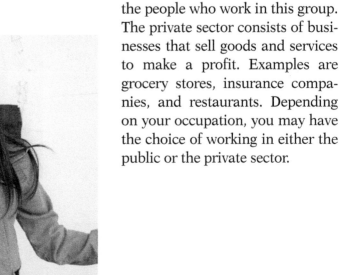
SUCCEED IN SCHOOL

Ask Your Teacher
Know when your teachers are available to meet with you and other students. Make an appointment with your teacher to discuss your progress in the class and any other concerns that you may have. Create a list of questions you want to ask your teacher before you attend the meeting.

When people work, they help their families, their communities, and themselves. Work fulfills several important human needs:

- **Money** Most people work to make money to pay for the goods and services they need and want. Food, housing, transportation, medical care, and education are just some of the things people need to survive. But people also work so that they can afford luxuries, the things that add to one's comfort but are not absolutely necessary, such as movies, sporting goods, and vacations.

- **Self-Fulfillment** People also work to feel good about themselves. Many people enjoy what they do and would not trade their work for another job, even if it paid more money. Work gives people a sense of pride. They feel valued when others depend on them and respect the work that they do. Being good at what you do can help you build confidence in who you are.

- **Philanthropy** Philanthropy means goodwill toward fellow humans, or an active effort to promote human welfare. Making a positive contribution to society is another reason why people may choose to work in a particular field. You may choose to become an environmental scientist because you are concerned about the state of the natural world. You may choose to become a teacher because you want to help children learn and grow. Devoting yourself to a cause that has a positive effect on the world around you gives you a sense of purpose and meaning.

- **Companionship** Finally, people work to be around others. Many people develop strong friendships at work and gain a sense of belonging. They enjoy being in an environment with people who have similar interests and goals.

The Work World

The more you know about the world of work, the better your chances are of finding a career that's right for you. The world of work consists of two major categories: the public sector and the private sector. The public sector is funded by taxes and made up of local, state, and federal government agencies. Teachers, police officers, and firefighters are some of the people who work in this group. The private sector consists of businesses that sell goods and services to make a profit. Examples are grocery stores, insurance companies, and restaurants. Depending on your occupation, you may have the choice of working in either the public or the private sector.

Types of Businesses

Most private sector businesses are small businesses. *What might be the benefits and drawbacks of working in a very small business?*

Types of Private Sector Businesses

Businesses in the private sector range from very small businesses with one employee to large companies with thousands of employees. There are three main types of businesses in the United States:

- **Sole or Individual Proprietorships** These businesses are owned and controlled by one person—the proprietor—who receives the profits if the business succeeds but loses money if it fails.
- **Partnerships** These businesses are owned and controlled by two or more people who share profits and risks.
- **Corporations** Corporations are owned by many people, called shareholders, who share in the profits and lose money if the business does not do well.

Entrepreneurship

There are millions of businesses in the United States, each started by an **entrepreneur**, someone who sets up and operates a business. Entrepreneurs are perceptive people. They follow business trends and discover needs other companies do not address. Once an entrepreneur decides that the possible rewards outweigh the downsides of a potential business, he or she accepts the challenge to build a new company from scratch. With their new ideas and their willingness to take risks, entrepreneurs create the proprietorships, partnerships and corporations that give millions of people a place to work.

Entrepreneurship provides the satisfaction of being one's own boss and the possibility of earning large sums of money. However, entrepreneurs risk losing the money they invest in the business. The failure rate of a new business is high, especially during its first years. Most entrepreneurs work long hours to keep their businesses profitable.

Employment Options

Both the public and the private sectors offer full-time, part-time, and temporary employment options. Most full-time jobs require seven or eight hours of work each day, five days a week, although some full-time jobs require more hours per week. Part-time positions, such as after-school jobs, vary and can range from one to 40 hours a week. Temporary jobs can be either full-time or part-time, but they only last a certain number of days.

✓ Reading Check **Recall** How does work fulfill human needs?

The School-Work Connection

School and paid work have several things in common. Learning in school can be hard work. Like work, school requires practice and commitment, even when you would rather be somewhere else. Most skills learned in school are necessary to succeed at work. Employers want to hire people who are committed to learning, work hard, and have good attendance records.

There are also differences between school and paid work. In school, students spread their efforts across a variety of subject areas. In the workplace, people try to choose jobs that allow them to work in areas that they like and in which they do well.

Another difference between school and work is that employers pay wages and require people to do a good job in return for those wages.

How I See It

WORK ETHIC

Sarah, 18

I never gave much thought about my work ethic until I worked as a waitress in a local restaurant. I didn't think about trying my best until I saw how hard my coworker Francesca worked. She helped everyone, rarely called in sick, and was always positive. I asked her how she did it, and she told me that she never really thought about her work ethic either! She said that her parents raised her to always give everything she did her all, no matter what. Now, I always try to follow her example.

Critical Thinking
Sarah suggests that having a work ethic means working hard all the time no matter what kind of day you are having. Do you agree? Why or why not?

©Hero/age fotostock

Because of this, employers often have less patience than teachers have. When a worker fails to show up at work, somebody else has to do his or her job. In the workplace, people who do not meet expectations often lose their jobs. Those who have not performed well in past jobs may not be considered for future ones.

Many jobs require lifelong learning. **Lifelong learning** means keeping skills and knowledge up-to-date throughout your life. Some companies provide or help pay for employee training and education. Wherever you work, it will be important to keep your skills and knowledge current, or up to date. In other words, you will need to become a lifelong learner.

Prepare for Your Career

Some teens have planned every step of their career paths before they enter high school. They have charted out the courses they will take, the activities they will join, and the training or education they will need for their first job. For most teens, however, career plans are much less clear-cut. In fact, career planning may seem of little use before your senior year of high school. Technology and social trends change the job market rapidly, and jobs that look appealing now may be drastically different when you enter the workforce.

Yet it is this unpredictability that makes some preparation essential. You want to be ready for whatever the future brings. These strategies can help:

- **Gain a variety of experiences.** You may be surprised at the different learning experiences that are open to young teens. From attending a science camp to volunteering in a soup kitchen, the more you learn about the world, the more you learn about yourself. For example, one teen discovered a real empathy for older adults when she went on rounds with her mother, a home health aide.

- **Focus on goals and priorities.** What do you want to accomplish in your lifetime? What matters to you? For many people, the answers to these questions develop over time. Each career path brings its own rewards. Staying aware of your values and expectations can help you decide which path to take and when, or whether, to change course.

> ### Experiences
> You can share your enthusiasm and knowledge with others to help them gain a variety of experiences. *Why might it be important for students to learn about ecology at a young age?*

Health & Wellness TIPS

Prioritize Health

Do not get so caught up in school, work, and activities that you forget to take care of yourself! If you do not take care of your body, you lower your defenses to stress and illness. Keep these guidelines in mind:

- ▶ Eat balanced meals at regular intervals.
- ▶ Exercise for 45 minutes 3–5 times a week.
- ▶ Get at least 8 hours of sleep every night.

Digital Vision/Alamy

- **Develop transferable skills.** These are "seed" abilities that can be grown and used in numerous job situations. For example, developing time management skills now can help you do your chores, finish your homework and still have time to play basketball after school. These same skills help a head cook perfectly time a five-course meal and help a teacher decide how two students can share a computer so that both finish an assignment on time.
- **Look at general trends.** You cannot always predict what a job will be like in the future, but you can make assumptions based on trends in society. You know that global events have a growing effect on the local job market, for instance. This can help you decide whether to consider jobs in a certain field.
- **Ask an expert on careers.** A school counselor or job recruiter, can help you discover what skills are always in demand. Use this information to analyze the classes you are taking. How are your classes helping you learn these skills? Make a list of future classes that would help you gain necessary workplace skills.

◄ **Trends**

You can read business periodicals to gain a better sense of global matters and market trends in many career fields. *Based on what you know about global matters and market trends, what kinds of career fields are you thinking of pursuing?*

Section 3.1

After You Read

Review Key Concepts

1. **Describe** what it means to be an entrepreneur?
2. **Explain** why you should develop transferable skills?

Practice Academic Skills

English Language Arts

3. Consult a career guide and look up jobs that appeal to you. Choose three jobs you are interested in, and list the benefits and drawbacks of each.

Social Studies

4. Interview a person in your community who works with the public. For example, you may interview a police officer, firefighter, or store clerk. Find out if this person's beliefs and values have helped him or her succeed in that job.

 **Check Your Answers** Go to connected.mcgraw-hill.com to check your answers.

Section 3.2

Investigating Careers

Reading Guide

Before You Read

Preview Determine the topics of the Reading Check questions throughout this section. Then, write a short paragraph predicting what you think the section will be about.

Read to Learn

Key Concepts

- **Summarize** why it is important to consider skills, interests and lifestyle before choosing a career.
- **Identify** five different strategies for researching career options.
- **Describe** the benefits of experiencing a career firsthand.
- **Explain** why some occupations will no longer exist in the future.

Main Idea

Understanding your own interests, skills, and aptitudes and exploring the variety of careers available to you will help you make a career decision.

Content Vocabulary

◇ skill
◇ aptitude
◇ career cluster
◇ exploratory interview
◇ fringe benefit
◇ mentor
◇ job shadowing
◇ internship
◇ cooperative program

Academic Vocabulary

You will find these words in your reading and on your tests. Use the glossary to look up their definitions if necessary.

▢ route
▢ proficient

Graphic Organizer

Fill in a graphic organizer like the one below with the different ways you can explore careers firsthand.

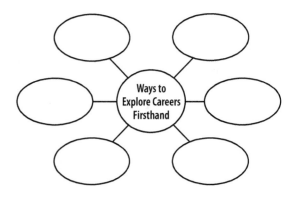

Ways to Explore Careers Firsthand

 Graphic Organizer Go to **connected.mcgraw-hill.com** to download this graphic organizer.

Take a Personal Inventory

As You Read

Connect As you read, think about how you like to spend your free time. How can your activities help you find a career you will enjoy?

◆ Vocabulary

You can find definitions in the glossary at the back of this book.

Current research shows most people change careers several times in their lifetime. Now is a good time to do some detective work and learn as much as possible about careers you might enjoy. Once you have an idea of the sort of work you would like to do, you can use career information as a road map, choosing your destinations and determining the best route, or course of action, to reach your workplace goals.

To understand your possibilities in the working world, start by looking at yourself. The more you know about your skills, interests and desired lifestyle, the easier it will be to pick your career path.

Skills and interests are two very different things. An interest is something you like to do, and a **skill** is the ability to do a certain task well. A person may be interested in an occupation but may not be willing to invest the time and effort to develop the skills needed to succeed at it. Another person may have natural talent but may not be interested in using these skills for paid work. While people usually learn to enjoy the activities they can do well more and more over time, this is not always the case. Ideally, you should choose an occupation that suits both your skill-sets and interests.

Interests

To help identify interests that could lead to a career, ask yourself which activities you enjoy most and which you think you would enjoy doing more than 2,000 hours each year. This is the average number of hours people spend at work in a year.

You might be surprised to find out that your answers to the questions are different. Some activities seem interesting but lose their attraction when you have to do them constantly. Nola, for example, loves camping and working outdoors at her uncle's ranch, yet she has no desire to work outside in the snow, rain, or extreme heat. She decided that, for her, outdoor activities were hobbies to enjoy rather than occupations.

➤ Hobbies

Hobbies you have now can lead to a career later in life. *Which of your hobbies could lead to a future career? Explain.*

moodboard/Corbis

Skills

You develop a skill if you practice it enough. Some people become proficient, or well advanced, at a task more quickly than others, however. An **aptitude** is a natural tendency or talent that makes it easy for each of us to learn certain skills. Students may possess different aptitude levels in school subjects, athletics, mechanical ability, public speaking, leadership, and the ability to understand the feelings of others. To get a complete picture of your natural talents, list every skill that seems to come easily to you. If you are struggling with this list, you can identify your aptitudes through school activities and career aptitude tests. Family members and friends can also help you identify less obvious aptitudes you may have that could lead to a career. Pat chose accounting as a career goal for several reasons, including her aptitude for mathematics and her excellent memory for details.

 Talent

Discovering your talents will help you choose a career path. *What talents do you have?*

Lifestyle

As you consider a career path, think about the kind of adult life you want to have. What things are most important to you? The type of work you choose will affect many aspects of your life, including the money you make, the place where you live, and the way you spend your work and leisure hours. For example, some careers may pay well, but will require you to work long hours and live in a large city. If living in a rural setting is more important to you than a large paycheck, you may want to consider another career path.

✓ **Reading Check** **Differentiate** How do interests, skills and aptitudes differ?

Research Career Paths

As you begin to explore career options, you may feel overwhelmed by the number of available opportunities. You could spend years researching every single one. So how do you know where to begin?

One way to narrow your search is to use a career cluster system. A **career cluster** is a large grouping of occupations that have certain characteristics in common. The U.S. Department of Education has organized careers into 16 different career clusters (see **Figure 3.1**).

Ben Blankenburg/Corbis

Figure 3.1 **Career Clusters**

Career Characteristics The U.S. Department of Education groups careers into 16 career clusters based on similar job characteristics. *How might career clusters help you explore careers?*

Career Cluster	Job Examples
1. Agriculture, Food, and Natural Resources	1. farmer, ecologist, veterinarian, biochemist
2. Architecture and Construction	2. contractor, architect, plumber, building inspector
3. Arts, Audio/Video Technology and Communications	3. graphic designer, musician, actor, journalist, filmmaker
4. Business, Management, and Administration	4. executive assistant, receptionist, bookkeeper, business owner
5. Education and Training	5. teacher, trainer, principal, counselor, librarian
6. Finance	6. bank teller, tax preparer, stockbroker, financial planner
7. Government and Public Administration	7. soldier, postal worker, city manager, nonprofit director
8. Health Science	8. pediatrician, registered nurse, dentist, physical therapist
9. Hospitality and Tourism	9. chef, hotel manager, translator, tour guide
10. Human Services	10. social worker, psychologist, child care worker
11. Information Technology	11. Web designer, software engineer, technical writer
12. Law, Public Safety, Corrections and Security	12. attorney, police officer, firefighter, paralegal
13. Manufacturing	13. production supervisor, manufacturing engineer, welding technician, quality technician
14. Marketing, Sales, and Service	14. sales associate, retail buyer, customer service representative
15. Science, Technology, Engineering and Mathematics	15. lab technician, marine biologist, electrical engineer, cryptanalyst
16. Transportation, Distribution, and Logistics	16. pilot, railroad conductor, truck driver, automotive mechanic

A career cluster system is an efficient method of exploring occupations. The jobs associated with each career cluster often require the same types of skills. If you have the skills necessary for success in one occupation, there probably will be other occupations in the same cluster that suit your skill set and appeal to you. The career cluster system helps you focus on an occupation yet remain flexible to pursue a variety of job opportunities.

Career clusters also identify areas of academic emphasis for different occupations. You may now be studying a wide variety of subjects in school, but eventually you will need to narrow your studies to gain the necessary skills to succeed in certain occupations. Career clusters can help you focus your education.

You can receive information about career clusters and career opportunities from private companies, associations, and government agencies such as the U.S. Department of Labor. Your teachers, guidance counselors, librarians, and media specialists can help you gain access to these valuable resources.

Reference Works and Other Useful Materials

Your school and local library resources can help you explore careers and plan for the future. Many libraries have career information centers. You can search the catalog or database to find reference books, journals, magazines, DVDs and other media sources of career information. The U.S. Department of Labor, among other organizations, publishes many materials. Two especially helpful resources are the *Occupational Outlook Handbook and the Guide for Occupational Exploration.* The *Occupational Outlook Handbook* describes the type of work, the required training or education, and the future outlook for many careers. The *Guide for Occupational Exploration* groups careers into categories, such as careers that involve working with food, and describes many occupations within each category.

Online Career Research

The Internet offers an almost unlimited amount of career information. Web sites set up by companies, schools and colleges, and youth and trade organizations can be helpful in your career exploration. Company profile directories can also be found online, so you can read in-depth, current information about companies in all industries.

The U.S. government also offers valuable career information online, including information from the *Occupational Outlook Handbook* and the *Carrer Outlook*. The Occupational Information Network (O*NET) is another helpful resource. It provides information you can use to research career clusters and occupations and to determine which occupations match your skills and interests.

Exploratory Interviews

Once you have done the initial research and have a list of occupations that you find interesting, you may want to talk to people who do these jobs every day. Ask your family members, friends, neighbors, teachers and career counselors to help you locate people who work in your field of interest. Call each of these people to request an exploratory interview. An **exploratory interview** is a short, informal talk with someone who works in a career that appeals to you. Do not be nervous about asking people for interviews! People who love their jobs are often more than willing to talk about them, and are happy to help others who share their interests.

To get the most out of the interview, think about what you still do not know about your potential career. Prepare a list of questions to help guide the interview. You will probably want to ask your interviewee how he or she got started in his or her career. Questions such as "What do you like most about your job?" and "What do you do during a typical workday?" can also help you get a good feel for the career. At the close of the interview, ask your interviewee if he or she has any advice or words of wisdom for someone who chooses this career path.

SUCCEED IN SCHOOL

School Library

Librarians and media center specialists can offer you assistance in conducting research and finding the most helpful reading materials. They may also be able to help you with online tutorials and other learning programs.

Building Character?!

Respect Rob and a group of his classmates are discussing their favorite professional athletes. One of his classmates strongly disagrees with Rob's opinion and argues with Rob. Rob really wants his classmate to understand and respect his position but does not want to argue with him. How should Rob deal with his classmate?

You Make the Call

Should Rob try to prove his point? Or, should Rob tell him that they should respect each other's differing opinions?

Categories to Consider

As you gather up-to-date information about jobs, workers, employers, and educational opportunities, consider these categories of information to make the best career choice:

- **Required Education or Training** Educational requirements range from short-term, on-the-job training to as many as ten years of college and a doctorate degree. Most employers require some post-high-school education or training for job applicants.
- **Compensation** Earnings vary greatly among occupations and employers. Some jobs include regular pay increases based on the length of time a worker is employed. Employees can earn wages on an hourly rate of pay, or they may earn a fixed annual salary.
- **Employer Benefits** It is important to consider the fringe benefits offered with a job when comparing the income of two jobs. A **fringe benefit** is a service or product you receive for little or at no cost to you. They can include paid vacation time, sick leave, child care, health insurance, continuing education and retirement programs.
- **Nature of Work** This refers to the actual activities you do on a job, including the equipment used and the supervision received. It also includes whether you work alone or as part of a team.

TAKE CHARGE!

Attend a Job Fair

You can learn a lot about career opportunities at a job fair. Job fairs feature companies that are knowledgeable about the future opportunities in their field, and are looking to hire employees. When talking to company representatives at a job fair, keep these points in mind:

- **Prepare** Find out which companies will be at the job fair, and think about what you want to know about them. Create a list of questions to ask.
- **Wear Appropriate Attire** Remember that company representatives are more likely to take time to talk with you if you look professional.
- **Be Confident and Courteous** Approach a company's booth, smile, and introduce yourself. Ask if the representatives have time to answer your questions. Then, ask your questions in a courteous manner.
- **Get Names** After learning more about a company, you may decide you want to explore their career offerings further. Make sure to note the names and positions of the representatives you talk to. You may want to follow up about a possible internship.

Real-World Skills

Career Guidebook
Research and compile a career guidebook that others could use to find a job. Address methods of finding jobs and ways to learn more about specific industries. Make your career guidebook available to the career center at your school so other students can benefit from your research.

- **Working Conditions** Working conditions refer to the environment in which you work. Will you work inside or outside? Will you work alone, or with other people? Other conditions include work schedules, chances of job-related injury, and perhaps travel requirements. Do you want a job with regular hours or would you be willing to work extended shifts, nights, weekends, or holidays?

- **Job Outlook** Job outlook refers to the future opportunities in an occupation. Most job opportunities are created because of new industries or the retirement of existing workers. Other job opportunities may come about because there is a shortage of skilled applicants for necessary positions. When this happens, employers are willing to hire people that do not have the typical experience or education the position usually requires.

✓ **Reading Check** **Describe** How do career clusters help you research careers?

Experience Careers Firsthand

The best way to learn about a job is to try it out. Field trips are visits to job locations that provide a broad overview of what a certain career involves. If you are interested in publishing, for example, you might take a tour of a newspaper facility. You can learn every major step in the process, from writing room to printing press and discover jobs along the way that you never knew existed. Some tours may allow you to lend a hand in certain stages of the process.

If your schedule allows it, working part-time will enable you to observe a career from the inside. You can gain valuable experience, make personal contacts and put some money in your pocket at the same time. Students can benefit from developing special relationships with experienced workers. A **mentor**, or an informal teacher or guide, demonstrates correct work behavior, shares knowledge, and helps new employees adjust to the workplace. You can learn a lot by working closely with a mentor. Job shadowing, internships, and vocational programs are some other good ways to discover what careers you might enjoy.

▲ **Working Conditions**

Working conditions vary from job to job. Some occupations require working evening hours or overnight. *What jobs can you think of that require late hours or overnight shifts?*

Community Connections

Volunteer

Volunteering is a great way to learn about a career while giving back to the community. Hospitals, parks, and museums are just a few of the places you can volunteer. Non-profit organizations in your community are also great places to volunteer. Your experiences can help you develop important workplace skills while learning about important social issues.

Ingram Publishing

Job Shadowing

Did you ever wonder how much you could learn if you could see what a person actually does at work? Following a worker for a few days on the job is called **job shadowing**. The individual you observe follows a regular workday while providing a sample of the real work done on the job. You stay nearby and quiet, like a shadow. The person being shadowed may take time to answer questions and listen to your comments. Job shadowing can provide valuable information about the education and training needed for various jobs.

Because job shadowing is an individual experience, you will need permission from a parent or guardian and from the person you are shadowing. You may also need permission from your school. Some schools permit students to do job shadowing as a school-related activity. If so, you may receive credit for shadowing and for reports you write about your experiences. Ask your teachers or counselor about shadowing opportunities.

HOW TO . . . Try Out Careers

You have tried to determine which career is right for you. You have completed an inventory of your skills and interests, and you have interviewed and shadowed people in the workforce. What happens if you begin a job in your career path and realize it is not what you thought it would be? What if you are not enjoying yourself or the work is too stressful? What if your priorities change, for example, and you realize having time off is more important to you than having a high-paying job?

Keep your options open. If you change your mind about your career, do not feel as if you failed or that you are locked into one occupation. People in all stages of life change careers for a variety of reasons. What is important is to keep your options open, think about your interests, and figure out what you want to do next.

Time your change wisely. If you decide to leave a job, think carefully about how and when to do so. If you need the money, you may want to stick with your job until you find something new.

©RubberBall/Alamy

Internships

An **internship** is a short-term job or work project that usually requires formal commitment. Internships provide students with opportunities to do actual work, though generally without pay or benefits. Interns benefit from a broad range of hands-on experiences. Many interns spend time working in several departments of a company, learning which aspects of an occupation they like best while developing vital job skills.

Internships can also lead to full-time, paying positions. An employer is more likely to hire someone who knows the company well than someone who does not know company policies and processes. Even when a company does not have job openings, an internship will look good on your résumé and you will have developed contacts who can help you find a permanent job elsewhere.

It may surprise you to learn that internships are not just for the typical office environment. You can find internship programs at many museums, zoos, film production companies, landscaping architecture firms, national parks, and other unexpected places.

Consider your employer. Whether you need the job or not, it is always wise to leave on good terms with your employer. Let your employer know you will be leaving at least three weeks in advance, and continue to work hard for your remaining time. If you make a good impression, you can use your employer as a reference for future jobs.

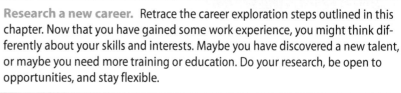

Research a new career. Retrace the career exploration steps outlined in this chapter. Now that you have gained some work experience, you might think differently about your skills and interests. Maybe you have discovered a new talent, or maybe you need more training or education. Do your research, be open to opportunities, and stay flexible.

Ask the right questions. Before you take a new job, think about the questions you wish you had asked yourself before taking the last one. You might ask yourself: Is the job rewarding? Is there opportunity for growth? Is the salary acceptable? Do the benefits meet my needs? Do the job requirements meet my talents and skills? Will I be comfortable working in this environment?

Robert Daly/Getty Images

New Careers

If you are good with languages and enjoy new experiences, you may find job opportunities in another country. *If a student is planning on pursuing an international career, what kind of skills might he or she consider developing?*

Cooperative Education

You can also get first hand experience through a vocational education program. These programs help you learn job skills while you are still in school. A **cooperative program** is an arrangement in which schools partner with local businesses. The students perform jobs that use the knowledge and skills they have learned in their school classes. They get class credit for working. A student who studies accounting may work part-time as a bookkeeper for a small company. A student who studies drafting may be placed with an architectural design firm. Some high schools create school-based businesses. Students learn marketing and retailing in class, and then get to apply their knowledge by working at the store.

✓ **Reading Check** **List** In what ways can you gain firsthand experience in a career?

Looking Toward the Future

The job market is constantly changing with increasing speed. To make smart career decisions now, you need reliable information about future job openings and industries. Some occupations will be eliminated because of changes in technology. Other jobs will be added because of new inventions and new ways of doing things. You will probably work at a job that does not even exist today!

Today's job market is very different from that of just 15 years ago. Job growth in industries that produce goods has slowed. The increasing number of service jobs, however, will likely continue. The service industry includes jobs in the media, healthcare, leisure, hotels, transportation, education, banking, government, retail, insurance and restaurants. Job opportunities in these areas are expected to grow over the next decade to meet the demands of a growing population.

With the growth in the global economy, and advances in communication technology, more and more careers will involve working with other countries. You may collaborate with people overseas on a project. Or you may decide to work in another country to experience a different environment and culture. English teachers, civil engineers and healthcare workers are just a few of the jobs that are in high demand. Above all else, good communication skills are needed to work with people from another country. The ability to respect and get along with many different types of people will also take you a long way.

Career opportunities will be unlimited for people who are willing to continue learning and can adjust to change.

Section 3.2

After You Read

Review Key Concepts

1. **Explain** how you can identify interests that could lead to a career.
2. **Identify** the categories you should consider when evaluating a specific career.
3. **List** three ways that a mentor helps a new employee.
4. **Identify** areas of job growth.

Practice Academic Skills

 **English Language Arts**

5. What kind of job appeals to you? Think of a job you find interesting, and write a brief letter to a potential employer outlining your skills. Be sure to emphasize how those skills make you a good candidate for employment.

 Social Studies

6. Interview someone who has a job that interests you. Ask the person to describe the job, emphasizing how the job has changed over time. Then, write a paragraph about how your understanding and appreciation of the job have changed after learning more about it.

Check Your Answers Go to connected. mcgraw-hill.com to check your answers.

Exploring Careers

Landscape Architect

JUPITERIMAGES/Comstock Images/Alamy

What Does a Landscape Architect Do?

Landscape architects design and plan attractive outdoor areas, such as golf courses, recreational areas, and gardens for buildings, roads, and walkways. They plan the location of flowers, shrubs, and trees, and the restoration of places like wetlands, mining sites, streams, and forests that have been disturbed by people.

Skills To work as a landscape architect you should enjoy nature and working with your hands. Creativity, strong analytical skills, and the ability to communicate both orally and in writing is important. Landscape architects also use all kinds of computer software to create presentations and to draft and design projects.

Education and Training Most states require that landscape architects be licensed. License requirements involve obtaining a degree in landscape architecture, gaining work experience, and passing an exam. College courses that you are likely to take include surveying, landscape design, construction and ecology, and urban and regional planning.

Job Outlook New construction spurred by a growing population ensures that the demand for landscape architects will increase faster than the average for all occupations. However, in places that face slow real estate sales and construction activity, fewer jobs may be available.

Critical Thinking Imagine that you have been employed to design the landscape for an attractive shopping center, using plants and construction materials available in your local environment. Write a paragraph describing what features and materials you might include.

Career Cluster
Architecture and Construction

Landscape architects work in the Architecture and Construction career cluster. Here are some of the other jobs in this career cluster:

- Surveyor
- Biologist
- Carpenter
- Hazardous Material Remover
- Photogrammetrist
- Cartographer
- Drywall Installer
- Civil Engineer
- Architect
- Conservation Scientist
- Electrician
- Drafter
- Hydrologist
- Urban and Regional Planner
- Interior Designer
- Specification Writer
- Cost Estimator
- Construction Manager
- Mason
- Environmental Engineer

Explore Further Research this career cluster. Choose a career in this cluster that appeals to you and write a career profile.

CHAPTER SUMMARY

Section 3.1
Work and You

People work to benefit themselves, their families and their communities. Most businesses are classified as a sole proprietorship, a partnership, or a corporation. School and work have some common features, but they are very different in some ways. Lifelong learning is important in today's rapidly changing workplace. You can prepare for your future career by gaining a wide variety of experiences and developing transferable skills.

Section 3.2
Investigating Careers

People tend to make better career decisions when they understand their interests, skills, desired lifestyles and aptitudes. You can research careers using a career cluster system, exploratory interviews and print and online resources. Experiencing a career firsthand is one of the best ways to learn about it. Internships and cooperative education programs help you get real-world experience. The job market is constantly changing so continuous learning is extremely important.

Vocabulary Review

1. Use these content and academic vocabulary terms to create a crossword puzzle on graph paper. Use the definitions as clues.

Content Vocabulary
◇ job (p. 63)
◇ occupation (p. 63)
◇ career (p. 63)
◇ entrepreneur (p. 65)
◇ lifelong learning (p. 67)
◇ skill (p. 70)
◇ aptitude (p. 71)

◇ career cluster (p. 71)
◇ exploratory interview (p. 73)
◇ fringe benefit (p. 74)
◇ mentor (p. 75)
◇ job shadowing (p. 76)
◇ internship (p. 77)
◇ cooperative program (p. 78)

Academic Vocabulary
▢ philanthropy (p. 64)
▢ current (p. 67)
▢ route (p. 70)
▢ proficient (p. 71)

Review Key Concepts

2. Identify the four major reasons people work.
3. Describe the connection between school and work.
4. Summarize why it is important to consider skills, interests, and lifestyle before choosing a career.
5. Identify five different strategies for researching career options.
6. Describe the benefits of experiencing a career firsthand.
7. Explain why some occupations will no longer exist in the future.

Critical Thinking

8. Compare and contrast List similarities between job fairs and online job searches. How are they different? Which strategy do you think would be more valuable to someone seeking a job? Why?
9. Apply Name the various resources available to plan a career path. Then, summarize your personal skills and interests. How would you use this information to prepare your career path?
10. Judge What are the benefits and drawbacks of taking an unpaid job?
11. Draw conclusions How are your school experiences helping prepare you to be an effective employee?

ACTIVE LEARNING

12. Job Interview Follow your teacher's instructions to form pairs. Role-play a short job interview with a partner. One of you should act as the employer, and the other should act as the potential employee. The interview can be for any job you and your partner choose to research. However, the questions asked by the employer and the responses given by the potential employee should focus on the required skills and duties of the job. You should each write your own parts, but can help each other if you are struggling to come up with appropriate questions and responses. Be sure to keep your tone and behavior formal and respectful throughout the entire interview.

Family & Community Connections

13. Changing Careers Interview an adult who has made a career change. Ask the person to describe his or her current and past careers. What did he or she enjoy most about his or her past career? What does he or she enjoy most about the new career? Ask what it was about the previous career that led to the desire for a change. Find out if the transition was difficult, and if he or she is happier with the new career. Why, or why not? After you have finished your interview, compare and contrast the two careers you discussed. Write a paragraph about the relationship between the two. Are they both part of the same career cluster? What are the differences between them? Finally, explain the reasons you think most people change careers. Do you think most career changes occur between two careers in the same cluster?

Real-World Skills and Applications

Leadership Skills

14. Research an Organization Research a student or community organization in an area of interest to you, such as a school or local newspaper. Write a few paragraphs describing the organization and the roles and responsibilities of its leaders. Then, consider the skills necessary to leaders of the organization. Describe ways in which the responsibilities can be further split up among organization leaders and members. Also, list ways that people can develop the necessary skills to meet the tasks of their specific jobs.

Financial Literacy

15. The Job Search Cost Suppose you are looking for a new job and need to go on a number of interviews. You buy new clothes that cost $57.63 total. You end up taking 8 bus trips to get to and from your interviews and each trip costs $1.25. How much money overall do you spend searching for a job?

Information Literacy

16. Career Skills Choose a job of interest to you, and research the required academic or technical skills for the job. Use the *Occupational Outlook Handbook* available from the U.S. Department of Labor or another source to gather information. Which skills do you already possess? Which do you need to learn? How will you go about acquiring the necessary skills you do not already possess?

Academic Skills

English Language Arts

17. Nominate a Mentor Imagine you are nominating someone for "Mentor of the Year." Write a letter explaining the reasons for your nomination. Describe the traits that make the person a good mentor. If you have trouble thinking of mentors, consider your teachers, coaches, classmates, and counselors.

Science

18. Water as a Solid What happens to water as it freezes and melts? Use this experiment to find out.

Procedure Place one ice cube in a glass and fill the glass with water until it overflows. Wait for the ice to melt without disturbing the glass. Note the effect.

Analysis Note the distance between the top of the glass and the water level and reach a conclusion about the effect of melting ice.

Mathematics

19. Weekly Expenses Suppose you spend $22.00 a week on food, $35.00 a week on clothing, and $33.00 dollars a week on entertainment. You do not have a car so you ride the bus to get to work. If you also spend $30.00 a week on transportation, how many hours per week do you need to work if you make $8.50 an hour and 15 percent of this is taken out for taxes?

Math Concept **Division** In a division problem, the number that is divided is called the dividend. The number by which another number is divided is called the divisor.

Starting Hint First, add together your weekly expenses to discover how much money you spend per week. Then, find out how much you actually make per hour after taxes. Divide your weekly expenses by your hourly take-home pay to find how many hours per week you must work.

 For math help, go to the Math Appendix at the back of the book.

Standardized Test Practice

ENGLISH WORD PROBLEMS
Directions Read the paragraph. Then, choose which sentence should be removed.

Test-Taking Tip When reading a question with multiple answer choices, try to think of the answer before looking at the choices. If your answer is not an option, eliminate the choices you feel are incorrect and take an educated guess among the choices that remain.

20. (1) I can either take the 12:20 bus or the 1:15 bus. (2) The 12:20 bus is usually more crowded, but I would like to arrive as soon as possible. (3) The weather is very nice today. (4) I was late last time, and I don't want to be late again.
a) sentence 1
b) sentence 2
c) sentence 3
d) sentence 4

Chapter 4

Workplace Skills

Section 4.1
Employability Skills

Section 4.2
Navigating the Workplace

Chapter Objectives

Section 4.1

- **Distinguish** task-specific skills from transferable skills.
- **Explain** how academic skills are used in the workplace.
- **Identify** the seven employability skills necessary for success in the workplace.

Section 4.2

- **Describe** the personal characteristics of an ideal employee.
- **List** four issues you may encounter in the workplace.
- **Explain** why mastering employability skills is critical in today's job market.

⬥ Explore the Photo

It is never too early to start developing the characteristics of an ideal employee. *What characteristics do you think you should start developing now to make you a model employee in the future?*

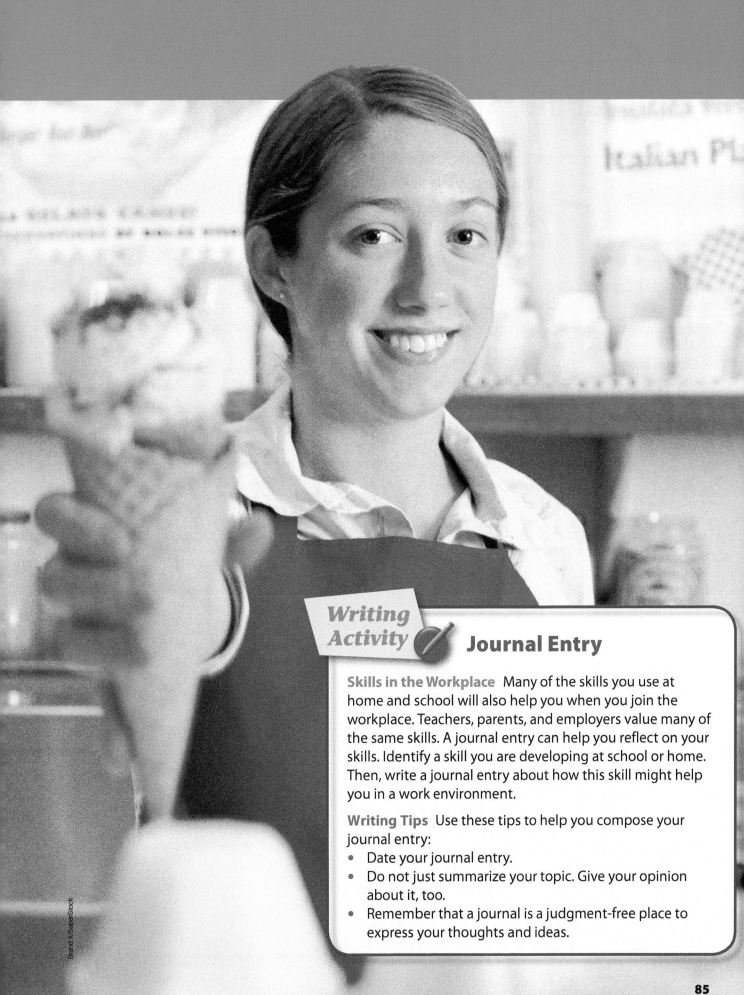

Writing Activity

Journal Entry

Skills in the Workplace Many of the skills you use at home and school will also help you when you join the workplace. Teachers, parents, and employers value many of the same skills. A journal entry can help you reflect on your skills. Identify a skill you are developing at school or home. Then, write a journal entry about how this skill might help you in a work environment.

Writing Tips Use these tips to help you compose your journal entry:

- Date your journal entry.
- Do not just summarize your topic. Give your opinion about it, too.
- Remember that a journal is a judgment-free place to express your thoughts and ideas.

Section 4.1

Employability Skills

Before You Read

What You Want to Know Write a list of what you want to know about this section. As you read, write down the heads in this section that provide the information.

Read to Learn

Key Concepts

- **Distinguish** task-specific skills from transferable skills.
- **Explain** how academic skills are used in the workplace.
- **Identify** the seven employability skills necessary for success in the workplace.

Main Idea

Employers need workers with many different kinds of skills. Developing strong academic and employability skills will help you to become a valued employee.

Content Vocabulary

◇ transferable skill
◇ academic skill
◇ thinking skill
◇ problem solving
◇ teamwork
◇ work ethic

Academic Vocabulary

You will find these words in your reading and on your tests. Use the glossary to look up their definitions if necessary.

☐ implement
☐ obtain

Graphic Organizer

As you read, record the academic skills critical for workplace success. Use a graphic organizer like the one below to organize your information.

Academic Skills

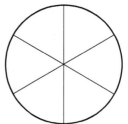

 Graphic Organizer Go to **connectED.mcgraw-hill.com** to download this graphic organizer.

Skills for Success in the Workplace

Thinking about your future and what will be required of you at work can be scary. It is normal to question whether you have the skills to be a successful employee.

Skills are things you know how to do. They are the result of knowledge combined with experience. Skills include tasks you are good at, or even ways of behaving. Some skills you use only for specific tasks. For example, knowing how to drive a car, how to water a plant, or how to give correct change are task-specific skills. A skill that you can use in many different situations is called a **transferable skill**. Writing, getting along with people, time management, and making decisions are all transferable skills. For example, you can use your writing skills to write an essay for a language arts class or to send an e-mail to a coworker or friend.

Today's jobs require a combination of skills. Employers are looking for people who work well with others and who are capable of doing many things well. To prepare for your future, you should master a wide range of transferable skills. The skills you learn at home and in school form the foundation you need to succeed at work. Practicing these skills every day is the most effective way to develop them. Communication skills, math skills, thinking skills, and interpersonal skills will be especially critical in helping you adapt to and succeed in a new job.

✓ **Reading Check** **Explain** What are skills, and how do you develop them?

As You Read

Connect Think about skills a person would be able to use in many different situations. What multi-purpose skills do you have?

◇ **Vocabulary**

You can find definitions in the glossary at the back of this book.

Fotosearch Premium/Getty Images

◀ **Skills in Action**

Many skills you learn in school are skills you will use on the job. *What skills is this person using?*

Academic Skills

Each of the competencies in reading, writing, mathematics, and science is known as a core **academic skill**. Speaking and listening are basic communication skills. These skills are the tools, or building blocks, for learning. You will need the skills you learn in school to succeed in just about every workplace you can think of, from an accounting firm to a mechanic's garage.

Reading Skills

Workers need to be able to understand what they read, summarize the information, and apply it to their jobs. You use reading skills to read and interpret written text, including newspapers, magazines, instruction manuals, encyclopedias, dictionaries, and maps. Most jobs require a variety of reading skills. Higher-level jobs may also call for the ability to read financial reports, technical journals, architectural plans, or legal documents.

Writing Skills

At work, writing skills are used to communicate information, ideas, thoughts, and messages in written form. All occupations require the completion of job applications, business forms, and correspondence, such as written letters and e-mail. Higher-level jobs may also require the ability to take notes and write reports, speeches, and journal articles. The widespread use of computer-based communication has resulted in an increased need for clear writing skills and good grammar.

Math Skills

As an employee, you will likely be expected to know how to add, subtract, multiply, and divide. You also might have to work with decimals, fractions, and percentages and know how to use a calculator. A combination of math and reading skills is needed to figure out such things as wages, credit card expenses, bank statements, and budgets.

Science Skills

Science skills help you understand everyday physical and chemical reactions that occur at home and at work. Sandy used her knowledge of chemistry and her reading and math skills to develop a set of safety procedures for handling chemicals at work. She used her writing skills to document the new procedures. All four skills helped her research the situation,

Science You Can Use

Workplace Ergonomics

Use this experiment to experience the effects the angle of your keyboard has on the strain placed on your hands and wrists.

Procedure Type on a keyboard for five minutes. Then, change the angle of the keyboard and type for an additional five minutes. Note the effect of the keyboard angle on your hands and wrists. Is one position more comfortable than the other?

Analysis Note the angles of the keyboard and the strain each places on your hands and wrists. Consider the accompanying positions of your wrists and reach a conclusion about what is best for you while typing.

communicate the procedures to others, and calculate what it would cost to implement, or carry out, the new procedures. But you do not need to be in a scientific field to benefit from science. Loggers, for example, need to have a basic understanding of physics to protect themselves on the job and ensure that the trees they cut fall in the right direction.

Speaking Skills

Speaking skills are needed to organize ideas and communicate to individuals, small groups, and large groups. Much verbal communication in the workplace takes place in person, over the phone, through e-mail, and in meetings. Verbal communication is most effective when you present information in an organized way and in a clear voice. In any organization, you will need to talk to coworkers and communicate issues and ideas to your supervisors. If you get promoted, you may have people who work under your direction. Speaking skills are important in all three types of work relationships.

Corbis Premium RF/Alamy

Listening Skills

Effective listening skills help you understand another person's entire message. People do not always say everything that they are thinking or feeling. Besides the words being said, an effective listener pays attention to the speaker's tone of voice and body language. This allows the listener to discover the hidden messages, the feelings and attitudes the speaker does not say aloud.

When listening to others, it is important to show them that you understand what they are saying, whether you agree with them or not. When people are focused on getting their own ideas across, they often fail to hear what someone else is saying.

Ingenuity

Combining your academic abilities with problem-solving skills helps prepare you for challenging careers. *Why might employers value inventive employees?*

✓ **Reading Check** **Understand** What are the core academic skills, and why are they important?

How I See It

Simon, 17

I used to think geometry was pretty useless. I told my older sister that school does not teach you anything you will ever need to know in the real world. She laughed and said she felt the same way until she started using geometry every day as an architectural intern. She told me that architects spend years studying geometry to learn how to construct houses and buildings. Now, I try harder to see how each of my classes could help me in life. In English I am reading poetry from the Middle Ages. I know that if I can understand that stuff, I can understand anything!

Critical Thinking
List the courses you are currently taking. Explain how each of these courses might strengthen your problem-solving, creative thinking, logical thinking, and interpersonal skills.

Workplace Skills

Besides core academic skills and communication skills, there are other abilities that most employers will expect their employees to have. Workplace skills are skills that help you learn to effectively perform a job quickly. Developing these skills greatly increases your employability.

Technology Skills

Knowing your way around a computer and other current technologies is essential. These skills will prepare you for the modern workplace that relies on many different forms of technology to get things done. Whether you become an astronomer, a mechanic, an English teacher, or a bookkeeper, you can expect to use multiple forms of technology every day. To be successful in your profession, you will need to keep up with the many changes and advances in technology throughout your career. Take advantage of opportunities now and in the future to learn and update your technology skills.

Information Skills

Knowing how to obtain, or gain by planned action, information when you need it is very important in every workplace. You need to know exactly what you are looking for, and where you can locate it. You should also be able to determine whether a source provides facts or misleading opinions. With so many different sources of information on the Internet, it can be difficult to tell the difference between truth and fiction.

Analyzing and processing information are other information skills you will need. An effective employee must be able to make sense of his or her research and effectively communicate it to his or her employer, coworkers, and customers. This is especially important in today's diverse workplace.

Building Character

Politeness Sam works at a fast-food restaurant. One day the restaurant is short-staffed and the staff struggles to wait on the customers quickly. Near the end of Sam's shift, a customer rudely complains about the amount of time he has been waiting to order. Sam has been working as hard as she can and is upset by his comment. How should she handle the situation?

You Make the Call

Should Sam apologize, even though the wait is not her fault? Should she ignore the comment and continue with the transaction? Or, should she let the rude customer know he can go somewhere else if he does not like the service?

Interpersonal Skills

Interpersonal skills are people skills. Many employees deal with people from different backgrounds, cultures, and experiences every day. Because they must be able to work effectively in teams, teach others, or serve customers, employees need to get along with a wide variety of personalities.

People that have good interpersonal skills communicate clearly and thoughtfully consider the ideas and feelings of others. They make others feel respected and appreciated, which creates a positive working environment.

Thinking Skills

Each of the mental skills you use to learn, make decisions, analyze, and solve problems is commonly referred to as a **thinking skill**. Workers need to be able to think creatively and make the best decisions possible based on sound reasoning and facts. Using thinking skills to suggest a solution to a problem is called **problem solving**. Employers do not have time to make every little decision it takes to run a company. They want employees that can think on their feet and resolve small problems before they become big issues. Both everyday and long-term decisions call for thinking skills.

Teamwork Skills

How does playing on a soccer team, organizing a recycling drive, or working with your family to prepare a meal relate to your future work and adult roles? Teamwork skills are central to all these things. **Teamwork** occurs when members of a group work together to reach a common goal. Members cooperate rather than compete. Working cooperatively allows people to achieve goals that one person could not accomplish alone, while building trust and friendship with their teammates.

Whether as an employee or as a family member, you need teamwork skills. For example, teamwork skills help you work cooperatively with family members to plan a family trip or paint the kitchen. Teamwork skills are also used when employees work together to accomplish a task, such as serving customers quickly or cleaning a store after closing.

People with good teamwork skills can work through conflicts that might arise among team members. Conflict resolution techniques allow the team to discuss and solve problems, strengthen relationships, and make better team decisions. Left unresolved, conflict can be a major obstacle to a successful team.

▼ Technology Skills

Learning new technology is important in getting and keeping a job. *You might already know a lot about computers, but are there any other technological skills you might need to develop for a future career?*

Randy Faris/Corbis

Leadership Skills

Leadership skills are essential in the workplace. Leaders often motivate others with their positive attitude, enthusiasm, and work ethic. **Work ethic** means working hard, being honest, and staying committed to your work responsibilities. To set group goals and delegate tasks, leaders must be skilled at listening and working with others. Antonio is a leader at school. He organized a group of students to create the school's float in the city parade. He solved many scheduling difficulties and found two party stores that were willing to donate decorations when they ran over budget. Because of his leadership, the students were able to complete the job on time and won first prize.

There are many kinds of leaders. Some lead quietly, preferring to lead by example. Others are more vocal, frequently giving encouragement. Some leaders become involved in every part of a job, and others prefer to stay in the background until they are needed. Regardless of their leadership style, good leaders set a positive example for others to follow. They encourage tolerance and understanding. They help others in the group accept and appreciate all who contribute.

HOW TO . . . Be a Team Player

What do a promising athlete and a preschooler have in common? Both need to learn how to play well with others. The same is true of workers. Employers realize that in this competitive, global economy, valuable employees are people who fit in with existing team members and work together to add to a company's success. The following guidelines can help you become an effective team member.

Be Results-Oriented Focus on making progress, not taking credit or placing blame. With this perspective, put aside personality disputes and individual pride. Understand that you are only one part of the team and that everyone needs to work together to be successful.

Appreciate Diversity Respect each team member's cultural background and personal qualities. View these traits as assets. Each person's background and personality influence how he or she meets needs, solves problems, and deals with the world. Encourage others to bring these skills to the job and find ways to use them.

Image Source

Leadership does not always mean that you are the head of a team. Team members who actively lead from within a group make the whole team more effective. Team members who hold supportive roles can show their leadership skills in many ways.

- **Example** When the official team leader delegates a task to each person on the team, supportive members show leadership by doing the best work they are able to do. Having a good work ethic as a member of the team is leading by example. This helps motivate other members in the team to work hard, as well.

- **Initiative** A team member shows leadership when he or she takes the initiative to solve any problems that might derail the task he or she has been assigned.

- **Active Support** When team members lose sight of the common goal, a team can become divided and ineffective. Team members show leadership skills by staying focused on the common goal. They support and motivate other team members, as well as the team leader.

- **Outspokenness** When team members are able to express their opinions, they can help the whole team reach their goal in the best way possible. If a team member has an idea about the direction a team is headed, he or she shows leadership by voicing it to the official leader and the rest of the team.

Keep an Eye on the Big Picture Ask yourself "How does my contribution affect your contribution?" Seeing this relationship can help you decide how to direct efforts to best achieve goals. This might mean knowing whose job must be done first and pitching in to help do it. Or, it might mean seeing how the project could affect a company's ability to stay competitive in the future.

Understand Human Nature Recognize when someone needs praise, support, or even gentle criticism. Deliver this message in a way that inspires others to give their best. Remind yourself that everyone makes mistakes and that there is often more than one way to accomplish a particular task.

Be Positive Remember, it is not always easy to work in a group, but being optimistic and encouraging will make the task at hand much easier. The most effective team members are those who hope for the best and find the positive even in negative situations.

Communication Skills

Whether you are speaking to one person or a crowd, you want listeners to understand your message. To get your point across to listeners, you need to be clear about your message and how you say it.

Making sure your body language and your words say the same thing is important to effective communication. Body language, messages you send with your face and body, can communicate something different than your verbal message. When this happens, you risk sending a mixed message. A mixed message, such as smiling while speaking angrily, is confusing to listeners and hinders good communication. Successful employees avoid sending mixed messages.

Effective communicators in the workplace use assertive communication, which means they say what they mean in a firm, but positive, way. People are more likely to pay attention to what assertive speakers have to say and take them seriously. On the other hand, aggressive communication is overly forceful. It is seen as negative and tends to push others away. A third style of communication, passive communication, is the opposite of aggressive communication. Passive communicators are too timid to say what they mean. They tend to follow the crowd rather than stating their own ideas. Often, passive communicators fail to gain the respect of others.

Section 4.1

After You Read

Review Key Concepts

1. **Summarize** what employers are looking for when they hire new employees.
2. **Explain** when you might need to use a combination of reading and math skills in the work place.
3. **Identify** the combination of skills effective leaders possess.

Practice Academic Skills

 English Language Arts

4. Assume the role of a school newspaper reporter. Write a short article about teamwork skills in action. You might write about someone who displays excellent teamwork skills, or you might discuss skills that are essential to members of a team.

Social Studies

5. Interview an employer about skills he or she considers important when evaluating job applicants. Ask what he or she finds more valuable: transferable skills, such as the ability to get along with others, or skills more specific to the job. Share your findings with your class.

 **Check Your Answers** Go to connectED. mcgraw-hill.com to check your answers.

Section 4.2

Navigating the Workplace

Reading Guide

Before You Read

Stay Engaged One way to stay engaged when reading is to turn each of the headings into a question, and then read the section to find the answers. For example, Workplace Issues might be, "What are some workplace issues?"

Read to Learn

Key Concepts

- **Describe** the personal characteristics of an ideal employee.
- **List** four issues you may encounter in the workplace.
- **Explain** why mastering employability skills is critical in today's job market.

Main Idea

Employees with positive characteristics and work habits are more successful at completing tasks and dealing with workplace challenges than those without such qualities.

Content Vocabulary

◇ discrimination
◇ harassment
◇ downsizing

Academic Vocabulary

You will find these words in your reading and on your tests. Use the glossary to look up these definitions if necessary.

☐ address
☐ resolve

Graphic Organizer

As you read, identify the four issues you may encounter in the workplace. Use a graphic organizer like the one below to organize your information.

 Graphic Organizer Go to **connectED.mcgraw-hill.com** to download this graphic organizer.

As You Read

Connect Think about the characteristics that employers value. How many of these characteristics can be used to describe you?

Health & Wellness TIPS

Positive Attitude

Your mental health can influence your physical health. Studies show that keeping a positive attitude increases energy, wards off illness, and leads to a longer, healthier life. Keep these tips in mind:

▶ Look for the positive in every situation.

▶ Use positive affirmations to ward off negative thoughts.

Employee Characteristics

"Most people I fire are let go because they do not get along with others," says Nelson Ruiz. "Everybody has to cooperate with each other or the work doesn't get done, and I lose a lot of money."

Employers do not just expect employees to have appropriate skills. They also want the people they hire to have certain personal traits or characteristics. Most of these traits are the same ones that help you at school or in social situations. At work, these traits increase your effectiveness and lead to positive employer-employee relationships.

- **Positive Attitude** Your attitude is your way of looking at the world and the people in it. People with a positive attitude usually get along well with others and tend to be cheerful and enthusiastic most of the time. They complete tasks they do not like without complaining or trying to avoid them.

- **Initiative** Most employers expect their employees to take initiative. Taking initiative means doing what needs to be done without being asked. That could mean restocking shelves when business is slow, developing a training guide to help new employees, or volunteering to help a coworker meet an upcoming deadline. Your willingness to find and complete tasks that need to be done will be recognized by your employer and increase your value as an employee.

- **Honesty** Be honest with your employer and coworkers. Being honest includes not stealing money or property and being truthful about the time you spend on the job. Misusing time on the job by arriving late, taking long breaks, conducting personal business on company time, and stopping work early can be costly for employers. Dishonesty can also damage your reputation and make it hard to advance in your career. Think about how your actions would appear to someone you admire.

Positive Attitude

Employees who keep a positive attitude are more likely to be recognized by their employers. *What strategies have you used to stay positive in tough situations?*

Flint/Corbis

Professionalism

Following your employer's dress code and maintaining your work wardrobe help show others you are a professional. *Why is it important for employees to look professional?*

- **Flexibility** Flexible employees are willing to help with different tasks or learn new skills and technology. Flexibility allows workers to adapt to new situations, deadlines, or unexpected problems.
- **Work Ethic** Employees with a good work ethic are willing to do tasks that need to be done. They put their best effort into everything they do and they are likely to be recognized by their employers for having the company's interests in mind.
- **Responsibility** Responsible employees show up for work on time, ready to work. Employers can depend on them to finish their work correctly and efficiently and to not waste time or money. Responsible employees do their fair share of a job when working with others, and do not try to blame others for their mistakes.
- **Professionalism** Employees show professionalism in several ways. It is reflected in their appearance when they dress neatly and appropriately. It is reflected in their behavior when they treat others with respect and consideration. Successful employees choose to look and act their best so that they represent the company well.

✓ **Reading Check** **Explain** Why do employers consider a person's personal characteristics before hiring him or her?

Workplace Issues

Workplaces are not perfect. From time to time problems come up and need to be addressed. If handled positively, the issues are resolved, the working environment improves, and work gets done. Your workplace skills and characteristics can help you manage the workplace issues that you might encounter.

Building Character ?!

Trustworthiness Ricky was reprimanded by his supervisor for failing to show up for his shift, which Ricky's friend Erik promised he would cover. This was the second time Erik did not keep his word. What options does Ricky have in approaching Erik about his trustworthiness? What can he say to help Erik understand his actions?

You Make the Call
Should Ricky tell Erik that he can no longer be his friend? Or, should Ricky explain how Erik has become untrustworthy?

Criticism

Constructive criticism is an employer's means of evaluating what you are doing and letting you know what you can do to improve your tasks. If you want to improve your work performance and progress in your career, it is important to learn how to **address**, or deal with, criticism in a professional way. Here are some suggestions that can help you handle criticism.

- **Listen to the criticism.** While you listen, think honestly about your performance. Do not become defensive, blame coworkers, or sulk. Getting defensive will keep you from being honest with yourself, and will prevent you from learning and growing as an employee.
- **Understand the criticism.** Ask your employer to clarify the problem with your performance, if necessary. What exactly do you need to do better or in a different way? Find out what results he or she would like to see.
- **Make a plan.** Depending on the problem, you may need to break the solution into steps and take one step at a time. List the steps needed to meet your improvement goal.
- **Take action.** Stay focused and follow your list of improvement steps. Talk to your manager if you need support along the way.

Conflict

Conflicts can occur among people who have differing ideas or goals. Many conflicts are small and are quickly resolved. Others are serious and take time and effort to resolve.

Many work conflicts occur when an employee feels a need to be in control of certain situations that are not part of his or her job description. This can create a power struggle. Power struggles, or conflicts over roles and responsibilities, often disrupt the work environment for everyone. Other common causes of conflict are personality differences, poor communication, and jealousy.

Vocabulary

You can find definitions in the glossary at the back of this book.

SUCCEED IN SCHOOL

Making Mistakes

Realize that making mistakes is part of the learning process. If you make a mistake the first time you try to solve a problem or work on an assignment, do not give up. Double-check each step you took and continue working until you get the correct answer.

Criticism

By listening to criticism, you learn how to be a better employee. *What have you learned from another's criticism?*

Blend Images/John Fedele/Getty Images

Employee Discrimination

Diverse employees contribute different viewpoints in the workplace. *How might you benefit from working with a diverse group of people?*

If you are ever involved in a conflict, avoid complaining to your boss right away. Instead, schedule a time with the other people involved to talk things out, using the conflict resolution strategies described in Chapter 7. Working together to **resolve**, or find a solution to, a conflict can be a valuable experience. You strengthen many of the skills you need in the workplace, and you help strengthen relationships at work.

Discrimination

Every employee has a legal right to fair treatment. Even so, some employees suffer **discrimination**, unequal treatment based on factors such as race, religion, nationality, gender (male or female), age, or physical appearance.

Various state and federal laws make it illegal for employers to engage in discrimination.

- Two acts, the Rehabilitation Act of 1973 and the Americans with Disabilities Act of 1990, protect the rights of individuals with disabilities such as visual or hearing impairment, mental illness, or paralysis. These two acts make sure that employers provide wheelchair ramps and other job accommodations so that workers with disabilities can do their jobs.
- The Age Discrimination in Employment Act of 1967 protects the rights of workers who are 40 years of age or older.
- The Civil Rights Act of 1964 prohibits discrimination by employers on the basis of race, color, religion, gender, or national origin.
- The Equal Pay Act of 1963 requires that employers pay men and women equally for performing the same job under similar working conditions.

These laws protect both employees on the job and people who are applying for jobs. Know your rights. If you notice illegal or inappropriate workplace practices, you should voice your concerns immediately.

Digital Vision/Alamy

> ## Community Connections
>
> **Work Well with Others**
>
> Working well with people from other cultures is an important skill for an employee to have. People from different cultures bring unique ideas to their work. This encourages creativity. Help your work community by creating an environment that allows employees to share ideas freely.

TAKE CHARGE!

Solve Problems

Workplace problems or issues that you do not know how to solve can be frustrating. They might cause you to react quickly instead of clearly thinking through the problem. These steps will help you develop ways to solve your problems.

- **Be Clear** Verify, or confirm the truth, that your problem is not simply the result of a misunderstanding.
- **Get Advice** Talk to people you trust about similar problems they may have encountered at work and ask how they resolved them.
- **Talk to Each Other** Calmly and rationally approach the individual to discuss how you can work together to resolve the problem. Listen carefully to what the person has to say.
- **Find a Suitable Resolution** Remember, successful resolution usually involves a compromise.

Real-World Skills

Perform a Problem Role-play a problem-and-solution situation with a classmate. Prepare a five-minute presentation for the class. Stage a problem or misunderstanding, and then show how the problem is identified and resolved. Remember to use the given strategies. Then, ask class members to suggest other ways the problem might have been resolved.

Harassment in the Workplace

Behavior that is unwelcome and disturbing to others is called **harassment**. Persistent teasing, insults, bullying, and stalking are all forms of harassment. Sexual harassment consists of disturbing comments or conduct with sexual overtones. It includes unwanted and inappropriate touching, gestures, and jokes. Spreading sexual rumors and pressuring someone for dates are other examples of sexual harassment. Both men and women can be victims of sexual harassment in the workplace.

Any kind of harassment is unacceptable. When you constantly feel uncomfortable or afraid in the workplace, it can be nearly impossible to concentrate on your job. Your work will likely suffer as a result of the harassment.

When another person's behavior first makes you uncomfortable, you may choose to ignore it or stay away from that individual. If that is not possible, or if the actions continue, speak up! A confident and assertive response may be all that is needed to stop the harassment. First, let the harasser know that the behavior is offensive and needs to stop. Write down what happened, noting the date, time, and place. If the harassment continues, document each occurrence and tell a trusted supervisor or human resources representative. When harassment happens at work, your employer has the responsibility to make it stop. Remember that you have the right to work free from harassment.

✓ **Reading Check** **Identify** What are three common causes of conflict at work?

Skills for a Changing World

In past generations, many people took jobs when they were young and continued to work for the same company until they retired. Today the workplace is very different. You can expect to change jobs numerous times before you retire.

Some of these job changes will be your choice. Another company may offer you a higher salary or better job title. You may move away from the area because another family member lands an excellent job elsewhere. Or you may find you are not happy with your career choice and decide to try a new career that will better suit your interests, skills, and desired lifestyle.

At other times, job changes may be forced upon you, especially if a company moves work overseas or downsizes. **Downsizing** occurs when a company eliminates jobs to save money. Downsizing affects everyone in the workplace. Some employees lose their jobs, and others are given additional responsibilities to make up for the lost man power.

In such an unstable environment, how can you make sure that most of your future job changes are up to you? Master and continuously update your employability skills. These skills will help you stay employed in a changing job market.

Section 4.2

After You Read

Review Key Concepts

1. **Define** initiative and what can result from it.
2. **List** four things a person can do to handle criticism from his or her employer.
3. **Explain** why downsizing occurs and how it affects employees.

Practice Academic Skills

English Language Arts

4. Read a story in which a character is teased or harassed. How does the character overcome the problem? Do you think the character's solution would work in other situations? Why or why not?

Social Studies

5. In a small group, create a workplace scene in which one of several employees is not an effective team-member. Demonstrate how communication skills can be used to encourage teamwork. When you are finished, perform your scene for the class.

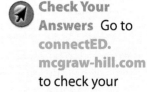 **Check Your Answers** Go to connectED. mcgraw-hill.com to check your answers.

Exploring Careers

Retail Buyer

What Does a Retail Buyer Do?

Retail buyers purchase goods, such as clothing, furniture, or electronics for resale. In other words, they shop for a living! Retail buyers consider price, quality, availability, and reliability when choosing goods. They try to get the best deals for their companies: high-quality goods at a low cost.

Skills Retail buyers should be good at planning and quick decision-making. They should be resourceful, and have good judgment and self-confidence. Marketing skills, leadership skills, and the ability to predict trends and identify products that will sell are also very important.

Education and Training Large stores prefer that applicants have a bachelor's degree with a business emphasis. Most trainees begin by selling goods, managing sales workers, checking bills, and keeping track of stock. Trainees are given more buying-related tasks as they progress.

Job Outlook Employment of retail buyers is expected to be very competitive, because there will be little job growth. As companies merge, individual buying departments are cut. Also, the largest retail stores are getting rid of local buying departments and are keeping the work at company headquarters.

Critical Thinking Choose a business in your city that hires retail buyers. Think of the reasons why you would be a great fit for the position. Then, write a paragraph detailing those reasons. Be sure to explain why you want to work for the specific business as a retail buyer.

Career Cluster

Marketing, Sales, and Service

Retail buyers work in the Retail/Wholesale Sales and Service career cluster. Here are some of the other jobs in this career cluster:

- Purchasing Manager
- Purchasing Buyer
- Procurement Clerk
- Wholesale Buyer
- Purchasing Agent
- Advertising Manager
- Promotions Manager
- Public Relations Manager
- Food Service Manager
- Insurance Sales Agent
- Lodging Manager
- Sales Representative
- Sales Engineer

Explore Further Research this career cluster. Choose a career in this cluster that appeals to you and write a career profile.

CHAPTER SUMMARY

Section 4.1
Employability Skills

Today's jobs require a variety of employability skills. Transferable skills such as writing, getting along with others, and making decisions are skills that you can use in many different situations. Workplace skills are skills that help you quickly adapt to a job and foster your success. Leadership styles vary, but good leaders motivate others and encourage tolerance and understanding. Teamwork skills help employees work through conflicts and accomplish goals.

Section 4.2
Navigating the Workplace

Employers look for specific characteristics in potential employees that make them productive workers. Employability skills and personal characteristics can help workers deal with workplace issues such as criticism, conflict, discrimination, and harassment. In today's rapidly changing job market, it is extremely important to master and continually update your employability skills. You can expect to change jobs numerous times before you retire.

Vocabulary Review

1. Create a fill-in-the-blank sentence for each of these vocabulary items. The sentence should contain enough information to help determine the missing word.

Content Vocabulary
◇ transferable skill (p. 87)
◇ academic skill (p. 88)
◇ thinking skill (p. 91)
◇ problem solving (p. 91)
◇ teamwork (p. 91)
◇ work ethic (p. 92)
◇ discrimination (p. 99)
◇ harassment (p. 100)
◇ downsizing (p. 101)

Academic Vocabulary
▫ implement (p. 89)
▫ obtain (p. 90)
▫ address (p. 98)
▫ resolve (p. 99)

Review Key Concepts

2. **Distinguish** task-specific skills from transferable skills.
3. **Explain** how academic skills are used in the workplace.
4. **Identify** the seven employability skills necessary for success in the workplace.
5. **Describe** the personal characteristics of an ideal employee.
6. **List** four issues you may encounter in the workplace.
7. **Explain** why mastering employability skills is critical in today's job market.

Critical Thinking

8. **Analyze** Your teacher asks you to organize an Earth Day project for the class. Which academic and workplace skills might help you achieve this goal? Why?
9. **Describe** Your friend has a job interview scheduled for next week. How might you advise him to show professionalism at the appointment?
10. **Evaluate** You need to hire an administrative assistant. What three skills or personal characteristics should he or she have above all others? Why?
11. **Predict** What might happen to employees who are unable to deal with criticism in the workplace?

 **ACTIVE LEARNING**

 Family & Community Connections

12. Personal Growth Think of a job that you find interesting. What skills are necessary for that job? Reflect on the academic, employability, communication, and personal skills you have recently read about. Make a list of the skills that you think would be useful in your chosen workplace. Create a second list of skills that are necessary for a good employee to have. Compare your two lists, and note the skills that you already have. Then highlight the skills  that you would need to gain or improve to be ready for the job. Then, list the steps you can take to practice and improve those skills.

13. Learn from Experience Talk to a trusted adult, such as a parent, teacher, or coach about a problem he or she encountered in the workplace. Ask the adult to describe the problem and what caused it. Then, ask him or her to tell you how the problem was resolved. Did he or she attempt to solve the problem by pointing it out to a supervisor or someone else in the workplace, or through some other means? Was the attempt to solve the problem successful? Was it a solution that lasted, or was it only temporary? After talking, consider how you would have acted if you were faced with the same situation. Do you think the way the person handled the problem was the best way? Why or why not? If you do not agree with his or her actions, suggest another way of attempting to solve the problem.

Real-World Skills and Applications

Leadership Skills

14. Defend Your Opinion Think of students in your school who display good leadership skills. For example, consider the captain of the soccer team or the editor of the yearbook. Describe the skills that make the students good leaders. Would these students be effective leaders in the workplace? Why or why not? If not, describe the skills the students lack that are essential to good leadership in the workplace.

Financial Literacy

15. Paid Vacation You are given two weeks of paid vacation as a bonus after finishing an important project at work. You make $12 an hour after taxes, and you work 40 hours per week. Will you be paid enough during your time off to afford a trip that will cost you $550? If so, how much money will you have left? If not, how much money do you need to save?

Cooperative Learning

16. Experience Helps Develop Skills Follow your teacher's instructions to form groups. Think of school activities that encourage young people to develop teamwork skills. You might consider clubs, teams, or the school newspaper. Do you think these activities do a better job of teaching cooperation or competition? Why? Can you think of another way to teach cooperation that is more effective? If so, describe it and the reasons you think it is a better method.

Brand X/SuperStock

Academic Skills

English Language Arts

17. Constructive Feedback Write a dialogue between an employer and an employee in which the employer provides constructive criticism. The employee should respond in a professional manner. Use language that sounds real and appropriate to the people talking. Write with accurate grammar and spelling. Remember to use quotation marks appropriately.

Social Studies

18. Valuable Qualities Interview a local coach or club leader about his or her team members. Ask the person to describe the qualities that the most valuable team members exhibit. How do their behaviors affect other team members? Write a paragraph about how these qualities might also be valued in the workplace.

Mathematics

19. Calculate the Cost When an employee misses a day of work, his or her company loses time and money. Say an employee costs an employer $150 each day the employee does not show up for work. During the course of a year, the employee does not show up for work two days every month. At the end of the year, how much has the employee cost the company in lost productivity?

Math Concept **Multiplication** In a multiplication problem, the numbers that are being multiplied together are called factors. The result of multiplying two or more factors together is called the product.

Starting Hint First calculate the number of days the employee would miss for the entire year. Then, multiply that number by $150.

 For math help, go to the Math Appendix at the back of the book.

Standardized Test Practice

MATH WORD PROBLEMS
Directions Read the word problem. Then, determine the answer.

Test-Taking Tip To solve math word problems, first note the information you need to solve the problem. Then, set up equations to find this information. Look for key words that indicate math operations. Solve multiple equations in the correct order.

20. An employer has lost $700,000 and needs to close one of its four branches. The workforce will be downsized from 550 employees to 500 employees. Expressed as a percentage, approximately how many members of the original workforce will lose their jobs?

Chapter 5

Entering the World of Work

Section 5.1
The Job Application Process

Section 5.2
Your New Job

Chapter Objectives

Section 5.1

- **Outline** the process of applying for a job.
- **Compare and contrast** résumés and portfolios.
- **Summarize** how to prepare for a job interview.
- **Explain** how to follow up after a job interview.

Section 5.2

- **Describe** the basic responsibilities of a new employee.
- **Identify** strategies for balancing work and family.
- **Recognize** the factors that lead to job success.

©Sam Edwards/age fotostock

Writing Activity

Topic Sentence

Introduce Yourself Cover letters are one way to introduce yourself to an employer and make a good first impression. Many employers only have time to briefly scan cover letters and résumés. Therefore, your letter should begin with a topic sentence that will grab an employer's attention. Think about your work experience and skills. Then, write a topic sentence that introduces you to an employer.

Writing Tips Use these tips to write an effective topic sentence:
- Use words and phrases that catch the reader's attention.
- Make sure you include only important information in the topic sentence.
- Remember, a topic sentence should briefly introduce or summarize your experience and skills.

Apply for a Job

Many people get their first jobs during their teen years. *What advice would you give this teen about applying for a job?*

The Job Application Process

Reading Guide

Before You Read

Preview Look through the images and photo captions in this section. Write one or two sentences predicting what you think the section will be about.

Read to Learn

Key Concepts

- **Outline** the process of applying for a job.
- **Compare and contrast** résumés and portfolios.
- **Summarize** how to prepare for a job interview.
- **Explain** how to follow up after a job interview.

Main Idea

Learning how to apply for a job, create a résumé, and impress a job interviewer are important skills needed for entering the world of work.

Content Vocabulary

◇ networking
◇ résumé
◇ chronological résumé
◇ skills résumé
◇ cover letter
◇ portfolio
◇ interview

Academic Vocabulary

You will find these words in your reading and on your tests. Use the glossary to look up their definitions if necessary.

▢ relevant
▢ indicate

Graphic Organizer

As you read, list the information that can be found on a résumé. Use a graphic organizer like the one below to organize your information.

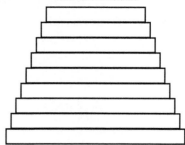

Contents of a Résumé

 Graphic Organizer Go to **connectED.mcgraw-hill.com** to download this graphic organizer.

Applying for a Job

Ryan thought he could get a job any time he wanted. After all, he was on the football team and had just been elected class president. However, after applying at several places for a summer job, he had not had any success. No job offers came his way.

Getting a job can be challenging. The employer wants the best person for the job, and you want a job you can do well and that pays a fair wage. A job offer is a two-way agreement that benefits both the employer and you, the employee.

Once you have one or more job leads, or information about specific job openings, you can apply for a job. The job application process is important in getting the job you want and should not be taken lightly.

Employers have several ways of getting the information they need to choose the best person for the job. Most employers start by asking you to fill out an application form, either on paper or online. Many employers also ask you to submit a résumé and cover letter. For some jobs, you may have to take a blood or urine test to check for illegal drug use. Other tests may include a performance test to see how well you can do a particular task, such as keying text or proofreading. Some employers also conduct background checks, which inform them of any criminal convictions you might have. Some employers do credit checks, which let them know if you are responsible and pay your bills on time. Many employers also search for your name on the Internet to see what sort of information they can learn from social media accounts you may have. This may give the employer an idea of your level of professionalism. For most jobs, you will also need to arrange a personal meeting with the employer. The way you provide employers with the information they want often determines whether you get the job or not.

As You Read

Connect Think about a summer job that interests you. What do you think this employer would like to know about you before hiring you?

Vocabulary

You can find definitions in the glossary at the back of this book.

Networking

Networking, or making use of personal connections to achieve your goals, is one of the best ways to get a job. Many people credit someone else with helping them find work. Some help by serving as references. Others help by encouraging people to explore career opportunities in a given area. They may be able to answer your questions or put you in contact with someone who can. Personal connections also allow employers to verify a job applicant's skills, experience, and positive attitude before offering a job to the individual.

✓ **Reading Check** **Give Examples** In what ways do employers get the information they need to choose the right person for the job?

> **Performance Tests**
>
> Find out what performance tests an employer requires, and brush up on your skills before applying. *What kinds of skills might be tested on a performance test?*

Fancy Collection/SuperStock

Résumés, Portfolios, and Cover Letters

Résumés, portfolios, and cover letters introduce you to future employers. A **résumé** provides a brief history of your work experience and education. It is a critical tool to help you get your foot in the door. Often your résumé is the first contact the employer will have with you. You want your résumé to look professional, stand out, and highlight your skills and competencies. Your résumé should:

- Be honest.
- Be error free.
- Be clear and concise.
- Use action words.
- Be printed on high-quality paper.
- Focus on skills, achievements, and accomplishments.
- Use keywords that correspond with the position you are seeking.

Prepare a Résumé

Most employers review résumés before choosing which applicants they want to meet in person. Your résumé highlights your interests and skills and includes some personal information. There are two kinds of résumés: chronological résumés and skills résumés.

A **chronological résumé** lists your work experience and employment history in chronological order, that is, by date. This type of résumé is excellent for highlighting the education and experience you have in a field. A chronological résumé is shown in **Figure 5.1**.

A **skills résumé** organizes your experience according to specific skills or functions. This format works well if you are changing careers or entering a field for the first time because it highlights transferable skills and abilities and downplays unrelated work experience.

If an employer is looking for someone who has a specific skill, the reviewer will eliminate résumés that fail to identify the requested skill.

An electronic résumé is a chronological or skill-based résumé that is formatted for electronic submission. Electronic résumés are usually created in plain text, without any formatting such as boldface, indents, bullets, or underlines.

Skills Résumés

You can list skills you have developed on the job and in your classes. *What skills do you think this student can mention on her résumé?*

Hero Images/Getty Images

Figure 5.1   **Using a Résumé**

Chronological Résumé   A résumé identifies work experience, accomplishments, and your educational background. *What work experience and accomplishments would you put on your résumé?*

James Smith
123 Main Street, Springfield, IN 55555
(555) 555–5555

CAREER OBJECTIVE   A paid position as a preschool teacher assistant.

WORK EXPERIENCE AND ACCOMPLISHMENTS

- Three years of experience babysitting for five families
- Two years as an assistant coach for Little League baseball and helping care for my two younger brothers
- Class president of Family, Career and Community Leaders of America (FCCLA)
- Completed Red Cross CPR and first aid training courses
- Sophomore student at Hayes High School, currently on the honor roll

EDUCATION AND TRAINING

Present   Hayes High School, 23 Oak Street, Springfield, Indiana

2006   Red Cross CPR Training Program Certificate of Completion

SCHOOL ACTIVITIES

- Active member of FCCLA for two years, current class president
- Manager of junior varsity football team
- Member of National Honor Society

COMMUNITY ACTIVITIES

- Assistant coach for Little League baseball, Springfield Recreation Department

REFERENCES

References available upon request

After-School Programs

Some communities offer after-school and summer programs that help students increase their academic skills. Check your local newspaper or school bulletin board to see if these services are available in your area.

Building Character ?!

Professionalism Over the past two weeks you submitted several job applications. Your friend, Tristan, posted a photo on your social networking site a few days ago that he thinks is funny. You're worried, though, that if employers see your profile page, they may think it's unprofessional. Tristan has sent you a text message asking if you've seen the photo. If you delete it from your profile, Tristan will know. How can you explain your situation to Tristan without him becoming upset?

You Make the Call

It's hard to control what others post on your social media profiles. How can you set up better guidelines for yourself and your friends in order to appear professional to employers who happen to see your social networking sites?

The Contents of a Résumé

Include these items in the contents of your résumé:

- **Personal Information** Write your name, address, and telephone number. If you have a temporary or school address, you will want to include a permanent address and phone number as well. Do not include other personal information (marital status, height, weight, health, interests, or hobbies) unless you think it is relevant, or related, to the job. Keep it simple. Adding unessential information only clutters up your résumé and detracts from the essential information.

- **Job Objective** Include a job objective if you are seeking a specific job. You may be willing to accept various jobs in a company, especially if you are a new graduate with little experience. If you decide not to list your job objective, you can use the cover letter to relate your résumé to the specific job for which you are applying. A cover letter tells the employer that you are applying for a position in the company.

- **Education** List your degrees, schools attended, dates of study, and major field of study. Include related educational experience that may be relevant to the job, such as certification, licensure, advanced training, intensive seminars, and summer study programs. Do not list individual classes on your résumé. If you have special classes that relate directly to the job you are applying for, list them in your cover letter.

- **Awards and Honors** List awards and honors that are related to the job or indicate excellence. In addition, you may want to list special qualifications that relate to the job, such as fluency in a foreign language. Highlight this information prominently. Pack a persuasive punch by displaying your best qualifications up front.

- **Work Experience** If you use the chronological résumé format, you will list the title of your last job first, dates worked, and a brief description of your duties. Do not clutter your résumé with needless detail or irrelevant jobs. You can elaborate on specific duties in your cover letter and when you speak with the employer.

- **Skills and Abilities** If you use the skills-based résumé format, categorize your accomplishments and work experience by types of skills and abilities, such as attention to detail or interpersonal skills. After each heading, describe how you have demonstrated these skills and abilities in school and on the job. If you use the chronological résumé format, highlight your skills and abilities in the descriptions of your job duties and accomplishments.

- **Campus and Community Activities** List activities that show leadership abilities and a willingness to make a contribution to the community.

- **Professional Memberships and Activities** List professional memberships, speeches you have given, or research projects you have been involved in.

- **References** References can be provided upon request. However, make sure that you have contacted the individuals you plan to use for references. Include, if possible, former employers and teachers.

Write a Cover Letter

Generally, a résumé is sent with a cover letter, although some employers do not require a cover letter. The cover letter is the first thing a potential employer sees, and it can make a powerful impression. If you are going to get the great job you want, you need to write a great cover letter. Think of a cover letter as an introduction: a piece of paper that conveys a smile, a confident hello, and a nice, firm handshake. Here are some tips for creating a cover letter that is professional and gets the attention you want:

- **Keep it short.** Your cover letter should be no more than one page.
- **Make it look professional.** Use word-processing software to write your cover letter, and print it on a laser printer. Use white or buff-colored paper. Include your name, address, phone number, and e-mail address at the top of the page.
- **Explain why you are writing.** Start your letter with one sentence describing where you heard of the opening. "Joan Wright suggested I contact you regarding a position in your marketing department" or, "I am writing to apply for the position you advertised in the *Sun City Journal.*"
- **Introduce yourself.** Give a short description of your professional abilities and background. Refer to your attached résumé: "As you will see in the attached résumé, I am an experienced editor with a background in newspapers, magazines, and textbooks." Then highlight one or two specific accomplishments.
- **Sell yourself.** Your cover letter should leave the reader thinking, "This person is exactly what we are looking for." Focus on what you can do for the company. Relate your skills to the skills and responsibilities mentioned in the job listing. If the ad mentions solving problems, relate a problem you solved at school or work. If the ad mentions specific skills or knowledge required, mention your mastery of these in your letter. Be sure these skills are included on your résumé.

Wavebreakmedia Ltd/Getty Images

References

Former employers, teachers, and the parents of friends can be good references. *Whom would you include in your list of references?*

Math You Can Use

Take-Home Pay

Ivan works at a pizza restaurant. He makes $8.50 an hour. Every time Ivan is paid, 25 percent of his income is taken out in taxes. Ivan works 15 hours a week. How much money will Ivan make after taxes in one week?

Math Concept **Percents** Percentages can be calculated by multiplying a number by the "other" percent. So, instead of multiplying by 0.25, multiply by 0.75 to figure out in one step what the number will be.

Starting Hint Ivan has to pay 25 percent in taxes. That means he takes home 75 percent of his income. Divide that percent by 100 to get a decimal number. Then, multiply it by his weekly income.

 For math help, go to the Math Appendix at the back of the book.

- **Provide all requested information.** If the Help Wanted ad asked for "salary requirements" or "salary history," be sure to include this information in your cover letter. However, you do not have to give specific numbers. It is okay to say, "My current hourly wage is in the range of $10 per hour." If the employer does not ask for salary information, do not offer any.

- **Ask for an interview.** You have sold yourself, now wrap it up. Be confident, but not pushy. "If you agree that I would be an asset to your company, please call me at [insert your phone number]. I am available for an interview at your convenience." Finally, thank the person. "Thank you for your consideration. I look forward to hearing from you soon." Always close your letter with a "Sincerely," followed by your full name and signature.

- **Check for errors.** Read and reread your letter to make sure each sentence is correctly worded and there are no errors in spelling, punctuation, or grammar. Make sure that you have spelled your potential employer's name correctly. Also make sure that you have used his or her correct job title. Do not rely on your computer's spell checker or grammar checker. A spell checker will not detect if you typed "tot he" instead of "to the."

- **Have a friend or family member review your letter.** It is a good idea to have someone else read your letter once you have finished it. He or she may be able to offer suggestions for improvement, or might notice a spelling error that you missed.

Create a Portfolio

Some employers want to see a career **portfolio**, a collection of work samples demonstrating your skills. The work samples, or photographs and copies of the samples, are placed in a folder to protect them. They may include writing samples, artwork, or photographs of visual displays or models.

Instead of putting your samples in a folder, you can place your collection on a CD, DVD, flash drive, personal Web site, or professional social networking site. A computer-generated, or electronic, portfolio is another way to show your skills. An electronic portfolio helps you demonstrate a variety of skills you have mastered. For example, you might include an audio file documenting your fluency in another language or your debating skills. Or you might create a digital video spotlighting your theatrical talents. Portfolios are also very valuable tools when applying for scholarships. In addition to showcasing your skills, a well-presented portfolio can impress a selection committee and give you an edge on the competition.

✓ Reading Check **Evaluate** What is the purpose of a résumé?

Interview for a Job

An **interview** is a meeting between a job applicant and an employer. It is the employer's chance to meet you and learn more about you and your specific job skills. The time you spend with an interviewer may play a major role in the course of your life. Unfortunately, many people fail to prepare for an interview and have no idea what they will say or how they will act.

The way you present yourself when applying and interviewing for a job usually determines whether you will get the job or not. You can expect to be judged by the first impression you make. Employers tend to rate highly those candidates who are prepared, who appear genuine and enthusiastic, and who share the same values as the company. The following tips can also help prepare you for a successful interview:

- **Dress appropriately.** You will never get a second chance to make a good first impression. Nonverbal communication is 90 percent of communication, so dressing appropriately is of the utmost importance. Every job is different, and you should wear clothing that is appropriate for the job for which you are applying. In most situations, you will be safe if you wear clean, pressed, conservative business clothes in neutral colors. Pay special attention to grooming. Keep make-up light and wear very little jewelry. Make certain your nails and hair are clean, trimmed, and neat. Avoid carrying a large purse, backpack, books, or coat. Simply carry a pad of paper, a pen, and extra copies of your résumé and letters of reference in a small folder.

- **Be on time.** Make certain you write down the date and time of your interview. A good first impression is important and lasting. If you arrive late, you have already said a great deal about yourself. Make certain you know where to go and the time of the interview. Allow time for travel arrangements and parking.

- **Be poised and relaxed.** Avoid nervous habits such as tapping your pencil, playing with your hair, or covering your mouth with your hand. Avoid littering your speech with verbal clutter such as "you know," "um," and "like." Do not smoke, chew gum, fidget, or bite your nails. Most career development centers or public speaking classes will videotape you while being interviewed. It is excellent experience, and you can identify any annoying or distracting personal habits.

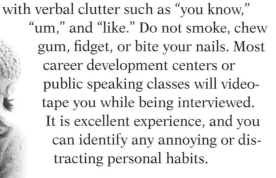

Rainer Holz/zefa/Corbis

◀ **Career Portfolio**

Your portfolio is a reflection of you. Make sure it contains your best work organized in an attractive manner.
What kinds of jobs might require you to submit a portfolio?

- **Maintain good eye contact.** Look your interviewer in the eye and speak with confidence. Your eyes reveal much about you; use them to show interest, confidence, poise, and sincerity. Relax and take a deep breath. You are relating to another person, not giving a speech to a large crowd. Look at the interviewer, and watch for body cues that indicate, or signal, understanding and rapport. Use other nonverbal techniques to reinforce your confidence, such as a firm handshake and poised demeanor.
- **Convey maturity.** Interviewers evaluate maturity by observing your ability to remain poised in different situations throughout the interview. Exhibit the ability to tolerate differences of opinion. Give examples of how you have assumed responsibility with little supervision. Employers greatly value maturity in their workers, because mature workers are less disruptive, require less training, and are more productive and successful than immature workers.
- **Avoid being too familiar.** Familiarity can be a barrier to a professional interview. Make the effort to know your interviewers' titles and the correct pronunciation of their names prior to the interview. Address them by their last name unless asked to do otherwise and never sit down or enter a room before your interviewers, unless directed to do so.
- **Be professional.** Reliability, an excellent appearance, and proper business manners are all part of professionalism. Do not ramble, or talk too much about your personal life. For example, "Tell me about yourself" is not an invitation to discuss your personal life. Also, never bad-mouth your former employers. This is unprofessional and says more about you than about them.
- **Answer questions fully.** Be clear, concise, and direct. Even if the interviewer is easygoing and friendly, remember why you are there.
- **Be prepared.** Successful interviews are the result of good preparation. Preparation will give you the information you need, and more importantly, the confidence to succeed.

Presentation

First impressions are lasting impressions. *What can you do to make sure your first impression is a good one?*

Caia Images/Glow Images

- **Know the company.** Your ability to convince an employer that you understand and are interested in the field you are interviewing to enter is important. Show that you have knowledge about the company and the industry. What products or services does the company offer? How is it doing? What is the competition? Demonstrate your understanding of the company: "I understand that your sportswear doubled in sales last year. According to current retail journals, this is in response to the company's marketing of its exercise clothes as the new action clothes for sports and casual wear."

- **Find out about the position before you interview.** Ask the personnel office to send you a job description. Use information from the job description to determine what the company is looking for in applicants for the position. You will likely be asked the common question, "Why are you interested in this job?" Be prepared to answer with a reference to the company. A sample answer: "Your store has opened up several new branches in the last two years, so I believe that there is great opportunity in your organization. I also feel that I have the necessary skills and personal qualities to make a contribution."

- **Relate your experiences to the job.** Use every question as an opportunity to show how the skills you have relate to the job. Use examples of school, previous jobs, internships, volunteer work, leadership in clubs, and experiences growing up to indicate that you have the personal qualities, aptitude, and skills needed at this new job. You want to get the point across that you are hard working, honest, dependable, loyal, a team player, and mature. You might mention holding demanding part-time jobs while going to school, working in the family business, being president of your business club, or handling the high-pressured job of working in customer service at a department store during holidays.

> **Research**

Learning as much as you can about a company can help make an interview go smoothly and demonstrate your interest in the business. *What resources can you use to learn about a company that interests you?*

Banana Stock/Photolibrary

Eat Breakfast

There is a reason breakfast is called the most important meal of the day. It is hard to stay awake and focus when you are hungry. Eating a good breakfast can help you feel physically and mentally energized all day long. The following breakfasts will help get you going in the morning:

▶ Two scrambled eggs, wheat toast, and fruit slices or juice

▶ Cereal with sliced fruit and milk

▶ Yogurt with fruit and granola

- **Focus on what you can do for the company.** Do not ask about benefits, salary, or vacations until you are offered the job. This implies a "what can this company do for me" attitude. Be careful about appearing arrogant or displaying a know-it-all attitude. You are there to show how you can contribute to the organization.

- **Stress your skills.** When considering job applicants, employers look for both job-specific skills and general workplace skills. Job-specific skills are the skills necessary to do the particular job, such as balancing a budget or programming a computer. General workplace skills are transferable from school to job and from job to job. These include communication skills, listening skills, problem-solving skills, technology skills, decision-making skills, organizing skills, planning skills, teamwork skills, social skills, and adaptability skills. All jobs require general workplace skills; not all jobs require fully developed job-specific skills. If the employer offers on-the-job training, you may only need to demonstrate that you have the basic skills required to start the job.

- **Be honest.** Do not overstate your accomplishments or grade point average or exaggerate your experience. Many employers check the background of promising applicants. While it is important to be confident and stress your strengths, it is equally important to always be honest. If you have not had a particular kind of experience, say so, but also indicate your willingness to learn new skills.

How I See It

TRUTHFULNESS   Karla, 16

At an interview for a data entry position, I was asked about specific computer software. I have some computer experience, but I didn't know about some of the software programs they asked me about. If I exaggerated my experience in the job interview, it might increase my chances of getting the job. But if I got the job, it would become clear that my computer skills were not what I said they were. Instead of leading the interviewer to believe I was more experienced, I chose to be honest.

Critical Thinking
Karla was honest about her lack of knowledge about certain computer software. How could you turn a lack of experience or knowledge into something positive?

- **Show a positive attitude.** Employers want people who believe in themselves and their skills, who want to work, who want to work for them, and who have a positive attitude. An interviewee with a positive attitude shows poise, self-confidence, decisiveness, and has a tendency to be more extroverted. Employers usually choose candidates who are enthusiastic about their lives and their careers, because people perform best when they are doing what they like to do. One step toward developing a positive, enthusiastic outlook is to surround yourself with supportive, positive people.

- **Practice interviewing.** Like any skill, the more you practice the better you will be. Consider videotaping a practice interview. Most campuses have this service available through the career center or media department. It is also very helpful to practice being interviewed by a friend. Rehearse questions and be prepared. Make certain that you communicate your skills, abilities, and talents. Answer questions directly and relate the skills that you have learned. Expect open-ended questions such as, "What are your strengths?" "What are your weaknesses?" "Tell me about your best work experience," and "What are your career goals?" Decide in advance what information and skills are relevant to the job and reveal your strengths. For example, "I learned to get along with a variety of people when I worked for the park service."

- **Close the interview on a positive note.** Follow-up begins as you end your interview. If it is unclear to you what will happen next, ask. If an employer asks you to take initiative in any way, do it! The employer may be testing your interest in the company. Thank the interviewer for his or her time, shake hands, and say that you are looking forward to hearing from him or her.

✓ **Reading Check** **Explain** How should you present yourself in an interview?

Follow Up

Following up after a job interview is as important as the preparation you do beforehand. According to a recent survey, fifteen percent of hiring managers say they would not hire a person who did not send a thank-you letter after the interview. Thirty-two percent say they might still consider the applicant, but would think less of him or her.

After thanking your interviewer for his or her time, your letter should remind the interviewer of your qualifications and restate your wish to work for the company.

Send your thank-you letter within three days of the interview. This shows the interviewer that you are efficient and very interested in the job. Thank-you letters can be e-mailed, though most employers prefer handwritten or typed letters. Remember to include your telephone number and e-mail address.

Even if you decide you are not interested in the job, send a letter to thank the interviewer for the time he or she spent with you. He or she may be able to recommend you for another position in the company, or know of a position in another company that would suit you.

If you told the interviewer you would follow up with a phone call, make the call when you said you would. When the interviewer answers the phone, state your name and when your interview took place. Then ask if a decision has been made about the job. If the employer has not made a decision, ask when a decision might be made. If the employer has already hired someone for the job, kindly thank him or her again for taking time to consider you for the position.

If you do not get the job, keep looking and learning. Going through the process of applying and interviewing for a job is educational in itself. Make a list of what you think you did well, and what you would have done differently. If you thought the interview went very well, and cannot identify areas where you need to improve, try sending a brief e-mail to the person who interviewed you. He or she may be willing to give you a few pointers or explain why they chose another candidate. You can also discuss your interview with a family member. He or she may be able to provide the insight you need to improve. Remember to use your notes to prepare for future interviews.

Section 5.1

After You Read

Review Key Concepts

1. **Explain** why networking is important.
2. **Distinguish** how chronological and skills résumés are different.
3. **Describe** what you should consider when you dress for a job interview.
4. **Discuss** what should be included in a follow-up letter.

Practice Academic Skills

Check Your Answers Go to connectED. mcgraw-hill.com to check your answers.

English Language Arts

5. Create a cover letter for a well-known figure describing why he or she is qualified for a job. For example, Madame Curie might apply for a job as a physicist. Follow the tips mentioned in the chapter to make sure you include all the relevant information.

Social Studies

6. Interviewers may be easygoing and friendly. They may call you by your first name and sit before you do. Explain in a paragraph why you must avoid being too familiar in a job interview even if the interviewer is easygoing.

Your New Job

Before You Read

Preview Scan the headings and boldface words that appear in this section. Write one or two sentences predicting what you think the section will be about.

Read to Learn

Key Concepts

- **Describe** the basic responsibilities of a new employee.
- **Identify** strategies for balancing work and family.
- **Recognize** the factors that lead to job success.

Main Idea

Balancing the responsibilities of a job and personal time are key factors in getting job satisfaction.

Content Vocabulary

◇ stress
◇ flextime
◇ job sharing
◇ telecommute
◇ benefit

Academic Vocabulary

You will find these words in your reading and on your tests. Use the glossary to look up their definitions if necessary.

☐ compress
☐ accumulate

Graphic Organizer

As you read, record the causes of positive and negative stress as well as their results. Use a graphic organizer like the one below to organize your information.

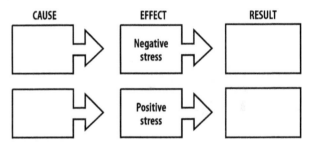

 Graphic Organizer Go to **connectED.mcgraw-hill.com** to download this graphic organizer.

Starting a New Job

The interview went well, you got the job, and you start work next week. Now what? What can you do to prepare? What will your employer expect of you your first day on the job? What can you expect from your employer?

Look the Part

How you appear to your employer and to any customers and coworkers is important. The clothing and accessories you wear must be appropriate for the workplace. One way to find out what to wear is to ask about a dress code. Some jobs require a uniform, and others allow more casual wear. If your job involves meeting the public, it is especially important to choose clothing that is clean and neat.

When creating a work wardrobe, select easy-care items that can be coordinated with each other. This is easy to do when you choose basic colors such as black, navy, and khaki instead of bright colors or flashy patterns. If you wear jewelry, keep it simple and not too large. Avoid trendy clothing.

If you work with or around machinery, choose clothing that fits well and does not have fringe or drawstrings. Loose clothing, scarves, and drawstrings can get caught in the machinery and cause personal injury as well as damage to the machinery. Accessories can also get caught on or fall in machinery. If you are not sure which accessories are safe to wear in your workplace, talk to your employer. You may find it is better to leave these items at home.

Stay Safe on the Job

Many people are injured on the job every year. Part of your job is to make sure you are not one of them. The government, employers, and employees all have a part to play in preventing work accidents.

The federal Occupational Safety and Health Administration (OSHA), a branch of the U.S. Department of Labor, sets job safety standards and inspects job sites. Its goal is to make sure employers provide a place of employment free from safety and health hazards. These hazards include:

- Exposure to Toxic Chemicals
- Excessive Noise Levels
- Mechanical Dangers
- Heat or Cold Stress
- Unsanitary Conditions

As You Read

Connect Think about how you prepare for a new school year. How might preparing for a new job be similar?

▼ **Prepare for Work**

It is always important to dress appropriately for the kind of job you have. *What kinds of clothes do you or someone you know wear to work?*

Dave and Les Jacobs/Blend Images LLC

Getting along with coworkers can sometimes be a challenge. Here are some suggestions you can use to build and maintain positive relationships at work:

- **Respect Others** Understand and appreciate people's differences. Someday, you may be the one in need of some extra understanding, tolerance, and respect.
- **Focus on the Job** If you dislike someone at work, separate your personal feelings from the job requirements and learn to work together.
- **Stay Neutral** By taking sides in a dispute, you may strengthen your friendship with one person, but damage your working relationships with others.
- **Keep a Sense of Humor** Try to laugh when the joke is on you. People tend to like and respect people who can laugh at themselves.

Real-World Skills

Present to the Class Follow your teacher's instructions to form into groups. As a group, choose one of the suggestions for achieving workplace harmony to present to the class. Your presentation should focus on why the suggestion is important, how it could be implemented, and how it would result in harmony.

The employer's role is to provide a safe workplace, supply equipment and materials needed to do the job safely, teach employees how to use the equipment and materials, inform employees when conditions are hazardous, and keep records of job-related illnesses and injuries. The employer is also expected to follow policies for conservation and environmental protection. The U.S. Environmental Protection Agency (EPA) sets standards for workplace environments, including the safe disposal of hazardous wastes.

Your role as an employee is to learn and follow the safety regulations of your employer and OSHA. This includes learning to perform your job safely, knowing how to operate and maintain tools and equipment safely, and reporting unsafe conditions or practices immediately to your supervisor. Failure to follow these guidelines can result in human errors that may affect both you and others.

Make Sound Decisions

You will make many decisions during your career. The chances of making good ones can be increased if you follow the sound decision-making process (see Chapter 2). The process, a series of steps involved in making a choice, can be used in a variety of workplace situations. Decisions ranging from choosing what to wear to selecting the kind of tool needed to do a certain job safely require critical-thinking skills. These skills can help you analyze problems and deal with them effectively.

✓ **Reading Check** **Describe** What are the basic responsibilities of an employer?

Safety Check

Workplace Dangers
The safety standards for a job in a factory are different from those for a job in an office. Remember that every job has hazards that should be avoided by following certain safety precautions.

Write About It
Think of possible jobs you are interested in. Research the types of hazards and safety rules one of them has. Write a paragraph about what you find.

Balance Work and Your Personal Life

◆ **Vocabulary**

You can find definitions in the glossary at the back of this book.

Sandra starts her new job next week. She knows that being successful will take hard work, and she knows that, like most jobs, her job will include a certain degree of stress.

Stress is the pressure people feel as the result of their ability or inability to meet the expectations of others and themselves. Stress can result in a variety of physical reactions or symptoms, such as sweaty palms, the feeling of butterflies in the stomach, loss of appetite or overeating, sleep difficulties, and headaches.

Stress can be either positive or negative. The cause and the intensity of stress determine whether stress is a positive or negative force in your life. Sad events and crises, such as the death of a loved one, a serious illness, or the loss of a job, cause feelings of negative stress. Happy events, such as a wedding, graduation, or job promotion, result in positive stress. Positive stress is usually connected with a sense of accomplishment and, if kept at a low level, can improve your performance. However, too much stress decreases performance levels. This is why balance is so important.

Balance Work and Family

Because employees are expected to work hard, meet deadlines, and interact with coworkers and supervisors, they often have difficulty balancing their commitments to their jobs, family, and friends.

Some companies help employees deal with the challenges of work and family by allowing flexible work schedules, or flextime. **Flextime** lets workers adjust their daily work schedules to meet family needs as long as the workers put in the required number of hours on the job.

A few companies allow employees to compress, or squeeze together, each work week. This is called a compressed week. Instead of working five 8-hour days, an employee can choose to work four 10-hour days or even three 12-hour days! The work day is long, but this makes the weekend longer, too. Depending on a family's schedule, compressing the work week can increase quality time with family members. Employers find that workers who have more control over their schedules tend to be more productive and miss less work than workers who do not have that option.

For some people who do not need a full-time salary, working part-time may be a good choice. In some work situations, **job sharing** is allowed, in which two part-time workers share one full-time job, splitting the hours and the pay.

An increasing number of employees **telecommute**, which is when people work at home and communicate with customers and coworkers by phone, fax, and computer. This allows them to be home for important family events. Telecommuting also saves people the time they would spend in traffic and the money they would spend on transportation to and from the workplace.

Health & Wellness TIPS

Avoid Office Injuries

Desk jobs can be dangerous. For example, improper use of computers can lead to injury. Common injuries include wrist, head, shoulder, and back strain. Use the following tips to stay healthy at work:

▶ Keep wrists straight when using the computer mouse.
▶ Stand up and move around once every hour.
▶ When seated, sit up straight.

Find Personal Time

Several strategies decrease the stress of balancing work and family.

- **Set and prioritize activities.** Identify the activities that are most important to you. Which activities are enjoyable and help promote your health and well-being?

- **Budget time.** When planning your schedule, set aside a certain amount of time for your hobbies, school events, and activities with your family and friends. Distractions can frequently interrupt whatever task you are doing. Try to focus on completing one thing at a time. Turn off the TV, put down your cell phone, and set aside the tablet. Designate times where you allow yourself to check your social networking sites, play video games, watch TV, and catch up on e-mails and text messages. You will get more done without these interruptions.

- **Avoid overload.** Do not fill your schedule with work-related activities and major family commitments. You need some downtime in your schedule to stay healthy and balanced. Before getting a part-time job, Julie used to babysit for a neighbor. Now that she is working, she cannot babysit as much as she used to. If she did, she would not have any time to enjoy family activities.

Take Advantage of Benefits

Some companies refund the money parents pay for child care, or provide onsite child care facilities. A company may offer other benefits. A **benefit**, or reward for employment besides salary, may include health insurance, personal financial savings plans or retirement plans, and paid vacations. Vacations offer employees opportunities to release stress and time to be with their family and friends. Paid vacations are usually available to new employees once they have completed six months or a year of work. Some employers also increase employees' vacation time as they accumulate, or slowly gain, years on the job. Another benefit, an employee assistance program, provides confidential counseling services to workers.

✓ **Reading Check** **Recall** What are some ways employees can make time for their personal lives?

Telecommute

Many people who telecommute work from home. Others work from satellite offices. *What might be some benefits of telecommuting?*

©JGI/Jamie Grill/Blend Images LLC

Aim for Success

Studies show successful employees are usually in jobs that they like and find satisfying. You will be most successful if you:

- Enjoy the work that you do.
- Feel comfortable and safe in the work environment.
- Have the tools and equipment you need to do the job well.
- Earn wages and benefits that are appropriate for your skills.
- Get recognition for performing well.
- Can voice opinions and suggestions.
- Have the opportunity for personal development and learning.
- Work at a job that is compatible with your skills and interests.
- Have the opportunity for advancement.
- Enjoy a good relationship with your manager and coworkers.

Section 5.2

After You Read

Review Key Concepts

1. **Identify** things you should consider when planning your work wardrobe.
2. **List** three types of alternate work schedules that help employees balance their lives.
3. **Explain** why it is important to enjoy your job.

Practice Academic Skills

English Language Arts

4. Make a plan to start your own business. Describe your business in a few short paragraphs, including the goods or services you will provide. Explain how you will attain the necessary resources, and any research, training, or other preparation required.

Social Studies

5. The way you maintain a balanced life is a reflection of your sense of self. Interview a parent or friend about how he or she balances work and family. Write a paragraph explaining how you balance school, work, and family obligations in a similar or different manner.

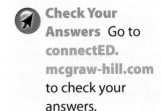

Check Your Answers Go to connectED. mcgraw-hill.com to check your answers.

CHAPTER SUMMARY

Section 5.1
The Job Application Process

The application process is an important part of getting a job. A cover letter introduces you to an employer and serves as your first impression. A résumé summarizes your qualifications, work experience, education, interests, and skills. Career portfolios can be used to demonstrate certain skills to prospective employers. A successful interview requires planning and preparation. Following up after an interview can determine whether you are offered a job or not.

Section 5.2
Your New Job

New employees should dress appropriately for the workplace, and familiarize themselves with the safety regulations of their employer and OSHA. You can use several strategies to decrease the stress of balancing work and family commitments. You will be most successful in a job if you are comfortable in the work environment, have the tools you need to do your job, earn wages that are appropriate for your position, and have the opportunity for personal development.

Vocabulary Review

1. Write a sentence using two or more of these content and academic vocabulary terms. The sentence should clearly show how the terms are related.

Content Vocabulary
◇ networking (p. 109)
◇ résumé (p. 110)
◇ chronological résumé (p. 110)
◇ skills résumé (p. 110)
◇ cover letter (p. 112)
◇ portfolio (p. 114)
◇ interview (p. 115)
◇ stress (p. 124)
◇ flextime (p. 124)
◇ job sharing (p. 124)
◇ telecommute (p. 124)
◇ benefit (p. 125)

Academic Vocabulary
■ relevant (p. 112)
■ indicate (p. 116)
■ compress (p. 124)
■ accumulate (p. 125)

Review Key Concepts

2. **Outline** the process of applying for a job.
3. **Compare and contrast** résumés and portfolios.
4. **Summarize** how to prepare for a job interview.
5. **Explain** how to follow up after a job interview.
6. **Describe** the basic responsibilities of a new employee.
7. **Identify** strategies for balancing work and family.
8. **Recognize** the factors that lead to job success.

Critical Thinking

9. **Create** You have been asked to submit a portfolio for a possible summer job at an advertising company. What items should you include? Explain your answer.
10. **Analyze** In which of these careers might flextime work best: schoolteacher, day care provider, mechanic, writer, receptionist, or hairdresser? Explain your choices.
11. **Determine** You are preparing to reenter the world of work after spending several years raising a family. Would you submit a chronological résumé or a skills-based résumé? Explain your reasoning.

 ACTIVE LEARNING

12. Prioritize Your Activities Make a list of the activities you enjoy in your free time. For example, you may like to read, watch television, browse social media, go hiking, draw, and spend time with friends. Now rank your activities according to how much they promote your health or well-being. For example, you may value hiking more than watching television because hiking is enjoyable exercise while watching television does not provide any exercise. You may prefer drawing to hiking because you want to improve enough to get into art school. Create an after-school schedule that budgets time for your favorite activities. Be sure the time you plan for each activity reflects its ranking in your list.

 **Family & Community Connections**

13. Safety on the Job Each year, more than 4 million people are injured at the workplace or develop job-related illnesses. More than 5,000 people die as a result of their injuries. Interview a local employer about safety on the job. Ask him or her to describe the risks of the workplace. How does he or she manage those risks? For example, a factory manager may restrict use of heavy machinery to experienced employees only. Restaurant managers ensure that employees wash their hands or wear gloves, and practice safe food-handling techniques. Make one list of the potential dangers of the job and another list of the safeguards to help protect employees. When you have finished your interview, think about other dangers in this workplace. Write two paragraphs describing these dangers. What precautions would you take to protect employees against them?

Real-World Skills and Applications

Leadership Skills

14. Interview Techniques Act as an employer and interview a partner who is applying for a job at your company. After a few minutes, stop the interview and give your partner tips on how he or she can improve his or her interview technique. For example, you might suggest that your partner is too familiar or not formal enough. Switch roles and repeat the exercise.

Financial Literacy

15. Weigh Your Options You are offered two jobs. Chen's Movie Theater pays $9.00 an hour and wants to schedule you to work 15 hours a week. Johnny's Comics pays $7.50 an hour and wants to schedule you to work 22 hours a week. With which job would you earn more money per week? How much more would you earn?

Technology Skills

16. Create a Résumé Think of a job you would like to have, and use a computer program to create a résumé listing the job objective as well as your relevant skills, hobbies, and accomplishments. Also, be sure to list your education, prior work experience, and references. You may choose to create a chronological résumé or a skills résumé.

©Sam Edwards/age fotostock

Academic Skills

English Language Arts

17. Follow Up You have just completed a job interview. Write a one-page thank-you letter to the employer to express your thanks for the interview and to restate your interest in the job. Remember to use formal language and to include your telephone number and e-mail address.

Science

18. Workplace Comfort Ergonomics is the study of the work environment for comfort and efficiency. If you work with a computer, improper placement of the monitor can cause strain on your neck and eyes. Place a monitor so that you have to look up to see it and type for five minutes. Lower the monitor so that you can look straight ahead and type for five more minutes. Note how your neck and eyes feel after each placement of the monitor. What would be the effect of placing the monitor even lower?

Mathematics

19. Compare Values After all the hard work you put into creating your résumé, you find that you have three job offers. After considering the positives and negatives of each job, you are equally interested in all three. You decide to base your decision on the distance you must travel to get to work. Job A requires a 1.61 mile trip. Job B requires a 1.16 mile trip. Job C requires a 1.611 mile trip. List the jobs in order of closest to farthest that you must travel.

Math Concept **Decimals** The first place after the decimal is the tenths place. Next is the hundredths place and last is the thousandths. When comparing decimals, look at each place individually.

Starting Hint First rewrite the numbers so they have the same amount of place values after the decimal. Thus, 1.61 will become 1.610 and 1.16 will become 1.160. 1.611 can remain the same.

 For math help, go to the Math Appendix at the back of the book.

Standardized Test Practice

RATIO
Directions Read the problem. Then, calculate the correct answer.

Test-Taking Tip In a math word problem, first identify the information you need to solve the problem. Then, convert this information into a mathematical equation necessary to solve the problem. After solving the equation, translate the numbers back into words. Present your answer in the wording of the question.

20. You are looking at a map that uses a scale of 2 inches to represent 30 miles. You want to find the distance between your house and the office building where your job interview will take place. The distance on the map between your house and the office is 5 inches. How many miles are between your house and the office building?

Life Skills Project

Career Map and Ladder

In this project you will create a career map that establishes a path to achieve a career goal that interests you. You will also design a career ladder, a visual representation of the sequence of jobs to progress through to achieve your career goal.

My Journal

If you completed the journal entry from page 58, refer to it to see if your thoughts have changed after reading the unit.

Project Assignment

In this project you will:
- Research a career that interests you.
- Identify and interview an adult in your community who is knowledgeable about the career that interests you.
- Prepare a career map and a career ladder that you will share with your class.

STEP 1 Choose a Career

Select a career that interests you. Research that outlines the steps you must follow to succeed in this career. Write a summary of your research:
- Describe the training and other qualifications required for advancement.

The Skills Behind the Project

Life Skills

Key personal and relationship skills you will use in this project include:
- Researching
- Listening patiently
- Thinking critically

- Identify the skills you need to develop to become successful in this career. Include skills specific to the job as well as transferable skills, including academic skills.
- Outline the steps you must go through to gain experiences, build networks, and achieve employment.

Analytical Skills
- Examine a complex situation.
- Use problem-solving techniques.
- Make informed predictions.

STEP 2 Plan Your Interview

Use the results of your research to write a list of interview questions to ask an adult in your community who is knowledgeable about your chosen career. Your questions might include:
- What are the best things about working in this career?
- What are the biggest challenges of this career?
- What steps can I take to achieve this career goal?
- If you wanted to achieve this career goal, how would you go about doing it?
- What advice would you give a young person who is interested in this career?

130

Life Skills Project Checklist

Plan	☑ Conduct research.
	☑ Write a summary of your research.
	☑ Plan and write interview questions.
	☑ Interview an adult in your community and write a summary of what you learned.
	☑ Use your research and the results of your interview to plan and create a career map that visually and chronologically describes the education and training, skills, and experiences you would need to achieve this career goal.
	☑ Design a career ladder that shows the sequence of jobs you plan to progress through in order to achieve your ultimate career goal.
Present	☑ Present your career map and ladder to your class.
	☑ Invite the students in your class to ask you any questions they may have. Answer these questions.
	☑ When students ask you questions, demonstrate in your answers that you respect their perspectives.
	☑ Turn in your career map and ladder, your interview questions, and the notes from your interview to your teacher.
Academic Skills	☑ Communicate effectively.
	☑ Use creativity.
	☑ Express your ideas clearly.
	☑ Demonstrate listening skills.

STEP 3 Connect to Your Community

Interview an adult in your community who is knowledgeable about the career or in a field related to the career in which you are interested. Review your research summary and outline with the person. Conduct your interview using the questions you prepared in Step 2. Take notes during the interview and transcribe them after the interview.

Communication Skills

- Ask open-ended questions that cannot be answered with "yes" or "no."
- Listen attentively.
- Show enthusiasm for and interest in what the speaker is saying.

STEP 4 Share What You Have Learned

Use the Life Skills Project Checklist to plan and create a career map and ladder and share what you have learned with your class.

STEP 5 Evaluate Your Life Skills and Academic Skills

Your project will be evaluated based on:
- Content and creativity of your career ladder.
- Clarity of your presentation.
- Speaking and listening skills.

 Evaluation Rubric Go to **connectED.mcgraw-hill.com** for a rubric you can use to evaluate your final project.

UNIT 3

Building Relationship Skills

Chapter 6 Communication with Others
Chapter 7 Conflict Resolution
Chapter 8 Dealing with Peer Pressure

Unit Life Skills Project Preview

Healthy Relationships

In this unit you will learn how to relate to others in positive ways. In the life skills project you will define what healthy relationships mean to you.

 My Journal

Choosing Friends Write a journal entry about one of the topics below. This will help you prepare for the project at the end of this unit.

- Identify the qualities that you would like a true friend to have.
- Describe how you would handle a conflict, such as a difference of opinion, with a friend or family member.
- Explain how you can speak to other people in a way that communicates respect for them and for yourself.

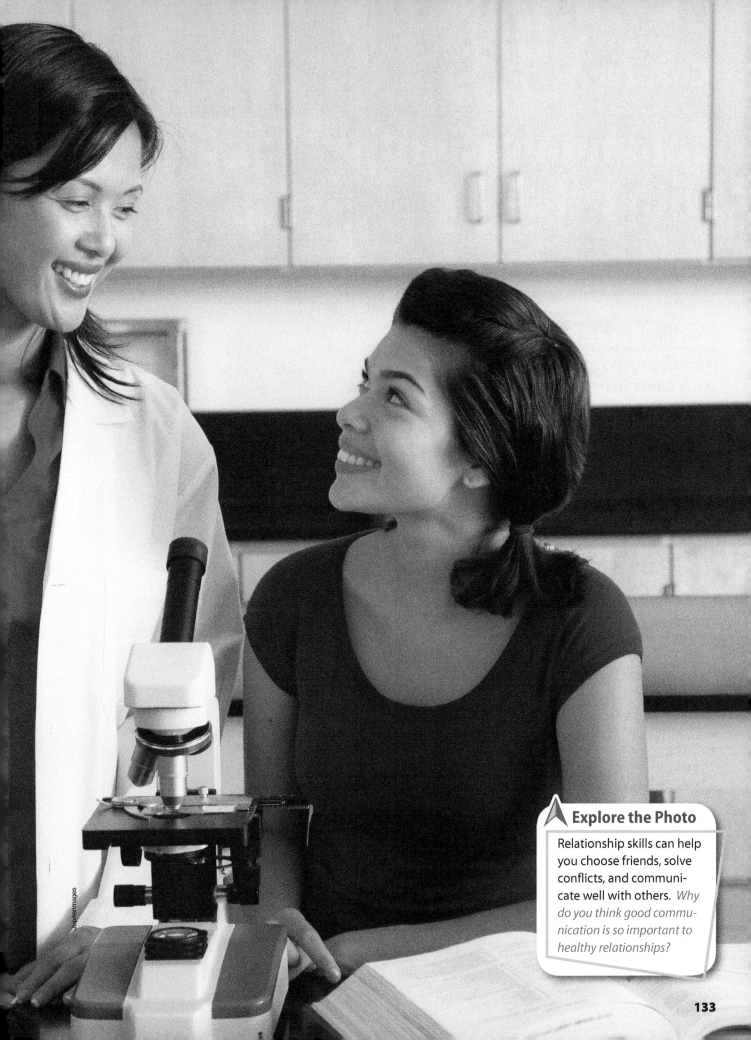

Explore the Photo

Relationship skills can help you choose friends, solve conflicts, and communicate well with others. *Why do you think good communication is so important to healthy relationships?*

Chapter 6

Communication with Others

Section 6.1
Speaking, Writing, and Listening Skills

Section 6.2
Communicating Respect

Chapter Objectives

Section 6.1
- **Compare and contrast** verbal and nonverbal communication.
- **List** four strategies for speaking effectively.
- **Describe** how to listen actively.

Section 6.2
- **Explain** how to communicate with respect.
- **Describe** how to overcome communication roadblocks.

Banana Stock/PhotoLibrary

Writing Activity Paragraph Development

Communication Skills Communication is an important skill for academic success. It is easier to complete your assignments if you ask for help when you encounter a problem.

Observe a conversation between two people at a restaurant or in a library. Write a descriptive paragraph about your observations and include details such as facial expressions, body postures, and hand gestures the subjects displayed throughout their conversation.

Writing Tips Follow these steps to write a strong paragraph:
- Write a topic sentence that clearly expresses the main idea of the paragraph.
- Each sentence should have at least one detail that supports the main idea.
- Make sure all of your sentences are linked clearly and logically to one another.

Section 6.1

Speaking, Writing, and Listening Skills

Before You Read

Preview Read the key terms and headings in this section. Write one or two sentences predicting what you think the section will be about.

Read to Learn

Key Concepts
- **Compare and contrast** verbal and nonverbal communication.
- **List** four strategies for speaking effectively.
- **Describe** how to listen actively.

Main Idea
Speaking well, reading nonverbal signals, and listening actively are important skills for communicating with others.

Content Vocabulary
◇ communication
◇ verbal communication
◇ nonverbal communication
◇ enunciate
◇ body language
◇ active listening

Academic Vocabulary
You will find these words in your reading and on your tests. Use the glossary to look up their definitions if necessary.
☐ appropriate
☐ minimize

Graphic Organizer
As you read, list techniques for effective speaking, writing, and listening. Use a chart like the one below to organize your information.

Techniques for Effective Communication

Speaking	Writing	Listening

 Graphic Organizer Go to **connectED.mcgraw-hill.com** to download this graphic organizer.

What Is Communication?

Every second of every day, people all over the world send messages to each other. A message is any thought or feeling that you share with another person. You send messages when you speak, write, or even move, and you receive messages when you read, watch, or listen. In the time it takes you to read this sentence, millions of facts, opinions, and feelings will have been communicated in person, over the phone, through the mail or by e-mail.

Communication is the process of sending and receiving messages. Good communication is the foundation of strong relationships. Communication skills help you reach your goals, speak up for yourself, build friendships, and succeed in your career. Communication is a valuable skill, and like any skill it requires practice.

Verbal and Nonverbal Communication

People communicate and express themselves verbally and nonverbally. **Verbal communication** is communication using words, both spoken and written. Communication takes place without words, too. People send many messages through facial expressions, posture, eye contact, touch, gestures, and more. Communication without words is called **nonverbal communication**. Most communication is a mixture of verbal and nonverbal messages.

Verbal Communication

Communication is successful when your message is received as you intended it. You can speak well by organizing your thoughts, paying attention to your delivery, and relating to your listeners.

- **Organize your thoughts.** Before you talk, organize your thoughts in your mind or on paper. Make sure you know your main point so that the person you are talking to can follow your ideas. Be aware of your feelings before you speak. Think twice before saying anything that you might later regret.

As You Read

Connect Think about the different ways people send messages. How many ways do you communicate with your friends?

Vocabulary

You can find definitions in the glossary at the back of this book.

Nicole Katano/Jupiter Images

> **Positive Communication**
>
> Good communication is a skill that needs to be learned and practiced. *How can you tell that these two people are communicating well?*

Tact Juan's class is making presentations on important figures in U.S. history. His best friend Stephen finishes his presentation and asks Juan what he thinks of it. Juan feels that Stephen's presentation lacked adequate research and was not well organized. What options does Juan have for answering Stephen's question? What can Juan say without hurting Stephen's feelings?

You Make the Call

Should Juan make his friend happy by saying that the presentation was great? Should Juan be honest and say that he did not like Stephen's presentation?

- **Enunciate.** To **enunciate** (ē-ˈnən(t)-sē͏̠ˌāt) is to speak each sound clearly and distinctly. Enunciating is especially important when speaking to a group. Speak up so that others can hear you. Keep in mind that speaking very quickly or slowly may cause people to tune out.
- **Avoid making assumptions.** Do not assume that you know what other people think, how they feel, or what they want. Ask them, and let them speak for themselves. Likewise, do not assume that others know what you think, how you feel, or what you want. Share your experiences and feelings, and speak for yourself.
- **Relate to your listeners.** Speaking is a way of relating to others. Think about what is appropriate, or suitable for the setting, such as home or school. Tailor your communication to fit your listeners and the occasion. Find a balance between talking and listening. If you do all of the talking, your listener might feel that you are not interested in his or her point of view.
- **Check for understanding.** Check that your audience understands what you are saying. Ask questions. If your audience looks confused, you may not be getting your point across effectively. Try expressing your ideas in a different way. A positive attitude gets better results than a negative attitude. No one likes to hear others whine, complain, or criticize all the time. Express thanks and appreciation, especially to friends and family.
- **Pick the right time.** Choosing the right time to communicate is also important for good communication. Pick a time when listeners are interested in communicating with you. Communication can be difficult when one person in the conversation is tired, frustrated, angry, or distracted.

TAKE CHARGE!

Make Effective Presentations

There are several steps that you can take to make an effective presentation. The following steps will help you improve your presentation skills.

- **Speak with Confidence** Practice and preparation can help you feel more confident and less afraid.
- **Prepare Your Mind** Choose the key points you need to remember, and create an organized outline for your presentation.
- **Prepare Your Body** Get plenty of rest the night before, eat lightly, and avoid caffeine.
- **Make Eye Contact** Make eye contact with one member of the audience at a time and pretend that you are speaking to that person one on one.
- **Breathe** Take pauses between your major points to breathe in through your nose and out through your mouth.

Real-World Skills

Express Yourself Through Your Movements Use appropriate body language to communicate your points. Prepare a five-minute presentation for your class on a topic that interests you. Focus on one key point. Give the presentation, using the guidelines above. Survey the class to see whether you effectively communicated your key points.

◄ **Nonverbal Communication**

Smiling, making eye contact, and standing close to another person are ways of showing interest. *What other nonverbal communication do you see here? What do you think it means?*

Nonverbal Communication

You send many messages without ever speaking a word. All forms of nonverbal communication—gestures, facial expressions, posture, eye contact, physical distance, and even your appearance—communicate your thoughts and feelings. You can use nonverbal communication to make your message stronger. You can also learn to "read" other people's nonverbal communication to help you understand their thoughts and feelings.

- **Body Language** **Body language** is the use of gestures and other body movements to communicate. You can use hand gestures to emphasize a key point or show excitement. A clenched fist might show others that you are determined, angry, or hostile.

- **Posture** The way you hold your body is an important part of nonverbal communication. Your posture conveys an attitude. Standing or sitting comfortably upright as you talk shows interest and confidence. So does walking with your shoulders back and head up. Stooped shoulders and a bowed head suggest that you lack confidence or feel sad.

- **Facial Expressions** Facial expressions can encourage or discourage communication. A smile attracts others and makes them feel at ease. Facial expressions also reveal a lot about how you really feel. If a friend said everything was fine but had a sad or angry facial expression, what would you think?

- **Eye Contact** Looking into another person's eyes shows that you are friendly, confident, and interested in the speaker. However, be aware that in some cultures looking directly into the listener's eyes can be a sign of disrespect.

SUCCEED IN SCHOOL

Create a Study Buddy List Create a list of classmates' telephone numbers and e-mail addresses. Add the list to your homework binder or keep it in a place where it is readily available. If you are absent from class or do not understand something in an assignment, you can call a classmate for the information you need.

Reduce Stress

Stress can have an effect on your quality of life and well-being. Stress can also affect your ability to communicate with others. Use these tips to help reduce stress:

▶ Exercise frequently and eat nutritious foods.

▶ Get enough sleep.

▶ Talk to friends and family about problems.

- **Tone of Voice** The way you speak is just as important as the words you use. Your emotions can come through in your tone of voice. Strive to use a tone and inflection (pitch and loudness) that accurately conveys your message. Controlling your emotions makes it easier for you to achieve the right tone and for people to understand what you are saying.

- **Physical Distance** The space between you and another person often sends a message without words. Usually, the closer the relationship, the less distance people put between each other when they speak. However, people in conflict often stand close when sending messages of aggression.

- **Appearance** Your appearance sends messages, too. A clean and healthy appearance sends a message that you respect and care about yourself. It also shows respect for others. What does your personal appearance say about you?

✓ **Reading Check** **Explain** What is the difference between verbal and nonverbal communication?

Writing Effectively

Writing is another important skill for personal and career success. Whether you are writing an e-mail or filling out a job application, you will need writing skills to communicate your ideas and present yourself well. You can improve your writing skills by practicing clarity, organization, and revision.

How I See It

PEER PRESSURE
John, 18

Sometimes I feel insecure and have a hard time just being myself. In my school there is a lot of pressure to act a certain way, look a certain way, and have the right clothes. I want to be liked, and I like to look good, but to me it is more important to be healthy, to exercise, and eat the right foods. I know that I have a lot going for me, and I do not want to hurt myself or my body.

My best friend and my mom help me a lot when I feel unsure of myself. If you have someone in your life who loves you, it makes you want to take care of yourself. You need to believe that you are worth something. Having my first job helped, too. I felt independent, and I felt like I had a purpose. It was an awesome feeling. To me, it is important to remind myself that I don't have to be a follower all the time. I can be a leader, too.

Critical Thinking
John suggests that one way to deal with peer pressure is to be a leader, not a follower. Do you agree? Why or why not?

- **Be clear.** Clarity is the foundation of good writing because it helps people understand your message. How can you be clear? Focus on your main point. Be concise and direct, without a lot of extra words. This is especially important in business writing, such as e-mail.

- **Organize your thoughts.** Just as with speaking, it is important to organize your thoughts in your mind or on paper before you write. Organizing your thoughts helps your reader and makes the writing process much easier. One good organizing strategy is outlining, which helps you put your ideas in a logical order. Outlining also helps you decide which of your ideas are main points and which of your ideas are minor points or examples.

- **Rewrite and revise.** Rewriting and revising is an important part of writing. J.K. Rowling wrote ten versions of the first chapter in *Harry Potter and the Sorcerer's Stone* before she was ready to publish. Writing is work! Start with a first draft, then reread. Reword sentences to make them clearer. Take out words and phrases that do not support your point. Rearrange ideas if necessary. Check your spelling, grammar, and punctuation.

✓ **Reading Check** **Explain** How can you improve your writing skills?

Active Listening

Active listening is just as important to communication as speaking. **Active listening** is listening and responding with full attention to what another person says. Listening is the most overlooked communication skill. It may also be the hardest.

Concentrate

The first part of listening actively is concentrating on the speaker. Focus on understanding what he or she is actually saying, rather than what you expect him or her to say. Pay attention to the speaker's body language, which can help you figure out what he or she needs to communicate. Try to **minimize**, or greatly reduce, distractions such as noise or daydreams that make it hard to concentrate on the speaker.

▼ Active Listening

Active listening helps people connect and build relationships. *How can you show a speaker that you are paying attention?*

Jupiterimages

Keep an Open Mind

Keep an open mind, even if you and the speaker disagree. Temporarily set aside any prejudice or opinions you may have about the topic at hand. Otherwise, you might be too busy planning what you are going to say next to catch important points. Try not to judge a message before the speaker is done. You may miss areas of agreement that could foster better understanding and communication.

Give Feedback

The second part of active listening is giving verbal and nonverbal feedback to the speaker. Verbal feedback might be a simple "Yes" or "I see," or it might be a question or statement. Try rephrasing in your own words what you think the speaker said. This shows the speaker that you understand and helps you remember what you heard. Rephrasing is very helpful for step-by-step instructions.

Nonverbal feedback includes maintaining eye contact, nodding your head to show you understand, or shaking your head when you do not understand. Responses like these show the speaker whether the message is getting through.

Section 6.1

After You Read

Review Key Concepts

1. **Define** enunciate.
2. **Explain** the importance of outlining.
3. **Describe** types of verbal and nonverbal feedback.

Practice Academic Skills

 **English Language Arts**

4. Write down your own opinion of your active listening skills. Then ask friends and family members their opinion. Gather suggestions on how you could listen better. Then write a list of strategies you will use to become a better listener. Revise your list to make each strategy clear and to cut extra words.

 **Social Studies**

5. Your communication style, or way of expressing yourself, is part of your identity. Write about your communication style. How do you speak to others? Are you loud or quiet? Fast or slow? Emotional or reserved? Explain how you think you developed your communication style. What influenced it?

 **Check Your Answers** Go to connectED.mcgraw-hill.com to check your answers.

Communicating Respect

Reading Guide

Before You Read

Preview Look at the photos and read their captions. Write one or two sentences predicting what the section will be about.

Read to Learn

Key Concepts

- **Explain** how to communicate with respect.
- **Describe** how to overcome communication roadblocks.

Main Idea

Respect is belief in the worth of someone or something. You can communicate respect for others and for yourself through your words and actions.

Content Vocabulary

◇ respect
◇ self-respect
◇ rapport
◇ tact

◇ empathy
◇ assertiveness
◇ stereotype
◇ prejudice

Academic Vocabulary

You will find these words in your reading and on your tests. Use the glossary to look up their definitions if necessary.

☐ occur   ☐ establish

Graphic Organizer

As you read, write strategies you can use to show respect for yourself and others. Use a chart like the one below to organize your information.

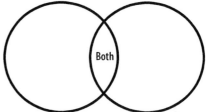

Respect for Myself   Respect for Others

Both

Graphic Organizer Go to **connectED.mcgraw-hill.com** to download this graphic organizer

Respect Yourself and Others

As You Read

Connect Think about the ways in which you communicate with your family and friends. Why is both respect and self-respect important for effective communication?

Respect is an important part of effective communication. **Respect** is belief in the equal worth of others. You show respect for others when you honor their thoughts, feelings, bodies, and property. You show respect when you treat them as they wish to be treated.

Self-respect is also an important part of effective communication. **Self-respect** is a belief in your own worth. You show self-respect when you treat your own thoughts, feelings, body, and property as valuable. You show self-respect when you avoid what could hurt you physically or emotionally. You also show self-respect when you develop your skills and abilities and choose kind friends.

Respectful Communication

Good communication can occur, or take place, when people send verbal and nonverbal messages of respect. When you respect another person, you are willing to consider his or her point of view, even if you do not agree with it. You consider the feelings of others before speaking and listen with an open mind to what they have to say. When you respect yourself, you expect others to consider your point of view and listen to what you have to say. You treat others with kindness and openness and expect the same in return.

Kindness and Openness

Kindness and openness make communication easier and more positive. Kindness means accepting people for who they are and not judging them harshly.

Openness is a generous attitude toward others. Open people share their thoughts, feelings, and experiences and are interested in other people's thoughts, feelings, and experiences, too. Open people are willing to consider different ideas and points of view. Closed people think that other people's ideas are wrong or stupid and display a know-it-all attitude. Open people realize that they can always learn something from others.

Show Interest in Others

Do you take an interest in your classmates' opinions? Do you remember what people share with you? Taking an interest in others is an important way to show them respect.

The key to good conversation is to show interest in other people. Here are some ways to start a conversation:

- **Encourage others to talk.** Ask open-ended questions that require more than a "yes" or "no" answer. For example, you might start a question with, "What do you think of ...?" This will encourage the other person to share with you.
- **Listen actively.** Pay attention and respond to what the other person says. Nod your head, maintain eye contact, and make occasional positive comments.
- **Be friendly.** Smile and be enthusiastic in what you say.

Vocabulary

You can find definitions in the glossary at the back of this book.

Use Cell Phones Safely

It is never a good idea to use a cell phone or to text while riding a bike or driving. Do you think hands-free cell phone use while driving is safe? Why or why not?

Write About It

Research your state's cell phone use while driving laws and share this information with your class. Do you consider your state's laws fair? Why or why not?

Figure 6.1   **Communicating Respect**

Be a Team Player Even if you do not play a sport, the rules of good sportsmanship can help you communicate respect in every aspect of life. *Why is good sportsmanship important?*

Encourage Others
Give others the same encouragement you would like to have from them.

Communicate Positive Messages
Speak positively not only about members of your own group but also about the opposing groups.

Share What You Know
Help others to learn new skills.

Solve Conflicts Assertively Discuss problems with others to find solutions that work for everyone involved.

SUCCEED IN SCHOOL

Media Tour Arrange a media center or library tour with your school's librarian. Ask the librarian to show you where resources are located and the rules concerning media and technology use. Collect any handouts regarding library rules and regulations.

Building Rapport

To communicate well, try to build rapport with your listener. **Rapport** (ra-ˈpȯr) is harmony or understanding among people. It is the feeling of being listened to and accepted. One way to establish, or set up, rapport is to put other people at ease. Show interest in them by involving them in the conversation. Call them by name and make them feel comfortable. Ask questions or ask for their opinions on a topic and give them time to respond. If you act relaxed and comfortable, others will react in the same way, too.

Tact and Empathy

You do not have to agree with other people but you do have to listen to show respect. The way you disagree makes a big difference. Use tact. **Tact** is the ability to communicate something difficult without hurting another person's feelings. Saying "I hear your point of view but I see things differently" is much more tactful than blurting out "You don't know what you are talking about!"

To be tactful, you need empathy. **Empathy** is the ability to understand what someone else is experiencing. You empathize by putting yourself in another person's place and trying to see things from his or her point of view. When you show empathy for others, they are more likely to show empathy for you. This creates feelings of mutual respect.

Assertiveness

Have you ever been afraid to express your feelings? Many people feel uncomfortable saying what they think or asking for what they want. When people are passive, they do not stand up for themselves. They are afraid to say something that might make others angry. Passive people often end up following the crowd whether or not the crowd is making good decisions.

Other people are aggressive and have the need to be in control. They are often viewed as pushy and rude, concerned mostly with their own needs and wants. They fail to respect the rights of others, and they may try to get their way by bullying people who do not stand up to them. Most people are turned off by aggressive people.

Individuals who communicate with assertiveness are neither passive nor aggressive. **Assertiveness** is standing up for yourself and your beliefs in firm but positive way. Assertive people do not bully others, but they do not give in either. They state their opinions and respectfully listen to other people's opinions. When opinions differ, they try to reach an agreement that works for everyone.

▼ Assertiveness

When you are assertive, you stand up for yourself without disrespecting others. You can say no and mean it. *What is the difference between assertiveness and aggressiveness?*

Masterfile

Show Respect and Character

You show respect through what you do as well as what you say. Respect your community and the environment by doing your part to take care of them. Stay informed about community issues and help your neighbors and people in need when you can. Driving safely and keeping noise levels low are other ways to show respect in your community.

You show respect at home when you act with consideration for the feelings of family members and when you clean up after yourself without being asked. At home and school, you can show respect by following rules, telling the truth, listening to adults with consideration, treating others' property with care, and taking responsibility for your actions instead of blaming others.

✓ Reading Check **Explain** What is respect?

Math You Can Use

Calculate Gross Profit

You decide to start your own after-school cleaning business. You charge $7.50 an hour for cleaning services. If you use 75 cents' worth of cleaning supplies for every two hours worked, what is your gross profit on every eight hours of work?

Math Concept **Order of Operations** Do all operations within grouping symbols first. Multiply and divide in order from left to right, and then add and subtract in order from left to right.

Starting Hint Calculate how much you earn for eight hours' work (your gross pay). Then calculate the cost of eight hours' worth of cleaning supplies and subtract this from your gross pay. This is your gross profit.

For math help, go to the Math Appendix at the back of the book.

Overcoming Communication Roadblocks

Negative attitudes make communication nearly impossible. Common forms of negativity include:

- **Gossip and Lies** People often use rumors and lies to gain unfair power over other people. This kind of hurtful talk can destroy relationships.
- **Insults, Threats, and Accusations** Aggressive tactics can scare or anger others. The listener may withdraw or lash out.
- **Nagging and Preaching** No one likes to be lectured. Comments such as "You should exercise, like I do" or "How many times do I have to tell you to clean your room?" turn listeners off.
- **A Know-It-All Attitude** No one is all-knowing. Having a superior attitude drives people away.
- **A Poor-Me Attitude** Some people feel that they have a harder life than everyone else. This can show as anger and resentment.
- **Sarcasm** When you use a tone of voice that expresses the opposite of what your words seem to say, you are using sarcasm. Sarcasm is a type of humor, but it can be unkind when it is used to hurt someone else. For example, saying "you are so smart" in a sarcastic tone sends the message that "you are not smart."

Become aware of negative patterns like these. Focus on solving problems rather than blaming others or proving that you are right. Try to understand issues from the other person's point of view. Show kindness, even if the other person has negative attitudes.

Stereotypes and Prejudice

Stereotypes and prejudice are the biggest communication road-blocks of all. A **stereotype** is the belief that an entire group of people are alike in certain ways. People who hold stereotypes do not see others as individuals. Every group has stereotypes about them. People with disabilities, the homeless, and people from different cultures often have to battle stereotypes. Older adults and teens are sometimes stereotyped as well.

Stereotypes can lead to prejudice. When people dislike or hurt others because of their differences, they show prejudice. **Prejudice** is an unfair opinion made without knowledge of the facts. Prejudice often is directed against people because of their race, religion, gender (male or female), age, amount of money, or disabilities. Prejudice causes distrust and hate. People on the receiving end of prejudice often respond with anger, frustration, despair, and sometimes develop prejudices of their own because of unfair treatment.

Overcome Stereotypes and Prejudices

We learn stereotypes and prejudices from our friends and family, from the media, and from our own experiences. A first step to overcoming stereotypes and prejudice is getting to know a wide range of people in your community. Treat others like you want to be treated. Learn how much people around the world have in common. Knowledge and understanding can help eliminate stereotypes and prejudice.

Section 6.2

After You Read

Review Key Concepts

1. **Explain** how to communicate with respect.
2. **Describe** how to overcome communication roadblocks.

Practice Academic Skills

English Language Arts

3. Reread the description of passive, aggressive, and assertive behavior and explain which one best describes you. What might you want to change about your behavior? Are there some situations in which you find it hard to be assertive? What steps could you take to become more assertive in the future? Summarize your ideas in a one-page essay.

Social Studies

4. You can show respect at school by treating others as equals and by treating others' property with care. How else can you show respect at school? Brainstorm ideas and then write a one-page "Policy for Respect" that clearly explains how you think students, teachers, and staff should act and talk to show respect for one another.

 Check Your Answers Go to connectED. mcgraw-hill.com to check your answers.

Community Connections

Global Interaction

Good communication is an essential part of living in an increasingly interconnected world. Miscommunication can have negative consequences. For this reason, it is very important to understand the nuances, or subtle differences, in how other cultures communicate both verbally and nonverbally.

Chapter 6 — Review and Applications

CHAPTER SUMMARY

Section 6.1
Speaking, Writing, and Listening Skills

Verbal communication includes writing and speaking. Nonverbal communication reveals feelings and attitudes and includes body language and facial expressions. Written communication can take many forms. Speaking and writing involve focusing on a clear message, considering the listener, and using words effectively. Active listening involves concentrating on the speaker and giving feedback.

Section 6.2
Communicating Respect

Respect is a belief in the worth of others. Self-respect is a belief in your own worth. You show respect through your words and actions. You show respect by being open to other points of view, showing interest in others, and treating others with tact and empathy. You also show respect for yourself by being assertive. Keep communication respectful by learning to recognize and overcome communication roadblocks, such as negative attitudes and stereotypes.

Vocabulary Review

1. Use each of these content and academic vocabulary words in a sentence.

Content Vocabulary
◇ communication (p. 137)
◇ verbal communication (p. 137)
◇ nonverbal communication (p. 137)
◇ enunciate (p. 138)
◇ body language (p. 139)
◇ active listening (p. 141)
◇ respect (p. 144)
◇ self-respect (p. 144)
◇ rapport (p. 146)
◇ tact (p. 146)
◇ empathy (p. 146)
◇ assertiveness (p. 146)
◇ stereotype (p. 148)
◇ prejudice (p. 148)

Academic Vocabulary
■ appropriate (p. 138)
■ minimize (p. 141)
■ occur (p. 144)
■ establish (p. 146)

Review Key Concepts

2. Compare and contrast verbal and nonverbal communication.
3. List four strategies for speaking effectively.
4. Describe how to listen actively.
5. Explain how to communicate with respect.
6. Describe how to overcome communication roadblocks.

Critical Thinking

7. Analyze Imagine that a friend looks angry but says that everything is fine. Which message would you believe? Why?
8. Predict What is likely to happen if one person in a conversation has a know-it-all attitude? Why?
9. Evaluate Consider this statement: "When you show empathy for others, they are more likely to show empathy for you." Do you agree or disagree? Why?
10. Critique Stand in front of a full-length mirror. What message do you think your posture conveys? What can you do to look more confident?
11. Construct Write a letter to a friend. Then change the organization and punctuation of the sentences. Has your tone changed? Has the meaning changed? How?

 **ACTIVE LEARNING**

 **Family & Community Connections**

12. Practice Active Listening Practice concentrating and giving feedback during a conversation with a classmate, friend, or family member. Make eye contact with the speaker. Pay attention to his or her body language, intonation, speed, and volume, and try to figure out what message these nonverbal cues are sending. Use your own body language and facial expressions to respond to the speaker. React to the speaker with comments or questions that show you have understood. After the conversation, write a paragraph describing the experience. Did active listening feel different? If so, how? Did it contribute to a positive experience? If so, how? If not, why not?

13. Investigate Similarities A stereotype is the belief that an entire group of people fit a fixed common pattern, meaning that they are all alike in certain ways. Stereotypes can lead to prejudice, an unfair or biased opinion about a group of people. However, people who are different from each other have many similarities. Interview a friend or neighbor who is different from you in some way, such as race, age, or gender. What similarities do you notice between yourself and the person? Interview a second friend or neighbor who is different from you in another way. If the first person you interviewed was much older than you, for example, the second person you interview should be of a different race, religion, or gender. What do the two of you have in common? In what way are all three of you alike? Present your findings to the class.

Real-World Skills and Applications

Leadership Skills

14. Community Involvement Describe a volunteer project you could organize to clean up a local park, recreation center, or other community property. Write down why the project is important, how you would organize it, what tasks it would involve, what people and resources you would need, and how you would publicize the event. Brainstorm possible local donors or businesses that might sponsor the event. If possible, carry out your idea.

Financial Literacy

15. Time Is Money You talk on your cell phone for three hours every week. You are considering two cell phone plans. The first plan allows you to talk for 450 minutes per month for $39.99; the second plan gives you 900 minutes per month for $59.99. For both plans, each additional minute costs ten cents. Which plan is the best for you?

Information Literacy

16. Analyze Advertising Ads are a form of persuasive communication. Analyze an ad. Who is the target audience? What strategies does the ad use to make you feel you should buy the product? What persuasive words does the ad use? What emotional message do the images send? What does the ad suggest that the product will do for you? Is this realistic? Summarize your findings.

Banana Stock/PhotoLibrary

Academic Skills

English Language Arts

17. Practice Presentation Skills Write a five-minute oral presentation on a subject that interests you. Begin with a thesis statement that describes your main point. Organize the presentation around three supporting points. Include facts and examples for each supporting point. Conclude by restating your thesis. Practice your speech in front of a mirror. Then present your speech to the class.

Social Studies

18. Research Communication in Different Cultures Conduct research about verbal and nonverbal communication customs in a culture of your choice. How do people speak with one another in this culture? How are facial expressions, body language, and personal distance used? Share your findings with the class.

Mathematics

19. Calculate Salary Workers with excellent communication skills can earn more at their jobs than workers without these skills. If the average salary for an office manager is $35,930 and the average salary for an office manager with excellent communication skills is $42,050, how much more does the manager with excellent communication skills earn? Express your answer as a percentage.

Math Concept **Calculate Percentages** A percent is a ratio that compares a number to 100.

Starting Hint Subtract the lower salary from the higher salary to find the difference. Then divide this difference by the lower salary to determine the difference as a percentage.

 For math help, go to the Math Appendix at the back of the book.

Standardized Test Practice

READING COMPREHENSION
Directions Read the passage, and then answer the question on a separate piece of paper.

Test-Taking Tip Read the passage carefully, identifying key statements as you read. Answer the question based only on what you just read in the passage, not based on your previous knowledge.

20. Interference, such as the television, phone, or a radio, can disrupt communication. People who want to communicate well try to eliminate interference first.

According to this passage, why do people who want to communicate well try to eliminate interference first?

Chapter 7

Conflict Resolution

Section 7.1
Preventing Conflict

Section 7.2
Working Through Conflicts

Chapter Objectives

Section 7.1

- **Determine** what causes conflict.
- **Identify** strategies for managing anger.
- **Describe** the guidelines you should follow when negotiating.

Section 7.2

- **Compare** your two options when faced with a conflict.
- **List** the steps in the conflict resolution process.
- **Suggest** ways to deal with bullies.

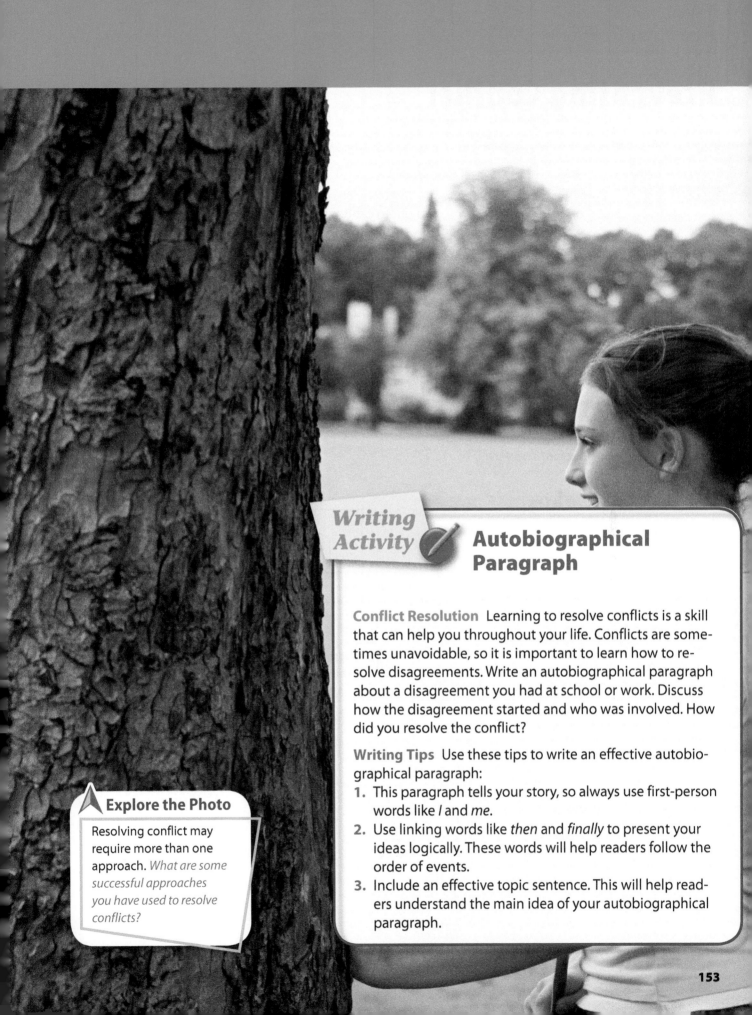

Writing Activity

Autobiographical Paragraph

Conflict Resolution Learning to resolve conflicts is a skill that can help you throughout your life. Conflicts are sometimes unavoidable, so it is important to learn how to resolve disagreements. Write an autobiographical paragraph about a disagreement you had at school or work. Discuss how the disagreement started and who was involved. How did you resolve the conflict?

Writing Tips Use these tips to write an effective autobiographical paragraph:

1. This paragraph tells your story, so always use first-person words like *I* and *me*.
2. Use linking words like *then* and *finally* to present your ideas logically. These words will help readers follow the order of events.
3. Include an effective topic sentence. This will help readers understand the main idea of your autobiographical paragraph.

Explore the Photo

Resolving conflict may require more than one approach. *What are some successful approaches you have used to resolve conflicts?*

Preventing Conflict

Before You Read

Predict Before starting the section, browse the content by reading headings, bold terms, and photo captions. Do they help you predict the information in the section?

Read to Learn

Key Concepts

- **Determine** what causes conflict.
- **Identify** strategies for managing anger.
- **Describe** the guidelines you should follow when negotiating.

Main Idea

When faced with different types of conflict, take steps to control your anger and be willing to negotiate.

Content Vocabulary

◇ conflict
◇ external conflict
◇ internal conflict
◇ tolerance
◇ negotiate

Academic Vocabulary

You will find these words in your reading and on your tests. Use the glossary to look up their definitions if necessary.

▢ constructive
▢ invaluable

Graphic Organizer

As you read, record the nine causes of conflict. Use a graphic organizer like the one below to organize your information.

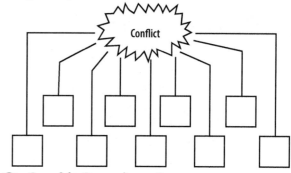

 Graphic Organizer Go to **connectED.mcgraw-hill.com** to download this graphic organizer.

Understand Conflict

People are different, with different thoughts and emotions. Sometimes these differences can create conflicts. A **conflict** is a disagreement or fight between people with opposing points of view. It can involve individuals or groups, such as friends, family members, community organizations, or even nations. Many conflicts are easily resolved. Others become never-ending struggles or turn into physical fights. When violence occurs, it is usually because the people involved don't know how they can settle their differences in more constructive, or positive and useful, ways. Fortunately, a conflict does not have to end in violence.

As You Read

Connect Think about the conflicts you have faced. How many were the result of a misunderstanding? What did you learn from them?

Types of Conflict

People experience two types of conflict: external conflict and internal conflict. A disagreement between family members, friends, or community members is an **external conflict**. Whenever one person's wants, needs, or values clash with those of another person, an external conflict can occur.

A conflict may also be an **internal conflict**, which is a struggle inside your heart or your head. For example, Marcus found out his friend Christine had been plagiarizing, or copying, reports for school. Marcus strongly felt what Christine was doing was wrong, but he worried she would hate him if he brought it up. He did not know what to do about his feelings. It felt like a tug-of-war in his head. Should he keep quiet and continue to lose respect for his friend? Or should he speak to Christine and risk losing her friendship?

If people in conflict use destructive tactics to try to resolve a problem, the outcome is likely to be negative. But not all conflicts need to end poorly. Positive outcomes are possible if each person involved approaches the conflict with mutual respect, an honest effort to listen, and a commitment to finding a solution.

Successful conflict resolution can actually bring people closer together. Marcus finally decided to speak to Christine. He found out that she plagiarized the reports because she was unsure of her writing skills. Marcus worked with Christine on her next report. He helped her improve her writing skills, and his caring actions reinforced their friendship.

Vocabulary

You can find definitions in the glossary at the back of this book.

> ➤ **Understand Conflict**
>
> Conflict often arises in friendship. Think about conflicts you have had with your friends and ways they can be resolved. *Why do you think it is important to resolve conflicts in constructive ways?*

©Radius Images/Corbis

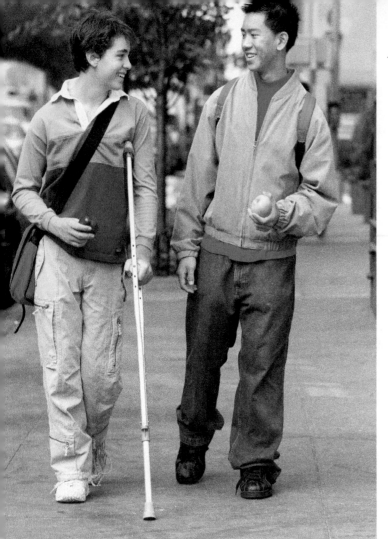

Don't let conflict ruin an important friendship. Think about what you respect and admire about each other, and work together to resolve your problem. *How do you feel after resolving a conflict with a friend? Explain.*

Causes of Conflict

Have you ever argued with someone and later could not remember what caused the conflict to begin with? No matter how small, every conflict has a cause. Some big conflicts, such as international problems, have many causes. Understanding the cause of a conflict can help you respond to it. In general, conflicts are caused by the following:

Personality Differences

Differences help make life exciting and fun, but they can also create conflict. Perhaps you like being around large groups of people, but your friend feels uncomfortable in groups. As a result, conflict over what to do when you get together may be an occasional part of your friendship. Thankfully, these sorts of disagreements are usually brief, and easily forgotten.

Specific Situations

Sometimes a specific situation can cause conflict. Say three teens have to share the same bathroom. If all three have to be ready for school at the same time, you can see how this situation can lead to conflict! The teens cannot control the fact that they must share a bathroom. But they can control how they deal with the situation.

Emotion

Has someone ever gotten extremely angry with you for something trivial you did or said? It is common for people to overreact to small issues when they are stressed out, hurt, hungry, exhausted, or just having a bad day. Their anger may actually have very little to do with you. Take these things into consideration before you respond to someone who has lashed out at you unfairly. Let the person know you did not mean to offend him or her. Do not attempt to "talk sense" to someone who is not in a logical frame of mind. As long as one person remains calm and logical, issues like this are easily defused.

Safety Check

Prevent Road Rage

Anger can be dangerous for drivers. Getting frustrated while behind the wheel can cause a person to drive aggressively and erratically. Driving at very high speeds, failing to signal, and cutting off other drivers are just some of the dangerous things drivers with road rage do.

Write About It

Write a paragraph describing techniques you can use to help control your anger while driving. How might these techniques reduce the likelihood of road rage in others?

Ken Karp/McGraw-Hill Education

Power Issues

Power struggles often take place when different people try to control a situation. Many arguments in families with teens are the result of power struggles. Say a teen disagrees with her parents' rules. To assert her independence, she may ignore her weekend curfew. In response, her parents may ground her, or take away other privileges to show that they are the ones in control.

Jealousy and Insecurity

Conflict that begins without an obvious cause is usually the result of one person's jealousy or insecurity. Many bullies are unhappy with themselves, so they put others down and push them around to gain a sense of control and importance. They tend to pick on those who seem weaker, or who have something they want.

Cultural Differences

Some social practices that are acceptable in one culture are not acceptable in another. For example, in some cultures, looking another person directly in the eye is considered an act of hostility. In others it is considered a sign of confidence and respect. If not familiar with another culture's customs, a person can easily offend or be offended by someone of that culture. Conflict and prejudice may arise from simple misunderstanding.

Disrespect

Treating a person or a person's property with disrespect is another common cause of conflict. When someone feels he or she has been treated poorly or unfairly, anger builds and he or she may seek revenge. If not dealt with in a positive manner, this sort of situation can get out of hand very quickly, leading to an endless cycle of violence.

Drugs and Alcohol

Drugs and alcohol can trigger conflict or cause existing conflicts to escalate because they impair a person's judgment. Some people get very aggressive when under the influence of drugs or alcohol and start fights without cause. Avoid conflict by avoiding those who use these substances.

Poor Communication

Misheard statements, unclear directions, and rumors are just some of the communication mistakes that can lead to conflict. It is smart to rephrase directions and double-check plans to be certain everyone involved is on the same page. Otherwise, a simple misunderstanding can turn into a full-blown "I said–you said" argument and cause future mistrust. Rumors often become more fiction than fact the more they are repeated and lead to hurt feelings and resentment. These are the beginnings of conflict. Save yourself from unnecessary drama by refusing to start rumors or pass along those you hear.

✓ **Reading Check** **Identify** What are the two types of conflict?

Community Connections

Cultural Knowledge

Learn the customs of people from other cultures that you frequently encounter. Understanding a person's background can help you avoid offending him or her. It can also help you understand some of the mistakes he or she may make in communicating with you.

Building Character?!

Proactive Support Your friend Camisha receives threatening e-mails several times a week from a schoolmate. The e-mails really upset Camisha, but she does not think she is technically being bullied because the threats are not made in person. In fact, the schoolmate never talks to her. What, if anything, should you do to help?

You Make the Call

Should you tell Camisha to delete the e-mails and hope that they stop? Should you convince her to tell a trusted adult about the threats? Or, should you ignore the situation since Camisha is trying to shrug it off? Explain.

SUCCEED IN SCHOOL

Fun Is Important

Having fun is an important part of living a balanced life. Fun activities help relieve building stress so you can think clearly and function at your best in school.

Avoid Conflict

The best way to deal with conflict is to prevent it from starting in the first place. This feat is much simpler than it seems.

Respect and Tolerance

Did you know that you can prevent many conflicts simply by showing others respect? When you show respect, you show you value another person as an individual. You also make it more likely the person will respect you. People who respect each other tend to listen with an open mind. They consider the views and feelings of one another, and honor each other's basic values.

Tolerance is also vital to prevent and resolve conflict. **Tolerance** is the ability to accept and respect other people's customs and beliefs. People who are willing to accept others as they are tend to have fewer conflicts than people who are not accepting of others. Tolerance helps you understand that people have a right to behave and express themselves in ways different from your own, as long as they do not hurt others in the process. You need to be willing to accept all people and learn to understand their points of view.

Tolerance also involves getting along with people of all generations. Teens sometimes find it hard to get along with older adults because they have different ways of talking, dressing, and acting. You are deserving of respect, but so are they. Show older adults the respect you would like to be shown. Remember, you will be an older adult someday, too.

How I See It

PEACEFUL SOLUTIONS
Gretchen, 15

When my older brother was in high school he got into a lot of fights and was expelled from school. I saw firsthand how hard this was on my brother and my family. My brother always tells me to learn from his mistakes by choosing friends who are involved in positive activities, like sports or community work. He says fighting got him nowhere, so I should try to stop conflicts before they start and walk away from situations that could turn violent. It was hard at first, but leaving all the drama behind and joining the track team has helped me focus in school. My grades have gone up, and I feel really good about myself now!

Critical Thinking Gretchen's story suggests that people with positive outlets are more likely to deal with difficult situations in positive, nonviolent ways. Do you agree? Why or why not?

Anger Management

Everyone gets angry at times. When people are angry or annoyed, they may walk away or use a harsh tone of voice. Other times, they may yell, argue, or start a fight. If you learn to manage, or control, your anger, you can redirect these surges of anger energy to reach your goal.

When anger is not controlled, conflict becomes worse. Dwelling on how angry you are doesn't help defuse your anger. Instead, your anger can build and lead to rage. At this stage, you may no longer be able to think clearly. The ancient martial art of jujitsu (jū-jit-sū) teaches those who practice the art to remain calm, to empty themselves of anger, and to gain the advantage in a conflict by using their opponent's tendency to strike out in blind rage. This type of self-control is not just for martial artists. You can develop these techniques to control your anger and prevent conflicts from getting out of hand.

Pent-Up Anger

Anger can take two forms. The first form of anger is often called pent-up anger. It builds over time, and if not released in a healthy way, pent-up anger can explode when you least expect it. When you feel anger or frustration building inside, release these feelings in a positive and productive way.

- **Exercise.** Go for a walk, play basketball, clean your room or lift weights. Getting your heart going will help you release building energy and emotional tension. This stress-relieving action will allow you to clear your head and think about the situation logically.
- **Talk it out.** Talk about your feelings with a good friend, or write about them in a journal. Getting things off your chest reduces anger and frustration. A friend can help you view things in a new way, and help you find a positive solution. Seeing your problem in black and white may also help you see your problem (and a positive solution) more clearly.
- **Get space.** Remember where you are when you get angry. If you are in a public place, respect the people around you that are not involved in the situation. It is never okay to yell at a retail clerk, or restaurant staff. You will look foolish and cause others unnecessary stress. You will also feel even worse than you felt before. Find a private place where you can let your emotions out. Listen to soothing music. Cry or yell if you need to.
- **Meditate.** Close your eyes and sit quietly for a while. Push everything out of your mind. If your heart is racing, try to bring it down to a slow, steady pace. Focus on your breathing. Breathe in through your nose for five slow counts, then breathe out of your mouth for five slow counts. This may feel silly at first, but it really works!

▲ Anger Management

Strenuous exercise is a great way to put "anger energy" to work. You will feel better and more in control of your emotions when done. *What kind of exercise do you do to channel "anger energy"?*

Health & Wellness

Work Off Stress

Exercise decreases stress by reducing the production of stress hormones. It also works against your body's natural response to stress. Try these tips to combat stress:

- ▶ Choose an activity you truly enjoy.
- ▶ Forget your troubles and focus on exercising.
- ▶ Exercise with a friend to keep motivated.

Michael Krinke/Getty Images

Hot Anger

The second form of anger can be called hot anger and occurs suddenly when conflict flares between you and another person. To deal with hot anger, and prevent a situation from getting out of hand, try these suggestions:

- **Breathe deeply.** Pull air in through your nose and let it flow evenly and slowly out through your mouth. Do this at least three times before responding. This helps slow your heart rate and gives you time to think.
- **Count to ten.** Before reacting, slowly count to ten. This gives you a chance to collect yourself and prevents your emotions from taking control.
- **Self-talk.** Tell yourself, "I am calm. I am in control of my actions. I choose to be focused. I choose to be relaxed."
- **Redirect your energy.** Think of your anger as energy. Instead of fighting with someone, you can use this energy to get things done and positively resolve an issue.
- **Picture a calming place or person.** Positive thoughts help put a situation into perspective.
- **Walk away.** If feel you can not control your anger, remove yourself from the situation immediately. It is best to escape a situation until you are ready to deal with it calmly.

✓ **Reading Check** **Explain** What are respect and tolerance, and how do they prevent conflict?

Negotiation

Ashley worked hard all summer so she could save enough money to buy a new stereo. When they heard of her plans, Ashley's parents told her she needed to put all of her earnings into the bank to save for college. Instead of fighting with her parents about it, Ashley asked them to set a time when they could negotiate an agreement about how to spend the money.

To **negotiate** is to deal or bargain with another person. Negotiation involves talking, listening, considering the other person's point of view, and compromising if necessary. The goal of negotiation is to achieve a win-win solution. This means that all parties are happy with the outcome. Negotiation is an invaluable, or extremely useful and valuable, tool in preventing full-blown conflict.

Keep the following guidelines in mind when you are negotiating to solve a problem:

- **Choose the right time.** Pick a time that works for everyone. Avoid meeting if you feel rushed or impatient. If you have to rush through the discussion, you may miss facts that you need to reach a satisfying conclusion.

- **Choose the right place.** Choose a quiet place so that the person you need to talk to is not distracted by the television or other people's conversations.

- **Keep an open mind.** Listen carefully to each person and consider all points of view. If you show others respect, they are more likely to show you respect and listen to your points.

- **Seek a win-win solution.** Instead of making sure you get everything you want out of the negotiation, work with others to find a solution that makes everyone happy. If you are happy with the results of a negotiation, but others are not, the issue will likely come up again later. Since negotiation did not work for all involved the first time, the issue is more likely to turn into a full-blown conflict.

Learning to negotiate can help you resolve problems before they turn into big conflicts. In Ashley's case, negotiation kept Ashley and her parents from fighting about the money. They all agreed some of the money would be put aside for her college education, and the rest could be spent on the stereo.

Section 7.1

After You Read

Review Key Concepts

1. **Define** conflict.
2. **Explain** the importance of controlling your anger.
3. **Describe** negotiation and its role in preventing conflict.

Practice Academic Skills

English Language Arts

4. Think of an example of an external conflict and an example of an internal conflict. Write two paragraphs describing the differences and similarities between the two examples. Which type of conflict do you think is more challenging to resolve? Explain.

Social Studies

5. Interview a friend, family member, teacher, or coach about conflicts he or she faces. Does the person face internal or external conflicts more often? What causes most of these conflicts? For example, is poor communication involved?

 Check Your Answers Go to connectED. mcgraw-hill.com to check your answers.

Working Through Conflicts

Before You Read

Two-Column Notes Two-column notes are a useful way to study and organize what you have read. Divide a piece of paper into two-columns. In the left column, write down main ideas. In the right column, list supporting details.

Read to Learn

Key Concepts

- **Compare** your two options when faced with a conflict.
- **List** the steps in the conflict resolution process.
- **Suggest** ways to deal with bullies.

Main Idea

Most conflicts can be resolved through communication and cooperation. Other conflicts cannot be resolved but can still be dealt with in productive ways.

Content Vocabulary

◇ escalate
◇ conflict resolution
◇ compromise
◇ mediation
◇ peer mediator

Academic Vocabulary

You will find these words in your reading and on your tests. Use the glossary to look up their definitions if necessary.

▢ deadlock
▢ instill

Graphic Organizer

As you read, record the questions you can ask to decide how to respond to conflict. Use a graphic organizer like the one below to organize your information.

 Graphic Organizer Go to connectED.mcgraw-hill.com to download this graphic organizer.

Respond to Conflict

When a conflict develops, you have two choices. You can either face it or ignore it. Before deciding which action to take, ask yourself these questions:

- **Are you in danger?** Your personal safety should be your first concern. If a situation looks like it might turn into a physical conflict, your best bet would be to walk away. Leaving a potentially dangerous situation is a positive choice, not a sign of cowardice.
- **Who is involved?** If the other person is someone you do not know well, you might decide it is best to ignore the situation. If it involves someone you care about, try to communicate your feelings in a calm and reasonable way.
- **What is the cause?** If the person is upset because of something you know you did or said, apologize and correct your mistake if possible. It is best to address a situation while it is still small. Otherwise that person's anger can grow and you may find yourself in the middle of a major conflict.
- **What outcome do you expect?** If you feel bringing up a problem will only make it worse, it is better to ignore it until both people cool off.

In some cases, people let conflicts **escalate**, or grow into disagreements that are destructive or unsafe to everyone concerned. Some teens think that becoming involved in a conflict may prove they are tough and fearless. Unfortunately, getting out of a difficult conflict is not as easy as getting into one. You can suffer legal consequences, lose friends, and lose your family's trust if you engage in violent conflicts.

✓ **Reading Check**   **Describe** What are your options when a conflict develops?

As You Read

Connect Think about a conflict you walked away from. Why did you decide to ignore the conflict?

◇ **Vocabulary**

You can find definitions in the glossary at the back of this book.

Avoid Conflict

Sometimes walking away is the best choice. *When is walking away from a conflict a positive action?*

Resolve Conflict

Whether a conflict is unavoidable or tests your pride or values, you can still resolve it peacefully. **Conflict resolution**, the process of settling a conflict through cooperation and problem solving, is a proven approach. Conflict resolution lets people involved in a dispute work out a solution to their problem without resorting to violence or losing face. Resolving conflicts takes work, but anyone can learn the necessary problem-solving and communication skills.

I Love Images/PhotoLibrary

The Conflict Resolution Process

For the conflict resolution process to work, the people involved have to want to solve their problem. They must be open to negotiation and willing to brainstorm with the other people involved to bring the conflict to an end.

Follow these steps to resolve conflicts:

1. **Accept responsibility for your role in the conflict.** Be willing to apologize if you see you have unfairly hurt another person. Accepting your mistake and wanting to correct it are signs of maturity.

2. **Define the problem.** Each person takes a turn describing the problem from his or her point of view. Everyone listens with respect until it is his or her turn to speak.

3. **Suggest a solution.** After considering all points of view, each person suggests a solution to the problem.

4. **Evaluate each solution.** Each person identifies the parts of each solution that he or she agrees with or cannot accept.

5. **Compromise.** If the parties are close to an agreement, they may compromise. **Compromise** means giving in on some points of disagreement and getting your way on others.

6. **Brainstorm.** If individuals cannot compromise, they brainstorm different ways to approach the problem and try again to reach a compromise.

HOW TO . . . . Deal with Bullies

Bullies use continual taunts, threats, and physical violence to intimidate others. Most bullying occurs at school, which can make it hard to concentrate. Cyberbullying is bullying that occurs through the use of electronic technology. It is hard to escape cyperbullying because it reaches a person anytime of the day or night—even when the victim is alone. Bullies are not open to conflict resolution. Follow these guidelines to deal with bullies.

Show Confidence Bullies choose easy targets. If you show that you are not likely to be bothered by their aggression, they usually look elsewhere. Show postive self-esteem: Carry yourself with pride, look people in the eye, and be friendly to others.

Ignore Verbal Abuse Show no reaction to insults or cruel jokes aimed at you. Bullying is like a game that takes two or more to play. If you do not go along, the game ends.

Stand Up for Yourself Tell—do not ask—the bully to stop the hurtful behavior. Avoid criticizing, name-calling, or other emotional responses, which only encourage and provoke further attacks. Then leave calmly.

7. **Take a break.** If negotiating is not going well, it is okay to work at it another time. Pressuring others to agree to a solution because you are tired or out of time or no longer making progress will only make things worse in the long run. Suggest a future time and place to continue the process.

8. **Seek help.** If no solution can be reached, you can ask a mediator, a neutral third party, to listen to your problem and make suggestions to resolve it.

Mediation

Sometimes people cannot resolve an issue on their own using either negotiation or conflict resolution. A deadlock is a situation in which no further progress is possible in a dispute. Deadlocks usually occur when two or more people refuse to compromise. To resolve a deadlock, they may need mediation.

During **mediation**, a neutral third party is used to help reach a solution that is agreeable to everyone. Mediators are trained to withhold judgment and to be careful listeners. They ask questions of both parties and respond to questions fairly and calmly. Mediators do not make decisions for other people. Instead, they help those involved in a conflict to evaluate, assess, and decide for themselves.

Health & Wellness TIPS

Prevent Cyberbullying

Cyberbullying can happen 24 hours a day, seven days a week. If you have a better understanding of social media sites, you may be able to protect yourself and others. Use these tips to prevent cyberbullying:

▶ Adjust privacy settings on social media sites so only your trusted friends and family see your posts.

▶ Think before you post anything embarrassing or hurtful. What you put on the Internet can never be erased.

▶ Confide in an adult immediately if you are being cyberbullied.

Stand Up for Others There is strength in numbers. Come forward to defend someone who is being abused, and encourage others to do the same. Bullies often back down when faced with a show of real power—the power of people with courage. They see that their actions make them unpopular.

Talk to an Adult Tell a parent, teacher, or other trusted adult if you are bothered by a bully. Take a friend if you need support. Adults' intervention may not be needed at that point. If the bullying continues or escalates, however, they will be ready to act. Parents need to be made aware of any intimidation or inappropriate physical contact by one sibling to another.

Put Safety Before Possessions If a bully demands money, shoes, or any other thing you own, hand it over. Your physical well-being is more important than any material items. Report the incident to an adult.

(tr)PhotoAlto/SuperStock, (c)©Tetra Images/Tetra Images/Corbis

TAKE CHARGE!

Forgive and Forget

We all make mistakes. Think about the choices you have when another person's mistake upsets you. Sometimes the only way you can improve the situation is by forgiving the other person. These steps can help you forgive others:

- **Put Yourself in Another's Place** Have you ever been forgiven for a mistake? Remember what a relief it was? Share that feeling with others by forgiving people who have made mistakes.
- **Accept Apologies** It takes a lot for a person to admit that he was wrong and to apologize. When people apologize to you, show respect for their courage by accepting their apologies graciously.
- **Let Go of the Past** Avoid holding grudges against people. Once you have forgiven them, wipe the slate clean and move on.

Real-World Skills

Act It Out You might be surprised by how much you can express through pantomime. Follow your teacher's instructions to form into pairs. Without using words, perform a mistake, an apology, and an act of forgiveness. Then, survey the class to see how effectively you used pantomime to perform the situation.

Many schools have instituted peer mediation programs to help resolve conflicts. A **peer mediator** is a young person who listens to both parties in conflict and helps them find a solution. Schools with peer mediation programs tend to have more cooperation, fewer fights, and less overall violence. Many families and communities now use mediation to resolve disagreements and prevent violence. When people resolve differences peacefully, everyone benefits.

Agreeing to Disagree

Not every honest discussion will result in agreement. You may never agree with your parents about which music is best, but you can realize that no matter what you say, you will not change their minds. Some people involved in conflicts realize that it is pointless to continue to argue, so they shake hands and agree to disagree. This means that each person does not completely accept the views of the other person, but both people decide that they will tolerate one another's views.

Most conflicts can be resolved if people are willing to talk, cooperate, and work toward positive solutions. Learn as much as you can about conflict resolution, mediation, and agreeing to disagree, to do your part to bring about peace at home, at school, and in your community.

✓ **Reading Check** **Explain** How would you describe conflict resolution?

SUCCEED IN SCHOOL

Prepare a Speech

Before you give a speech, it is important to prepare what you will say. You might want to write out the main points of your speech in the order you want to present them. You will also want to prepare an introduction and strong conclusion to your presentation.

When Talking It Out Is Not an Option

Mediation and the conflict resolution process are not options when you are dealing with a bully. Through continual taunts and physical aggression, bullies can make life miserable for others. Unfortunately, bullies are not open to conflict resolution because the conflict is really within themselves.

Bullies are motivated by many reasons. Some may be unhappy and insecure. Others are jealous of the person they target. Still others struggle with other personal issues. Humiliating those who are weaker or different gives them a sense of importance. Bullies may believe they are earning respect, but it is only fear and resentment that they instill, or inspire, in their victims. For some, the abuse confirms the low opinion they hold of themselves. They need help dealing with their insecurity and anger.

Most bullies will eventually leave you alone if you show confidence and ignore their verbal abuse. They are looking for any sort of reaction, and if you do not give them one, they will eventually find an easier target. If you are being bullied by e-mail, ask your service provider to help you block the bully's messages.

If a bully does not stop harassing you, you need to get help. Talk to a trusted adult. A parent, teacher, guidance counselor, or a coach may be able to help.

Safety Check

Report Cyberbullying

It can be difficult to track a cyberbully, but if you see or learn of cyberbullying, you can take steps to report it. First, don't respond to cyberbullying. Keep any evidence by printing it out or taking a screenshot. Inform the parties involved. This can include social media sites, online service providers, law enforcement, and schools.

Write About It

Think of any time where you have experienced, or know someone who has experienced being bullied through the Internet or text messages. Write a paragraph about how you would report that instance of cyberbullying.

Section 7.2

After You Read

Review Key Concepts

1. **Explain** why you should not let a conflict escalate.
2. **Summarize** how a mediator helps people resolve their conflicts.
3. **Explain** why bullies are not open to conflict resolution.

Practice Academic Skills

English Language Arts

4. Read a story in which a character struggles with a conflict. Describe the conflict and how the character deals with it. Is the response successful? Could the character have worked through the conflict in a better way? If so, how?

Social Studies

5. You have been asked to select peer mediators for your school. What qualities would you look for in a peer mediator? Why? Remember that mediators should assist but not make decisions for other people.

 Check Your Answers Go to connectED. mcgraw-hill.com to check your answers.

Correctional Officer

What Does a Correctional Officer Do?

Correctional officers work in jails and prisons. Their job is to make sure that inmates are orderly and obey rules. In jails, correctional officers supervise people who are waiting for their trials to begin. In prisons, they maintain security and order.

Skills Good judgment and the ability to think and act quickly are critical. Good communication skills are also valuable. Correctional officers must usually meet certain levels of physical fitness, eyesight, and hearing. Candidates should be willing and able to work with prison inmates.

Education and Training A high school diploma is required. Most states require some college. The Federal Bureau of Prisons requires at least a bachelor's degree or a combination of a degree and three years full-time experience. Most states provide on-the-job training with an experienced officer.

Job Outlook Job opportunities are excellent. The demand for officers is growing because the prison population is increasing. Most of the jobs are in state correctional institutions and in rural areas. One key to promotion is continuing education.

JUPITERIMAGES/Thinkstock/Alamy

Critical Thinking Research and find at least three articles about correctional officers and their job responsibilities. In your own words, summarize their job responsibilities. Then, write a paragraph comparing and contrasting the responsibilities of each officer.

Career Cluster — Law, Public Safety, Corrections and Security

Correctional officers work in the Law, Public Safety, Corrections and Security career cluster. Here are some of the other jobs in this cluster:

- Police Officer
- Police Detective and Investigator
- Probation Officer
- Correctional Treatment Specialist
- Jailer
- Warden
- Security Officer
- Gaming Surveillance Officer
- Youth Services Worker
- Program Counselor
- Fire Fighter
- Dispatcher
- Park Ranger
- Judge
- Paralegal
- Attorney
- Private Investigator
- Loss Prevention Specialist

Explore Further Research this career cluster. Choose a career in this cluster that appeals to you and write a career profile.

Chapter 7 · Review and Applications

CHAPTER SUMMARY

Section 7.1
Preventing Conflict

A conflict is a disagreement or fight between people with opposing points of view. Conflict is a part of everyday life. Some conflicts are settled easily, while others may last indefinitely. Conflicts are caused by a variety of factors. What creates conflict for one person may not matter to someone else. People who are tolerant and can control their anger are better able to prevent conflict. Negotiation is one way to prevent a disagreement from escalating into a full-blown conflict.

Section 7.2
Working Through Conflicts

When responding to conflict, think of your safety first. The conflict resolution process is a proven method for successfully resolving conflicts. When disagreeing parties are deadlocked, they may need mediation. Some people agree to disagree to end unnecessary conflict. Conflict resolution and mediation strategies do not work when dealing with bullies. Instead you should show confidence, ignore verbal abuse, stand up for yourself and others, and tell an adult if the bully becomes physical.

Vocabulary Review

1. Write a paragraph using five or more of these content and academic vocabulary terms. The paragraph should clearly show how the terms are related.

Content Vocabulary
◇ conflict (p. 155)
◇ external conflict (p. 155)
◇ internal conflict (p. 155)
◇ tolerance (p. 158)
◇ negotiate (p. 160)
◇ escalate (p. 163)
◇ conflict resolution (p. 163)
◇ compromise (p. 164)
◇ mediation (p. 165)
◇ peer mediator (p. 166)

Academic Vocabulary
▪ constructive (p. 155)
▪ invaluable (p. 160)
▪ deadlock (p. 165)
▪ instill (p. 167)

Review Key Concepts

2. **Determine** what causes conflict.
3. **Identify** strategies for managing anger.
4. **Describe** the guidelines you should follow when negotiating.
5. **Compare** your two options when faced with a conflict.
6. **List** the steps in the conflict resolution process.
7. **Suggest** ways to deal with bullies.

Critical Thinking

8. **Apply** The prom committee has been struggling with power issues and has asked you to be its peer mediator. How might you help the committee resolve its problems?
9. **Demonstrate** You have plans tonight and want to trade chores with your brother, but he is unwilling. How can you resolve this problem fairly?
10. **Compare and Contrast** Compare the ways you dealt with conflict a few years ago with how you deal with conflict today. Have your conflict resolution skills improved? Explain.
11. **Plan** Your friend is the favorite target of a bully at school. What can you do to help your friend avoid the bully's abuse?

ACTIVE LEARNING

Family & Community Connections

12. Conflict Resolution Follow your teacher's instructions to form into pairs. With your partner, write and perform a scene in which you use the conflict resolution process to resolve a problem. For example, you might portray two students who disagree on the topic for a group science project. Remember to display these steps: accept responsibility for your role in the conflict; define the problem; suggest a solution; evaluate each solution; compromise; brainstorm; take a break; seek help. You may choose to solve the problem in a  manner that does not require following all of the steps. Present your scene to your classmates, and ask them to evaluate how well you used the steps in the process.

13. Resolution Problems Ask a friend or family member about an external conflict he or she has experienced. Have him or her describe the cause of the conflict and the manner in which it was resolved. Was the attempt at a solution successful? If so, what was the key to the successful resolution? Note which conflict resolution steps the person followed and which he or she did not. Were the steps that he or she followed necessary? Were some steps ignored? If so, why? For example, compromise would be difficult if only one person was willing to give in on some points of disagreement. Likewise, it would be pointless to suggest a solution to someone who was not willing to listen to another person's ideas. If an additional problem made following the steps difficult, brainstorm ways to deal with this problem should it come up again. Present your findings to the class.

Real-World Skills and Applications

Leadership Skills

14. Control Your Emotions Think about situations at school and in the workplace that can cause hot anger. Why is it important to manage your emotions in these types of situations? Why do you think it is important for a leader to be able to manage his or her anger? What suggestions would you give teens for managing their emotions so that they can work effectively with others?

Financial Literacy

15. Gym Membership You want to join a gym to help reduce your stress level, but you want to spend as little money as possible. You like Gym A and Gym B equally. Gym A requires a start-up fee of $34.95 and charges a monthly rate of $19.95. Gym B requires no start-up fee but charges $24.95 per month. Which gym is cheaper for a year of membership? By how much is it cheaper?

Cooperative Learning

16. Negotiation With a partner, create a comic book depicting two or more teens who resolve a problem by negotiating. Remember that negotiation involves choosing the right time and the right place to have a productive discussion. Share your comic book with the class.

Academic Skills

English Language Arts

17. Research Road Rage When anger turns into rage, it often becomes difficult to think clearly and make wise decisions. Research the issue of road rage. Then, use your findings to write an informational essay that explains the consequences of road rage and some proper responses.

Science

18. Breathe Deeply People often do not breathe as effectively as they could. Use this activity to try a breathing technique that should restore your natural breathing when you are out of breath or upset.

Procedure Breathe in slowly through your nose. Then, breathe out through your mouth for twice as long as you breathed in. Use this breathing technique for a few minutes.

Analysis After using the breathing technique for a few minutes, write a paragraph about it and how it makes you feel.

Mathematics

19. Compromise You are going on a hike with your friend. You want to hike for two and one-half hours, but your friend says he is really tired so he only wants to hike for 45 minutes. You suggest that you both compromise and split the difference. What amount of time should you suggest as a compromise?

Math Concept **Averages** In order to find the average of a group of numbers, add all the numbers together and divide this sum, or total, by the quantity of numbers you have added.

Starting Hint Convert the 2½ hours you want to spend hiking into minutes. There are 60 minutes in an hour, so 150 minutes would equal 2.5 hours (60×2.5). Add 150 minutes to the 45 minutes your friend wants to spend hiking.

 For math help, go to the Math Appendix at the back of the book.

Standardized Test Practice

READING COMPREHENSION
Directions Read the paragraph. Then choose the correct answer.

Test-Taking Tip If there is no guessing penalty and you do not know the answer to a multiple-choice question, do not leave it unanswered! First eliminate the answers you know are wrong. Then take an educated guess between the remaining options. Do not continually change your answer. Your time will be better spent on other questions.

For the conflict resolution process to work, everyone involved has to want to solve the problem. Each person must be open to compromise and willing to brainstorm to bring the conflict to an end. If unable to resolve the problem on their own, the involved parties may want to seek outside help to mediate the situation.

20. Which approach is not part of the conflict resolution process?
a) Compromise
b) Meditate
c) Seek help
d) Brainstorm

Chapter 8

You and Your Peers

Section 8.1
Dealing with Peer Pressure

Section 8.2
Enjoying Friendships

Chapter Objectives

Section 8.1

- **Compare and contrast** negative and positive peer pressure.
- **Identify** three ways you can respond to negative peer pressure.

Section 8.2

- **Describe** the benefits of friendship with those who are different from you.
- **List** the qualities of a true friend.
- **Summarize** your major responsibilities when hanging out with friends.
- **Explain** why friendships end.

Aldo Murillo/Getty Images

172

Writing Activity

Personal Letter

Cultivate Friendships Personal letters can help maintain friendships. They let friends know you are thinking of them while also giving them news about your own life. Write a personal letter to a friend you have not seen in a while. Include information about recent events in your life, and ask specific questions about events in your friend's life.

Writing Tips Use these tips to write a personal letter:
- Personal letters typically have five parts—the heading, the greeting, the body, the complimentary close, and the signature line.
- Remember to proofread your letter for spelling and grammatical errors.
- Sign the letter yourself to make it more personal and friendly.

Explore the Photo

Surround yourself with people who have positive attitudes to help you develop self-confidence and a positive self-image. *How do you and your friends reflect positive attitudes?*

Dealing with Peer Pressure

Reading Guide

Before You Read

Prior Knowledge Look over the Key Concepts in this section's Reading Guide. Write down what you already know about each concept and what you want to find out by reading the section. As you read, find examples for both categories.

Read to Learn

Key Concepts

- **Compare** and contrast negative and positive peer pressure.
- **Identify** three ways you can respond to negative peer pressure.

Main Idea

It is important to understand the difference between positive and negative peer pressure and to find ways to respond to negative peer pressure.

Content Vocabulary

◇ peer
◇ peer pressure
◇ manipulation
◇ refusal skill

Academic Vocabulary

You will find these words in your reading and on your tests. Use the glossary to look up their definitions if necessary.

☐ beneficial
☐ abstract

Graphic Organizer

As you read, record the different types of manipulation techniques. Use a graphic organizer like the one below to organize your information. Examples of each technique are provided.

Technique	Example
1.	"I thought I could count on you."
2.	"If you don't, I'll tell everyone."
3.	"What are you, chicken?"
4.	"Come on, everybody's doing it."
5.	"We only ask cool people to join us."

 Graphic Organizer Go to **connectED.mcgraw-hill.com** to download this graphic organizer.

Recognizing Peer Pressure

A **peer** is a person of the same age group. The clothes you wear, places you go, and activities you choose are often influenced by your peers. Peers can even affect the way you act and the things you say. The pressure you feel to do what others your age are doing is called **peer pressure**. People of all ages are influenced by their peers, but teens are especially sensitive to their peers' opinions. Teens want to fit in, which can make peer pressure hard to resist.

Positive Peer Pressure

Have you ever been influenced by friends to do something positive for yourself, others, or your community? Positive peer pressure is what you feel when people your age encourage you to do something worthwhile. When a good friend encourages you to study for a big test, you are experiencing positive peer pressure. The same is true when you pressure a friend to eat healthfully and get in shape.

True friends do not ask each other to do things that are wrong or hurtful to themselves or anyone else. Positive peer pressure supports your values and beliefs, and it almost always results in positive consequences for everyone involved.

Role Models

A person you admire and learn behavior and attitudes from is called a role model. A role model influences your thinking by providing you with an example to imitate. Athletes, musicians, actors, and other celebrities are role models to many, but family members and friends can also be role models. You can be a positive role model to someone who looks up to you and follows your actions.

As You Read

Connect Think about the ways your peers influence you. How have they had a positive influence on your daily activities? What, if any, negative influence have they had?

Vocabulary

You can find definitions in the glossary at the back of this book.

Inspire Others

It is an honor when someone sees you as a role model. By being a positive role model, you can inspire others around you. *How can you be a positive role model for others?*

Alistair Berg/Getty Images

Manipulation

Manipulation comes in many forms and can result in serious troubles. *How can you avoid being manipulated?*

Community Connections

Community Pride

Showing community pride means working to make your community a better place to live, work, and play. Disposing of your own trash properly is one simple way to show community pride. Working with others on community projects, like cleaning a park or school yard, is another.

Good role models are a positive influence on those whose lives they touch. They inspire you to work harder, to think about your future, and to develop **beneficial** behaviors, or behaviors that are to your advantage.

Role models can also serve as good examples of what not to do. A teen whose role models do not use tobacco, alcohol, or other drugs may be positively influenced to follow their lead. Unfortunately, not all role models are positive ones. Some people, including a number of celebrities and athletes, may exemplify behavior that is not positive.

Negative Peer Pressure

When you hear someone say "everybody's doing it", how do you feel? Do you think true friends say things like this to each other? This is just one of the phrases people say when they are using negative peer pressure. Negative peer pressure is what you feel when your peers try to persuade you to do something you do not feel is right, or something that has negative consequences. Some peers may try to persuade you to do something to hurt others or to do something unhealthy, dangerous, or illegal, such as use tobacco, alcohol, or other drugs. They may urge you to try something you feel you are not ready for or that goes against your better judgment.

People who use negative peer pressure often know that what they are pressuring others to do is wrong. Convincing friends to join them fills their own needs, not the needs of their friends, and makes them feel important and in control.

Chris Windsor/Getty Images

Manipulation

People sometimes pressure others through **manipulation**, a dishonest way to control or influence someone. People who manipulate others aim to get what they want, regardless of the consequences. To get others to do what they want, manipulators use the following techniques:

- **Challenge your courage.** They may cluck at you to shame you: "What are you, chicken?" They may tease you by comparing you to something they consider weak or less-than-intimidating: "My 90-year-old grandma could do this! Quit being a little baby!"
- **Appeal to your desire to belong.** Besides the familiar statement "Come on, everybody's doing it," other appeals include "Only losers say no".
- **Use flattery.** Manipulators will flatter or praise you insincerely: "We only ask people we think are cool to join us."
- **Appeal to your guilt.** "Man, I thought I could count on you!" is an example of manipulation with guilt.
- **Threaten or blackmail.** Some manipulators may threaten violence or other acts of sabotage if you do not do what they want. "If you don't, I'll tell everyone" is a typical threat.

How do you feel when people try to manipulate you into doing things that are wrong? Watch out for so-called friends who constantly push you to prove yourself by doing things you feel are wrong. True friends will not pressure you to do something you do not want to do. In the same way, your peers should be able to count on you to respect their values and beliefs and to not manipulate them.

How I See It

TRUE FRIENDS
Emily, 16

When my family and I moved to a new town two years ago, I had a hard time finding a new group of friends. I hung out with my neighbor, but she always pressured me into doing stuff I really didn't want to do. I didn't really like this "friend" of mine, but I figured hanging out with her was better than being alone. One day I saw a flyer about tryouts for the girls' soccer team. I used to play soccer at my old school, so I decided to try out. Instead of supporting me, my neighbor said it was lame and called me a wanna-be. I went to the tryouts anyway. I made the team, but best of all, I found a group of friends who accept me just as I am. They never pressure me to do things I don't agree with, or expect me to be anything but myself.

Critical Thinking
Emily suggests that true friends are accepting and supportive, and make others feel comfortable. Do you agree or disagree with her?

Bullying

Bullying is aggressive, unwanted behavior involving an imbalance of power. Bullying may have serious, lifelong problems for the bully and the kid who is bullied.

Here's how to identify bullying behaviors:

- Look for a power imbalance. Bullies use their power. They access embarrassing information, use physical strength, as well as popularity to cause harm to others.
- Look for repeated actions. Bullies behave in the same manner repeatedly, or have the possibility of repeating the behavior.

Bullies pick on others as a way to gain power, to get their way, or to feel important. There are three main types of bullying.

- Verbal bullying. This involves name-calling, teasing, spreading rumors, making inappropriate sexual comments, or threatening to cause harm to another person.
- Social bullying involves hurting another's relationships or reputation. This can also include embarrassing someone in public and spreading rumors.
- Physical bullying is when a bully harms someone's body or possessions. This involves tripping, pushing, spitting, hitting, kicking, pinching, stealing or breaking someone's possessions. When bullies use these tactics to get others to do what they want, they are using negative peer pressure.

Most bullying occurs during school hours, but a large amount takes place on the playgroup or the bus. The amount of bullying occurring on the Internet is on the rise.

Cyberbullying is bullying that happens through electronic technology. This includes hurtful text messages, e-mails, rumors or embarrassing information posted to social media and other Web sites.

You do not have to let bullying get the best of you. Sometimes appearing confident and telling the bully to stop is enough to make a bully back down. Other times, ignoring the bully makes the pressure go away. Whenever bullying gets out of hand, tell an adult. Do not bully back. Fighting back just satisfies a bully and can make the harassment worse.

If you are being cyberbullied or know someone who is, do not respond to the bully. Keep a copy of all cyberbullying as evidence. Block the bully from your social media and other devices. Report the cyberbullying immediately to your parents or guardians, online service providers, law enforcement, and schools.

Gangs

A gang is a group of people who associate with one another because they have something in common and are looking for acceptance. Not all teen groups are bad. However, many gangs are involved in illegal activities, and they use negative peer pressure to convince others in their group to go along with it.

There are many alternatives to joining a gang. If you are lonely or bored, search out a youth group, sports team, volunteer opportunities, or other activities in your neighborhood or community. If peers are negatively pressuring you, think about starting a group that works for positive change, such as a group that tutors young children or collects items for a homeless shelter. Talk to adults and local businesses to sponsor sports, music, or art events for teens who do not participate in gangs.

If you are harassed by gang members, seek help. A family member, community group, school counselor, or police officer can help protect you and give you support.

✓ **Reading Check** **Explain** What is peer pressure, and how can it influence your life?

SUCCEED IN SCHOOL

Attendance

Try to be at school every day. If you attend classes, you will not miss the important information your teachers present each day. You will also be better prepared for tests and quizzes.

Responding to Negative Peer Pressure

Standing up to negative peer pressure is one of the most important skills you can learn. It can be very difficult to say no to friends when you want to be part of a group. You may be afraid of hurting someone's feelings or losing a friendship. You may fear being laughed at or excluded.

Possible Responses

How you respond to negative peer pressure is up to you. You can give up your self-control, or you can decide to be the one who is in charge of your life.

TAKE CHARGE!

Stand Up for Yourself

There are several steps you can take to prevent others from taking advantage of you. Use these tips to stand up for yourself without resorting to manipulative tactics.

- **Know What You Want** This is the time to change difficult to understand, or abstract, concepts like respect, into concrete actions. Identify specific actions or behaviors that need to be changed or put into action.
- **Prepare Yourself** Rehearse a situation you expect to encounter with a friend. Have your friend give responses designed to weaken your position.
- **Speak with Conviction** Politely state exactly what you want, and do not apologize or weaken your message with appeasing phrases such as, "It would be nice if . . ." or "Could you . . .?"
- **Keep Your Body "On Message"** Stand up straight and use eye contact to show determination.
- **Refuse To Be Ignored** Finish your thought, even if you have to repeat it when someone tries to interrupt.
- **Compromise** Decide in advance what compromises would be satisfactory. Would you change some of your habits if other people agree to change theirs?

Real-World Skills

Demonstrate Assertiveness Think of a situation in which teen peers make decisions together, such as dividing the tasks of a group project. Use the techniques discussed here to demonstrate an assertive response from a teen who feels taken advantage of while working on a group project. In class, discuss how this response prevents manipulation.

Direct eye contact, a serious facial expression, hand gestures, a firm tone of voice, and upright posture send the message that you really mean no when being pressured to do something you know is wrong for you. *Why do you think these silent messages convey no to another person?*

Passive Response

Giving in to peer pressure is a passive response. So is backing down instead of standing up for your needs and wants. You may know someone who is passive and thinks he or she wins friends by going along with whatever other people are doing. Instead, this person is viewed as a pushover who is not worthy of respect.

Aggressive Response

Hostile responses that violate the rights of others are aggressive responses. Even though aggressive people think they will get their way and be seen as powerful and popular, this approach often backfires. People either tend to avoid those who are aggressive or jump in and fight back.

Assertive Response

When you respond assertively to peer pressure, you stand up for your rights in firm but positive ways. You directly and honestly state your thoughts and feelings. You show that you mean what you say. Most people respect others who show the courage to be true to themselves.

Developing Refusal Skills

What if a friend tries to convince you to do something you do not want to do or that goes against your values? If you say yes to something that does not feel right, you will end up feeling disappointed in yourself. Saying yes to something risky may harm you physically and emotionally. It also may hurt the people you care about most.

Learning refusal skills can help. A **refusal skill** is a basic communication skill you can use to say no effectively. Use these skills to say no without feeling guilty or uncomfortable. People will respect you for your honesty and firmness.

- **Say no and *mean* it.** If you are pressured to do something you do not believe is right, say no with conviction. If you seem to waver, the other person may try to change your mind. Use eye contact to show you mean what you say. If the other person will

Know When to Leave

You may encounter situations where events get out of hand or people do not follow your values or standards of behavior. When this happens, leave the scene. Call your parents or guardians, other relatives, a taxi, or the police, and ask for a ride home.

Write About It

Think about a story you have read or a movie you have seen where a character had to leave an uncomfortable or unsafe situation. Write a paragraph in your journal describing the situation.

Ken Karp/McGraw-Hill Education

not take no for an answer, repeat your refusal and your reason for it. Practice saying no in front of a mirror until you sound and look like you really mean it.

- **Offer alternatives.** If a friend presses you to do something that makes you uncomfortable, suggest another activity that is acceptable to you.
- **Take action.** Back up your words with actions. If someone is pressuring you to act against your better judgment, make it clear that you will not do it. If that does not work, just leave an uncomfortable situation. It is okay to say, "I'm going home."

Developing Confidence

Doing what you believe is right can be especially hard when peers pressure you to make certain decisions. Decisions about the friends you keep, the clothes you wear, and how you treat your body can be particularly difficult.

When you are struggling with peer pressure, remember that it is your life, not someone else's. Rather than letting others pressure you into behavior you may regret, start now to follow your own values and dreams. Most people will respect you more as you become more confident and show that you respect yourself. Individuals who stand up for what is right for themselves and others are the ones who are most admired in the long run.

Section 8.1

After You Read

Review Key Concepts

1. **Describe** the influences a role model might have on your life.
2. **Explain** refusal skills and how they can help you avoid peer pressure.

Practice Academic Skills

**English Language Arts**

3. Read a story in which a character responds to negative peer pressure. Is the response passive, aggressive, or assertive? Write a paragraph describing the peer pressure, the character's response, and how you think the response could be improved.

Social Studies

4. Follow your teacher's instructions to form into groups. Create an activity for young children that teaches them how to respond effectively to bullying. You might create a board game or crossword puzzle, for example. Activities should present a variety of bullying situations that require different responses.

 Check Your Answers Go to connectED. mcgraw-hill.com to check your answers.

Enjoying Friendships

Before You Read

Preview Understanding causes and effects can help clarify connections. A cause is an event or action that makes something happen. An effect is a result of a cause. Ask yourself, "Why does this happen?" to help you recognize cause-and-effect relationships in this section.

Read to Learn

Key Concepts

- **Describe** the benefits of friendship with those who are different from you.
- **List** the qualities of a true friend.
- **Summarize** your major responsibilities when hanging out with friends.
- **Explain** why friendships end.

Main Idea

Friendships are valuable and should be cherished and respected, but not every friendship will last a lifetime.

Content Vocabulary

◇ clique
◇ acquaintance
◇ dependable
◇ infatuation

Academic Vocabulary

You will find these words in your reading and on your tests. Use the glossary to look up their definitions if necessary.

☐ perspective
☐ empathy

Graphic Organizer

As you read, record ways to make new friends, strengthen a friendship, and end a friendship. Use a graphic organizer like the one below to organize your information.

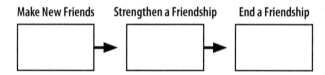

Make New Friends	Strengthen a Friendship	End a Friendship

 Graphic Organizer Go to **connectED.mcgraw-hill.com** to download this graphic organizer.

Your Friends

Think about the friends you have. How are they different than you? Although most of your friends are probably around your age and similar to you in many ways, not all of them have to be. A variety of friends makes life interesting.

Peer Friendships

Your peers are likely the people you associate with the most. They have the most in common with you at this point in your life. There is no rule about the number of peer friendships you should have. Some people are happy with one or two close friends. Others prefer to have many friends. Some teens struggle to be popular, even to the point of doing things they should not do. Their quest for popularity can cause them to focus on status instead of substance, and cost them their true friends.

Cliques

In any setting where people gather, they tend to move into groups in which they feel comfortable. There is nothing wrong with that. Many teens, as well as adults, form groups to feel a sense of belonging.

Unfortunately, some groups form cliques. A **clique** is a group that excludes others from its circle of friendship. Only by the group's approval can someone be a part of the group. The basis for acceptance is often superficial, based on external qualities such as their appearance, their clothing, where they live, or the amount of money they have to spend. The members of a clique reject people they think do not fit in. When this kind of rejection occurs, people get hurt.

Perhaps you have been in a clique and have seen someone rejected by the group. Maybe you have been the one excluded. Avoid groups that treat others cruelly. This may mean forming your own circle of friends who do not judge others. If the exclusive clique mentality comes up in your group, challenge it.

As You Read

Connect What do you have in common with your friends? What are the differences between you?

Vocabulary
You can find definitions in the glossary at the back of this book.

> **Choose Friends Wisely**
>
> Some popular teens seem to choose friends based on looks. Remember, true friendships are not based on appearances. *Why do you think that true friendships are not based on appearances?*

Sharing your time and knowledge is a great way to give back to your community. For example, you might teach a friend a skill you have or tutor someone struggling with a subject at school. You can also join Big Brothers Big Sisters, an organization that helps younger children find positive role models. Sharing your time and knowledge with others strengthens your community.

Friends of Different Ages

Having friends in different age groups may broaden your understanding of people, including yourself. These kinds of friendships can help you gain insight into your own thoughts, feelings, and actions.

Younger Friends

Although most of your friends are probably other teens, children can be good companions, too. Since you are older, your attention is special to them. They may look up to you and see you as both a friend and a role model. You might teach them a skill or just sit and talk with them. Children who do not have positive parental figures can especially benefit from your friendship and guidance.

You may find you like being a guiding force, which could lead you to a career as a teacher, child care worker, or therapist later on.

Older Friends

Sometimes it is hard to think of adults as anything more than authority figures who talk only about rules and standards of behavior. But whether it is a new skill or words of advice, the adults in your life have much they can offer you. They have faced many of the same problems and obstacles you now face. They have stories from their own teen years that may help you put your own problems in perspective. And, they can give you tried and true advice for overcoming these obstacles.

Diverse Friends

Friends can come in different ages, shapes, colors, and from many different walks of life. Spending time with friends from a variety of backgrounds and experiences makes you a more well-rounded and interesting person. People who have different qualities than you do bring out different parts of your personality. Someone from a different background or culture can give you a new perspective, or particular evaluation of a situation or facts. You may discover things about yourself you never knew before, or view certain aspects of life in a completely new way.

✓ Reading Check **Evaluate** Compare the benefits of younger friends and older friends to the benefits of peer friendships.

Focus on Friendships

Some people form childhood friendships that last a lifetime. Even if they eventually move far apart, they manage to stay in touch through the years. Other people make new friends as they move to high school and beyond. Whatever the case may be, friends enjoy the time they spend together. They listen to one another and offer each other advice and support. True friends stick up for each other and stick by each other in good times and bad.

Qualities of True Friends

Qualities you may want in a friend vary depending on the degree of friendship. An **acquaintance** is a person you may know, but who is not a personal friend. For example, a neighbor down the street or someone you say hello to at school may be an acquaintance. In time, the person may become a friend, someone you know well and like to spend time with. A friendship generally goes through stages on the way to becoming a close relationship.

You may have known some of your friends for as long as you can remember. Other friendships may have recently developed. Regardless of how you met, or how long you have known each other, the following qualities are generally true of all good friends:

- **Caring** Friends care about each other. They accept each other's weaknesses and focus on their strengths. They value and show consideration for one another's feelings.
- **Dependable** Friends who can be counted on and who keep their word are **dependable**.
- **Loyal** Real friends stick by each other. They like you for who you are, not for what you have or what you can do for them. They will take your side if you need support. A true friend believes in you and is there when you need him or her.
- **Respectful** Your true friends respect your values and never ask you to go against these values. They respect your position on sensitive issues. They may not always agree with you, but they hold your opinion in high regard and are willing to hear you out.
- **Empathetic** Good friends have empathy, or the ability to understand what others are experiencing. They are able to put themselves in your place and to see things from your point of view.
- **Forgiving** Good friends understand that everyone, even best friends, make mistakes. They forgive the mistakes of their friends, and do not hold grudges. They also apologize when they make mistakes.

Building ?! Character

Loyalty Emily and Jia were best friends in middle school, but they have grown apart since entering high school. Recently, Emily has been hanging out with a new group of friends. She really likes them, but sometimes she feels uncomfortable because they make fun of Jia's clothes. How can Emily keep her new friends but still stick up for Jia?

You Make the Call

Should Emily stick up for Jia? Or, should Emily keep quiet and go along with her new friends?

▶ **Loyalty**

If you expect loyalty from friends, you must be loyal to them, also. *When have you shown loyalty to your friends?*

Fancy Collection / SuperStock

Making New Friends

Making friends seems to come naturally to young children. Strangers sharing a sandbox can be best friends within minutes. For many teens, however, making friends can be awkward and stressful. It can be especially difficult for those who are going to a new school.

Making friends begins with self-confidence. When you believe in yourself, and your ability to contribute to a friendship, you are more likely to be friendly and open with people you do not know. Remind yourself that you are likeable, that you have traits and abilities others will enjoy.

Even people who seem to have a natural talent for meeting new people do not do it without effort. Remember that your facial expressions can reveal a lot about you. Make an effort to appear pleasant and open. A friendly smile goes a long way. If you walk around with a frown or negative expression, others will steer clear. Practice conversation starters with a family member to build confidence. Resolve to start a conversation with at least one new person every week. Some of the best friendships have begun with something as simple as "Did you see that?" or a comment about homework.

HOW TO . . . Make New Friends

Friends can be a great source of support and help. Friends can also share your interests and goals. Whether you are the new kid or not, these pointers can help you reach out and make new friends.

Be Positive Do you enjoy the company of people who always complain or feel sorry for themselves? Avoid behaviors and attitudes like these because they drive away potential friends. Also, remember to smile. People are more willing to begin a friendship with someone who appears positive.

Strive for Friendship, Not Popularity To win friends, some teens focus on what they think are the keys to popularity. This could mean wearing certain clothes or using certain language. Actually, popular teens attract people through their personalities. You can do the same.

Get Involved Getting involved in an activity is one of the easiest ways to make new friends. Think of activities or hobbies you enjoy. Then, look for clubs, groups, or organizations where you can join other people with similar interests.

(t)Realistic Reflections; (b)Ilene MacDonald/Alamy

Strengthening Friendships

Remember, friendships take effort. People with lifelong friendships know how to give as well as take. This involves spending time with your friends, listening to what they have to say, and offering them help when they need it. To have a friend is to be a friend. When you have a friend whom you consider a good and true friend, it is worth the effort to maintain the friendship. Do not take your friends for granted. Friendships grow stronger as friends continue to show the qualities that helped them become friends in the first place.

If you always seem to have trouble keeping friendships, ask yourself the question, "Why did it end?" Did you do something to cause the friendship to dissolve? Did you choose manipulative or superficial friends? It is important to identify the causes of past problems so that you can avoid them in future friendships. For example, some teens with low self-esteem try to be friends with anyone, at any cost. They need to work at developing a positive self-image, so they will make better choices in the future.

✓ **Reading Check** **Contrast** What is the difference between an acquaintance and a true friend?

Extend an Invitation Instead of waiting to be asked, take the first step. You may be surprised to learn that the other person was hoping you would reach out. If someone turns you down, try not to worry. This happens to everyone. Just try later with another person.

Lend a Hand What makes a better impression than offering help? Ask first to be sure the person needs or wants your help. Whether the problem is understanding algebra or fitting a wheelchair through a doorway, give help in the spirit of service, not superiority.

Keep Expectations Realistic Even the closest of friends may not share the same goals, values, or interests. In fact, the contrast can help keep relationships fresh. Do not let differences in things like musical tastes or favorite foods stop you from developing a friendship. Likewise, give people space. Do not overwhelm potential friends with constant demands on their time or energy. Give your friendships room and time to grow.

Hanging Out with Friends

Hanging out with friends becomes more and more important during adolescence. Generally, teens like to be in mixed-gender groups, which means both males and females. There is less pressure in group situations than in one-on-one dating situations. There are more people to keep the conversation going, so there are few awkward silences. Without the nervousness of a date, you can relax and have a good time. You can get to know everyone better at your own pace, without being rushed into pairing off with one particular person.

Places to Go, Things to Do

Some communities offer plenty of fun places to go and things to do. Other communities have fewer options. Activity costs and transportation can also restrict what many teens are able to do. In such cases, creative thinking helps. Carpool with a friend who has a driver's license, use public transportation, or ask a willing parent to drive. An afternoon or evening spent watching DVDs at a friend's house, playing board games, skateboarding, scrapbooking, making jewelry, or preparing a meal can be as much fun as going out. Where do you like to go with your friends? What activities could you plan for a day with your friends?

Your Responsibilities

When you spend time with others in a group, do not forget that you have some important responsibilities. The choices you make affect your friends, family, and community, as well as yourself.

Responsibilities to the Community

Remember that other people visit the same places you go with your friends. When you and your friends gather in community places, think about how your actions affect others. For example, what might happen to a restaurant if a large group of people routinely took up table space and ordered only soft drinks? Without a chance to make enough money to pay its expenses, the restaurant would go out of business. It is also important to be careful about the language you use in parks, malls, and other areas where young children are present.

▼ Fun with Friends

Even the simplest activities can be fun when you are with friends. *How do you spend time with your friends?*

TAKE CHARGE!

Be Responsible

When you show people that you are responsible, they will learn to respect your maturity, and you can gain their trust. Use these tips to show that you are responsible.

- **Follow Through** When you agree to do something, take responsibility for the entire task. Remember that others trust and rely on you to come through as promised.
- **Back It Up** You choose which words to say, and you decide which actions you will take. Take responsibility for yourself by standing behind all that you say and do.
- **Step Up to the Challenge** Leaders are responsible for their groups, but group members are responsible for working with their leaders. Let your parents or guardians, teachers, and coaches know that you would like to help them with their responsibilities.

Real-World Skills

Reflect on Responsibility Think of tasks that you are responsible for at home, school, or work. Then, write a few paragraphs addressing how you fulfill your responsibilities, why the tasks are important, and how you have stepped up to meet the challenges.

Responsibilities to Family

Parents and guardians need to know where you are going, with whom you are going, and when you will be home. They ask for this information and make rules because they are responsible for your safety and well-being. Show you care about your family by following the rules they set. Breaking rules can cause family members to worry and lose trust in you. If you disagree with a rule, talk it over with your parents or guardians. You might find there is room for compromise.

Responsibilities to Friends

By meeting them on time and treating them as you would like to be treated, you show your friends that you respect them. When you are out, stay with your friends. Never leave your group or let another friend leave alone. Instead, leave together so that everyone returns home safely, and by curfew. If you are out with a mixed-gender group, aim to have an equal number of females and males.

Personal Responsibilities

Going out with people of the opposite gender involves other responsibilities and decisions. You must make decisions about your personal conduct ahead of time. Set standards of behavior and keep them in mind while you are out with your friends.

Any time you hang out with your friends, difficult situations might arise. Your friends might pressure you to do something that goes against your standards of behavior. In these cases, use your refusal skills. If you cannot convince your friends to change their minds, leave. Your true friends will respect you for sticking to your values.

Take a Break

If you are struggling to focus while studying, take a 10-minute break. Going for a brief, brisk walk can help you reduce stress and feel more alert. If it is too late in the evening to go for a walk, try calling a friend for a set time limit.

Safety Away from Home

Whether you are alone or with friends in a crowd, keep safety in mind. Act confident. Always look as if you know where you are going, even if you are lost. Carry personal identification and emergency contact numbers, and make sure someone at home knows where you are and when you will be home. Also, learn where the police and fire stations are located. Here are some other street smarts to keep in mind:

- **Use the buddy system.** There is safety in numbers. Go places with friends whenever you can.
- **Use well-traveled routes.** Do not take risky shortcuts or travel through isolated areas. Be aware of your surroundings, and stay in well-lit areas. Try to walk in the middle of the sidewalk and not next to buildings.
- **Make a plan in case you become lost.** If you are in a public area and are separated from your friends or family, do not wander around looking for them. In advance, designate a specific place to meet them in case you become lost.
- **Ignore strangers.** If anyone attempts to verbally harass you, keep walking. Responding can make the situation worse.
- **Do not get into strangers' cars.** If someone tries to force you into a car, scream to get attention and fight to escape. Some experts suggest that you yell, "Fire!" instead of "Help!" People are more likely to pay attention if they think there is a fire.
- **Watch your belongings.** Keep your personal items with you to prevent others from taking your identification or money. Do not leave your drink unattended in public, and do not accept food or drinks from people you do not know well. Drugs can be slipped into your drink without your knowledge, and some drugs are designed to be odorless and tasteless.
- **Trust your instincts.** If a situation does not feel right to you, leave quickly.

➤ Look Out for Your Friends

True friends consider each other's safety when they hang out together. *How do your friends look out for each other?*

Healthy relationships with the opposite sex are based on respect. *How can friends of the opposite gender show respect for each other?*

Dating

Adolescence is the time when most people develop an interest in romantic relationships. Because teens mature at different rates, not all of them will develop an interest in the opposite sex at the same time. You probably know someone who is so involved in a relationship that he or she rarely spends time with old friends. You probably also know at least one person who prefers to spend time with friends and is not even slightly interested in dating. Some teens are interested in dating, and others are not. If you are not ready for that step, do not force it. Holding off on a one-to-one relationship until you are ready is completely normal.

Infatuation

Have you ever had a huge crush on a celebrity, or even a classmate you did not know very well? You probably found yourself daydreaming about this person often, and struggled to keep your mind on schoolwork, or anything else, for that matter. What you experienced is **infatuation**, an intense attraction to another person that may or may not be one-sided.

Infatuation can feel like love because it is very powerful and emotional, but it is unrealistic. Infatuation is usually based on superficial qualities such as physical attraction or popularity. When you are infatuated, you are in love with what you imagine the other person is like. You are so caught up in the wonderful feelings you are experiencing that you ignore your crush's negative traits and the important differences between you.

Infatuation seldom lasts long. Once the initial emotional rush is over, you begin to see things more clearly. You begin to see your crush's negative traits and shortcomings, and you may realize that you have very little in common with him or her. Once a crush is over, you may even wonder why you ever felt the way you did.

Digital Vision/Alamy

Science You Can Use

The Science of Emotions

You know your body language often reflects the emotional state you are in. But did you know that the reverse is also true? Your expression can actually affect your mood and the moods of others.

Procedure Cut 12 pictures out of old magazines or newspapers that all show one emotion. You can choose sadness, joy, anger, or fear. Find a family member or friend who does not know the purpose of this experiment. Ask this person to rate on a scale of 1–10 how **sad** he or she is. Do the same for **happy, angry,** and **anxious.** Now show your family member or friend your first picture. Direct him or her to look at and imitate the expression shown in the picture for 10 seconds. Use a stopwatch if you have one. Repeat this procedure for the rest of the pictures. Now ask your partner to rate on a scale of 1–10 how **depressed** he or she feels. Do the same for **joyful, annoyed,** and **upset.**

Analysis Do you notice any changes in your partner's emotional state after imitating the expressions in the pictures? What does that reveal about the connection between emotions and the body?

Mature Love

Mature love can start as a sudden, strong attraction or develop from a close friendship. Where infatuation is more superficial and short-lived, mature love is meaningful and lasting. Much like a strong friendship, people who are in love show each other caring, dependability, loyalty, respect, empathy, and forgiveness. They share interests and life goals and want to work toward these goals together. Physical attraction is part of love, but it is not the main focus.

✓ **Reading Check** **Explain** What are the benefits of hanging out in mixed-gender groups?

When Friendships End

Not all friendships last forever. People are constantly moving, growing, and changing. Though some friendships last a lifetime, many end abruptly or slowly fade away. Some friendships that seem to have faded may grow strong again at another time, sometimes many years later. What exactly causes friendships to end or fade?

- **Distance** Some friendships end because one person moves away and there are fewer opportunities to keep in touch. In these cases, remaining emotionally close takes work. Long-distance friendships can survive with a great deal of effort.
- **Conflict** Some friendships end because of conflict or misunderstandings. Most fights can be resolved with an apology, but failing to stand up for your friend or failing to keep secrets can cost you his or her trust and quickly end the friendship.
- **Jealousy** Feelings of jealousy and possessiveness can end a friendship. Not allowing your friend to spend time with other people because you feel threatened may cause him or her to feel smothered and want space.
- **Changing Interests** Friends that used to enjoy the same things may find they have less and less in common with each other. Changing interests, goals, and experiences may cause people to grow apart because they find it hard to relate to one another. Friendships that are based on core values rather than shared activities are more likely to survive diverging paths.
- **Deliberate Action** If a friend is physically or emotionally abusive, causes you serious problems, or is unpleasant to be around, you need to end the friendship. Unhealthy or destructive friendships can prevent you from reaching your potential, and are not the kind you want to keep.

Ending a Friendship

If you must deliberately end a friendship, do it with sensitivity. Ending a friendship is difficult for both parties, but it does not have to create hostility between you. You can still remain cordial if you are tactful in your approach.

- **The Gradual Approach.** One way to end a friendship is to ease out of the relationship. You can distance yourself by finding other activities that gradually take more of your time. Joining an athletic team, volunteering, accepting a part-time job, and spending more time with other friends can be effective ways of stepping back from the relationship.
- **The Direct Approach.** In the case of a friendship that is especially unhealthy or destructive, you may need to be direct, but kind, in your actions. Consistently ignoring your friend's question "Is anything wrong?" will hurt him or her even more than the truth. Explain why you need to end the friendship. Focus on how you feel, not on the other person, by using "I" messages, or statements that begin with the word "I." For example, you might say, "I don't feel comfortable around people who use drugs," or "I don't like putting down other people." Giving reasons rather than blaming the other person takes a good deal of courage. However, doing so can help you end a friendship in the most positive way possible.

Health & Wellness TIPS

Healthy Friendships

Strong, healthy friendships can enrich and improve your life, but unhealthy friendships can have the opposite effect. To make sure someone is your true friend, watch out for these signs:

- ▶ A friend should not try to control or manipulate you.
- ▶ He or she should not discourage you from starting new friendships.
- ▶ He or she should not try to embarrass you in front of others.

Handling Rejection

If a friendship or relationship ends against your wishes, understand that these are not lifetime commitments and this simply happens sometimes. Everyone experiences rejection at some point. You may feel sad or angry for a while, and you may even blame yourself. In time, these negative feelings will fade. As you move on to other friendships, you can take what that relationship taught you about friendship and yourself with you.

> **Rejection**

Not everyone you want to be friends with will share your feelings. Appreciating yourself will help you move on and make new friends. *What strategy can you think of that might help you move forward after being rejected?*

©Tetra Images/Alamy

If feelings of rejection are difficult to deal with, here are some ideas to consider:

- **Share your feelings.** Talk with a friend or family member, and be open to advice and suggestions.
- **Be kind to yourself.** Just because you were not the one to end your friendship does not mean you are a bad person or not good enough. The friendship may have simply outgrown itself, and your friend responded first.
- **Appreciate yourself.** On bad days, make a list of your positive points and refer to your list when you need a boost.
- **Evaluate your actions.** Think about your behavior toward the other person. Did you do something that was hurtful? If so, learn to behave differently so that future friendships will not end this way.
- **Do not spread rumors or gossip.** Avoid making negative comments to peers or on social networking sites about the person who hurt you. That kind of behavior only makes you look bad, and discourages new friendships.
- **Move on.** Focus on other friends and activities. In time, it will all be just a distant memory.

Section 8.2

After You Read

Review Key Concepts

1. **Explain** what cliques are, and why should you avoid them.
2. **Explain** what "To have a friend is to be a friend" means.
3. **Describe** four strategies for staying safe when away from home.
4. **Identify** strategies that can help you cope with rejection.

Check Your Answers Go to connectED.mcgraw-hill.com to check your answers.

Practice Academic Skills

English Language Arts

5. Choose a topic for a newspaper article such as "What Works in Friendship" or "When a Friendship Must End." Write the article, providing tips on sustaining or ending a friendship in a positive way. Read the article to your class.

Social Studies

6. Create a plan to entertain friends at your home for little cost. What activities will you make available? Share your plan with your friends and make adjustments based on their feedback. If possible, implement your plan.

Chapter 8

CHAPTER SUMMARY

Section 8.1
Dealing with Peer Pressure

Peer pressure may be positive or negative. Positive role models encourage you to be your best. Negative peer pressure includes manipulation tactics that encourage you to go against your better judgment. If you are tempted to join a gang, search out a youth group, a sports team, or other activities in your community instead. When you respond assertively to peer pressure, you stand up for your rights firmly and positively. Refusal skills help you say no without feeling guilty or uncomfortable.

Section 8.2
Enjoying Friendships

You can learn a lot from friends who differ from you. There are many ways to make new friends. When spending time with others in a group, you have important responsibilities to yourself, to your friends, to your family, and to your community. Many people experience feelings of infatuation, but true love is a different thing. Friendships can end for a variety of reasons. If you end a friendship, do so with sensitivity. Almost everyone experiences rejection at some point. You can take steps to overcome rejection.

Vocabulary Review

1. Write each of the vocabulary terms below on an index card, and the definitions on separate index cards. Work in pairs or small groups to match each term to its definition.

Content Vocabulary
◇ peer (p. 175)
◇ peer pressure (p. 175)
◇ manipulation (p. 177)
◇ refusal skill (p. 180)
◇ clique (p. 183)
◇ acquaintance (p. 185)
◇ dependable (p. 185)
◇ infatuation (p. 191)

Academic Vocabulary
▢ beneficial (p. 176)
▢ abstract (p. 179)
▢ perspective (p. 184)
▢ empathy (p. 185)

Review Key Concepts

2. **Compare and contrast** negative peer pressure and positive peer pressure.
3. **Identify** three ways you can respond to negative peer pressure.
4. **Describe** the benefits of friendship with those who are different from you.
5. **List** the qualities of a true friend.
6. **Summarize** your major responsibilities when hanging out with friends.
7. **Explain** why friendships end.

Critical Thinking

8. **Evaluate** Think about a family member or friend who has served as a role model for you. Make a list describing this person's qualities, and write a paragraph describing the positive effect this person has had in your life.
9. **Analyze** Observe responses to peer pressure among your friends and acquaintances. Which responses were the most effective? Which were the least effective? Explain.
10. **Plan** You want to hang out with a group of your friends, but some of your friends do not have transportation and others cannot afford to go out. How might you still get together?
11. **Remember** Think about a friend from your past. What did you learn from that person that you can carry over to other friendships?

 **ACTIVE LEARNING**

12. Make New Friends Pretend that you have just moved to a new community. You do not know anyone in your new school or neighborhood, and it seems like everyone you meet already has a circle of friends. It can be difficult to make new friends in a situation such as this. With a partner, role-play a situation in which you could make new friends. Remember that self-confidence often helps people make friends. Keeping a positive attitude, getting involved in activities, extending invitations, helping others, and keeping expectations realistic also often result in new friendships. Role-play a scenario for the class. Then, ask other students for feedback.

 **Family & Community Connections**

13. Plan a Service Project Follow your teacher's instructions to form into groups. Then, plan a service project you can conduct in your community. First, think of needs within your community that interest you or would benefit from volunteers. For example, if you know of young children struggling in school, you might think about organizing or volunteering at an after-school tutoring program. You might want to organize a food and clothing drive or volunteer at a homeless shelter. If you are having trouble identifying volunteer opportunities, contact your city's chamber of commerce. Once you have identified needs within your community that you would like to address, plan a service project to help you do so. Outline the necessary steps that will result in helpful change, and present your plans to the class.

Real-World Skills and Applications

Leadership Skills

14. Community Resources Research community resources that provide positive alternatives to gangs for young people. These might include community recreation centers, school-related clubs, sports teams, and service organizations. Choose two such resources and describe them for the class, noting their benefits as well as any requirements to become involved. Be sure to explain why you are interested in the resources you choose.

Financial Literacy

15. Compare Activities You and a friend go out to dinner and to see a movie. Your bill for dinner is $13.78 and your friend's bill is $11.44. The movie tickets cost $9.50 each. How much more do you spend combined than you would have if you had made dinner at home for $18.65 and rented two movies for $6.99?

Technology Skills

16. Interview a Role Model Think of a person in your life whom you admire. Record an interview with that person and then create a video or a podcast about him or her based on your interview. Describe how his or her behavior has influenced you. Show your video to the class and play an excerpt of your role model speaking that supports a point in your video.

Aldo Murillo/Getty Images

Academic Skills

 English Language Arts

17. Short Story Write a short story with two different endings that is about a teen responding to negative peer pressure. In the first ending, describe the consequences of giving in to negative peer pressure. In the second ending, describe what happens when the teen successfully resists the pressure. Show the effect of each choice on the teen's friends and family.

 Social Studies

18. Cross-Cultural Understanding Read print and online sources about teen friendships in other cultures around the world. Compare the friendships of teens in other cultures to your own friendships. What do all of these friendships have in common? How do they differ? What, if any, influence do parents have on teen friendships in each of these cultures? Do they sound like your parents or guardians?

 Mathematics

19. Calculate Long-Term Costs You want to show a friend who is pressuring you to smoke cigarettes that it is not financially worth it. If one package of cigarettes costs $6.35, calculate the cost of smoking one package of cigarettes a day for 2 years. Now calculate the cost of smoking one package of cigarettes a day for 10 years.

Math Concept **Multiplication by Ten** When multiplying a number by ten, simply move the decimal to the right one place.

Starting Hint To solve the problem, first find out how many days in a year there are. Then calculate the cost of smoking one package of cigarettes a day for a year. Multiply that cost by 2 to find out how much smoking for two years would cost. Multiply the one-year cost by 10 to find out how much smoking for 10 years would cost.

 For math help, go to the Math Appendix at the back of the book.

Standardized Test Practice

MATH WORD PROBLEMS
Directions Read the problem. Then, choose the correct answer.

Test-Taking Tip Try to solve the problem on your own and then find your answer among the choices. If the problem is too difficult to solve this way, you can work backwards, trying each possible answer.

20. You have decided to buy movie tickets for yourself and two friends. You pay $23.97 for all three movie tickets. Each ticket is the same price. How much does each ticket cost?
a) $7.95
b) $6.99
c) $7.99
d) $8.25

Life Skills Project

Healthy Relationships

In this project you will reflect on your own experiences and interview an adult to define what a healthy relationship means to you.

 My Journal

If you completed the journal entry from page 132, refer to it to see if your thoughts have changed after reading the unit.

Project Assignment

In this project you will:
- Research the qualities of healthy relationships.
- Identify and interview an adult in your community who enjoys a healthy relationship, such as a supportive friendship or happy marriage.
- Prepare a presentation to share what you have learned with your class.

The Skills Behind the Project

Life Skills

Key personal and relationship skills you will use in this project include:
- Thinking independently.
- Making healthy choices.
- Communicating respectfully

STEP 1 Analyze Relationships

Use research and independent reflection on your own experience to analyze healthy relationships. What makes a relationship healthy or unhealthy, and why? Write a summary of your research to:
- Define the qualities of a healthy relationship.
- Describe how people in a healthy relationship communicate with each other.
- Explain how people in a positive relationship handle conflicts.
- Identify what people can do to make a healthy relationship last.

Writing Skills
- Use complete sentences.
- Use correct spelling and grammar.
- Organize your interview questions in the order you want to ask them.

STEP 2 Plan Your Interview

Use the results of your research to write a list of interview questions to ask an adult in your community about healthy relationships. You questions might include:
- What does a healthy relationship mean to you?
- How can you tell if a relationship is healthy or unhealthy?

Creatas/PhotoLibrary

Life Skills Project Checklist

Plan	☑ Use research and independent thinking to reflect on the qualities of healthy relationships.
	☑ Plan and write your interview questions.
	☑ Interview an adult in your community and write a summary of what you learned.
	☑ Plan and write your speech.
Present	☑ Make a presentation to the class to discuss the results of your research and your interview.
	☑ Invite students to ask any questions they may have. Answer these questions.
	☑ When students ask you questions, demonstrate in your answers that you respect their perspectives.
	☑ Turn in the summary of your research, your interview questions, and the notes from the interview to your teacher.
Academic Skills	☑ Communicate effectively
	☑ Speak clearly and concisely
	☑ Adapt and modify language to suit different purposes
	☑ Thoughtfully express your ideas

- What role does communication play in a healthy relationship?
- What do you think keeps your own relationships strong?
- How do you resolve conflicts in your relationship?
- Have your close relationships ever gone through a difficult time? If so, how did you solve the problem?

STEP 3 Connect with Your Community

Identify an adult in your community who enjoys a healthy relationship, such as a supportive friendship or a happy marriage. Conduct your interview using the questions you prepared in Step 2. Take notes during the interview and write a summary of the interview.

Interviewing Skills
- Record interview responses and take notes.
- Listen attentively.
- Write in complete sentences and use correct spelling and grammar when you transcribe your notes.

STEP 4 Share What You Have Learned

Use the Life Skills Project Checklist to plan and give a speech to share what you have learned with your classmates.

Speaking Skills
- Speak clearly and concisely.
- Be sensitive to the needs of your audience.
- Use standard English to communicate.

STEP 5 Evaluate Your Life Skills and Academic Skills

Your project will be evaluated based on:
- Content and organization of your information.
- Proper use of standard English.
- Mechanics—presentation and neatness.
- Speaking and listening skills

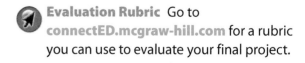 **Evaluation Rubric** Go to **connectED.mcgraw-hill.com** for a rubric you can use to evaluate your final project.

UNIT 4

Relating to Family and Children

Chapter 9 **Building Strong Families**

Chapter 10 **Family Challenges**

Chapter 11 **Child Development and Care**

Chapter 12 **Understanding Parenting**

Unit Life Skills Project Preview

Learn Parenting Skills

In this unit you will learn about different types of families and caring for family members. In this unit's life skills project, you will show how positive parenting skills can help build strong families.

 My Journal

Parenting and Families Write a journal entry about one of these topics. This will help you prepare for the project at the end of this unit.

- List resources you could use to learn more about parenting.
- Identify how each family member can help contribute to a strong family relationship.
- Determine what you would need to know about children before becoming a parent.

Explore the Photo

Spending quality time with every member of your family strengthens the family bond. *What are some activities you can do together as a family?*

Building Strong Families

Section 9.1
The Anatomy of a Family

Section 9.2
Family Dynamics

Chapter Objectives

Section 9.1
- **Identify** the functions of families.
- **Describe** the various types of families.
- **Outline** the family life cycle.

Section 9.2
- **Explain** the purpose of roles and how they are learned.
- **Identify** four strategies for getting along with your family members.
- **Describe** the characteristics of strong families.

Writing Activity — Poem

The Meaning of Family Family life can be fun, but it can also be challenging. Writing poetry is one way to channel and control your feelings about your family. Since poetry does not have spelling or grammatical rules, you can express your thoughts and emotions in a way that makes sense to you.

Write a short poem discussing what family means to you. Include vivid sensory details in your poem.

Writing Tips Use these tips to write a poem:
- Freewrite as a way to develop and direct your thoughts.
- Choose precise words that develop the meaning and style of your poem.
- Use specific imagery and vivid descriptions to bring your poem to life.

▲ Explore the Photo

A happy family is one that works together. *What are the benefits of a strong, happy family?*

Section 9.1

The Anatomy of a Family

Before You Read

Stay Engaged One way to stay engaged when reading is to turn each of the headings into a question, and then read the section to find the answers.

Read to Learn

Key Concepts

- **Identify** the functions of families.
- **Describe** the various types of families.
- **Outline** the family life cycle.

Main Idea

Although there are many different types of families, each family has a similar life cycle and fulfills the same important functions.

Content Vocabulary

◇ society
◇ social skills
◇ nuclear family
◇ single-parent family
◇ blended family
◇ extended family
◇ adoptive family
◇ foster family
◇ culture
◇ tradition
◇ family life cycle
◇ empty nest

Academic Vocabulary

You will find these words in your reading and on your tests. Use the glossary to look up their definitions if necessary.

▢ function
▢ unique

Graphic Organizer

As you read, write notes about the five stages of the family cycle. Use a graphic organizer like the one below to organize your information.

Family Life Cycle

1.
2.
3.
4.
5.

 Graphic Organizer Go to **connectED.mcgraw-hill.com** to download this graphic organizer.

The Importance of Families

Picture your family as a human body, a structure of connected bones from the skull to the toes. Although every bone is different, each bone is important. Like your skeleton, family members are healthier and more effective when they all work together. Family members laugh and learn together. They enjoy each other's company, and help one another through tough times.

Without families there would not be communities, cities, or countries. This is because families are the building blocks for society. **Society** is a group of people who have developed patterns of relationships from being around one another. Families teach children all the skills they need to become independent adults, including how to relate to others and be productive members of society. Once grown, many of these children will raise children of their own, and pass on the same values and lessons they learned.

Families provide the physical, emotional, social and moral support their members need to grow and develop into independent, well-adjusted adults.

Physical Needs

A physical need is something that your body must have to function, or work, properly. People cannot survive without food, sleep, shelter and clothing. Families provide for these basic physical needs. Family members also protect each other. They treat each other's minor injuries and take their children to the doctor for serious illnesses and vaccinations that will protect them from diseases. Families also set rules that will prevent children and other family members from encountering dangerous situations.

Emotional Support

Family members provide each other with love and affection. They believe in one another, supporting each other's goals and celebrating achievements. Families also help each other through difficult times. When something goes wrong, family members are often the first people to provide support. Problems are more manageable when you do not have to deal with them alone.

Social Skills and Moral Values

Parents also help their children learn **social skills**, or ways of relating to other people. Young family members learn how to take care of themselves and how to get along with others. They learn which of their actions are acceptable, which actions are not acceptable, and discover the responsibilities they have to the world around themselves. By example and through direct instruction, parents teach children right from wrong and what is most important in life.

✓ **Reading Check** **Compare** How is a family like the human body?

As You Read

Connect As you read this section, think about how your family spends time together. How does spending time together help your family function?

Vocabulary

You can find definitions in the glossary at the back of this book.

Safety Check

Make an Escape Plan

When you are relaxing at home, your family can be at risk of the unexpected danger of a fire. This is especially true if everyone is asleep. By making, and practicing, a fire escape plan, your family can be ready to respond if a fire strikes your home.

Write About It

Research steps that your local fire department suggests for a family fire escape plan. Write a paragraph explaining how your family can create and practice a fire escape plan for your home.

Types of Families

Family life has changed drastically over the years. In the early 1900s, many people still lived and worked on farms, and few of today's conveniences had been invented. Simple daily tasks such as preparing dinner or doing laundry were extremely time-consuming. Having a large family was important, because it meant more help with household and family tasks. Sharing the workload saved time and helped family members bond.

Today, life is changing faster than ever, and so are families. No family remains exactly the same over the years. Children grow up, and parents grow older. Some changes, however, are not simply the result of passing years. They are a result of social trends, such as divorce, remarriage, and the economic shift from farming to industry. Because of these trends, families today tend to include fewer family members.

Family Structure

Families come in all sizes, shapes, and personalities. They differ in who the family members are and how these individuals are related. These characteristics make each family unique, or one of a kind. Which family type describes your family?

- **Couples** When two people get married, they form a new family. The partners form a close bond and rely on each other for love and support.
- **Nuclear Families** A **nuclear family** consists of a mother, a father, and their children. In nuclear families, parents share household and child-raising responsibilities. Children in a nuclear family benefit from the attention and support of both parents. They can also learn what it means to be a mother or father firsthand.
- **Single-Parent Families** In a **single-parent family**, one parent raises the children. The parent may be divorced, widowed, or never married. Most single parents treasure the close one-on-one relationships they have with their children. However, many single parents are also the sole providers of income and child care. They often struggle with time, energy, and money as they raise their children.

Impact Your Family

When you include family members in activities, you can build positive relationships. *How do the actions of your family members positively affect you?*

©Hero/Corbis/Glow Images

TAKE CHARGE!

Strengthen Your Relationship with a Stepparent

In blended families, misunderstandings may develop because stepparents, teens, and younger children do not know each other well. You can help smooth out bumps in the getting-to-know-you phase by keeping these communication points in mind:

- **Put Yourself in Your Stepparent's Place** How would you act if you were the new stepparent?
- **Listen with an Open Mind** That means listening without cross-examining or ridiculing your stepparent. This helps you avoid jumping to conclusions that you might regret later.
- **Ask for Clarification** Are you unclear about what your stepparent expects of you? To prevent confusion, politely ask for an explanation.
- **Talk out Disagreements Calmly** Remember, it is impossible to erase an ugly word that was said in anger.
- **Stepparents Have Feelings Too** Treat your stepparent with kindness and respect, and your stepparent will treat you the same way.

Real-World Skills

Solve a Problem with a Stepparent Role-play with a classmate a disagreement between a teen and a stepparent. Choose a subject such as household chores. Prepare a five-minute presentation for the class in which the disagreement is resolved. Remember to use the communication points. Ask class members for feedback on improving use of the points.

- **Blended Families** A **blended family** is a husband and wife, at least one of whom has children from a former relationship. A blended family can include the children of both spouses. It also may include children the couple have together. Both adults and children in a blended family have to adjust to new routines and relationships. This takes time and understanding.
- **Extended Families** An **extended family** is a family that includes relatives other than parents and their children. Grandparents, aunts, uncles, and cousins are all part of the extended family. Some extended families live in the same household, but they usually live in different homes.
- **Adoptive Families** An **adoptive family** is a family with a child who was made part of the family through legal action. The child is not born to the parents, but has the same rights that a child born into the family has. An adopted child usually takes the family's last name. An adopted child is a permanent part of the family.
- **Foster Families** A **foster family** is a family that takes care of children on a short-term basis. The children are not related to the foster parents but are cared for as family members. Some foster children are waiting to be adopted. Other foster children need a place to live until the problems of their birth parents are resolved.

Family Culture

Do you know a family that is similar to your own? You may think this family is just like yours, but if you spent a day with that family, you could find dozens of differences. A family may have the same structure yours does. But every family has its own unique traditions and ways of doing things. Families are shaped by their cultural background as well as the individual personalities of family members.

Cultural Background

Everything that defines the identity of a specific group of people, including their common traits and customs, is called **culture**. Cultural influences include what you eat, wear, and believe in and how you act.

Families who value their cultural history usually make a point of carrying on its traditions and beliefs. A **tradition** is a custom passed from one generation to another. Parents encourage their children to learn traditional ways and to respect their cultural heritage. At the same time, they teach their children to respect and appreciate other cultures.

Family Personality

Your best friend's family may have the same structure yours does. You may both share the same cultural background. But some of your values and the way your family members interact can still be completely different. A family's personality is like a culture within a culture. Differences in family personality include:

- **Differences in Atmosphere** The atmosphere in a family's home can be loud and crazy, laid-back and friendly, or formal and distant. Family members can be very affectionate with one another, or more reserved. Some families tease one another a lot, while others are more serious and straightforward.
- **Differences in Traditions and Rituals** Individual families have different traditions and rituals. For one family, birthdays may be cause for a party. Another family may choose to celebrate birthdays with family-only dinners.
- **Differences in Values** The Tanner family values athletic achievement. They support any talent or interest a family member has in a sport. Most of their extra income is spent on sporting goods and events. Athletic trophies are displayed proudly in their home. The Holmes family believes it is important to encourage educational activities. This family spends much of its spare time and money attending museums. Most of the family members like to read, and they display books as if they were trophies.

✓ Reading Check **Describe** How has family life changed since the 1900s? Why?

Math You Can Use

Calculate Interest

Mr. and Mrs. Yuen are saving money to help pay for their son's college expenses. They opened an account that pays them 5% annual interest by depositing $2,000.00. After one year, they earned $100.00 in interest. How much money will they have saved after three years?

Math Concept **Interest** To calculate earned interest, multiply the amount of money in the savings account by the annual interest rate. That number is the additional money earned over the course of one year.

Starting Hint First, add the $100.00 to the initial amount in the savings to figure out how much money was in the savings account after one year. Then, calculate the interest paid after two years.

Math For math help, go to the Math Appendix at the back of the book.

The Family Life Cycle

Although social trends and changes have affected today's families, most families still go through certain predictable stages from their beginning as a couple until their final years. The process families go through as they grow and change is called the **family life cycle**. Some researchers label the stages of the family life cycle differently. However, the basic pattern remains the same. Knowing about the family life cycle will help you better understand your current and future family.

- **Beginning Stage** The first stage begins with a couple. The two people learn to rely on each other, yet keep their individuality. The couple's major tasks include setting up a home, setting goals for the future, and learning to act as a team.

- **Parenting Stage** During this period, new members (children) are added to the family. When children are young, most parents are involved with home and family life. They have less time for themselves as a couple. Great amounts of time, attention, and money are required to care for the children's needs.

- **Launching Stage** In this stage, teens and young adults begin to leave the family home. They assume work and household responsibilities of their own.

- **Middle Years Stage** This stage allows parents to focus on being a couple once more. Having an **empty nest**, or a home children have left to be on their own, allows couples more time to enjoy hobbies, community activities, and volunteer work. There can be an adjustment period once grown children leave the home.

> **Build Family Bonds**
>
> Special activities can help family members develop strong bonds with one another. *What special activities might a family enjoy doing together?*

- **Retirement Stage** For many people, the final stage of the family cycle involves retirement from a job. During this stage of life, people have time to reflect on the past and share with others what they have learned over their lifetimes. Many older adults remain active, spending time with children, grandchildren, and friends. They take advantage of their new found free time to enjoy hobbies and travel. Money, age-related health issues, and declining ability to live independently may be major concerns during this stage.

Though most families go through the family life cycle stages in order, not all do. There are variations of these stages. For example, some couples do not have children, some marry at an older age and have children later in life, and some couples separate and divorce. Other couples find themselves parenting one or more grandchildren as they enter the middle years stage or the retirement stage. Some couples have their adult children move back in with them, with or without their own children. Further, by choice or because of financial need, an increasing number of retirement-age people are continuing to hold either full-time or part-time jobs.

Section 9.1

After You Read

Review Key Concepts

1. **Explain** the term *society* and how children learn to be a part of it.
2. **Describe** differences among family personalities that make each family unique.
3. **List** two possible variations of the typical stages in a family life cycle.

Practice Academic Skills

English Language Arts

4. Research current information about adopting a child or becoming a foster parent in your state. Note the requirements of adoption and foster parenting, as well as the legal processes. Report your findings to the class.

Social Studies

5. Develop a brief list of interview questions to ask a grandparent or older family member about his or her experiences in each stage of the family life cycle. Conduct the interview. What answers surprised you?

Check Your Answers Go to connectED.mcgraw-hill.com to check your answers.

Section 9.2

Family Dynamics

Before You Read

Check for Understanding If you run into questions in the text, or have questions of your own about the material, try to answer them. This will help you get the most out of the material.

Read to Learn

Key Concepts

- **Explain** the purpose of roles and how they are learned.
- **Identify** four strategies for getting along with your family members.
- **Describe** the characteristics of strong families.

Main Idea

Learning family roles and understanding how to get along with family members will help you create and maintain strong family relationships.

Content Vocabulary

◇ role
◇ sibling
◇ age span
◇ sibling rivalry

Academic Vocabulary

You will find these words in your reading and on your tests. Use the glossary to look up their definitions if necessary.

☐ consensus
☐ conscious

Graphic Organizer

As you read, record the five tips for organizing a successful family meeting. Use a graphic organizer like the one below to organize your information.

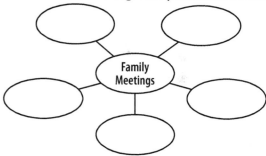

 Graphic Organizer Go to **connectED.mcgraw-hill.com** to download this graphic organizer.

Family Roles and Responsibilities

As You Read

Connect As you read, think about how you act with friends. How do you act with teachers? How and why does your behavior change?

Vocabulary

You can find definitions in the glossary at the back of this book

A **role** is an expected pattern of behavior. It is linked to a person's place in society. All family members have specific roles. Some roles like son, daughter, younger brother or older sister, come with a person's position in the family. They are given roles, or roles that are automatically acquired. Other roles, such as employee, at-home parent, or soccer player, are chosen roles, and refer to the way the person chooses to spend his or her time. Everyone has more than one role. You might be a son, a younger brother, and a grandson all in one. You also might be a friend, a baseball team member, and a paper carrier outside the family.

Think about the way your behavior changes to suit different situations and expectations. The way you act with a friend is not the same way that you act with a teacher or parent. Roles help people know how to act in different situations.

Like values, you learn roles through examples and direct teaching. Families provide much of this information when their children are young. Parents and other older family members serve as role models for relationships. For example, children learn the expected behaviors and responsibilities of a wife, husband, mother and father by watching the way their parents interact with them and each other.

Individual Responsibilities

With a role comes responsibility. For a family to function effectively, every member must do his or her part to help out. Major responsibilities fall primarily on the parents and other adult family members. These responsibilities include providing for basic needs such as food, shelter, clothing, healthcare and education. Parents are also responsible for setting limits and maintaining rules regarding behavior, health, and safety.

Share Family Responsibilities

Being willing to help out with a variety of responsibilities helps you learn more about what is involved in making a family function well. *What chores can you do to help your family function?*

Somos Images/Corbis

Children have responsibilities as well. Maybe you help with cleaning and grocery shopping. Perhaps you take care of your younger sibling after school. A **sibling** is a brother or sister. You may feel like you have way too many household responsibilities, but take a closer look at your family. Evaluate how responsibilities are divided. What are each person's roles inside and outside the home? What responsibilities go with each role? In your family, who pays the bills, keeps the car running, cooks the meals, cares for sick family members, and does laundry? When you look at the bigger picture, you may find that you really do not have that many obligations after all! With so many things to be done, every person can and should do some things to help. Remember that chores are not punishment. Chores are tasks that everyone must do to keep the home in order. When you share these tasks, you not only help the family run more efficiently but also develop life skills you will need as an adult.

Family Meetings

One of the best ways to ensure that family members share household responsibilities is to build consensus, or come to a decision agreeable to everyone. What skills do you think are required for successful consensus building?

Meeting regularly to discuss problems, assign chores, and celebrate good news can also help family members get along and strengthen their bonds. The following tips can help you plan a successful family meeting:

- **Set a date.** Make sure everyone knows the time and place for the meeting. Every family member should be included in the meetings. If someone cannot attend the meeting, find another time to meet.
- **Appoint a meeting leader.** A meeting leader helps guide the discussion and keep everyone on track. Rotate the responsibility so that everyone has a chance to lead.
- **Give everyone a chance to speak.** Any family member, even the youngest child, should be allowed to voice their concerns or suggestions. If people are talking over one another, try passing a talking stick or other object from one speaker to another. The only person that should be speaking is the person that holds the stick.
- **Avoid the blame game.** Attacking or blaming other family members for their actions creates a negative environment. Instead of bringing up what a family member did wrong, list what the person did right and then build on it.
- **Make meetings fun.** Serve a favorite snack or dessert. Have some soft, relaxing music during the meeting. Perhaps family members could rotate turns choosing their favorite music.

✓ **Reading Check** **Describe** In what ways might a person have more than one role in life?

Getting Along in Your Family

SUCCEED IN SCHOOL

Sibling Rivalry

Sometimes you might find yourself competing with your brother or sister at school. It is important to realize that you have your own unique gifts and that not everyone, even in the same family, has the same strengths. Make a list of what you do well and add to the list as things come to mind.

Getting along presents challenges in every family. Think about all the ways family members are different: age, gender, personality, and life experiences. Add differing interests, abilities, and responsibilities, and you have quite a mix of people. These differences can cause miscommunication and conflict.

What can you do to improve family relationships? You can probably do more than you realize. You can start by controlling your own attitudes and actions. Many teenagers react to events without considering the consequences of their words and actions. This careless approach often hurts others and can pull a family apart. If you think about each situation first, you will make better choices. Talk through problems without an "I win, you lose" attitude.

You and Your Parents

As teens move toward more independence, their relationships with their parents may change or feel like a roller coaster. Some have difficulty finding ways to get along and stay close. Think about your own family. How do you maintain strong relationships with your parents or guardians? Do your relationships periodically change?

Increase Your Understanding

How well do you really know your parents or guardians? What have their lives been like? What responsibilities and problems do they have? Understanding means learning about the reasons behind your parents' beliefs and actions. Maybe they are strict with you because they are trying to protect you from problems they had at your age.

Understanding also depends on how well your parents know you. If you do not share your thoughts and feelings with them, how can they understand you? Find time when you can talk to your parents or guardians. Jared and his mom talk as they walk the dog in the evening. Carmen has become closer to her dad and stepmother by talking with them during mealtime each night.

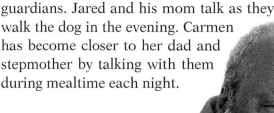

Comstock/Corbis

Family Support

Strong families share good times and stick together through times of trouble. *How might a family show its strengths?*

How I See It

Micah, 14

My brother Sean is an amazing basketball player. He is the star of the team and gets a lot of attention because of it. Sometimes it felt like my parents had one child, and Sean was the center of the entire family! I would get so jealous and angry I couldn't even look him in the eye. Then one day I heard my mother telling her friend what a great musician I am. I felt so stupid. I realized that my parents pay for my lessons and go to all my concerts. They even missed one of Sean's games for my last recital. Sean and I are good at different things, and my parents are proud of us both.

Critical Thinking
Micah suggests that parents can be equally proud of two very different siblings. Do you agree or disagree? Explain.

Show Respect

Unfortunately, it is easy for disrespect to creep into a family. Disrespectful words and actions often result in anger and hurt feelings. When that happens, everyone's happiness suffers. Try making mental movies of how you interact with your parents or guardians. What message do your words give? What does your tone of voice or body language say about you and your feelings? How can you change your words and actions so that they show respect?

Act Responsibly

Teens who are responsible are often given more privileges. Here are some ways you can demonstrate of responsibility:

- Be honest with your parents and admit mistakes when you make them.
- Complete your chores at home without constant reminders.
- Tell your parents where you are when you are away from home.
- Call your parents as soon as you know you are going to be late. Do not wait until you have exceeded your curfew.
- Do your best in school.
- Watch out for your younger brothers or sisters, whether your parents ask you to or not.

Show Appreciation

How often do you give a friend a compliment or say thank you? Appreciation is just as important in families, but it is often overlooked. A willing smile, an offer of help, or even a request for advice can show that you realize how much your parents and guardians help you.

You and Your Siblings

Understanding, respect, responsibility, and appreciation are traits of all healthy relationships, including your relationships with your siblings. How well you get along with your siblings depends on many factors. Sharing common interests can help you get along. The **age span**, or the number of years between siblings, also plays a part. Siblings who are close in age often have more in common than those who are many years apart. Being close in age is not a guarantee that siblings will be or will remain close to one another. Some older siblings are overly protective of the younger ones. Others feel frustrated when a younger brother or sister hangs around and asks questions all the time. Try to figure out what your sibling thinks and feels. Then you can find better ways to get along.

HOW TO... Make Time for One Another

Have you ever watched television sitcoms from the 1950s or 1960s? They often showed families eating meals together every day. It was an ideal, but it was also more likely to happen then than now. Today, parents and children are busier than ever. Families cannot assume they will naturally spend time together relaxing over a meal or playing together at a park. Instead, they must set aside time to spend together and take advantage of every occasion they are together.

Have Fun with Family Chores Making meals and cleaning are some tasks that families do together. Add an enjoyable element that helps you appreciate one another's company. Listen to music while you prepare meals or clean the house. Take turns telling why you like certain songs.

Start New Traditions Traditions do not have to be elaborate, just fun. Consider making dinner from scratch on weekends. Visit a farmers' market every Saturday morning, or have a family game night. A new tradition can be a treat for the entire family if it is something you look forward to every week.

RoyMcMahon/Corbis

Sibling Rivalry

Sibling rivalry, or competition for the love and attention of parents, is common. Have you ever felt that unfairness was a problem in your family? Do you keep track of gifts, awards, privileges, and compliments that each sibling receives? Try not to fall into this trap. Every situation is different. If you were a parent, how would you keep track of everything you said to, bought for, or rewarded to each child? It is impossible!

When you feel competitive, remember that you have your own special qualities and abilities. They may not be the same as those of your siblings, but that does not matter. Discover what you do well, and develop those skills. Remember, too, that your parents have the ability to love more than one child.

✓ Reading Check **Summarize** What can a person do to improve family relationships?

Take Advantage of Passing Moments You can talk with family members while riding to school or waiting in line at a store. Listen carefully when someone shares an opinion or a funny story. You might gain insight into a family member's interests and concerns. Those moments may become fond memories.

Volunteer as a Family Look for volunteer activities that call for a family effort. For example, your family might collect food for a food drive or visit a nursing home. You learn to be charitable by seeing your family in action. Ask or remind your parents or guardians to help your entire family find ways to volunteer.

Spend Time with Individual Family Members You will not be able to include family members in every activity. Special bonds can still form when siblings spend time together without parents or when you share time with only one parent.

Make Togetherness a Priority The bottom line is that spending time together must be seen as important. Carve family time out of busy schedules, even if it means giving up other activities.

Building Family Strengths

What does it take to have a strong family? Researchers have identified some characteristics of strong, successful, loving families. No family will have all the characteristics, and certainly not at all times. However, strong families do not just happen. It takes time and effort from everyone to make and keep a family strong. You can positively affect your family relationships through the actions you take. You can help make your family strong by doing the following:

- **Have a positive attitude about life and family.** Family members who look for the best in one another have great potential for getting along. They believe that if they work together, they can achieve family goals.
- **Arrange to spend time together.** This includes quality time spent either in a group or one on one.
- **Show appreciation and love for one another.** A hug, a compliment, a card or note of thanks, a task done without asking—these are all actions of loving family members.
- **Share beliefs, values, and goals.** The family's daily actions reflect what it considers important. A family teaches a sense of right and wrong. Members share their hopes and dreams.
- **Stay committed to one another.** Family members care about one another's well-being and happiness for a lifetime. They are willing to work out difficulties among themselves.
- **Show consideration and respect for one another.** This includes respecting one another's privacy and space and accepting differences of opinion.
- **Be tolerant and forgiving.** No one is perfect. Strong families may have their differences. They may even quarrel, but they are successful in working out solutions.
- **Share traditions and family history.** Old family stories, daily and seasonal rituals, photo albums, and special mementos link the family to its past. Creating new traditions is valuable, too. The children will someday base their traditions on their own experiences.
- **Take time for laughter and play.** The ability to laugh together, even in rough times, can mean a lot. Strong families know that their time together is valuable. Activities such as a picnic or a soccer game in the yard or at a nearby park can bring family members closer.

Siblings

Older siblings often are special people in the eyes of their younger brothers and sisters. *Why might younger brothers and sisters look up to older siblings?*

Masterfile

Pulling Together

When you think about all of the things that combine to make families strong, there is one last point to remember. People need the support, love, and friendship of their family. Friends can drift apart, but parents and siblings share a bond like no other. This goes for grandparents as well.

Make a conscious, or deliberate, effort of thinking of yourself as part of the whole family. Think of "us" instead of just "me." This can help you remember that your actions affect other members of your family. Living under one roof can be stressful. However, it is worth the effort to ensure that relationships with your family members can tolerate the ups and downs of day-to-day living. If you wipe up a spill, then no one will slip on it and fall. If you phone your grandfather or your grandmother, his or her day will be brighter, and you will have a closer relationship with your family members.

If you want your family members to be there when you need them someday, then it is well worth your effort to work toward building strong family ties now. You get out of family relationships what you put into them. Be an example for others to follow. Begin now with a personal commitment to family strength. A little investment on your part produces great reward: relationships that last a lifetime.

Section 9.2

After You Read

Review Key Concepts

1. **List** five tips for holding a successful family meeting.
2. **Describe** sibling rivalry, and how a person can avoid it.
3. **Explain** why it is important for family members to pull together.

Practice Academic Skills

English Language Arts

4. Imagine you are the parent of a teen your age. Write a letter to the teen explaining your reasons for making a decision or taking an action that the teen thinks is unfair.

Social Studies

5. Follow your teacher's instructions to form into groups. Then, act out a scene in which two or more siblings are engaged in sibling rivalry. Ask classmates for suggestions on how to solve the problem, and discuss why those solutions might work.

 Check Your Answers Go to **connectED. mcgraw-hill.com** to check your answers.

Computer Programmer

What Does a Computer Programmer Do?

Computer programmers create programs that tell computers how to work. Video games are examples of computer programs. So are Internet browsers. Engineers and analysts tell programmers what the software should do. Then, programmers convert these ideas into instructions that the computer understands. They also repair and modify existing programs.

Skills Computer programmers should be able to think logically and pay close attention to detail. They should also be patient, persistent, and able to work under pressure. Problem-solving skills and creativity are important. Because programmers often work on teams, they should have good communication skills.

Education and Training Most computer programmers have a bachelor's degree. However, some may only need a two-year degree or certificate. Programmers often major in computer science or business. Technology changes quickly, so programmers should update their skills on an ongoing basis.

Job Outlook Computer programming jobs are expected to decline slowly. Those with the most education and experience with a variety of programming languages and tools will have the best prospects.

Critical Thinking Think about your typical daily activities. How many times do you encounter computers at home, at school, or in your community? What functions are these computers performing? Write a paragraph identifying at least four industries that use computers. Why might these industries need computer programmers?

Career Cluster

Information Technology
Computer Programmers work in the Information Technology career cluster. Here are some of the other jobs in this career cluster:

- Network Administrator
- Multimedia Author
- Webmaster
- Statistician
- Data Analyst
- Technical Writer
- Maintenance Technician
- Mathematician
- Operating System Engineer
- Help Desk Technician
- Software Engineer
- Customer Liaison
- Systems Analyst
- Commercial Designer
- Business Analyst
- Digital Media Specialist
- Network Technician
- Applications Analyst

Explore Further Research this career cluster. Choose a career in this cluster that appeals to you and write a career profile.

JGI/drr.net

Chapter 9 — Review and Applications

CHAPTER SUMMARY

Section 9.1
The Anatomy of a Family

Families provide for members' physical and emotional needs. The family unit is also where children first learn social skills and moral values. There are many different family structures, cultures, and personalities, but all families share the same basic functions. Social trends and changes have affected today's families, though most families go through the same predictable stages of change. This is called the family life cycle.

Section 9.2
Family Dynamics

From young to old, every member of a family fulfills several roles and has many responsibilities. Strong families have common characteristics that foster family bonds. Showing understanding, respect, responsibility, and appreciation can help you improve relationships with your family members. Spending quality time with family members can help you build relationships that last a lifetime.

Vocabulary Review

1. Write a memo introducing yourself to the rest of the class. Use four content vocabulary words and at least one academic vocabulary word in your memo.

Content Vocabulary
◇ society (p. 205)
◇ social skill (p. 205)
◇ nuclear family (p. 206)
◇ single-parent family (p. 206)
◇ blended family (p. 207)
◇ extended family (p. 207)
◇ adoptive family (p. 207)
◇ foster family (p. 207)
◇ culture (p. 208)
◇ tradition (p. 208)
◇ family life cycle (p. 209)
◇ empty nest (p. 209)
◇ role (p. 212)
◇ sibling (p. 213)
◇ age span (p. 216)
◇ sibling rivalry (p. 217)

Academic Vocabulary
▪ function (p. 205)
▪ unique (p. 206)
▪ consensus (p. 213)
▪ conscious (p. 219)

Review Key Concepts

2. **Identify** the functions of families.
3. **Describe** the various types of families.
4. **Outline** the family life cycle.
5. **Explain** the purpose of roles and how they are learned.
6. **Identify** four strategies for getting along with your family members.
7. **Describe** the characteristics of strong families.

Critical Thinking

8. **Analyze** Which types of families have you observed among your friends and acquaintances? What characteristics of strong families do they share?
9. **Making Generalizations** Which stage in the family life cycle do you think is the most important? Which do you think is the most difficult for adults? Explain.
10. **Compare** Think about the roles you currently fill in your family and the roles of your other family members. Compare and contrast the similarities and differences you see.
11. **Consider** Think about your own family situation. How can you make your family stronger through your own actions?

ACTIVE LEARNING

Family & Community Connections

12. Build a Stronger Family Respecting other family members and spending quality time with them helps strengthen family ties. But, you can do many other things to strengthen your family. Follow your teacher's instructions to form groups. In groups, write a list of things each of your families do that strengthen them. Then, make a list of things your families could do to become stronger. Which item on these

lists do you think is most important for a strong family? How can your family become stronger in that area? Act on your suggestions and share your results with the rest of the class.

13. Family Meeting Sharing household responsibilities helps a home run smoothly. It also prevents any one member from doing an unfair amount of work. One of the best ways to ensure that family members share responsibilities is to divide them in a way that everyone finds agreeable. One way to do this is through a family meeting. Consider the responsibilities in your household and the way they are divided. Think of a better way they could be divided. Then, plan a meeting to discuss your proposed change. If you think the responsibilities are already divided fairly, plan a meeting to ask others' opinions. Remember to consult other family members when setting a date. Provide an outline of what you will discuss. Also include tips to make the meeting go smoothly. Then, have the meeting at the set time.

Real-World Skills and Applications

Leadership Skills	**14. Understanding** When your parents understand how you feel and what you need, it can improve your relationship with them. But understanding starts with good communication. Think of a few things you would like your parents to know about you. Also think of different ways you could share this information. Then, take the initiative to have discussions with your parents that will teach them more about you.
Financial Literacy	**15. The Cost of Kids** Suppose a young couple that takes in foster children is trying to decide whether they can afford to support another child. They currently take care of two foster children, and they spend approximately $1,450 per month doing so. If they receive an additional $825 each month from the government, can they afford to support one more child? If so, by how much?
Information Literacy	**16. Changing Families** According to the U.S. Census Bureau, there were 40,365 nuclear families living in the United States in 1950. This number rose to 58,410 in 2010. The number of single-parent families rose from 4,144 in 1950 to 20,423 in 2010. Record this information using a line graph or a bar graph. What can you conclude from the information? Make a generalization about the change in each type of family.

Academic Skills

 English Language Arts

17. Compare Cultures Read about a family whose culture is different from yours. The family may live in a different country or simply follow different traditions. Write a brief essay comparing the traditions and beliefs of the family to those of yours. You may want to first describe some traditions and beliefs that are important to your family, and then describe those that are important to the other family.

 Science

18. Probability Probability is the chance of something happening. The probability of a flipped coin landing with the heads side up rather than the tails side is 50:50.
Procedure Flip a coin twenty times, and record which side it lands on each time. Record an H when the coin lands with the heads side up and a T when it lands with the tails side up.
Analysis Total the number of Hs and Ts. Based on your findings would you say probability is a guarantee? Why or why not?

 Mathematics

19. Families of All Types Imagine that you need to gather information for a paper about types of families in specific regions. In your own town, you find that in a given year there are 652 single-parent families. There are 73 more couples with children in your town than there are single-parent families. How many blended families are there if there are 233 fewer blended families than couples with children?

Math Concept **Addition and Subtraction** The numbers added together in an addition problem are called addends. The answer of a subtraction problem is called a difference.

Starting Hint First, find the amount of couples in your town. Add the number of additional couples with children to the number of single-parent families. Then, subtract the number of blended families from the number of couples.

 For math help, go to the Math Appendix at the back of the book.

 ## Standardized Test Practice

MULTIPLE CHOICE
Read the question. Then choose the correct answer.

Test-Taking Tip When answering a multiple-choice question, scan the possible answers and eliminate the ones you know are incorrect. Then, if you still do not know the answer, make an educated guess among the choices that remain.

20. Identify which of the following terms does not describe a type of family.
a) Nuclear
b) Adoptive
c) Extended
d) Compressed

Chapter 10

Family Challenges

Section 10.1

Changes in the Family

Section 10.2

Abuse and Addiction in the Family

Chapter Objectives

Section 10.1

- **Identify** specific changes in circumstances that affect families.
- **Summarize** strategies for adjusting to changes in family structure.
- **Describe** how people react to and adjust to death.

Section 10.2

- **Describe** how substance addiction affects individuals and their families.
- **Identify** the most common types of physical and mental abuse.
- **Name** sources of help for families dealing with addiction or abuse.

Burke/Trioio Productions/Jupiter Images

Writing Activity

Persuasive Paragraph

Substance Abuse Drug addiction is one of the most challenging situations a family can face. When one member of a family uses drugs, the entire family is affected. Encouraging others to avoid substance abuse is one way to prevent this problem. You can use a persuasive essay to convince others to agree with your viewpoint. Write a persuasive paragraph convincing young students to stay away from drugs and alcohol.

Writing Tips Use these tips to write a persuasive paragraph:

- Clearly state your position in the first sentence of your paragraph.
- Understand the views of the opposition, and use information that counters their stance.
- Use logical reasoning and examples in your essay.

Explore the Photo

Family structures and circumstances will change over time. *How has your family, or another that you are familiar with, changed over time?*

Section 10.1

Changes in the Family

Reading Guide

Before You Read

Preview Read the topics of the Reading Check questions. Write one or two sentences predicting what you think the section will be about.

Read to Learn

Key Concepts

- **Identify** specific changes in circumstances that affect families.
- **Summarize** strategies for adjusting to changes in family structure.
- **Describe** how people react to and adjust to death.

Main Idea

Understanding change and strategies for dealing with change can help you deal with any challenges your family may face.

Content Vocabulary

◇ financial
◇ creditor
◇ credit rating
◇ grief
◇ closure

Academic Vocabulary

You will find these words in your reading and on your tests. Use the glossary to look up their definitions if necessary.

☐ incur
☐ upset

Graphic Organizer

As you read, record ways you can help your family adjust to a move and unemployment. Use a graphic organizer like the one below to organize your information.

	A Move	Unemployment
How I Can Help My Family Adjust		

 Graphic Organizer Go to **connectED.mcgraw-hill.com** to download this graphic organizer.

Changes in Circumstances

Whether expected or unexpected, change is a part of life. Some changes are exciting. For example, say your older sister graduates from college and moves into her first apartment. Suddenly the room you shared with her is all yours. Or perhaps your dad gets a new job that gives him a higher salary and more vacation time. Your family might have more barbeques and take more trips than you used to.

Other changes are more difficult and stressful. Say you have an older brother who develops a serious health problem, for example. Your family would probably be very worried about his health and your mom might take a second job to help with the additional bills. She may no longer be able to attend your softball games or have time to help your sister with her homework.

Changes and the joy and challenges they bring are part of life's normal ups and downs. Families adjust to most changes fairly easily. However, when a family experiences major problems, some family members may have difficulty coping. Knowing what to expect in certain situations can help family members deal effectively with the challenges they will face.

Moving

Karen placed the last box into the moving truck and looked at her childhood home. Her mother had accepted a job in another town 200 miles away, which meant that the family had to move. "I just made the basketball team this year, and now we're moving," thought Karen. "This is so unfair!"

Moving affects every member in a family. How might Karen's mother be affected by her new job? What issues related to the move might her father have? What fears might her siblings have? Moving to a new community can be both challenging and exciting. Most moves involve adjusting to a new school, finding your way in unfamiliar surroundings, and getting to know new people. Feeling strange about a new community is perfectly normal. Usually the feeling disappears once you develop a new routine.

As You Read

Connect As you read this section, think about your family's home life. How would it affect you if a grandparent came to live in your home?

Find Help

When you need advice about a problem you are experiencing, you may not need to go far to find help. Sometimes an understanding family member can keep your problem confidential and help you work things out. *Think about a family member you would go to for advice. Why would you go to him or her?*

Comstock Images/Getty Images

TAKE CHARGE!

Whether you have moved to a new community or just want to meet someone new, try these tips for making new friends:

- **Look Friendly** Smiling at people will give you a friendly appearance.
- **Take the First Step** Do not wait for others to make friends with you. Make the first move to let others know you want to get to know them.
- **Make a Call or Write an E-Mail** Contact someone you talked with in class or during lunch.
- **Sign Up for Activities** Try out for a part in a play, for instance. Chances are there will be other teens involved who are looking to make friends, too.
- **Help New Students Feel at Home** Ask new students about themselves, and show them around the school or community.

Real-World Skills

Review Your Friendships
Take some time and think about your current friendships. How did you meet? Who made the first move? How did the friendship begin and eventually evolve into what it is today? Write several paragraphs on how you can use experiences with your current friendships to make new friends.

Visiting your new neighborhood before you move can help reduce feelings of anxiety. If this is not a possibility, you can go online to find out more about the area, including local points of interest. You can fit in more quickly at a new school by signing up for a sport or other activity you enjoy. That makes it easier to meet other teens with similar interests. Be friendly and show interest in others in your new community. Soon it can feel as though you have lived there your entire life.

Financial Problems

Vocabulary

You can find definitions in the glossary at the back of this book.

Financial, or money-related, problems can be triggered by many things. A family member may lose a job. Others may struggle with finances after a natural disaster or serious illness in the family. They may not be able to pay the expensive medical or repair bills they incur, or become subject to. Additions to the family can also be more expensive than parents expect. Meeting a child's basic medical and daycare needs can be costly. Many families routinely struggle with financial problems simply because they spend more than they earn.

There are some effective strategies that can help families deal with financial problems.

- **Prepare.** Preparing for potential financial trouble is the best way to prevent it. Experts suggest saving up to three months of living expenses. These savings can help a family through hard times.
- **Spend less.** Put off buying new clothes. Mending the clothes you have or buying "gently used" items at thrift and consignment stores can help cut costs. Cutting back on restaurants can also help a lot. Meals made at home usually cost less than prepared food, especially if you watch grocers' ads to find the best buys.

Another way to reduce spending is to take advantage of free and low-cost entertainment. Check out books and videos from the library instead of renting or buying them. Trade games with your friends instead of buying new ones. Check your community center's calendar for free events such as concerts in the park.

- **Show maturity.** Maturity goes a long way when finances are tight. Putting other family members' needs ahead of your own wants helps everyone get through tough situations more easily. Although it may be stressful at the time, learning to handle financial resources carefully makes teens better money managers as adults.

- **Develop a payment plan.** A **creditor** is a person or company to whom you owe money. When a bill is overdue, most creditors are willing to help you make a new arrangement for payment, as long as you let them know you intend to pay your debt. This can protect your **credit rating**, a record that shows your ability and willingness to pay your debts.

- **Find help.** Sometimes a family cannot solve its financial problems alone. Many communities offer classes that provide money-managing strategies. Credit counselors are another good source of advice. They help people create plans to control spending and get out of debt. In some situations, they work with creditors to arrange realistic payment schedules. Credit counselors can be found in telephone or online directories under Consumer Credit Counseling Services.

Unemployment

Of all the reasons for financial problems, unemployment is one of the hardest on families. This is because losing income is only a part of the problem. When a person suffers a job loss, he often experiences feelings of low self-esteem, anger, and frustration. He may feel as though he has failed both himself and his family. The longer a person is unemployed, the more depressed and irritable he becomes. Some people withdraw from others, and some turn to alcohol or other substances to dull their feelings. This makes the person feel worse. It also adds emotional stress to the financial stress a family is already struggling with.

Masterfile

Cope with Financial Problems

Consumer credit counseling is one of many ways that families can learn to cope with financial problems. *Why might a family go to consumer credit counseling?*

Most people who lose their jobs eventually find new ones. In the meantime, older children can help their families cope with the emotional and financial strain unemployment brings. If he or she is old enough, a teen can get an after-school or weekend job to contribute to the family's income. While a parent is looking for a job, teens can look after their younger siblings, run errands, and help with cleaning or yard work. Above all else, showing support and understanding is the most important thing you can do to help an unemployed family member. A parent often feels bad about not being able to provide for his or her family. Complaints and blame only deepen the hurt. Help your family member by showing respect, love, and support.

Health Problems

When a family member becomes seriously ill or disabled, it can lead to many changes in the family's routines and schedules. Family members may need to make adjustments so that the person with the illness or disability can receive proper care. Parents or guardians may need to decrease their working hours to help provide care. Children may need to pitch in and do extra household chores.

When one family member is physically or mentally unwell, the whole family experiences worry and stress. Not knowing if a loved one will completely recover from injury or illness can cause loss of sleep, changes in appetite, and an inability to focus on work or school. Serious illnesses or disabilities can also cause financial problems for a family, even if the unwell person is not the main source of the family's income. A family member who takes time off from work to help with care often loses income. Medical bills can also add up quickly.

All of this financial and emotional stress can cause feelings of anger and resentment in family members. If not careful, they may lash out at one another out of frustration and make a very difficult situation even worse.

Communication and cooperation can help families deal with health problems. Learning about a family member's illness or disability can help you better understand his or her daily and long-term physical and emotional needs. Doctors, clinics, libraries, and Web sites offer valuable information. People who have had similar difficulties can provide advice and support. Becoming well informed and showing an attitude of understanding, direction, and compassion can help the family stay strong.

Natural Disasters

Families all over the world have been victims of natural disasters. Earthquakes, hurricanes, tornadoes, floods, and fires are just some of the disasters that can occur, with or without warning. Homes or entire communities, including workplaces and schools, may be damaged or destroyed.

The first concern in any disaster is physical safety. Families should install smoke detectors in their homes and regularly test them to make sure they work. It is also wise to put together emergency supply kits that include bottled water, flashlights, first-aid kits, non-perishable foods, and a can opener. These items can help in many different disaster situations. Families can also practice emergency responses and evacuation plans.

Planning for life after a disaster is also important. The loss of a home, and perhaps a job due to the loss of a workplace, can seriously affect family finances. Some family members may also need substantial time and emotional support to overcome the effects of a disaster. Government agencies, private organizations, and religious groups often provide some money, clothing, food, counseling, and temporary shelter to victims of disaster. But families should make sure they have enough insurance to pay for repairs and long-term needs until they are back on their feet. A family may not be able to predict a disaster, but if they prepare for it, they will be able to recover quickly.

Homelessness

Homelessness, having no permanent place to live, is a problem all over the world. Some families lose their homes because of natural disasters. But many others lose their homes because of financial troubles or job loss. This problem has become more common in recent years. Many communities have agencies, such as the Salvation Army and the Red Cross, that can provide temporary shelter for people who lose their homes.

✓ Reading Check

Assess What are four actions you can take to help your family through expected or unexpected changes?

Health & Wellness TIPS

Take Care of Yourself

Having a seriously ill family member can be stressful for the entire family. During this time, remember to take care of your own health, too. Practice these tips to support your physical and emotional well-being:

► Reduce your stress level by exercising or keeping a journal.

► Communicate openly with others about your feelings.

► Make sure your family shares caretaking responsibilities fairly.

▼ Cope with Natural Disasters

Homelessness is often the result of natural disasters. For some families, their homes, possessions, and finances are destroyed. *How are these people helping one another cope with a disaster?*

Changes in Family Structure

Most changes to a family's structure are expected and follow the pattern of the family life cycle. Parents have children, children grow up, parents grow older, and grown children leave the home one by one to start families of their own. Other changes are less expected and require more adjustment time.

New Family Members

Many families experience change because of a new addition. The new family member may be a new brother or sister or may be a cousin who has come to live with you while attending a local college. Or your mother or father may have gotten remarried. Any time a family adds another member, everyone needs to make adjustments.

It is only natural to feel a little stress, insecurity, and resentment when your daily routine is upset, or turned upside down. You do not have to see a new family member as a negative. You can view the change as a way to learn more about yourself and your family. Thinking of ways to value a new addition to your family makes it easier to see the change as a positive experience.

New Siblings

A new brother or sister can shake up everyone's daily routine. New babies rarely sleep through the night and require a lot of attention. Your parents may be tired and unable to spend as much time with you as before. You may also have to take on new chores to help your parents deal with the demands of new infant care.

It is natural for older siblings to feel a bit jealous and hurt by the temporary loss of their parents' attention. But spending time with your new sibling can help you see a baby as a blessing, not a burden. Take part in the care of your new brother or sister. Your parents will be thankful for the help. Plus, loving and entertaining a new baby can be more fun than you ever imagined.

Change Your Perspective

Having a grandparent come to stay with your family can be a blessing in disguise. *What are some of the benefits of having a grandparent around every day?*

Grandparents

A grandparent may join your household because of financial or health reasons. A grandparent may also move in with a family to help with child care. Having yet another adult in your home telling you what to do can be frustrating. But grandparents have much to offer their grandchildren. A grandparent can teach you new skills and traditions, and is a great source of family history.

Fuse/Getty Images

How I See It

Carrie, 17

When my father married my stepmother, Shirley, three years after my parents' divorce, I felt like he was betraying our family. I refused to talk to Shirley. One day, my father told me that he didn't expect me to love Shirley but that he did want me to give her a chance. He explained that Shirley didn't cause the divorce, and it was unfair of me to take my frustrations out on her. I'm still upset about the divorce, but I realize he is right. I'm trying to be nicer to Shirley.

Critical Thinking
Carrie suggests that stepparents need respect and understanding. Do you agree or disagree? Explain.

Stepparents

It can take up to three to five years for a family to adjust to a new stepparent. A new parent may have different rules, values, and ideas about discipline than you are used to. You may not understand these values and rules, and may resent having a new authority figure in your life. Competition is another common problem. When a new stepparent feels left out, or not valued as much as his or her new stepchildren, jealousy and competition for attention can occur.

If a new stepparent has children from a previous marriage, they may join the household as well. This can cause tension, or strained relationships, as the new siblings adjust to their new roles. An oldest child may suddenly have an older stepsister, for example, and no longer have the same kind of influence as before. Tension and jealousy can also occur if a parent shows favoritism to his or her child over a stepchild.

A new stepparent can be a positive thing, however. A stepparent who is involved in your life, and takes the time to talk with you and teach you new things, can raise your self-esteem. If both of your birth parents are very involved in your life, a stepparent still has much to offer. Maybe your real mom is a great cook and has taught you how to cook. Your stepmother may not cook as well, but may be good at sports and can give you tips that will help you make the volleyball team.

Stepbrothers and stepsisters can also make a positive difference in your life. If you are an only child, having a new family member around your age can make family events more fun. Perhaps you always wanted a little brother or sister. Gaining younger stepsiblings gives you a chance to be the role model they look to for advice.

As you look for the positive attributes of your new family members, make an effort to make them feel appreciated and welcome. Remember, they too may be finding it difficult to adjust to their new family structure.

Extended Stays

When a family member or friend comes to live with you for a few weeks or months, it may take time to adjust. A cousin may need to stay with your family while his or her parents are going through a rough patch. A family friend could live with your family while attending a local college. You might have to give up some privacy and share a bathroom or even your room. However, having an older relative or friend around means you can get advice from someone closer to your age, not just your parents or guardians. A person on an extended stay may also be able to help you with your homework, teach you new skills, or introduce you to new books and music.

Teenage Pregnancy

Having a child is a life-changing event. This is especially true when the pregnancy is unplanned and the parents are still teenagers. Parenthood involves many responsibilities, and they are best handled when the parents are independent adults who have prepared for them. However, this is not always the case.

Teen parents and their families face many challenges. Teen parents usually experience financial difficulties, and they often find child care to be overwhelming. Many teen parents give up their dreams, such as a college education, to meet the responsibilities of parenthood. The families of teen parents are also affected. Many teen parents continue to live with their families because they need help with child care and cannot afford housing costs. Despite the difficulties, however, some teens make parenthood work with great effort, sacrifice, and the support of their families.

Separation and Divorce

When parents separate or divorce, usually one parent moves out of the family home. Some couples separate for a period of time but then resolve their differences and get back together. In other cases, they decide to end the relationship and divorce, which causes major changes in family life.

The children of parents who separate or divorce often go through a difficult time of emotional adjustment. They may think their behavior caused the breakup and blame themselves. For this reason, they need to receive loving support from both parents and reassurance that this is not the case. Children cope best with divorce when they have stability. This means there are few changes in the rest of their lives. It can mean living in the same home, going to the same school, and spending time with the same friends.

Parents can make mistakes when a separation or divorce process involves bitter feelings. They may make negative comments about each other to their children or want the children to take sides. Children may feel torn between parents who are going through a separation or divorce. For them, this is the most stressful part of the breakup. To lessen the effects of divorce, children need to know that it is all right to love both parents equally after a divorce.

Building Character ?!

Empathy Every Monday and Wednesday, Jacob manages a food and clothing drive at his high school. Jacob does not have a car, so his parents help him transport the items to local families. Jacob's parents are often tired after working all day and caring for his siblings. They do not always have the energy to help with Jacob's drive. How can Jacob show empathy for his parents?

You Make the Call

Showing empathy means seeing things from another person's point of view. How might Jacob continue to manage the food and clothing drive while showing empathy for his parents?

Feelings of guilt, rage, rejection, and helplessness are common reactions to divorce. To remain strong and positive, spend time with both parents and share your feelings with them. You have the right to express how your parents' actions make you feel. If you are unsure about how to talk to your parents about what you feel, talk to a trusted adult. First talking things out with a teacher, school counselor, or religious leader can help you find the words to describe the emotions you are experiencing. Adjusting after a divorce takes a lot of time, emotional healing, and special effort.

✓ **Reading Check** **Identify** What are the most common reactions to changes in family structure?

Death

Death is as natural as birth. When a person has lived a long life, death is the next natural step. Family members and friends find comfort in the fact that their loved one lived a full and long life. Emotionally, they are often as prepared as possible for the event. They have been expecting it. Unfortunately, not everyone dies in this way. Some people lose their lives suddenly, because of accident or illness.

Whenever death occurs, it is natural to experience **grief**, emotions and physical feelings that can be very painful. The closer you were to the person, the greater your sense of loss. The person's age and the circumstances of the death can also affect the level of your grief. Though every death is difficult to deal with, family members are struck hardest by sudden deaths, because they did not expect them and were not able to prepare for them.

People handle grief in different ways. Some need to talk to friends and family members and express intense emotions. Others need to process their emotions alone. Family members need to respect one another's grieving process and allow others to mourn in their own way for as long as appropriate. Participating in or attending a funeral or memorial service can help people accept the reality of death. For some, the funeral provides the **closure**, or finality, that helps them deal with the reality of the loss.

Conflict among family members is common because of increased emotional stress during this period. However, families can also grow closer and stronger as a result of loss. Sharing emotions and memories with one another and with good friends can ease family members' pain and help them cope with loss. Talking to a counselor who specializes in this type of therapy can also help you through the grieving process.

 Divorce

It is normal for children to feel grief, anger, fear, and frustration when they learn their parents are divorcing. Children should remember that the divorce is not their fault.

Why might children feel that a divorce is their fault?

©Fabrice Lerouge/SuperStock

Suicide

Suicide is one of the most common causes of death among teenagers. A suicidal person may be overwhelmed by the problems in his life. He may believe there is no hope for future happiness.

When a death is caused by suicide, family members face loss, unanswered questions, and guilt. Family members may feel they are to blame in some way. They may go over and over what they should have said or done, thinking they could have prevented the tragedy somehow. With so many questions remaining, closure can be extremely difficult.

Warning signs for suicide include severe depression and frequent mood swings. The person considering suicide may withdraw from people and activities he or she once enjoyed. He or she may give away special possessions, act irrationally, or talk about death often. Sudden happiness after a long period of depression can indicate that a decision to commit suicide has been reached.

If you recognize these warning signs and suspect that someone you know is suicidal, do not be afraid to show that you care. Seek help from a responsible adult right away. If you have suicidal thoughts yourself, get help immediately!

Section 10.1

After You Read

Review Key Concepts

1. **Describe** why unemployment is one of the hardest financial problems for families to confront.

2. **Define** the word tension, and give an example of how new family members might cause it.

3. **Explain** why a person should attend the funeral or memorial service of a loved one.

Check Your Answers Go to connectED. mcgraw-hill.com to check your answers.

Practice Academic Skills

English Language Arts

4. Suppose that an older, disabled family member is coming to live with your family. Describe specific ways you and your other family members can make the transition as simple as possible while providing care and comfort to your older relative.

Social Studies

5. People handle grief in different ways. Describe some of the things people do to deal with the grief they experience when a loved one dies. How do these techniques help people deal with loss?

Section 10.2

Abuse and Addiction in the Family

Reading Guide

Before You Read

Preview Examine the images and features. Then, write one or two sentences predicting what you think the section will be about.

Read to Learn

Key Concepts

- **Describe** how substance addiction affects individuals and their families.
- **Identify** the most common types of physical and mental abuse.
- **Name** sources of help for families dealing with addiction or abuse.

Main Idea

Addiction and abuse can destroy both individuals and their families. Families dealing with these problems can turn to numerous sources for help.

Content Vocabulary

◇ addiction
◇ alcoholism
◇ alcoholic
◇ crisis
◇ emotional abuse
◇ domestic violence
◇ neglect

Academic Vocabulary

You will find these words in your reading and on your tests. Use the glossary to look up their definitions if necessary.

☐ view
☐ neglect

Graphic Organizer

As you read, record solutions to drug/alcohol addiction and emotional/physical abuse. Use a graphic organizer like the one below to organize your information.

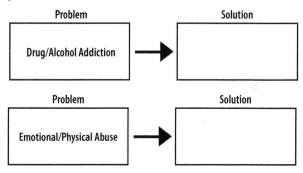

 Graphic Organizer Go to connectED.mcgraw-hill.com to download this graphic organizer.

Addiction

Few forces are as destructive to individuals and families as drugs and alcohol. People who use drugs or alcohol can develop an addiction. An **addiction** is a dependence on a particular substance or action. It is a mental or physical need to have a substance despite the personal cost. People addicted to drugs or alcohol will do almost anything, even commit crimes, to obtain the substance they crave.

As You Read

Connect Think about how you and your family members view the use of drugs and alcohol. Do you have similar or different opinions? Explain.

Vocabulary

You can find definitions in the glossary at the back of this book.

Alcoholism

Alcohol is one of the most commonly abused substances. **Alcoholism** is physical and mental dependence on alcohol. Someone who is addicted to alcohol is called an **alcoholic**. Many people who regularly drink large amounts of alcohol do not believe they are alcoholics. They may say they only drink to be social. Their friends and family members may view, or see, things differently, however. These people have witnessed the gradual changes in the alcoholic's personality and behavior.

Symptoms of alcoholism can include:

- Drinking often, sometimes alone.
- Drinking to deal with difficult situations.
- Missing commitments, such as work or family events.
- Blacking out, or not remembering events that took place while drinking.
- Experiencing extreme mood swings.

TAKE CHARGE!

How to Help Someone Who Abuses Alcohol

If you are concerned about someone close to you who is abusing alcohol, these guidelines can help:

- **Express Concern** Let the person know you are concerned and willing to help. Speak calmly and call the problem by its name: alcoholism.
- **Do Not Be an Enabler** Do not cover up or make excuses for the drinker. Set boundaries. Not setting boundaries just enables the person to continue drinking without facing the consequences.
- **Seek Help** Let the person know that help is available. Provide information about community resources and their locations. Talk to a trusted adult, and encourage your friend or family member to seek assistance.
- **Remain Safe** Never argue with someone who has been drinking, as he or she may react violently. Also, refuse if the person offers to drive you somewhere. You do not want anyone to become a victim in a drunk-driving accident.

Real-World Skills

Informational Pamphlet
Follow your teacher's instructions for forming into small groups. Work together to list signs of alcoholism. Then, have each group member research a different organization or program available to help alcoholics. Compile your findings into a pamphlet. Make the pamphlet available to your school so that other students can benefit from your research.

◀ **Drug Abuse**

Facing a drug problem requires courage from the person abusing drugs and other family members. *What qualities might help a person overcome drug abuse? Explain.*

Drug Addiction

It is no secret that illegal drugs can cause serious problems. But did you know that prescription drugs can also be addictive? When medications for injury or illness are misused, the user can develop a physical or emotional dependence on them. Serious health problems, and even death, can result from substance abuse.

Symptoms of drug use include:

- Difficulty focusing.
- Missing work or school often.
- Aggressive or attention-seeking behaviors.
- Mood swings.
- Poor coordination.
- Slurred speech.
- Unhealthy appearance.

Effects on the Family and Society

Substance abuse can put a family on the fast track to a crisis. A **crisis** ('kri-ses) is a situation that has reached a critical phase. A crisis causes great emotional stress and hardship. The situation is so overwhelming that a family's usual coping methods are not enough.

Whether young or old, people with a substance abuse problem can make life difficult for their families. They may neglect, or give little attention to, their responsibilities and act irrationally or violently. Their behavior often causes other family members to live in tension and fear, never knowing how the addicted person will act. Abusers usually deny they have a problem, which makes it discouraging for family members who try to help them. The abuser's denial can cause anger, frustration, stress, and pain for a family.

When teens use alcohol and other drugs, they face serious consequences that can affect them for life. Long-lasting physical, mental, and emotional problems can interfere with how well teens perform in school or at work. They may frequently fight with parents or guardians and show a "don't care" attitude. Because their use of alcohol and other drugs is against the law, they may face serious legal troubles.

Building Character?!

Support Nadia's friend Megan seems extremely unhappy lately. She confides to Nadia that her mom has been drinking heavily since she and Megan's dad divorced. Megan feels as though the divorce and her mom's drinking are somehow her fault. Megan warns Nadia not to tell anyone about the situation. How can Nadia support Megan during this difficult time?

You Make the Call

Should Nadia keep Megan's secret, or tell someone that Megan needs help? How can Nadia help Megan cope with her mother's alcoholism and her role in the situation?

Somos/Veer/Getty Images

Crime

Substance abuse affects society as well. Drug abusers may be violent and may physically harm others. They may drive a car under the influence and seriously injure or kill another person or themselves. Many crimes are committed by addicts who steal money and objects to pay for drugs. Some addicts will even steal from friends and family members to feed their addictions. When a family member commits a crime, the rest of the family suffers.

Have you, or someone you know, been a victim of crime? It can happen to anyone. Children, teens, older adults, and people with disabilities are often at high risk. Victims of crime can become emotionally scarred. Family and friends need to rally around the victim and give support. If you become aware of a crime, talk to an adult you trust and report the crime to the police.

If the person who commited the crime is a family member, the best approach is to obtain legal help. It can take a lot of work to shift the person's life back on track. Family support is extremely important.

HOW TO... Break the Silence of Abuse

If you or someone you know is being abused, you need to seek help immediately. Silence will not make the abuse go away. It will only allow the abuse to continue and possibly get worse. By seeking help now, you may prevent the abuse from happening to another innocent victim.

Acknowledge the Problem The first step in breaking the silence of abuse is to acknowledge the abuse, or accept that the abuse happened. This may be especially difficult for people being abused by a trusted adult, such as a parent. It is never easy to accept that someone who is supposed to love, protect, and care for you is hurting you.

Do Not Accept the Blame Victims of abuse often think they did something wrong to deserve the abuse. Abusers often encourage this belief. Abusers might urge their victims to be silent about the abuse, threatening trouble or physical attack if anyone finds out. Remember that abuse is never the victim's fault and the best course of action is to seek help.

DreamPictures/Blend Images LLC

Solutions

Prevention is the best solution to the problem of drug abuse. If you do not start using alcohol or any other drug, you will not develop a problem. That means resisting pressure from peers to try drugs and avoiding places where drugs will be available. Refusing drugs might seem hard at times, but doing so can prevent a lifetime of problems and heartache.

When your family's well-being is threatened by one member's drug use or alcohol abuse, all of the family members need help. Seeking help from a counselor, a therapist, or support groups, such as Al-Anon, Alateen, Alcoholics Anonymous, or Narcotics Anonymous, is a way of caring for your family.

✓ **Reading Check** **Explain** Why are drugs and alcohol so potentially harmful to individuals and their families?

Community Connections

Promote School Safety

You can build a safe environment in your school by taking part in school clubs and events. This can help you see beyond the differences you may have with others and teach you to respect and value each other. You can also join or create a nonviolence club in your school to help prevent teen violence.

Confide in a Trusted Adult Talk to someone you can trust: a family member, a school counselor or teacher, a doctor, or someone who works in a place of worship. Counselors are trained to work with people who have been abused. They know how to help. If you feel you cannot report the abuse face to face, try calling or even sending an e-mail.

Call a Help Line If you cannot discuss the problem with an adult you know, call a crisis help line. Sometimes it is easier to talk with someone you do not know. Telephone books list local child abuse and family violence help lines.

Call the Police Safety of the victim is the primary concern. In cases of physical or sexual abuse, the police should be contacted immediately. You can contact them yourself or ask an adult you trust to make the call for you. The police can remove the abuser from the situation and provide the victim with sources for support and counseling.

(b)Ausloser/zefa/Corbis; (tr)Steve Smith/Getty Images

Violence in the Home

Sometimes a family member harms or threatens to harm another's physical or mental health. This abuse can be directed toward any member of a family, including children, older family members, or one's husband or wife. Abuse takes various forms but generally falls into one of two categories: emotional abuse or physical abuse.

Emotional Abuse

Emotional abuse is the wrong or harmful treatment of someone's emotional health. It causes invisible, but permanent, damage to the victim's self-esteem. Emotional abuse can cause a person to feel worthless. A person who feels worthless tends to make poor choices throughout his or her life that support this feeling.

There are several types of emotional abuse, including:

- **Threats** An abuser may threaten the victim with violent or horrible punishments.
- **Rejection** This usually includes negative and hurtful comments and put-downs. Ignoring or being mentally unavailable to a victim is another form of rejection.
- **Isolation** To maintain control of their victims, some abusers prevent normal contact with others. A spouse may be prevented from working. A child may not be allowed to have friends.
- **Corruption** An abuser may teach a victim to be antisocial or violent.

Physical Abuse

When physical force is used to harm a family member, it is called **domestic violence**. Violent outbursts damage property and hurt people and animals. They can even kill. But physical abuse is not always violent. **Neglect**, another form of abuse, occurs when people fail to meet the needs of their children or the disabled adults in their care. For example, a child who spends long periods of time without food or adult attention and supervision suffers from neglect. If he or she gets hungry or hurt, no one is around to help. Sexual abuse is yet another form of physical abuse. When a child is forced or lured into sexual activity by an adult, it can cause both physical harm and long-term emotional damage.

Cycles of Abuse

There is no excuse for any kind of abuse or neglect. Every type of abuse is wrong and severely damaging to the victim and his or her family. Causes of abuse usually have little, if anything, to do with a victim's actions. Even if an action triggers the abuse, the action is not the cause of abuse. Many violent adults were abused as children, and they often lack skills to cope with anger, fear, or stress. They may have had abuse as a model, and the cycle can continue within the family until someone seeks help. Many child abusers lack basic parenting skills and cannot make responsible child guidance decisions.

When you observe instances of abuse or neglect, contact the police. *Why is it important to report instances of abuse or neglect to the police?*

Low self-esteem, marital conflict, and employment problems can also lead to an adult's abusive behavior. The same is true for drug or alcohol abuse, neither of which is an excuse for the behavior. Abuse is never excusable. In many cases, abuse is almost certain to be repeated.

Solutions

Anyone who is abused can benefit from professional help. An abused person must find someone who will listen and provide shelter if needed. Some teens run away from abusive situations. Unfortunately, running away can turn out to be just as dangerous or even worse than staying in the home. Strangers may take advantage of runaways and abuse them.

Many communities provide safe shelter for victims of abuse. You can locate a safe shelter by calling 911 (or the emergency number in your area). You can also ask for a referral at a hospital emergency room or from various community organizations.

Prevention of abuse and neglect starts with respect for each family member. Learning about child development and parenting skills and reducing stress can also help prevent abuse. Community outreach programs link family members with people who will listen and help guide them.

Dangers of Running Away

If you learn that someone intends to run away from home, talk to him or her about it. Teens who run away often face new, more dangerous problems, such as kidnapping, drug abuse, and the challenges of living on the streets.

Write About It

Research the signs that a teen might run away. What solutions could you come up with to convince the teen not to run away? Share your findings with the rest of the class.

✓ **Reading Check** **Contrast** How is emotional abuse different from physical abuse?

Sources of Support

Most families have to deal with unexpected changes and challenges. Through love, care, and support for one another, family members are better able to cope with stress and crisis. At times, however, family members may need to seek help from outside groups or people.

S. Olsson/PhotoAlto

Extended Family Often another family member who understands the problem can help. The person's support and fresh perspective may help you find a solution.

Trusted Adults Outside the Family Sometimes it is wise to talk with someone outside the family who is not involved in the situation, such as a teacher, counselor, religious leader, family physician, or trusted neighbor.

Friends Close friends may be able to offer emotional support and help you clarify your problem. They may suggest that you seek counseling.

Support Groups Members of support groups share similar experiences. They meet to discuss specific problems, solutions, and sources of help.

Community Organizations and Agencies Look for a guide to human services on the Internet, in the telephone directory, or at the library. Many of these services are provided for free or for little cost.

Law Enforcement Agencies When a person is abused or neglected, immediate action must be taken to stop the abuse. A police officer can stop the abuser and help the victim seek support. You must report the abuse before you can obtain police help.

Section 10.2

After You Read

Review Key Concepts

1. **List** the symptoms of alcoholism and drug addiction.
2. **Summarize** the cycle of abuse.
3. **Explain** how law enforcement agencies can help someone who is abused or neglected.

 Check Your Answers Go to connectED.mcgraw-hill.com to check your answers.

Practice Academic Skills

 **English Language Arts**

4. What other kinds of addiction exist? Gambling and food can be addictive, for example. Choose an addiction and research its causes and effects. Summarize your findings in several paragraphs. Include recommendations to help people confront the addiction.

 **Social Studies**

5. Many support groups are available to help people suffering from alcohol or drug abuse. Use print or online sources to research one of these groups. Write a short description of the group's goals, techniques, and history. Then, share your findings with the class.

Chapter 10 Review and Applications

CHAPTER SUMMARY

Section 10.1
Changes in the Family

Change is a part of life. Some changes are very positive and exciting. Other changes, such as the loss of a family member, are upsetting or unexpected and can create a family crisis. A crisis may affect family members in different ways. There are many positive strategies you can use to cope with changes in your family's structure or circumstances. Although most families can deal with these changes and issues, outside help is sometimes necessary and is usually helpful.

Section 10.2
Abuse and Addiction in the Family

Few forces are as destructive to individuals and families as drugs and alcohol. Substance abuse affects society as well. Addicts may steal from others to support their addictions, or hurt others while under the influence of drugs or alcohol. Family support is essential when dealing with addictive behaviors. There is no excuse for domestic violence. Abuse can do long-term damage to any member of a family. Seek professional help if you or anyone you know is suffering from physical or emotional abuse.

Vocabulary Review

1. Write each of the vocabulary terms below on an index card, and write the definitions on separate index cards. Work in pairs or small groups to match each term with its definition.

Content Vocabulary
◇ financial (p. 228)
◇ creditor (p. 229)
◇ credit rating (p. 229)
◇ grief (p. 235)
◇ closure (p. 235)
◇ addiction (p. 238)

◇ alcoholism (p. 238)
◇ alcoholic (p. 238)
◇ crisis (p. 239)
◇ emotional abuse (p. 242)
◇ domestic violence (p. 242)
◇ neglect (p. 242)

Academic Vocabulary
▢ incur (p. 228)
▢ upset (p. 232)
▢ view (p. 238)
▢ neglect (p. 239)

Review Key Concepts

2. **Identify** specific changes in circumstances that affect families.
3. **Summarize** strategies for adjusting to changes in family structure.
4. **Describe** how people react to and adjust to death.
5. **Describe** how substance addiction affects individuals and their families.
6. **Identify** the most common types of physical and mental abuse.
7. **Name** sources of help for families dealing with addiction or abuse.

Critical Thinking

8. **Judge** Some people think homelessness is always caused by substance abuse, unwillingness to work, or other faults of the homeless person. How would you respond to this position? Explain.
9. **Draw Conclusions** What three actions could parents take to help their children adjust to a separation or divorce?
10. **Generalize** Which two sources of help do you think would be most beneficial for families trying to cope with the challenges of the cycle of abuse? Why?
11. **Predict** If you took the time to learn about a family member's illness or disability, how do you think that would make your family member feel? Explain.

ACTIVE LEARNING

12. Create a Welcome Program Although it can be exciting, moving to a new community can also be challenging. Moving often involves adjusting to a new school as well as getting to know new neighbors. Follow your teacher's instructions for forming into groups. With your group, create a welcome program for teens who have just moved into your community. Consider clubs and teams that will help them become involved in their new neighborhood. Also include information about local entertainment, school activities, and community resources. Once you are finished, share your program with the rest of the class and any students who recently moved to your area.

Family & Community Connections

13. New Family Members Living with new family members can be difficult, but it can also be rewarding. When a sibling returns from living away from home or when a stepparent, grandparent, or other extended relative moves in, your daily routine can change. Talk to a friend or neighbor who has recently had a change in his or her household. Ask him or her to describe the situation. Have your friend consider the following questions: What do you like and dislike about having this new person living with you? How has your life changed since he or she moved into your house? Did the new addition affect individual family members differently? How? Do you still wish the change had never happened? After you talk to your friend, share what you have learned with the rest of the class.

Real-World Skills and Applications

Leadership Skills

14. Raise Awareness Suicide is a leading cause of death among teenagers. Some teenagers cannot overcome their depression, while others feel they can no longer take the pressures of school and family. Research the issue of suicide, and then create a poster that lists the warning signs that a teen may be thinking of suicide. Include resources the teen can turn to for help. Then, hang the poster in an area of your school where students will see it.

Financial Literacy

15. Financial Strategies Financial problems can occur unexpectedly. The loss of a job, natural disasters, and serious illness are just a few of the things that can trigger financial problems. However, financial problems can be solved. Describe three strategies that can help families deal with financial problems. They can be tips on how to prevent financial problems or tips on how to deal with financial problems.

Cooperative Learning

16. Planning for Natural Disasters Natural disasters often occur without warning. Thus, it is important to be prepared for them. Some common natural disasters are earthquakes, floods, tornadoes, and wildfires. What natural disasters is your community at risk for? Choose one, and work with a partner to research it. Together, list ways that families can prepare for this natural disaster.

Academic Skills

English Language Arts

17. Literature and Life Read a short story in which a family goes through a difficult time, such as the loss of a job, a natural disaster, serious illness, or divorce. Then, write a short essay comparing the way that family handled the problem with other approaches it might have taken. Consider other stories you have read and movies you have seen. Also think about real-life experiences you have had or heard about.

Social Studies

18. Separation and Divorce Use print or online sources to research options for families going through a separation or divorce. What resources are available to families who want to try to stay together? What resources are available to families who want to make a separation or divorce as smooth as possible? Which resources appear to be most plentiful or easily found? Why do you think this is?

Mathematics

19. Commute Time You live two miles from school and ride your bike there every morning. It takes you 13 minutes to ride to school. Your family plans to move in with your grandparents. You will soon live five and one-half miles from school. If you travel at the same speed, how long will it take you to ride your bike to school from your new house?

Math Concept **Proportion** A proportion is an equation with two equal ratios. To solve a proportion, cross multiply. Then, divide to solve for the unknown.

Starting Hint First, set up a proportion. You know it takes 13 minutes to travel two miles ($\frac{13}{2}$), and you want to know the time it will take to travel five and one-half miles ($\frac{x}{5.5}$). Cross multiply, or multiply the top half of each proportion with the bottom half of the other proportion, to solve for the unknown value.

 For math help, go to the Math Appendix at the back of the book.

Standardized Test Practice

SHORT ANSWER PROBLEMS
Directions Read the problem. Then, answer the prompt.

Test-Taking Tip When answering short answer questions, spend some time organizing your responses before writing them in the answer space provided. Doing so can help you reduce the time you need to spend on revision.

20. Briefly describe the four types of emotional abuse.

Chapter 11

Child Development and Care

Section 11.1
How Children Grow

Section 11.2
Caring for Children

Chapter Objectives

Section 11.1
- **Describe** the six areas of child development.
- **List** the stages of child development.
- **Explain** the special needs of children with disabilities.

Section 11.2
- **Identify** the basic responsibilities of a caregiver.
- **Describe** the safety precautions you should take while caring for a child.
- **Outline** the steps you should follow when responding to an emergency.

Writing Activity

Describe an Event

Early Memories Some memories from your childhood may be very clear, especially "firsts." For example, you might recall your first day of school or the first time you rode a bike without training wheels. Perhaps you remember the first time you met someone who became a good friend. Write a paragraph describing a memorable first achievement or moment in your life.

Writing Tips These tips can help you write a descriptive paragraph:

- Think about touch, taste, smell, sight, and sound. Use details from as many of your senses as you can to liven up your description.
- Use action verbs rather than passive verbs such as *is*, *was*, *were*, and *had been* to make your description interesting.
- Be sure to include details about how the event made you feel. Were you happy, sad, frightened, or something else?

Explore the Photo

Siblings often spend much time together when they are young. *What activities do you or your friends do with siblings?*

Section 11.1

How Children Grow

Before You Read

Look It Up As you read this section, keep a dictionary handy. If you hear or read a word that you do not know, look it up in the dictionary. Before long, this practice will become a habit. You will be surprised at how many new words you learn!

Read to Learn

Key Concepts

- **Describe** the six areas of child development.
- **List** the stages of child development.
- **Explain** the special needs of children with disabilities.

Main Idea

Knowing the areas and stages of children's physical, mental, emotional, and social development can help you to understand their needs.

Content Vocabulary

◇ motor skill
◇ large motor skill
◇ small motor skill
◇ hand-eye coordination
◇ gene
◇ developmental milestone
◇ parallel play
◇ conscience
◇ cooperative play
◇ puberty
◇ acne

Academic Vocabulary

You will find these in your reading and on your tests. Use the glossary to look up their definitions if necessary.

▢ praise
▢ correspond

Graphic Organizer

As you read, identify and describe the two factors that affect a person's development. Use a graphic organizer like the one below to organize your information.

What Influences Development?

Influence	Description

 Graphic Organizer Go to **connectED.mcgraw-hill.com** to download this graphic organizer.

A Look at Child Development

As a child gets older, he or she is able to do more and more complex things. This process of change is called child development. Development is different than growth. Growth only means getting bigger in size. Although changes in adults tend to occur slowly, children grow and develop rapidly. Many changes occur very quickly, from month to month or even from week to week. In a very short time, children learn many skills, including walking, talking, and solving problems. These developmental changes, as well as certain influential factors, create unique individuals.

Developmental Areas

When you learn to ride a bike, you need to learn how to balance, how to control your speed, and how to stop. All of these tasks require specific physical skills. You also have to understand bike safety, which requires intelligence. If you ride with friends, you need social skills. Almost everything you do requires many skills, all of which fall into six developmental areas.

Physical Development

The growth of the body and the strength and coordination of muscles are all part of physical development. A **motor skill** is an ability that depends on the use and control of muscles. Walking, jumping, and throwing a ball all involve large motor skills. A **large motor skill** is the movement and control of the back, legs, shoulders, and arms. Writing or picking a flower requires small motor skills. A **small motor skill** is the movement and control of smaller body parts, such as the hands and fingers. Physical development also includes the development of **hand-eye coordination**, which is the ability of the eyes and the hand and arm muscles to work together to make complex movements. When you hit a baseball with a bat, you are using hand-eye coordination.

As You Read

Connect Think about your favorite sport or hobby. What skills do you use when you participate in this sport or hobby?

◇ Vocabulary

You can find definitions in the glossary at the back of this book.

▼ Personality Traits

Photo albums keep a record of how you have changed over the years. *What traits do you have now that you had as an infant?*

Shutterstock/India Picture

Discover Learning Styles

Each student has his or her own way of learning. Some students learn best when they hear their teacher speaking. Other students learn more when they read something from a book. Still others learn best when they touch or have hands-on assignments. Ask your teacher or guidance counselor how you can determine which way of learning is most effective for you.

Building Character?!

Gratitude Ms. Gazowski, a language arts teacher, recognized Tamika's talent for writing even though she was shy. She encouraged Tamika to write more and suggested that she join the drama club to build confidence in herself. Now Tamika is writing frequently and even got a role in the school play. How can Tamika express her gratitude to her teacher in a meaningful way?

You Make the Call

Should Tamika send Ms. Gazowski an e-mail, send her a card, or give her tickets to the school play? How can Tamika best express her gratitude to Ms. Gazowski for her encouragement?

Intellectual Development

Intellectual development involves the ability to think, understand and reason. Infants use their senses to understand the world. Sensory experiences including bright colors, a range of sounds, and interesting smells and textures help them learn. Hands-on experiences and toys that promote learning and creativity help young children discover how things work. By the time they are seven years old, most children begin to think logically. They are able to sort objects into broad categories. Matching games and other activities that involve sorting objects helps them strengthen their logic skills. When they are twelve, most children begin to think in an abstract way. This means they are able to use their imaginations to predict what might happen in the future. They start to identify the causes of past events and experiences, and can solve problems with thought alone.

Language Development

The more you talk to or read to a child, the better. Children learn the rules of language by listening to the people around them. New worlds open to a child once he or she learns to communicate with words. He or she can share ideas, and be truly understood. Many types of growth and development are enhanced once a child learns to communicate with words.

Emotional Development

Infants show emotions through body movements, facial expressions, and sounds, such as cooing or crying. As children grow older, they experience a wider range of emotions. They need help identifying these feelings. They also need to learn how to express their emotions in socially acceptable ways.

Social Development

Children demonstrate their social development through their interactions with others. Sharing, getting along, and making friends all require social skills. Social development begins at birth. Babies enjoy the love and attention they get from their parents and others. When children learn what it is to feel loved and wanted, they want more. They naturally seek out people and positive attention. Smiles and praise, or expressions of approval, from others encourage children to repeat good behaviors. Frowns and scoldings help children learn to avoid other actions. In this way, children learn how they should act around other people.

Moral Development

Moral development involves an understanding of right and wrong. Very young children do not understand the difference between right and wrong. They depend on their parents to tell them whether an action is good or bad. Through instruction and by modeling moral behavior, parents and other adults help children build character. Parental guidance continues through the teen years and into young adulthood.

Developmental Influences

No one is just like you. Even if you have an identical twin, each of you is different in some ways. Heredity and your environment work together to shape you into a one-of-a-kind individual.

Heredity

Heredity refers to all of the traits a person inherits from parents, grandparents, and other relatives. These traits are passed on through genes. A **gene** is the basic unit of heredity. Genes determine a person's body type and the color of his or her hair, skin, and eyes. A person also may inherit certain talents, such as musical or athletic talent, and personality traits, such as shyness.

Environment

Environment is what surrounds a person and affects his or her development and behavior. It includes family, friends, home, school, and the community. It even includes technology, such as computers, mobile devices, television, and video games.

Although heredity is permanent, environmental influences are also strong. For example, praise, encouragement, and support from family members are crucial to developing healthy self-esteem. Children who feel good about themselves are better able to complete challenging tasks. They are also likely to be successful in future relationships and in the workplace. On the other hand, children who are not encouraged often feel insecure and are afraid to try new things.

Culture and traditions also influence a child's development. Culture influences parents' and caregivers' roles and what and how children are taught. What differences do you see between your family and that of a friend from a different culture? What similarities do you see?

✓ Reading Check

Contrast What is the difference between growth in a child and child development?

⋁ Influence of Culture

Heredity and culture contribute to a child's development. *What other influences help shape your personality?*

Developmental Stages

Knowing how children grow can help you better understand yourself and those around you. You will be more prepared to care for children, whether they are your siblings, younger relatives, neighbors, or ultimately your own children should you choose to become a parent later in your life.

Your development began before you were born, in the prenatal stage of life. During this period, you developed from a single cell into a baby capable of surviving in the outside world. Since birth, you have continued through several developmental stages to become who you are today. The developmental stages **correspond**, or relate, to a person's age, beginning in infancy and continuing through young adulthood.

▼ **Development of Infants**

Infants younger than six months are more than what they seem. They can learn and communicate, and they develop at a rapid pace. *How would you help an infant younger than six months learn and communicate?*

For most people, development in all areas follows a general and progressive sequence. As people develop, they accomplish certain developmental milestones. A **developmental milestone** is a skill achieved at a particular stage of life. For example, before you could walk, you had to learn to stand. Walking and standing are developmental milestones. Everyone proceeds through developmental stages in the same sequence, but the rate of progress differs from person to person. For example, you may have learned to stand two months earlier than your best friend did.

Young Infants

Infants younger than six months of age can do many things. Newborn infants look at faces and can recognize primary caregivers' voices. A few months after birth, their neck muscles strengthen, allowing them to hold up their head. Soon they learn to kick their legs and roll from their stomach to their back. Young infants communicate by cooing, laughing, and crying.

Frare/Davis Photography/Brand X Pictures/Getty Images

Older Infants

The period between 6 and 12 months of age is an exciting time because infants make many changes. Older infants can eat solid foods and drink from a cup. They learn to sit alone, crawl, and stand. Some may even begin to walk.

At this stage, infants interact more with their caregivers. They also begin to play (see **Figure 11.1** on page 258). They raise their arms to be picked up and can recognize close family members. They also imitate others' actions and facial expressions and listen to others speak. Infants this age spend much of their time looking and reaching for objects. They explore many objects by putting them in their mouths, so they must be supervised closely. Older infants enjoy music, picture books, and simple games, such as peekaboo. Their language has developed from cooing to babbling, and they usually speak their first word by the time they turn one.

Young Toddlers

After infancy, children become toddlers. Young toddlers, those between 12 and 24 months of age, master quite a few skills before their second birthday. Not only are they eating table foods, but they also can hold their own spoon to eat and may use a straw to drink. They can walk, climb steps without help, and run, although they may do so clumsily. Increased coordination in their arms and hands allows them to roll a ball, turn pages of a book, and scribble with crayons or markers.

Young toddlers are very curious people. They enjoy exploring their surroundings, which means they need to be monitored constantly. They want independence, so young toddlers may tell adults no when adults try to do something for them. Although they may push adults away and want to do many tasks for themselves, young toddlers still need love, care, direction, and comfort from their parents and caregivers.

Older Toddlers

Children round out their toddler years with increased physical energy. They run, jump, walk on tiptoes, climb, pedal a tricycle, and throw and catch balls. At times, they seem as if they'll never stop moving! Between 24 and 36 months, many children become toilet trained. They can also wash their own hands and dress themselves. Although many older toddlers have trouble sharing, they are interested in other children and may play with them. Older toddlers will often engage in **parallel play**, in which they play alongside other children but not with them. Their increased vocabulary helps them interact with parents and caregivers. Older toddlers can ask questions and use longer sentences to express their thoughts and feelings. Gradually, with help from parents and caregivers, they develop a **conscience**, an inner sense of right or wrong. A developing conscience helps children monitor their own behavior.

Health & Wellness TIPS

Limit TV Time

Carefully selected television programs can provide fun and interesting ways to help children learn. Watching too much television, however, can harm children's health. These tips can help you reduce TV time:

▶ Limit TV viewing to less than ten hours a week.
▶ Encourage reading, playing, and exercising.
▶ Turn the TV off when TV time is over.

Preschoolers

By the time they are three to five years old, or preschool age, children's large motor skills are well developed. Their fine motor skills are becoming more refined, allowing them to cut paper with scissors, draw shapes, print their own name, and shape clay into recognizable forms. During the preschool years, children develop the skills they need for school. They learn the alphabet and how to count. Their vocabulary continues to grow, and they learn that printed symbols have meaning.

Their increased vocabulary helps preschoolers express their feelings. Preschoolers can experience many emotions, such as jealousy, curiosity, fear, joy, and affection. They have a sense of right and wrong and are beginning to understand that adults set rules that they need to follow. During the preschool years, children move from parallel play to **cooperative play**, in which they play with other children and learn to share, take turns, solve problems, and control their emotions. These early play experiences build important social skills that are needed throughout life.

HOW TO . . . Handle Tantrums

For every skill young children learn, it seems another one is denied them. Life seems unfair, and they react the only way they know how: screaming, thrashing, and throwing things. A tantrum is an early attempt at problem solving. Parents and caregivers need to address tantrums in an appropriate manner, or this bad behavior can become a pattern for children to get what they want. As a teen, you have learned better ways to deal with problems, and you can help children deal with theirs. Try a few of these techniques the next time a child throws a tantrum.

Ignore the Tantrum Ignoring a tantrum shows the child you are not giving in. Make sure children cannot hurt themselves, others, or anyone's possessions. This teaches them how to behave in public, share, and deal with frustrations in a nonphysical manner. Biting is not uncommon and is inappropriate.

Steve Cole/Getty Images

Maintain the Rules Giving in only teaches children that poor behavior gets results. Likewise, do not reward children for stopping the tantrum by giving them what was wanted.

School-Age Children

When children reach five years of age, they enter the school-age stage of life. During this time, they begin to spend more time away from home. They spend time at school and in structured activities outside of school, such as swim lessons and art classes. These activities foster their independence, help them develop a sense of self, and teach them skills they will use later in life.

School-age children can ride bicycles and participate in activities that require skilled movements, such as team-related sports. Their fine motor skills have become more refined, which allows them to write and draw more precisely.

During this stage, children can read and do arithmetic, reason, and problem solve. Because they face increased academic pressure, they can also experience stress. They may worry about school or family life, and they can be sensitive and easily suffer embarrassment. Their range of feelings increases, and friendships become more complex. School-age children learn teamwork and compromise and can consider others' feelings. They understand right and wrong and generally want to do what is right.

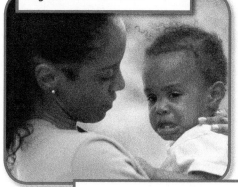

Distract the Child Become involved with a game or other activity. This shows that you are not bothered and encourages the child to join you in something more enjoyable.

Hold the Child Sometimes a firm but gentle embrace gives the comfort that an angry or frightened child needs.

Remove the Audience If you are in a public place, find a quiet spot away from "center stage." Attention from others can encourage the child and put pressure on you to end the tantrum. You might resort to actions that only make the situation worse.

Stay Calm This teaches children that you are in control. It shows control of the situation and gives them a sense of security. Children learn trust when they see that you keep your word, even when they don't like it. They see that you care about them even after they behave poorly.

(l)Stockbyte/EyeWire/Photodisc Collection/Getty Images; (r)Blend Images/Alamy

Figure11.1

Importance of Play

Children at Work Experts agree that play is a child's work. Play nurtures all areas of children's development and allows children to explore their world. Jean Piaget, a noted child expert, describes three stages of play: sensorimotor play, symbolic play, and games with rules. *What games might a three-year-old enjoy?*

Sensorimotor Play
Infancy to 24 Months
Infants and young toddlers experiment with movement. Once they master coordination, they enjoy playing with objects that respond to them. For example, they shake rattles to hear a sound or push a ball to watch it roll.

Symbolic or Pretend Play
24 Months to 6 Years
In this type of play, children pretend by taking on roles. They may play house, pretending to be parents, siblings, or even pets. As their experiences grow, so do their imaginations. Soon they take on roles of construction workers, princesses, or doctors. This fantasy play helps them understand reality.

Games with Rules
School-Age Children
Because older school-age children understand cooperation and teamwork, they are able to play more complicated games with rules. These games can be formal games, such as sports, or games the children create on their own.

Adolescents

The period of adolescence is a time when teens experience many changes in preparation for adulthood. Adolescence begins with **puberty**, the set of changes that result in a physically mature body that is able to reproduce. These changes are most noticeable in teens' voices and appearance. Their bodies begin to look like those of adults and their voices become deeper. Some awkward changes may also be taking place, including acne. **Acne** is a skin problem that develops when pores in the skin become blocked with oil, dead skin cells, and bacteria. This causes pimples on the face, back, and chest. The physical changes brought on by puberty can also affect emotions. Many teens experience mood swings, or sudden changes in behavior that feel like an emotional roller coaster.

Teens have the ability to reason and think of alternatives to problems or actions, which helps them deal with social situations and academic work. During adolescence, friendships become stronger, and some may even develop into romantic relationships. Although friends are important at this stage of development, the family remains a stable base for teens.

✓ **Reading Check** **Give Examples** Identify one developmental milestone from each of the six stages of child development.

Special Needs

Not all children follow the typical pattern of development. Many children have physical impairments, emotional problems or learning disabilities. These children have to work harder than other children to master certain physical or mental skills. For this reason, children with special needs may not be independent as soon as other children. A few will need assistance for their entire lives. The support a child needs depends upon the type and severity of his or her disability.

➤ **Children with Special Needs**

Children with special needs might need extra help with schoolwork to succeed. *How can parents and caregivers help promote self-esteem in children with special needs?*

PhotoAlto/SuperStock

- **Physical Disabilities** Some children with special needs have health-related conditions that can affect their ability to function in some way. Some have problems with movement, and may find it difficult to walk, write, talk, or even breathe. Others may have vision or hearing issues that can make learning more difficult.
- **Learning Disabilities** Children with learning disabilities often struggle with language concepts and reading. These children often need extra guidance and unique lesson plans to succeed. Children with certain learning disabilities may be competent or even clever in other areas, however. Students who struggle with reading may be able to do highly advanced mathematics, for example.
- **Emotional Problems** Some children have an emotional disability that affects their behavior in a negative way. These children may have difficulty following directions. They may find it difficult to understand or get along with others. Children with emotional problems may isolate themselves or lash out at others out of frustration.

Children with special needs require additional guidance from parents, caregivers, teachers, and sometimes health professionals to reach their full potential. These children want to be treated just like other children. They have the same basic needs for praise, support, and encouragement as anyone else.

Section 11.1

After You Read

Review Key Concepts

1. **Compare** large motor skills and small motor skills.
2. **Identify** the difference between parallel play and cooperative play.
3. **List** reasons a child may not follow the typical pattern of development.

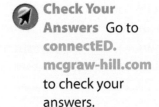

Check Your Answers Go to connectED.mcgraw-hill.com to check your answers.

Practice Academic Skills

English Language Arts

4. Write a persuasive essay encouraging people to learn more about how children grow. In your essay, discuss some of the ideas you learned from this chapter. Be sure to include reasons why it is beneficial to be knowledgeable about child growth and development.

Social Studies

5. Both heredity and environment act as developmental influences. Together, they shape people into one-of-a-kind individuals. Briefly describe the difference between heredity and environment and how each influences personal identity.

Section 11.2

Caring for Children

Before You Read

Prior Knowledge Look over the key concepts at the beginning of the section. Write down what you already know about each concept and what you hope to learn by reading the section. As you read, find examples for both categories.

Read to Learn

Key Concepts

- **Identify** the basic responsibilities of a caregiver.
- **Describe** the safety precautions you should take while caring for a child.
- **Outline** the steps you should follow when responding to an emergency.

Main Idea

Understanding the responsibilities of a caregiver, including how to respond to emergencies, keeps children safe, healthy, and happy.

Content Vocabulary

◇ nightmare
◇ night terror
◇ childproof
◇ poison control center
◇ concussion
◇ shock
◇ cardiopulmonary resuscitation (CPR)

Academic Vocabulary

You will find these words in your reading and on your tests. Use the glossary to look up their definitions if necessary.

☐ sensory
☐ indicate

Graphic Organizer

As you read, identify the tasks involved in caring for children. Use a graphic organizer like the one below to organize your information.

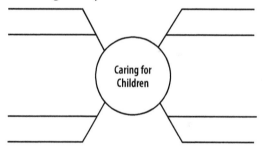

 Graphic Organizer Go to **connectED.mcgraw-hill.com** to download this graphic organizer.

As You Read

Connect Think about the different ways young children communicate. Why is it important to understand typical needs and wants when caring for a child or infant?

Providing Care

Caring for children includes playing with them, dressing them, feeding them, bathing them, and putting them to bed. Caring for children also means protecting them, guiding their behavior, and promoting their self-esteem.

Many parents need others to care for their children while they are at work or taking some time for themselves. Often teens take jobs caring for infants, toddlers, or young children. Some have already had practice babysitting younger siblings. For others, it is a new experience. Teenagers who take child care responsibilities seriously are highly valued and can become regular caregivers. Whether you are an experienced babysitter or just starting out, caring for children can be both fun and profitable.

Manage Behavior

One of the greatest challenges any caregiver faces is behavior management. Children of different ages have different needs, and they behave differently to have their needs met.

Infants

Infants have many physical needs. When they cry, caregivers need to find out what is troubling them. Is the infant too cold or too warm? The baby may be hungry or sick or need a clean diaper. Changing diapers is a necessary part of infant care. To change a diaper, make sure all necessary supplies are nearby before you begin. Never leave an infant alone on a changing table. It is too easy for the child to fall off. If an infant has a dry diaper and is not interested in food, he or she may be crying to be held. Try holding the baby while walking or rock the baby in a chair. Always support the head and neck when holding infants.

Be a Positive Influence

Teens can be a positive influence to the young children they care for. *How can you be a positive influence on young children you might care for?*

©Hero/Corbis/Glow Images

How I See It

Corey, 15

My nephew Joe's birthday is coming up next week. I don't have a little brother, so I wasn't sure what I should get him. I don't have much money to spend, either. My friend Paul told me about how much his little brother likes to cook, so Paul got him a cookbook for kids. That made me think about the kinds of things Joe likes to do. Every time I visit, Joe wants me to play a board game with him, go to the park with him, or take him to the pet shop to look at the animals. After a lot of thought, I decided to make him "Corey-Coupons" that he can use whenever he wants to go to the pet shop, park, or game room. I think he's really going to like my gift this year!

Critical Thinking Although Corey did not spend any money on his gift for Joe, the gift still has a "cost." What is this cost?

Toddlers

The behavior of toddlers is different from that of infants. Trying to find out what they need still requires a bit of guesswork, but many toddlers are able to help by pointing at what they want. Toddlers are also fond of exploring. Unfortunately, they tend to get into things that can be hazardous, and many like to climb, which can lead to falls. You need to watch them every moment and provide safe play activities and toys.

Preschoolers

Preschoolers can do more for themselves. They can let you know when they are hungry, tired, sick, or hurt. Preschoolers mostly need the attention of their caregiver. They enjoy when you read to, play with, and talk to them. Preschoolers can get extremely upset when their parents leave. You can help them look forward to the time they spend with you. Play their favorite games with them, or bring some age-appropriate games or craft supplies of your own.

School-Age Children

Caring for older children requires different skills. Some children may feel they are old enough to take care of themselves. Be friendly to them and show a sincere interest in their ideas and activities. Sometimes older children are jealous of the attention you give to their younger siblings. They may misbehave to get your attention. If a child deliberately misbehaves, remain calm and discipline the child. The most effective discipline has a clear connection to the misbehavior. For example, if a child bumps into others with a bicycle after being told not to, you might take the bicycle away. Be fair, but firm. You can be friendly and still be in charge.

Entertain Children

Children like to be entertained. Keeping children involved in activities also keep them out of trouble. School-age children usually have favorite activities or games that you can play with them. Yet if you ask a younger child, "What do you want to do?" he or she may not know. These ideas for simple, low-cost fun activities can help you keep a child active.

⬦ Vocabulary

You can find definitions in the glossary at the back of this book.

- **Fascinate infants with simple, sensory experiences.** Sensory means related to one or more of the five senses. Take time and help them safely explore things that draw their interest. Let them feel the cool smoothness of a metal wind chime, hear its music, and watch it sway in the breeze.
- **Play peekaboo with infants.** Slowly lower a stuffed toy down one side of a chair and pop it up (making appropriate popping noises) on the other. Repeat and cheer when the child turns to see it appear again.
- **Make mealtime fun.** For years parents have made train noises as a spoonful of strained peas "pulls in" to a child's mouth. You can make the train a honking car, airplane, or rumbling truck.
- **Play pretend with toddlers.** Pretend to be cats, dogs, or jungle or farm animals. Toddlers are also great imitators. Teach them dance steps but do not expect coordination.
- **Make play out of work.** Encourage toddlers' can-do spirit and channel their energy by giving them "jobs." They can wash socks in tubs of water or dust chair legs.
- **Explore nature.** Most toddlers and preschoolers enjoy nature activities. Pick wildflowers. Gather acorns. Compare colors of autumn leaves. Watch ants at work. Feel different types of grasses and leaves.
- **Encourage preschoolers' imagination.** Play dress-up or make-believe. Help with props but leave the story line to them. You might help set up a diner and write the menu as they dictate it. Take turns playing the grouchy customer, the clumsy waiter, or the master chef.
- **Create prints.** Use textured fabric pieces, rubber stamps, plastic cookie-cutters, sponge pieces, and leaves to make impressions in clay. You can also dip the materials in paint to make prints.

⌄ Learning Through Play

Many fun activities can actually promote the healthy social, emotional, physical, or intellectual development of young children. *What areas of development does playing with sand promote?*

Design Pics/Kristy-Anne Glubish

Clothing

Most young children and all infants need help getting dressed. As a general rule, dress infants in one more layer than you would wear. Infants lose body heat more easily than adults do, but they are also sensitive to overheating. Most baby clothes have snaps from the neck to the toes and are easy to put on. Pullover garments can be a bit tricky, however. If the neck opening is large, put the opening around the baby's face first, and then pull it over the back of the head. If the opening is small, scrunch the fabric into a loop and slip it over the back of the baby's head. Stretch the garment forward, down, and away from the baby's face and ears. Put the baby's fist into the armhole and pull the arm through with the other hand.

Toddlers and young preschoolers are very mobile, and their clothing can become dirty quickly. Help them choose clothing that allows movement and can be cleaned easily. Offer clothing that is appropriate for the weather, and the activity. Because many children at this age are learning to use the toilet, they need clothes they can remove easily and quickly. Pants with elastic in the waist are a better choice than those with buttons.

Older preschoolers and school-age children can dress themselves, but may need help tying their shoes. Because children this age have definite likes and dislikes, allow them several clothing options.

Mealtime and Snacks

When you care for children, you may be responsible for feeding them. Find out what food should be served, when to serve it, and how much to serve. Also, it is extremely important to ask parents or guardians about any food allergies or special diets. If a child is allergic to a food, he or she can go into anaphylactic (ˌa-nə-fə-ˈlak-tik) shock. This is a life-threatening condition that makes it difficult to breathe.

Infants

When caring for an infant, you may need to feed him or her with a bottle of breast milk or formula. Before feeding, put a bib on the infant to protect his or her clothing. To feed a baby breast milk, put the bag of frozen milk under cool running water just until the milk has thawed. Increase the temperature of the water from cool, to room temperature, to warm, and then hot. Stop before the water is steaming so that it does not burn the baby's mouth. You can feed an infant formula at room temperature, or you can warm it by placing the bottle in warm water for several minutes. Never warm a bottle in a microwave oven. The liquid can become dangerously hot. Check the breast milk or formula's temperature by shaking a drop out on the inside of your wrist. It should feel warm, not hot.

Math You Can Use

Unit Conversion

Since your parents are going to be gone for one week, they have asked you to care for your younger brother. You are to feed him 20 fluid ounces of milk every day. How many cups of milk is that in one day? How many cups in one week? How many gallons is it in one day and in one week?

Math Concept Unit Conversions There are eight fluid ounces in one cup and 128 fluid ounces in one gallon. One gallon has 16 cups.

Starting Hint To figure out how many cups of milk are needed in one day, divide the total fluid ounces of milk used in one day by the amount of fluid ounces in one cup.

 For math help, go to the Math Appendix at the back of the book.

When you feed an infant, hold the infant upright and hold the bottle while the infant eats. You will need to burp the baby during and after eating. This will prevent the baby from developing painful gas or spitting up.

Older infants may eat baby cereal or baby food. Be prepared for messiness. The child is likely to play with the food, as well as eat it. Have a sense of humor and make mealtimes fun.

Toddlers

Toddlers need the support of a high chair, but unlike infants they can eat some regular food. They like simple foods in small, bite-size pieces they can pick up with their fingers. Cereal pieces, chunks of banana, cooked carrot slices and other foods that break up easily in the mouth are best. Never give young children hard candy, raw carrots or any other food that might cause choking.

Preschoolers

Preschoolers may lack good manners, but they are somewhat skilled at eating. Avoid serving foods that are high in fat and sugar. Simple foods such as milk, crackers, fresh fruit, and vegetable sticks are popular and healthful snacks for preschoolers. If you are not sure about a child's allergies, do not offer eggs, milk, soy, wheat, fish, citrus fruit, peanut butter or anything else that includes nuts! These are the most common food allergies in children.

Bath Time

Bath time is a great way to end the day. Warm water helps children relax and transition into bedtime. Whether you are caring for a toddler or a preschooler, bathtub safety is very important. Use a bathtub mat to prevent falls. Also, you should never leave a young child alone in the bath, not even for a minute. A child can drown in as little as 1 inch of water.

Toddlers often want to wash themselves. By the time they are two, most children can wash, rinse, and dry themselves fairly well. They may need help reaching tough to get to places like the back. By age three, children can wash by themselves, though they still need supervision. Bath toys or simple plastic containers can make bath time more fun for toddlers and young children.

Bananastock/Jupiter Images

Bedtime

Bedtime is often a challenge. Toddlers, preschoolers, and young school-age children may not want to go to bed. They will protest bedtime by crying, climbing out of bed, making excuses to get up for water or restroom visits, and refusing to return to bed. Ask parents or guardians what the bedtime routine is and stick to it. Putting on pajamas, brushing teeth, and listening to a quiet story can help prepare children physically and emotionally for bed.

A sleeping child is still in your care. Be sure to stay close by in case the child needs your attention. Many children experience bedwetting during the night and need a change of pajamas and bedding. A child may experience a **nightmare**, or bad dream, and need your help and comfort. Occasionally, a child may experience a **night terror**, a type of sleep disorder that is more intense than a nightmare. These often occur when a child has a high fever or illness. Children experiencing night terrors might scream, cry, and act confused while still asleep. For nightmares and night terrors, stay with the child and provide comfort until he or she falls back asleep. If the child is asleep, do not wake him or her. Simply provide comfort until the child quiets down.

✓ **Reading Check** **Describe** What should you consider before feeding an infant, toddler, or preschooler?

TAKE CHARGE!

Become an Expert Child Care Provider

Babysitting can be an excellent way to earn money and learn more about child care. You can become a trustworthy, in-demand care provider by following these steps:

- **Get Training** Babysitter training clinics teach babysitting activities and safety skills. This knowledge will make you more comfortable and reassure adults.
- **Learn About the Family** Find out the date, time, number of children and ages, how long you will be needed, and transportation details. Agree on your fee.
- **Inform Your Parents** Tell your family the clients' name, address, and phone number.
- **Arrive Early** Arrive 15 minutes early. Get to know the children and the home's layout. Ask about allergies, medications, and mealtime and bedtime routines.
- **Get Emergency Information** Have the parents write down emergency numbers for you, including a number at which the parents can be reached.
- **Stay Focused on the Children** You have been hired to watch the children, so leave personal calls and television for when you get home.

Real-World Skills

Gain Confidence in Your Babysitting Skills Review babysitter training materials on Web sites such as the American Red Cross. Then, work in pairs to create a five-minute role-play of an interview between a parent and a prospective babysitter. The babysitter should explain his or her qualifications and gain information about the assignment while the parent expresses concerns. Ask class members for suggestions to improve your presentation.

Safety Check

Plant Safety

Many people like to keep houseplants in their homes. These look nice, but it is important to choose plants carefully. Pets like to chew on plants, and small children put almost anything in their mouths. Some plants are poisonous and can harm pets and children.

Write About It

Make a plan for a safe garden. The Internet and libraries have information about poisonous plants, so you will know which ones to avoid. Write a paragraph or draw a garden map showing child- and pet-friendly plants.

Create a Safe Environment

Being in charge of a child is an enormous responsibility. Chances are it is the biggest responsibility you have ever had. Whether you are caring for a younger sibling or your neighbor's toddler, you are in charge of the child's safety and welfare. It is extremely important to provide a safe environment for children. You should also know how to respond to any emergency you may encounter while caring for a child.

Safety in the Home

When caring for small children, think about how they see things. Anticipating children's natural curiosity can prevent accidents. Take steps to identify possible hazards and remove them, or **childproof** the home, to help ensure children's safety.

- **Hazardous Objects and Furniture** Check for debris, objects, furniture, or equipment that could hurt a crawling baby. Remove from tables any heavy items that infants or toddlers might pull off. Put away small items they might choke on. Also, it is good to pad any sharp table corners and the corners of other furniture to avoid accidents.

- **Stairways** Monitoring the use of stairs is an absolute must. Infants and young toddlers often attempt to climb stairs. Keep them away from stairs, lock any gates at stairways, and provide temporary gating when necessary. Remind older toddlers and preschoolers to hold on to a handrail to prevent falls on stairs.

- **Doors and Windows** Keep windows and exterior doors locked at all times. This is especially important in an apartment building or home with more than one story. Doors should never be opened to strangers, even if they appear to be friendly. Children should never indicate, or point out, to strangers that they are home without their parents or guardians.

- **Chemicals and Matches** Many ordinary household products are poisonous and can cause death. Common poisons include insecticides, cleaning supplies, and medicines. Chemicals and medications should be in locked cabinets, well out of reach of children. Swallowing chemicals is extremely dangerous, but damage can also be caused when chemicals are inhaled into the lungs or if they come into contact with skin or eyes. Be alert to signs of poisoning, such as coughing, stomach pain, dizziness, rashes or burns, vomiting, unconsciousness, and swelling in the mouth or esophagus, which causes choking and breathing difficulty. If you think a child has been poisoned, immediately call 911 and a poison control center in your area. A **poison control center** gives advice on treatment for poisoning. Its staff will tell you what emergency action to take.

- **Constant Supervision** Accidents can happen in the blink of an eye! This is why you should never leave children alone in any room, especially a bathroom. They may lock themselves inside, open medicine cabinets, or fall into toilets or tubs containing water.

When bathing children, never leave them alone. Most drownings of small children occur in bathtubs. In the kitchen, be sure to keep children away from ranges, heaters, hot-water faucets, knives and other sharp utensils, heavy pot covers, and hot drinks.

Toy Safety

Children enjoy toys of all types. Although they can be fun to play with, toys may also be safety hazards. Before giving a toy to a child, make sure it is clean, unbreakable, free of sharp edges, and too large to swallow. Loose eyes or buttons on stuffed animals can be extremely dangerous. Any object that can pass through a tube of toilet tissue is too small to give to children younger than three years of age.

Toys should also be age appropriate. For example, clay is an appropriate choice for preschoolers. It is not appropriate for infants, who may put it in their mouths and get sick. Some loud toys can scare small children and even permanently damage hearing. Toys with long strings or cords may cause choking and should not be placed in cribs or playpens where children might become tangled in them.

Toy safety is important for older children, too. Check to see that their toys are in good working condition with no broken pieces or sharp edges. Broken toys can cause serious injuries. Also, provide children with safety equipment for activities such as biking or inline skating.

Outdoor Safety

Most children enjoy playing outdoors, but they must be supervised at all times when outside. In some cases, you can remain inside and watch children who are playing in an enclosed backyard. Other outdoor areas, such as playgrounds, require extra caution. When choosing a playground, select one that has a soft surface, such as shredded tires, beneath the equipment. Make sure to keep children off playground equipment that has peeling paint, is developmentally inappropriate, or is broken. Keep children away from the edges of a play area, and other areas where suspicious people may be lurking. Playground outings should always be supervised by a teen or adult caregiver.

Streets are dangerous areas for children. Never let children play in streets or roads. If older children need to cross the street, explain to them how to cross safely and monitor them as they do. Bicycle safety rules need to be established before children ride.

Wading or swimming pools are another type of outdoor danger. Although they are lots of fun, pools can also be deadly.

Safe Play Areas

Taking a child to a nearby playground can be a lot of fun for both of you. *What safe playgrounds are available in your community?*

©PhotosIndia.com LLC/Alamy

Self-Control Seth and his friend, Jared, were skateboarding at the park. Jared had just started down a ramp when a classmate, Mike, skated down the same ramp. The two crashed, and Jared seemed hurt. Seth approached Mike and seemed ready to punch him for hurting Jared. Jared said he was okay, and warned Seth to calm down. How can Seth show self-control in this situation?

You Make the Call

How might Seth deal with his feelings and the actions he might take in this situation? Should he go ahead and hit Mike for being careless? Should he listen to Jared and calm down before doing anything?

Community Connections

Health Fair

One step you can take to increase knowledge in your community about first aid is to organize a school health fair. With help from teachers and students, you can set up booths with information about first aid, safety, and other topics of interest to people in your area.

If you are taking children to a pool, do not take your eyes off them for even a minute. Children who are inexperienced swimmers, or who get cramps while swimming, can easily drown within seconds. Swim activities, as well as other outdoor activities, also can cause sun-related problems, such as sunburns. Be sure to apply waterproof sunblock to children before they swim or play outdoors. Reapply sunblock as often as the container suggests.

✓ **Reading Check** **Determine** What steps should you take to protect a small child in his or her home environment?

Accidents and Emergencies

Would you know what to do if a child fell from a swing or into a swimming pool? The action you take can be the difference between a minor injury and a more serious injury.

To prepare yourself for dealing with an emergency while providing care for children, commit these suggestions to memory:

1. **Remain calm.** Breathe deeply and focus your thoughts on actions you need to take. Also, try to keep the child calm by speaking in a soothing, controlled manner. The child will pattern his or her behavior after yours.

2. **Assess the situation.** Is this a minor or major injury? Is the child burned, bleeding, or unconscious? Can you handle the situation by yourself, or do you need to call for help?

3. **Call for assistance.** If the child is seriously injured, call 911 or your local emergency number for help. If eye pupils are different sizes, if the child vomits, or if the child just wants to sleep after an injury, he or she may have a **concussion**, or a type of head injury. Keep the child awake until help arrives! If the child appears abnormally cold, he or she could be going into shock. **Shock** is a physical condition characterized by inadequate blood flow and can be very serious. In this case, use a blanket, jacket, or large towel to cover the child. If the child is overheated, he or she may be experiencing sunstroke. Make sure the child has adequate fluids and has a chance to cool down naturally. Providing shade can help.

4. **Give the minimum necessary first-aid treatment.** Knowing what you should not do in an emergency is as important as knowing what you should do. Some injuries, such as broken bones, can be made worse by moving an injured person. Only treat injuries if you know how!

Classes that provide instruction in basic emergency care, or first aid classes, can teach you how to treat minor injuries and how to respond to serious ones. You can also take a class to learn **cardiopulmonary resuscitation (CPR)** a rescue technique used to keep a person's heart and lungs functioning until medical care arrives. These classes are offered in schools and through the American Red Cross and other community agencies.

Respond to Fire

Most families should have an escape plan and at least one fire extinguisher. Before you do anything else, make sure you know the fastest escape route and where the fire extinguisher is stored. The following tips will help you and the children in your care remain safe in case of fire:

- If a fire starts in the oven, turn off the oven and close it. If a fire starts in a frying pan, put a frying pan cover on it. Do not pour water on a grease fire! This may cause the fire to spread. If the fire is out of control, leave the house and call for help.
- If there is smoke in the home, cover your nose and mouth with a wet cloth and do the same for the children. Tell the children to crawl under the smoke as they escape the home.
- Before leaving a room, touch the door. If it is hot, do not open it. Find another exit. If you are unable to escape, stand by a window and signal for help.
- Never stop to take personal belongings or to call 911 while escaping. Wait to call until you are safely outside.
- If you are in an apartment building, locate the nearest stairway marked "Fire Exit," or a fire escape if a stairway is not accessible. Never use an elevator in a fire.
- If clothing is on fire, stop, drop, and roll until the flames are out.

Section 11.2

After You Read

Review Key Concepts

1. **Give** three examples of how you might entertain children you are babysitting.
2. **Explain** why you would want to see things from a child's perspective.
3. **Identify** the signs of a concussion, and how you should respond to a child with a concussion.

Practice Academic Skills

English Language Arts

4. Using a catalog or the Internet, choose one toy you think would be safe for an infant, one for a toddler, and one for a preschooler. Write a short description of each toy and explain what makes the toy safe.

Social Studies

5. Children of different ages have different needs and behave differently to have those needs met. Describe the different needs that caretakers should meet in infants, toddlers, preschoolers, and school-age children.

Check Your Answers Go to connectED.mcgraw-hill.com to check your answers.

Early Childhood Teacher

What Does an Early Childhood Teacher Do?

Early childhood teachers are like learning coaches. They help students learn and apply new concepts. Early childhood teachers introduce three- to five- year-old children to mathematics, language arts, science, and social studies. They use games, music, artwork, films, books, computers, and other engaging tools to teach basic skills.

Skills Teachers must know the subjects they teach. They should be organized, dependable, patient, and creative. Teachers also should be able to work with others and communicate effectively with other teachers, support staff, parents, and members of the community.

Education and Training Education programs for early childhood teachers include courses designed for those preparing to teach. Many states also offer professional development schools. These schools allow the student to experience a year of teaching under expert guidance. Students enter these one-year programs after they have a bachelor's degree.

Job Outlook Employment of early childhood teachers is projected to grow at an average rate. Job prospects are favorable, with many opportunites in lower income urban and rural school districts. A master's degree, national certification, or acting as a mentor can result in a pay raise.

Critical Thinking Think about your experiences at school when you were younger. Write a paragraph explaining how an early childhood teacher could help a child learn and grow based on your experiences. Make sure to discuss at least one way that a teacher could interest a child in learning.

Career Cluster

Education and Training

Early childhood teachers work in the Education and Training career cluster. Here are some of the other jobs in this career cluster:

- Kindergarten Teacher
- Elementary School Teacher
- Middle School Teacher
- Secondary School Teacher
- Postsecondary Teacher
- Counselor
- Teacher Assistant
- Education Administrator
- Librarian
- Writer
- Editor
- Childcare Worker
- Public Relation Specialist
- Social Worker
- Coach
- Umpire

Explore Further Research this career cluster. Choose a career in this cluster that appeals to you and write a career profile.

Image Source/Getty Images

CHAPTER SUMMARY

Section 11.1
How Children Grow

Both heredity and environment influence a child's growth and development. As children grow older, they reach certain developmental milestones. Play nurtures all areas of children's development and allows children to explore the world. Tantrums need to be addressed immediately so they do not become a pattern. A child with special needs requires assistance to reach his or her full potential, but he or she has the same basic needs as other children.

Section 11.2
Caring for Children

Children of different ages require different behavior management techniques. A successful caregiver knows how to prepare and serve children healthful meals and snacks. Following regular routines can help when preparing children for bedtime. Childproofing the home helps keep children safe. Infants, toddlers, and preschoolers should never be unsupervised. Caregivers must know what not to do, as well as what to do, in case of an emergency or accident.

Vocabulary Review

1. Write your own definition for each content and academic vocabulary term.

Content Vocabulary
◇ motor skill (p. 251)
◇ large motor skill (p. 251)
◇ small motor skill (p. 251)
◇ hand-eye coordination (p. 251)
◇ gene (p. 253)
◇ developmental milestone (p. 254)
◇ parallel play (p. 255)

◇ conscience (p. 255)
◇ cooperative play (p. 256)
◇ puberty (p. 259)
◇ acne (p. 259)
◇ nightmare (p. 267)
◇ night terror (p. 267)
◇ childproof (p. 268)
◇ poison control center (p. 268)
◇ concussion (p. 270)

◇ shock (p. 270)
◇ cardiopulmonary resuscitation (CPR) (p. 270)

Academic Vocabulary
▪ praise (p. 252)
▪ correspond (p. 254)
▪ sensory (p. 264)
▪ indicate (p. 268)

Review Key Concepts

2. Describe the six areas of development.
3. List the stages of child development.
4. Explain the special needs of children with disabilities.
5. Identify the basic responsibilities of a caregiver.
6. Describe the safety precautions you should take while caring for a child.
7. Outline the steps you should follow when responding to an emergency.

Critical Thinking

8. Evaluate Heredity and environment play important parts in a child's development. Which do you think is the most influential? Explain your answer.
9. Analyze Parents and caregivers play an important role in a child's moral development. How might they encourage the child to learn moral behaviors?
10. Plan You babysit for a family of three children. One child is seven, one is three, and the third child is six months old. What activities can you plan to entertain the children?
11. Organize Relatives have just had a baby and will need to childproof their home. Write down ideas to help them prepare their home.

ACTIVE LEARNING

Family & Community Connections

12. Meal Planning Imagine that you have been hired to care for two preschoolers every afternoon for the next week. Think of five different activities you can do with them to keep them entertained. Then identify five creative and healthful snacks you might serve each day, without repeating any of them. Remember that preschoolers should not eat foods that are high in sugar and fat. Also, remember that you should avoid feeding children eggs, milk,  soy, wheat, fish, citrus fruit, peanut butter, or anything else that includes nuts unless you are sure they are not allergic to these foods. Share your menu and play plan with the class.

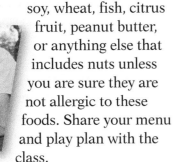

13. Emergency Escape Plan Knowing what to do in an accident or emergency can help you remain calm and be more helpful to those around you. In the case of a fire, it is particularly important to be aware of the layout of the house, the options for exiting, the quickest way out, and the location of any fire extinguishers. Draw a floor plan of your home or a home where you care for children. Show the location of doors, windows, stairways, and outside fire escapes, if applicable. Also, mark the locations of any fire extinguishers. Work with family members to diagram a plan for escape in the event of a fire or other emergency. You should plan the quickest route out of the house or apartment as well as alternate routes. Post your diagram on the refrigerator where every family member can see it.

Real-World Skills and Applications

Leadership Skills

14. Emergency Training Demonstrate your knowledge of how a person should respond when faced with an emergency. Describe how to apply the four suggestions in the text to an emergency situation of your choice. Outline an emergency response training session and then present it to the class. Feel free to use drawings, diagrams, or other props to help train your classmates in emergency response. During or after your presentation, field questions from the rest of the class.

Financial Literacy

15. First Aid A basic first-aid kit containing three gauze pads, scissors, a roll of adhesive tape, and 50 adhesive bandages costs $9.95. Separately, you can buy three gauze pads for $0.99, a pair of scissors for $1.99, a roll of adhesive tape for $2.25, and 25 adhesive bandages for $2.65. How much more or less will it cost you to buy the items separately than to buy the first-aid kit?

Technology Skills

16. Child Care Products Use print or Internet sources to research modern products that help people care for children. For example, you may research baby monitors or car seats. Make a list of three products you think are particularly helpful and briefly describe each. Or invent a realistic product of your own that would aid in child care. When you are finished, share your descriptions of existing products or a detailed drawing and description of your invention with the rest of the class.

Somos Images/Corbis

Academic Skills

 ### English Language Arts

17. Activities for Children Read a few parenting magazines or Web sites that describe activities for young children. Then, based on what you know about development and play, rate the activities on a scale from one to five, with one being the best. Share your ratings with the class, and explain why you rated each activity the way you did.

 ### Science

18. The Weight of Sugar The sugar in many popular drinks is unhealthy. It also has different properties than its sugar-free counterparts.

Procedure Fill a sink up with water. Place one can of diet soda and one can of regular soda in the sink. Note what happens to the two cans.

Analysis Does one can act differently than the other when placed in water? What does it do? Why do you think this is?

 ### Mathematics

19. Fraction of a Fraction Your baby sister, Robin, loves peas. She usually eats ½ cup of mashed peas twice a day. But yesterday she ate more of other foods, and only ate half of her ½ cup of peas in the morning and ⅗ of her ½ cup of peas at night. When Robin eats her full ½ cup serving of peas twice a day, she eats 1 cup of peas. How much less did she eat yesterday than she usually eats?

Math Concept **Multiplying Fractions** To multiply fractions, first multiply their numerators and then multiply their denominators. A numerator is the top half of a fraction, and a denominator is the bottom half of a fraction.

Starting Hint First, multiply ½ by ½ cup to find the amount of peas your sister Robin ate in the morning. Use the same strategy to find out the amount of peas she ate at night.

 For math help, go to the Math Appendix at the back of the book.

Standardized Test Practice

MULTIPLE CHOICE
Directions Read the question and select the best answer from the choices.

Test-Taking Tip Multiple-choice questions often prompt you to select the best answer. They may present you with answers that seem partially true. The best answer is the one that is completely true and can be supported by information from the text.

20. "After struggling through my math test, I realized that I should of studied harder." Which of the following is the best revision of this sentence?
a) I should have studied harder for my test.
b) After struggling through my math test, I realized that I failed.
c) After struggling through my math test, I realized that I should have studied harder.
d) If I had studied harder, I would have done better.

Chapter 12

Understanding Parenting

Section 12.1
Considering Parenthood

Section 12.2
Caring for Children

Chapter Objectives

Section 12.1

- **List** the questions couples should consider before deciding to have children.
- **Describe** lifestyle, financial, and career changes related to parenthood.
- **Identify** the challenges of teenage parenting.

Section 12.2

- **Summarize** the needs of children and how parents can meet them.
- **Describe** five effective behavior management techniques.
- **Identify** five ways parents can handle their emotions.

Henglein and Steets/Getty Images

Writing Activity

Dialogue

Parenting Responsibilities Becoming a parent involves many important, life-changing responsibilities. Imagine that your cousin recently had a child. Write a dialogue between you and the new mother or father discussing the new challenges and responsibilities he or she is facing with the new child in the house. Be sure to include in your dialogue how your cousin is coping with some of the challenges.

Writing Tips Use these tips to write your dialogue:
- Let the people in your dialogue express themselves and their purpose through the words you write.
- Use language that sounds real and appropriate to the people talking.
- Use quotation marks appropriately.

Explore the Photo

Becoming a parent can bring many changes and new experiences to your lives. *Why might you choose to become a parent?*

Considering Parenthood

Before You Read

Understanding It is normal to have questions as you read. Many of them will be answered as you continue. If they are not, write them down and ask your teacher.

Read to Learn

Key Concepts

- **List** the questions couples should consider before deciding to have children.
- **Describe** lifestyle, financial, and career changes related to parenthood.
- **Identify** the challenges of teenage parenting.

Main Idea

Parenting involves many demanding responsibilities that affect your lifestyle, finances, and career.

Content Vocabulary

◇ parenting
◇ fidelity

Academic Vocabulary

You will find these words in your reading and on your tests. Use the glossary to look up their definitions if necessary.

▢ reflect
▢ accommodate

Graphic Organizer

As you read, identify the four main costs of raising a child. Use a graphic organizer like the one below to organize your information.

 Graphic Organizer Go to **connectED.mcgraw-hill.com** to download this graphic organizer.

The Decision to Have Children

How old were your grandparents when they had children? Chances are they began their families at a young age. In the past, it was common for couples to marry and have children shortly after high school. Today, couples often wait until they are older, with established careers, before becoming parents.

Parenting is the process of caring for children and guiding their growth and development. The choice to have a child is a major life decision. A child needs much physical care, financial support, love, attention, and guidance until adulthood. Wise couples know that once they become parents, they must put the needs and wants of their children first.

Reasons People Have Children

People have children for various reasons. Unfortunately, not all of them are good ones. For example, some people may feel pressure from family members. Their parents may be eager for grandchildren. Friends that have children may constantly talk about the joys of being parents. A couple that does not have children may begin to feel like they are missing something, or they might feel selfish. These are not the right reasons to have a child. Perhaps the most important reason to have a child is that two people in a loving, committed relationship want to share their love and time with a child.

People considering parenthood should take a close look at what parenting involves. Making a careful decision to have a child will benefit both you and your child. People should learn about the myths and realities of parenting. If either member of a couple has any doubts, then they should wait to have children. Children deserve to be born to parents who are ready for parenthood.

As You Read

Connect Think about the responsibilities of a life-long commitment. Why is it important to carefully consider these responsibilities before making such commitments?

Vocabulary

You can find definitions in the glossary at the back of this book.

Path of Success

Couples who finish school before starting a family have a head start on a successful life for themselves and their children. *How would finishing school be helpful for raising children?*

Fairness Corinna and her brother, Teo, each need the family computer to do their homework. Corinna gets home from school first and wants to get on the computer right away. She has to write a short story for English class. Teo arrives and says he needs to do Internet research for a history report. What is a fair solution for sharing the computer time?

You Make the Call

Should Corinna use the computer first until she is finished with her short story? Or should Teo use the computer first? What do you think would be a fair solution?

Parenthood Readiness

What if everyone had to pass a test before becoming a parent? Unlike driving a car, there is no test, license, or training required for parenting. For some people, parenthood happens with little or no preparation. Before deciding to have children, couples need to ask themselves the following questions and **reflect**, or think quietly and calmly, about their answers.

- Do we really want children? Are our reasons sound?
- Are we mature enough to be parents?
- Have we completed our education?
- Is our relationship as a couple mature and stable? Will it be able to withstand the challenges of parenthood?
- Do we have a good understanding of the principles of child growth and development?
- Are we ready to meet a baby's emotional and physical needs?
- Do we have enough money to support a family?
- Are we willing and able to make the long-term personal sacrifices needed to care for another person?
- When is the best time to start a family? What will happen to our future plans and career goals if we have a child now?

✓ **Reading Check** **Conclude** Why is the decision to have children important?

Changes That Come with Children

When a child is born or adopted into a family, parents have the unique experience of getting to know and love a new family member. They also have the added responsibility of taking care of a child.

Having a child is not something you can just walk away from, emotionally, legally, or morally. You can quit a job or end a friendship. You can move away to a foreign country or change your hair color every day of the week. The decision to become a parent, however, is a permanent one. A child's birth changes the lives of the parents, and their families, forever.

◄ **Preparing for Parenthood**

The responsibilities of parenting are different from responsibilities you have as a student. As a parent, you must take care of your child's needs in addition to your own. *What items would you need to purchase to take care of a new baby?*

JUPITERIMAGES/Creatas/Alamy

Lifestyle Changes

A child brings many changes and adjustments to daily life. For example, a newborn infant must be fed every few hours, every day, around the clock. In addition, an infant needs diapering, bathing, positive interactions with others, love, comfort, and constant supervision. When you add a job and necessary household tasks such as laundry to this list, it is easy to see why new parents have little time for themselves or each other. Movies, dinners out, and other entertaining activities the couple used to enjoy are often put on hold to care for the baby.

Financial Changes

Have you ever thought about how much money it costs your parents to raise you? Parents generally want to give their child every advantage possible. Since you were an infant, your parents have provided you with clothing, food, health care, and shelter. If you attended a day care or preschool, they paid the bills. They probably purchased toys, books, and school supplies for you. If you ever played a sport, participated in an after-school activity, or went to camp, they likely paid the fees for you. Add all of these costs, and it is easy to see why parents must make financial sacrifices to meet their child's needs. Estimates set the cost of raising a child at two and a half to three times the family's yearly income at the time the child is born.

Career Changes

Having children also affects parents' careers. To keep up with parenting tasks, parents need to adjust their schedules to accommodate, or fit, their children's schedules. People who travel a lot for work or who have long work hours often find that their jobs interfere with their roles as parents. Many of these people seek ways to reduce their working hours. This might mean turning down promotions. Other parents look for new jobs that are less demanding or closer to home. Some decide to take lower-paying jobs because these jobs allow them more time and energy for raising children.

If child care is not available or affordable, one parent may work from home or stop working entirely to care for the children. This will affect the household income. Career plans may have to be put on hold until the children are old enough to go to school.

✓ **Reading Check** **Summarize** How does having a child affect the lives of the parents?

Financial *Literacy*

Child Care Costs

Mr. and Mrs. Moore both work part-time jobs. Mr. Moore is paid $15.00 an hour, while Mrs. Moore is paid $19.00 an hour. They each work 22 hours a week. Child care for their son, Dylan, costs $12.00 an hour. How many hours of child care a month can the Moores afford without spending more than one-fifth of their monthly income?

Math Concept Fractions A fraction is part of an entire object. The numerator is the top number of the fraction, and the denominator is the bottom number. The numerator tells how many parts of the whole object are used.

Starting Hint First, figure out how much money the Moores make in one month. Then, take that number and divide it by five. This will tell you how much of their income the Moores can spend on child care.

 For math help, go to the Math Appendix at the back of the book.

Challenges of Teen Parenthood

Think about your plans for yourself and your future. Where do you want to be five years from now? How about ten years from now? Do you think having a child would fit into your plans? Adolescence is a full-time job. Life becomes extremely complicated when you add a baby.

Under the best of circumstances, parenthood is full of challenges. When the parents are teens, they usually lack the money, education, emotional maturity, and skills to raise children. The time, energy, and money needed to raise a child are far greater than most teens can even imagine.

Many teens get pregnant each year in the United States. Many teens want to have a child to have someone love them. However, a child cannot give unconditional love until he or she is older. Parents must give, rather than receive, love. While parenting can be rewarding, it is also very demanding. Even some mature adults find the challenges of parenthood difficult. Teen pregnancy can cause health risks for the baby and the mother. It also can cause education challenges, financial issues, and emotional and social stress for both parents, their families, and society.

It is important to remember that a pregnancy will affect both parents. The father has rights and responsibilities. Even though the father can physically walk away from parenthood more easily than the mother, the law requires him to provide child support until the child turns 18. Many teen parents drop out of school and never return. It is hard to get a high-paying job without an education. This can make it more difficult to meet the financial responsibilities of having a child.

How I See It

TEEN PREGNANCY
Maddie, 16

Between school, swim practice, art classes, babysitting, and finding time for friends, my life is so crazy these days! I am planning to become a mural artist after I graduate, so I'm trying to put together a portfolio that will get me a scholarship at a well-known art school.

I really love kids, so I definitely want children someday. But I know from babysitting my neighbor's daughter that children need a *lot* of care and attention. If I had a baby now, I wouldn't have much time for my art, my schoolwork, or even my friends. Money that I usually spend on art supplies and movies with my friends would have to be spent on things like baby food and diapers instead. There is no way I'm taking any chances that could result in an unplanned pregnancy. My goals and my friends are much too important for me to risk.

Critical Thinking
Maddie suggests that having a baby as a teenager will prevent her from achieving her goals. Do you agree? Why or why not?

Because child care takes up so much time and effort, many teen parents are often too busy or exhausted to see their friends. They may begin to feel trapped by their new responsibilities. Compared to their peers who do not have children, teen parents have been found to have very high levels of stress.

Take Responsibility

What does it mean to be sexually responsible? It means thinking about the outcome of your decisions and actions. It means knowing your values and living by them. Values are the principles a person considers important and the rules he or she uses to guide his or her life. Values include trust, self-respect, respect for others, commitment, and loyalty.

Most people want sexual activity to be special. They want their strong feelings of attraction to go along with a strong bond to one beloved person. They want a sexual relationship based on fidelity. **Fidelity** is faithfulness to an obligation, duty, or trust. Choosing abstinence from sexual activity provides a way to show your responsibility. It also shows respect for yourself and others.

Parenthood is a challenging and rewarding time of life, but it can be especially challenging for teens. When people wait to have children until they are physically, emotionally, and financially prepared, it helps assure a bright future for both the children and the parents.

Section 12.1

After You Read

Review Key Concepts

1. **Identify** reasons why people decide to have children.
2. **List** ways that having a baby can affect the lifestyle of the parents.
3. **Describe** how teen pregnancy can affect the education and career of the parents.

Practice Academic Skills

English Language Arts

4. Consider the changes that come with children and then write a short essay briefly describing those changes. In your essay, mention the three general areas of change that come with children, as well as examples of each general change.

Social Studies

5. In the past, it was common for couples to marry and have children shortly after high school. Ask your parents how old they were when you were born. How old were your grandparents when your parents were born? Which generation was younger when they had kids? Write a paragraph to summarize your findings.

Check Your Answers Go to connectED. mcgraw-hill.com to check your answers.

Section 12.2

Caring for Children

Before You Read

Pace Yourself Short blocks of concentrated reading repeated frequently are more effective than one long session. Focus on reading for 10 minutes. Take a short break. Then read for another 10 minutes.

Read to Learn

Key Concepts

- **Summarize** the needs of children and how parents can meet them.
- **Describe** five effective behavior management techniques.
- **Identify** five ways parents can handle their emotions.

Main Idea

Teaching children discipline and proper behavior are among the most important and challenging tasks of a parent.

Content Vocabulary

◇ vaccine
◇ nurturing
◇ discipline

Academic Vocabulary

You will find these words in your reading and on your tests. Use the glossary to look up their definitions if necessary.

▪ model
▪ deliberate

Graphic Organizer

As you read, identify ways to practice positive parenting. Use a graphic organizer like the one below to organize your information.

Positive Parenting Practices

1.
2.
3.
4.
5.

Graphic Organizer Go to **connectED.mcgraw-hill.com** to download this graphic organizer.

Parenting Responsibilities

Many people only see the charming side of babies and have little or no understanding of what parenting involves. Parenting is incredibly demanding work. Baby portraits do not show the hours of feeding, cleaning, watching, and sleepless nights that help keep the baby happy.

Parenting Education

Parenting requires knowledge of child growth and development. It also requires teaching, counseling, and even first-aid skills. Large amounts of patience, understanding, and a sense of humor are needed, too. Unfortunately, many parents learn these difficult skills by trial and error. Taking time to learn them before you have children can help.

Many schools, hospitals, and community groups offer classes in parenting and child development. People can also gain parenting skills by working with or caring for children, and by observing the interactions of responsible parents and their children. After they have children, people can continue their education by reading books, magazine articles, and online information about parenting. Your own parents also may be a wealth of information.

Meeting Children's Needs

Think about an infant or young child you know. What needs does the child have? Who meets his or her needs? All children have basic needs, and their parents or guardians must meet them. Food, clothing, and shelter are a few of the physical needs of children. Children also need plenty of rest, play, exercise, and medical care. Medical care includes regular checkups and vaccines. A **vaccine** is a small amount of dead germs introduced to the body so that the body can recognize danger and build resistance to a disease. Parents are responsible for making sure their children get the vaccines they need at the right times. Many states require all children to have vaccines for certain diseases, such as polio and chicken pox, before they enter school. Some states also require that children in child care centers have certain vaccines. For a schedule of what vaccines a child should receive, and when, visit the Web site of the Centers for Disease Control and Prevention.

Children also need **nurturing**, which means the giving of love, affection, attention, and encouragement. This fulfills children's emotional and social needs. Nurturing makes children feel secure and accepted and gives them a sense of worth and confidence. It also helps them relate well to others. Children who learn to be comfortable with themselves can reach out to others more easily.

As You Read

Connect Think about the time and effort involved in parenting. Why is parenting so demanding?

Vocabulary

You can find definitions in the glossary at the back of this book.

Parental Resources

Even simple parenting tasks can be challenging. *What kinds of resources would you use to help prepare for parenting?*

Masterfile

Science You Can Use

Invent New Vaccines

There are many vaccines that exist to protect people from different diseases. However, there are still many diseases that do not have vaccines.

Procedure Follow your teacher's instructions to form into pairs. Brainstorm diseases that do not currently have vaccines. You may need to conduct research using reliable Internet or library sources. Pick two to three diseases that you would like to see vaccines created for.

Analysis Write a paragraph about each disease that you chose. Explain their symptoms and why they need vaccines.

Children begin learning as soon as they are born. Caregivers must be prepared to teach, and provide tools and learning opportunities, to meet the developmental needs of children. Parents and caregivers can create a nurturing environment for children in several ways. Simple activities help children develop healthy bodies and brains. Talk, read, and listen to children from the time they are born. Provide opportunities for children to play and learn. Library story hours, children's museums, community-owned zoos, and petting farms help meet children's intellectual needs. Remember that children learn using all five of their senses.

It is not necessary to spend a lot of money to provide learning opportunities. A walk in the park will use a child's senses of sight and sound. The child can also touch and smell the flowers. All of these simple activities stimulate a child's brain development.

✓ Reading Check **Describe** What is parenting, and why is it demanding?

Behavior Management

When people compliment you for doing what is right, you feel good and want to continue doing the right thing. This same idea is behind positive parenting. **Discipline** is the process of helping children learn to behave in acceptable ways. Many people think of discipline only in terms of punishment. Effective discipline is more like guidance. Guidance means using firmness and understanding to help children learn how to behave. It helps children learn to get along with others and control their own feelings. Gradually, children begin to see why certain actions are right or wrong. They learn how to take responsibility for their behavior.

Here are some ways to practice positive parenting:

- **Give Praise** Children feel good about themselves when they receive genuine praise for appropriate behavior. They are also more likely to continue the behavior.
- **Set Good Examples** Young children model, or imitate, what adults say and do. Modeling appropriate behavior often works better than long explanations about how a child should act.
- **Be Consistent** Make your words match your actions. When someone says one thing and does another, children become confused and lose confidence in the person.
- **Set Clear Limits** By setting clear limits for behavior, children learn what is acceptable, appropriate, and safe for them to do. Limits should keep children from hurting themselves, other people, or property.

- **Give Effective Direction** Children need age-appropriate explanations. When they have done something wrong, children need to know why it is wrong and what should be done instead. Messages must match a child's age and level of understanding. For example, with a younger child you might say, "Pet the dog," along with a simple demonstration. With an older child you could say, "It hurts the dog when you pull his ears. You have to be gentle to play with him."

Also, be sure that you have the child's attention. You may need to stoop down or sit beside a young child to make eye contact. Use positive statements whenever possible. For example, "Please walk," is better than "Don't run." Be clear and specific. A young child can only remember one direction at a time. As children get older, they are able to understand and remember multiple directions at one time. For example, a two-year-old can only remember "Pick up your socks." However, you could tell a three-year-old, "Please pick up your socks and put them in the laundry room."

▲ Show Your Child

Children are great imitators. They learn best by being shown what to do, rather than by simply being told. *How might this knowledge affect your behavior around children?*

TAKE CHARGE!

Build Interest in Reading

Children enjoy having stories read to them. The experience builds their critical thinking, comprehension, and memory skills. It also shows them that you value reading. Share the fun of reading by using these steps:

- **Get Close** Let the child sit on your lap or cuddle next to you as you read. Children who feel comfortable and safe are more receptive to learning.
- **Use Voices and Sounds** Make stories more interesting by varying the tone of your voice, using different voices for different characters, and adding sound effects.
- **Point Things Out** As you read, point to the words. This helps the child see that reading moves left to right and shows that speech is made up of individual sounds and words. Point out pictures, shapes, colors, and numbers.
- **Read It Again** Repetitive reading helps a child recognize and remember words.

Real-World Skills

Read Aloud Choose a children's story, such as *Little Red Riding Hood*, and make notes about how you would read it to a young child using the steps. Read the story to the whole class as though you were reading to a toddler. Ask class members for suggestions to improve your use of the steps.

JGI/Jamie Grill/Getty Images

Shaken Baby Syndrome

Occasionally, overwhelmed parents or caregivers attempt to quiet a crying infant by shaking it. Shaken baby syndrome is the name given to the brain injury that may occur when an infant is violently shaken. Serious injuries caused by shaking may include blindness, mental retardation, cerebral palsy, and even death.

Write About It

Research the situations that may lead parents or caregivers to shake infants and the initial symptoms of shaken baby syndrome. What solutions could you come up with to help parents and protect infants? Share your findings.

Dealing with Misbehavior

Even the best children misbehave from time to time, and wise parents and caregivers are prepared to respond in an appropriate way. Caregivers should agree on discipline methods beforehand so that they respond in similar ways each time a child misbehaves. If you react differently each time a child acts a certain way, he or she may become confused. When you always have the same reaction to a behavior, the child connects the behavior to your actions. Consistency shows that caregivers mean what they say.

Discipline should be immediate and fit the misbehavior. The goal is to help children learn suitable behavior. Knowing when to punish misbehavior can be tricky. A mistake is not misbehavior. Do not become angry with a child who drops a glass of juice because she lacks coordination. Instead, teach her how to carry a glass, and help her clean up the spill. A young child who draws on a wall may be experimenting with a new tool or trying out a big drawing board. In this case, you need to explain, not punish. If a child leaves something undone, ask him or her to return to the task to finish it.

Misbehavior that is deliberate, or done on purpose, calls for a reaction that fits the child's level of understanding and the misbehavior. There are different ways to deal with misbehavior. You can take away a privilege, such as not allowing a child to go outdoors to play.

HOW TO . . . Be a Positive Example

You may already be someone's role model without even knowing it. Even if you are not a parent, you can influence a child's growth and development. Children naturally imitate the speech, actions, and attitudes of older family members. Encouraging children to follow your good example not only benefits them but also helps you. Setting a positive example now is good practice for when you start your own family as an adult.

Be Consistent As often as possible, make your words match your actions and your actions match your values. Children can tell when someone says one thing and does another. They may become confused and lose confidence in the person.

Point to Other Role Models Tell children why you admire your role models. Perhaps a parent taught you the importance of honesty, or you learned a solid work ethic from a favorite athlete.

Photomondo/Getty Images

Having the child sit quietly for a few minutes is another option. Caregivers can also ignore misbehavior. For example, if a child cries because he or she wants a toy at the store, caregivers can simply say, "No, we aren't buying toys today." The child will learn that crying for something does not get the toy or the caregivers' attention.

It is important that parents continue to show the child that he or she is loved, but that some actions are not acceptable. Be prepared to repeat your instructions and explanations many times. Young children may not realize that what applies to one situation also applies to another, similar situation. Above all, discipline should never be an outlet for an adult's anger or abuse. Overly aggressive physical and verbal responses to acts of misbehavior often occur because parents become frustrated with the responsibilities of parenthood, or with each other.

✓ Reading Check **Explain** What is discipline, and how should parents discipline their children?

Sources of Help

Caring for children is both physically and emotionally demanding. Anyone who cares for children needs some time away on a regular basis. Many couples share the duties of child care so that the responsibility does not fall on one adult.

SUCCEED IN SCHOOL

Determine Progress
Once you determine what success means to you, set goals to achieve that success. Break these goals into steps that will help you gauge your progress.

Give Reasons for Your Actions Examples work best when a child connects your behavior to your values. Enforcing a bedtime may seem unfair until you explain that you are respecting a parent's rule and how that rule is good for the child. Knowing your motives also helps you make sure they are good ones.

Admit Your Mistakes Would you trust someone who claims to never make mistakes? Children do not either. Letting children know that you sometimes getting things wrong shows them that you do not have to be perfect to do well.

Respect Their Limitations Expect no more than children are capable of. To you, generosity may mean giving half your lunch to a classmate. To a five-year-old, it means parting with one cracker from a whole box. As the child grows socially and emotionally, the child's ability to understand giving will grow as well. These are behaviors instilled in children by example or by loving direction. You also started with these same small steps.

(l)Image Source/Alamy Images; (r)©Greatstock Photographic Library/Alamy

Couples need time to themselves, too. If a paid babysitter is not an option, family members and friends may be willing to help out with short-term child care. Also, consider taking turns with other parents to care for each other's children. Some churches or other organizations will sponsor a "Mother's Day Out" where free child care is offered for an afternoon or a day.

Sometimes parents need help communicating with each other about parenting issues. They may disagree about how to handle a situation or behavior. There are many ways that children can be successfully raised. When caregivers are open to each other's opinions, issues can be resolved calmly and quickly. Most communities have state and local agencies that can help parents. Doctors, schools, places of worship, and support groups are also sources of help.

If your emotions threaten to put a child at risk of physical or emotional harm, stop and do the following:

- If you are holding an infant, put the infant down in a safe place. Never shake or hit an infant!
- Take several deep breaths. Then count slowly to ten.
- Have someone look after the child while you take a walk.
- Call a parent, a friend, relative, or religious leader. Ask how he or she deals with a child while frustrated, fatigued, or angry.
- Check the Internet or phone book for social service and mental health agencies or crisis hotlines. Call and ask for help.

Section 12.2

After You Read

Review Key Concepts

1. **Describe** how caregivers can provide tools and learning opportunities to meet the developmental needs of children.
2. **Summarize** how parents can give effective direction to children.
3. **Explain** why it is important for caregivers to have time away from the children and list ways they might create time for themselves.

Check Your Answers Go to connectED. mcgraw-hill.com to check your answers.

Practice Academic Skills

English Language Arts

4. Use print or online resources to research recommended and required vaccines in your community and state. Look for the most current information about vaccines. Discuss your findings with the class.

Social Studies

5. Parenting requires knowledge of child growth and development. It also requires teaching, counseling, and first-aid skills. Research schools, hospitals, and community groups that offer classes in parenting and child development in your community. Create a chart to share your results with the class.

Chapter 12 Review and Applications

Chapter 12

CHAPTER SUMMARY

Section 12.1
Considering Parenthood

Having children is a major life decision, and should not be taken lightly. People have children for many reasons, but not all of them are good ones. Parenting is incredibly demanding and comes with many responsibilities. Parenthood often results in lifestyle, financial, and career changes. Teen parents usually lack the money, education, emotional maturity, and skills to raise children. The happiest and healthiest children are those born to parents who honestly want and are ready for them.

Section 12.2
Caring for Children

Discipline is an important part of raising a child. It does not always mean punishment. Parents encourage good behavior by setting good examples, praising children for good behavior, setting clear limits, and giving effective directions. Good discipline is immediate and fits the misbehavior. It is important to remember that small children do not always know right from wrong. Parents must stay calm and be patient. Many communities have resources that can help parents deal with the responsibilities of parenting.

Vocabulary Review

1. Write a sentence using two or more of these vocabulary terms. The sentence should clearly show how the terms are related.

Content Vocabulary
◇ parenting (p. 279)
◇ fidelity (p. 283)
◇ vaccine (p. 285)
◇ nurturing (p. 285)
◇ discipline (p. 286)

Academic Vocabulary
■ reflect (p. 280)
■ accommodate (p. 281)
■ model (p. 286)
■ deliberate (p. 288)

Review Key Concepts

2. List the questions couples should consider before deciding to have children.
3. Describe lifestyle, financial, and career changes related to parenthood.
4. Identify the challenges of teenage parenting.
5. Summarize the needs of children and how parents can meet them.
6. Describe five effective behavior management techniques.
7. Identify five ways parents can handle their emotions.

Critical Thinking

8. Generalize When do you think is the ideal time for a married couple to have children? Why?
9. Role Play How would you respond to a teen who says, "Babies are so cute. I want one of my own to play with"?
10. Predict Think of some personal sacrifices that parents often make. Which of the sacrifices would be most difficult for you at this stage of your life?
11. Judge What do you think would be the hardest part of disciplining a child? Why?

ACTIVE LEARNING

Family & Community Connections

12. Discipline Techniques Discipline is the process of helping children learn to behave in acceptable ways. The most effective discipline is guidance. It helps children learn to get along with others and control their own feelings. When children misbehave, they should be given guidance about why their behavior was inappropriate and how they should have acted. Deliberate misbehavior on the part of a child should be met with a reaction that matches that child's level of understanding as well as the misbehavior. Create three scenarios involving  a preschooler who misbehaves. With a partner, demonstrate appropriate discipline techniques that address the behavior. Ask classmates for feedback.

13. Parenting Experiences Having a baby is a lifelong commitment. A child needs much physical care, financial support, love, attention, and guidance until adulthood. Raising a child can be difficult, especially when that child misbehaves. Further, many changes come with parenthood. Not only do new parents go through lifestyle changes, they also experience financial and career changes. However, children also can be a source of joy and fulfillment. Not only do they bring difficult changes, they also bring extremely fulfilling changes. Interview family members about their parenting experiences. Which were the most rewarding to them? Which were the most challenging? Ask family members to describe some of the most extreme changes that took place upon becoming parents. Ask: "Which were most difficult?" Which were most rewarding?" Write a summary of your findings.

Real-World Skills and Applications

Leadership Skills

14. Teach Parenting Skills Interview a peer mediator, school counselor, or mental health worker about ways that communication and conflict resolution skills can be used in parenting situations. Share your findings with the class in the form of an instructive presentation. When you are finished, ask for questions from the rest of the class. Do your best to answer them using the information you gained in your interview as well as the information from this text.

Financial Literacy

15. Parenting Prices Assume an infant consumes 3 ounces of formula every 2 hours, 24 hours a day. The infant's formula costs $4.95 for 12 ounces. Determine the cost of baby formula for the infant for one week. What is the cost of baby formula for the infant for a year?

Cooperative Learning Skills

16. Sources of Help Parents often need ways to find relief from the constant supervision required to raise a child and keep that child safe. For example, they may hire a babysitter. How can parents best go about finding this help? Work with a partner to brainstorm ideas. Make sure to provide options for parents who cannot afford a babysitter.

Henglein and Steets/Getty Images

Academic Skills

 English Language Arts

17. Positive Parenting Visit your school library or a community library and ask a librarian to recommend a book that teaches positive parenting skills. Read the book and discuss what you learned with your classmates. Write a report about the usefulness of the book. Did it offer good advice? Point out what you think are the most helpful tips discussed in the book.

 Social Studies

18. Demonstrate Parenting Review the five tips provided in the text for positive parenting and briefly describe each. Then, choose one and give an example of how to put the tip into practice. Create a scenario that would allow you to practice this positive parenting skill.

 Mathematics

19. Child Care There are 656 students at Elwood Elementary School. Many of those children have parents who work full-time. Only 377 students take advantage of the after-school program at the elementary school, where they are supervised by adults so their parents do not have to leave work early. What percentage of the students does not take advantage of the after-school program?

Math Concept **Percentage** To find percentage, divide the part by the overall number and multiply that result by 100.

Starting Hint First, find the number of students that do not take advantage of the after-school program. Then, find what percent of the overall students that number is.

 For math help, go to the Math Appendix at the back of the book.

 ## Standardized Test Practice

READING COMPREHENSION
Directions Read the paragraph. Then, choose the correct answer.

Test-Taking Tip When taking a multiple-choice test, skip a question if you are stuck on it. Once you finish the questions you are more sure about, you may return to those you skipped and work on them.

Young children have many needs. In addition to regular meals, clothing, and medical care, children also need to be nurtured. This means that they receive the affection, encouragement, love, and attention they need to become confident and happy people.

20. According to the text, what is nurturing?
   a) Savings account
   b) Discipline
   c) The giving of love, affection, attention, and encouragement
   d) The giving of praise and blame

Learn Parenting Skills

In this project you will identify a parenting role model. You will interview your role model about things you should know before becoming a parent. You will then create a handbook with tips for parents that will help them to build a strong family.

My Journal

If you completed the journal entry from page 200, refer to it to see if your thoughts have changed after reading the unit.

Project Assignment

In this project you will:
- Choose a person you believe can teach you good parenting skills.
- Identify four good parenting qualities this person possesses.
- Interview the parent about their parenting skills and how they contribute to a strong family, and then create a parenting handbook.

STEP 1 Create Interview Questions About Parenting

What qualities do you think make a good parent? How do these qualities build a strong family?

The Skills Behind the Project

Life Skills

Key personal and relationship skills you will use in this project include:
- Evaluating the qualities of a good parent.
- Understanding connections between parenting and strong families.

You might think good parents treat their children with respect, explain what is right or wrong, and provide emotional support. By doing these actions, the parents are fostering a relationship of trust and security with their child. Use complete sentences to write a list of at least four questions that can help you learn about parenting from a parenting role model.

Writing Skills
- Organize your thoughts.
- Use correct spelling and grammar.
- Consider your audience.

STEP 2 Choose a Parent Role Model

Choose a parent role model. The parent you choose as a role model can be anyone in your community. A possible parent to talk to might include a:
- Friend
- Teacher
- Religious Leader
- Neighbor
- Counselor
- Child Care Worker
- Relative

Masterfile

Life Skills Project Checklist

Plan	☑ Use research and independent thinking to reflect on the qualities of good parents and strong families.
	☑ Plan and write your interview questions.
	☑ Interview an adult in your community and write a summary of what you learned.
	☑ Make a handbook that illustrates with words and pictures the parenting skills you learned from your parent role model.
	☑ In your handbook, list one skill per page. Include an example of how the skill might be used and an explanation of how the skill helps build a strong family.
Present	☑ Make a presentation to the class to share your handbook and discuss what you learned.
	☑ Invite students to ask any questions they may have. Answer these questions and demonstrate that you respect the students' perspectives.
	☑ Turn in your handbook and the questions and answers from your interview to your teacher.
Academic Skills	☑ Be creative in writing and illustrating the content of the handbook.
	☑ Arrange your presentation so the audience can view your handbook as you discuss it.
	☑ Communicate effectively.

STEP 3 Connect with Your Community

Arrange to speak with the parent role model you chose in Step 2. Use the questions you wrote in Step 1 to interview the parent. Questions should focus on the positive parenting qualities you identified in your role model. How does the parent use this quality to strengthen his or her family? Accurately record the answers to your questions in complete sentences.

Interpersonal Skills

- Be polite. Do not interrupt the parent while he or she is talking.
- Listen attentively.
- Ask additional questions to better understand the parent's answers.

STEP 4 Share What You Have Learned

Use the Life Skills Project Checklist to plan and give an oral report to share what you have learned with your classmates.

STEP 5 Evaluate Your Life Skills and Academic Skills

Your project will be evaluated based on:
- Content and organization of your information.
- Mechanics—presentation and neatness.
- Speaking and listening skills.

Evaluation Rubric Go to **connectED.mcgraw-hill.com** for a rubric you can use to evaluate your final project.

Managing Your Life

Chapter 13 Be a Responsible Consumer

Chapter 14 Your Health

Unit Life Skills Project Preview

Manage Yourself

In this unit you will learn about managing your life. In your life skills project you will create a report card for yourself that evaluates the areas of your life that you manage well and identifies areas where you have room for improvement.

My Journal

Take a Closer Look Write a journal entry about one of these topics. This will help you prepare for the project at the end of this unit.

- Describe an area of your life where you excel. For instance, you may excel in sports, friendships, or musical ability.
- Identify three areas of your life where you are challenged. For instance, you may be challenged in writing papers, eating healthfully, or organization.
- Explain how you might evaluate how well a person manages his or her life.

Christopher Futcher/Getty Images

Explore the Photo

Think about the various challenges and successes you have had in your life. *How can you use your success to overcome your challenges?*

Be a Responsible Consumer

Section 13.1
Making Consumer Choices

Section 13.2
Living with Technology

Chapter Objectives

Section 13.1
- **Identify** factors that influence consumer choices.
- **Summarize** the rights and responsibilities of consumers.
- **Outline** the steps for creating a budget.
- **Describe** procedures for using savings and checking accounts.
- **Recall** the benefits and costs of credit.

Section 13.2
- **Recognize** the benefits and drawbacks of technology.
- **Identify** strategies for technology management.

Writing Activity

Create an Advertisement

Use a Budget Planner Deciding what to buy depends on your budget. It might seem simple to spend only as much money as you have, but many people go into debt by overspending. They need to budget their purchases. Since advertisements persuade, they are one way to convince people to create and stick to a budget. Write a print, radio, or television advertisement convincing consumers to purchase a personal budget planner.

Writing Tips Use these tips to write an advertisement:
- Address why budgets are important and how a personal budget planner can help people spend wisely.
- Use language and factual information that will appeal to consumers.
- Use short sentences that allow the consumer to focus on your message.

Explore the Photo

There are many different products and service choices that exist for consumers. *What factors might influence the choices you make as a consumer?*

Section 13.1

Making Consumer Choices

Before You Read

Create an Outline Use this section's headings to create an outline. Add supporting information to create Level 2, 3, and 4 details. Use the outline to predict what you are about to learn.

Read to Learn

Key Concepts
- **Identify** factors that influence consumer choices.
- **Summarize** the rights and responsibilities of consumers.
- **Outline** the steps for creating a budget.
- **Describe** procedures for using savings and checking accounts.
- **Recall** the benefits and costs of credit.

Main Idea
Understanding factors that affect consumer purchasing can help you decide which goods and services to buy.

Content Vocabulary
◇ consumer
◇ income
◇ impulse purchase
◇ comparison shopping
◇ redress
◇ warranty
◇ budget
◇ expense
◇ interest
◇ endorse

Academic Vocabulary
You will find these words in your reading and on your tests. Use the glossary to look up their definitions if necessary.
▢ sole
▢ slight

Graphic Organizer
As you read, record the six factors that influence what you buy. Use a graphic organizer like the one below to organize your information.

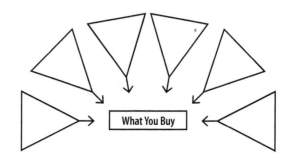

What You Buy

 Graphic Organizer Go to **connectED.mcgraw-hill.com** to download this graphic organizer.

Become a Smart Shopper

What was the last thing you bought? Maybe it was the haircut you received yesterday or the video game you picked up last weekend. Any time you pay for something, you are a consumer. A **consumer** is someone who buys and uses goods and services produced by others. Making good decisions is the basis of being a smart consumer. You can learn the skills you need to make good decisions. As a teen, you are among a group of highly active consumers, whose total annual spending is in the billions of dollars! No matter how much money you spend, you will be more satisfied with your purchases if you make wise shopping decisions.

You, The Consumer

How can you determine the right products and services to buy? How can you get the best price? Like any consumer, you want the most value for your money. To become a smart shopper, you need to realize that each purchase involves a choice affected by many factors, including the following:

- **Income** Whether it is from a paycheck or an allowance, your **income**, or the amount of money that you receive, is the single most important factor that affects what you buy.
- **Environment** Your environment may affect your purchases. If you live in a cold climate, you need different kinds of clothing than people who live in a hot climate do.
- **Personal Interests and Values** You choose to spend money on goods and services that you value and that interest you. Clothing often falls into this category.
- **Family and Culture** Each family and culture has certain customs and traditions that influence how people shop and what people purchase.
- **Advertising** Most advertising is designed to tempt you to buy something. Clever ads can make it easy to lose control of your purchasing decisions.
- **Peer Pressure** Keep in mind that you, not your friends, know what you need, want, and can afford.

As You Read

Connect Think about the last purchase you made. What factors influenced your decision?

Vocabulary

You can find definitions in the glossary at the back of this book.

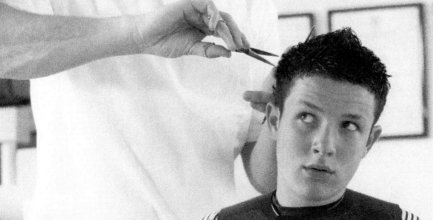

◄ **Consumers**

You are a consumer not only when you buy goods but also when you purchase services, such as a haircut. *How would you, as a consumer, get the most value out of your money for a service like a haircut?*

JUPITERIMAGES/BananaStock/Alamy

Plan Before You Shop

Have you ever bought something and later decided it was not at all what you wanted? This is a common problem for many shoppers. One way to gain control of what you buy, and to be pleased with the results, is to develop a shopping plan.

Know Your Wants and Needs

The most important part of a shopping plan is deciding what to buy. Make your decisions based on your needs and wants with your values and resources in mind. For example, say you need a baseball glove. You know if you buy the glove, you will not have enough money to pay for a movie Friday night. You might buy the glove and skip the movie because you value your performance on the baseball team more than a few hours of entertainment.

A shopping plan can help you resist an **impulse purchase**, an item you buy without thinking it through. Felicia saw some earrings she liked and immediately bought them. When she got home, she realized the earrings did not match any of her outfits. The money Felicia impulsively spent on earrings was money she could have saved for something she really needed.

Find Consumer Information

Smart consumers research the products they plan to buy. Most manufacturers provide valuable information about their products online or in print. Other consumers are also excellent sources of information. Ask friends and relatives about their experiences with certain goods or services. Consumer magazines, such as *Consumer Reports*, test and rate different brands for quality, safety, and price. Check for them at local libraries or at newsstands. You can use the consumer information they provide for **comparison shopping**, or comparing products, prices, and services to get the most value for the money.

Consumer Choices

Many of the choices consumers make reflect their interests. *How do your interests affect the way you spend your money?*

PNC/Getty Images

TAKE CHARGE!

Buyer Beware

Be smart with your money. You are more likely to be happy with your purchases if you consider these tips before making a purchase.

- **Examine the Product** Make sure there are no chips, dents, stains, or tears in the product. Just because it is in the store does not mean that it is in perfect condition.
- **Compare Prices** Check the price of the item. You may be able to find it for a better price elsewhere.
- **Look at the Brand** Store brands may have the same quality as name brands, but at a lower cost.
- **Read the Label** Labels can give information that may affect your buying decisions. For example, does the garment require dry cleaning?
- **Look at the Warranty** If the product has a warranty, read it carefully and fully understand all of its conditions.

Government and consumer organizations tend to provide the most reliable consumer information. The Consumer Product Safety Commission is a government agency that provides information about the safety of various products. The Better Business Bureau (BBB) is an organization supported by businesses that follow ethical practices. You can use the BBB Web site to locate a reputable place of business near you.

Know When to Buy

Knowing when to shop can be as important as deciding what to buy. Smart shoppers plan their purchases to coincide with sales. For instance, end-of-season summer clothing sales are often held in July or August. Sales also occur around major national holidays.

Product advertisements in print, online, or on the radio can alert you to sales, which help save you money. Read and listen to all ads carefully. Some ads can be misleading. They may show products that are not actually price-reduced. Do not rely on them as your sole, or only, source of information.

Know Where to Buy

Today's consumers have more shopping options than ever before. Deciding where to shop depends on what you want to buy and the price you are willing to pay. Depending on where you live, you might have some or all of the following shopping options:

- **Department Stores** Department stores sell a variety of products, from clothing and makeup to small appliances and furniture. Many department stores also offer a number of customer services, such as gift wrapping and delivery.

Smart Shopper

Smart shoppers search for the lowest price before they purchase an item. *What techniques do you use to compare prices?*

• **Mail-Order Companies** These companies sell items you can order from a catalog and have sent to you. Remember to add shipping and handling fees, and in some cases sales tax, to mail-order items. You may also have to pay shipping fees if you return items.

• **Specialty Stores** Whether it is sporting goods, stationery, or shoes, specialty stores usually sell one type of merchandise. They offer a wide selection of these products but sometimes charge more than other stores.

• **Discount Stores** Discount stores buy products in large quantities and limit the number of customer services. One benefit of discount stores is lower prices.

• **Factory Outlets** These manufacturer-owned stores sell products directly to shoppers. Prices are usually lower than those at department stores. Some items may be seconds with slight, or small, imperfections. Other items may be discontinued.

• **Warehouse Clubs** These warehouse-sized stores can charge lower prices than most supermarkets or department stores because they buy in bulk and offer little or no services. They charge a membership fee.

• **Electronic Shopping** Television shopping channels and the Internet provide many shopping opportunities. Generally, you need a credit card for electronic shopping. Some Web sites will accept personal checks.

• **Other Shopping Alternatives** Thrift stores, garage and yard sales, flea markets, auctions, and swap meets often sell merchandise for low prices. These shopping options usually have no customer service, and items are sold as-is, which means they might have flaws. As-is items are generally nonreturnable.

✓ **Reading Check** **Identify** What should you take into consideration when developing a shopping plan?

Your Consumer Rights and Responsibilities

Consumers have both rights and responsibilities in the marketplace. State and federal laws protect consumers' interests, or rights. At the same time, consumers have a duty to respect the interests of manufacturers and shop owners.

Your Rights as a Consumer

Have you ever returned an item to a store because it did not work or was broken? If so, you practiced one of your consumer rights. As a consumer, you have seven major rights:

- **The Right to Safety** Consumers are protected against sales of products that endanger life or safety.
- **The Right to Be Informed** Consumers should be protected against dishonest advertising, labeling, or sales practices. Businesses must give consumers honest and relevant facts about goods and services.
- **The Right to Choose** There should be a choice of goods and services available at fair and competitive prices. Businesses are forbidden to take actions that limit competition.
- **The Right to Be Heard** Consumers have a right to speak out about consumer laws.
- **The Right to Redress** The right to have a wrong corrected quickly and fairly is called **redress**.
- **The Right to Consumer Education** All consumers are entitled to information about consumer issues.
- **The Right to Service** Consumers have the right to expect courtesy, convenience, and responsiveness from a business.

Building Character ?!

Honesty Lisa has worked at an ice cream shop all school year to save enough money for the prom dress of her dreams. While shopping for a prom dress, Lisa notices that she got makeup on one of the dresses she tried on that did not fit her. She only has enough money to buy one dress. What should she do?

You Make the Call

Should Lisa tell the store clerk about the makeup and risk having to pay for the dress that does not fit her? Or, should she put it back on the rack without saying anything? Write a paragraph explaining what you think Lisa should do, and why.

Your Responsibilities as a Consumer

With every right, there is a responsibility. For example, with your right to information about products and their safety is your responsibility to learn about products and to use them safely, according to the manufacturers' directions. Some other responsibilities include the following:

- **Be Fair and Honest** As a consumer, you are expected to take care of merchandise you handle or try on. You are also required to pay for your purchases. If you do not pay, you are stealing, which is punishable by the law, and you can be sent to jail.

▶ **Merchandise Returns**

Be calm and polite when returning an unsatisfactory item to a store. Most problems between consumers and businesses can be resolved easily. *Why might keeping a calm and polite attitude produce positive results when there is a problem?*

Purestock/SuperStock

- **Pay Attention** When you go to the check out counter to pay, you should watch the register to make sure the price is correct. If you paid with cash, count the change you get back. If you receive too much change, you are responsible for returning it.
- **Save Paperwork** It is your responsibility to furnish, or provide, these materials as proof of purchase if you return an item.

Resolve Your Consumer Problems

Have you ever paid for a service that was not performed correctly? Or have you ever paid for a product and later found out the store overcharged you? Most consumer problems involve refunding a customer's money or replacing a purchased product. Whenever you need to resolve a consumer problem, the following steps may prove helpful:

▲ Product Information

Always review your product information after you purchase an item and file it for future use. *Why might it be important to keep your product information for future use?*

- **Check Your Warranty** A **warranty** is a guarantee that a product will work properly for a specific length of time unless misused or mishandled by the consumer. If your problem is covered by a warranty, follow the warranty instructions for service. If the product has no warranty, or if the problem is not covered in the warranty, take the product and your records to the store's customer service department. If your problem is not resolved, politely ask to speak to the manager.
- **Write to the Manufacturer** If your trip to the store does not resolve the problem, put your complaint in writing. Briefly state the problem and the solution you think is fair. Include your name, address, e-mail, and telephone number, as well as copies of your receipt and warranty.
- **Take Further Action** If your letter does not bring results, you may contact the Better Business Bureau to help you resolve the problem. As a last resort, you may choose to go to small claims court. In this type of court, you present your complaint before a judge, and the business involved must respond within a certain period of time.

✓ **Reading Check** **Identify** What rights do consumers have?

A. Minde/PhotoAlto

Manage Your Money

Money is an important resource that must be managed. Some people manage money with ease. They seem to make smart purchases and save money with very little effort. For others, money management requires discipline. Saving money for a future goal means cutting back on spending, which can be difficult. A budget can help. See **Figure 13.1** below.

Figure 13.1 **Understanding Your Paycheck**

Exploring Your Pay Stub When budgeting, it is important to understand your paycheck. When you are paid, look at the pay stub carefully and make sure it is correct. *Why is it important to confirm that the information on your pay stub is correct?*

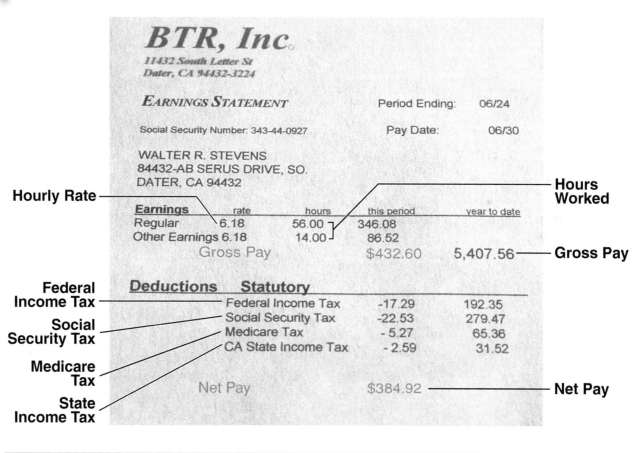

Hours Worked	This is the number of hours you worked during a pay period.
Gross Pay	This is the total amount of money you earned during the pay period.
Deductions	These are monies subtracted from your gross pay. Tax deductions for federal, state, and local income taxes may be included. Other government deductions known as Social Security and Medicare use the abbreviation FICA.
Net Pay	This is the amount of your check.

Create a Budget

A **budget** is a plan for spending and saving the money you have available. When you make a budget, you make a plan for saving and spending your money in ways that will fulfill your needs and wants and help you meet a goal.

To make the best use of your budget, first identify all of your expenses. An **expense** is a good or service you purchase. Then take steps to make your budget a reality.

1. Using paper and pencil or a computer spreadsheet program, list your expenses in order of importance, deciding which are needs and which are wants.
2. Write down the estimated cost of each of your expenses.
3. Record expected income during the period of your budget. For example, if your budget is for one month, write down all of the money you will receive in that time.
4. Subtract the total cost of your necessary expenses from your income. Do you have enough money to pay for all of these items? If not, you will need to cut back on your spending. If you have money left over after paying for your necessary items, you can purchase a non-essential item if you want. Keep your personal goals in mind. You may find saving any remaining money will be better for you in the long run.
5. Review your budget now and again to see how it is working. If you allowed too much or too little for some budgeted items, adjust your plan. If you forgot one or more expenses, include these as you update your budget.

▼ **Manage Money**

Managing money is easier when you keep a simple financial record and update it frequently. *How do you keep track of your expenses?*

✓ **Reading Check** **Draw Conclusions** Why is it important to create a budget?

Use Financial Services

Financial institutions such as banks, credit unions, and savings and loan associations, offer checking and savings accounts. These accounts help you manage your money while keeping it safe. Financial institutions offer a variety of services. Some services are free, some cost money, and some actually earn money. Before opening an account, compare the fees and services of different institutions. Is the free checking really free?

Ingram Publishing/SuperStock

Commercial National Bank			DEPOSIT TICKET
			70-4
			711

Commercial National Bank

Member Midwest Financial Group, Inc.
ANYTOWN, USA

DATE _____ *Oct. 22* _____ 20 *16*
DEPOSITS MAY NOT BE AVAILABLE FOR IMMEDIATE WITHDRAWAL

SIGN HERE FOR LESS CASH IN TELLER'S PRESENCE

JANE SMITH
12235 LAKE FOREST DR.
ANYTOWN, USA

099:5600 250000: 223 0007 289394

CASH	CURRENCY	15	00
	COIN		
CHECKS LIST CHECKS SINGLY	70-8/711	27	63
TOTAL CHECKS FROM OTHER SIDE			
TOTAL		42	63
LESS CASH RECEIVED			
NET DEPOSIT		42	63

CHECKS AND OTHER ITEMS ARE RECEIVED FOR DEPOSIT SUBJECT
TO THE PROVISIONS OF THE UNIFORM COMMERCIAL CODE OR ANY
APPLICABLE COLLECTION AGREEMENT.

◄ **Making Deposits**

Some banks require a deposit slip each time you deposit money. *What kind of information might be asked for on a deposit slip?*

Savings Accounts

Saving money is extremely important. Many people open a savings account to save for a major goal, such as a college education, a vacation, or a car. People also save for retirement and costly emergencies, such as home repairs.

You can earn money simply by putting your money in a savings account. Savings accounts earn **interest**, or money a financial institution pays customers at regular intervals. The interest is a certain percentage of the amount in your savings. For example, if you have $500 in a savings account that earns one percent interest, you would earn $5 during one interest period.

You may deposit cash or checks into your savings account using a deposit slip. Before depositing a check, you must **endorse** it, or sign your name on the back. This transfers your right to the check over to the bank, which deposits it in your account. You can withdraw money from your savings account whenever you need it. However, you must maintain a certain amount in the account to keep it open. To take out money, complete a withdrawal slip.

Checking Accounts

Checking accounts allow you to pay with checks instead of cash. A check is a written order to a financial institution to pay a specific amount of money. To write checks, you must first deposit money in your account. Checking accounts are convenient. Carrying cash can be unsafe, and cash sent through the mail can be stolen. Bills are often paid using checks.

When you open a checking account, you agree to certain terms, or rules. One term is to pay any charges applied to your account. You also agree to not write checks for more money than you have available. If you write checks for more money than you have in your account, the account will be overdrawn. Institutions charge a fee for overdrawn, or bounced, checks. They may also send a check back to the business that presented it for payment, causing you embarrassment and additional charges. For these reasons, it makes sense to keep careful track of your account.

Community Connections

Recycled Treasures

Do you want to get rid of unwanted clutter and raise money to benefit a school or community club? Organize a yard sale or garage sale! Your friends and family members can help you gather donated items, advertise the sale, and help out during the event.

Use a Checkbook

You receive a checkbook when you open a checking account. A checkbook contains two important features:

- **Checks** Always fill these out in ink, as needed. Write the date and name of the person or business you are paying. Then write the amount, first in figures and then in words. Make sure the amount in figures is the same as the amount written in words. Sign the check.
- **Check Register** This small booklet is used to keep a record of your account. Each time you make a deposit or withdrawal of any type, you record the date, the amount, and the check number if the withdrawal was by check. Then adjust your balance, or the total amount in your account. To adjust the balance for deposits, add the deposit to the balance in your register. To adjust for withdrawals, subtract the withdrawal from the balance showing. The result is your new balance. Be sure to double-check all calculations.

Use Debit and ATM Cards

Many people with bank accounts use debit cards and automatic teller machine (ATM) cards. A debit card can be used to make a deposit or withdraw cash from an ATM machine. A debit card can also be used to make a purchase in a store. An ATM card can only be used for ATM withdrawals and deposits. When you use a debit or ATM card to withdraw cash or to make purchases, you are using your own money at your financial institution. When you use a debit card to make a purchase, the amount of your purchase is transferred electronically from your checking account to the store's account.

Many people use debit cards in place of cash or checks. Always make sure to keep your receipts from purchases or withdrawals and record them in your checkbook register. Compare the receipts with the information on your monthly statement. This will help you check the accuracy of your statement, as well as identify any unauthorized purchases. If your card is lost or stolen, you may be responsible for charges made on the card. Report a lost or stolen debit card to your bank immediately!

Read Account Statements

Your financial institution will keep records of your account and send them to you. These records, called statements, list checks that have been paid, deposits that have been made, and fees that have been charged. Most banks allow you to view your statements online. Keep all statements and any check copies sent to you. They serve as proof of purchases you have made.

When you receive your statement you need to reconcile your account, or make sure your own records and the bank statement are in agreement. This process is similar to balancing your check register. See **Figure 13.2** on p. 311.

✓ **Reading Check** **Explain** What are the benefits of using checking and savings accounts?

SUCCEED IN SCHOOL

Public Speaking Anxiety

Some people get extremely nervous when they have to present a project or paper to the whole class. To help reduce anxiety, practice your speech several times before you present it. Try giving your speech in front of a mirror or a friend who will give you constructive feedback. This will help you get used to speaking in front of an audience. The day of your presentation, take a deep breath before speaking and focus on speaking at a moderate pace.

Figure 13.2

Reconciling Bank Statements

Double check It is important to reconcile your account with each statement. *What might happen if you do not compare your records to the bank statement on a regular basis?*

Follow these steps to reconcile your checkbook register with your account statement:

STEP 1 Write down the last balance shown on your checking account statement.

STEP 2 Total the deposits you have made that do not appear on the statement. Add this total to the amount that appears on your statement.

STEP 3 Make a list of checks that you have written that do not appear on the statement. These are called outstanding checks. Total all of these checks.

STEP 4 Subtract the total of your outstanding checks from the total you reached in Step 2. This amount should be the same as the balance in your checkbook register.

Understand Credit

Credit allows people to buy things now and pay for them later. Sometimes using credit is a good decision. For example, it would take most people years to save enough cash to cover the entire cost of a college education. Using credit makes large purchases possible.

Types of Credit

Consumers have several credit options:

- **Cash Loans** Usually used to pay for large items, cash loans are commonly used in purchases such as cars or homes. With loans, you borrow money from financial institutions or loan companies and pay the loan back in specific amounts.
- **Sales Credit** Using this method allows you to charge a purchase and pay the store for it over time.
- **Credit Cards** The most widely used type of credit, credit cards can be used to pay for goods and services in person, over the phone, or online. Financial institutions that issue credit cards require minimum monthly payments.

Costs of Credit

Using credit costs money. In addition to the money you owe, you pay the lender interest. Unless you pay the total of your credit card bill on time each month, you must pay interest. The interest is usually high. That is how credit card companies make money. Additional fees are charged if payments are not made on time.

Purestock/SuperStock

Control Credit Card Use

Credit is easy to obtain and easy to use. Unfortunately, it is also easy to misuse. Credit card bills can quickly increase, and people can sink into serious financial trouble. For this reason, you should use credit only when necessary. Whether the credit card belongs to you or your parents or guardians, the following tips can help you keep the credit card bill low:

- **Set limits.** Use your budget or talk to your parents or guardians to determine how much you can spend. Then stick to your limit.
- **Save your receipts.** Total your receipts after shopping to make sure you have not overspent. Verify the credit card statement's accuracy using the receipts. If you notice charges you did not make, contact the creditor immediately.
- **Keep your card to yourself.** Never let friends use your card, even if they say they will pay you back. Also, make sure to keep your passwords private. If your card is lost or stolen, contact the credit card company immediately.
- **Get help.** If you overcharge, be honest with your parents or guardians. Tackling credit card debt is not easy, but if you avoid dealing with the problem your bill will only increase with interest and late fees.

Section 13.1

After You Read

Review Key Concepts

1. **Recall** where a consumer can find information about a product.
2. **List** the steps you should take to resolve a consumer problem.
3. **Name** the first step in creating a budget.
4. **Tell** how to deposit or withdraw money from a savings account.
5. **Explain** why using credit costs money.

 Check Your Answers Go to connectED.mcgraw-hill.com to check your answers.

Practice Academic Skills

 **English Language Arts**

6. Imagine you purchased a computer that stopped working after only one week. The warranty does not cover the problem, and the store manager will not refund your money. Write a letter of complaint to the manufacturer to resolve the problem.

Social Studies

7. Bring at least three advertisements from mailings, newspapers, magazines, and other print sources to class. Do any of the ads specifically target teenagers? How can you tell? How do you think the ads persuade adolescent consumers?

Living with Technology

Before You Read

Pace Yourself Short blocks of concentrated reading can be more effective than one long session, when they are repeated frequently. Focus on reading for 10 minutes. Take a short break. Then read for another 10 minutes.

Read to Learn

Key Concepts
- **Recognize** the benefits and drawbacks of technology.
- **Identify** strategies for technology management.

Main Idea

Since there are benefits and drawbacks of using technology, it is important to know how to manage technology in your life.

Content Vocabulary

◇ technology
◇ video teleconferencing
◇ cost-effective
◇ hybrid
◇ obsolete
◇ identity theft
◇ telemarketing
◇ fraud
◇ repetitive stress injury

Academic Vocabulary

You will find these words in your reading and on your tests. Use the glossary to look up their definitions if necessary.

☐ decline
☐ exploit

Graphic Organizer

As you read, record both the benefits and drawbacks of technology. Use graphic organizers like the ones below to organize your information.

Benefits of Technology	Drawbacks of Technology

 Graphic Organizer Go to **connectED.mcgraw-hill.com** to download this graphic organizer.

Technology Is Everywhere

As You Read

Connect When you get ready for school, do you use a hairdryer? How do you get to school? Think about the technology you use every day. How would your life be different if this technology had never been invented?

Imagine a world in which phones, tablets, televisions, and computers do not exist. There are no cameras, no stereos, no DVD players, no MP3 players, and no movies. It is not unlike the world a little more than a century ago. Today, it is hard to imagine a life without technology. **Technology**, the application of science to help people meet needs and wants, is everywhere. It includes time-saving, energy-saving, and life-saving devices.

Although new advances continually occur, technology itself is not new. Technology has been advancing for thousands of years, from simple stone tools to complex spacecraft. Throughout history, technology has affected the lifestyle of many people in positive ways, and it will continue to do so. The effect of technology can be complicated. Your role as a technology user is to understand the benefits and drawbacks of this important resource.

Vocabulary

You can find definitions in the glossary at the back of this book.

Benefits of Technology

Tamika used to spend hours writing assigned essays. Each assignment meant piles of wadded up drafts in her trash can. This year has been different. Tamika learned to use her computer's word processing software. She can now delete and rewrite words with no wasted paper, and the printed assignments are much neater than her handwritten versions. By using technology, Tamika is saving energy, time, and money, and her grades reflect the change.

Like Tamika, many people experience the benefits of technology every day. Technology positively affects almost all aspects of life.

TAKE CHARGE!

Put Your Technology Skills to Work

Your technology skills are valuable and can earn you extra money. If you are computer savvy, you may be able to help people who lack computer skills. Better yet, you can get paid for your assistance. The following list includes just a few of the ways you might market your technological services.

- **Install Software Programs** People often need help setting up computers and installing new software.
- **Create Web Sites** Many people do not know how to create Web sites. You can get them started and enhance the Web sites with photos and graphics. You can also write material for the sites.
- **Publish Newsletters** Many community groups need help designing and publishing newsletters.
- **Tutor Senior Citizens and Other Students** Share your computer knowledge with others.

Real-World Skills

Market Your Computer Services To become a software services provider, think about additional computer skills you should learn to be successful. Write a newspaper advertisement, create a Web site, or design a poster describing your services. Display your poster or ad in a five-minute marketing presentation for the class. Ask class members for suggestions to improve the presentation.

New Technology

Thinking about future technology can be exciting. The creativity of scientists, engineers, designers, and others results in many new products. *How have new technologies affected your lifestyle?*

Transportation

Technology has changed how we travel. Early automobiles did not have air conditioning, radios, power windows, or even turn signals. Today, these items are common vehicle features, as are MP3, CD, and DVD players. Safety is another important automobile feature. Most vehicles today are equipped with air bags that inflate in a car crash to protect the driver and passengers. Global positioning systems (GPS) in vehicles inform emergency personnel of a car's location in case of emergency and give drivers directions and shopping and restaurant options in any state. To conserve energy and reduce pollution, a consumer can drive a **hybrid**, a vehicle that uses a combination of electricity and fuel.

Communication

With telephones, cell phones, e-mail, instant messaging, and fax machines, people today have more communication methods than ever before. They can learn about events as they unfold around the world, thanks to television, radio, and Internet news. Businesses have also benefited from communication technology. In the past, people had to travel to do business with distant companies. Today they can use **video teleconferencing**, a technology that enables people in different locations to see and hear each other at the same time. Compared with face-to-face meetings, this method of meeting is often faster and more **cost-effective**, or less expensive, for the benefits produced.

Science You Can Use

Design Communications Technology

Today, much communication takes place using electronic devices, such as computers and cell phones.

Procedure Work with a partner to brainstorm a new type of communications technology. Or, think of ways to improve the features of an existing technology, such as instant messaging or voicemail. Identify the communication problem you want to solve.

Analysis Write a report explaining how the suggested improvements to the communications technology would be useful and effective for users of the technology.

Home and Community Safety

Technology helps protect people, their property, and their communities. Many homes have alarms to detect unauthorized entry, smoke, and carbon monoxide. Business owners use video cameras to record shoplifters. Police officers have computers in their vehicles that allow them to access information about criminal suspects.

Modern weather technology helps communities around the world predict natural disasters such as hurricanes, flash floods, and tornadoes. Communication technology helps spread severe weather warnings based on these predictions, saving thousands of lives every year. Using satellites, radar, and seismographs, scientists are learning how to predict landslides and earthquakes more accurately. New designs allow buildings to flex and move when earthquakes strike, preserving these buildings and the people inside.

Health Care

Technology is helping people live healthier and longer lives. Computerized tomography (CT) and magnetic resonance imaging (MRI) scans allow doctors to "see" inside a person's body without having to conduct surgery. Tiny pill-sized cameras can be swallowed by a patient to show problems in the intestines. These tools and others like them allow doctors to detect many diseases early. Patients receive treatment earlier, which greatly improves their chances of recovery. Surgical procedures are performed using scopes with microscopic cameras and other technology-rich equipment. At home, people can use the Internet to gather information about specific medical conditions and healthy lifestyle practices.

Home Management

Do you use a washing machine to wash clothes, or do you wash your clothes by hand? If you use a washing machine, you are benefiting from technology. Washing machines today are sophisticated. Some front loaders have a multitude of features and are extremely energy and water efficient. Other devices in the home save people time and energy. Smart refrigerators track their contents and print grocery lists. Newer microwaves can read package information to program themselves. With home monitoring systems, people can control their home's appliances and lighting from just about anywhere in the world.

Tim Burkitt/FEMA

Entertainment

Satellite television and radio, gaming stations, and home theaters with high-definition picture quality and surround sound provide endless hours of entertainment at home with just the touch of a button. Outside the home, global positioning systems are used for geocaching, a real-life treasure-seeking game. With wireless technology, it is possible to surf the Internet while hanging out in cybercafés. Amusement parks are also using virtual reality technology to create more thrilling rides for park goers.

Banking and Shopping

With online shopping and banking, people save the time they used to spend traveling to businesses. Debit cards can be used to check your balance and make deposits and withdrawals at an ATM. Debit and credit cards can be used to make purchases quickly in person, over the phone, or online. Self-scan registers allow customers to pay for store items without ever talking to a cashier. How has modern technology affected your shopping experiences?

Education

Technology has made education more accessible. People can take courses online without ever sitting in a classroom. They can learn at home and begin "class" whenever it fits into their schedules. With audio and video technology, students can view live, long-distance demonstrations from experts such as engineers, teachers, and doctors.

The Drawbacks of Technology

"I cannot believe it," Matt complained to his friend Alex. "I just bought the latest graphics software to finish my class project, and it will not run on my old computer! I have to upgrade my computer or use someone else's program. So much for modern technology!"

Almost everyone has complained about technology at some point. Although it helps people in many ways, technology has some serious disadvantages. Have you ever bought a device and had trouble figuring out how to use it? Perhaps you have experienced being out of range with your cell phone or have lost information on your computer when your hard drive crashed. If so, you are familiar with the frustration technology can cause.

▶ **Technology and Free Time**

Technology has changed how many people choose to spend their leisure time. *In what ways has technology affected how you and your family spend your free time?*

ATM Safety

ATMs make it easy for bank customers to deposit or withdraw money. They can use an ATM even when the bank is closed. However, using an ATM safely is important and can help prevent you from being robbed.

Write About It

Research the safe use of ATMs. What tips could you give to parents and friends about using ATMs safely? Write a paragraph covering the basics of informed, safe use of ATMs.

Rapid Change

Many people experience frustration because of the rapid changes in technology. Quickly learning new technology to keep up with the changes can be difficult. Broken devices, computer viruses, and power outages can also cause frustration.

The cost of technology is a drawback for many people. The newest devices are often expensive. Rapid changes in technology also affect people's budgets. Quickly changing technology often means devices are quickly **obsolete**, or out of date and no longer useful. A software program you buy today can be obsolete in just a couple of years, which might mean you have to buy a new program.

Identity Theft

Using today's technology, a thief can steal your identity without your knowledge. **Identity theft**, or stealing and illegally using someone else's personal information, is a concern for anyone who uses a computer or has a bank account. Identity thieves use many methods to find out a person's name, date of birth, and Social Security or bank account numbers. With this information, thieves can raid savings accounts and run up debts in the victim's name. Many people do not realize that they have been the victim of identity theft until a collection agency calls them.

HOW TO ... Protect Your Identity

From dumpster diving to installing computer programs that "spy" on your Internet use, identity thieves will do just about anything to steal your personal information. Fortunately, a few simple steps can help you keep your identity safe and secure.

Secure Your Mail Drop mail in a public collection box, rather than leaving it in your house or apartment mailbox. If you go on vacation, ask a trusted friend to pick up your mail while you are gone or ask for it to be held at the post office.

Watch the Mail for Regular Bills Contact utility or credit card companies if bills are late, or ask for an online billing option. Always look them over right after receiving them to check for any unusual charges.

Properly Dispose of Documents Tear or shred papers such as bills and bank statements. Make sure to tear and shred any other documents that have personally identifiable information also.

(l)Onoky Photography/SuperStock; (r)PNC/Brand X/Corbis

Privacy Issues

Technology has raised other privacy concerns. Some phone calls can be illegally tapped, which means you should be careful about what you say on the phone.

Also, if you make online purchases, visit certain websites or register for certain services online, some of your personal information may be sold to online advertisers or telemarketers. **Telemarketing**, or selling over the telephone, is a highly profitable business. Some online marketers may flood your e-mail with solicitations, however, and some telemarketers may continue to call though you repeatedly decline, or refuse, their offers. Set up your Web mail program to block e-mails from people you do not know. Contact the National Do Not Call Registry to prevent telemarketers from calling you.

Scams

Although most online advertisers and telemarketers are honest, some are scam artists. They tell lies to steal money or valuables, which is **fraud**. People who commit fraud are skilled at sounding believable. They might use phrases such as, "free bonus," "valuable prizes," "get rich quick" and "only if you act right away" to motivate you to give them money. You may believe you are buying a product or giving money to a charity, when in reality the scam artist is stealing your money.

Choose Creative Passwords Letter and number combinations make the best passwords. Do not choose obvious words and numbers. Birth dates and names of family members are not the best choices.

Keep Personal Information Private Give personal information only when initiating contact with reputable companies like the cable or phone company. Never give this information to someone who calls or e-mails and asks for it.

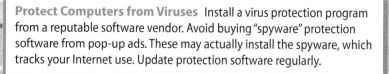

Protect Computers from Viruses Install a virus protection program from a reputable software vendor. Avoid buying "spyware" protection software from pop-up ads. These may actually install the spyware, which tracks your Internet use. Update protection software regularly.

Secure Wireless Computer Connections Strangers can read your files and steal your information if your wireless home network is not secure. Most wireless equipment comes with built-in security features that you need to turn on.

When you receive a solicitation, be cautious about the information you share. Personal information can be used for illegal means. When in doubt, the best way to handle the situation is to delete the e-mail or say "No, thank you," and hang up the phone.

Health Risks

Technology can also negatively affect a person's health. Too much time spent working on a computer or playing video games can result in back pain, eyestrain, and hand and wrist injuries. Even a very young child who spends many hours clicking a mouse or pushing video game buttons can suffer from a **repetitive stress injury**, a joint injury caused by repeated motions. General health also suffers when people choose television, video games, or the computer over physical activities.

In addition to the physical health risks of technology overuse, there are emotional risks. The increased use of technology can cause isolation. Hours spent watching television, surfing the Internet, and playing video games means hours away from family and friends. This isolation can negatively affect people's social and emotional health. How can you lessen your technology use and increase face-to-face time with the people you care about?

✓ Reading Check **Recall** What is technology, and what is your role as a technology user?

Manage Technology

Technology is a resource, and despite its drawbacks, it is here to stay. Like any other resource, technology needs to be managed. People who manage technology well enjoy its benefits and experience fewer of its disadvantages.

The following strategies can help you stay in control of the technology in your life:

- **Practice healthy habits.** Avoid working at the computer or playing video games for hours at a time. Take breaks often to walk around or stretch. When sitting at the computer, sit up straight, with your feet flat on the floor. When you are not using electronics, be active. Swim, ride a bike, jog, or take a walk.
- **Take time to learn.** Take available classes. By keeping up your technology skills, you are more likely to use technology successfully, without feeling frustrated or overwhelmed. Read current magazine articles and books, and talk to tech-savvy friends and family members.

New Technology

Many high-tech products released have bugs, defects, omissions, or design flaws. *Would you purchase a high-tech product on the first day it is released? Why or why not?*

Health & Wellness

TIPS

Social Interaction

Using the computer, playing video games, and watching television can be entertaining and educational. It is important, though, to balance those screen-watching activities with ones that involve social interaction. These tips can help:

▶ Limit weekly "screen time" to ten hours or less.

▶ Organize family activities, such as swimming or camping.

▶ Join school clubs and teams.

- **Be a smart shopper.** Before buying a high-tech product, ask yourself the following questions: How will it improve my life? How often will I use it? Can I justify the expense? Do I want it just because my friends have it? You might find that the device you thought you needed is not that important. If you decide you do need it, research the product to find the best buy. Read consumer magazines and product reviews. If possible, wait a few months to buy the product. Many consumers who buy the latest device to hit the shelves end up frustrated with the product's bugs, or defects. Waiting gives the manufacturer time to fix the bugs.

- **Protect your privacy.** Losing control of your personal information can cost you and your family money. Always keep your personal information private. The tips in this chapter's How To... feature on pages 318 and 319 can help protect you from identity theft and other Internet crimes. If you have a cell phone that has an option to enter a code before use, this can prevent others from accessing your personal information in your phone.

- **Make time for others.** The latest technical devices may be cool, but they can not replace people. Family and friends bring comfort and joys that technology cannot. Make time for the people you care about. Doing so will prevent isolation and help strengthen your relationships.

- **Remember your values.** Will your use of technology hurt you or anyone else? Disrespectful chat room or e-mail messages can hurt friendships and turn arguments into fights. How does the technology you use affect the environment? The growing problem of e-waste is a concern to everyone. Investigate ways to reuse or recycle old equipment. It is up to you to make the best possible use of present and future technology.

How I See It

E-MANNERS

Desmond, 17

A good friend sent me an e-mail that made me really mad. He was really out of line. So I immediately began writing a response because I was so angry. As I finished drafting the message, I realized that I had written things that were just as hurtful. Plus, my e-mail said things I would *never* say to my friend in person. So, I decided to hold off on sending it. I saved the draft and read it the next day when I was calmer. I was so glad I waited! Some of the things I wrote could have made the situation worse and could have hurt our friendship. I deleted it. You can apologize to someone you hurt, but once the words are out there, they can never be taken back.

Critical Thinking
Desmond suggests that it is important to not send e-mails while you are angry. Do you agree? Why or why not?

Internet Safety

Millions of people regularly go online to exchange e-mail, surf the Internet, post and read messages on bulletin boards, view and post videos, and join chat rooms. This Internet community is like any other community. There are good people, and people who want to **exploit** others, or use others for selfish purposes. The two groups can be harder to distinguish on the Internet. How can teens stay safe from sexual predators and others who try to take criminal advantage of their trust?

Help protect yourself from online predators by following these guidelines:

- **Get permission first.** These general words of wisdom apply to almost anything you do on the Internet, from logging on to sending pictures of yourself or your home. Parents and guardians and many of your teachers may not have grown up with the Internet, but they have life experience and can often spot potential dangers that teens might not see.

- **Choose usernames thoughtfully.** Consider the impression your name might make on people who do not know you. What might people assume about "Crazy Carleen" compared with "Egghead" or "Sports Fan 27"?

- **Keep passwords private.** Keep your passwords private from everyone except your parents or guardians. No one, not even your best friend, should be able to access your passwords.

- **Monitor discussion groups before joining.** Get a feel for the topics and personalities. If they make you uncomfortable, find another group.

- **Do not give out personal information.** Information such as your address, telephone number, parents' or guardians' workplace addresses and phone numbers, and the name and location of your school should be kept private.

- **Keep your image private.** Do not send photos to people you "meet" online. Do not post photos to Web sites without your parents' or guardians' approval.

- **Say no to face-to-face meetings.** Never agree to meet in person anyone you meet online. If someone suggests that you meet, discuss it with your parents or guardians.

▲ Internet Safety

The Internet is not always safe just because you do not encounter people or businesses face-to-face. *Why is it important to follow safe practices when on the Internet?*

Jupiter Images

- **Word messages carefully.** Replies to blog postings, Websites, and discussion groups can be read by all members. Carefully word your responses to avoid revealing information that you would not want a stranger to know about you or your family. The same goes for e-mail.
- **Resist peer pressure.** Peers can exert the same pressure online as they do in person. Politely but firmly tell fellow chatters if their talk offends you. If you receive a hostile response, leave the chat room.
- **Be alert to signs of imposters.** Someone may claim to like the same music as you do. Another person may use teen slang heavily. Try stating something you know is false. Does the other person go along? Maybe he or she is just a polite teen, or maybe the "teen" is not a teen. Tell a trusted adult if you have suspicions.
- **Resist the temptation to create a public profile.** It may seem like fun to create a public profile that displays your photo, age, gender, hobbies, and interests. However, these profiles can be viewed by anyone on the Web. They can make you the target of harassment or worse, even if you do not post your name and address or other information that could lead to an attempt to make physical contact. To be safe and avoid potential hassles, it is better not to have a public profile.
- **Get help.** Tell your parents or guardians if you come across any information that makes you feel uncomfortable.

Section 13.2

After You Read

Review Key Concepts

1. **Describe** some of the drawbacks that result from the rapid change of technology.
2. **List** healthy habits you can practice while using technology.

Practice Academic Skills

English Language Arts

3. Think of a technology device you would like to buy. Research the device using consumer magazines and the manufacturer's Web site. Visit a retail store that sells the product, and ask a salesperson for his or her recommendations and opinions. What are the drawbacks of owning the product? What are the benefits? How can you get the most value for your money?

Social Studies

4. Research advice to reduce the risk of repetitive stress injuries while using technology. Choose several tips to implement at home. Ask your family to also follow the suggestions. Share reasons with the class why you chose the advice you did.

Check Your Answers Go to connectED. mcgraw-hill.com to check your answers.

What Does an Investment Advisor Do?

Investment advisors, also called financial planners, provide advice to individuals and businesses about a broad range of financial subjects. These subjects include investments, retirement planning, and tax management. Advisors may buy and sell financial products such as stocks, bonds, and mutual funds, on behalf of their clients.

Skills Investment advisors have an interest in finance and a desire to help others succeed financially. They should be able to work long hours under pressure. Investment advisors should have people skills, since a large part of their job includes communicating with clients.

Education and Training There are no specific licensure requirements for personal financial advisors. However, those taking courses for the title usually have licensure credentials in their existing financial position. Many advisors earn a Certified Financial Planner credential. This requires that they pass an exam, have three years of experience in a related field, and possess an accredited college degree.

Job Outlook Employment in the investments industry is projected to rise more than 40 percent until 2016, compared to an 11 percent increase across all industries. Job competition is expected to be lively. Those with four-year degrees will have the best prospects.

Critical Thinking Find an investment company either online or located in your area. Call the company's human resources department and ask for a job description of an investment advisor. Then, write a paragraph speculating about an investment advisor's typical day.

Career Cluster

Finance

Investment advisors work in the Finance career cluster. Here are some of the other jobs in this career cluster:

- Credit Analyst
- Financial Examiner
- Loan Officer
- Stockbroker
- Customer Service Representative
- Tax Preparer
- Actuary
- Insurance Agent
- Accountant
- Claims Examiner
- Auditor
- Financial Manager
- Development Officer
- Real Estate Broker
- Budget Analyst
- Insurance Underwriter
- Securities, Commodities, and Financial Services Salesperson
- Brokerage Clerk

Explore Further Research this career cluster. Choose a career in this cluster that appeals to you and write a career profile.

Chapter 13 Review and Applications

CHAPTER SUMMARY

Section 13.1
Making Consumer Choices

Every purchase involves a choice that is influenced by many factors. Consumers have certain responsibilities and rights that are protected by law. Good money management means not spending more than you earn. A budget helps you make the most of your money. Before opening a savings or checking account, compare fees and services of different institutions. Credit allows you to buy now and pay later.

Section 13.2
Living with Technology

Technology includes time-saving, energy-saving, and life-saving devices. Technology positively affects almost all aspects of life. Technology also has some serious disadvantages. Identify theft is one of the major disadvantages of technology. Technology is a resource that needs to be managed. People who manage technology well enjoy its benefits and experience fewer of its disadvantages.

Vocabulary Review

1. Some words, such as *slight* and *sole*, have many meanings. Choose one of these words and write one sentence using the verb form, one using the noun form, and one using the adjective form.

Content Vocabulary
◇ consumer (p. 301)
◇ income (p. 301)
◇ impulse purchase (p. 302)
◇ comparison shopping (p. 302)
◇ redress (p. 305)
◇ warranty (p. 306)
◇ budget (p. 308)
◇ expense (p. 308)
◇ interest (p. 309)
◇ endorse (p. 309)

◇ technology (p. 314)
◇ hybrid (p. 315)
◇ video teleconferencing (p. 315)
◇ cost-effective (p. 315)
◇ obsolete (p. 318)
◇ identify theft (p. 318)
◇ telemarketing (p. 319)
◇ fraud (p. 319)
◇ repetitive stress injury (p. 320)

Academic Vocabulary
▢ sole (p. 303)
▢ slight (p. 304)
▢ decline (p. 319)
▢ exploit (p. 322)

Review Key Concepts

2. **Identify** factors that influence consumer choices.
3. **Summarize** the rights and responsibilities of consumers.
4. **Outline** the steps for creating a budget.
5. **Describe** procedures for using savings and checking accounts.
6. **Recall** the benefits and costs of credit.
7. **Recognize** the benefits and drawbacks of technology.
8. **Identify** strategies for technology management.

Critical Thinking

9. **Compare** Think of two similar purchases you made in the past year, such as two clothing items. Which would you consider the better buy? Why?
10. **Generalize** Imagine you were going to spend a week in a remote area, and could only take clothes and food with you. Which technology device would you miss the most? Explain.
11. **Defend** Some experts blame technology for people's weight problems. Take a stand either with or against these experts. Defend your position.

ACTIVE
LEARNING

12. Compare Checking Options Checking accounts offered by banks, credit unions, and savings and loan companies can help you manage your money in a safe place. Although cash may sometimes be necessary, paying with checks is a safe alternative. Carrying cash can be unsafe, and cash sent through the mail can be stolen. Find advertisements for checking accounts offered by a local financial institution. Compare the costs and features of each type of checking account offered. Select the account that you think best fits your needs. Share your reasons for your selection with the rest of the class.

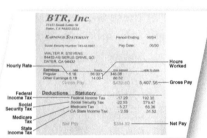

Family & Community Connections

13. Plan a Donation Drive The recent rise in electronic waste is partly due to the short life span of electronics. Electronic waste comes in the form of computers, television sets, cell phones, telephones, and radios, just to name a few. These products contain materials such as cadmium, mercury, and lead, which can be dangerous to humans and the environment. Properly recycling e-waste can reduce the amount of harmful substances that go into landfills. Rather than discarding electronics, you can also donate old electronics so that they will be reused. Find a local charity organization that could use these donations. As a class, plan an e-donation drive for the charity. Design a pamphlet to educate your community about electronic waste. Create posters to advertise the e-donation drive.

Real-World Skills and Applications

Leadership Skills

14. Practice Your Consumer Rights With a partner, act out a scenario in which a consumer is unhappy with a purchase and is trying to resolve the problem with a store manager. Use the presentation as a way to show your classmates effective techniques consumers can use to solve problems. After you finish, ask your classmates for feedback.

Financial Literacy

15. Cell Phone Plan Options You send text messages on your cell phone more often than you make calls. Plan 1 costs $55.95 per month and includes 450 minutes and 500 text messages. Plan 2 costs $59.95 per month and includes 500 minutes and 750 text messages. Additional text messages cost 10 cents per message. If you send 600 messages per month and talk for just 200 minutes, which plan is cheaper for your usage?

Information Literacy

16. Rate the Source Consumer magazines, such as *Consumer Reports*, test and rate different brands for quality, safety, and price. You can find consumer magazines at your local or school library or a newsstand. Read an article of your choice in a consumer magazine. Then research the same product on the company's Web site. Which source of information do you think would be more helpful when considering a major purchase? Why?

Academic Skills

 English Language Arts

17. Future Technologies Research the technologies that were available to people 200 years ago. Then think of the amazing technological developments that have occurred in your lifetime. Consider how much things have changed in a relatively short amount of time. Now imagine you have been transported in time 200 years into the future. Using your imagination, write a letter to your family describing the types of technology that are available to you.

 Social Studies

18. Technology Consider a relatively recent technological development, such as the cellular phone, hybrid car, or GPS device. Briefly explain the development, and state whether it benefits society on the whole. Are there more benefits than drawbacks to the development? What are they? In what ways does this technology need to improve?

 Mathematics

19. Interest Gain You can earn money by putting your money in a savings account. Savings accounts slowly earn interest at regular intervals. Say you make $200 working as a lifeguard every other weekend this summer. Calculate the total amount of money you will have in your savings account after one interest period if you open an account that earns 2 percent simple interest.

Math Concept **Interest** There are two different kinds of interest, simple interest and compound interest. With simple interest, only the principal, which is $200 in this case, earns interest.

Starting Hint First, convert the two percent interest rate into a decimal by dividing it by 100, or by simply moving the decimal two places to the left. Then multiply this number by the amount you put in the bank to find the interest you will earn.

 For math help, go to the Math Appendix at the back of the book.

Standardized Test Practice

MATH WORD PROBLEMS
Directions Read the problem. Then, choose the correct answer.

Test-Taking Tip When attempting a word problem, first find the necessary information. Identify the question being asked and the information necessary to answer that question. You can ignore everything else in the problem.

20. You pay three bills one day with checks for a total of $67.88. You also use your debit card to purchase a pair of shoes for $35.95 and lunch for $5.63. Lastly, you deposit a $20.00 check that you received for your birthday. How much less money do you have in your account than you did when the day started?

a) $225.22
b) $89.46
c) $46.30
d) $129.46

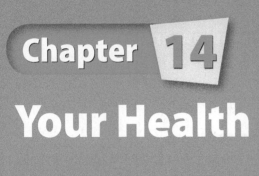

Chapter 14

Your Health

Section 14.1
Staying Healthy and Fit

Section 14.2
Health Risks

Chapter Objectives

Section 14.1
- **Describe** the two major categories of health.
- **Identify** five factors in physical health.
- **Explain** the causes and effects of emotional stress.

Section 14.2
- **Identify** factors that influence one's weight.
- **Summarize** the negative effects of frequently abused illegal and legal drugs.
- **Describe** the potential risks associated with sexual activity.
- **Recognize** steps you can take to protect and promote your health and well-being.

Writing Activity

Compare and Contrast

Staying Fit Eating right and exercising are key elements to good health. The secret to staying fit for life is to find healthy habits that work for you. There are lots of ways to keep your body healthy. By comparing and contrasting different forms of exercise, you will find healthy methods that work for you. Write a short essay comparing and contrasting the different types of exercise.

Writing Tips Use these tips to write a compare and contrast essay.

- Choose two types of exercise with distinct similarities and differences.
- Your first paragraph should include a thesis statement that introduces the main point of your paper.
- Remember to fully address the similarities and differences of each form of exercise in your paper.

△ Explore the Photo

Exercise is one part of having good physical health. *What kinds of healthy physical activities do you enjoy?*

Section 14.1

Staying Healthy and Fit

Before You Read

Preview Read the topics of the reading check questions in this section. Write one or two sentences predicting what you think the section will be about.

Read to Learn

Key Concepts

- **Describe** the two major categories of health.
- **Identify** five factors in physical health.
- **Explain** the causes and effects of emotional stress.

Main Idea

Wellness means adopting positive habits and attitudes that promote better physical and mental health. Healthy people actively seek ways to keep their bodies, minds, and social lives fit and strong.

Content Vocabulary

◇ wellness
◇ grooming
◇ acne
◇ dandruff
◇ plaque
◇ stress

Academic Vocabulary

You will find these words in your reading and on your tests. Use the glossary to look up their definitions if necessary.

☐ vigorous
☐ attentive

Graphic Organizer

As you read, record four elements of fitness and three exercise program tips. Use a graphic organizer like the one below to organize your information.

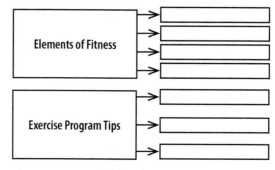

 Graphic Organizer Go to **connectED.mcgraw-hill.com** to download this graphic organizer.

Health and Wellness

What does good health mean? Some people might reply, "not being sick" or "feeling good." Others may say, "being happy." They would all be partly right. Health can refer to the condition of your body or your mind. There are two major categories of health:

- **Physical health,** or the condition of your body.
- **Mental and emotional health,** which is reflected in your thinking processes, attitudes, feelings, and relationships with others.

Physical, mental, and emotional health are interrelated. All are affected by your day-to-day actions and decisions. For instance, one night you might not get much sleep. The next day you may be irritable, do poorly on a math test, and have an argument with your best friend. How would you rate your overall health, or wellness, that day?

Wellness is a positive approach to life based on healthy attitudes and actions. When you feel healthy and good about life in general, you may not think about what you did to make that attitude happen. When you feel down or out of sorts, however, maintaining a positive attitude and taking positive actions to improve your physical, emotional, or social health takes serious effort.

Wellness is more than the absence of illness. It means adopting habits and behaviors that promote better health and the highest quality of life possible.

✓ Reading Check **Recall** What is wellness and how does it relate to health?

Physical Health

Your everyday activities, such as sleeping, grooming, eating, and exercising, all contribute to your physical health. When you enjoy physical health, you have energy to engage in the activities you need and want to do every day. You also look and feel your best.

As You Read

Connect Think about the ways you keep your body, mind, and social life healthy. Which of these three health components could you improve upon?

◆ Vocabulary

You can find definitions in the glossary at the back of this book.

> **Positive Attitude**
>
> Studies show that people with positive attitudes do not get sick as often as people with negative attitudes. *How else can thinking positively benefit you?*

Bananastock/usa.stockfood.com

Sleep

Have you ever wondered what your body does during the night? While you sleep, your body repairs itself, removes waste products from cells, and builds a supply of energy for action the next day.

You may think that you can accomplish more if you sleep less. But when you do not get enough sleep, everything requires more effort. It is hard to concentrate when you are tired, and you are more likely to make mistakes. Your need for sleep actually increases as you move into adolescence. Teens should aim for about nine hours of sleep a night. You will feel a lot better the next day, and will be more likely to accomplish everything you want to do!

Personal Hygiene

Grooming refers to the personal care routine you follow to keep yourself clean and well-groomed. Not everyone is born with natural good looks, but anyone can be attractive by making the most of what he or she has. Cleanliness is vital for your health and appearance. As you read about grooming and cleanliness, think about how your own grooming routine measures up.

Skin

Your skin covers and protects your body. It warns you about heat, cold, and pain. It produces oils to keep itself soft, and moisture in the form of perspiration to help regulate your body temperature.

Everyone perspires. Perspiration is a natural body process that regulates body temperature. Your body contains glands called sweat glands. These glands are located everywhere hair grows.

> **Improve Your Sleep**

Relaxing activities, such as reading, help calm you and prepare you for sleep. *How can you improve your sleep?*

Chev Wilkinson/Photolibrary

When you perspire, skin bacteria react with the perspiration and produce an odor. You can prevent perspiration-caused body odor by using deodorant or antiperspirant every day. Take a bath or shower as part of your daily routine. Soap and water remove dirt, dried skin, excess oil, and surface bacteria that can cause body odors and infections.

When you wash your face there are things you can do to help make it as clean as possible:

- Wet your face completely by splashing it with warm water.
- Lather cleanser or facial soap between your clean hands. Use your fingertips or face brush to gently massage your face, using a circular motion.
- Start at the forehead, move down the nose, lather the cheeks, and then move down to your neck.
- Rinse the cleanser or soap off by repeatedly splashing cool water over your face. Spend more time rinsing than cleansing.
- Use a clean soft towel to blot, not forcefully rub, your face.

Acne **Acne** is a skin problem that develops when glands below the pores (tiny openings) in the skin become blocked. The oils that normally move through your pores to soften the skin are trapped beneath them. As more oil becomes trapped, blackheads and whiteheads develop. Often these areas become irritated or infected with bacteria and develop into pimples, or acne. Despite what you might think, there is no medical evidence linking food items such as chocolate, cola drinks, or potato chips to acne.

Most teens develop acne. The condition most commonly appears on the face, upper chest, and back. The best treatment for mild cases of acne is to wash your face twice daily. Shower right after exercising, and keep telephone receivers, cell phones, and pillowcases clean to reduce outbreaks. You can also blot your skin with a tissue between washings to remove built-up oil. Over-the-counter acne medicine, available without a doctor's prescription, may also help. Avoid picking at and squeezing the pimples. This injures the skin, spreads bacteria, and can leave lifelong scars. Serious cases of acne need to be treated by a dermatologist, a doctor specializing in skin problems.

▲ Skin Care

Take the time to wash your face thoroughly, especially before bedtime. *Why is it important to wash your face before bedtime?*

Blend Images/SuperStock

Hair

Did you know that hair reflects your general health? Attractive hair begins inside the body. A poor diet, emotional stress, or even a bad cold can alter the appearance and texture of your hair. It can turn dull and brittle within weeks if you do not take proper care of yourself, both physically and mentally.

How often do you need to shampoo your hair? Many teens have so much natural oil in their hair that they need to shampoo it every day, while others need to shampoo it less often. Wash your hair often enough to keep it looking clean.

Dandruff is scales and flakes on the scalp, and it can be a problem for many teens. To help control dandruff, keep your hair clean. Special dandruff shampoos available over the counter can be effective. Keep combs, brushes, and other hair-care items clean, and change your pillowcases often. Avoid scratching your scalp with sharp combs or fingernails. If dandruff is severe and does not improve, a dermatologist may be helpful.

HOW TO . . . Protect Your Skin

Bright, sunny weather and exercise seem to go together. In fact, exposure to sunlight is a proven promoter of good mental health. A bit of sunlight throughout the week helps your skin manufacture vitamin D. However, the sun can damage skin as well. Ultraviolet (UV) rays, a type of solar energy that affects the cells, are responsible for a so-called healthy tan. This is actually a sign of skin cells under stress. These rays can lead to burns and wrinkles. They can also change cells' genetic makeup, leading to skin cancer. These tips can help you enjoy the sun safely.

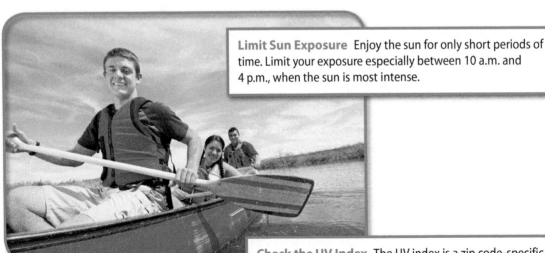

Limit Sun Exposure Enjoy the sun for only short periods of time. Limit your exposure especially between 10 a.m. and 4 p.m., when the sun is most intense.

Check the UV Index The UV index is a zip code-specific prediction of the strength of the UV rays for the following day. It is often mentioned in local weather forecasts. An index of 5 or greater indicates a high intensity. Avoiding the sun altogether on these days may be a good idea.

Imagesource/Photolibrary

Teeth

Good dental hygiene is important for healthy teeth, fresh breath, and an attractive smile. Brushing your teeth helps remove most stains and decay-causing plaque. **Plaque**, a sticky film that clings to your teeth, is formed by the food, bacteria, and air in your mouth. Together, plaque and sugar combine to form acid, which eats away your tooth enamel and forms cavities. Sugary and starchy foods feed the bacteria in plaque.

Fight plaque and prevent tooth decay by following these simple tips:

- **Brush regularly.** Brush after eating and before bed to remove any plaque clinging to your teeth. Try a specialized mouthwash to loosen plaque before brushing.
- **Floss regularly.** Dental floss removes food particles between your teeth that a toothbrush cannot reach. Floss your teeth every day.
- **Drink water.** The liquids you drink, along with your saliva, help rinse plaque-promoting sugar and starch from your mouth.
- **See a dentist regularly.** A dentist can find and fix minor problems before they become major ones.

Health & Wellness TIPS

Healthy Teeth

One of the first things you notice about someone is his or her smile. A dazzling smile requires excellent dental health, including healthy teeth and gums. Keep your teeth healthy by using these simple steps:

- ▶ Use a toothbrush with soft bristles.
- ▶ Use short back-and-forth brushstrokes.
- ▶ Replace your toothbrush every three months.

Use Strong Sunscreen Choose a sunscreen lotion with a sun protection factor (SPF) of 15 or more. The SPF indicates the amount of time the sunscreen protects you from UV rays. A 15 SPF lotion protects your skin about 15 times longer than if you did not use it. Apply it liberally, and reapply it often. A more effective option is sunblock, which reflects the sun completely.

Clothing as Protection Clothing is a physical sunblock. Wide-brimmed hats and long-sleeved, tightly woven garments are basic cover-ups. Clothing labeled "sun protective" has an ultraviolet protection factor (UPF) of 15 or more, meaning it allows one fifteenth of UV rays to penetrate. Some specially treated fabrics have a UPF of 50 or higher.

Know Your Skin Some people tan and burn more easily than others. You may know from experience if you fall into this group. Respect your body's limits. Also, seek medical advice on any changes in moles or freckles.

Care for Your Skin All Year The sun can be a concern in the winter if you spend a lot of time outdoors, especially if sunlight is reflected onto your skin by snow. That is added reason to wear gloves and scarves, even if it does not feel that cold. Colder, drier winter air can also dry skin. Include skin lotion in your daily hygiene routine.

Exercise

People who are more physically active and maintain a healthy weight over their life span tend to have fewer health problems, more energy, and a better mental outlook. Exercise also helps your body's organs function more efficiently.

To benefit the most from exercise, make it a regular habit. It is easier to stick with an exercise program if you stay active and have fun at the same time. Make a date with a friend to play tennis, hike, shoot baskets, bike, or go dancing. Plan to meet at least twice a week to exercise together. Make sure to try different activities to avoid boredom and improve your overall fitness.

Your Exercise Program

The ideal exercise program should include four elements of fitness, but you do not need to work on all four elements every day.

- **Heart and Lungs** Your heart, lungs, and blood vessels deliver oxygen to every part of your body. You can train them to work more efficiently with regular aerobic exercise. Aerobic exercise is any vigorous activity that causes your heart to beat faster for a sustained amount of time. Jumping rope, dancing, cycling, swimming, and walking at a fast pace are healthful aerobic exercises.
- **Muscular Endurance** The ability of your muscles to work continuously over a long time is called muscular endurance. Most aerobic activity improves your muscular endurance.
- **Muscular Strength** Strength enables your muscles to push or pull with force. Having strong muscles can also improve your posture and help prevent injury. Weight lifting, leg lifts, and push-ups are examples of weight-bearing exercises. They increase the strength of your muscles, bones, and joints.
- **Flexibility** You should be able to move your muscles and joints easily, without pain or stiffness. Slow, gentle stretching exercises help improve flexibility.

◀ Aerobic Activity

Aerobic activity not only helps strengthen the heart but also helps relieve stress and burns calories. *What types of aerobic activity do you engage in?*

rubberball/Getty Images

How I See It

Rosa, 14

Before I became a runner, I often had trouble keeping up on hikes and long walks. Then my best friend convinced me to go walking with her every day after school. The first day was *tough*. But after only a week of exercising regularly, I started to feel really good. Within two weeks I cut back on the sugary foods I used to eat for energy, because I had more energy than before. After a month, I was able to jog every other block. I have so much more energy and endurance these days, thanks to my regular workouts. Now when I go hiking with friends, I'm usually in the front of the group. I can even run for three miles without stopping!

> **Critical Thinking**
> Rosa suggests that eating less junk food and exercising noticeably improved her health. How could you improve the nutrition and exercise habits you have?

Follow the tips to plan a personal exercise program:

- **Strength Building** Exercises that strengthen the muscles are known as resistance or strength training. Include a strength-building session two to three times a week. Work all the major muscle groups: chest, stomach, back, legs, and arms. Allow at least 48 hours between strength workouts to rest your muscles and build new tissue. Increasing muscle mass will help your body burn the calories you consume faster. That makes it easier to control your weight.

- **Stretching** Perform stretching exercises several times a week. Stretching exercises help improve your flexibility, circulation, posture, and coordination. It also helps ease stress. Ideally, you should warm up your muscles by jogging in place or doing jumping jacks, then stretch for at least ten minutes before a workout to help prevent injury. You should stretch for another ten minutes after a workout to help prevent your muscles from tightening up and slowing your recovery. Stretching for five minutes before going to bed is also beneficial because it can relax you, allowing you to fall asleep quickly.

- **Aerobic Exercise** Most health experts recommend performing aerobic exercise every day for at least 30 to 45 minutes. If you cannot block out 45 minutes in your schedule for a workout, do not worry. Some studies show that getting 45 minutes of aerobic exercise in total throughout the day may have the same benefits of a regular 45-minute workout. You might walk your dog for 15 minutes in the morning, do three five-minute laps around the block during your lunch hour, and jump rope for 15 minutes after school.

Keep a Fitness Log

You may keep a record of how you spend your money or how many hours you babysit in a month, so why not keep a record of your eating and exercise habits? People who keep fitness records are often more successful in staying fit than those who do not. You are not always aware of the habits you develop, some of which may be poor. A fitness record can help you identify and correct poor habits.

Try keeping a fitness record for at least a week. List the foods and beverages, along with the amounts, that you consume. Note the place and time you eat and drink. Comment on how you feel and your mood at the time. List your physical activities and the length of time you do them.

After a week, take a look at your record. You will probably see some patterns emerging. Are you pleased with what you see? Are you exercising enough? What would you continue to do the same? What changes would you make?

Workout Safety

When you are exercising or playing a sport, remember that safety comes first! If you overdo your workouts or ignore simple safety precautions, you may develop an injury that could sideline you for weeks. The following guidelines can help prevent exercise-related injuries:

- **Pick a safe place and time to exercise.** Surfaces with some cushioning, such as a track, are better for running than hard surfaces, like concrete. On hot days when you may become dehydrated, try to exercise in the early morning or early evening when it is cooler, and take a water bottle on your runs.
- **Warm up.** Start each exercise session with a warm-up period, which prepares your body for more vigorous, or forceful and energetic, activity. It also helps prevent injury. Begin by stretching for 5 to 10 minutes. Then start a light and easy version of the activity you are planning to do before beginning more intense exercise.
- **Hydrate.** Remember to drink plenty of water before, during, and after any vigorous exercise. If you exercise intensely for more than 45 minutes, you should drink a sports drink.
- **Follow the rules of the sport.** When bicycling, for example, ride on the right side of the road with traffic, not against it. When skating, avoid parking lots, streets, and other areas with traffic.
- **Wear a helmet.** This is especially important for sports such as football, hockey, baseball, biking, skateboarding, and inline skating.
- **Use eye protection.** The eye gear offering the most protection is made from a plastic called polycarbonate, which has been tested especially for sports use. Goggles are often worn for racquet sports, soccer, basketball, snowboarding, street hockey, baseball and softball.
- **Wear a mouth guard.** Mouth guards protect your mouth, teeth, and tongue if you play a contact sport or other sport for which head injury is a risk.
- **Protect your bones and joints.** Wrist, knee, and elbow guards are important gear for inline skating and skateboarding.

- **Stay off the phone.** Any time you are involved in an active sport such as biking or skateboarding, do not use a cell phone! The sport requires your full attention. Losing your focus can result in a serious accident.
- **Cool down.** After you have exercised, end each session with a cool down period to allow your heart rate to slow and return to normal. A cool down lets you gradually slow your body down rather than bring it to a sudden halt. Walking at a slower pace is a good way to cool down. After your cool down, stretch again to help prevent soreness.

Balanced Nutrition

Exercise and good nutrition are a powerful combination. Like a machine, your body needs the right kind of fuel to function efficiently. Eating a variety of foods keeps you well nourished and gives you the energy you need to grow, stay active and keep on top of your schedule.

Throughout the normal life cycle of childhood, adolescence, adulthood, and finally old age, dietary needs change. Establishing good food habits now can minimize illness later. Infancy and adolescence are the most rapid growth periods; therefore, teens have an increased need for most nutrients. Although older adults continue to need the same nutrients, they need them in smaller amounts.

Teens should try to eat a healthful, well-balanced diet every day. The Dietary Guidelines for Americans do not recommend that teens diet. Instead, teens should consistently eat a healthful diet and exercise regularly. See Chapter 16 for more information on the Dietary Guidelines for Americans and how to use them in your daily life. Any teens that are concerned about their weight should talk to their doctor.

Regular Checkups

To maintain your physical health, it makes good sense to seek regular medical checkups. Checkups give you the chance to talk to a doctor about any health problems or questions you may have. As part of a medical exam, your doctor may ask questions about your general health. Unusual fatigue, unexplained weight loss, ongoing pain, blurred vision and sores that do not heal are red flags. These physical conditions might be the result of lack of sleep or over-activity, or they may be signs of a serious illness.

Somos Images LLC/Alamy

◭ Safe Workouts

A balanced exercise program will not be effective if it is not safe. *How can these teens keep their workouts safe?*

Health & Wellness

TIPS

Safe Weight Loss

If you want to lose a substantial amount of weight, you should consult a doctor first. The doctor can recommend a weight loss plan that is safe and realistic. With a safe plan, dieters can:

▶ Eat real food, not special liquids or powders.
▶ Include foods from all the food groups.
▶ Stick to a regular exercise program.

Doctors can usually identify and handle small problems before they turn into major ones. *Why is it important to handle small problems before they turn into major ones?*

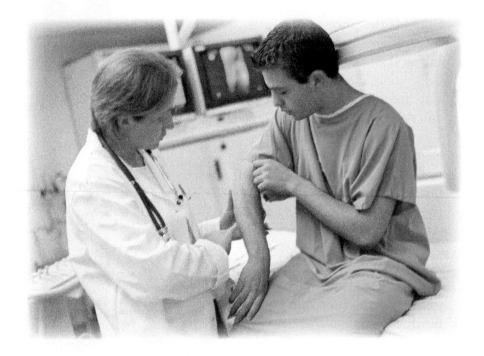

Your doctor is experienced at diagnosing serious illnesses, including different types of cancer. He or she can teach you how to perform self-examinations so that you can find signs of cancer early. For example, a self-examination of your skin might reveal recent changes in the size or coloration of the skin around a mole or birthmark. Your doctor should examine the change to eliminate the possibility of skin cancer. Females should examine their breasts and males should examine their testicles for any thickening or lumps. Testicular examinations are particularly important because testicular cancer is one of the most common forms of cancer in teen males. Screening for cancer is important because early detection increases the chance for successful treatment.

✓ **Reading Check** **Describe** How do exercise and balanced nutrition contribute to a person's overall wellness?

Mental and Emotional Health

Between school, after-school activities, homework, and family responsibilities it is not always easy to find time for yourself. However, taking care of your mental and emotional well-being is just as important as taking care of your physical health. Feelings affect health more than you might think. For example, overeating or avoiding food when you are unhappy or bored can cause you to gain or lose weight.

People with good mental and emotional health have positive attitudes about themselves and life in general. They are able to cope with change, face problems, and handle anger and disappointment. Emotionally healthy people are open-minded, confident, sensitive to the needs and feelings of others, and able to work toward goals.

In your everyday activities, you need to strike a balance between your mental, emotional, and physical health. If one of these areas is seriously out of balance, the other areas often suffer, too.

Mark Thornton/Brand X/Corbis

Stress

Stress is mental, emotional, or physical strain. Everyone has to deal with stress. Anyone who moves to a new city or school experiences stress. Family problems can trigger stress. Trying to meet a deadline for school can cause stress.

Stress is not entirely negative. When you prepare for a major sports event or test in class, it is natural to feel a certain amount of stress. The stress you feel compels you to work harder to succeed. When the event or test is over, the stress you felt usually vanishes. On the other hand, too much stress can cause emotional strain and even lead to long-term health problems.

How do you know when you are suffering from an overload of stress? Your body gives you physical and emotional signals. For example, physical clues may include a racing heart or sweating hands if you are scared or nervous. Other physical signs of stress can include headaches, tightness in your shoulders or neck, tiredness, overeating, and irritability. Signs of emotional stress can include edginess, feelings of frustration, and crying.

Physical and emotional reactions to stress are warning signals. They could be warning you of serious problems. When you recognize signs of stress in yourself, you need to find healthy ways to reduce it.

Strategies for Coping with Stress

There is no doubt that just being a teen is stressful. You have to balance many things in your life, such as homework and tests, a changing body, parents, friends, sports, and other after-school activities. And for many teens, there are additional stressors, such as parents going through a divorce, or pressure to fit in with the "in crowd." Too much stress can take a toll on your emotional and physical health. Fortunately, you can take positive action to get a handle on stress.

SUCCEED IN SCHOOL

Manage Stress

Talk to your teacher or guidance counselor if you need help managing your stress levels. He or she may be able to teach you a set of stress reduction skills or provide resources for you to develop your own.

Michael Stuckey/Comstock/Corbis

Keep a Balance

Hobbies are important to maintaining balance in your life. *How do you keep your life balanced?*

- **Exercise regularly.** Exercise releases endorphins, your body's natural stress relievers. Take a walk, swim some laps, or ride your bike for 60 minutes each day.
- **Eat for health.** While stress may lead you to indulge in fast foods and comfort foods, such as cookies and chips, these foods do you more harm than good. Instead, keep your blood sugar stable with regular meals and healthy snacks such as fruit, yogurt, and vegetable sticks.
- **Get plenty of sleep.** When well rested, you are better able to tackle what life throws at you. Health experts recommend that teens sleep about nine hours each night.
- **Avoid caffeine.** Caffeine, which is found in chocolate and many sodas, teas, and coffee, can increase feelings of anxiety. This, in turn, can make you feel more stressed.
- **Prioritize activities.** You can reduce the number of activities you choose to do. Figure out which activities you truly enjoy and stick to only those. Make sure that the things you choose to do are those that have the highest priority.
- **Talk it out.** Talk about your problems with an adult or trusted friend. Sometimes just letting out your fears or frustrations can do wonders for your stress level.
- **Be realistic.** Do not put pressure on yourself to be perfect. After all, no one is perfect. Do your best and make a promise to yourself to accept yourself at your best, not at a level of perfection.

▲ Depression

People who suffer from depression feel alone and overwhelmed. Counselors, teachers, caring adults, and friends can help teens feel better about themselves and their life. *How would you help a friend who was suffering from depression?*

Depression

Depression is not uncommon in teens. With all of the physical, emotional, and social changes adolescence brings, many teens feel unsettled and insecure. Unrealistic academic, social, or family expectations can overwhelm teens. When things go wrong at home or school and they find themselves falling short of the high standards that have been set, many teens may feel worthless or rejected. Major events such as illness or divorce only make things worse. Recent surveys suggest that as many as one in five teens suffers from serious depression.

©Eric Simard/Alamy

Preventing Suicide

Every teen experiences a certain amount of stress, disappointment, and confusion. Sometimes these feelings can be overwhelming, causing some people to view suicide, or taking their own life, as a solution.

People who are considering suicide need help, and it is important for others to know the warning signs of suicide. Be concerned if a friend or family member who has been under stress or has been depressed says, "You won't have to worry about me anymore." This person may also display dramatic changes in personality and appearance and may give away prized personal belongings.

What can you do if you suspect someone is considering suicide? Be attentive, or pay special attention to what this person says by listening carefully and asking questions. Suggest that many problems have solutions that are not obvious at the moment. Encourage the person to get help by speaking with a counselor, a trusted adult friend, a parent, or a well-liked teacher. If the person refuses help, seek a trusted adult yourself and request help for your friend immediately. Above all, do not dismiss the person's remarks and actions as unimportant.

Section 14.1

After You Read

Review Key Concepts

1. **Describe** physical health and mental and emotional health, and how they are related to one another.
2. **Identify** the four elements of fitness that an ideal fitness program provides.
3. **List** strategies for dealing with stress.

Practice Academic Skills

English Language Arts

4. Develop a one-minute commercial designed to encourage the general public to become more fitness conscious. Videotape the commercial and present it to your class for feedback.

Social Studies

5. Health is the condition of your body and your mind and includes physical health, mental and emotional health, and social health. Write a brief essay identifying ways you can meet your needs for physical, mental, emotional, and social health.

Check Your Answers Go to connectED. mcgraw-hill.com to check your answers.

Section 14.2

Health Risks

Before You Read

What You Want to Know Write a list of what you want to know about health risks. As you read, write down the heads in this section that provide that information.

Read to Learn

Key Concepts
- **Identify** factors that influence one's weight.
- **Summarize** the negative effects of frequently abused illegal and legal drugs.
- **Describe** the potential risks associated with sexual activity.
- **Recognize** steps you can take to protect and promote your health and well-being.

Main Idea
You will be healthier if you manage your weight and abstain from drugs and sexual activity.

Content Vocabulary
◇ basal metabolic rate (BMR)
◇ anorexia nervosa
◇ bulimia nervosa
◇ addiction
◇ stimulant
◇ depressant
◇ hallucinogen
◇ anabolic steroid
◇ sexually transmitted infection (STI)
◇ abstinence
◇ acquired immunodeficiency syndrome (AIDS)

Academic Vocabulary
You will find these words in your reading and on your tests. Use the glossary to look up their definitions if necessary.
▢ acuity
▢ adverse

Graphic Organizer
As you read, record four risks related to tobacco. Use a graphic organizer like the one below to organize your information.

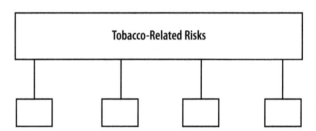

Tobacco-Related Risks

 Graphic Organizer Go to connectED.mcgraw-hill.com to download this graphic organizer.

Maintain a Healthy Weight

Your weight is not the result of any single factor. One person can eat an unbelievable amount of food every day and never seem to gain a pound, and another person may have to struggle just to stay at the same weight. Although weight management is hard work, it is important to your health. Thousands of people die each year due to poor diet and lack of physical activity (see Chapter 16). Now that is a reason to eat right and exercise!

Factors Affecting Weight

Your weight is affected by your metabolic rate, your genetic makeup, your body composition, your physical activity, and the food you eat. Each of these factors influences the number of pounds that registers when you step on a scale:

- **Your Basic Energy Needs** Your **basal metabolic rate (BMR)** is the rate at which your body uses energy when you are inactive. Your body is always working for you. It needs energy to make your heart beat, to breathe, and to keep your body warm. It also cools your body down, sends messages to your brain, and produces thousands of body chemicals. Your basal metabolism consumes about 60 percent of your body's energy needs. Adults generally use about 1,200 calories per day for body processes. Teens use more energy because they are growing.

- **Genetic Makeup** Your genetic makeup is what you inherit from your family. It helps determine your skin and hair color, your height, your size, and your body shape. Genetics also affect your basal metabolism. Remember, though, that genetics are only a part of the puzzle. You still make decisions every day about what you eat and how much you exercise.

- **Body Composition** Your body is made up of lean tissue (muscle, organs, bone and connectivie tissue) and body fat. Exercise develops muscles. Muscles burn more calories than fat tissue but take up less space. So if you develop muscles through exercise, you can improve your health and appearance.

As You Read

Connect Think about how you manage your weight. What tips would you give others to help them manage their weight?

Vocabulary

You can find definitions in the glossary at the back of this book.

Genetic Traits

Body shape and size are genetic traits. *What genetic traits have you inherited?*

Blend Images/Alamy

Math You Can Use

Finding a Healthy Weight Range

Body mass index (BMI) is a measure of body weight relative to height. William is a 16-year-old male who weighs 182 pounds and is 6 feet tall. A healthy BMI for boys in this age range is about 17 to 24. What is William's BMI? Is he in the healthy range for his age group?

Math Concept **Multi-Step Problems** When solving problems with more than one step, think through the steps before you start.

Starting Hint Use this formula to determine William's body mass index: BMI = weight (in pounds) × 703 / height (in inches)^2.

Math For math help, go to the Math Appendix at the back of the book.

- **Physical Activity** When you move your body, you use energy. Active people use more energy than inactive people. Physical activity generally accounts for 30 to 40 percent of your energy needs. When you are physically active, you increase your basal metabolic rate for at least 24 hours after exercise. While sleeping, your exercise routine is still working for you!
- **Food** Food's nutrients supply energy, so it is important to eat healthful foods, and to eat at regular times throughout the day. When you go too long without food, your body lacks the fuel it needs. People who skip meals usually make up for the missing calories by overeating later.

Eating Disorders

It is normal for teens to be concerned about their weight, but sometimes those concerns get out of control. Obsession about food, combined with mental and emotional problems, may indicate an eating disorder. Eating disorders can be identified by extreme eating behaviors that eventually cause sickness; deterioration of the body, hair, and teeth; and even death. Anorexia nervosa, bulimia nervosa, and binge eating, are the most common eating disorders.

Anorexia Nervosa **Anorexia nervosa** is a disorder characterized by self-starvation. People with this eating disorder have a strong, and often irrational, fear of being overweight. Anorexics eat little and become extremely thin, yet they still think they look fat and weigh too much.

Bulimia Nervosa People with **bulimia nervosa** eat large quantities of food in a short period of time and then purge. They may induce vomiting, abuse laxatives, or overexercise to keep from gaining weight.

Binge Eating Disorders The main symptom of binge eating disorders is compulsive overeating. People who binge may be overeating due to low self-esteem, stress, or mental or physical abuse.

Eating disorders carry a number of severe health risks, including severe dehydration, sleep problems, heart-related problems, and muscle-tone loss. They can also cause a reduction in mental acuity, or sharpness. People suffering from eating disorders need medical help and qualified counseling immediately. Although recovery takes time, early diagnosis greatly improves the chances of recovery.

Signs of Eating Disorders

People with eating disorders need help to overcome them. To identify an eating disorder, look for the following signs:

- Obsessing over weight, weight loss, calories, or food
- Chewing gum excessively
- Going to the bathroom immediately after eating
- Eating excessive amounts of food and not gaining weight
- Gaining an extreme amount of weight in a very short period of time
- Pretending to eat by moving food around on a plate
- Overexercising
- Vomiting or using laxatives
- Stealing, hiding, or hoarding food

If you recognize any of these signs in someone you care about, get help! Talk to a parent, teacher, counselor, or other trusted adult. People who develop eating disorders usually cannot get well on their own. They need medical help for a healthy recovery. This may include counseling, nutritional guidance, or a doctor's care.

✓ **Reading Check** **Paraphrase** What are eating disorders and why are they dangerous?

Drugs

Making wise decisions is a critical part of becoming an adult. It is hard enough to make certain choices when you are alert and in control. It becomes much harder if you use illegal drugs that alter your judgment.

When under the influence of drugs, people are more likely to take deadly risks and do things they will regret. Relationships with friends and family members are strained and sometimes permanently damaged. The local community can also be affected. Drug abuse is a factor in many crimes, and in increased health care costs.

Tobacco, alcohol, inhalants, stimulants, marijuana, and steroids are among the most commonly abused drugs. Although different, they all have one thing in common: These drugs affect the user's feelings, behavior, and outlook on life. They also can cause serious damage to your physical and mental health.

▼ **Self Image**

People with eating disorders often think they are overweight, even when they are not. *How could you help a friend who mistakenly thought he or she was overweight to overcome self-doubt?*

©Ted Foxx/Alamy

Community Connections

Anti-Smoking Campaign

You can help alert people to the dangers of secondhand smoke by organizing an anti-smoking campaign at your school. Students can create posters with colorful art and clever slogans about the risks of secondhand smoke. Interest local media in airing stories about your campaign.

Fun Without Alcohol

Alcohol can cause people to behave violently and irresponsibly. Friends who avoid alcohol have fun without harming themselves or others. *How do you celebrate without alcohol at a gathering?*

Tobacco

Tobacco is the number one preventable cause of death in the United States. Tobacco seems harmless enough, but it causes more deaths than illegal drugs, alcohol, motor vehicle injuries, suicides, and murders combined. Each year, more than 400,000 people die from a tobacco-related illness. Over 80 percent of these people began smoking as teenagers.

Many teens start smoking as a way to assert their independence, or fit in with a certain crowd. When so many media sources glamorize smoking, it can be hard to resist. Unfortunately, it is even harder to quit once you have started.

Consider the following risks related to tobacco:

- **Addiction** An **addiction** is a dependence upon a particular substance or action. Cigarettes, cigars, pipes, and chewing tobacco (smokeless tobacco) all contain nicotine, an addictive drug. Many tobacco users crave greater amounts of nicotine and will use more tobacco products over time.
- **Health Problems** Studies show that tobacco causes lung cancer and cancers of the throat, mouth, bladder, larynx (voice box), kidney, lung, pancreas, stomach, and others. Tobacco use is the cause of other serious health problems such as emphysema, heart disease, high blood pressure, and stroke.
- **Stress** Some people claim that smoking calms their nerves. In reality, smoking releases a substance that creates physical stress rather than relaxation.
- **Secondhand Smoke** The smoke given off by a burning cigar, cigarette, or pipe is secondhand smoke. It is a danger to your health. To promote personal health, some states have passed laws that ban smoking in public places.

SOMOS/SuperStock

TAKE CHARGE!

Saying "No"

Teens have heard the message about saying "no" to drugs for years, but good advice is useless without realistic strategies to carry it out. Here are some practical tips for staying substance-free:

- **Choose Friends Wisely** Your friends can both positively and negatively influence your life. Look for positive, confident people who do not use drugs.
- **Choose Activities Carefully** Negative peer pressure can undermine the best of intentions. Avoid places and events where you think drugs will be available.
- **Know the Facts** Knowing the dangers of drug use can strengthen your commitment to stay drug-free.
- **Find Ways to Solve Problems** Many people use drugs to escape their problems, but drug use often becomes a bigger problem than the one they tried to escape. Face problems and work out solutions. Ask your family, friends, teachers, or counselors for help if you need it.
- **Remember What Is at Stake** Remind yourself of things that you could lose by using drugs—like family, friends, or a scholarship.

Real-World Skills

Solving Problems Think about a problem faced by teens you know, such as worries about grades or family problems. Write a paragraph about how you could rely on problem-solving skills, and the support of friends and family, to find a solution to problems instead of resorting to drug use.

Alcohol

Why is it against the law for anyone under the age of 21 to drink? Alcohol consumption interferes with your natural growth and development. As a teen, you risk serious harm to your health if you drink.

Alcohol is a depressant that reaches the brain in a matter of minutes. Over time, drinking destroys brain cells, which cannot be repaired or replaced like other cells in the body. As a result, the brain cannot function properly. Body movements, speech, vision, and good judgment are dramatically altered. Recent studies show that even casual use of alcohol during adolescence can cause long-term damage to your memory, learning capacity, and attention span.

You can become addicted to alcohol more rapidly than adults do because your body is still developing. Teens who begin drinking at age 15 or younger are four times more likely to become alcoholic than those who wait until they are of legal age. Excessive use of alcohol can cause serious damage to nearly every part of your body. Heavy consumption of alcohol can lead to high blood pressure, heart disease, liver disease, and intestinal cancer.

People have many ways of persuading you to drink. They may tell you that everyone's doing it, or that drinking will make you look cool. They may say that drinking will help you relax and forget your problems. The truth is that drinking can cause you to look foolish. It cannot help you deal with problems. Problems remain after the alcohol has worn off.

Inhalants

An inhalant is a substance with dangerous fumes that are sniffed to produce a mind-altering high. More than a thousand household and commercial products can be abused by sniffing or "huffing." Huffing is inhaling through the mouth. Glue, hair spray, nail polish, and spray paints are a few examples of inhalants.

What is wrong with inhaling these products? Inhalants contain volatile solvents that starve your body of oxygen, which causes your heart to beat more rapidly. Sniffing highly concentrated inhalants can cause dizziness, headaches, vomiting, loss of coordination, memory loss, and even heart failure or death.

Illegal Drugs

Illegal drugs are not prescribed for medical purposes, and they are dangerous to use. They can have adverse, or harmful, psychological effects (confusion, depression, or anxiety) and physical effects (blurred vision, tremors, sweating, or chills). Taking illegal drugs gives an intense sensation or "rush," which lasts only a short time. However, the long-term effects are serious. To maintain that rush, you need more drugs, more often. You become mentally and physically addicted.

It is illegal to buy, sell, or possess some drugs no matter how old you are. If a person is found guilty of an illegal drug charge, he or she can be suspended from school, placed under court supervision, or sent to jail. You have to ask yourself, is it worth the physical damage, the psychological problems, and the legal consequences?

▼ **Effects of Drug Use**

When friends choose to sell and use drugs, you may have to choose new friends. *How might this teen's life be affected if he stays friends with teens who use drugs?*

Aaron Roeth Photography

Stimulants A **stimulant** increases a person's heart rate, speeds up the central nervous system, increases breathing rates, and raises blood pressure. Illegal stimulants include cocaine, crack cocaine, methamphetamines, and ecstasy. They give a short-term rush followed by a crash, or sense of coming down.

Depressants A **depressant** reduces blood pressure and slows heart and breathing rates. It results in a loss of coordination, poor attention span, mood changes, and extreme anxiety. Examples of depressants include barbiturates, such as sleeping pills and tranquilizers, such as anxiety-reducing drugs.

Marijuana Marijuana is a drug made from the hemp plant. It is the most commonly used illicit drug in the United States. There are numerous street names for marijuana, including pot, weed, grass, ganja, and reed. Marijuana is rapidly absorbed by the body and has dangerous effects. The short-term effects of marijuana use include loss of motivation, memory loss, and learning difficulties. Long-term use can lead to serious health problems, such as lung cancer.

Hallucinogens A **hallucinogen** is a street drug that distorts the user's thoughts, moods, and senses. PCP and LSD are hallucinogens. Hallucinogens change the way your brain functions and can affect your self-control. People under the influence of hallucinogens may think they are hearing voices, seeing images, or feeling sensations that do not really exist. Hallucinogens can cause heart and lung failure and induce a coma.

Anabolic Steroids An **anabolic steroid** is a manufactured substance that alters body characteristics. Anabolic refers to muscle building, and steroids are simply a class of drugs. Athletes and others have abused anabolic steroids to enhance performance and to improve their physical appearance. The major side effects of abusing anabolic steroids include cancer, increased aggressiveness, and severe mood swings.

Prescription and Over-the-Counter Drugs

Prescription and over-the-counter (OTC) drugs are beneficial in treating many health conditions. OTC drugs are those sold without a prescription. Everyone responds to these drugs differently. That is why it is important to follow your doctor's and pharmacist's directions for prescription and OTC drugs. What can you do to avoid misusing medicine?

- **Stay away from others' medications.** Do not use a drug prescribed for someone else. You do not know how your body will react to it.
- **Follow the directions.** Take the amount prescribed by your doctor or the dosage listed on the OTC drug label, not more or less. If you are taking a prescription, use all of the medicine.

- **Never mix drugs and alcohol.** Drugs, even OTC drugs, should never be mixed with alcohol. Alcohol can severely change the beneficial effects of any drug and cause serious physical harm.
- **Obtain a doctor's approval for supplements.** OTC products such as diet pills and herbal supplements can also be dangerous to your health. These products should not be used unless advised by your doctor.

Detect Drug Abuse

Drugs affect the lives of many people and may affect one of your friends or family members. Drug abuse may be a problem if someone you care about is:

- Acting strangely or showing erratic behavior.
- In trouble at school or work.
- In conflict with family and friends.
- Hanging around with others who use drugs.
- Not taking care of his or her responsibilities.
- Letting go of activities, friendships, and hobbies.

▲ Over-the-Counter Drugs

Read all information on boxes, bottles, and inserts of OTC products and note any side effects. *Why is it important to read all the information with OTC products?*

Reaching Out for Help

Alcohol and drug abuse can and should be treated. There are many kinds of addictions, and many communities offer counseling services, support groups, treatment services, and interventionists to help people beat their addictions and change their lives. Organizations such as Alcoholics Anonymous, Alateen, and Al-Anon help alcohol users and their family and friends. Narcotics Anonymous is helpful to people dealing with drug abuse, and Gamblers Anonymous can help those with a gambling addiction. People struggling with food addictions can contact Overeaters Anonymous.

Drug treatment centers offer a safe place to withdraw from drug use. Some of these centers provide medications to help with the physical and psychological effects of withdrawal. Drug counselors can also help people adjust to a life without drugs. Some counselors use behavioral change strategies to help a person become drug-free.

✓ **Reading Check** **Describe** What are the signs that someone you care about is abusing drugs?

Sex-Related Risks

Giving in to sexual pressures as a teen can have serious emotional and physical consequences. Those who engage in sexual activity too soon may develop low self-esteem, trust issues, or have difficulty committing in future relationships. Sexual activity can also be physically harmful, resulting in an unheathy pregnancy, sexually transmitted infection, or HIV and AIDS.

Sexually Transmitted Diseases

A **sexually transmitted infection (STI)** is an illness passed from one person to another through sexual contact. STIs are also referred to as sexually transmitted diseases, or STDs. There are numerous STIs, including chlamydia, gonorrhea, syphilis, pelvic inflammatory disease, human papillomavirus (HPV) and herpes. Symptoms and complications range from feelings of discomfort to permanent physical or mental damage, and sometimes death. Symptoms are not always obvious, and if symptoms do appear, they may be confused with symptoms of other diseases. Some people transmit STIs because they do not realize they have an infection.

Though some STIs can be treated with antibiotics, others, like herpes, have no cure. Your body cannot build up immunity (resistance) to STIs. The only way to be absolutely certain you will not contract an STI is to practice abstinence from sexual activity. **Abstinence** is a deliberate decision to avoid high-risk behaviors, including sexual activity and the use of tobacco, alcohol, and other drugs. An important benefit of abstinence is that you maintain a healthy sense of self-respect. Abstinence puts you in charge of your body and your future.

Abstinence

True friends will understand your choice to abstain from sexual activity *How might your choice affect your friends' choices?*

Hero/Corbis/Glow Images

AIDS and HIV

Acquired immunodeficiency syndrome (AIDS) is a life-threatening STI that interferes with the body's natural ability to fight infection. The virus that causes AIDS is called the human immuno-deficiency virus (HIV). This virus invades and kills the cells of the immune system. The body then has no way to defend itself from other life-threatening infections and diseases.

The U.S. Centers for Disease Control and Prevention (CDC) esti-mates that about 1 million people in the United States are living with HIV or AIDS. About 40,000 new cases occur each year.

HIV is spread from one person to another by the exchange of body fluids during sexual activity. It is also transmitted by unclean needles. HIV has been spreading rapidly among teens. HIV carriers do not always show symptoms, so you cannot identify who does or does not have the disease. Also, because there is a time lag between initial infection with HIV and the onset of AIDS, an infected teen may not show signs of AIDS until he or she is 20 years old or older. For your own protection, it is important to guard against HIV and AIDS by avoiding illegal drugs and by practicing sexual abstinence.

There is no cure for AIDS, so it is in your best interest to become knowledgeable about it. You can obtain information about HIV, AIDS, and other STIs from the CDC, state health departments, and commu-nity health organizations.

Negative Effects of Early Pregnancy

Teen pregnancy can create harmful health risks for both young mothers and their children. A teen girl's body is still developing and may not be able to support and nourish an unborn child. Many preg-nant teens receive inadequate prenatal care, or care received dur-ing pregnancy. Their children are often born with low birth weights, which can lead to health problems later on, as well as other physical and mental disabilities. The majority of teenage mothers are unmar-ried, which often creates emotional and financial problems for young children and their mothers.

Many teen parents choose to keep their babies, despite a lack of money, education, and emotional maturity. Raising children is a major challenge for mature adults. For teens, the demands of parent-ing are overwhelming and can negatively affect the rest of their lives. Many teen mothers and fathers are unable to pursue their education, which would open doors to higher-paying jobs. While their friends are enjoying the freedom and fun of being teenagers, teen parents often feel trapped by having become parents too soon.

✓ **Reading Check** **Identify** What is HIV and how is it related to AIDS?

Your Health Is in Your Hands

Who is ultimately responsible for your health? Your family? Your doctor? The answer is you. To do the best job possible, it is important to stay informed about good health practices and strategies for avoiding the dangers you will confront.

Health and Wellness Resources

Everyone has health-related concerns or questions from time to time. Government and community resources can provide you with health and wellness information to help guide your decisions. You can obtain reliable health maintenance information by checking with your doctor or searching Web sites and publications from government agencies, such as the U.S. Food and Drug Administration and the U.S. Department of Health and Human Services.

Professional health organizations, such as the American Medical Association, the American Heart Association, and the American Cancer Society, also help people understand different health issues. Community-level organizations, such as health clinics and your own doctor, are local resources you can use to keep your life on a healthy track.

Influence

You are more influential than you may think. *How might your behavior affect your friends?*

Image Source

Avoiding Health Risks

What can you do to avoid high-risk behaviors? Try to develop friendships with people who share your interests and values and who will not pressure you into sexual activity or drug use. Consider joining a school service organization, or pursue your interests in sports or the arts. Keep in mind that when you are busy doing positive things, risky activities seem less appealing.

There are refusal strategies that you can use to help you live by your values. You can use these tips in any situation that feels wrong to you:

- Say "no" in a firm voice.
- Explain why by saying you feel the activity goes against your values or beliefs.
- Offer safe, healthful alternatives to the situation.
- Stand your ground. Make it clear that you will not back down.
- Leave. If the other person continues to pressure you, simply walk away.

Taking a firm stand to protect yourself against the dangerous effects of high-risk behaviors is one of the most important things you can do in your life. By doing so, you show that you value your health, wellness, and self.

Section 14.2

After You Read

Review Key Concepts

1. **Explain** why it is important to maintain a healthy weight.
2. **Recall** the reasons alcohol consumption is especially dangerous for teens.
3. **Describe** the physical, mental, and emotional effects of teen pregnancy.
4. **Identify** choices you can make to avoid high-risk behaviors.

Check Your Answers Go to connectED. mcgraw-hill.com to check your answers.

Practice Academic Skills

English Language Arts

5. Use reliable print and online resources to learn about the AIDS epidemic in Africa. In what ways is the international community addressing the problem? What medical advancements have been made? Summarize your findings in a brief report.

Social Studies

6. Your genetic makeup is what you inherit from your family. Explain how your genetic makeup affects your weight. How can your sense of self be affected by your genetic makeup?

CHAPTER SUMMARY

Section 14.1
Staying Healthy and Fit

Physical, mental and emotional health are all inter-related. You can take active measures to promote your wellness. A good personal care routine is important to your health. Forming good nutrition and exercise habits now can benefit you throughout your lifetime. Regular checkups are an important part of maintaining your physical health. There are many strategies for coping with stress. If you suffer from extreme depression, seek help immediately.

Section 14.2
Health Risks

Understand the factors that determine weight to manage your weight more effectively. Eating disorders result in severe health problems. Drugs have many negative physical and psychological effects. STIs can cause serious physical and mental harm. Teen pregnancy is unhealthy for both mother and child. Abstinence is the only guaranteed way to avoid STIs and the risk of pregnancy. Refusing risky activities shows others that you respect your health and yourself.

Vocabulary Review

1. Use at least five of these content and academic vocabulary terms in a short essay about personal hygiene.

Content Vocabulary
◇ wellness (p. 331)
◇ grooming (p. 332)
◇ acne (p. 333)
◇ dandruff (p. 334)
◇ plaque (p. 335)
◇ stress (p. 341)
◇ basal metabolic rate (BMR) (p. 345)

◇ anorexia nervosa (p. 346)
◇ bulimia nervosa (p. 346)
◇ addiction (p. 348)
◇ stimulant (p. 351)
◇ depressant (p. 351)
◇ hallucinogen (p. 351)
◇ anabolic steroid (p. 351)
◇ sexually transmitted infection (STI) (p. 353)

◇ abstinence (p. 353)
◇ acquired immunodeficiency syndrome (AIDS) (p. 354)

Academic Vocabulary
■ vigorous (p. 338)
■ attentive (p. 343)
■ acuity (p. 346)
■ adverse (p. 350)

Review Key Concepts

2. **Describe** the two major categories of health.
3. **Identify** five factors in physical health.
4. **Explain** the causes and effects of emotional stress.
5. **Identify** factors that influence one's weight.
6. **Summarize** the negative effects of frequently abused illegal and legal drugs.
7. **Describe** the potential risks associated with sexual activity.
8. **Recognize** steps you can take to protect and promote your health and well-being.

Critical Thinking

9. **Predict** You plan to address a group about the importance of establishing good lifelong health practices. What will you say to influence their behavior both now and in the future?
10. **Compare** Imagine two people, one with good grooming practices, and one with poor grooming practices. What effects do poor grooming practices have on a person's life?
11. **Make Connections** In addition to fear of being overweight, suggest other reasons people might develop eating disorders. How can our society help prevent eating disorders?

ACTIVE LEARNING

12. Product Warnings Many household products are dangerous if inhaled. Doing so may cause dizziness, headaches, vomiting, loss of coordination, memory loss, and even heart failure or death. Follow your teacher's instructions to form groups. Research the dangers of household chemicals, using reliable print or Internet sources. These dangers may result from inhaling the chemicals, drinking them, or even touching them. Using art supplies or computer graphics software, create a poster that warns young children about the dangers of household chemicals. When you are finished, present your poster to your class and ask if any of your classmates can think of alternatives to the potentially dangerous chemicals included on your poster.

Family & Community Connections

13. Attitudes About Steroids Some people, such as professional athletes, have abused anabolic steroids to enhance their performance and to improve their physical appearance. However, anabolic steroids can have serious side effects. Use of steroids may cause cancer, increased aggressiveness, and severe mood swings. As steroids have such harmful possible side effects, those who choose to use steroids do so at a great risk. Interview a local gym owner, a sports coach, an athletic director, or some of your classmates who are athletes to find out their knowledge and attitudes about steroids. Ask them what they know about the dangers of using steroids and what they think about steroid use. Write a short article based on your findings. When you are finished, share your article with the class.

Real-World Skills and Applications

Leadership Skills

14. Show Your Concern Imagine a friend has written you telling you he has been taking steroids in order to enhance his performance on the baseball team. You became concerned because of what you have heard about steroids. Write a letter to him explaining your concerns and offering alternatives to his steroid use.

Financial Literacy

15. Hygiene Expenses Suppose you use one bottle of shampoo per month. You have a coupon to get one bottle of shampoo free for every ten you buy. Each bottle costs $7.45. You use one bottle of conditioner every two months. Each bottle of conditioner costs $8.99, but you have no coupons for them. How much money will you spend on shampoo and conditioner in one year?

Technology Skills

16. Exercise Technology Use reliable print or Internet sources to research heart rate monitors. Look for information about what heart rate monitors do as well as how they can be helpful in keeping you fit. Research the various models available, their special features, and their prices. When you are finished, share your information with the rest of the class.

Academic Skills

English Language Arts

17. Create a Guide Cleanliness is vital for your health and appearance. In addition to your hair and teeth, you should also keep your skin clean. Create a how-to pamphlet explaining proper skin care techniques for teens. Include information about available skin care products and their use.

Science

18. Safe Cleaning Options Many household cleaners can be dangerous. Use this experiment to try a safe alternative to the cleaners many people use.

Procedure Pour ¼ cup of white vinegar and 1 teaspoon of salt into a bowl. Dip a penny halfway in the solution for 20 seconds.

Analysis What happens to the penny? Briefly describe the results.

Mathematics

19. Compare Ratios Suppose that a class of 25 students begins to exercise daily. Of the 25 students, 16 begin to get higher grades. A different class of 22 students begins to exercise daily, but only 10 begin to get higher grades. Is the ratio of students in the first class with improved grades to total students equal to the same ratio in the second class?

 Ratio A ratio is a comparison of two numbers. You can write the two numbers in a ratio separated by a colon, such as 16:25. You can also show the two numbers in a ratio as a fraction, such as $^{16}/_{25}$.

Starting Hint To compare two ratios, first write the ratios as fractions. Then cross multiply the fractions. The fractions are equal if their cross products are equal.

For math help, go to the Math Appendix at the back of the book.

Standardized Test Practice

MULTIPLE-CHOICE QUESTIONS
Directions Read the question. Then, choose the correct answer.

Test-Taking Tip Once you choose an answer for a multiple-choice question, do not change it unless you misread the question. Your first choice is usually the correct one.

20. Which of the following is a type of hallucinogen?
a) marijuana
b) PCP
c) alcohol
d) tobacco

Manage Yourself

In this project you will create a report card for yourself that evaluates the areas in your life that you manage well, and where you have room for improvement.

My Journal

If you completed the journal entry from page 296, refer to it to see if your thoughts have changed after reading the unit.

Project Assignment

In this project you will:
- Reflect on the different areas of your life and your management skills for each one.
- Identify and interview an adult in your community who helps to manage other people, whether professionally or personally.
- Prepare a report card for yourself on your management skills.

The Skills Behind the Project

Life Skills

Key personal and relationship skills you will use in this project include:
- Practicing self-awareness.
- Making healthy choices.
- Gathering and consolidating information.

STEP 1 Analyze Your Life-Management Skills

Use the information in the chapters as well as independent reflection to analyze your ability to manage these areas of your life:
- Being a responsible consumer
- Managing your money
- Living with technology
- Your physical health
- Your emotional and social health

Write a summary of your self evaluation to:
- Identify specific areas in your life where you believe you excel.
- List the specific areas where you are challenged.
- Explain why you think these specific areas may be challenging to you.
- Describe steps you can take to improve your habits.

Analytical Skills
- Research and gather information.
- Use facts and personal reflection to identify your strengths and weaknesses.
- Ask thoughtful interview questions.

STEP 2 Write Interview Questions

Identify a person in your community who helps people to manage their lives. This person

Life Skills Project Checklist

Plan	☑ Use independent thinking and the information in the unit to analyze your life management abilities.
	☑ Interview an adult in your community and write a summary of what you learned.
	☑ Create a report card for yourself that evaluates your life management skills.
Present	☑ Make a presentation to discuss what you learned about life management.
	☑ Invite the students in your class to ask you any questions they may have. Answer these questions.
	☑ When students ask you questions, demonstrate in your answers that you respect their perspectives.
	☑ Turn in the summary of your research, your interview notes, and your report card.
Academic Skills	☑ Use research to gather information.
	☑ Communicate effectively.
	☑ Adapt and modify language to suit different purposes.

can be a counselor, life coach, financial planner, technology expert, nutritionist, personal trainer, or anyone else in your neighborhood who works with people to manage their lives. Arrange to interview that person. Then write interview questions about strategies for managing your life.

STEP 3 Connect to Your Community

Interview the person in your community you have chosen in Step 2. Ask this person about the skills he or she uses to be successful. Share the summary you wrote and ask for advice on how to build on your strengths and improve your weaknesses. Take notes during the interview, and write a summary of the interview.

Listening Skills
- Make eye contact.
- Ask additional questions to ensure your understanding.
- React appropriately to humor, interesting facts, and personal anecdotes.

STEP 4 Create Your Own Report Card

Use the Life Skills Project Checklist to plan and create your report card to share what you have learned with your classmates.

STEP 5 Evaluate Your Life Skills and Academic Skills

Your project will be evaluated based on:
- Content and organization of your information.
- Objectivity about yourself.
- Mechanics–presentation and neatness.
- Quality of writing.

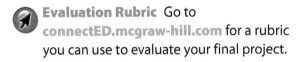
Evaluation Rubric Go to **connectED.mcgraw-hill.com** for a rubric you can use to evaluate your final project.

Food and Nutrition

Chapter 15   How Nutrients Work

Chapter 16   Guidelines for Healthy Eating

Chapter 17   Meal Planning

Unit Life Skills Project Preview

Research Food Choices

In this unit you will learn about food and nutrition. In your unit thematic project you will create a visual representation that shows foods with varying degrees of nutrient density.

 My Journal

Reflect On Your Eating Habits Write a journal entry about one of these topics. This will help you prepare for the unit project at the end of the unit.

- Describe your favorite meal and explain why you enjoy it.
- List three to five fast food items you eat regularly, and give suggestions for healthy substitutions.
- Imagine that food can talk, and stage a debate between an apple and a bag of potato chips about which is the better snack and why.

Explore the Photo

Many activities have unhealthy foods associated with them. *What are some ways that you can enjoy those activities while remaining healthy?*

Chapter 15

How Nutrients Work

Section 15.1
Nutrients at Work

Section 15.2
The Process of Digestion

Chapter Objectives

Section 15.1
- **List** the three primary nutrient functions.
- **Describe** the two types of carbohydrates.
- **Summarize** the role of proteins in the body.
- **Identify** three main types of fat and in which foods they are found.
- **Explain** why vitamins, minerals, phytochemicals, and water are essential nutrients.

Section 15.2
- **Describe** the process of digestion.
- **Relate** calorie intake to energy.
- **Compare** the effects of nutrient-rich foods to nutrient-deficient foods.

▲ **Explore the Photo**

Eating nutritious food is a good way to stay healthy. *What kinds of nutritious foods do you enjoy eating?*

Purestock/SuperStock

Writing Activity

Write an Explanation

Nutrients Nutrients are an essential part of a healthy diet and a healthy body. Your body relies on nutrients for energy and growth. Healthful foods like whole grains, fruits, vegetables, milk, meat, beans, and oils contain the nutrients your body needs. Briefly scan Section 15.1. Then, write an explanation that describes how eating nutritious foods can benefit your health.

Writing Tips Use these tips to write an explanation:
- Take notes about how nutrients help your body function as you skim the section.
- Remember, your paper should answer the question, "Why are nutrients important?"
- Strengthen your explanation by mentioning what might happen if your body does *not* get the nutrients it needs.

Nutrients at Work

Before You Read

Preview Read the boldface words and main headings. Write one or two sentences predicting what you think the section will be about.

Read to Learn

Key Concepts

- **List** the three primary nutrient functions.
- **Describe** the two types of carbohydrates.
- **Summarize** the role of proteins in the body.
- **Identify** three main types of fat and in which foods they are found.
- **Explain** why vitamins, minerals, phytochemicals, and water are essential nutrients.

Main Idea

The human body needs a variety of nutrients to function effectively.

Content Vocabulary

- ◇ nutrient
- ◇ carbohydrate
- ◇ fiber
- ◇ protein
- ◇ amino acids
- ◇ complete protein
- ◇ incomplete protein
- ◇ cholesterol
- ◇ high-density lipoprotein
- ◇ low-density lipoprotein
- ◇ phytochemicals

Academic Vocabulary

You will find these words in your reading and on your tests. Use the glossary to look up their definitions if necessary.

- ▢ minute
- ▢ trace

Graphic Organizer

As you read, record the six categories of nutrients. Use a graphic organizer like the one below to organize your information.

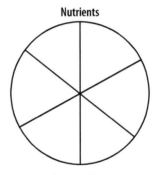

Nutrients

 Graphic Organizer Go to **connectED.mcgraw-hill.com** to download this graphic organizer.

Nutrients

Think about how you feel today. Do you feel energized? Are you alert and able to concentrate in class? If so, you can thank the food you ate this morning or at lunch. You can also credit your diet with the condition of your hair and skin. Your body relies on the nutrients found in food for good health and proper functioning. When you are well nourished, you tend to feel better, grow properly, and perform at your best.

A substance found in food that keeps your body in good working order is called a **nutrient**. Your body needs nutrients for energy. Nutrients are also necessary for growth and to repair your body's cells. Finally, nutrients help your body maintain basic functions, such as digestion, blood circulation, and breathing.

Scientists have identified more than 40 nutrients that are essential for good health. Each of these nutrients performs a different task. Though some nutrients cannot effectively perform their tasks without the presence of other nutrients, no single nutrient can do the work of another. Nutrients work together as a team to keep you alert and help your body systems run smoothly.

Nutrients are grouped into six categories: carbohydrates, proteins, fats, vitamins, minerals, and water. Each nutrient category has unique functions. Some nutrients do not work without the presence of others. For example, calcium in milk cannot be absorbed by your body without vitamin D.

✓ Reading Check **Generalize** How do nutrients work independently and together?

As You Read

Connect Think about how you feel after eating certain foods. Which foods make you feel healthy and energized? What nutrients are in these foods?

◆ **Vocabulary**

You can find definitions in the glossary at the back of this book.

Think Color

Vegetables and fruits of different colors contain different important nutrients. Be sure to eat a variety. *What kinds of fruits and vegetables do you and your family eat?*

xefstock/Getty Images

Tame Your Sweet Tooth

Most people enjoy sweets. Cookies, cakes, and other high-calorie, high-fat desserts contribute to weight gain though. When you crave a sweet treat, try one of the following low-calorie options:

- **Fresh and Fruity Parfaits** Try layering sliced fruit with a sugar-free, flavored gelatin.
- **Low-Fat or Fat-Free Yogurt** Either plain or topped with fresh fruit, this snack will give you protein and calcium.
- **Fruit Smoothies** Use different combinations of your favorite fruits and fruit juices to make a nutritious and tasty treat!
- **Low-Fat Fig Cookies** Try these sweet-tasting, fruit-filled snacks when you crave a cookie.

Real-World Skills

Try It Follow your teacher's instructions to form into pairs. Then, brainstorm other low-calorie sweet treats that you can eat. Try using the options listed, as well as any you and your partner came up with, the next time you crave a sweet treat. Remember to note how your cravings change after you have had the low-calorie sweets.

Carbohydrates

A **carbohydrate** is a nutrient that provides your body with most of its energy. The two main types of carbohydrates are simple carbohydrates and complex carbohydrates. Sugars, which are simple carbohydrates, can be either natural or refined. Refined sugar is sugar that has been removed from its plant source. Candy and soft drinks contain refined sugar, but most do not provide you with other nutrients. Fruits, vegetables, and milk contain natural sugars, as well as other important nutrients.

Starches are complex carbohydrates that are broken down into single sugars when digested. These are used to make energy. Breads, cereals, pasta, rice, dry beans, and some vegetables, such as potatoes and corn, contain starch and other nutrients.

Many complex carbohydrates also contain **fiber**, or plant material that does not break down during digestion. Although fiber is not a nutrient, it is an important part of healthful eating. Insoluble fiber comes from grains. It helps move food through the body and helps eliminate waste. Soluble fiber, which is found in fruit and other foods containing pectin, helps reduce the risk of heart disease.

Where can you find fiber? The cereal you ate this morning probably contains some fiber, as do the fruits and vegetables you ate with lunch or as a snack. Other sources of fiber include whole-grain bread, oatmeal, whole-wheat crackers, and popcorn.

✓ **Reading Check** **Recall** What is a carbohydrate, and what types of food are carbohydrates?

Proteins

Think about your muscles, hair, skin, and nails. What do they have in common? What feature do they share with your vital organs? The answer: they are all made of protein. The nutrient used to build, maintain, and repair body tissues is called a **protein**. Protein is especially important during your teen years to help you grow and develop.

Protein foods are made up of chemical compounds called **amino acids**, which are known as the body's building blocks. Every type of protein food contains a different combination of amino acids that helps your body function. Your body makes all but nine of the amino acids that you need. Those nine are called essential amino acids. Because your body cannot make these amino acids, the food you eat has to supply them.

A food from an animal source that has all nine of the essential amino acids your body needs is called a **complete protein**. Meat, fish, poultry, milk products, eggs, and other foods from animal sources are complete proteins. Foods from soybeans, such as tofu, are also complete proteins.

An **incomplete protein** lacks one or more of the nine essential amino acids. Plant foods such as grains, dry beans and peas, nuts, seeds, and vegetables contain incomplete proteins. Eating a variety of foods from plant sources daily can provide all the essential amino acids you need, however.

Some incomplete proteins work together to form complete proteins. For example, when eaten together, beans and rice form a complete protein. You can also make complete proteins by combining a complete and an incomplete protein. For example, when you eat milk with your cereal, the complete proteins in the milk fill in for the missing amino acids in the cereal. To make sure that your body gets enough complete proteins, you should eat a wide variety of foods each day.

> ✓ **Reading Check**
>
> **Describe** What are amino acids, and how does your body obtain them?

Pixtal/AGE Fotostock

Food Banks

Each of us has some control over eating a healthful diet. Help improve menu choices for others in your community by donating food items to your local food bank. If possible, organize a school-wide food drive to collect items for the food bank.

▼ **Complete Proteins**

Protein can be found in a wide variety of animal sources and some vegetable sources. *Which of these foods provide complete proteins? Which of these foods do you eat on a regular basis?*

Fats

Though eating too much solid fat can increase your risk for heart disease, a small amount of fat is vital to good health. Fats help regulate body temperature, cushion vital organs, and provide substances your body needs for normal growth and healthy skin. Fats are the most concentrated form of food energy you eat, and they store your body's energy for you to use later. Fat works as a partner with other nutrients in your food. Some vitamins need to dissolve in fat before they can be carried to other parts of the body that need them.

Foods such as butter, margarine, sour cream, and salad oil are fats you can easily see. Fats you may not see as easily are called hidden fats and are found in meat, fish, egg yolks, whole milk, cheese, nuts, and processed foods such as doughnuts. There are three main types of fat: saturated fat, unsaturated fat, and trans fat.

Saturated Fats

Saturated fats are solid at room temperature and should be used sparingly. You can find saturated fats in animal foods, such as meat, poultry, egg yolks, and whole-milk dairy products. Saturated fats are also found in tropical oils, such as coconut and palm oil. Saturated fats raise the level of harmful cholesterol in your blood. This increase in cholesterol can lead to heart health issues.

Unsaturated Fats

Unsaturated fats are liquid at room temperature and can be found mainly in vegetable, olive, and nut oils. Avocados, nuts, and olives also have unsaturated fat. Try to use these fats instead of saturated fats in your cooking. Unsaturated fats actually help *lower* the cholesterol level in your blood. Omega-3 is an unsaturated fatty acid that is especially good for your heart. You can find it in salmon and other fatty fish, walnuts, and canola oil.

Unsaturated and Saturated Fats

Try to limit the amount of saturated, or solid, fats you eat. *What substitutions can you make for the saturated fats shown here?*

John Thoeming/McGraw-Hill Education

Trans Fats

Food manufacturers can turn liquid oils into solid ones. This process is called hydrogenation (hī-ˌdrä-jə-ˈnā-shən). Stick margarine, for example, is made from hydrogenated vegetable oil. Hydrogenation forms trans-fatty acids, also known as trans fats. Trans fats can be found in some vegetable shortenings, French fries, doughnuts, fried foods, salad dressings, and many processed foods, such as crackers and cookies. If you see the words *hydrogenated*, *partially hydrogenated*, or *vegetable shortening* on a food label, this means the product contains trans fat. Though they are made from unsaturated fats, trans fats function like saturated fats in the body. They tend to raise blood cholesterol levels and have been linked to heart disease.

Cholesterol

Cholesterol is a soft, fat-like, waxy substance found in the bloodstream and in all of your body's cells. Despite its bad reputation, it is needed for several important bodily functions. Cholesterol aids in digesting fat, making vitamin D, building cells, and building some hormones.

Cholesterol travels in your bloodstream with proteins. Together, they form two types of lipoproteins. **High-density lipoprotein** (HDL) is often called good cholesterol. It removes any excess cholesterol from your blood and artery walls and takes it to your liver, where it cannot harm your body. **Low-density lipoprotein** (LDL) is often called bad cholesterol. This is because too much of it can build up on the walls of your arteries, which carry blood and oxygen to the heart. If enough cholesterol builds up, it clogs the arteries so blood and oxygen cannot reach the heart, causing a heart attack. High cholesterol also causes stroke and high blood pressure.

Your liver makes all the cholesterol your body needs. You get additional cholesterol from some foods, however. All foods from animal sources contain cholesterol. Fruits, vegetables, and foods from other plant sources do not have any cholesterol.

The fat you eat also has an effect on your blood cholesterol levels. This is because the liver uses fats as fuel to make cholesterol. Each type of fat affects cholesterol in a different way. Saturated fats and trans fats tend to raise the level of LDL (bad) cholesterol in the bloodstream. Unsaturated fats may lower LDL (bad) cholesterol and raise levels of HDL (good) cholesterol in the bloodstream. This is why it is important to check the fat content on nutrition labels and limit the saturated and trans fats in your eating plan.

✓ **Reading Check**) **Conclude** How can fats help the body?

Vitamin Supplements

Vitamin supplements are not a substitute for good nutrition. *Why might vitamin supplements not be a substitute for good nutrition?*

Building Character ?!

Willpower José and his friends go out for pizza after seeing a movie. José has been dieting successfully for two weeks and planned to hit the salad bar. But his friends order a large sausage and pepperoni pizza and he is tempted by the flavorful aroma. Plus, he skipped the buttered popcorn at the movies, so he is really hungry. What steps, if any, can José take to strengthen his willpower?

You Make the Call

Should José break his diet, just for today? Or should he stick to his diet and his weight-loss goal by having salad? How can he fight the temptation to break his diet?

Essential Elements

Vitamins and minerals are micronutrients. This means that only **minute** (mī-¹nüt), or very small, amounts are needed for normal body function. Though a little goes a long way with most vitamins and minerals, they are just as essential to your health and wellness as carbohydrates, fats, and protein. In fact, without vitamins and minerals, carbohydrates, proteins, and fats could not do their work.

Vitamins

Vitamins trigger many of your body processes. They function like spark plugs in an engine by setting off chemical reactions in your body's cells. Each vitamin regulates a different process. Their roles are very specific, and one cannot substitute for another. Your body requires a variety of vitamins each day, and generally you get all the vitamins you need when you eat an assortment of healthful foods. If vitamins are consistently absent, cellular slowdowns and other problems will eventually affect the way your body operates. Vitamins fit into two categories:

Fat-Soluble Vitamins Vitamins A, D, E, and K are absorbed with the help of fats. Your body can store fat-soluble vitamins. However, too much of these vitamins can be harmful to your health. For example, too much vitamin D can cause nausea, confusion, weight loss, and muscle weakness. See **Figure 15.1**.

Water-Soluble Vitamins Vitamin C and the B vitamins dissolve in water and easily pass out of the body as waste. You need a frequent supply of these vitamins, but, again, too much at once may be harmful. Water-soluble vitamins are shown in **Figure 15.2** on page 373.

Figure 15.1 **Fat-Soluble Vitamins**

A Variety of Vitamins The key to good nutrition is to eat a variety of foods.
How do you get a variety of healthy foods in your diet?

Vitamin	Where It Is Found	What It Does
Vitamin A	Dark green, leafy vegetables (spinach, kale); deep yellow and orange fruits and vegetables (cantaloupe, carrots, sweet potatoes, apricots); liver; milk, cheese, and eggs	Helps keep skin and hair healthy; aids night vision; builds strong bones and teeth
Vitamin D	Milk that has been fortified with vitamin D, egg yolks, salmon, liver	Helps build strong bones and teeth; helps the body use calcium and phosphorus
Vitamin E	Whole-grain breads and cereals; dark green, leafy vegetables; dry beans and peas; nuts and seeds; vegetable oils, margarine; liver	Helps form red blood cells, muscles, and other tissues
Vitamin K	Dark green, leafy vegetables; cabbage	Helps blood to clot

Figure 15.2 | Water-Soluble Vitamins

Water at Work Make sure to drink water when you eat foods that contain water-soluble vitamins. *What water-soluble vitamins did your breakfast foods provide today?*

Vitamin	Where It Is Found	What It Does
B-complex vitamins (riboflavin, niacin, B_6, B_{12}, thiamine)	Whole-grain and enriched breads and cereals; dry beans and peas; peanut butter; nuts; meat, poultry, and fish; eggs and milk	Helps the body use carbohydrates, fats, and proteins; helps produce energy in cells; helps maintain healthy nervous system, muscles, and tissues
Folate	Fruits; enriched and whole wheat breads; dark green, leafy vegetables; liver; dry beans and peas	Helps build red blood cells and DNA
Vitamin C	Citrus fruits (oranges, grapefruit, etc.), strawberries, broccoli, tomatoes, potatoes	Helps maintain bones, teeth, and blood vessels; helps heal wounds

Minerals

Like vitamins, minerals also have certain jobs to perform. Minerals are an essential part of your bones, teeth, and internal organs, and they help regulate body functions. To work efficiently, your body needs at least 16 minerals each day. Your body needs trace, or very small, amounts of some minerals and larger amounts of others. When you eat a variety of foods every day, you usually get the minerals you need.

Calcium is an especially important mineral for teens because it helps teens develop strong bones and teeth. Most of the body's calcium is stored in your bones. Bone mass accumulates rapidly when you are a teen, creating a strong bone structure. Many people who do not get enough calcium when they are young risk developing osteoporosis, or brittle bones, later in life. It is important that you get enough calcium now so that your bones remain strong for a lifetime. Drinking milk and eating milk products is a good way to get the right amount of calcium. See **Figure 15.3** on page 374.

Iron is also an important mineral. It helps red blood cells carry oxygen to your cells. Without enough iron, you can develop a condition known as anemia. Anemia can make you feel tired and weak.

Water

Water feeds and cleanses your body, as well as helping to dissolve vitamins. *How do you supply your body with sufficient water each day?*

rubberball/Getty

Figure 15.3 **Important Minerals**

Mighty Minerals Your body may need only trace amounts of certain minerals, but that small amount is vital to good health. *How might you provide your body with the minerals it needs?*

Mineral	Where It Is Found	What It Does
Calcium	Milk and milk products; dark green, leafy vegetables; dry beans and peas; sardines and salmon (eaten with bones)	Builds and maintains strong bones and teeth; helps heart, muscles, and nerves work properly; helps blood to clot
Magnesium	Whole-grain products; green vegetables; dry beans and peas; nuts and seeds	Helps build bones; helps nerves and muscles work normally; contributes to proper heart function
Phosphorus	Meat, poultry, fish, and eggs; dry beans and peas; nuts; milk and milk products	Builds and maintains strong bones and teeth; helps body use carbohydrates, fats, and proteins
Iodine	Saltwater fish, iodized salt	Helps produce substances needed for growth; helps regulate rate at which body uses energy
Iron	Red meats, liver, and egg yolks; dark green, leafy vegetables; dry beans and peas; nuts; whole-grain and enriched breads and cereals; dried fruits (raisins)	Helps red blood cells carry oxygen to all parts of the body; helps cells use oxygen
Sodium	Salt, many foods	Helps maintain fluid balance in body; helps muscle and nerve action
Zinc	Meat, liver, poultry, and fish; milk products; dry beans and peas; whole-grain breads and cereals	Promotes normal growth; helps wounds heal; helps body use carbohydrates, proteins, and fats
Potassium	Oranges and orange juice; bananas; dried fruits; dry beans and peas; peanut butter; meats	Works with sodium to help maintain fluid balance in body; helps heart and muscles work properly; helps regulate blood pressure

Health & Wellness TIPS

Prevent Dehydration

Water is a large part of who we are. It makes up about two thirds of our body weight, and our brains are about seventy percent water. Use these tips to avoid dehydration:

▶ Drink plain water, not sugary or caffeinated sodas.

▶ Drink water before, during, and after exercise.

▶ Drink six to eight 8-ounce servings of water each day.

Phytochemicals

Phytochemicals are substances that plants produce naturally to protect themselves from harm. They do the same for you by improving your body's immunity, which helps you fight diseases, such as heart disease and cancer. As an added bonus, they give many foods their attractive color. You can find phytochemicals in fruits, vegetables, dry beans, nuts, and whole grains. Some phytochemicals are now available as dietary supplements. Many researchers, though, feel these are not as effective as eating foods with phytochemicals.

Water

Water is an essential nutrient. It makes up most of your body weight, and you could not survive long without it. Water helps regulate body functions and carry other nutrients to your cells. It also helps carry waste from your body.

Think about the last time you exercised outside or in physical education class. Did you sweat? Perspiring is how your body regulates its temperature, and water helps it do so. Water even keeps your nasal passages from drying out. Moist nasal passages help trap germs and keep them from entering your body.

Getting the right amount of water is important. The average person needs eight to twelve glasses of water each day. Foods with high water content, such as fruits and vegetables, provide some of the water you need. Liquids you drink, such as milk and juice, provide more water. Sports drinks also contain water but should not be a main source of water. Sports drinks contain ingredients that may be harmful to your body if you are not engaged in rigorous or prolonged physical activity. When you exercise or perspire a lot, you need to drink additional water to prevent dehydration. Experts recommend drinking four cups of water for every hour of moderate to intense exercise. Many experts say that if you feel thirsty, you have waited too long to drink fluids.

Section 15.1

After You Read

Review Key Concepts

1. **Define** nutrient and identify the six categories of nutrients.
2. **Explain** the importance of fiber to the body.
3. **Contrast** complete proteins and incomplete proteins.
4. **Define** cholesterol and explain how too much cholesterol can affect your health.
5. **Identify** the two types of vitamins and provide examples of each.

 Check Your Answers Go to connectED. mcgraw-hill.com to check your answers.

Practice Academic Skills

English Language Arts

6. Write a children's story incorporating a healthful food, such as broccoli. Emphasize the role the food plays in the body's functioning. The goal of the story should be to convince children that healthful food is good for them. Share your story with younger children.

Social Studies

7. Read print and Internet sources to find out more information about phytochemicals. You might visit your school or community library. List various foods that contain phytochemicals and summarize their health benefits. When you are finished, share your summary with your class.

Section 15.2

The Process of Digestion

Before You Read

Preview Read the content vocabulary and academic vocabulary words. Write one or two sentences predicting what you think the section will be about.

Read to Learn

Key Concepts

- **Describe** the process of digestion.
- **Relate** calorie intake to energy.
- **Compare** the effects of nutrient-rich foods to nutrient-deficient foods.

Main Idea

Your body has specialized methods of processing and disposing of the calories and nutrients you consume.

Content Vocabulary

◇ calorie
◇ nutrient density
◇ deficiency

Academic Vocabulary

You will find these words in your reading and on your tests. Use the glossary to look up their definitions if necessary.

☐ obtain
☐ fatigue

Graphic Organizer

As you read, record the definition and the sources of calories. Use a graphic organizer like the one below to organize your information.

Calories

Definition:	
Sources:	

Graphic Organizer Go to **connectED.mcgraw-hill.com** to download this graphic organizer.

The Digestive System

To get nutrients from food, your body must first digest it. When food enters your mouth, your teeth break it into small pieces. This releases the food's flavor. Your tongue pushes the food around in your mouth, and your saliva combines with the food. The chemicals in saliva, along with chewing, begin to break down the food. The path food takes through the digestive system can be seen in **Figure 15.4**. Any undigested food is eliminated as body waste.

✓ Reading Check **Explain** How does saliva help the digestion process?

As You Read

Connect Think about the appearance and smell of your favorite foods. When you see or smell food, how does your body respond?

Energy and Calories

You need energy for schoolwork and other activities, such as getting dressed, playing sports, or doing chores. Even when you sleep, your body uses energy. You need energy for normal body processes, such as breathing and pumping blood. Your body gets its energy from the carbohydrates, proteins, and fats in the food you eat.

A **calorie** is a unit for measuring energy. Calories are used to measure both the energy you obtain, or gain, from food and the energy you use when you are active.

◇ Vocabulary

You can find definitions in the glossary at the back of this book.

Figure 15.4 The Digestive System

From Food to Fuel Food moves from the mouth through the esophagus to the stomach, where digestive juices break it down further. Food remains in the stomach about three to five hours. From the stomach, food moves to the small intestine, where nutrients are absorbed into the bloodstream. Unneeded nutrients and undigested food become body waste. *Why might it not be beneficial to overeat at meals?*

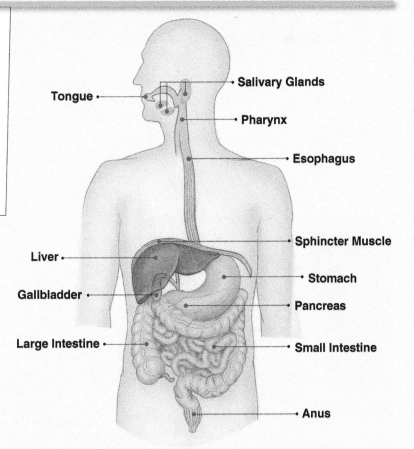

- Tongue
- Salivary Glands
- Pharynx
- Esophagus
- Liver
- Sphincter Muscle
- Stomach
- Gallbladder
- Pancreas
- Large Intestine
- Small Intestine
- Anus

The amount of calories you need each day depends on your level

The amount of calories you need each day depends on your level of activity and your basal metabolic rate (BMR). Your BMR is the rate at which your body uses energy for body processes. A person with a high BMR uses more calories when resting than someone with a low BMR. BMR differs from person to person depending on age, gender, body type and size, and genetic makeup.

The number of calories you take in should balance with the amount you burn. If you take in more calories than you need, you will gain weight. On average, adults use about 1,200 calories just for body processes. Teens need more energy because they are growing.

Sources of Calories

Where your calories come from is important. The energy in foods comes from fats, carbohydrates, and proteins. Fat is the most concentrated source of energy, with 9 calories per gram. (A gram is a metric unit of weight.) You do not want to eat large amounts of fat for your energy needs. Most of your energy needs will be met by carbohydrates and proteins.

Most nutritionists recommend that teens should get 45 to 65 percent of their calories from carbohydrates. Ten to 35 percent of their calories should come from proteins. Fats should comprise about 25 percent of a teen's daily calories.

✓ **Reading Check** **Describe** How should you determine how many calories to eat each day?

HOW TO ... Maintain A Healthy Weight

Modern nutrition science is learning more about what constitutes a healthy weight. Finding your healthy weight can be a challenge, as new findings shape scientific opinion. The best advice is to talk to your family health care provider. He or she can give you information to help with each of these steps.

Learn Your Healthy Weight Range Health experts are developing increasingly exact methods to determine a healthy weight for any one person. Besides looking at traditional height and weight charts, learn your body mass index (BMI). BMI uses a formula that compares weight to height to find what percentage of weight is fat, which many experts believe is a more important factor than weight alone.

Give Yourself Room to Grow Remember that young teens are in the early stages of a great and somewhat unpredictable period of physical growth. What now looks like excess weight may look just right after a growth spurt in a few months. Likewise, an underdeveloped body may be on the verge of filling out.

©JGI/Blend Images LLC

Nutrient Density

When making food choices, think about nutrient density. **Nutrient density** is the amount of nutrients in a food item in relation to the number of calories.

Candy, potato chips, and sugary soft drinks have low nutrient density. They increase your calorie count but contribute few essential nutrients. Which foods do you think have high nutrient density? If you answered fruits, vegetables, whole grains, lean meats, fish, poultry, and low-fat milk, you would be correct. These foods supply energy and important nutrients, such as proteins, and minerals, and fiber.

You can still eat foods with low nutrient density, but eat them sparingly. If you eat mainly low-nutrient foods, you not only miss out on good nutrition but also may experience weight problems, difficulty concentrating, or illnesses brought on by the lack of necessary vitamins or minerals. Food fuels your body, and you want to give it the best fuel possible.

Math You Can Use

Sources of Calories

Suppose your daily caloric intake is 2,000 calories. One 8-ounce bag of potato chips contains 452 calories from carbohydrates, 749 calories from fat, and 41.7 calories from protein. Use these numbers to calculate what percentage of your total daily caloric intake comes just from the carbohydrates, fat, and protein in the potato chips.

Math Concept **Percentage** To determine what percent *A* is of *B*, divide *A* by *B*. Then, multiply the answer by 100, round to the nearest whole number, and add the percent sign after the number.

Starting Hint To figure out what percent of your daily caloric intake comes from carbohydrates, divide the calories from carbohydrates by the total amount of calories you consume in one day.

Math For math help, go to the Math Appendix at the back of the book.

Choose Your Course of Action Are your eating and activity habits helping you reach and maintain a healthy weight? If not, will you change them? If you choose to gain or lose weight, will you pay as much attention to nutrition as to the numbers on a scale? What role will exercise play?

Calculate Calories Once you identify your healthy weight range, you need to know how many calories you need to maintain it. Compare your calorie needs with your current caloric intake. You can learn this by reading nutrition labels and keeping track of what you eat in a food diary.

Be Firm After you have decided on a healthy weight and a plan to reach it, be firm with yourself in following the plan. If you miss a few workouts or forget to eat nutritious food, do not be too hard on yourself. Get back to your plan and learn to make it a regular part of your life.

Food Diary

Breakfast
²/₃ c. oatmeal
¹/₂ c. milk
banana

Snack
8 oz. yogurt
¹/₃ c. low-fat granola

Lunch
3 oz. turkey
2 slices whole grain bread
¹/₂ tomato
lettuce
1 slice cheese
mustard
¹/₂ c. carrot sticks
2 small cookies

Comstock/Getty Images

Light and Healthy Recipe

Marinated Vegetables

Yield
4–6 servings (1 cup each)

Nutrition Analysis
Per Serving: 160 calories, 6 g total fat, 0.5 g saturated fat, 0 g trans fat, 0 mg cholesterol, 230 mg sodium, 22 g total carbohydrate, 5 g dietary fiber, 9 g sugars, 4 g protein

Vegetable Directions

Vegetable Ingredients
2–3 small zucchini
½ lb. snow peas
1 cup broccoli florets
1 cup cauliflower florets
⅓ lb. baby carrots
½ cup water
1 can (15 oz.) baby corn on cob
1 lb. grape tomatoes

1. Peel zucchini and cut into ½-inch bias slices.
2. String and cut snow peas in half diagonally
3. Remove stems of broccoli and cauliflower, using only the florets.
4. Place carrots in a large glass bowl with a small amount of water (about ½ cup). Cover with a paper towel. Heat in microwave for 3 minutes on high. Remove bowl; add snow peas along with cauliflower and broccoli florets; return to microwave for an additional 2 minutes or until crisp-tender.
5. Remove vegetables from microwave. Drain. Rinse vegetables with cold water to stop cooking process; drain vegetables well.
6. Place in a large bowl. Add zucchini, baby corn, and tomatoes.
7. Pour marinade over all; toss gently to coat vegetables.
8. Cover and chill for at least 2 hours or overnight.

Marinade Directions

Marinade Ingredients
2 Tbsp. olive oil
1 tsp. lemon zest
2 Tbsp. water
3 Tbsp. lemon juice
2 Tbsp. minced garlic
2 tsp. fresh oregano
½ tsp. fresh rosemary
1 Tbsp. sugar
½ tsp. salt
¼ tsp. pepper

1. In a small bowl, whisk together oil, lemon zest, water, and lemon juice.
2. Add garlic, oregano, rosemary, and sugar; whisk to combine.
3. Just before serving, add salt and pepper to taste. Toss gently.

Foodcollection.com/Alamy

Deficiencies in Nutrition

When your body does not receive enough nutrients, a **deficiency**, or shortage, occurs. The symptoms, or effects, of the deficiency depend on its seriousness.

Symptoms of a nutrition deficiency may not seem serious. People may feel tired, have difficulty concentrating, have frequent colds, gain weight, or lose weight. However, more serious symptoms of a nutrition deficiency can occur, such as hair loss, brittle nails, skin problems, nervousness, and *fatigue*, or extreme exhaustion.

Nutritional deficiencies are more common than you might expect, even among people who think they eat well. Even though many people eat plenty of food, their diets often lack many important vitamins and minerals. To keep your body in top shape and avoid deficiencies, it is important to eat a variety of foods from every food group.

Health & Wellness TIPS

Prevent Anemia

Iron deficiency anemia is a common ailment in teens. Anemia can make you feel irritable and exhausted. It can make it difficult to concentrate. To avoid anemia, you can:

▶ Eat iron-rich foods.

▶ Increase iron absorption by getting enough vitamin C.

▶ Take iron-enriched multivitamins, if your doctor recommends them.

Section 15.2

After You Read

Review Key Concepts

1. **Identify** the twelve major muscles and organs that make up the digestive system.
2. **Explain** what determines your basal metabolic rate (BMR).
3. **Describe** the symptoms of a nutrition deficiency.

Practice Academic Skills

 **English Language Arts**

4. Use reliable print or Internet sources to research the average number of calories someone your age burns during ordinary activities (breathing, walking to class, etc.) and during various physical activities (bike riding, running, etc.). Write a summary of your average daily activity and use the information from your research to estimate the amount of calories you burn in an average day.

 **Social Studies**

5. Research the effects of deficiencies of a few specific nutrients, including micronutrients. For example, what are the effects of a deficiency of vitamin D? List the effects of a deficiency of the nutrients you research as well as foods that are good sources of those nutrients.

 Check Your Answers Go to connectED.mcgraw-hill.com to check your answers.

Exploring Careers

EMT/Paramedic

What Does an EMT/Paramedic Do?

Emergency medical technicians (EMTs) and paramedics transport and provide emergency care for sick and injured people in an emergency. EMTs and paramedics generally work in teams. At the medical facility, EMTs and paramedics help transfer patients to the emergency department and report their observations to the staff.

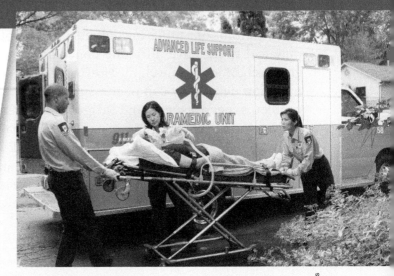

Paul Burns/Getty Images

Skills EMTs and paramedics should be emotionally stable and should have good dexterity, agility, and physical coordination. They need to be able to lift and carry heavy loads. Job-specific skills are learned through training and education courses.

Education and Training Generally, a high school diploma is required to enter a training program to become an EMT or paramedic. Workers must complete a formal training and certification process. Training is offered at progressive levels: EMT-Basic, EMT-Intermediate, and EMT-Paramedic.

Job Outlook Employment for EMTs and paramedics is expected to grow faster than the average for all occupations through 2016. Job prospects should be good, particularly in cities and with private ambulance services. EMTs and paramedics who have advanced education and certifications will likely enjoy the most favorable job outlook.

Critical Thinking Think about the job duties and skills of an EMT/paramedic. How do your personality, skills, and desire to help other people relate to the duties and skills of an EMT/paramedic? Write a paragraph explaining how you are or are not a good fit for an EMT/paramedic.

Career Cluster

Health Science

EMTs and paramedics work in the Health Science career cluster. Here are some of the other jobs in this career cluster:

- Speech Pathologist
- Radiographer
- Physician
- Physician Assistant
- Medical Biller
- Microbiologist
- Registered Nurse
- Audiologist
- Optometrist
- Chiropractor
- Pharmacist
- Sonographer
- Medical Records Administrator
- Biostatistician
- Industrial Hygienist
- Health Educator
- Nurse
- Nursing Aide

Explore Further Research this career cluster. Choose a career in this cluster that appeals to you, and write a career profile.

CHAPTER SUMMARY

Section 15.1
Nutrients at Work

Six categories of nutrients work together to help your body function effectively. Each nutrient performs a unique task. Fiber is not a nutrient, but it is an important part of healthful eating. Incomplete proteins can work together to form the complete proteins your body needs. Small amounts of fat and cholesterol are important for good health, though trans fats and saturated fats should be used sparingly. Vitamins, minerals, and phytochemicals help regulate body functions and prevent disease. You need a variety of these elements for good health. Water is an essential nutrient.

Section 15.2
The Process of Digestion

Digestion begins when you chew food and continues as food is transported through the body. You get energy from the food you eat, and energy is measured in calories. Your basal metabolic rate (BMR) is the rate at which your body uses energy for body processes. To meet nutritional needs, eat a variety of nutrient-dense foods each day. Though fat provides energy, most of your calories should come from carbohydrates and protein foods. Foods that have low nutrient density should not be eaten often because they are poor fuel for your body. Nutritional deficiencies can cause health problems.

Vocabulary Review

1. Use at least six of these vocabulary terms in a short essay about your daily diet.

Content Vocabulary
◇ nutrient (p. 367)
◇ carbohydrate (p. 368)
◇ fiber (p. 368)
◇ protein (p. 369)
◇ amino acids (p. 369)
◇ complete protein (p. 369)
◇ incomplete protein (p. 369)

◇ cholesterol (p. 371)
◇ high-density lipoprotein (p. 371)
◇ low-density lipoprotein (p. 371)
◇ phytochemicals (p. 374)
◇ calorie (p. 377)
◇ nutrient density (p. 379)
◇ deficiency (p. 381)

Academic Vocabulary
■ minute (p. 372)
■ trace (p. 373)
■ obtain (p. 377)
■ fatigue (p. 381)

Review Key Concepts

2. List the three primary nutrient functions.
3. Describe the two types of carbohydrates.
4. Summarize the role of proteins in the body.
5. Identify three main types of fat and in which foods they are found.
6. Explain why vitamins, minerals, phytochemicals, and water are essential nutrients.
7. Describe the process of digestion.
8. Relate calorie intake to energy.
9. Compare the effects of nutrient-rich foods to nutrient-deficient foods.

Critical Thinking

10. Role Play How would you respond to a friend who thinks sugar is harmful and refuses to eat fruit because it contains sugar?
11. Draw Conclusions Many professional athletes follow strict diets. How do you think food affects their athletic performance? How might their diets change if they were to stop competing?

 ACTIVE LEARNING

 **Family & Community Connections**

12. Create a Vitamin Mural Vitamins regulate many different processes in your body. Vitamins are micronutrients, which means that only very small amounts are necessary for normal body function. Vitamins are found in many foods you eat every day. Yet few people know which foods are the best sources of certain important vitamins. As a class, create a mural depicting different foods classified according to vitamin content. For example, carrots would be grouped with other foods labeled as vitamin A. Include groups for vitamins A, D, E, K, B, and C. Also include a group for folate. Somewhere on your mural, note foods that contain many different important vitamins. Be sure your mural includes colorful, attractive art. The information should be easy to understand.

13. Create an Advertisement Calcium helps teens develop strong bones and teeth. Some teens do not get enough calcium in their diets, though. A lack of calcium as a teen can lead to health risks later in life, including osteoporosis. Use reliable print or Internet sources to research the recommended daily intake of calcium. Then, research foods that contain calcium. Ask your family members to estimate how much of these foods they eat per day. How many of your family members meet the recommended daily intake? How many of them fall short of the recommended daily intake? Follow your teacher's instructions to form groups. In your group, work with your classmates to create a public-service advertisement that encourages teens to eat calcium-rich foods. Include the percentages from your research of people who do not meet the recommended daily calcium intake in your advertisement. Explain what can happen if you do not get enough calcium.

Real-World Skills and Applications

Leadership Skills

14. Create a Meal Plan Show your classmates how easy it can be to get the necessary nutrition you need to be healthy. Create a menu for breakfast, lunch, dinner, and one snack. Each meal should include a variety of necessary vitamins, minerals, fats, proteins, and carbohydrates. Aim to make your meals appetizing as well as easy to prepare.

Financial Literacy

15. Supermarket Shopping On a trip to the supermarket, you buy a carton of blueberries for $4.65. You also buy a bag of carrots for $3.99. You buy a bunch of bananas for $6.53 and two avocados for 99 cents each. If you pay with a $20.00 bill, how much change will you receive?

Information Literacy

16. The Purification Process Water is an essential nutrient. Without it, you could not survive for long. Use reliable print or Internet sources to research the water cycle. When you are finished, create a poster showing the cycle, and share your information with the class.

Academic Skills

 English Language Arts

17. Expand Your Diet Research diets from other cultures. How do the diets compare with yours? What are the nutritional differences? Would it benefit you to incorporate foods from other cultures into your diet? If so, what specific foods will benefit your health? Write a paragraph to answer these questions.

 Science

18. Evaporation Use this experiment to see one part of the water cycle in action. Monitoring evaporation on a small scale can help you understand it on a large scale.

Procedure Place a small drop of water on a flat, dry surface. Leave it undisturbed until it evaporates. Keep track of the time it takes for the drop to evaporate.

Analysis How long did it take the water to evaporate? How can this help explain the existence of large bodies of water over a period of time?

 Mathematics

19. Evaporation Rates The water cycle is the system that describes how water is evaporated, is held in the atmosphere, and then falls back to earth as rain. Suppose you leave a one-gallon bowl of water outside one day. Suppose the water will naturally evaporate at a rate of ⅛ gallon every 12 hours. If it is raining outside and the bowl catches 0.5 gallons of water in a 24-hour period, how much water is remaining in the bowl after one day?

Math Concept **Fractions** To multiply fractions, multiply their numerators by each other and multiply their denominators by each other. A whole number can be written as a fraction by making it the numerator of a fraction with a denominator of 1.

Starting Hint First multiply ⅛ of a gallon by 2 in order to find the amount of water that will evaporate in one day, or 24 hours. Then, subtract that amount from the gallon you began with.

Math For math help, go to the Math Appendix at the back of the book.

 Standardized Test Practice

SHORT ANSWER
Directions Read the question. Then, write a short response.

Test-Taking Tip When taking a test with short answer questions, be sure to read the questions carefully so that you will answer everything they ask. Some short answer questions have multiple parts.

20. Although vitamins are necessary for normal body function, getting too much of certain vitamins can be harmful to one's health. Briefly outline the negative effects of getting too much vitamin D.

Chapter 16

Guidelines for Healthy Eating

Section 16.1
Dietary Guidelines for Americans and MyPlate

Section 16.2
The Dietary Guidelines and Your Lifestyle

Chapter Objectives

Section 16.1

- **Recall** the questions you should ask when considering food information.
- **Summarize** the recommendations of the Dietary Guidelines for Americans.
- **Explain** the key ideas represented by MyPlate.

Section 16.2

- **Identify** factors that influence individual food choices.
- **Give** five examples of special nutritional needs.
- **Clarify** seven common food myths.

Cause-and-Effect Essay

Lifestyles The habits you form result in consequences that can be positive or negative. For example, regularly watching too much television can lead to weight gain, which in turn can lead to low energy and health problems. Writing a cause-and-effect essay will help you understand how the choices you make impact your life. Write a cause-and-effect essay detailing how a healthful or unhealthful lifestyle is the result of specific causes and effects.

Writing Tips Use these tips to write a cause-and-effect essay or paragraph:

- Create an outline to help you organize your thoughts.
- Use supporting details to illustrate specific causes and effects of a healthful or unhealthful lifestyle.
- Use appropriate transitions between paragraphs.

▲ Explore the Photo

Eating healthful food should be a goal whether you are eating at home or in a restaurant. *What kinds of healthful foods do you eat when you go to a restaurant?*

Dietary Guidelines for Americans and MyPlate

Before You Read

What You Want to Know Write a list of what you want to know about the Dietary Guidelines for Americans and MyPlate. As you read, write down the heads in this section that provide this information.

Read to Learn

Key Concepts
- **Recall** the questions you should ask when considering food information.
- **Summarize** the recommendations of the Dietary Guidelines for Americans.
- **Explain** the key ideas represented by MyPlate.

Main Idea

Asking the right questions and using appropriate resources will help you select healthful foods and avoid unhealthful foods.

Content Vocabulary

◇ Dietary Guidelines for Americans
◇ nutrient-dense
◇ sedentary
◇ obesity
◇ MyPlate

Academic Vocabulary

You will find these words in your reading and on your tests. Use the glossary to look up their definitions if necessary.
- consistent
- counteract

Graphic Organizer

As you read, record ways to handle food safely. Use a graphic organizer like the one below to organize your information.

How to Handle Food Safely

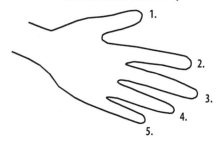

1.
2.
3.
4.
5.

 Graphic Organizer Go to **connectED.mcgraw-hill.com** to download this graphic organizer.

Eating, Exercising, and Good Health

How do food and exercise fit into your life? Do you regularly eat fried or fast foods and get most of your exercise operating the controls on the television remote? Or do you exercise for at least 60 minutes every day and eat a variety of foods? The answers to these questions may reveal a lot about your overall health now and throughout life.

The choices you make today will affect your health in the future. Establishing good eating and exercise habits can help you avoid heart disease, diabetes, and some forms of cancer. But exactly what eating and exercise habits should you maintain? Fortunately, there is plenty of information out there that can assist you in making wise choices.

Question Information

There is a wealth of health and nutrition information in print, online, and on television. Unfortunately, it is not consistent, or free from variation or contradiction. Before deciding whether food information is reliable and accurate, ask the following questions:

- **Where did the information come from?** Rely on experts, such as registered dietitians, health care professionals, researchers in the nutrition field, family and consumer science teachers, and professional organizations, such as the American Dietetic Association.
- **Could the statements be false?** Many businesses make false claims to persuade you to purchase their products. On the other hand, statements by health organizations, such as the American Heart Association or the American Cancer Society, are meant to educate the public about health issues of interest. They base their information on scientific research.

✓ **Reading Check** **Determine** Why is it important to pay attention to the foods you eat and how much exercise you get?

The Dietary Guidelines

The federal government also provides material to guide you as you make food and exercise decisions. The **Dietary Guidelines for Americans** include scientifically-based advice for making smart food choices, balancing food choices and physical activity, and getting the most nutrition out of your calories. These guidelines are updated and published by the U.S. Department of Agriculture (USDA) and the U.S. Department of Health and Human Services (HHS) every five years. The Dietary Guidelines are suggestions for healthy people age two and older. They are not for infants and toddlers because their nutrition needs are age-specific to early growth.

As You Read

Connect As you read this section, think about your exercise patterns. How can choosing to ride a bike instead of driving affect your health?

Vocabulary

You can find definitions in the glossary at the back of this book.

SUCCEED IN SCHOOL

Two-Column Notes

Two-column notes are a useful way to study and organize what you have read. Divide a piece of paper into two columns. In the left column, write down main ideas. In the right column, list supporting details.

Make Calories Count

Though many people consume more calories than they need, they still do not get the recommended amount of nutrients they need for good health. Many teens, for example, tend to eat too many high-calorie foods that contain a lot of saturated fat, trans fats, cholesterol, refined flour, sugar, and sodium. They do not get enough calcium, potassium, magnesium, vitamin E, or fiber in their daily diets.

To get the nutrients you need while staying within your recommended calorie range, choose nutrient-dense foods and beverages from the basic food groups. A **nutrient-dense** food is a food that provides high amounts of vitamins and minerals for relatively few calories. Whole grains, fruits, vegetables, low-fat milk and milk products, beans, and lean meats are all nutrient-dense foods.

Play Sports

Playing sports is a good way to get exercise, maintain your health, and be with your friends at the same time. *What sports do you play with your friends or family members?*

Manage Your Weight

Balancing calories from foods and beverages with the calories used in physical activity is the key to maintaining a healthy weight. Many teens take in too many calories and lead a **sedentary**, or inactive, lifestyle. This way of life can lead to **obesity**, or being seriously overweight as a result of excess body fat. Experts estimate that nearly 16 percent of adolescents are overweight. This is a concern because excess body fat increases the risk of many illnesses, including type 2 diabetes, heart disease, arthritis, respiratory problems, and certain cancers.

Get Regular Physical Activity

Regular physical activity promotes health, well-being, and a healthy body weight. Teens should be physically active for at least 60 minutes every day or almost every day. This includes aerobic activities, such as walking, skating, playing a sport, mowing the lawn, or raking leaves. These activities burn excess calories and improve the health of your heart and lungs. Resistance exercises are also important. These exercises build strength and endurance, and increase the number of calories you burn while at rest. Finally, stretching is important because it reduces the risk of injury.

BananaStock/Getty Images

Choose the Right Foods

The ideal eating plan is rich in foods containing high amounts of fiber, vitamins, minerals, and phytochemicals. Vegetables, fruits, whole grain products, and low-fat milk and milk products are excellent sources of these nutrients. These foods are also low in fat and calories. Calcium-rich milk increases bone mass and reduces the risk of osteoporosis and broken bones later in life. Whole grain products, fruits, and vegetables have fiber, which protects against heart disease. People who regularly eat generous amounts of yellow, dark green, red, and orange vegetables and fruits also reduce their risk of many diseases and illnesses.

Limit Fats

As you learned in Chapter 15, fat is an important component of a healthy diet. It helps supply energy and is important for many body functions. Eating a moderate amount of unsaturated fat, such as olive oil, is beneficial to your health. Limit foods that are high in saturated fats, trans fats, and cholesterol, however. They are linked to heart disease.

Saturated fats should make up no more than 10 percent of your daily calories. Cholesterol intake should be less than 300 milligrams per day. As a general rule, you should reduce the amount of stick margarine, butter, and other solid fats that you use.

Limit Added Sugar

Many popular foods, such as soft drinks, cookies, and sweetened cereals, contain high amounts of added sugar. Foods with added sugars should be eaten sparingly, because they are usually high in calories and low in nutrients. Too much sugar can lead to weight gain and tooth decay. Read food labels carefully to make sure that added sugars are not one of the first few ingredients on the list. Examples of added sugars include sucrose, glucose, fructose, maltose, corn syrup, and high-fructose corn syrup. If an ingredient ends with *ose*, it is a sugar.

Reduce Sodium and Increase Potassium

Sodium, or salt, helps the body maintain a balance of fluid, and it helps regulate blood pressure. Too much sodium can cause unhealthy conditions, such as high blood pressure, heart attack, and kidney disease. Some foods contain sodium naturally. But chances are most of the sodium you consume comes from processed foods. To keep your sodium intake at a healthy level, choose and prepare foods with little salt. Also eat plenty of potassium-rich foods, such as vine fruits, root vegetables, and leafy green vegetables. Potassium helps counteract, or neutralize, sodium's effects on blood pressure.

Avoid Alcohol

Teens should avoid beer, wine, and other alcoholic beverages. Alcohol has calories, but almost no nutrients. Drinking alcohol has a negative effect on a person's coordination and judgment. This can make the user a danger to himself or herself and others.

Alcohol also has serious long-term effects. Recent studies indicate that exposure to alcohol interrupts key processes of brain development during adolescence. This interference has long-lasting negative effects on a person's memory, learning capacity, and attention span. Teens who begin drinking at age 15 or younger are also four times more likely to become alcoholics than those who do not drink until they are of legal age. Heavy use of alcohol leads to high blood pressure, heart disease, liver disease, and intestinal cancer.

HOW TO . . .   Lower the Fat

Many people have trouble following the Dietary Guidelines when it comes to limiting fats. Once you know what types of fats to avoid, it will be easier for you to limit your fats. Follow these tips to reduce fat consumption.

Cut Fat in Poultry and Meat Choose lean ground meat and poultry and reduced-fat versions of luncheon meat and sausage. Trim visible fat and remove skin from poultry and fish before or after cooking. Eat fish often, especially those that contain fish oil, such as salmon.

Choose Lower-Fat Dairy Foods High-fat dairy foods often have low-fat versions. A reduced-fat variety of sour cream has about 10 fewer grams of fat than regular sour cream. Also look for low-fat substitutes. Buttermilk, which tastes similar to sour cream, contains only 1 gram of fat.

Choose Nutritious Snacks To satisfy a sweet tooth, instead of eating a brownie, which has about 10 grams of fat, choose fresh fruit, which has none. When you crave a crunchy snack, choose a small bag of low-fat pretzels instead of potato chips.

(l)Purestock/SuperStock; (b)Pixtal/AGE Fotostock

Handle Food Safely

Keeping food free from harmful bacteria and other hazards is vital to healthful eating. The following guidelines can help you prepare, handle, and store food safely:

- **Wash** your hands with soap and warm water before preparing, handling, and eating food.
- **Clean** food-contact surfaces to avoid spreading bacteria.
- **Use** different, clean cutting boards for preparing different types of food.
- **Wash** fruits and vegetables thoroughly before eating.
- **Chill** perishable foods promptly and thaw frozen foods properly. Make sure food is not left on the counter.

✓ **Reading Check** **Identify** What are the Dietary Guidelines for Americans, and who created them?

Use Low-Fat Condiments Dress up a sandwich with salsa, relish, horseradish, or wasabi (the Japanese version of horseradish). Make potato salad with more vinegar and less mayonnaise. Explore ethnic condiments, such as chutneys (spicy fruit relishes) and hoisin, a spicy Asian ketchup.

Reduce Fat in Baking Learn tips for cutting the fat in baked recipes, such as using applesauce to replace oil. Start by following specially developed low-fat recipes, applying principles of low-fat cooking as you gain experience.

Spice Up Your Foods Experiment with a wide variety of herbs, spices, and other seasonings. Try salads with fruit vinegars instead of oily dressings. Toss pasta with an herb blend.

Learn Cooking and Menu Terms How a food is described can be a clue to how it is prepared. Learn terms that denote high- and low-fat methods. Roasted vegetables are a lower-fat choice than scalloped vegetables, which are served in a cream sauce and topped with breadcrumbs.

(l and r) Copyright © FoodCollection

Figure 16.1 **MyPlate**

A Visual Tool MyPlate provides a visual tool that uses shape, color, and words to help people understand the food groups and make smart dietary choices. Think about how MyPlate relates to the items you put on your plate when you eat. *What can you do to eat more healthfully?*

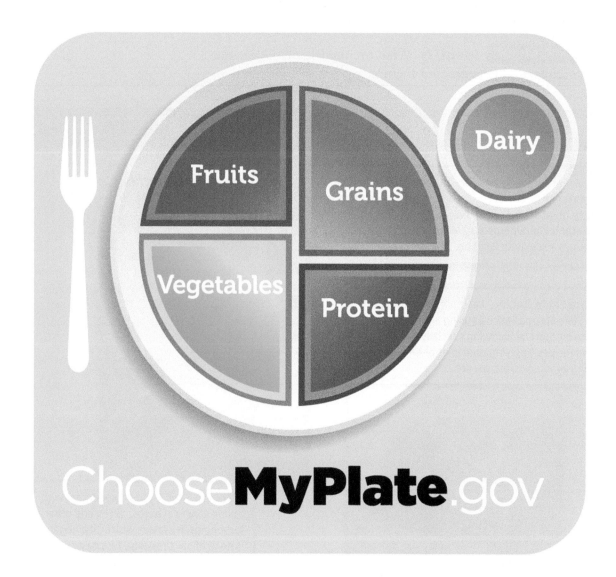

MyPlate

MyPlate is an easy-to-use food guidance system developed by the U.S. Department of Agriculture (USDA). MyPlate was developed to help people make smart choices about nutrition and fitness.

MyPlate is shown in **Figure 16.1**. MyPlate is organized to look like a dinner plate, with a glass on the side, labeled dairy. The plate is divided into four sections. Each section is labeled with a food group. The size of each section provides guidance in selecting how much food you should eat from each food group. For example, based on MyPlate, your overall diet should contain more vegetables and grains than proteins, fruits, and dairy. When you create a weekly menu, keep in mind that the overall eating plan should contain more vegetables and grains than other foods.

MyPlate shows the five food groups, which include Protein (or meats and beans), Vegetables, Fruits, Grains, and Dairy. Four of the food groups are shown on MyPlate. Dairy is shown alongside the plate in a cup. MyPlate does not include oils or fats. Oils and fats are not a food group. They should be consumed in small amounts. See **Figure 16.2** on page 396. You should select foods from each food group on a daily basis in order to get the nutrients you need.

Visit the MyPlate Web site, **www.ChooseMyPlate.gov**, for free food and exercise recommendations.

Eat the Right Amount

How much food do you need each day? These estimates apply if you are 14-18 years old and get 30 minutes of daily physical activity beyond normal activities.

- **Grains** Females need 6 ounces and males need 8 ounces, or the equivalent. At least half of daily grains should be whole.
- **Vegetables** Females need 2½ cups and males need 3 cups.
- **Fruit** Females need 1½ cups and males need 2 cups.
- **Dairy** Females and males need 3 cups or the equivalent.
- **Protein Foods** Females need 5 ounces and males need 6½ ounces, or the equivalent.

TAKE CHARGE!

Create a Nutrition Plan

Whether you want to gain weight or get in shape for a sport, planning nutritious meals can help.

- **Determine Your Energy Needs** Use MyPlate to decide what amount of caloric intake you need. Your end goal will determine this number.
- **Eat Nutritious Foods** No matter what your goal is, you should always provide your body with the vitamins and minerals it needs.
- **Plan Meals** To make your nutrition plan easier to follow, plan out your meals and snacks a week in advance. Be flexible and choose a variety of meals.
- **Embrace a New Healthy Lifestyle** Think of your nutrition plan as a lifestyle change and not a diet. This will help you accept eating healthfully as a permanent change.

Real-World Skills

Put Your Plan to Work Think about your nutritional needs and goals. Create a weekly nutrition plan that will help you reach your goal. Plan out breakfasts, lunches, and dinners. Show your plan to your parents or guardians and ask for their input and meal ideas. Then, try out your plan the following week.

Figure 16.2   **MyPlate's Five Food Groups Plus Oils**

The Five Food Groups   Foods are grouped into food groups because their nutrient content is similar. *How can you be sure that you are getting all of the nutrients your body needs?*

Grain Group

The Grain Group includes cereal, rice, pasta, breads, and grits.

Key Nutrients: Carbohydrates; B vitamins, especially thiamin, niacin, folate; minerals, including iron; fiber

Daily Amount: 6 to 8-ounce equivalents, at least half should be whole grain

1 Ounce Is: 1 slice of bread; 1 cup (250 mL) ready-to-eat cereal; ½ cup (125 mL) cooked cereal, rice, pasta, or grits; 1 small muffin; 1 small tortilla

Vegetable Group

The Vegetable Group includes broccoli, carrots, spinach, lettuce, asparagus, and beans.

Key Nutrients: Carbohydrates; vitamins, especially vitamins A and C and folate; minerals, including potassium; fiber

Daily Amount: 2½ to 3 cups

1 Cup Is: 2 cups (500 mL) raw leafy vegetables; 1 cup (250 mL) cooked or chopped raw vegetables; 1 cup (250 mL) vegetable juice

Fruit Group

The Fruit Group includes apples, oranges, tomatoes, avocados, blueberries, plums, and grapes.

Key Nutrients: Carbohydrates; vitamins, especially vitamins A and C and folate; minerals, especially potassium; fiber

Daily Amount: 1½ to 2 cups

1 Cup Is: 1 cup (250 mL) cut up cooked or raw fruit; 1 cup (250 mL) fruit juice; 1 large banana or orange; 1 small apple; ½ cup (125 mL) dried fruit

Dairy Group

The Dairy Group includes milk, yogurt, cheese, and some other dairy products.

Key Nutrients: Protein, calcium, some other minerals, vitamin B$_2$ (riboflavin), vitamin D

Daily Amount: 3 cups

1 Cup Is: 1 cup (250 mL) milk or yogurt; 1½ ounces (42 g) natural cheese; 2 ounces (56 g) processed cheese

Protein Foods Group

The Protein Foods Group includes all meats, poultry, fish, legumes, eggs, nuts, and seeds.

Key Nutrients: Protein, B vitamins (thiamin and niacin), iron, zinc

Daily Amount: 5 to 6½-ounce equivalents

1 Ounce Is: 1 ounce (28 g) cooked lean meat, poultry, or fish; ¼ cup (60 mL) cooked dry beans (legumes); 1 egg; 1 tablespoon (15 mL) peanut butter; ½ ounce (14 g) nuts or seeds

Oils

Healthful oils are not considered a food group. Some foods from the five food groups contain healthful oils. Healthful oils also include fish, vegetable, and olive oils; they are liquid at room temperature.

Key Nutrients: Fats (unsaturated), vitamin E

Daily Amount: 5 to 6 teaspoons (from fish, nuts, and some vegetable oils)

Figure 16.3

How Much Do You Eat?

Know Your Portions Knowing the size of a portion of food is an important step to proper nutrition. The column on the right shows the amount of food needed for a 2,000 calorie eating plan. *How closely do you follow the recommended portion sizes of foods?*

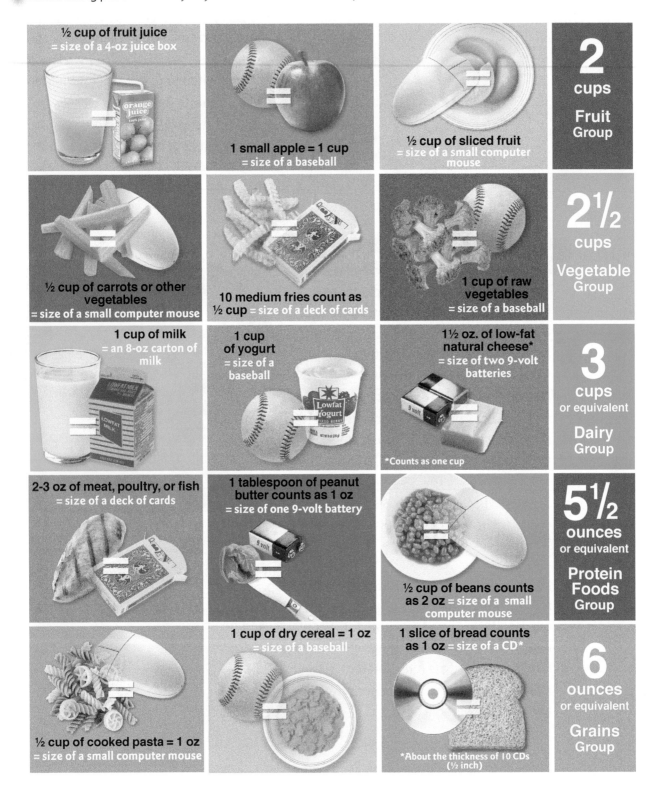

½ cup of fruit juice = size of a 4-oz juice box

1 small apple = 1 cup = size of a baseball

½ cup of sliced fruit = size of a small computer mouse

2 cups Fruit Group

½ cup of carrots or other vegetables = size of a small computer mouse

10 medium fries count as ½ cup = size of a deck of cards

1 cup of raw vegetables = size of a baseball

2½ cups Vegetable Group

1 cup of milk = an 8-oz carton of milk

1 cup of yogurt = size of a baseball

1½ oz. of low-fat natural cheese* = size of two 9-volt batteries

*Counts as one cup

3 cups or equivalent Dairy Group

2-3 oz of meat, poultry, or fish = size of a deck of cards

1 tablespoon of peanut butter counts as 1 oz = size of one 9-volt battery

½ cup of beans counts as 2 oz = size of a small computer mouse

5½ ounces or equivalent Protein Foods Group

½ cup of cooked pasta = 1 oz = size of a small computer mouse

1 cup of dry cereal = 1 oz = size of a baseball

1 slice of bread counts as 1 oz = size of a CD*

*About the thickness of 10 CDs (½ inch)

6 ounces or equivalent Grains Group

Figure 16.3 on page 398 shows how to compare what you eat with recommended daily amounts.

Again, the recommended daily amounts are just a general guide. Every person's calorie needs are different. Your calorie needs depend on your age, activity level, and whether you are trying to gain, maintain, or lose weight. If you are very active and want to maintain your current weight, for example, you may need larger amounts of food.

Visit the SuperTracker Web site, a feature of MyPlate, at **www. SuperTracker.usda.gov** to create a personalized nutrition and physical activity plan. If you enter your age, gender, activity level, height, and weight, the results will tell you how many calories you need every day. They will also show you how much of each food group you should eat each day. The SuperTracker Web site shows you how your favorite foods stack up nutritionally and helps you create a meal plan that will help you meet your nutrition goals.

Section 16.1

After You Read

Review Key Concepts

1. **Give** examples of the experts you can rely on for accurate food information.
2. **Explain** what a nutrient-dense food is and provide examples.
3. **Identify** the recommended daily amounts of each food group according to MyPlate.

Check Your Answers Go to connectED. mcgraw-hill.com to check your answers.

Practice Academic Skills

English Language Arts

4. Write a letter to parents outlining the Dietary Guideline recommendations. Request that parents provide their children with meals and snacks that follow these recommendations. Use language, tone, and techniques that will persuade parents to follow the guidelines.

Social Studies

5. Follow your teacher's instructions to form into groups. Discuss which of the recommendations in the Dietary Guidelines is the easiest for most teens to follow. Which is the hardest to follow? Why? Share your findings with the class and note whether other groups came to similar conclusions.

Section 16.2

The Dietary Guidelines and Your Lifestyle

Reading Guide

Before You Read

Preview Scan the photos in this section and read their captions. Write one or two sentences predicting what the section will be about.

Read to Learn

Key Concepts
- **Identify** factors that influence individual food choices.
- **Give** five examples of special nutritional needs.
- **Clarify** seven common food myths.

Main Idea

Understanding food myths, individual nutritional needs, and smart food choices can help you create a diet that will work for you.

Content Vocabulary

◇ diabetes
◇ insulin
◇ food allergy
◇ vegetarian
◇ vegan
◇ irradiated food
◇ food additive
◇ functional food
◇ dietary supplement

Academic Vocabulary

You will find these words in your reading and on your tests. Use the glossary to look up their definitions if necessary.

▢ strenuous   ▢ excess

Graphic Organizer

As you read this section, note the two types of food sensitivities listed in the text and explain how they can affect the body. Use a graphic organizer like the one below to organize your information.

Food Sensitivities ————

Graphic Organizer Go to connectED.mcgraw-hill.com to download this graphic organizer.

Individual Food Choices

Why do people make the food choices they do? Why might they select pasta rather than salad, or fish over beef? The following factors influence people's food choices and the way they feel about food.

Geographic Area Different regions of the country often feature their own foods' local availability and cultural traditions. Meals in New England may emphasize fish and baked beans, for example. Southern menus, on the other hand, might include barbecue and coleslaw. Also, the local resources of an area can factor into food choices. For example, fish and seafood are usually more available and affordable in coastal areas than in other areas of the country.

Religious Beliefs Many of the world's religions have guidelines concerning food and eating. For example, some religions restrict certain foods, some require foods to be prepared in certain ways, and some promote eating specific foods or fasting to observe religious holidays.

Family and Culture People tend to follow their family's food customs. Perhaps your grandparents always celebrated summer holidays by serving grilled food in the backyard. Now your parents carry on this tradition, and someday you may as well.

The Media Have you ever bought a food product after seeing a clever advertisement for it? Radio, television, and print advertisements can easily influence the foods you buy and eat. Some cooking programs also offer recipes and cooking methods that can influence your eating habits.

Technology Advances in technology allow people the convenience of microwavable and convection-oven foods and online ordering for restaurant takeout. Many people choose convenience foods over foods they need to prepare themselves.

✓ **Reading Check** **Draw Conclusions** How does geography affect the food choices that people make?

As You Read

Connect Think about how geography, weather, and family influence what you eat. How might your meal choices differ between July and January?

Healthy Eating

Coastal regions may have more seafood dishes than inland cuisines. *How can you incorporate healthy eating habits with the foods in your region?*

Image Source/Getty Images

Community Connections

Hometown Foods

Some geographic areas become identified with a particular food that is raised or sold there, such as Maine lobsters or Idaho potatoes. Think of a local food that is identified with your community. What do you know about this food? How has it contributed to the development of your community?

Safety Check

Dangers of Food Allergies

For people with food allergies, eating can be dangerous. Annually, about 30,000 people need emergency room treatment for food allergies. People allergic to foods such as milk, wheat, and peanuts can now make safer food selections, thanks to the 2006 Food Allergen Labeling and Consumer Protection Act.

Write About It

Research allergic reactions to peanuts, wheat, milk, or shellfish. In a paragraph, describe the symptoms, and explain what allergic individuals must do if exposed. Also, list ways that people can avoid being exposed to this allergen.

Special Nutritional Needs

Nutritional needs vary from one individual to the next. Your size, activity level, age, and other factors, such as any medical conditions you might have, determine what you need to eat to maintain good health.

Medical Conditions

Some medical problems, including high blood pressure, high cholesterol, and obesity, require people to follow special or modified diets. For example, doctors may suggest to people with high blood pressure that they consume less salt. Processed foods and table salt should be avoided. People who are obese or who have high cholesterol may need to greatly reduce the fat and animal products in their diets.

People who are obese or diabetic may need to regulate the portions and types of foods they eat. **Diabetes** is a condition in which the body cannot control blood sugar properly. The body does not respond to or make enough **insulin**, a chemical that helps blood sugar move into body cells. Without insulin, body cells cannot use blood sugar normally to provide energy. If not managed well, diabetes can damage many parts of the body. Regularly timed meals and snacks rich in whole grains, vegetables, and fruits can help people with diabetes control their blood sugar levels.

People with medical conditions that might be affected by food should consult health care professionals, such as physicians and dietitians, to obtain expert nutritional and medical advice.

Food Sensitivities

Some people have food intolerances. These conditions can cause severe digestive problems. You may know someone who is lactose-intolerant. This means that the person is unable to digest lactose, or the sugar contained in cow's milk. People with lactose intolerance often substitute lactose-free varieties or soy products for milk and other dairy products. They can also buy tablets that reduce lactose when added to milk.

Gluten intolerance is the inability to digest gluten, a protein found in wheat, rye, barley, and some oats. It is not a wheat allergy. In people with this intolerance, the protein damages the lining of the small intestine, making it difficult for the body to absorb nutrients. They must avoid foods with gluten to allow the small intestine to heal. Corn, beans, quinoa, and gluten-free flours help people with gluten intolerance get proper nutrition.

Food Allergies

A **food allergy** is a reaction of the body's immune system to ingested food. People allergic to food might break out in a rash, suffer stomach cramps, experience nausea, or have difficulty breathing after eating this food.

In some cases, even the tiniest amount of a food makes breathing so difficult that it can cause death. Other foods besides nuts that commonly cause allergic reactions include eggs, milk, wheat, fish, and shellfish. The only solution is to avoid the food.

Vegetarians

A **vegetarian** is someone who does not eat meat, poultry, or fish. Vegetarian meals typically consist of grains, beans, fruits, vegetables, and sometimes eggs and dairy products. Someone who does not eat any animal products, including dairy products or eggs, is a **vegan**.

Ideally, vegetarian meals are rich in fiber and complex carbohydrates. Because vegetarians do not eat animal proteins, they rely on plant sources, such as dry beans, peas, nuts, and soy products, for protein. Vegetarians should strive to eat a variety of foods to maintain a well-balanced diet. A well-planned vegetarian diet is often low in fat and cholesterol and high in fiber, which offers health benefits.

Vegetarian diets can be challenging. Some vegetarians eat too many processed carbohydrates and sugary, high-fat foods that do not provide the body with enough essential nutrients. Others do not know which vegetarian food combinations provide the complete proteins they need for proper nutrition. For this reason, it is important to get nutritional counseling before following a strict vegetarian or vegan diet.

Science You Can Use

The Science of Allergies

People who have food allergies have a wide range of reactions. The cause of food allergies is not completely known.

Procedure Follow your teacher's instructions to form into pairs. Discuss with your partner food sensitivities and food allergies. Identify foods that you believe result in the most severe reactions. Make sure to discuss what happens in people's bodies when they experience a reaction to certain foods.

Analysis Using reliable print or Internet sources, conduct research about various allergies and allergic reactions. Which foods are the most common causes of allergic reactions? Which foods tend to result in the most severe reactions? Create a chart comparing the most common allergens with regard to severity of reaction. Do you notice any common threads between these foods?

> ### Vegetarian Diet

If you are going to follow a vegetarian diet, you should obtain nutritional counseling from a dietitian to make sure your diet has a balance of nutrients. *What are some nutritious foods that vegetarians can eat?*

Ingram Publishing

Light and Healthy Recipe

Green Bean Salad

Yield
8 servings (1 cup each)

Nutrition Analysis
Per Serving: 300 calories, 28 g total fat, 2.5 g saturated fat, 0 g trans fat, 0 mg cholesterol, 630 mg sodium, 13 g total carbohydrate, 3 g dietary fiber, 4 g sugars, 1 g protein

Dressing Directions

Dressing Ingredients
1 whole garlic bulb, roasted
Vegetable oil spray
½ cup light olive oil, divided
2 Tbsp. fresh oregano, chopped
1 Tbsp. fresh chives, chopped
¼ tsp. salt
¼ tsp. black pepper

1. Preheat oven to 400°F (204°C).
2. Spray garlic bulb with vegetable oil spray. Place bulb on an ovenproof plate or container. Bake for 20 to 30 minutes until cloves feel soft and tender to the touch. Remove. Cool bulb enough to handle.
3. In the bowl of a food processor or blender, squeeze each clove of garlic. Process the garlic and 2 tablespoons olive oil until a smooth paste forms. Add vinegar and process until well blended.
4. With the food processor or blender running, add the remaining olive oil in a steady stream.
5. Add chopped oregano and chives. Mix well. Season with salt and pepper.

Salad Directions

Salad Ingredients
1 pound fresh, thin green beans, trimmed
1 medium Vidalia onion (or any sweet onion), thinly sliced (equal to 1½ cups)
1 can pitted black olives (15 ounces), halved vertically

1. In a large pot of boiling water, cook green beans about 2 minutes.
2. Remove beans with a large slotted spoon, and plunge into a large bowl of ice water to stop the cooking process. They should be crisp.
3. When beans are cool, drain in a colander and slice on the diagonal.
4. In a large bowl, gently toss together the cut green beans, thinly sliced onions, and black olives. Toss with dressing.
5. Serve at room temperature.

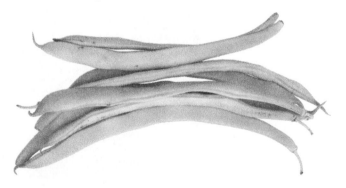

Athletes

Are the nutritional needs of competitive athletes different from those of people who exercise for health and enjoyment? The answer is no. Just like the average person, serious athletes need carbohydrates, protein, fat, vitamins, minerals, and water. However, athletes may need more of these nutrients.

Athletes must take extra care to drink plenty of fluids. This is because they are more active than the average person, and therefore perspire more than the average person. Everyone sweats when they are physically active. The perspiration evaporates from your skin to cool your body. Drinking fluids before, during, and after activities, even when you are not thirsty, replaces the fluids you lose to perspiration. Waiting until you are thirsty to drink is risky because thirst is an early sign of dehydration.

As a general rule, you should choose water when your workouts are shorter than an hour or not very strenuous, or demanding. For longer, more strenuous activities, drink sports beverages or fruit juices diluted to half-strength. These drinks provide important nutrients lost during exercise.

Along with water, athletes need plenty of energy, and the best source for energy is complex carbohydrates. You can increase your workout endurance by eating foods rich in complex carbohydrates, such as whole-grain breads and cereals.

✓ **Reading Check** **Generalize** What factors influence your nutritional needs?

How I See It

HEALTHY WEIGHT GAIN Frank, 16

As long as I can remember, I have always been skinny. My parents told me they thought I would gain weight once I was in high school because I ate a lot of potato chips, cookies, pizza, and hamburgers. But once I got to high school, I got even thinner!

I thought that being thin meant I was healthy. But last year I took a health class, and I learned that just because I did not show any weight gain, it did not mean that I was healthy. I found out the foods I ate were not providing the right kind of nutrients for building strong muscles and bones. So, I learned how to eat more nutritious food, started a strength-training program, and got more hours of sleep each night. It is now a year later, and I have been able to gain weight and muscle healthfully.

Critical Thinking Frank says that eating nutritious food, strength training, and getting plenty of rest all play a role in gaining weight healthfully. How could you improve these areas of your life?

Getting the Facts

You have probably heard this statement about food: "An apple a day keeps the doctor away." Because food is so important to people's health and way of life, they have a lot to say about it. Sometimes their statements are proven and true, but other times they are simply ideas and opinions that have been repeated until they sound true. This section will clear up some common food myths so that you can make informed decisions about what you eat.

Frozen Foods and Fresh Foods

Many frozen foods are just as nutritious as fresh foods, and some are even more nutritious. Frozen foods are processed right after being harvested, at the peak of their nutritive value. On the other hand, fresh produce that is transported long distances can age and lose nutrients.

Carbohydrate Intake and Weight

Eating too many chips, cookies, and other processed carbohydrates and not being active enough can be a bad combination. But whether they come from milk products, fats, meats, or any other food group, **excess**, or more than the needed amount of, calories are the true cause of weight gain. When you take in more calories than you expend in a day, your body stores whatever is not used as fat. That said, it is easy to overeat many processed carbohydrates because they are not as filling as unrefined carbohydrates, which contain more fiber. Choose whole grain foods, fruits, and vegetables instead of overly refined foods and soft drinks to avoid overeating.

Likewise, no one food can decrease fat in your body. The best way to lose weight is to eat in moderation from all of the food groups and exercise daily.

Exercise and Appetite

Although some people who exercise eat more to maintain their weight, exercise does not cause them to eat more. In fact, the opposite is often true. Many people reach for sugary snacks when depressed or when their energy levels are low. Because exercise increases a person's energy levels and improves a person's mood, it can actually cause some people to eat less.

Food Claims

When you read food claims, try to understand what is being said and what is not being said. Many claims can be made, but not all are reliable. *Why might a claim on a food label be unreliable?*

image100/SuperStock

Organic Foods

Perhaps while in the store you have noticed foods labeled natural or organic. Some people prefer these foods. Natural foods contain no artificial ingredients. Whereas many regular foods can contain preservatives to keep them fresh longer, natural foods do not. Organic foods are foods grown without the use of pesticides or artificial fertilizers. People choose natural and organic foods because they want to avoid consuming substances they feel are unhealthy.

Grocers usually charge more for natural and organic foods than regular foods. As with any food, compare the nutrition label to the labels of other foods to be sure you are getting the most nutrients for your money. You will find that most conventionally produced foods are just as nutritious as their organic versions, and that organic foods are as high in fat, sugars, and calories as regular foods.

Irradiated Foods

Some stores advertise irradiated foods. **Irradiated food** has gone through a process that destroys bacteria, mold, and insects by passing it through a field of radiant energy similar to X-rays. Irradiation extends the shelf life of foods and helps maintain their quality.

The irradiation process is controversial. Some people think that irradiated food is radioactive, but this is not true. Most of the radiant energy used in food passes through the food in much the same way as microwaves pass through foods. According to law, a food's label must state whether the food has been irradiated.

Additives

Have you ever wondered why ice cream is so smooth and creamy? Or why oil separates from some peanut butters and not others? The answer is a food additive. A **food additive** is a substance added to foods during processing to make them safer, more appealing, or more nutritious. Additives keep peanut butter from separating and make ice cream smooth. In these cases, the additives make the texture of the product more pleasing. Additives can also improve the flavor of products and increase a product's shelf life, or the length of time at which it can be stored. Some additives enrich food, or add back nutrients lost in processing. Other additives fortify food, or add nutrients that are not naturally present.

Perhaps you have noticed the words *calcium-fortified* on some cartons of orange juice. This juice is a **functional food**, or a food that provides benefits beyond basic nutrition. In this case, the manufacturer has added calcium to a product that is not a natural source of calcium to help ensure you get enough of this important mineral in your diet. Many of the foods you eat every day are functional foods. For example, most of the milk you drink is fortified with vitamins A and D to help you absorb more of milk's naturally present calcium.

All additives must pass rigid governmental tests for safety. Even so, some people choose not to eat foods that contain additives.

Dietary Supplements

Most health care professionals agree that you do not need to take dietary supplements if you eat a variety of healthful foods. **Dietary supplements** include pills, capsules, and powders that are taken in addition to, or to supplement, a person's diet. Dietary supplements include not only vitamins and minerals but also herbs and other botanical products.

Health care professionals may recommend dietary supplements for people who have special dietary needs. For example, pregnant women, or people recovering from an illness may need to take dietary supplements to increase nutrients or specific vitamins. If you cannot digest dairy products, your doctor might recommend an additional calcium supplement.

If your doctor recommends a supplement for you, read the label carefully to make sure you are getting the proper dosage. Check the expiration date and throw away expired supplements. Also, avoid taking megadoses, or large amounts, of dietary supplements. Often, it will simply pass through your system with no health benefit, but it is also possible for a large dose to lead to severe illness or death.

Section 16.2

After You Read

Review Key Concepts

1. **Identify** how technology can affect people's food choices.
2. **Recall** why people who are diabetic need to regulate the portions and types of foods they eat.
3. **Explain** how exercise can affect how much you eat.

Practice Academic Skills

**English Language Arts**

4. Read and analyze print advertisements for various food products. How might the ads influence people? Which ads seem to target teens specifically? Share your advertisements and analysis with your class.

**Social Studies**

5. Follow your teacher's instructions to form into groups. Research the benefits and drawbacks of natural and organic foods in comparison with foods produced in a traditional manner. Use online and print resources. After your group has finished, present your information to the rest of the class.

Check Your Answers Go to connectED. mcgraw-hill.com to check your answers.

CHAPTER SUMMARY

Section 16.1
Dietary Guidelines for Americans and MyPyramid

Before you accept information about nutrition as fact, consider the source. The Dietary Guidelines for Americans provide suggestions for a healthful lifestyle. MyPlate is a personalized way to approach healthful eating and physical activity. You can determine appropriate portion sizes by comparing certain foods next to common items.

Section 16.2
The Dietary Guidelines and Your Lifestyle

People's food choices depend on a number of factors. Nutritional needs vary from one person to another. Many people cannot digest certain foods without suffering annoying, painful, or even life-threatening side effects. Distinguishing between accurate and misleading nutritional information is important for a healthy lifestyle.

Vocabulary Review

1. Create a fill-in-the-blank sentence for each of these terms. Each sentence should contain enough information to help determine the missing word.

Content Vocabulary
◇ Dietary Guidelines for Americans (p. 389)
◇ nutrient-dense (p. 390)
◇ sedentary (p. 390)
◇ obesity (p. 390)
◇ MyPlate (p. 395)
◇ diabetes (p. 402)
◇ insulin (p. 402)
◇ food allergy (p. 402)
◇ vegetarian (p. 403)
◇ vegan (p. 403)
◇ irradiated food (p. 407)
◇ food additive (p. 407)
◇ functional food (p. 407)
◇ dietary supplement (p. 408)

Academic Vocabulary
▪ consistent (p. 389)
▪ counteract (p. 391)
▪ strenuous (p. 405)
▪ excess (p. 406)

Review Key Concepts

2. **Recall** the questions you should ask when considering food information.
3. **Summarize** the recommendations of the Dietary Guidelines for Americans.
4. **Explain** the key ideas represented by the MyPlate.
5. **Identify** factors that influence individual food choices.
6. **Give** five examples of special nutritional needs.
7. **Clarify** seven common food myths.

Critical Thinking

8. **Judge** Which of the recommendations in the Dietary Guidelines for Americans is the hardest for most teens to follow? Why? What strategies would make it easier to follow?
9. **Evaluate** Do you believe that teens today are more sedentary than they were a generation ago? Defend your response.
10. **Predict** Functional foods have captured people's interest. Describe some functional foods you expect to see in the future.
11. **Role Play** Describe how you would respond to a teen who says, "It does not matter what kinds of foods I eat. I get a lot of exercise, so I burn the calories no matter what."

ACTIVE LEARNING

Family & Community Connections

12. Regional Foods Use print or Internet sources to research regional foods of a certain part of the country. For example, you may research the regional food of the Southwest, southern California, the Midwest, or New England. You may even research a smaller geographic area, such as New Orleans or the Gulf Coast of Florida. In what ways do culture and food availability influence the cuisine? After you are finished, plan a meal that focuses on the foods and preparation techniques common to the area you researched. Use  the Dietary Guide lines for Americans to help you create as healthful a meal as possible. Share your research and your healthful meal plan with the class.

13. Food Allergies A food allergy is a reaction of the body's immune system to ingested food. People allergic to certain foods may break out in a rash, experience nausea, or even have trouble breathing after eating those foods. Peanuts, eggs, milk, wheat, strawberries, fish, and shellfish are some foods that commonly cause allergic reactions. Interview two people you know, such as family members, friends, teachers, neighbors, or coaches, who have allergies to certain foods. Ask them to discuss their allergies. How do their bodies react when eating certain foods? When they have a bad reaction, how do they address it? Have they ever gotten treatment in an attempt to reduce the severity of their allergies? Did the treatment help them in any way? Do their allergies pose a problem when dining out? Share your information with the class.

Real-World Skills and Applications

Leadership Skills

14. Provide Dietary Advice Imagine you work for a nutrition hotline that helps inform callers about the Dietary Guidelines for Americans. Take "calls" from classmates and answer their questions using the information from the chapter.

Financial Literacy

15. Compare Prices You go to the market to buy four bananas, three apples, and five carrots. Organic bananas cost 40 cents each, while bananas produced in a conventional manner cost 36 cents each. Organic apples cost $1.20 each, while conventionally produced apples cost 90 cents each. Organic carrots cost 69 cents each, while conventionally produced carrots cost 59 cents each. How much more will you spend if you buy all organic foods than if you buy all conventionally produced foods?

Technology Skills

16. Make a Food Plan Create a personalized daily food plan. Then consider how difficult you think it would be to follow the plan. Does the plan you have created differ much from the way you eat currently? If so, in what ways? What would be the most difficult part of the new plan for you to follow?

Corbis Super RF/Alamy

Academic Skills

English Language Arts

17. Explain Dehydration Use reliable print or Internet sources to research the warning signs and effects of dehydration. Then, create a public service announcement for television that addresses the issue of dehydration. Be sure to include guidelines for staying hydrated while exercising. Videotape your announcement and play it for your class.

Social Studies

18. Functional Foods Functional foods provide benefits beyond basic nutrition because of the added nutrients they contain. However, natural foods also contain great amounts of nutrients and phytochemicals. Given the variety of healthy food available in nature, why do you think people have developed functional foods? What is a functional food you would like to see developed?

Mathematics

19. Milkfat Andrew tries to follow the advice of MyPlate each day. He also knows that as long as he gets enough of each food group, he can eat those foods whenever he wants during the day. Andrew really loves milk, yogurt, and cheese. He ate his entire day's recommendation of milk products in one afternoon (three cups). Forty percent of the three cups was milk. If twenty-five percent of the milk Andrew drank was nonfat, how many cups of nonfat milk did he drink?

Math Concept **Percentage** To convert a percent to a decimal, simply divide the percent by 100.

Starting Hint First, find the amount of milk Andrew drank. You can do this by multiplying the original 3 cups of dairy products by forty percent. Multiply this answer by twenty-five percent to find the amount of nonfat milk he drank.

 For math help, go to the Math Appendix at the back of the book.

Standardized Test Practice

MATH WORD PROBLEMS
Directions Read the problem. Then, choose the correct answer.

Test-Taking Tip When answering a multiple-choice math word problem, first try to solve the problem before looking at the possible answers. Then, find your answer among the choices. If you cannot find your answer, you may be able to try each answer in the problem, if time allows.

20. Jessica made raspberry muffins and used ¾ cups raspberries, ⅛ cups sugar, and 1 ³⁄₁₆ cups flour. How many cups of those three ingredients did she use in all?
a) 2 cups
b) 2½ cups
c) 3³⁄₁₆ cups
d) 2¹⁄₁₆ cups

Meal Planning

Section 17.1
Planning Meals and Snacks

Section 17.2
Preparing Meals and Snacks

Chapter Objectives

Section 17.1
- **Identify** four things you should consider when planning a meal.
- **List** six ways families can save time when preparing a meal.
- **Compare** eating at home to eating at restaurants in terms of time, money, and health.
- **Describe** some healthful snacking strategies.

Section 17.2
- **Explain** the importance of teamwork when working in a food lab.
- **Outline** a step-by-step plan for preparing a perfectly timed meal.

Explore the Photo
Making a meal is more than following a recipe. You must plan what to serve, prepare it, and have it ready on time. *What management skills can help you plan a successful meal?*

Writing Activity — Step-by-Step Guide

Prepare a Meal Many teens lead very active lives and often feel too rushed to prepare their own meals. However, eating fast food and other convenience foods can lead to unhealthy weight gain. This is why it is important to know how to prepare your own meals. Writing a step-by-step guide will help you solidify your knowledge of how to complete a specific task.

Writing Tips Use these tips to write a step-by-step guide for preparing a meal:

- Before you begin writing, scan this section for tips on how to properly prepare a meal.
- Remember to record each step in the correct chronological sequence.
- Use transitional words like *first, next, then,* and *later* to help your reader understand the sequence of steps.

Section 17.1

Planning Meals and Snacks

Reading Guide

Before You Read

Think of an Example Look over the Key Concepts in this section. Think of an example of how or when you could use one of these skills. Thinking about how you might apply a skill can help you stay focused and retain knowledge.

Read to Learn

Key Concepts

- **Identify** four things you should consider when planning a meal.
- **List** six ways families can save time when preparing a meal.
- **Compare** eating at home to eating at restaurants in terms of time, money, and health.
- **Describe** some healthful snacking strategies.

Main Idea

There are several strategies you can use to eat healthfully and save time and money.

Content Vocabulary

◇ graze
◇ meal pattern
◇ convenience food

Academic Vocabulary

You will find these words in your reading and on your tests. Use the glossary to look up their definitions if necessary.

▢ primary
▢ incorporate

Graphic Organizer

As you read, record the elements that make a meal appealing. Use a graphic organizer like the one below to organize your information.

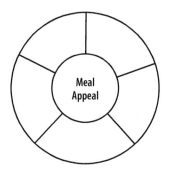

 Graphic Organizer Go to **connectED.mcgraw-hill.com** to download this graphic organizer.

Menu Planning Considerations

Food choices are a personal thing. Not only do people's ideas of what tastes good differ, but their needs differ as well. Your lifestyle, schedule, family, preferences, culture, and physical needs determine what, when, and how much you eat.

For many people, the primary, or main, focus is on how something tastes. The better a food tastes, the more likely it is that a person will eat it. Time and convenience are also great factors in food choices because of hectic schedules. Family members may have to juggle classes, job responsibilities, after-school activities, and volunteer work, leaving little time for regular meals. This means they may find it easier to eat on the fly, buy take-out foods for dinner, or order a pizza and make a quick salad at home. Finally, people take the cost of certain foods into consideration. Eating at restaurants all the time can be costly. Some people would eat lobster or steak every day if it were not so expensive.

Given all that there is to consider, planning a family meal requires a good deal of thought and management skills.

Meal Patterns

How does your family organize meals? Some sit together around a table to eat meals three times a day. Others tend to **graze**, with family members coming and going, each eating several small meals throughout the day. Over time, most people establish a **meal pattern**, or a way of grouping daily food choices into meals and snacks.

Think about your own meal patterns. Do you frequently skip meals? Most people skip a meal once in a while, but skipping meals as a habit is potentially unhealthy. Eventually, you may pay the price with fatigue and poor concentration. Skipping meals can also cause people to overeat later in the day, which can lead to an accumulation of unwanted calories.

As You Read

Connect Do you frequently skip meals? If so, what are your reasons? Do you lack hunger, time, or appealing food?

Vocabulary

You can find definitions in the glossary at the back of this book.

Morning Rush

Whether you sit to enjoy it, or eat on the go, breakfast is the most important meal of the day. *What foods do you normally choose for breakfast?*

FoodCollection/Stockfood

Mealtime is important in many cultures since it gives friends and family time to gather. By embracing different cuisine, you can appreciate other cultures. Visit ethnic food markets in your community to learn about foods and herbs that may be unfamiliar to you.

Meal Appeal

Imagine your favorite meal. What does it look like? Is it all white and beige or is it colorful? Does it have different shapes and flavors? Does it have a range of temperatures and textures? Many elements contribute to the appeal of a meal. The way something tastes is obviously important. But studies show that a meal that is appealing to the eye is more satisfying than a meal that tastes good but looks boring. When you are putting together a meal, think about the following elements:

- **Color** Combine different colors in a meal to make it visually interesting. Bright red tomato wedges, emerald green pepper slices, warm orange carrot sticks, and some wild rice or brown rice would definitely add visual interest to a chicken entrée.
- **Shape** Carrot and zucchini strips, bow-tie pasta, and a mound of cottage cheese offer contrasting shapes to a round beef patty.
- **Flavor** Experiment with different flavors in a meal to stimulate people's taste buds. Added flavors can come from herbs, spices, sauce, vinegar, a small drizzle of healthy oil, or a splash of citrus juice (lemon or lime). Combine a spicy main dish with a tongue-cooling side dish.
- **Texture** All meals should contain a variety of textures. If all of the foods in a meal were soft, you would feel as if you were eating baby food. Include crunchy or soft, and chunky, smooth, or chewy foods to incorporate texture in meals.
- **Temperature** Serving foods of different temperatures is yet another way to add appeal to a meal. Try a cool side salad with a warm main dish, or serve hot soup with a sandwich.

TAKE CHARGE!

Get a Good Start

Breakfast provides the fuel that gets you going in the morning. Teens who eat breakfast often do better in school and tend to eat healthier overall. You may not have time in the morning to prepare a traditional breakfast of eggs, toast, and juice, but you can still eat well on the go. Consider the following quick breakfast options:

- **Banana Toast** Peanut butter, banana slices, and raisins on whole-grain toast will keep you full until lunch.
- **Trail Mix** Toss dry cereal with nuts and dry fruit.
- **Fruit Smoothie** Blend fresh or frozen fruit with low- or non-fat yogurt.
- **Yogurt Mix** Mix low- or non-fat yogurt with fruit or whole grain cereal.
- **Whole Grain Low-Fat Cereal** Try adding fruit and low- or non-fat milk.
- **Instant Oatmeal** Add in fresh fruit for sweetness.

Real-World Skills

Try It Out Now that you have some nutritious breakfast ideas, try them out. Encourage family members to join you in eating healthier in the morning for one week. After one week, poll your family members on how the changes in their breakfasts made them feel. Share the results of your poll with the class.

Omelets can be stuffed with leftover meats or vegetables. They make a quick nutritious meal any time of the day. *How else can you use leftovers?*

Nutrition

A great meal does not just look and taste good. It also provides nutrient-dense foods. Use MyPlate to include the right variety and food-group amounts each day to match the energy and nutrient needs of the people you are feeding. Teens and physically active adults may need larger portions or different foods than younger siblings or grandparents.

When you select your food or help plan meals, try to incorporate, or fit in, more foods represented by the wide bands of color in MyPyramid. The results will be both delicious and healthful.

Food Budget

Whether families are buying food for meals or for snacks, they usually have to keep an eye on their spending. Food costs are a major part of a family budget.

By making wise food choices, you can make tasty, nutritious meals without overspending. For example, fruits and vegetables are less expensive when they are in season. Choosing whole foods instead of partially prepared or ready-to-eat items can also save money. Buying foods in bulk is yet another way to reduce costs.

Preparing larger portions with leftovers in mind can also be cost-effective. You can freeze leftovers for quick and handy meals, or transform them into new entrées. Leftover roast beef, for example, can be used in a stew or casserole, or to make sandwiches for lunch.

✓ **Reading Check** **Draw Conclusions** Why does meal planning require careful consideration?

Financial *Literacy*

A Food Budget

Lee currently spends $3.25 a day on coffee and $6.99 on lunch. He wants to create a food budget to save money, so he buys a coffee maker for $22.00 to make his own coffee. He also begins spending an average of $3.75 a day to buy food to make his lunch. With his new budget, how much money does Lee save at the end of 30 days?

Math Concept **Multiplication** When multiplying decimal numbers, multiply them as if they were whole numbers. Line up the numbers on the right, not by their decimal points. When finished multiplying all numbers, count the total number of decimal places in the multipliers. Then, use that number to move the decimal point that number of places from the right to the left.

Starting Hint Multiply $3.25 by 30 to figure out how much money Lee spends on coffee over 30 days. Do not forget to move the decimal point in the answer after you have completed the multiplication.

Math For math help, go to the Math Appendix at the back of the book.

Ingram Publishing/SuperStock

Dining Out

People tend to eat more calories when dining out because they are more likely to underestimate calories. They may also add unhealthful drinks and desserts. Use these tips to eat healthfully when dining out:

▶ Order salads without bacon bits, cheese, croutons, or mayonnaise-based items.

▶ Choose grilled or steamed food options instead of fried foods.

▶ If you want dessert, split it with a friend.

Mealtime Timesavers

The pressure to accomplish daily tasks can cause families to make unhealthy food choices. For example, it takes less time and effort to grab a quick meal at a fast-food restaurant than it does to shop at the supermarket for lean protein and salad ingredients to prepare at home. However, consistently choosing less nutritious food can lead to serious health issues, such as obesity, diabetes, and high blood pressure. No matter how busy you are, you are still responsible for your own health, and that includes selecting and preparing healthful food items.

Few people can spend a whole day in the kitchen to cook, except perhaps on weekends. However, families can still prepare nutritious meals by managing food preparation time effectively. How many of the following ideas does your family use?

- **Keep easy-to-fix foods on hand.** A few possibilities include cut vegetables, prepared pasta sauce, and salad ingredients.
- **Serve leftovers.** Leftovers are a great timesaver, and they can often be used as the basis for a different meal. For example, leftover spaghetti noodles or cooked rice can be combined with teriyaki sauce, chicken, and a bag of frozen stir-fry vegetables for a delicious and healthful dinner.
- **Use convenience foods.** Prepared or partially prepared foods are called **convenience foods**. Examples include salad greens in bags, precut fruit and vegetables, grated cheese, precut and cooked meat and poultry, and frozen dinners. One drawback to prepared foods is their higher cost.
- **Make meals ahead of time.** Some families prepare larger meals on the weekends, store the meals in the freezer, and heat them during the week. Casseroles and chili are examples of good make-ahead meals.
- **Use fast-cooking methods.** Microwaving, stir-frying, broiling, and indoor grilling are examples of fast-cooking methods. Cutting food into small pieces also helps it cook faster.
- **Create one-dish meals.** Try a chef's salad or casserole, or stuff a pita pocket with tuna salad and chopped vegetables.

✓ **Reading Check** **Explain** Why is there no excuse for not eating healthfully?

SUCCEED IN SCHOOL

Ask for Help

Talk to your teacher or guidance counselor if you need help identifying and developing good note-taking skills. He or she may be able to help you find additional assistance at your school, on the Internet, or in your community.

Meals Away from Home

Think about the meals you ate this week. How many did you eat away from home? Many people grab breakfast on the way to work or school. Even more eat lunch at school or at the workplace. They may eat dinner in a restaurant or order takeout several times every week.

Food consumed away from home is generally higher in fat, calories, and cholesterol, and lower in nutrients than foods made at home. Many restaurants also serve larger portions than most people need. Some restaurant portions are mega-sized, which can be four to eight times larger than suggested daily portions!

Light and Healthy Recipe

Chicken Salad Extraordinaire

Yield
4 servings (1 cup each)
or 8 wraps

Nutrition Analysis
Per Serving: 522 calories, 24 g total fat, 4 g saturated fat, 0 g trans fat, 61 mg cholesterol, 1,666 mg sodium, 43 g total carbohydrate, 4 g dietary fiber, 13 g sugars, 38 g protein

Salad Directions

Salad Ingredients
2 (12 oz.) cans chicken, white meat only, or precooked chicken, shredded
1 cup halved seedless red grapes
2 stalks celery
1 small onion
½ cup slivered almonds, toasted
2 cups chopped lettuce (optional)
4 8-inch tortillas (optional)

1. Drain canned chicken well or shred precooked chicken; place in a medium-sized bowl.
2. Wash grapes and pat dry with a paper towel. Cut grapes into halves; add to chicken.
3. In a food processor, using the chopping blade, finely chop celery and onions; add to chicken.
4. In a small frying pan, on a stove top or hot plate, add almonds and stir over medium heat 3–5 minutes until lightly toasted. Add to chicken.
5. Prepare dressing; mix with chicken mixture.
6. Chill and serve on bed of lettuce or wrap in tortilla.

Dressing Directions

Dressing Ingredients
½ cup light mayonnaise
1 Tbsp. garlic, minced
1 Tbsp. lemon juice
1 Tbsp. Worcestershire sauce
½ tsp. salt
¼ tsp. pepper

1. Combine all ingredients in a blender or whisk together in a bowl until smooth.

Eating every meal at home is impossible, so how can you eat out and maintain your health?

Choose wisely. Some restaurants have icons next to menu options to indicate that they are heart-healthy, low-fat, or low-sodium. If nutritional information is not available, however, you can still make smart choices. Choose items that are broiled, grilled, steamed, or stir-fried. Primavera means a dish is prepared with fresh vegetables. Steer clear of menu items that are breaded, creamed, deep-fried, scalloped, au gratin, or described as "rich." If you order a salad, choose a low-fat or "lite" dressing. Order the dressing on the side to make sure your salad is not drowning in it. Make a healthy beverage choice as well. Skip the soda and choose low-fat milk, juice, or water. Many fast-food restaurants now offer healthier selections, such as salads, low-fat meat options, yogurt, and low-fat, reduced-calorie sauces and salad dressings.

Control portions. Remember that portions served at restaurants are usually much larger than those served at home. Decide how much of your meal you will eat in advance, and stick to that plan. If you cannot keep yourself from picking at your meal once you have finished, have the waiter box it up for you before the bill comes.

HOW TO... Help with Family Meals

Sitting down with your family and eating a home-cooked, healthy meal is important. However, bringing everyone to the table is rarely easy. With working parents or guardians, after-school activities, and homework, eating on-the-go is often a necessity. Fortunately, there are ways you can help bring your family together to share a meal. Try these tips:

Create a Meal Plan Sometimes just deciding what to prepare makes family meals easier to accomplish. First, talk with your family and decide when everyone can meet for dinner. Then, choose a recipe for each meal. Choose recipes that are not too complicated. Those that have many ingredients or require a lot of kitchen time can be overwhelming, especially on a busy weeknight.

Make a Grocery List Once you have created your meal plan, make a grocery list. Find out which ingredients you have on hand. Then make a shopping list for the store. If the list is not too long and you live close to the store, offer to pick up the ingredients yourself. Ride your bike or walk, and you are also getting in some exercise! If this is not possible, offer to go along and help with the shopping.

Consider an appetizer. Many appetizers are the size of a reasonable meal. They are also less costly than most entrées. Choose an appetizer that has some protein foods in it to make sure it will be as filling and nutritious as a meal you would make at home. Make sure the appetizer is not deep-fried. A small deep-fried appetizer can have even more calories than a healthful entrée!

Share. Have your server ask the chef to divide an order and put it on two plates. For example, you could share an entrée and salad with a friend. Splitting a pizza is another great way to control portions. It also saves money.

Get it to go. If you are going straight home after dining out, take part of your meal home instead of cleaning your plate.

Push the bread basket away. Ask the waiter to remove tempting empty-calorie foods such as chips, crackers, or rolls from the table. If you fill up on these things, you will not have room for your more healthful and balanced meal.

✓ **Reading Check** **Identify** What strategies can you use to dine out and still maintain your health?

Help with Meal Preparation Depending on the meal, you can do part or all of the food preparation. If you are not able to do it all, you can prepare the kitchen for the "cook." Measure all ingredients, clear the kitchen counters of dirty dishes, and set the table. You also can prepare part of the main course or side dish. By pitching in, you help the meal reach the table faster.

Help Clean Up Some families are simply overwhelmed by the cleanup involved in making family meals. You can do your part by clearing the table, loading the dishwasher or washing dishes, and wiping down the counters and table. Be sure to store leftovers properly in the refrigerator or freezer.

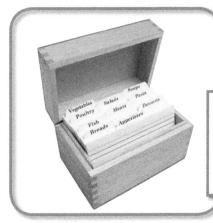

Put Together Family Recipes Each time your family enjoys a new recipe, add it to the recipe box or notebook. For example, you can copy the recipe or, if it is from a magazine or newspaper, cut it out and attach it to a note card or piece of paper. Having recipes on hand helps make meal planning a snap!

Building Character ?!

Courtesy Rebecca is trying to lead a healthy lifestyle. Rebecca's best friend, Chelsea, invites Rebecca to her house for her family's weekly cheeseburger and ice cream night. Although Rebecca wants to avoid eating unhealthy foods like cheeseburgers and ice cream, she does not want to hurt Chelsea's or her family's feelings by refusing the invitation.

You Make the Call

How can Rebecca stick to her healthy eating plan and still show courtesy toward Chelsea and her family? Does Rebecca have any options? If so, what are they?

▼ Make a Smoothie

Fresh fruit smoothies are healthy alternatives to ice cream. *What kinds of fruit might you use in a smoothie?*

Snacks

What is the first thing you do after you arrive home in the afternoon? Chances are you get a bite to eat. Snacking can be a healthful habit or an unhealthful one, depending on your choices.

Snacking can be good if you choose the right foods and are an active person who sometimes needs extra energy. Healthy snacks can keep your blood sugar and energy levels stable, and prevent you from over-eating at meals. Choosing snack foods high in fat and sugar can actually make you more tired than before after a short high-energy boost. They can also add excess calories which can negatively affect your health.

To make snacking part of a healthy lifestyle, follow these guidelines:

- **Do not snack when you are bored.** Substitute another activity for snacking when you are bored. Read a book, call a friend, play games, spend some time with your family pet, or develop a new hobby.
- **Munch snack-size portions.** Snacks are not meant to replace entire meals. Try putting snacks onto a small plate to make sure you are eating appropriate portions. Also, match your snack size to your energy needs. If you are physically active, eat a larger portion.
- **Make snacks a part of your daily meal plan.** Think about snacks as part of good nutrition. Instead of eating candy bars, cupcakes, and cookies, try snacking on fresh fruit with peanut butter or yogurt.
- **Turn off the television while eating.** When you are watching television, you lose track of how much you are eating.
- **Avoid eating snacks one hour or less before meals.** Snacks can interfere with your appetite at meals, where a variety of foods are usually available.
- **Plan ahead.** Try to keep nutritious snack foods on hand, such as air-popped popcorn, fresh fruit, low-fat cheese and crackers, and low-fat yogurt.

Pack a Healthful Snack

Packing a healthful snack is a great way to meet your calorie needs and squeeze in some good nutrition when eating on-the-go. When you prepare snacks, keep food safety guidelines and MyPlate in mind. The following healthful snack choices can be packed ahead of time in your backpack or in an insulated cooler:

- Fresh or dried fruit
- Apple slices with peanut butter
- Yogurt with low-fat granola or fruit
- Baby carrots
- A whole-grain bagel with low-fat cream cheese or peanut butter
- Low-fat cheese on crackers
- Hardboiled egg and an apple

Vending Machine Selections

You know you should snack healthfully, but it is not always easy. If you do not have time to stop at home or prepare a snack in advance, you have to eat on-the-go. And grabbing fast-food or prepackaged snacks from the nearest vending machine is a quick and easy solution. Unfortunately, these choices are often high in fat, calories, and sugar, and low in nutrients.

When hunger takes over, and you have to buy a snack from a vending machine, look for the following options:

- Low-fat or "light" popcorn
- Pretzels
- Nuts
- Dried fruit
- Water
- Low fat fig bars
- Trail mix
- Whole-grain cereal bars
- Cheese or peanut butter and crackers
- 100 percent juices
- Canned fruit in juice

Section 17.1

After You Read

Review Key Concepts

1. **Describe** negative effects of skipping a meal.
2. **Define** convenience food and provide examples.
3. **List** ways to eat fast food and maintain your health.
4. **Identify** activities you could substitute for snacking when you are bored.

Practice Academic Skills

English Language Arts

5. Write an article titled "Snacking the Healthy Way." Include information from this chapter as well as from other resources. Share your article with the class.

Social Studies

6. Fruits and vegetables are less expensive when they are in season. Choose one fruit and one vegetable and use reliable print or Internet sources to research the times they are in season as well as the areas in which they grow.

Check Your Answers Go to connectED. mcgraw-hill.com to check your answers.

Preparing Meals and Snacks

Before You Read

Helpful Memory Tools Successful readers use tricks to help them remember things. For example, the acronym HOMES is a memory aid where each letter stands for one of the five Great Lakes. You can also turn the information into a song or poem. As you read the section, look for opportunities to make up your own memory aids.

Read to Learn

Key Concepts

- **Explain** the importance of teamwork when working in a food lab.
- **Outline** a step-by-step plan for preparing a perfectly timed meal.

Main Idea

Organization and cooperation are just two of the skills necessary for proper meal preparation.

Content Vocabulary

◇ dovetail

Academic Vocabulary

You will find these words in your reading and on your tests. Use the glossary to look up their definitions if necessary.

▪ accurate
▪ major

Graphic Organizer

As you read, record the four food preparation steps. Use a graphic organizer like the one below to organize your information.

The Four Food Preparation Steps

1.

2.

3.

4.

Graphic Organizer Go to **connectED.mcgraw-hill.com** to download this graphic organizer.

Working in the Food Lab

When you work in the food lab at school, you will probably work as part of a group or team. This is an excellent opportunity to learn more about teamwork. Each person in the group is important, and you are each responsible for certain jobs. When one member of the team does not do a job correctly or on time, everyone else is effected. Working well as a team in the kitchen is important to your success.

Plan Your Work

Everyone needs a plan, and your food lab group is no exception. Your group will need to plan its supplies. For example, your teacher might ask you to list the ingredients and the amounts of food you need. Then your supplies will be added to the total grocery list for the lab. If your list is not accurate, or free from error, then your group will not have the supplies it needs.

Time is also an important part of your food lab plan. Because time in the lab is usually short, you need to plan your time wisely. Begin by listing the major, or most important, jobs in the order they need to be done. Estimate how long it will take to do each job. Do not forget to allow time for getting ready to cook. Before you can begin to prepare food, you will need to take the following steps:

1. Put on a clean apron, tie back long hair, roll up dangling sleeves, and, most importantly, wash your hands with soap and water.
2. Review your recipe.
3. Take out all of the equipment and ingredients you will need.
4. Finish any tasks you need to do before combining ingredients. Do you need to preheat the oven, grease baking pans, chop ingredients, or melt fat?

After you have listed all tasks, divide up the cooking responsibilities. Assign work fairly so that everyone has a comparable job. If someone has less responsibility this time, he or she can assume more next time.

As You Read

Connect Think about your favorite band, sports team, or other group. Which element of teamwork do you think is most important for this group's success?

◇ **Vocabulary**

You can find definitions in the glossary at the back of this book.

Design Pics/Monkey Business

▶ **Teamwork**

Good planning and teamwork help your work in the food lab go smoothly. *How can you improve your own work in the food lab?*

Figure 17.1 **Preparing a Meal**

Plan Ahead As a cook, make sure each dish is properly prepared and ready at the right time. *How can the habit of scheduling prepare you to make larger, more complicated meals?*

Getting a meal on the table is like conducting an orchestra. The conductor makes sure each musician plays the right notes at the right time. As a cook, you make sure each dish is properly prepared and ready at the right time. Unlike the conductor, however, you do not just oversee the production. You are involved. You have to keep a hand on the stirring spoon and an eye on the clock. It is almost like leading the band while playing an instrument. This kind of double duty takes a plan like the one outlined here.

Double Duty As a cook, you are involved in the production of the meal while you oversee its preparation.

STEP 1 **List the steps in each recipe and the time needed to complete each one.** Suppose a meal includes refrigerated crescent rolls. The first step, greasing the baking sheet, might take 1 minute. Separating and shaping the rolls might take 5 more minutes. Estimate times generously, especially when trying new skills or recipes.

STEP 2 **Next to the task times, list any added time needed for cooking.** The rolls mentioned in Step 1 might need 10 to 12 minutes to cook.

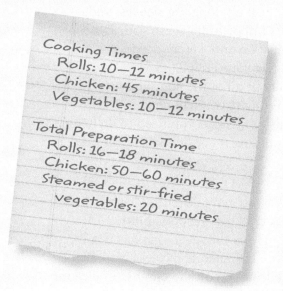

Cooking Times
Rolls: 10—12 minutes
Chicken: 45 minutes
Vegetables: 10—12 minutes

Total Preparation Time
Rolls: 16—18 minutes
Chicken: 50—60 minutes
Steamed or stir-fried
vegetables: 20 minutes

STEP 3 **Add the task and cooking times.** This total time will help you decide when to start each task. Total preparation time for the rolls would be 16 to 18 minutes.

STEP 4 **List tasks with flexible starting times.** Some tasks can be done in advance or fit in with others. You can set the table, for example, or wash a saucepan while you are waiting for part of the meal to finish cooking.

STEP 5   **Figure out the starting time.** Subtract the total time from the time at which the meal should be ready. Again, add a few minutes. To serve dinner at 6 p.m., roll preparation might start at 5:40 p.m.

STEP 6   **Make a schedule.** Put the tasks in order based on starting time, working backward from the time the meal should be ready. Fill gaps with tasks that have flexible starting times and others that can be dovetailed. If leftover soup is on the menu, for instance, you will need to reheat the soup while the rolls bake. Make adjustments to fit in any tasks that have the same starting time.

STEP 7   **Carry out the plan.** Check off tasks as you complete them so that nothing is forgotten. Note any problems that arise on your schedule to help improve the results next time.

Mealtime   6 p.m.
Preparation time   − 1 hour
              ————
Start time   5 p.m.

1. Prepare chicken for oven.
2. Set table.
3. Prepare vegetables.
4. Prepare rolls.
5. Put vegetables and rolls in serving dishes.
6. Put chicken on a platter.

Take Action

Plan and prepare a three-course meal of simple recipes, using the steps listed here. Was preparing the meal easier or harder when you put yourself on a schedule? How can the habit of scheduling prepare you to make larger, more complicated meals?

Carrying Out Your Plan

Before you go into the lab, know your assigned job. When you enter the lab, post the time plan where it can be seen. Follow the guidelines about dress, behavior, and lab rules for your safety and the safety of others. After you complete your work, volunteer to help someone else. If you see that something needs to be done, do it.

Cleaning Up

No one likes a big cleanup after preparing food. Cleaning as you go will help your group at the end of class. If food spills on the counter or floor, clean it up right away to prevent an accident, such as a slip or fall. Have a sink of warm, sudsy water ready. When you finish using a utensil, soak it in this water unless it is a sharp utensil. Wash sharp utensils separately, because you might cut yourself reaching for a sharp utensil such as a knife in the cloudy water. While you are waiting for something to cook, take advantage of these few moments to scrub and rinse utensils.

At the end of the lab period, wash any remaining dishes, wipe off tables and countertops, and sweep the floor. Always leave the food lab clean for the next group.

Evaluating Your Work

Evaluation is an important part of your lab experience. When you evaluate your work, you judge its quality, how it tastes, and what it looks like. Your evaluation might be in the form of a rating sheet given by your teacher. A rating sheet allows points for work well done. When evaluating teamwork, think about whether the job went as planned. Did team members perform all of their assigned tasks? Did anyone put forth an extra effort to help someone else? What could you do to improve? Your answers help you build on your success in future labs.

✓ **Reading Check** **Describe** What steps should you follow when working in a food lab?

Somos Images LLC/Alamy

➤ **Cleanup**

Do not forget to evaluate your cleanup tasks. *Why is cleanup an important final step in meal preparation?*

Working in Your Home Kitchen

Preparing food at home is similar to working in the food lab. In both cases, you probably have limited time. To be successful at home, plan to prepare and cook food as you did in the food lab. Organize your work and plan time for each task. Allow some extra time for unexpected delays. Often two or more family members work together. You will have to decide how to divide tasks.

Even when you work alone in the kitchen, you can still be efficient. Look for ways to dovetail tasks. **Dovetail** means skillfully fitting tasks together to make the best use of time. For example, you can wash salad greens during the time it takes water to boil for cooking pasta.

Planning a schedule is especially important when you are responsible for preparing an entire meal. Your goal is to have all foods ready at the same time. Start with the foods that take the longest to prepare and cook. For example, it may take you 15 minutes to put a casserole together and another 45 minutes to bake it. If you were also microwaving a frozen vegetable to go with the casserole, you would need to begin the casserole first. As you gain experience, you probably will not need to write out a schedule for simple meals. If meals are more complicated, you may want to jot down a rough time schedule.

Working in the kitchen requires a good deal of careful planning and preparation. But if you are organized, you will have more time to eat and enjoy yourself.

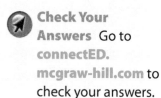

SUCCEED IN SCHOOL

Organize Your Schedule

Organizing your schedule and school assignments will help you reduce stress. You will be prepared to turn in your assignments on time and will avoid last minute rushing to complete all of your work.

Section 17.2

After You Read

Review Key Concepts

1. **List** the steps you should follow before preparing food in a food lab.
2. **Recall** ways that preparing food at home is similar to working in the food lab.

Practice Academic Skills

English Language Arts

3. Read an article on time management. Make a list of useful tips from the article. Which tips could be used in the kitchen? Is there a link between time management and meal patterns?

Social Studies

4. Think of a traditional meal you eat with your family. It may be a meal you have on a certain holiday, for example. Create a plan for cooking this meal that lists all tasks that need to be done as well as a schedule for preparation.

Check Your Answers Go to connectED. mcgraw-hill.com to check your answers.

Exploring Careers

Legislator

©Hill Street Studios/Blend Images LLC/Glow Images

What Does a Legislator Do?

Legislators establish government policy and develop laws, rules, and regulations. They are elected or appointed officials who either control units of government or make laws. Most state legislators work full time only when in session, usually for a few months a year, and work part time the rest of the year.

Skills Legislators must understand how to enact, review, and vote on laws. They must learn to hire division managers, and nominate others for government jobs. A legislator must comprehend how to make and keep a budget. All of these functions require the legislator to know how to compromise.

Education and Training Local voters elect most legislators. Taking part in volunteer work and helping to provide community services are good ways to establish community support. Those elected to legislator positions come from a variety of backgrounds, but must conform to age, residency, and citizenship regulations.

Job Outlook Although job prospects vary by state and region, overall prospects are favorable. In addition to brand new job openings resulting from population growth, workers who retire from the industry will also create many opportunities.

Critical Thinking Think about the job duties and skills of a legislator. Write a short speech that explains why voters should vote for you to become a legislator. What can you say that will persuade them to vote for you? Read your speech to the class.

Career Cluster
Government and Public Administration

Legislators work in the Government and Public Administration career cluster. Here are some of the other jobs in this career cluster:

- IRS Agent
- Foreign Service Officer
- Regional Planner
- Bank Examiner
- Cryptologist
- Intelligence Agent
- Soldier
- Sailor
- Legislative Aide
- Mayor
- City Council Member
- Chief of Staff
- City Manager
- Governor
- County Commissioner
- Policy Analyst
- Consul
- Ambassador
- Lobbyist

Explore Further Research this career cluster. Choose a career in this cluster that appeals to you and write a career profile.

Chapter 17 Review and Applications

CHAPTER SUMMARY

Section 17.1
Planning Meals and Snacks

Food choices depend upon a person's taste and personal needs. Many families have hectic or conflicting schedules that affect their food choices. Snacks can be an important part of a healthful food plan. You can use the elements of color, shape, flavor, temperature, and texture to increase the appeal of a meal or snack. Meal patterns may vary, but all meals and snacks can be nutritious. A variety of food preparation strategies can help you save time in the kitchen. If well chosen, meals eaten away from home can be just as nutritious as those prepared at home. Even vending machines provide healthful options.

Section 17.2
Preparing Meals and Snacks

Planning your work in the kitchen is important to successful meal preparation. Whether you are working in a food lab or at home, you will need to have effective time management and teamwork skills. Dovetailing tasks can help you save time in the kitchen. Cleaning up after preparing food is a necessary part of food preparation. If you clean as you go, you will save time in the long run. To improve your meal planning and preparation skills, you should always evaluate the results of your work. Taste, presentation, nutritional value, and efficiency in the kitchen should all be considered.

Vocabulary Review

1. Write a paragraph using at least five of these content and academic vocabulary terms. The paragraph should clearly show how the terms are related.

Content Vocabulary
◇ graze (p. 415)
◇ meal pattern (p. 415)
◇ convenience food (p. 418)
◇ dovetail (p. 429)

Academic Vocabulary
▢ primary (p. 415)
▢ incorporate (p. 417)
▢ accurate (p. 425)
▢ major (p. 425)

Review Key Concepts

2. **Identify** four things you should consider when planning a meal.
3. **List** six ways families can save time when preparing a meal.
4. **Compare** eating at home to eating at restaurants in terms of time, money, and health.
5. **Describe** some healthful snacking strategies.
6. **Explain** the importance of teamwork when working in a food lab.
7. **Outline** a step-by-step plan for preparing a perfectly timed meal.

Critical Thinking

8. **Compare** In your opinion, which element is the most important when creating meal appeal? Why is this element more important than others? Explain.
9. **Conclude** Why are convenience foods so appealing to people?
10. **Judge** What do you think is the hardest part of eating healthfully when you are away from home? Why?
11. **Role Play** What advice would you give to a friend who has trouble managing time in the food lab?

Family & Community
Connections

ACTIVE LEARNING

12. Analyze Menus How healthy is the food you eat? Gather several menus from local restaurants, including fast-food restaurants, at which you eat frequently. Then, analyze the food choices on the menus. Are there mainly healthy choices? Are there mainly unhealthy choices? With a partner, create a list of healthy dishes offered by each restaurant and explain what makes them wise choices. Create a second list of dishes that can be healthy with a few modifications. Note the necessary modifications next to each dish.

Create a third list of choices that should be avoided or only ordered rarely. Based on your findings, which of these restaurants offers the most healthful foods?

13. Plan and Prepare Planning a meal in detail well ahead of time can make the preparation of the meal much easier. Put together a step-by-step plan for cooking a special meal with a friend or family member. In your plan, be sure to note the approximate length of time it will take to prepare each item as well as the order in which the items should be prepared. If you will need to wait for something to cook, you might use the free time to wash utensils, start preparation of other items, or set places at the table. Also consider the food you plan to make. Plan an appealing, well-balanced, nutritious meal that is prepared in a healthful manner. When you are finished outlining your strategy, prepare your meal with your partner, each of you following his or her assigned roles.

Real-World Skills and Applications

Leadership Skills

14. Meal Appeal Outline for the class how the color, shape, flavor, and texture of the food you eat can make it more pleasing and satisfying. Describe the ways in which you can take each of those four elements into consideration to make your meals more interesting. Show an example of a boring, bland-looking meal, and point out specific ways it can be made more appealing.

Financial Literacy

15. Buy in Bulk Isabel uses four cups of rice per week. She can buy boxes of rice that contain four separately bagged two-cup packages for $5.95 per box. She can also buy bags of rice that contain 20 cups of rice for $12.95 per bag. How much cheaper is buying the bags of rice than buying the boxes of rice, in terms of price per cup? Round your answer to the nearest cent.

Cooperative Learning

16. Plan Weekly Meals With your family, create a schedule that includes one healthful family meal each day for a week. Be sure to consider the cost of the ingredients, the nutritional value of the foods you plan, the time it will take to prepare the meals, and the family members who will help prepare each meal.

Academic Skills

English Language Arts

17. Find Quick Meals Use magazines, newspapers, family cookbooks, and the Internet to collect a variety of quick one-dish meals. Try to find meals that are not only quick to prepare but also nutritious. Write a letter to your parent or guardian explaining the results of your research. Note which meals can be frozen to eat at a later time. Share the recipes with your family.

Science

18. Water Weight Certain foods absorb water when cooking or soaking in it. Use this experiment to see the effects of soaking rice in water.

Procedure Weigh a cup of rice. In the morning, combine it with two cups of water and let it soak until the late afternoon. Strain the rice and weigh it again.

Analysis What happened to the weight of the rice? Compare the weight of the rice before and after soaking.

Mathematics

19. A Variety of Vegetables You are trying to incorporate more vegetables into your diet. So you decide to serve at least two different vegetables as side dishes to a meal. You have carrots, broccoli, cauliflower, and snowpeas available. How many different combinations of the four vegetables are available to you, and what are they?

Math Concept **Combinations** A combination is a set of objects in which order is not important. To combine means to mix together different elements.

Starting Hint Each vegetable can be served with one, two, or all three of the other vegetables. Be careful not to repeat any options when you are thinking of combinations. If you are a visual learner, you could use a table to figure out all of the possible combinations.

 For math help, go to the Math Appendix at the back of the book.

 Standardized Test Practice

MATH WORD PROBLEMS
Directions Read the question. Then, choose the correct answer.

Test-Taking Tip When taking a multiple-choice test, it is a good idea to first glance over the test before beginning. You may want to see how many questions there are in all so that you can find out how much time you have to answer each question.

20. Joel is having a party and wants to buy enough food for his 16 expected guests and himself. He is ordering pizza and wants to have three slices available for each person. Each pizza contains 8 slices. How many pizzas does Joel need to order?
a) 6
b) 7
c) 8
d) 9

Research Food Choices

In this project you will create a visual showing images of foods from each of the five food groups and the oils category. These images will show nutrient-dense food choices as well as other less healthful choices. You will also interview an adult who makes healthful eating decisions and make a presentation to your class.

My Journal

If you completed the journal entry from page 362, refer to it to see if your thoughts have changed after reading the unit.

Project Assignment

In this project you will:

- Conduct research to gather information.
- Collect images of foods that illustrate varying degrees of nutrient density.
- Create a poster or storyboard that illustrates food choices in each food group and the oils category.
- Interview an adult who lives a healthful lifestyle.

The Skills Behind the Project

Life Skills

Key personal and relationship skills you will use in this project include:
- Researching.
- Relating to adults.
- Making healthy choices.

STEP 1   Research Food Choices

Use this text and other sources to research food choices from each of the five food groups and the oils category. As you conduct your research, save electronic files of photos of examples of various food choices. You will use these photos to create a visual, like a poster or a storyboard, that shows various food choices and identifies their degree of healthfulness. Write an essay explaining which food items you selected and why.

Writing Skills

- Use complete sentences.
- Include an introduction, a body, and a conclusion.
- Use transition words to ensure a smooth flow of ideas from paragraph to paragraph.

STEP 2   Write Interview Questions

Identify an adult in your community who lives a healthy lifestyle. This may be a doctor, nurse, a registered dietitian, a coach, or a personal trainer. Write a list of interview questions to ask this person. Your questions might include:

Life Skills Project Checklist

Plan	☑ Conduct research about food choices.
	☑ Write an essay about your research.
	☑ Interview an adult in your community who lives a healthful lifestyle.
	☑ Create a a poster or a storyboard that shows various food choices from each of the five food groups and the oils category and identifies their degree of healthfulness.
Present	☑ Make a presentation to your class to present your visual.
	☑ Invite the students in your class to ask you any questions they may have. Answer these questions.
	☑ When students ask you questions, demonstrate in your answers that you respect their perspectives.
	☑ Turn in the essay about your research, your notes from your interview, and your visual to your teacher.
Academic Skills	☑ Speak clearly and concisely.
	☑ Thoughtfully express your ideas.

- How often do you exercise?
- What is a typical breakfast, lunch, or dinner for you?
- Do you snack between meals? If yes, what kinds of snacks do you choose?
- When you want to treat yourself to a dessert, what kind do you choose?

STEP 3 Connect to Your Community

Contact the adult you identified in Step 2 and arrange to interview him or her. Bring your essay and share it with the person, and use the questions you wrote in Step 2. During your interview, ask for advice about making healthful food choices.

Interviewing Skills
- Take thorough notes.
- Listen attentively.
- Write in complete sentences and use correct spelling and grammar when you transcribe your notes.

STEP 4 Create Your Visual

Use the Life Skills Project Checklist to plan and create your visual and share what you have learned with your classmates.

STEP 5 Evaluate Your Life Skills and Academic Skills

Your project will be evaluated based on:
- Creativity and detail.
- Mechanics—presentation and neatness.
- Speaking and listening skills.

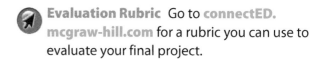

Evaluation Rubric Go to connectED. mcgraw-hill.com for a rubric you can use to evaluate your final project.

UNIT 7

Working in the Kitchen

Chapter 18 Food Shopping, Storage, and Sanitation

Chapter 19 Kitchen Equipment Selection and Safety

Chapter 20 Recipes and Measuring

Unit Life Skills Project Preview

Design Your Dream Kitchen

In this unit you will learn how to work safely and efficiently in a kitchen. In your life skills project you will design a kitchen that meets your needs and personal preferences.

 My Journal

Be Prepared Write a journal entry about one of these topics. This will help you prepare for the project at the end of this unit.

- Describe the problems you would face by preparing a peanut butter sandwich with no utensils.
- Explain the different ways you know if a food is not safe to eat.
- List the five most important appliances you believe are essential to the kitchen.

Explore the Photo

Cooking is a fun learning process, but it is important to be safe and organized at all times. *What are some of the dangers of not cleaning up properly during and after cooking?*

437

Chapter 18

Food Shopping, Storage, and Sanitation

Section 18.1
Shopping for Food

Section 18.2
Food Safety and Sanitation

Chapter Objectives

Section 18.1
- **Describe** what you should do to prepare for a shopping trip.
- **Explain** how to choose products based on brand, nutrition, and price.
- **Explain** how you can identify fresh, high-quality food products.

Section 18.2
- **Identify** the cause of foodborne illness.
- **Give examples** of personal cleanliness in the kitchen.
- **Describe** safe practices for preparing and serving food.

Writing Activity

Question & Answer Essay

Grocery Shopping Shopping for groceries can be intimidating. This is why it is important to plan before you go to the grocery store. Ask yourself a question related to grocery shopping, and answer it. For example, asking the question "What kinds of meals and snacks should I eat?" will help you create a grocery list. In this case, you would write a question-and-answer essay identifying what you would include on a grocery list.

Writing Tips Use these tips to write a question-and-answer essay:

- Review previous chapters for information about meal planning and wholesome meal options.
- Your first sentence should introduce the question your essay will answer.
- Each body paragraph should support your answer. In this case, each paragraph should illustrate why you would include a particular type of food on your grocery list.

Shop for Food

Shopping for food at a grocery store can take a lot of time and effort if you are not prepared. *How do you and your family prepare to go to the grocery store?*

Section 18.1

Shopping for Food

Reading Guide

Before You Read

Predict Before starting the section, browse it by reading headings, bold terms, and photo captions. Do they help you predict the information in the section?

Read to Learn

Key Concepts

- **Describe** what you should do to prepare for a shopping trip.
- **Explain** how to choose products based on brand, nutrition, and price.
- **Explain** how you can identify fresh, high-quality food products.

Main Idea

To successfully shop for groceries, it is important to choose appropriate types of foods, and be able to identify fresh and high-quality products.

Content Vocabulary

◇ impulse purchase
◇ staple
◇ comparison shopping
◇ unit price
◇ food product dating
◇ produce
◇ legume
◇ pasteurize
◇ homogenize

Academic Vocabulary

You will find these words in your reading and on your tests. Use the glossary to look up their definitions if necessary.

☐ disintegrate
☐ perishable

Graphic Organizer

As you read, note six ways you can stretch your food budget. Use a graphic organizer like the one below to organize your information.

How to Stretch Your Food Dollar
1.
2.
3.
4.
5.
6.

 Graphic Organizer Go to **connectED.mcgraw-hill.com** to download this graphic organizer.

Get Ready to Shop

Food shopping requires making many decisions. How many pounds of chicken should you buy for dinner? Should you get the name-brand cereal or the less expensive store-brand version? Should you buy salad dressing now or wait until it is on sale? With so many options and so many versions of the same product, shopping for groceries can be overwhelming. If you plan ahead, you will get the most out of your shopping experience.

Make a Shopping List

Have you ever gone shopping without a list and come back with items that you did not need? Perhaps you returned home from the store only to realize that you had forgotten something. A shopping list helps you plan your trip to the market so that you come home with what you need. A list also helps you stick to a budget and keeps you from making impulse purchases. An **impulse purchase** is an unnecessary item that is bought without much thought. Use the following tips to create a shopping list:

- **Keep a running list.** Find a handy spot in your kitchen to keep your shopping list and a pen or pencil. Family members can add to the list when they notice an item is running low. You can also keep a list in a notes application on your phone, tablet, or computer.
- **Plan weekly meals.** Look over recipes for upcoming meals, and add needed ingredients to your list. This will ensure that you have the ingredients you need for complete meals. This can also help you eat healthful, balanced meals throughout the week since your meals will be planned out in advance.
- **Take stock.** Before you head to the store, check the food that you have on hand, paying particular attention to staples. A **staple** is a food you are likely to use often, such as milk, eggs, pasta, rice, or bread.
- **Organize your list.** Group items according to the store's layout, and then shop in the order of your list. This will help save time.

> ## Update Your Grocery List

All family members can add to a shopping list if it is posted in a central location. *What else can younger family members do to help with food shopping?*

As You Read

Connect When you go shopping, do you use a list? Or do you buy items that look good?

Vocabulary

You can find definitions in the glossary at the back of this book.

Ken Karp/McGraw-Hill Education

Stretch Your Food Dollar

Most families have a food budget they need to follow. To stay within your budget, you must be organized. What can you do to help stretch your food dollars?

- **Scan newspapers for supermarket specials.** Planning meals around specials can help you save money. You can also compare advertised prices from several stores to find the lowest prices. Keep in mind that stores often advertise items at everyday prices, not sale prices. Be sure to look for the original price so that you choose items that are actually discounted.
- **Clip coupons.** Although coupons can help you save, coupon items may not always be the best buys. Use coupons for items you need and normally buy. Make sure the item with the coupon is less expensive than similar brands without a coupon. Follow your store's profile on social media because they may post coupons there, too.
- **Sign up for frequent-customer cards.** Some stores offer special savings to customers with these cards.
- **Take advantage of seasonal specials.** Fresh fruits and vegetables are usually less expensive when they are in season.
- **Buy in bulk.** When you buy in bulk, you buy larger quantities of an item to get a lower price. Before buying in bulk, be sure you will be able to eat all of the food before it spoils.
- **Shop on a full stomach.** If you are hungry when you shop, you are more likely to buy less healthful food or extra food that you do not need.

✓ **Reading Check** **Draw Conclusions** Why is it important to use a shopping list?

▲ Stick to Your Budget

Using a shopping list will help you stick to your budget. *How else can you stick to your budget?*

Community Connections

Surplus Food

Many food manufacturers, supermarkets, and restaurants across the country donate their excess food products to soup kitchens and food banks. You may be able to volunteer to stock shelves at food banks, help prepare or distribute foods, or organize a food donation drive.

Shopping for Food

Planning before shopping is important. However, even the best plan can **disintegrate**, or fall apart, once you get to the store if you are not careful. Colorful packaging, eye-catching displays, and coupon dispensers are designed to attract your attention. Products are often arranged in special end-of-aisle displays. These featured items are sometimes on sale, but not always.

Higher-priced and impulse items are typically placed at eye level or at the checkout stand so that you will be more likely to notice them and make a purchase. Some stores offer food samples. Store managers hope these samples and the store's pleasant background music will encourage customers to stay longer and buy more products. Try not to let these strategies distract you from your plan. You will be less likely to make unnecessary purchases this way.

Keep your grocery list handy as you shop. As you select items, cross them off the list. Some people use a calculator as they shop to track their spending and make sure they stay within their budget.

Read Labels

Food labels list information that will help you analyze the foods you eat or drink. By law, every food label must give the food's name and description, the weight of its contents, the ingredients listed from most to least, and Nutrition Facts (see **Figure 18.1** on page 444). Labels must also show the name of the manufacturer and note if allergens are in the product or processed on the same equipment. Read food labels carefully to help you make the most healthful choices.

How I See It

GROCERY SHOPPING TECHNIQUES
Lauren, 15

My family and I used to go grocery shopping before a meal so that we had the necessary ingredients. But we realized that because it was *before* the meal, we would only get food for that meal because we were hungry and in a rush to eat. So, this past weekend, we decided to go to the grocery store *after* we ate dinner. It turned out really well because we had a grocery list, which came from a meal plan we created. Having those steps helped us get all of the food we needed for the upcoming week in one trip. Since we were not as rushed, we were also able to find the best deals on the products we bought. Plus, we bought food for more than just the upcoming meal. This will cut down on how many trips we take to the grocery store and save us time and energy.

Critical Thinking Lauren says that it is important to create a meal plan and a shopping list from that plan before you go to the grocery store. How could you work this idea into your family's shopping routine?

Figure 18.1   **Nutrition Facts**

A Helpful Tool Nutrition information is located on the Nutrition Facts panel.
What information on the Nutrition Facts label do you look at before buying food?

Calories
The number of calories from a single serving is listed.

Trans Fat
The amount of trans fat, which functions like saturated fat in the body, is listed.

Nutrient Amounts
Only the nutrients related to today's most important health issues are listed.

Daily Values Footnote
Figures show the maximum amounts recommended for fat, saturated fat, cholesterol, and sodium.

Nutrition Facts

Serving Size 1/2 cup (114g)
Servings Per Container 4

Amount Per Serving	
Calories 90 Calories from Fat 27	
	% Daily Value*
Total Fat 3g	5%
Saturated Fat 0g	0%
Trans Fat 0g	
Cholesterol 0mg	0%
Sodium 300mg	13%
Total Carbohydrate 13g	4%
Dietary Fiber 3g	12%
Sugars 3g	
Protein 3g	

Vitamin A	80%	•	Vitamin C	60%
Calcium	4%	•	Iron	4%

*Percent Daily Values are based on a 2,000 calorie diet. Your daily values may be higher or lower depending on your calorie needs:

	Calories	2,000	2,500
Total Fat	Less than	65g	80g
Sat Fat	Less than	20g	25g
Cholesterol	Less than	300mg	300mg
Sodium	Less than	2,400mg	2,400mg
Total Carbohydrate		300g	375g
Fiber		25g	30g

Calories per gram:
Fat 9 • Carbohydrates 4 • Protein 4

Serving Size and Number of Servings
Servings are based on an average size and are not always the same size as those in MyPyramid.

Percent Daily Values
These percentages give you a good idea of how much one serving contributes nutritionally to a 2,000-calorie daily diet.

Calories-Per-Gram Conversion
Figures state the number of calories in one gram of fat, carbohydrates, and protein.

Science You Can Use

Brand Names vs. Generic Names

Most grocery stores carry national and store brands, as well as generic products. Similar products may have different ingredients and may taste different as a result.

Procedure Follow your teacher's instructions to form into small groups. Choose a product that everyone in the group has eaten. Make sure to mention if you have eaten a national brand, store brand, or generic product. Discuss the differences between the products.

Analysis Write a one- to two-paragraph report explaining the differences in one product between the national brand, store brand, and generic product versions.

Comparison Shop

Instead of choosing the first package you see, take time to do some comparison shopping. **Comparison shopping** is comparing prices of different forms, container sizes, and brands to get the best value for your money. When you compare different items, you can be sure you are buying what you want at a fair price.

- **Compare Brands** Scan the shelves of breakfast cereals, and notice the various brands. Is one brand better than another? You can only answer that by comparing national brands, store brands, and generic products.
- **Generic Products** These products are often less expensive than both national brands and store brands.

- **National Brands** Food companies produce many of the products you see on store shelves. National brands are sold in stores throughout the country and are advertised nationally on the radio, on television, and in magazines.
- **Store Brands** These products are produced and packaged for a particular chain of stores and carry the store's brand name. Store brands usually have prices that are lower than the prices of national brands. The quality is generally comparable to national brands.
- **Unit Pricing** Taking time to compare unit prices will help you get the most for your money. The **unit price** is the price per ounce, pound, or other unit of measure. Look for the unit price on the shelf near the item. The total price for the package is also given. If a store does not list unit prices, calculate them yourself. Divide the total cost of the package by the number of units (usually ounces or pounds) to find the cost per unit. Larger containers may cost less per unit than smaller containers. Buy a large size only if you can store it properly and use it all before it spoils.

SUCCEED IN SCHOOL

Ask for Explanations
When you feel completely lost trying to solve a problem, do not be afraid to ask for help. Have your teacher solve the problem with you, explaining each step out loud. By listening to each step in solving the problem, you can understand the thinking behind it so that you can later solve similar problems yourself.

✓ **Reading Check** **Describe** How should you organize your shopping?

Food Quality

Choosing the freshest and best-quality items can pose one of the biggest challenges as you shop. Foods that are past their peak have fewer nutrients than those that have not been sitting on store shelves as long. Also, if you buy overripe fruits and vegetables, most of it will likely spoil before you are able to use it. That wastes food and money. Some foods may be harmful to your health if they have passed their expiration date. Also, canned goods may not have the best quality if the can is dented or damaged. Be sure to inspect food carefully and look for dates before putting it in your basket.

Ken Karp/McGraw-Hill Education

▶ **Compare Products**

Comparing products enables you to get the most for your money and ensure quality.
What do you look for when you compare products?

Saving Leftovers

Leftover foods can provide additional tasty meals. To conserve nutrients and make sure those meals will not cause foodborne illness, follow these simple tips:

▶ **Refrigerate** leftovers within two hours.

▶ **Wash and dry** storage containers before filling.

▶ **Place** leftovers in shallow containers to chill rapidly.

Food Product Dating

One way to make sure you buy the freshest food possible is to check the date on the items. **Food product dating** is the process of dating food to indicate product freshness. You will see four types of dates stamped on product packages.

- **Sell-By Date** The sell-by date is the last day a product should be sold if the food is to remain fresh for home storage. This date is usually found on meat, milk, eggs, and other items that spoil quickly.
- **Packed-On Date** This date refers to the day the food was packaged. Bakery items usually have a packed-on date. This date tells the buyer the day the food was packaged. Food is at its peak quality on its packed-on date.
- **Best-If-Used-By Date** This date tells when you should use food for its best quality. A food item may still be safe to eat after this date, but the quality and nutritional content may not be at their best.
- **Expiration Date** This date indicates the last day a product should be eaten. After this date, the product may not be safe to eat. Products that have passed their expiration date should be thrown out.

How can you use product dating information? Buy the item with the latest possible sell-by date. If the sell-by date has passed, do not buy the product. Always choose the latest possible packed-on date for items that spoil quickly, such as meat, deli items, and baked foods. Refer to the best-if-used-by date when planning meals to make sure food is at its freshest. Throw out items when their expiration date passes. This way you will not think you have these ingredients when planning meals and forget to replace them or use them accidentally.

 Expiration Date

Always check the sell-by date before purchasing milk products. *Why is it important to check the sell-by date before purchasing milk products?*

JUPITERIMAGES/Comstock Images/Alamy

©Plush Studios/Blend Images LLC

A little time spent checking for signs of quality in produce can save you money. *Why is it important to check for signs of freshness or spoilage before purchasing fruit, vegetables, or produce?*

Buying Fruits and Vegetables

Knowing what to look for and what to avoid will help you buy the highest-quality and freshest fruits and vegetables, or **produce**.

- **Inspect produce for signs of freshness.** Fresh produce has certain telltale qualities. For example, heads of lettuce and cabbage should feel solid. Softness may be a sign that the produce is overripe. Celery, asparagus, and green beans should be crisp, not limp. Citrus fruit, squash, cucumbers, and tomatoes should feel heavy for their size.
- **Avoid bruised and wilted produce.** These are signs that produce has passed its peak of freshness or was not handled properly. These signs can also indicate that nutrients have been lost.
- **Do not buy root vegetables with sprouts.** When root vegetables, such as potatoes and onions, begin to show sprouts, it is a sign that they are past their peak.
- **Look for items in season.** Although items can be shipped to stores at any time of the year, try to buy items when they are in season. For example, acorn and butternut squash are in season in fall, and strawberries are in season during early summer. When produce is in season, it is more likely to have come from a local grower, and will be fresher because it has not spent a long time in shipment.
- **Never buy cans that are swollen, rusted, or dented.** These are warning signs of bacteria that can cause botulism, a serious food-borne illness. (See Section 18.2 for more information.)

Building Character ?!

Withhold Judgment
Ryan and his new friend Xavier go to the grocery store to buy food for an upcoming camping trip. They only have $30 to spend. Without looking at any prices, Xavier places several brand-name products in the shopping cart. He says they are better than the other products, even though he has never tried the others. Ryan is worried he will offend Xavier, but knows that in order to buy enough food for the trip, they will have to carefully watch their budget.

You Make the Call
Should Ryan avoid conflict and let his friend discover his error at the cash register? Or should Ryan try to convince Xavier not to judge a product by its packaging? Explain.

Buying Meat, Poultry, Seafood, and Legumes

Protein foods are perishable, meaning they spoil quickly. These suggestions can help you choose meat, poultry, seafood, and legumes:

- **Look at color.** Freshness of meat and poultry is indicated by color. Look for bright red beef and pinkish pork. You should also check for fat content. The percentage of lean meat on ground beef packages is a clue to the fat content. Poultry should be pinkish, without bruises or torn skin. Some chicken may appear yellow. This is caused by the food the chicken was fed.

- **Check the odor.** Raw meat should have little odor. You will immediately smell bad fish or meat. Fish should have a mild smell and be firm to the touch. Fresh fish should be refrigerated in the store. Frozen fish should feel solid and very cold.

- **Examine specific parts of seafoods.** The shells of clams, oysters, and mussels should be tightly closed. The gills of whole fish should be bright red, and the eyes should be clear, not cloudy.

- **Check for cracks on eggs.** Eggs are labeled by grade (AA or A) and size (medium, large, extra large, or jumbo). Open egg cartons to look for cracks and breaks.

- **Examine legumes.** A **legume** is a plant in which seeds grow in pods. Beans and peas are two types of legumes. They are available dry or canned. Make sure they are firm and uniform in size and color. Legumes need to be washed thoroughly before cooking.

Slip raw meat into a plastic bag to keep it from leaking or dripping onto other food items in your cart.

Buying Milk and Milk Products

There are many varieties of milk. Fresh milk is sold as whole milk (at least 3.25% milk fat) and with lower fat content (skim, 0.5%, 1%, 1.5%, and 2% milk fat). Fresh milk is labeled as pasteurized and homogenized. To **pasteurize** (ˈpas-chə-ˌrīz) is to heat milk to destroy harmful bacteria. To **homogenize** (hō-ˈmä-jə-ˌnīz) is to break up the fat particles and distribute them throughout the milk.

Before purchasing any milk product, check the package. If it is broken, the seals are disengaged, or the contents are leaking, do not buy the product. Also, check cheese labels carefully, and choose low-fat varieties.

If purchasing frozen milk products, such as ice cream or frozen yogurt, be sure the cartons are solidly frozen and very cold. The packaging should not be dented or discolored.

Check Meat

In addition to color, check the sell-by date, and do not buy meat that is expired. *How might you ensure that meat stays fresh after you have purchased it?*

Buying Grain Products

Grain products include bread, cereal, rice, and pasta. These products are made from a variety of grains, including wheat, oats, corn, barley, and rye.

- **Look for whole-grain products.** Select grain products that are enriched or that contain whole grain or bran. These will provide more nutrients. Whole-grain products should make up half of your grain intake. Try to select products that are labeled whole-grain. Examples of whole grains include whole wheat bread, brown rice, and old-fashioned oatmeal. Products labeled as multi-grain, stone-ground, 100% wheat, seven-grain, or bran do not necessarily mean whole-grain.
- **Check labels for sugar, sodium, and fat contents.** Do not assume that a cereal that sounds good for you necessarily is good for you. Many so-called healthy cereals contain added sugar or can be high in fat. It is important to read the label.
- **Look for holes or tears in the packaging.** If the packaging is damaged, the grain product may be stale or moldy.

Safety Check

Purchase Safe Foods

Food manufacturers and supermarkets try to make sure that the food you buy is safe. There are a number of steps you can follow to select safe food, handle it safely at the market, and keep it safe while taking it home.

Write About It

Use reliable Internet sources to research safety tips for food shopping and transportation. Draw up a safety checklist that can be used with a grocery-shopping list. Share your results with the class.

Section 18.1

After You Read

Review Key Concepts

1. **Explain** how scanning newspapers for supermarket specials may save you money.
2. **Identify** techniques that food stores use to encourage you to buy their foods.
3. **Define** food product dating, and identify the four types of dates stamped on product packages.

Practice Academic Skills

English Language Arts

4. Browse food store Web sites, noting the products available, their cost, and the delivery options. Based on your findings, write a brief essay describing the benefits and drawbacks of online grocery shopping.

Social Studies

5. Imagine you have been promoted to food store manager at a local supermarket. Your main job is to increase sales. Write a proposal describing the specific sales strategies you would use and why.

Check Your Answers Go to connectED.mcgraw-hill.com to check your answers.

Section 18.2

Food Safety and Sanitation

Reading Guide

Before You Read

Vocabulary To gain a better understanding of vocabulary, create a vocabulary journal. Divide a piece of paper into three columns. Label the first column "Term" and the second and third columns: "What is it?" and "What else is it like?" Write down each term, and answer the questions as you read the section.

Read to Learn
Key Concepts
- **Identify** the cause of foodborne illness.
- **Give examples** of personal cleanliness in the kitchen.
- **Describe** safe practices for preparing and serving food.

Main Idea
Understanding the cause of foodborne illness will help you apply clean and safe practices when preparing or serving food.

Content Vocabulary
◇ foodborne illness
◇ bacteria
◇ sanitize
◇ cross-contamination
◇ marinade

Academic Vocabulary
You will find these words in your reading and on your tests. Use the glossary to look up their definitions if necessary.
▪ refrain
▪ component

Graphic Organizer
As you read, record 12 tips for storing food safely. Use a graphic organizer like the one below to organize your information.

Store Food Safely

 Graphic Organizer Go to **connectED.mcgraw-hill.com** to download this graphic organizer.

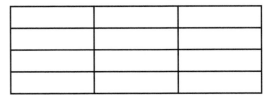

Foodborne Illness

Think about the safety guidelines that you typically follow in the kitchen. For how many seconds do you wash your hands before preparing your food? Do you keep raw meat and raw poultry separate from other foods? How do you check meat to be sure it is cooked thoroughly? There may seem to be an overwhelming amount of kitchen safety guidelines, but they are extremely important. Routinely taking basic precautions can prevent most food-related illnesses.

Health experts estimate that every minute of every day someone is stricken with foodborne illness, or food poisoning. **Foodborne illness** is a sickness caused by eating food that contains a contaminant. Parasites, fungi, viruses, and harmful chemicals are examples of contaminants that can make food unsafe, but most foodborne illnesses are caused by harmful bacteria.

Bacteria are one-celled living organisms so small that they can only be seen with a microscope. Eating small amounts of bacteria will not usually make you sick. But when there is food, moisture, and warmth, bacteria can multiply to harmful levels. Some bacteria such as Salmonella and E. coli can make a person extremely sick or can even cause death.

Simple precautions can prevent foodborne illness. Experts believe that 85 percent of all foodborne illness is avoidable. Taking the time to **sanitize**, or thoroughly clean, surfaces to get rid of bacteria is the first step in preventing foodborne illness. See **Figure 18.2** on page 452 for more details on kitchen sanitation.

✓ **Reading Check** **Explain** What causes a foodborne illness?

As You Read

Connect Have you ever gotten sick from something you ate? What was it, and what were your symptoms?

◆ **Vocabulary**

You can find definitions in the glossary at the back of this book.

➤ **Cleanup**

After cleaning countertops, wash towels in the washing machine using hot water to kill any bacteria. *How do you sanitize your kitchen?*

©Bananastock/Alamy

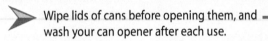

Figure 18.2 Sanitation in the Kitchen

Cleanliness Promotes Healthiness There are many simple ways to help keep your kitchen clean. *Why is it important to clean your sponges?*

Wipe lids of cans before opening them, and wash your can opener after each use.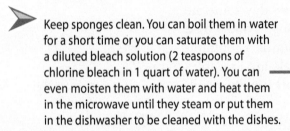

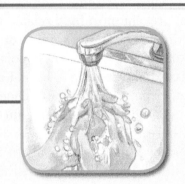

Keep sponges clean. You can boil them in water for a short time or you can saturate them with a diluted bleach solution (2 teaspoons of chlorine bleach in 1 quart of water). You can even moisten them with water and heat them in the microwave until they steam or put them in the dishwasher to be cleaned with the dishes.

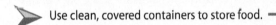
Use clean, covered containers to store food.

Run the garbage disposal immediately after placing food in it to keep it free from rotting food. Make sure your hands and utensils are completely out of the disposal before you turn on the disposal.

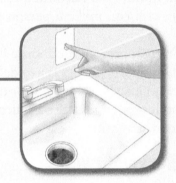

Wash knives, utensils, and countertops with hot, soapy water after each use. As an additional step, you can sanitize them with a bleach solution.

Use a stiff nylon brush and hot, soapy water to wash cutting boards after each use, particularly after cutting raw meat or poultry. Most cutting boards can be put into the dishwasher to be cleaned. Replace heavily scratched cutting boards, which are difficult to clean.

Use a clean spoon every time you taste food during cooking.

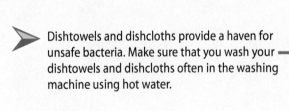

Dishtowels and dishcloths provide a haven for unsafe bacteria. Make sure that you wash your dishtowels and dishcloths often in the washing machine using hot water.

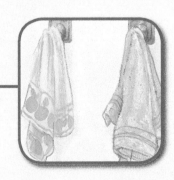

TAKE CHARGE!

Prevent Poisoning

Most kitchens are full of medications and cleaning products that contain potentially hazardous chemicals. To prevent poisoning in the kitchen, use the following guidelines:

- **Separate Food and Chemicals** Keep poisons, medications, and cleaning agents in a safe place away from food supplies.
- **Keep Original Containers and Labels** Household cleaners and other hazardous chemicals must be kept in their original containers to avoid confusion or misuse.
- **Read Directions** Read all warnings and directions, and follow them exactly.
- **Keep Chemicals Out of Reach** Store household cleaners and medicines out of the reach of children, in locked cabinets.
- **Do Not Mix** Some mixtures of household chemicals cause toxic chemical reactions.
- **Post Emergency Numbers** Keep the phone number for poison control posted near your telephone.

Personal Cleanliness

Imagine you are at a restaurant. As you pass the kitchen, you notice that some of an employee's hair is dangling into a plate of food. You spot another employee with dirty hands who is handling food. How would you feel about eating food prepared by these employees? The same feelings should apply to handling food in your own kitchen at home. It may not be a restaurant, but cleanliness still counts.

Personal cleanliness in the kitchen begins with clean hands. Before preparing food, always wash your hands thoroughly with soap and warm water, rubbing them together for at least 20 seconds. Dry your hands well. If you take a break from preparing food to use the restroom, make sure you wash your hands again. You will also need to wash your hands after handling anything dirty or potentially hazardous, such as cleaning solutions. If you have cuts or scrapes on your hands, wear plastic gloves while preparing food.

Other personal cleanliness tips include turning your face away from food to sneeze or cough, tying back your hair if it is long, and keeping your nails clean. You should refrain from, or keep yourself from, touching your hair while working in the kitchen. Also, always wear clean clothes to prevent dirt from transferring from your clothes to the food.

✓ **Reading Check** **Recall** During food preparation, when should you wash your hands?

Health & Wellness TIPS

Personal Hygiene
Preparing food can be fun. However, to help ensure that food you prepare is safe, keep yourself and the kitchen clean. Follow these simple tips for good personal hygiene:

▶ **Wash** hands thoroughly and often.

▶ **Use** paper towels once, and then throw them out.

▶ **Remove** rings and other jewelry before cooking, as dirt and bacteria can cling to them.

Safe Food Preparation and Service

Personal cleanliness and kitchen sanitation are not the only ways you can combat foodborne illness. The way you prepare and serve food is another important **component**, or part, of food safety.

The following cooking and reheating tips can help you prevent the spread of harmful bacteria:

- **Wash produce thoroughly.** Wash fresh fruits and vegetables under cold running water. Use a vegetable scrub brush while washing to loosen dirt on hard vegetables, such as potatoes or carrots.

HOW TO... Store Food Safely

Thanks to the work of people in many government and private agencies, your food supply, from farm to supermarket, is one of the safest in the world. To keep the chain going, take care of foods properly after you bring them home. You will need to store them to keep the food fresh and prevent it from spoiling. Start by buying only as much food as you can use before it begins to spoil. Then, store the food using these guidelines.

Keep Food Cold If you live far from the store, pack perishable groceries in coolers for the drive home. This is also a good idea for summer shopping.

Store Frozen First At home, put away frozen foods first, followed by the refrigerated foods. As you put away the cold foods, check the refrigerator and freezer temperatures. Refrigerators should be set between 32° and 40°F (0° to 5°C). Freezers should be 0°F (-18°C) or below.

Keep Cold Items Cold In the freezer, cluster frozen items together so that they act as ice packs for each other. In the refrigerator, leave space around items so that the cold air can circulate around them, keeping them cold.

Store Dry and Bulk Foods Put cans and boxes in cabinets. Store foods in their original packages until they are opened. Bulk foods are the exception. If you bought bulk foods in containers too large to store in cabinets, separate the contents into airtight containers. Then label the containers with the date, and put them away.

Store Food in Cool, Dry, and Dark Places This rules out spaces near a radiator, over the oven, and under the sink. Heat, moisture, and light can diminish the quality of the food.

Do not use soap or detergent. Be sure to wash all rinds or skins to prevent bacteria from spreading to the inside of the food after it is cut or peeled. Prewash any packaged salad mixes.

- **Use separate cutting boards for meat and vegetables.** When harmful bacteria are transferred from one food or surface to another, **cross-contamination** occurs. Wash cutting boards thoroughly between each use.
- **Thaw food safely.** Never thaw frozen meat, poultry, or seafood on the counter or in a sink of water. Thaw them overnight in the refrigerator. This prevents the outside of the meat from reaching a bacteria-friendly temperature.

Keep Foods Away From Hazards Besides the risk of contamination, there is the chance that someone may accidentally grab the cleansing powder instead of the garlic powder.

Clean Storage Spaces Often Bacteria thrive in dirt. Cleaning your storage areas will help eliminate this growth.

Follow Storage Directions on the Food Package Note whether the storage conditions need to change after the package has been opened. Also, pay attention to expiration and use-by dates. If no date appears, note the purchase date on the package.

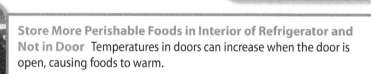

Store More Perishable Foods in Interior of Refrigerator and Not in Door Temperatures in doors can increase when the door is open, causing foods to warm.

Keep Track of Foods in Freezer If you use the freezer to stock up on foods on sale or to freeze foods at home, post a chart on the door listing what is inside. Include the foods, their amounts, purchase dates, and use-by dates. This way, you will not need to open the door to check your supplies. Update the chart as you use the foods.

Use Moisture-Proof Containers and Wraps to Extend Storage Time Heavy-duty aluminum foil, freezer bags, and sturdy plastic or glass containers are made for this purpose.

Use Only Packages and Wraps Intended for Food Aluminum foil, wax paper, plastic wrap, plastic bags, and plastic containers are safe choices. Seal them tightly to keep them from leaking.

(t)Nina Shannon/Getty Images; (c)Mark Dierker/McGraw-Hill Education; (b)Bob Coyle/McGraw-Hill Education

Light and Healthy Recipe

Banana Cream Trifle

Yield
4 servings (1 cup each)

Nutrition Analysis
Per Serving: 460 calories, 13 g total fat, 11 g saturated fat, 0 g trans fat, 10 mg cholesterol, 490 mg sodium, 78 g total carbohydrate, 3 g dietary fiber, 57 g sugars, 6 g protein

Ingredients

1 pkg. instant vanilla pudding

2 cups 2% milk

4 sheets cinnamon graham crackers

3 medium bananas

1 8 oz. tub non-dairy creamy whipped topping, light or fat-free

½ cup graham cracker crumbs

Maraschino cherries, for garnish (optional)

Directions

1. In a small bowl, combine pudding and milk. With an electric hand mixer, beat according to package directions.
2. Using two sheets of the graham crackers, break up into pieces, and layer in the bottom of a medium-size glass bowl. Using ⅓ of the pudding mixture, spread over graham crackers. Slice 1 banana and layer over pudding. Spread ⅓ of the whipped topping over bananas.
3. Repeat process twice, ending with whipped topping.
4. If desired, place 2–3 additional graham crackers in a small plastic sandwich bag and seal. Roll over crackers with a rolling pin to make cookie crumbs.
5. Sprinkle crumbs over whipped topping for garnish and decorate with cherries, if desired.
6. Refrigerate until ready to serve.

IMPORTANT: Both the pudding, prepared with milk, and the whipped topping must be stored in the refrigerator for food safety.

- **Wait before tasting.** Do not taste-test meat, poultry, eggs, or fish until they are thoroughly cooked.
- **Cook food until done.** Meat, poultry, and seafood should be cooked at an oven temperature of 325°F (163°C) or higher. Use a meat thermometer. Pork should be cooked to an internal temperature of 160°F (71°C), poultry to 180°F (82°C), ground meat to 160° to 165°F (71° to 74°C), and fish fillets to at least 145°F (63°C). Cook eggs until the yolks and whites are firm, not runny.
- **Finish cooking once you start.** Do not let interruptions stop you from finishing any food you have begun to cook. Never refrigerate partially cooked food to finish cooking later.
- **Heat leftovers properly.** When reheating leftovers, bring sauces, soups, and gravies to a boil. Heat other leftovers thoroughly to 165°F (74°C) or until hot throughout.

Serving delicious food is just one reward of preparing food. The following tips will help you serve delicious food safely.

- **Use sauces carefully.** Never brush foods you are ready to serve with a marinade that was used on raw foods. A **marinade** is a sauce used to flavor food, such as barbecue sauce.
- **Clean serving plates.** Never put cooked food on a plate that held raw meat, poultry, or seafood.
- **Serve food promptly.** Do not serve food that has been at room temperature for more than two hours.
- **Keep temperatures consistent.** Always keep hot food hot and cold food cold.

Section 18.2

After You Read

Review Key Concepts

1. **Identify** eight strategies for getting rid of bacteria in your kitchen.
2. **Explain** when you should wash your hands if you are working in the kitchen.
3. **Describe** how to prepare produce.

Practice Academic Skills

 **English Language Arts**

4. Plan a picnic or outdoor party. Brainstorm foods you would like to serve. Then write a brief essay describing how you would prepare and serve the food safely.

 **Social Studies**

5. Research the sanitation requirements of restaurants in your local community. Which requirements would benefit you in your home? How do the requirements compare with the guidelines in this chapter?

Check Your Answers Go to connectED. mcgraw-hill.com to check your answers.

What Does a Bookkeeping Clerk Do?

Bookkeeping clerks keep track of finances for a company. They update and maintain accounting records. Many bookkeeping clerks use accounting software, spreadsheets, and databases. The widespread use of computers has enabled them to take on more tasks, such as payroll and billing. Bookkeeping clerks work in an office environment.

Skills Bookkeeping clerks have a wide range of skills. They must be careful, organized, and detail-oriented. They should also have good analysis skills. Bookkeeping clerks use math every day, and they must be comfortable using computers to calculate and record data.

Education and Training Most bookkeeping clerks are required to have at least a high school degree. However, having some college education is becoming more important. An associate's degree in business or accounting is required for some positions. Bookkeeping clerks usually receive on-the-job training once they are hired.

Job Outlook Job prospects should be good as large numbers of bookkeeping clerks are expected to retire or transfer to other occupations. Clerks who can carry out a wider range of bookkeeping and accounting activities will be in greater demand than specialized clerks.

Critical Thinking Think of some different companies in your city or community. Explain why they would need bookkeeping clerks. Which of the companies would you prefer to work for, and why? Write a paragraph explaining your thoughts and ideas.

Career Cluster
Business, Management, and Administration

Bookkeeping clerks work in the Business, Management, and Administration career cluster. Here are some of the other jobs in this career cluster:

- Accountant
- Auditor
- Bill Collector
- Account Collector
- Billing Clerk
- Posting Clerk
- Machine Operator
- Brokerage Clerk
- Credit Authorizer
- Credit Checker
- Credit Clerk
- Payroll Clerk
- Timekeeping Clerk
- Procurement Clerk
- Teller

Explore Further Research this career cluster. Choose a career in this cluster that appeals to you and write a career profile.

Blend Images/Alamy

CHAPTER SUMMARY

Section 18.1
Shopping for Food

Organizing your food shopping will help you make good purchasing decisions. Making a shopping list can help you avoid impulse purchases and cut food costs. Knowledge of brands, labels, and unit pricing can help you comparison shop. Always check the label of a food before you buy it. Look for indicators of quality when buying perishable foods. Buy products well before their sell-by date.

Section 18.2
Food Safety and Sanitation

Bacteria cause foodborne illnesses, which can lead to serious physical symptoms or even death. Foodborne illnesses can be avoided by following proper sanitation procedures. Personal cleanliness is another important step in combating foodborne illness. Cleanliness begins with hand washing. Avoid cross-contamination. Food should be prepared, served, and stored properly.

Vocabulary Review

1. Label each of these content and academic vocabulary terms as a noun, verb, or adjective.

Content Vocabulary
- ◇ impulse purchase (p. 441)
- ◇ staple (p. 441)
- ◇ comparison shopping (p. 444)
- ◇ unit price (p. 445)
- ◇ food product dating (p. 446)
- ◇ produce (p. 447)
- ◇ legume (p. 448)
- ◇ pasteurize (p. 448)
- ◇ homogenize (p. 448)
- ◇ foodborne illness (p. 451)
- ◇ bacteria (p. 451)
- ◇ sanitize (p. 451)
- ◇ cross-contamination (p. 455)
- ◇ marinade (p. 457)

Academic Vocabulary
- ▪ disintegrate (p. 443)
- ▪ perishable (p. 448)
- ▪ refrain (p. 453)
- ▪ component (p. 454)

Review Key Concepts

2. Describe what you should do to prepare for a shopping trip.
3. Explain how to choose products based on brand, nutrition, and price.
4. Explain how you can identify fresh, high-quality food products.
5. Identify the cause of foodborne illness.
6. Give examples of personal cleanliness in the kitchen.
7. Describe safe practices for preparing and serving food.

Critical Thinking

8. Predict What could happen if you used the same platter for raw hamburgers and cooked hamburgers? What might the consequences be?
9. Role Play What advice would you give to teens who do the family grocery shopping?
10. Judge What assumptions do you think people make about different brands of products? Do people favor national brands over generic brands? Why or why not?
11. Draw Conclusions Why do you think storing food improperly impacts its freshness?

ACTIVE LEARNING

Family & Community Connections

12. Foodborne Illnesses Foodborne illness, also known as food poisoning, is caused by eating spoiled food or food containing harmful bacteria. Although health experts estimate that every minute of every day, someone is stricken with a foodborne illness, they also believe that 85 percent of all foodborne illness is avoidable. Washing your hands and sanitizing surfaces to get rid of bacteria are the first steps in preventing foodborne illness. Research the number of cases of foodborne illness in  the United States each year for the last five years. Draw a graph of the information. What conclusions can you draw from the information?

13. Buying Tips There are many approaches you might take and tips you can follow when you shop for food. With your teacher's permission, form into groups to outline tips on buying high-quality food. One student should be responsible for tips on buying produce, one for tips on buying protein foods, one for tips on buying dairy products, and one for tips on buying grain products. Read the information in the chapter, and ask your parents for tips they use. Outline the tips you collect, and explain them to the rest of your group. Note whether any tips are common to buying food of different types. Why do you think that there are differences in what you are looking for in various items? Discuss with your group which tips you already follow and which tips you were not aware of but will now follow. Write a report about the final decisions of your group.

Real-World Skills and Applications

Leadership Skills

14. Emergency Response Due to the nature of the equipment required for some cooking, injuries in the kitchen are a possibility. Knowing what to do if you have an injury while cooking can help keep you safe and calm if you or someone else ever gets injured. Research first-aid procedures for minor kitchen injuries such as burns and cuts. Present the procedures to your class using visual aids or first-aid supplies, if necessary.

Financial Literacy

15. Generic Product Savings A box of your favorite national brand cereal costs $4.95. A box of a generic brand of comparable cereal costs $2.99. You have a coupon for 20 percent off the national brand cereal. With your coupon, is the national brand still more expensive than the generic brand? If so, by how much?

Information Literacy

16. Create a Safety Poster Cleanliness is not the only way to combat foodborne illness. Preparing foods properly can also help prevent foodborne illness. Choose a food preparation guideline from this chapter, and create a poster to illustrate it. Display the poster in the foods lab or in your classroom.

Academic Skills

English Language Arts

17. Create a Brochure There are many things to consider when shopping for food. Shopping for specials and buying in bulk may help save money. Carefully checking the foods you buy will ensure that they are fresh. A smart and effective shopper needs to remember a lot. Create a brochure that will help teens remember important shopping information.

Social Studies

18. Analyze Store Layout Food stores usually place higher-priced and impulse items at eye level or at the checkout stand to make them more noticeable. Go to your local food store, and analyze the placement of products. How does the store use placement to sell more products? What types of products do they highlight?

Mathematics

19. Cooking Time Jacob has decided to help his family by cooking dinner every night for a week. Jacob determined that he could save time during the weekday evenings by preparing his family's meals in advance. He spent 6 hours on Saturday cooking food for the week. He spent 30 minutes on Sunday preparing food, 45 minutes on Monday, 10 minutes on Tuesday, 20 minutes each on Wednesday and Thursday, and 1 hour on Friday. What is the average time Jacob spent per day preparing food?

Math Concept **Averages** In order to find an average, divide the sum of a group of numbers by the amount of numbers in the group being used.

Starting Hint First, convert all values to minutes. Then, add up the total minutes Jacob spent preparing food and divide by the number of days.

 For math help, go to the Math Appendix at the back of the book.

Standardized Test Practice

SHORT ANSWER
Directions Read the question. Then, write a short response.

Test-Taking Tip Try not to leave an answer blank on a short-answer test. Although you may not get the exact answer, the work you provide may result in partial credit. You can ask your instructor if partial credit will be given.

20. Name the two types of brands food companies fall into, and briefly describe each one.

Chapter 19

Kitchen Equipment Selection and Safety

Section 19.1
Selecting Utensils and Cookware

Section 19.2
Appliance Selection and Safety

Chapter Objectives

Section 19.1

- **Explain** factors to consider when selecting kitchen equipment.
- **Classify** different kitchen utensils and provide an example of each type.
- **List** nine different types of cookware and explain their uses.

Section 19.2

- **Recall** nine types of small kitchen appliances and their functions.
- **Identify** four major kitchen appliances and safety measures for use.
- **Explain** the importance of keeping kitchen equipment clean.
- **Describe** ways to keep kitchens safe for children.

Renee Comet Photography, Inc./StockFood

Writing Activity

Explain a Viewpoint

Your Favorite Utensil Having the correct utensils on hand can make cooking a lot easier. What is your favorite utensil? Think about why you like this utensil. What is it used for? Is there a particular type of food you associate with this utensil? Writing a descriptive paragraph allows you to explain your viewpoint. Write a descriptive paragraph about your favorite type of utensil.

Writing Tips Use these tips to explain a viewpoint:
- Include a strong topic sentence.
- Orient the reader by presenting details in a logical order.
- Select precise transition words.

▲ Explore the Photo

Cooking and baking are easier when you use the right type of equipment. *What piece of kitchen equipment do you use most often?*

Section 19.1

Selecting Utensils and Cookware

Before You Read

Preview Read the photo captions and the content and academic vocabulary words in this section. Write one or two sentences predicting what you think the section will be about.

Read to Learn

Key Concepts

- **Explain** factors to consider when selecting kitchen equipment.
- **Classify** different kitchen utensils and provide an example of each type.
- **List** nine different types of cookware and explain their uses.

Main Idea

Knowing about different kinds of kitchen utensils and cookware makes it easier to choose the right kitchen equipment.

Content Vocabulary

◇ utensil
◇ serrated
◇ cookware

Academic Vocabulary

You will find these words in your reading and on your tests. Use the glossary to look up their definitions if necessary.

☐ pare   ☐ fine

Graphic Organizer

As you read, record notes about each type of cutting and chopping utensil. Use a graphic organizer like the one below to organize your information.

Cutting and Chopping Utensils

Type	Description	Purpose
Paring knife		
Utility knife		
Chef's knife		
Bread knife		
Cleaver		

 Graphic Organizer Go to connectED.mcgraw-hill.com to download this graphic organizer.

Selecting Kitchen Equipment

Setting up a new kitchen can be a lot of fun, but it takes careful planning. Your home kitchen does not need dozens of supplies for you to be a successful cook, but you do need to consider the kinds of foods you make or like to eat. Most people stock their kitchens with basic equipment that lets them perform many different food preparation tasks. The role of kitchen equipment is to simplify the task at hand.

Selecting kitchen equipment requires making decisions. Large equipment, such as ranges, refrigerators, and dishwashers, can be costly, so you have to consider these purchases carefully. Small equipment is less expensive, but you should still avoid spending money on clever gadgets you may not need or will use only once or twice. Another important consideration is quality. Do some research on appliances before you shop to get the best quality for your money.

There are many things to consider when choosing kitchen equipment. The following questions can help guide you.

- **How large is my kitchen?** If your kitchen is small, it probably has little cabinet and counter space. Think carefully about storage before you buy kitchen items.
- **What kinds of food do I like?** If you like Asian food, you might want to purchase a wok and an electric rice cooker or steamer. If hamburgers are your favorite, you might need an indoor or outdoor grill.
- **Do I need it?** If you can make a dish just as easily with equipment you have on hand, then the new item probably is not worth the money. Also, think about how often you will use the new equipment. If you will only want to use it once in a great while, pass it by.
- **Does quality count?** High-quality equipment may cost more, but it usually lasts longer with proper care.

✓ Reading Check **Explain** What is the role of basic kitchen equipment?

As You Read

Connect Imagine that you are moving into a new house with no kitchen equipment. What items would you select?

Health & Wellness TIPS

Nutrition Appeal

Many fruits and vegetables store most of their vitamins and minerals right in the peel. Peeling them can decrease their nutritional value. For the greatest nutritional value, follow these tips.

- ▶ Buy bright-looking fruit and vegetables.
- ▶ Buy enough produce for just a few days.
- ▶ Wash and scrub produce with a brush to remove pesticides.

Ariel Skelley/Getty Images

◀ Choose the Right Equipment

When selecting kitchen equipment, look for good construction for a fair price. *Why is it important to select kitchen equipment wisely?*

Figure 19.1 Knife Styles

A Purpose for Every Knife These are common knives for kitchen use.
What might some of these knives be used for?

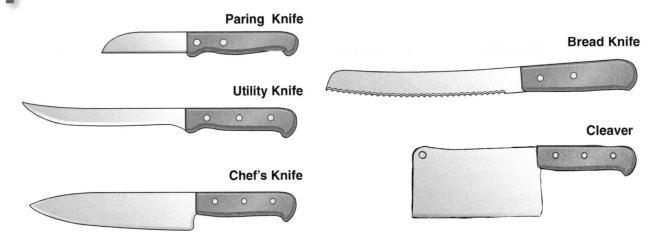

Paring Knife

Utility Knife

Chef's Knife

Bread Knife

Cleaver

Utensils

Vocabulary

You can find definitions in the glossary at the back of this book.

A **utensil** is a small cooking tool. If you have already done some cooking, you know how helpful utensils can be. Without the right tool for each job, it would be hard to measure, mix, or prepare food. Choose sturdy, well-made utensils and care for them properly so that they will last for a long time. If you have a dishwasher or microwave oven, try to choose utensils that are dishwasher and microwave safe.

Cutting and Chopping Utensils

Cutting and chopping tools are used to cut food. A good set of sharp knives is essential. If you can only afford two knives, purchase a good-quality slicing knife or chef's knife, and a knife with a saw-toothed blade for cutting things like bread. This type of blade is called **serrated**. See **Figure 19.1** for examples of these common knives used in the kitchen:

- **Paring knives** are used to *pare*, or peel, fruits and vegetables.
- **Utility knives** are all-purpose knives for cutting and slicing foods.
- **Chef's knives** are used for cutting, slicing, mincing, and dicing.
- **Bread knives** have serrated blades and are designed for slicing bread or baked goods.
- **Cleavers** are used for cutting through thick meats and bone.

Knife Safety

Dull knives are actually more dangerous than sharp knives. You have to push harder on a dull blade to make it cut and it may slip, so knives should be kept sharp. Always cut away from yourself. Use a cutting board; do not hold food in your hand to cut it. Do not use knives for opening cans, boxes, or for tightening screws. Make sure the handle is firmly attached to the blade with two or three rivets, or fasteners.

Measuring and Mixing Utensils

Have you ever seasoned a recipe by pouring salt directly from the shaker into the bowl without measuring it? Have you tried to mix thick cookie dough with a fork? If so, you probably know the value of measuring and mixing utensils.

Measuring utensils help you accurately measure ingredients for recipes. Mixing utensils make it easier to combine ingredients. Some mixing utensils can be helpful for a variety of tasks. Others can be used only for a specific task. See **Figure 19.2** below and **Figure 19.3** on page 468.

Other Kitchen Utensils

A variety of other tools can make work in the kitchen easier. See **Figure 19.4** on page 469 for examples. In addition to these, what other kitchen utensils does your family find helpful?

✓ Reading Check **Distinguish** What types of knives are useful in the kitchen, and which two are essential?

Figure 19.2 **Measuring Utensils**

The Right Tools Using the right measuring equipment helps ensure that your recipe will turn out right. *What might happen if you used an eating spoon instead of a measuring spoon when following a recipe?*

 Dry measuring cups are used to measure dry ingredients, such as flour and sugar. They usually come in sets: ¼ cup, ⅓ cup, ½ cup, and 1 cup. Sizes in a set of metric measures include 50 mL (milliliters), 125 mL, and 250 mL.

Liquid measuring cups are often clear plastic or glass. They have a spout for pouring and measurements marked on the side in cups, ounces, and milliliters. Common sizes are 1 cup, 2 cups, and 4 cups (250 mL, 500 mL, and 1,000 mL in metric).

 Measuring spoons are used for measuring smaller amounts of liquid and dry ingredients. The most common sizes are ¼ teaspoon, ½ teaspoon, 1 teaspoon, and 1 tablespoon. A set of small metric measures includes 1 mL, 2 mL, 5 mL, 15 mL, and 25 mL.

McGraw-Hill Education

Figure 19.3 **Mixing Utensils**

Combine Ingredients Mixing or combining ingredients often requires more than a simple bowl and spoon. *Which of these mixing tools might you use to make a cake?*

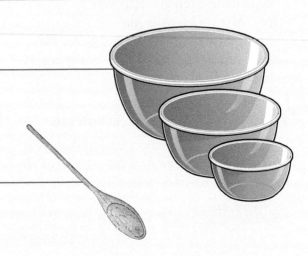

➤ **Mixing bowls** hold the ingredients that you mix and come in graduated sizes. They can be made of glass, plastic, or metal. They can also be used in a casual setting to serve food.

➤ **Mixing spoons** have long handles and are used to combine ingredients. They can be made of metal, wood, plastic, or silicone.

➤ **Plastic, silicone, and rubber scrapers** are used to mix ingredients together and to scrape bowls, pans, cans, and jars. They have a wide, flexible rubber blade.

➤ **Sifters** mix and add air to flour and other dry ingredients. They also break up any lumps in dry ingredients by forcing them through a **fine**, or thin, mesh screen.

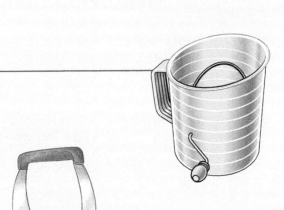

➤ **Pastry blenders** cut shortening into flour for pie crusts and biscuits.

➤ **Wire whisks** are used for beating and blending. Whisks are especially efficient for combining liquid ingredients and beating eggs.

➤ **Rotary beaters** are also known as hand beaters. When you want to mix dry and wet ingredients together, use a rotary beater. They are especially good for beating eggs and mixing thin batters, such as pancake or cake batter.

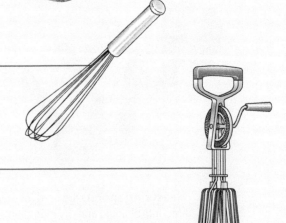

Figure 19.4

Other Kitchen Utensils

Make Your Work Easier Not having the right kinds of utensils can make food preparation difficult. *What piece of kitchen equipment do you think is the most important?*

> **Cutting boards** serve as a base for your cutting work, keeping knife blades sharp and counters in good shape. Clear plastic boards do not promote bacteria growth.

> **Graters** are used to shred and grate vegetables and cheeses. Check out photo-etched graters. They do an amazing job.

> **Kitchen shears** are sturdy scissors kept in the kitchen and used for cutting vegetables, pastry, poultry, and meat. Always wash shears with soap and warm water after each use.

> **Vegetable peelers** are used to pare vegetables and fruits. Some peelers have a blade that swivels for ease in paring.

Cutting Board

Kitchen Shears

Peeler

Grater

Colander

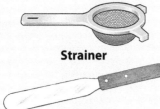

Strainer

Spatula

Slotted Spoon

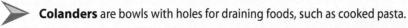

Turner

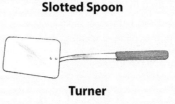

Tongs

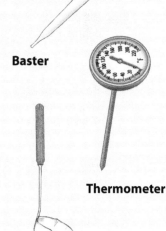

Baster

Thermometer

> **Colanders** are bowls with holes for draining foods, such as cooked pasta.

> **Strainers** are wire mesh baskets with handles used to strain liquids from solid foods, such as water from steamed vegetables. Strainers are available in different sizes of mesh.

> **Slotted spoons** are helpful for lifting solid food from liquid, like separating vegetables from their cooking juices.

> **Metal spatulas** have dull, narrow metal blades. They are useful in leveling dry ingredients, such as flour, in measuring cups.

> **Turners,** or wide spatulas, are used to lift and turn foods, such as pancakes or hamburgers.

> **Tongs** grasp or hold foods, such as a chicken drumstick or a corncob.

Ladle

> **Basters** are used for basting foods and are great for removing liquid.

> **Thermometers** are used to measure the temperature of food. Rapid-read thermometers can be placed in food at any time during cooking for an instant read.

> **Ladles** help spoon out hot soup and stews.

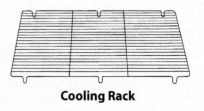

Cooling Rack

> **Cooling racks** are made of wire and allow air to circulate around hot baked products so that they cool evenly.

Figure 19.5

Cookware and Bakeware

Cooking and Baking Specific types of equipment are necessary for preparing cooked and baked dishes. *What type of bakeware do you use most often?*

▶ **Saucepans and stockpots** are deep pans. They come in a variety of sizes, usually measured in quarts or liters. Some have covers. Saucepans have one handle, and stockpots have two handles, one on each side.

▶ **Cake pans** come in different sizes and shapes. They can be used for baking many foods. Cake pans can be made of glass, metal, or silicone.

▶ **Loaf pans** come in different sizes and are used for breads and meatloaves. Loaf pans can be made of glass, metal, or silicone.

▶ **Casseroles,** or baking dishes, come in a variety of shapes and sizes. They are deep enough to hold a main-dish mixture and often have covers.

▶ **Skillets** are shallow pans and generally have long handles. They come in assorted sizes and sometimes have covers.

▶ **Pie pans** are round and come in different sizes and depths. Pie pans can be made of glass, metal, or silicone.

▶ **Baking sheets** are rectangular, low-sided pans. They are most often used for baking cookies and making sweets.

▶ **Muffin pans** have from 6 to 12 individual cups to hold muffins or cupcakes.

▶ **Custard cups** are made from heatproof glass. You can use them to bake custard or to microwave eggs.

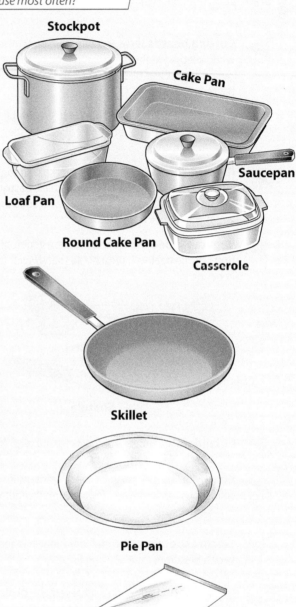

Stockpot

Cake Pan

Saucepan

Loaf Pan

Round Cake Pan

Casserole

Skillet

Pie Pan

Baking Sheet

Custard Cups

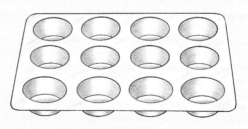

Muffin Pan

Cookware

Just about anything you prepare in the kitchen requires cookware. **Cookware** includes pots, pans, and other containers for use on top of the range, in the oven, or in the microwave. See **Figure 19.5** on page 470 for some examples. Cookware items can be made of metal, glass, silicone, aluminum, stainless steel, cast iron, enamel, ceramic, or plastic. Metal cookware should only be used on the stove or in the oven. Plastic cookware can only be used in the microwave. Most glass cookware can be used both in the oven and in the microwave. Check the label or bottom of all of your cookware to be certain it is safe for the way you plan to use it.

When buying cookware, be sure that the bottoms of pots and pans are heavy and flat, the handles are riveted to the pan, and the covers fit securely. If the handles are oven-safe (not plastic), the pan can be safely put into and used in the oven. Skillets are available with a non-stick finish or coating that keeps food from sticking to the cookware and makes it easier to clean.

Section 19.1

After You Read

Review Key Concepts

1. **Describe** how to determine if you need a piece of equipment.
2. **Explain** why measuring and mixing utensils are important.
3. **Identify** what you should look for when buying cookware for your kitchen.

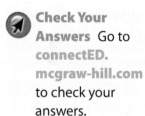 **Check Your Answers** Go to connectED. mcgraw-hill.com to check your answers.

Practice Academic Skills

 **English Language Arts**

4. Imagine you have an opportunity to purchase two small kitchen utensils. Which utensils would you choose to help you make the best use of your time in the kitchen? Write a one-page report to explain your decision. Include examples of the types of food you would prepare with these utensils.

 **Social Studies**

5. Use print or online resources to research ancient tools used in food preparation. Are any versions of those tools used today? What contemporary tools have taken the place of these ancient tools? How do the modern tools do the same job more efficiently? Prepare an oral presentation to share your findings with the class.

Appliance Selection and Safety

Before You Read

Understanding It is normal to have questions when you read. Write down questions while reading. Many of them will be answered as you continue. If they are not, you will have a list ready for your teacher when you finish.

Read to Learn

Key Concepts

- **Recall** nine types of small kitchen appliances and their functions.
- **Identify** four major kitchen appliances and safety measures for use.
- **Explain** the importance of keeping kitchen equipment clean.
- **Describe** ways to keep kitchens safe for children.

Main Idea

Kitchens can be hazardous, so it is important to keep your kitchen safe and clean. Always be sure to understand how to properly and safely use kitchen appliances.

Content Vocabulary

◇ immersible
◇ microwave

Academic Vocabulary

You will find these words in your reading and on your tests. Use the glossary to look up their definitions if necessary.

▢ mind
▢ anticipate

Graphic Organizer

As you read, record tips on cooking safely with a range. Use a graphic organizer like the one below to organize your information.

Cooking Safely with a Range

1.
2.
3.
4.

Graphic Organizer Go to connectED.mcgraw-hill.com to download this graphic organizer.

Small Kitchen Appliances

When you make toast, do you bake slices of bread in the oven, or do you put bread into a toaster? If you use a toaster, you are using a small kitchen appliance. There are hundreds of small appliances available today. Along with toasters, you can find mixers, coffeemakers, blenders, food processors, and indoor grills, just to name a few. Small appliances perform specific cooking tasks for you, such as toasting your bread, which can speed up your cooking time. Small appliances are generally powered by electricity. They are portable, so you can move them from place to place, which allows you to use and store them in different areas of your kitchen.

Some appliances are **immersible**, which means that the entire appliance can be put safely into water to be washed. On these appliances, the electrical unit has been sealed so that no water can enter it. Immersible appliances have the term "immersible" written on them. If you do not see the term, do not put the appliance in water. See **Figure 19.6** on page 474.

Using Small Appliances Safely

Many small appliances are so simple to use that people become careless with them. The result can be electrical shock, a burn, or a fire. Staying safe while using small appliances is not difficult, but it does require you to think about what you are doing. The following guidelines can help:

- **Follow instructions.** Before using an appliance, read the instruction manual so you know how to operate it correctly. Use an appliance only for its intended purpose. Keep the manual handy in case you need to refer to it in the future.
- **Use caution with blades.** Be careful when using or cleaning appliances with blades, such as food processors and blenders. Never put utensils or your hands near the blades while the appliance is running. When cleaning sharp blades, wash them separately and carefully. Be sure the appliance is unplugged before removing the blade.

Stockbyte/PhotoLibrary

As You Read

Connect Think about which small appliances you find most useful. Which appliances perform jobs that are time-consuming to do by hand?

Vocabulary

You can find definitions in the glossary at the back of this book.

Safety Guidelines

Kitchen appliances can save time when used correctly. *Why is it important to follow safety guidelines when using a kitchen appliance?*

Figure 19.6   **Small Kitchen Appliances**

Kitchen Helpers   Small kitchen appliances serve a variety of functions.
What types of small kitchen appliances do you use on a daily basis?

 Toasters brown and crisp slices of bread. Some can adjust for thicker breads, such as bagels or English muffins.

 Blenders have push-button or touch-pad controls and short blades that rotate quickly to blend, chop, mix, and purée. Handheld blenders, known as immersion blenders, blend foods directly in pots and bowls.

 Handheld mixers can be used for mixing cake batter and whipping cream, potatoes, or anything with a light to medium batter. They are lightweight, easy to manage, and convenient to store.

 Stand mixers are used for larger amounts or thicker batters and do not require you to hold either the mixer or the bowl.

 Food processors perform many cutting and mixing tasks using blades and disks.

 Electric skillets fry, roast, and simmer foods. The skillet's thermostatic controls regulate cooking temperatures. It also works to keep foods warm during an event.

 Toaster ovens take little time to preheat and are ideal for toasting bread and baking small amounts of food. Some toaster ovens have a broil feature.

 Slow cookers allow you to safely cook one-dish meals for several hours.

 Electric grills are grills with temperature controls that allow low-fat cooking, indoors or outside.

- **Keep cords under control.** Avoid letting appliance cords dangle over the edge of countertops or tables. You can trip and fall or accidentally jerk the appliance off the counter. Keep power cords away from heat, and never use an appliance with frayed power cords.
- **Make sure your hands are dry.** Dry your hands before touching any electrical equipment, and never plug in an appliance while standing on a wet surface.
- **Unplug with care.** Unplug power cords from outlets when not in use and before cleaning or attaching any parts. Always unplug a cord from the wall outlet before removing it from the appliance. Pull on the plug itself, not the cord.
- **Keep utensils out of toasters.** If bread becomes stuck in a toaster, unplug the toaster before trying to shake the bread loose. Do not stick a metal utensil in the toaster. This can cause electrocution.

✓ Reading Check **Identify** What are the benefits of small kitchen appliances?

Major Kitchen Appliances

Most kitchens are equipped with a few major appliances, such as a gas or electric range and a refrigerator. Additional large kitchen appliances include microwave ovens, convection ovens, dishwashers, freezers, trash compactors, and garbage disposals.

Large appliances are considered major purchases. The costs vary depending on the style, size, and features you choose, and whether you buy new or used appliances. When shopping for large kitchen appliances, compare the Energy Guide labels and look for safety and performance seals. Read and keep the owner's manuals. Each manual contains valuable information about your appliances.

Refrigerators

The function of a refrigerator is to keep perishable foods cold. Refrigerators are built in different ways. They can have a freezer at the top, the bottom, or on one side, or they can have no freezer at all. Sizes and features of refrigerators vary. People with smaller kitchens usually have a small refrigerator with few extra features. If you have more space, you can have a larger refrigerator, with features such as an ice and water dispenser. A large refrigerator can store more food, which means you can make fewer shopping trips. This is especially helpful if you live far from a grocery store.

Health & Wellness TIPS

Keep Your Refrigerator Healthy

Refrigerators keep food fresh and healthful. To do that, a refrigerator's temperature must be 40° Fahrenheit (4°C) or lower. Help your refrigerator protect food by following these simple steps:

▶ Use a refrigerator thermometer to check the temperature.

▶ Store meats in the refrigerator's coldest section.

▶ Clean the refrigerator often with hot, soapy water.

Kitchen Fire Safety

Most kitchen fires begin when a stove is left on and unattended. Your best kitchen fire safety tip is to stay in the kitchen when cooking. If a small fire does start on the stove, you can fight it by using a fire extinguisher.

Write About It

Research kitchen fire safety. Create a fire safety checklist for your kitchen. Include prevention tips, how to call for emergency help, and the steps for using a fire extinguisher. Share your results with the class.

Ranges

Standard ranges have a cooktop, an oven, and a broiler, and are powered by electricity or gas. Gas-range heating units are called burners. The gas flame on a burner is visible and can be raised or lowered quickly to control the heat flow. The heating units on electric ranges are called elements. When you turn on a heating element, it gradually becomes red. As it cools, it returns to gray or black. Be aware that heating elements retain heat long after you turn them off. Some ranges have a warning light that stays on until the cooktop is safe to touch. Older ranges often do not have this safety feature.

Cooking Safely with a Range

Being careless when using the range or oven may lead to fires and burns. If a grease fire starts inside a pan, smother it with a pan cover, salt, or baking soda. Do not use flour or water. Do not use water on a grease fire because the water spreads the flames. If the fire occurs in the oven, turn the oven controls off and close the door tightly to smother the flames. Always keep a fire extinguisher in the kitchen and know how to use it. Here are some additional tips:

- **Mind cooking food.** Mind, or pay attention to, any food you are cooking on the cooktop. Leaving food unattended is the main cause of kitchen fires.
- **Keep appliances clean.** Always make sure the oven and cooktop are clean. Grease and food left on surfaces can catch fire.
- **Keep pot handles inward.** Pot handles that stick out over the front edge of the range may cause injury. Also, be sure they are not over another gas flame or hot heating element.
- **Use a potholder.** Use potholders when removing anything from the oven or when moving pots. Make sure the potholder is dry. Wet dishtowels or potholders can cause steam burns.
- **Wear proper clothing.** Avoid wearing dangling jewelry or loose-fitting clothes that can become tangled on cookware handles or catch on fire. Long hair can also be dangerous near a stove. Tie hair back in a ponytail or put it up in a clip while cooking.
- **Keep flammables away from the range.** This includes towels, dishcloths, paper, cookbooks, and curtains.
- **Use utensils properly.** Flat-bottomed cookware and well-balanced cooking utensils that will not tip or spill work best. Also, use kitchen tongs, long-handled spatulas, or long silicone mitts to remove food from hot water and to turn frying food.
- **Open covers carefully.** Remove a pan cover by tilting the cover away from you so that the steam flows away from you.
- **Fry foods with caution.** Dry foods thoroughly before placing them into the hot fat, because fat can cause the water to pop and spatter. Cover skillets to keep hot fat in the pan.
- **Use cookware properly.** Do not put ovenproof glass dishes on hot burners or heating elements. The glass can easily shatter, scattering glass shards and destroying your meal.

Succeed in School

Three-Ring Binder

A three-ring binder is the easiest way to track and organize your notes and handouts. You can add, remove, or rearrange your notes to suit your needs.

Standard and Convection Ovens

There are two types of ovens: standard and convection. In standard ovens, the hot air rises naturally from the bottom to the top of the oven. Convection ovens have a fan in the back, which moves hot air around. The rapid air-flow equalizes temperatures throughout the oven. This helps food cook more evenly. This also allows most convection ovens to cook up to twice as fast as standard ovens. However, this is not true of all convection ovens. If you buy an oven, experimentation is key. You will have to check cooking times and compare them to the recipes you are preparing. Both types of ovens are available with a self-cleaning feature, which reduces food to ash so that it can be easily wiped away.

Microwave Ovens

Microwave ovens use energy waves called **microwaves** to heat food. A fan-like device called a stirrer distributes these waves throughout the oven, where they bounce off the walls and floor. Microwaves pass through glass, plastic, and paper. These microwaves are absorbed by the molecules in food and cause vibrations. This in turn produces friction, and the friction produces heat to cook the food. Rotating food during cooking allows the food to cook evenly in the microwave.

Cooking Safely with a Microwave

Microwaves are so easy to use you may forget that they can be the cause of injuries. Safe microwave cooking begins with the proper cookware. Choose microwave-safe plastic containers or cookware made of glass, microwave cookware, or microwave dishware to heat food in the microwave. Most dishes that are safe for the microwave will be marked as such. Special bags are also available for microwave cooking. Alternatively, you can use paper plates and paper towels as long as they are not made of recycled paper, which can catch fire. Never use anything made of metal or that has metal parts in a microwave oven! This includes aluminum foil. Metal will cause electrical sparks that can destroy the microwave and lead to a fire.

Community Connections

Kitchen Stores

Employees who work at kitchen stores are often food enthusiasts as well as knowledgeable salespeople. Next time you are out shopping and come across such a store, ask a salesperson to share his or her opinion on the relative value of different types of equipment or appliances.

When microwaving plastic containers and pouches, puncture or vent them to keep steam from building. If steam continues to build, it can cause the pouches or containers to burst. This can be dangerous as well as messy, and can ruin the food.

A process called superheating can cause another type of explosion. Superheating occurs when a liquid's container does not allow bubbles to form, causing the liquid to explode. To prevent superheating, heat liquids in a microwave a little at a time. Stop every few seconds to check the temperature.

Food cooked in a microwave continues to cook after the microwave timer goes off, which means it is still hot. Allow it a few minutes to cool slightly. Be careful when removing microwaved food. You can not always anticipate, or predict, whether the container will be as hot as the food, so use potholders.

Stay in the room while food is cooking in the microwave in case an emergency arises. If you see sparks inside the microwave, turn it off or unplug it immediately and seek help. If the microwave makes unusual sounds, tell an adult right away. Remember: No metal in microwaves!

✓ **Reading Check** **Summarize** What should you consider before purchasing a major kitchen appliance?

HOW TO... Grill Healthy Food

People have enjoyed the taste and aroma of grilling since they first learned to put food over fire. Quickly cooked with little added fat, grilled foods can also be nutritious. Remember these tips for safe and healthful outdoor cooking:

Assemble the Equipment Some items make grilling more successful. Fireproof mitts, long-handled brushes, and turning utensils are safety "must-haves." Wire baskets and metal rods, or skewers, let you grill small or delicate foods.

Practice Fire Prevention Flames can burn more than food. Always keep a fire extinguisher handy. Set the grill on a level surface, in a well-ventilated area, and away from anything that could catch fire. Trim fat from meat and poultry to prevent flare-ups caused by fat dripping onto coals. Keep a spray bottle of water for flare-up control.

©Robert Nicholas/age fotostock

Keep Kitchen Equipment Clean

When you cook, you have to clean. Keeping kitchen equipment clean helps prevent foodborne illness, helps your equipment last longer, and keeps you and your family well. The following supplies can help you keep your kitchen equipment spotless and sanitary:

- **Dishcloths and Sponges** Use these to wash dishes and to clean work surfaces. Wash dishcloths frequently. Wash sponges along with dishes in the dishwasher. Replace sponges if they contain difficult stains or are damaged.
- **Dishtowels** Use towels to dry dishes and other kitchen equipment, large and small. Wash and dry them frequently to prevent the build up of bacteria.
- **Cleaning Pads** These pads are helpful in removing stuck-on food from cookware and utensils. You can use plastic, fiber, or steel wool pads, but be sure to use plastic or fiber cleaning pads on nonstick surfaces. Refer to the product manual that came with your cookware if you have a question about cleaning tools.
- **Brushes** Vegetable brushes are useful in cleaning potato skins. Bottle brushes reach the insides of bottles and jars.

✓ **Reading Check** **Identify** Which supplies will help you keep kitchen equipment clean and sanitary?

Choose the Food Thin cuts of meat and poultry pieces cook quickly. Place fish in aluminum foil or a grill basket. To hasten cooking time without burning the food, keep the grill closed as much as possible. Note: If using bamboo skewers, make sure to soak them in water for 30 minutes before threading them with food. This prevents the skewers from burning.

Flavor for Health Grilled foods have a naturally smoky taste. Experiment with a rub (a blend of seasonings). Add fat only to keep certain foods from drying out. Vegetables may be lightly brushed with olive oil, and skinless chicken can be thinly coated with barbecue sauce. Try fish with low-fat salad dressing or a marinade.

Handle Meat Carefully Use tongs, rather than a fork, to move meat on and off a grill. Forks pierce the flesh, letting out natural fats and juices. Saving these flavorful fluids reduces the need for added fat or salty condiments. Make sure meat is cooked evenly on both sides. A rapid-read thermometer is a great tool when grilling.

(l)Michael Mahovlich/Masterfile; (r)Ingram Publishing

Light and Healthy Recipe

Asian Pasta Salad

Yield
6 servings (1 cup each)

Nutrition Analysis
Per Serving: 260 calories, 8 g total fat, .5 g saturated fat, 0 g trans fat, 0 mg cholesterol, 15 mg sodium, 40 g total carbohydrate, 7 g dietary fiber, 5 g sugars, 9 g protein

Salad Directions

Salad Ingredients
½ lb. fusilli pasta
1 red bell pepper
⅓ lb. snow peas, blanched
⅔ cup slivered almonds, toasted
3 scallions
1 can (5 oz.) sliced water chestnuts

1. Cook pasta according to package directions. Rinse pasta with cold water to stop cooking; drain well. Place in a large bowl.
2. Cut one pepper ring for garnish; cut remaining pepper in half, lengthwise. Remove white membrane and seeds; rinse well; pat dry with paper towel. Slice in julienne strips; set aside.
3. String snow peas; cut diagonally into two or three pieces, depending on size. Rinse in a wire mesh strainer or colander.
4. Place snow peas in a saucepan of boiling water for 2 minutes to blanch. Rinse in cold water to stop cooking; drain well; set aside.
5. Toast the almonds in a toaster oven or in a pan on low heat until lightly brown, 3–5 minutes; set aside.
6. Thinly slice scallions; drain water chestnuts.
7. To pasta, add red pepper, snow peas, scallions, water chestnuts, and ½ cup of the almonds, reserving remaining almonds for garnish.
8. Prepare dressing; toss with pasta ingredients.
9. Sprinkle with remaining almonds and garnish with pepper ring.
10. Serve at room temperature or refrigerate to chill.

Dressing Directions

Dressing Ingredients
1 Tbsp. gingerroot
⅓ cup light salad dressing
2 tsp. dry mustard
2 Tbsp. soy sauce

1. Freshly grate gingerroot.
2. With a wire whisk, combine gingerroot, salad dressing, mustard, and soy sauce until smooth.

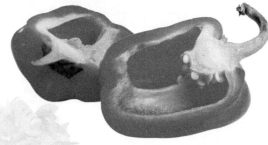

Keep the Kitchen Child-Safe

Many families enjoy preparing food together, but cooking with young children can be hazardous. Following a few simple guidelines can help everyone remain safe while enjoying special family time.

- **Supervise constantly.** When you are cooking with young children present, supervise them carefully. Keep them at a safe distance from hot items, such as the stove, toaster, or indoor grill. They might try to pull themselves up to stand on a hot, open oven door. Watch for young children when you move hot or heavy items.
- **Keep tempting objects out of reach.** Young children should never handle knives, cleaning products, or other hazardous chemicals. Electrical cords are also tempting to young children. Be sure to always use small appliances out of their reach.
- **Use placemats.** Very young children who are learning new motor skills present special challenges. Some might pull a table-cloth to stand, causing plates of hot food to spill on them. In this case, placemats would be a better choice of table covering.
- **Prevent falls.** To prevent falls, wipe up spills immediately. Close cabinet drawers and doors when not in use, and never leave anything on the floor where someone might trip over it. Use a sturdy step stool to reach high shelves instead of a chair or box.

Section 19.2

After You Read

Review Key Concepts

1. **Explain** what it means for an appliance to be immersible.
2. **Describe** superheating and how to prevent it when cooking in a microwave.
3. **List** the proper uses of cleaning supplies for kitchen equipment.
4. **Give** examples of dangerous situations young children may encounter in the kitchen.

Practice Academic Skills

 **English Language Arts**

5. Learn about the features of a gas range or electric range and how to use them. Write a short instruction manual for the appliance. Have classmates evaluate your instructions.

 **Social Studies**

6. List the kitchen equipment you have at home. Identify the equipment you feel is most or least helpful to your family. If you could replace three items, which would you replace? Why? What items would you choose to replace them?

 Check Your Answers Go to connectED. mcgraw-hill.com to check your answers.

Exploring Careers

Power Plant Dispatcher

What Does a Power Plant Dispatcher Do?

Power plant dispatchers control the flow of electricity to supply residential areas with electricity. Dispatchers monitor other distribution equipment and record readings. Dispatchers predict power needs, such as those caused by changes in the weather. They also handle emergencies and redirect the flow of power around affected areas.

Skills Strong computer and technical skills are generally preferred. Problem-solving and the ability to focus and pay constant attention are important. A basic understanding of science and math is also useful.

Education and Training Employers often seek recent high school graduates for entry-level power plant dispatcher positions. But a college or vocational school degree will allow more advancement opportunities. In addition to initial training, power plant dispatchers are expected to attend periodic training sessions to refresh their knowledge. This is especially important for nuclear power plant operators.

Job Outlook Job opportunities for power plant dispatchers are expected to be plentiful. This is due to the large number of retiring workers who must be replaced, the increased demand for energy, and new laws that pave the way for new plants.

Critical Thinking Review the job duties and needed skills of a power plant dispatcher. Write a paragraph explaining why you feel that you would be a good fit for the job. Make sure to explain how your traits make you a good fit.

Career Cluster

Transportation, Distribution, and Logistics

Power plant dispatchers work in the Transportation, Distribution, and Logistics career cluster. Here are some of the other jobs in this career cluster:

- Chemical Plant and System Operator
- Petroleum Pump System Operator
- Refinery Operator
- Refinery Gauger
- Stationary Engineer
- Boiler Operator
- Water Treatment Plant and System Operator
- Facility Maintenance Engineer
- Industrial Equipment Mechanic
- Industrial Electrician
- Mobile Equipment Maintenance Manager
- Electronic Technician
- Logistics Manager
- Logistics Analyst

Explore Further Research this career cluster. Choose a career in this cluster that appeals to you and write a career profile.

Masterfile

Chapter 19 Review and Applications

CHAPTER SUMMARY

Section 19.1
Selecting Utensils and Cookware

Research kitchen equipment before making decisions. You do not need a lot of equipment to be a successful cook, but you should have basic equipment that will let you perform many different food preparation tasks. Kitchen utensils allow you to cut, measure, and mix, as well as perform other food preparation tasks with accuracy. Just about anything you make in the kitchen requires some form of cookware. Some cookware can only be used on a stove or in a conventional or convection oven, some cookware can only be used in the microwave oven, and some cookware can be used in both.

Section 19.2
Appliance Selection and Safety

Selecting kitchen equipment requires careful consideration and decision making. Small kitchen appliances help make your food preparation time more efficient. Some small appliances are so simple that people become dangerously careless with them. Large kitchen appliances include refrigerators, ranges, and ovens. Proper use of kitchen appliances can prevent accidents, such as fires, burns, cuts, and bruises. Keeping kitchen equipment clean can make it last longer, and can help prevent foodborne illness. Following a few simple guidelines can help keep young children safe in the kitchen.

Vocabulary Review

1. Use each of these content and academic vocabulary words in a sentence. Then provide a real-life example of each.

Content Vocabulary
◇ utensil (p. 466)
◇ serrated (p. 466)
◇ cookware (p. 471)
◇ immersible (p. 473)
◇ microwave (p. 477)

Academic Vocabulary
▪ pare (p. 466)
▪ fine (p. 468)
▪ mind (p. 476)
▪ anticipate (p. 478)

Review Key Concepts

2. Explain factors to consider when selecting kitchen equipment.
3. Classify different kitchen utensils and provide an example of each type.
4. List nine different types of cookware and explain their uses.
5. Recall nine types of small kitchen appliances and their functions.
6. Identify four major kitchen appliances and safety measures for use.
7. Explain the importance of keeping kitchen equipment clean.
8. Describe ways to keep kitchens safe for children.

Critical Thinking

9. Evaluate You want to bake a cake for your friend's birthday. What utensils will you need?
10. Outline Write a list of things to consider when buying a refrigerator for the first time.
11. Apply You are babysitting your older sister's toddler for the day. How can you make sure the kitchen will be safe for him should you need to cook?

ACTIVE LEARNING

12. Critique Kitchen Utensils Select one small utensil to evaluate, such as a spatula, mixing spoon, rubber scraper, wire whisk, sifter, or vegetable peeler. Using catalogs, consumer publications, or actual items, compare and critique three different brands or designs of the utensil you chose. You can compare three tools made from different materials, such as wood, metal, or plastic, for example. If possible, try preparing food with each of these utensils. After you have finished, present your critique of the three tools to the class. Be sure to recommend one brand or design for each of the three utensils, and support your recommendation with information from your research and experience.

Family & Community Connections

13. Create an Advertisement There are hundreds of small kitchen appliances available today. Toasters, mixers, coffeemakers, blenders and food processors are just some of the small appliances you might see in a kitchen. Follow your teacher's instructions to form groups. Visit your local hardware or appliance store and ask if you can speak with a manager. Ask the manager which type of small appliance is the store's best seller, and which type of small appliance does not sell very well. Find out if he or she knows why one sells well and the other does not. Is it inexpensive or easy to clean, for example? Can another appliance do the same job? Imagine you work for an advertising company that has been hired to create a print advertisement for the small kitchen appliance that does not sell well. Working with your group, create an advertisement that showcases the appliance's use and features.

Real-World Skills and Applications

Leadership Skills

14. Direct an Emergency Response What would you do if a grease fire started in a pan while you were cooking in your kitchen? Enact a scene in which you respond to a grease fire in a safe, effective manner. When you are finished, ask the audience to provide feedback.

Financial Literacy

15. Compare Efficiency Suppose you are shopping for a refrigerator. One energy-efficient model costs $699.00 and will cost you just $4.96 in electricity bills per month. Another model only costs $495.00 but will cost you $14.57 in electricity bills per month. After how many months will you save enough on electricity bills with the energy-efficient model to offset the price difference between the two refrigerators?

Technology Skills

16. New Kitchen Technology Research new technology available in kitchen appliances, such as a refrigerator-oven combination. How is this new technology helpful? Are there any drawbacks to the new technology? If so, what are they? Present your findings to the class and explain your opinions on the new technology.

Academic Skills

 English Language Arts

17. Choose an Appliance Locate studies in a consumer magazine that compare the safety, features, and performance of different brands of the same small kitchen appliance, such as a toaster. Based on your reading, write a one-page essay to convince a potential buyer to purchase one brand over the others.

 Science

18. Water in Food How much water is in the food you eat? Use this experiment to discover the weight of water lost from an orange through evaporation.

Procedure Weigh a whole orange. Cut the orange into thin slices and place them on a paper towel to dry out overnight. Weigh the slices after they have dried. Repeat this procedure with apple slices.

Analysis Record the weight of the whole fruit and compare it to the weight of the dried fruit slices. Which has more water?

 Mathematics

19. Refrigerator Features Your local appliance store is having a major sale on large appliances this holiday weekend. Your refrigerator is broken, so you decide to replace it rather than pay for expensive repairs. You are shopping for a refrigerator among the 15 energy-efficient models at the store. Two-thirds of the store's refrigerators have built-in freezers. Of those with built-in freezers, 50 percent have automatic ice-makers. How many refrigerators have built-in freezers and automatic ice-makers?

 Fractions and Decimals Fractions and decimals both represent numbers that are not whole numbers. Fractions can be converted to equivalent decimals, and vice versa.

Starting Hint First, find the number of refrigerators with built-in freezers. To do this, multiply 15 by $\frac{2}{3}$. Then, find 50 percent of the refrigerators with built-in freezers.

 For math help, go to the Math Appendix at the back of the book.

Standardized Test Practice

SHORT ANSWER
Directions Read the question. Then write a short answer.

Test-Taking Tip It is a good idea to try to anticipate the types of questions that will be on a test when preparing for it. An easy way to do this while reading is to note the way the text is organized.

20. What is the difference between standard ovens and convection ovens? Briefly describe the two and explain how they are alike and how they are different.

Chapter 20

Recipes and Measuring

Section 20.1

Reading Recipes and Measuring Ingredients

Section 20.2

Altering Recipes

Chapter Objectives

Section 20.1

- **Identify** the questions you should ask to evaluate a recipe.
- **Explain** how to measure dry ingredients, liquid ingredients, and solid fats accurately.
- **Define** commonly used recipe terms.

Section 20.2

- **Explain** how to change the yield of a recipe.
- **List** examples of ingredient substitutions that work.
- **Identify** four things you can do to make a recipe more healthful.

©Hero/Corbis/GlowImages

Explore the Photo

Taking time to measure ingredients carefully can help make a recipe a success. *What measuring tools do you use when cooking?*

Writing Activity

Identify Purpose and Audience

Be Prepared Imagine that you need to explain how to make a certain dish to a person or group of people. Choose a dish and an audience. Then, highlight the most important part of your instructions for that audience. Identifying an appropriate purpose and audience will help you find effective ways to convey your message. Write a short paragraph identifying the purpose and audience of your recipe explanation.

Writing Tips Use these tips to get your message across to your intended audience:

- Determine if your purpose is to inform, persuade, entertain, or describe.
- Consider the aspects of a topic suitable for your audience.
- Explain how to make the dish.

Reading Recipes and Measuring Ingredients

Reading Guide

Before You Read

Be Organized A messy environment can be distracting. To lessen distractions, organize an area where you can read this section comfortably.

Read to Learn

Key Concepts

- **Identify** the questions you should ask to evaluate a recipe.
- **Explain** how to measure dry ingredients, liquid ingredients, and solid fats accurately.
- **Define** commonly used recipe terms.

Main Idea

Cooking and baking successfully requires that you know how to evaluate a recipe, measure ingredients accurately, and understand commonly used recipe terms.

Content Vocabulary

◇ recipe
◇ abbreviation
◇ customary measurement system
◇ metric system
◇ equivalent

Academic Vocabulary

You will find these words in your reading and on your tests. Use the glossary to look up these words if necessary.

☐ acquire
☐ adequate

Graphic Organizer

Record the questions to ask as you read a recipe. Use a graphic organizer like the one below to organize your information.

Questions to Ask as You Read a Recipe

1.
2.
3.
4.
5.
6.
7.
8.
9.

 Graphic Organizer Go to connectED.mcgraw-hill.com to download this graphic organizer.

Select a Recipe

A **recipe** lists ingredients and instructions for preparing a dish. Do you know where your favorite recipe came from? Perhaps the cookies you like best are made with a recipe handed down by your great-grandmother. Maybe your next-door neighbor has shared a barbecue recipe with your family, or a local restaurant owner gave you a recipe for lasagna.

Recipes are written by cookbook authors, chefs, food magazine and newspaper editors, family members, friends, and local charity and organizational groups. They are shown on television, posted on the Internet, shared between friends, and passed down from generation to generation. A well-written recipe includes:

- **Headnote** A headnote tells you any relevant information about the recipe. This may include the history or source of the dish or remarks about its flavor.
- **Ingredients** Recipes should include a list of ingredients with the amount of each ingredient. Ingredients should be presented in the order in which they will be used. This makes it easier to follow a recipe without forgetting an ingredient.
- **Prep** Pre-preparation steps describe what should be done to an ingredient before it is measured, such as chopping onion.
- **Instruction** Recipes should have clear directions explaining the cooking process step-by-step.
- **Equipment** The kitchen equipment you will need should also be included. A cake recipe, for example, may specify "a large bowl" for mixing, and "an 8 × 11 metal pan" for baking.
- **Temperature** It is important to include the temperature at which you will cook the dish and if preheating is necessary.
- **Time** The time it will take you to marinate, cook, or chill the food should be clearly noted.
- **Yield** The amount of food, or number of servings the recipe makes is another important piece of information.
- **Nutritional Information** You should also know the number of calories and grams of fat, sodium, and fiber per serving.

Most recipes will list the ingredients first, followed by the step-by-step directions. Some recipes incorporate the ingredient list right into the directions, however. This space-saving layout is most common on food packaging.

> **As You Read**
>
> **Connect** As you read this section, think about foods that your family prepares at holiday times. Describe some of the dishes and how they are made.

> ◆ **Vocabulary**
>
> You can find definitions in the glossary at the back of this book.

▶ Cookbook Recipe

Some cookbooks provide recipes for every mealtime dish, and others focus on one type of dish, such as grilled foods or desserts. *What kind of cookbooks do you and your family use?*

Alan Schroeder/Getty Images

Figure 20.1 Units of Measure

Measuring in Cooking Volume, weight, and temperature each have different units of measure. *Which measurements do you most often use when cooking?*

Type of Measurement	Customary Units and Abbreviations	Metric Units and Symbols
Volume	teaspoon (tsp.)	milliliter (mL)
	tablespoon (Tbsp.)	liter (L)
	fluid ounce (fl. oz.)	
	cup (c.)	
	pint (pt.)	
	quart (qt.)	
	gallon (gal.)	
Weight	ounce (oz.)	gram (g)
	pound (lb.)	kilogram (kg)
Temperature	degrees Fahrenheit (°F)	degrees Celsius (°C)

Experimenting with different recipes helps you to expand your food experiences and **acquire**, or develop, new tastes and favorites. As you read a recipe, ask yourself these questions:

- Does this recipe sound good? Are foods that I like included? Are there new foods I want to try?
- Does everyone who will share this meal like the ingredients?
- How long will it take to prepare the recipe? Do I have enough time?
- Do I have all of the equipment and ingredients I need to prepare the recipe?
- Do I understand all of the directions?
- Do I have the skills needed to do the job?

If you are less experienced in the kitchen, try to find recipes with fewer ingredients and fewer steps. They are usually easier to prepare.

✓ **Reading Check** **Describe** What information does a well-written recipe include?

Measure Ingredients

When you cook, you can choose to make something from scratch, which means to put all of the ingredients together on your own, or you can use a mix, which contains most or all of the ingredients you need in a store-bought package. Cooking from scratch may cost less than using convenience foods, but it also takes more time, energy, and kitchen skills. Whichever type of cooking you choose, you need to know how to measure and combine ingredients.

Building Character?!

Open-Mindedness Ravi invites Gabe over to his house for a traditional south Indian meal. Gabe has never eaten Indian food before. He is nervous that he will dislike it, which might offend Ravi and his family. How can Gabe overcome his unease and become more open-minded?

You Make the Call

Should Gabe agree to have dinner at Ravi's house and tell his hosts that he has never had Indian food before? Or, should Gabe turn down the invitation to avoid potentially offending Ravi and his family?

Measure Dry Ingredients

Sugar, flour, salt, and baking powder are examples of dry ingredients. When measuring ¼ cup (50 mL) of a dry ingredient, use a measuring cup. Make sure the cup is dry so the ingredient will not stick. Spoon the ingredient into the cup and heap it a little over the top. Level off the ingredients with the straight edge of a spatula or table knife. Use measuring spoons in the same way.

Keep the following points in mind when measuring:

- **Flour** Resist the urge to scoop your measuring cup into the whole container of flour. The tiny granules of flour tend to pack together in the container. Instead, spoon the flour into the cup. If the recipe calls for using sifted flour (flour you put through a screened utensil called a sifter to remove any lumps), sift the flour into the measuring cup. Do not tap the cup of flour. You may end up with extra flour.

- **Sugar** Put granulated sugar through a strainer if it is lumpy before you measure it. Overfill the cup a little and then run the back of a butter knife across the top to level it off. Pack brown sugar firmly into a measuring cup with a rubber scraper or spoon. Slightly overfill the cup and then level it off. Do not leave air pockets.

Measure Liquid Ingredients

Water, milk, and oil are examples of common liquid ingredients and are measured in clear measuring cups. For accurate measurement, put the cup on a flat surface and read the measurement at eye level. You can measure small amounts of liquid in measuring spoons. Simply fill the spoon to the brim.

Measure Fats

Sticks of margarine and butter have measurements marked on their wrappers to make it easier to measure the amounts needed. Each measurement line represents 1 tablespoon. Each stick equals ½ cup (125 mL). If you need just part of the stick, cut through the wrapper on the appropriate line. When using brands of butter that are in 8-oz. packages, you will need to measure or weigh the amount called for in the recipe.

Solid fats such as shortening or tub margarine can be measured in a dry measuring cup. First, pack the fat into the cup, trying to avoid any air pockets. Then, level it off. Use a plastic scraper to remove the fat from the cup.

Community Connections

Convert Measurements

Create a "Community Cookbook" by interviewing people in your community who want to share their recipes. Have them explain what they mean by "a pinch of salt" or a "dab of butter." Then, convert those ingredients into standard measurements.

Sift Flour

If a recipe calls for sifting, do not skip the step. *What might happen if you skip this step?*

Abbreviations and Equivalents

An **abbreviation** is a shortened form of a word. Abbreviations are commonly used in recipes to save space. Most recipes you will use are written using customary measurements, such as cups and tablespoons. The **customary measurement system** is the measurement system used in the United States. Other recipes use metric measurements, such as milliliters. The **metric system** is a system of weights and measures based on multiples of 10. This system is used outside of the United States. Use the correct measuring equipment, customary or metric, for the recipe you are following.

You will also find it helpful to know some basic equivalents. An **equivalent** is an amount that is equal to another amount. For example, 3 teaspoons are equal to, or the equivalent of, 1 tablespoon. Equivalents come in handy when you are preparing a recipe. They are also helpful when you do not have the right measuring tool or if you have already used the one needed. **Figure 20.2** lists some of the basic equivalents that will be helpful for you to know.

Figure 20.2 Equivalents

Units of Measurement Some food packages list both the metric volume of an ingredient and its equivalent in ounces. *Why would it be helpful to know both?*

Type of Measurement	Customary Units and Abbreviations	Metric Units and Symbols
Dash	Less than 1/8 tsp.	Less than 0.5 mL
¼ tsp.		1 mL
½ tsp.		2.5 mL
1 tsp.		5 mL
1 Tbsp.	3 tsp.	15 mL
1 fl. oz.	2 Tbsp.	30 mL
¼ c.	4 Tbsp. or 2 fl. oz.	50 mL
⅓ c.	5 Tbsp. + 1 tsp.	75 mL
½ c.	8 Tbsp. or 4 fl. oz.	125 mL
⅔ c.	10 Tbsp. + 2 tsp. or 6 fl. oz.	175 mL
1 c.	16 Tbsp. or 8 fl. oz.	250 mL
1 pt.	2 c. or 16 fl. oz.	500 mL
1 qt.	2 pt. or 4 c. or 32 fl. oz.	1 L (1,000 mL)
1 gal.	4 qt. or 16 c. or 128 fl. oz.	4 L
1 lb.	16 oz. (weight)	500 g
2 lb.	32 oz. (weight)	1 kg (1,000 g)

Figure 20.3 **Estimates of Common Ingredients**

Estimating in Cooking The more you cook, the more skilled you will become at estimating. *How often do you estimate amounts when cooking?*

☑ 1 cup chopped onion	=	1 large onion
☑ 1 cup chopped bell pepper	=	1 large bell pepper
☑ 1 cup chopped tomato	=	1 large tomato
☑ 1 cup chopped carrot	=	1 large carrot
☑ ½ cup of chopped celery	=	1 large rib of celery
☑ 1 teaspoon chopped garlic	=	1 large clove of garlic
☑ 3 tablespoons lemon juice	=	1 medium lemon
☑ 2 tablespoons lime juice	=	1 medium lime

☑ ⅓ cup orange juice	=	1 medium orange
☑ ½ cup mashed banana	=	1 medium banana
☑ 1 cup soft bread crumbs	=	2 slices of fresh bread
☑ 1 cup bread cubes	=	2 slices of fresh bread
☑ 2 cups shredded cheese	=	8 ounces of cheese
☑ 1 pound dry pasta	=	6 to 9 cups of cooked pasta, depending on the shape

Estimate Amounts

To celebrate her father's birthday, Sarah decided to make him dinner. The recipe Sarah wanted to make called for ¼ cup of chopped onion. Sarah looked in her refrigerator. "I have one onion," she noted. "Is that enough?" What do you think?

Deciding whether you have enough of certain ingredients to make a recipe can be tricky. In **Figure 20.3**, estimates are provided for some common ingredients. According to the chart, one onion will be adequate, or enough, for Sarah's recipe. Look at the figure to see other equivalents of common ingredients. Can you think of any others that could be added?

✓ **Reading Check** **Explain** Why should you know how to measure and combine ingredients?

Understand Recipe Terms

What do you think of when you see the words "coat" and "dice"? You probably picture a warm jacket, and the numbered cubes people roll to play board games. When cooking, however, these terms take on entirely different meanings. There are many words or terms that have a special meaning when they are used in food preparation. To prepare a recipe successfully, pay careful attention to the terms used in the recipe. This may include measurements, tools, or the way something must be cut or cooked. If you read a recipe too quickly you might even confuse cooking terms with the ingredients you need. A recipe that mentions "bread" or "cream" could be providing ingredients; or it could be giving directions for preparation.

See **Figure 20.4** on page 495, **Figure 20.5** on page 496, and **Figure 20.6** on page 497 for some examples of cutting terms, mixing terms, and other important cooking terms that can appear in recipes.

Ask Your Teacher

If you are experiencing problems in a particular subject, ask your teacher for additional help. He or she may be able to provide after-school tutoring or additional activities for you.

Knife Safety

Without proper knife skills, knives can be dangerous. Good knife skills and the right equipment can help you cut food properly and safely. Follow these guidelines to safely use knives.

- **Use sharp knives.** Sharp knives are actually safer than slightly dulled knives. You are more likely to press a dull knife harder into the food than you would need to press a sharp knife. This may cause the knife to slip and cause an accident.
- **Always use a cutting board.** Cutting directly on a kitchen counter or table can damage the surface and may cause the knife to slip.
- **Do not cut toward yourself.** When you use any type of blade, you should cut away from yourself. This includes holding food in your hand while cutting. If the knife slips or cuts faster than you expect, it can easily injure you.
- **Tuck your fingers under.** When you cut food with your fingers flat, there is a greater chance of accidentally cutting the tips of your fingers. When using one hand to hold food steady, tuck your fingers under. Because they are wider and positioned higher than your fingertips would be, your knuckles are less likely to get cut.
- **Keep the tip of the knife down.** When you are holding a knife, you should always point the blade down to prevent injuries to yourself or others. When cutting slippery foods like onions, keep the tip of the knife pressed to the cutting board and lift the blade up like a lever. Professional chefs use this technique because it both protects your fingers and allows you to chop faster. If you need to carry a knife across the kitchen, hold it loosely against your thigh with the blade tip facing the floor. When you are done using the knife, place it at the top of your cutting board with the blade facing away from you.

TAKE CHARGE!

Try Herbs and Spices

Herbs and spices can jazz up a dish without adding fat. Herbs are the fragrant leaves of plants. Spices come from the bark, buds, roots, fruit, seeds, or stems of plants and trees. When cooking with herbs and spices, keep these points in mind:

- **Do Not Overdo It** Too many herbs or spices in one dish can overpower the food. Use only a few herbs and spices to accent the flavor of the food.
- **Make Accurate Substitutions** If you are using dried herbs instead of fresh ones, you can use half as much dried herbs as fresh.
- **Pay Attention to the Time** For recipes with long cooking times, such as soup, add herbs, salt, and spices toward the end of cooking.
- **Cut Finely** Cut surfaces release more flavor.

Real-World Skills

Try It Out Follow your teacher's instructions to form into pairs. Then, discuss some of your favorite recipes with your partner. Pick at least one herb and one spice that you think would add to the flavor of one of your recipes. If you already use herbs and spices in your recipes, explain how they enhance the flavor.

Figure 20.4 **Cutting Terms**

Preparing Ingredients What is the difference between mincing and chopping or between dicing and cubing? At first glance, some of the differences may seem minor, but they make a significant difference in the appearance and texture of a dish. *How often do you use the different cutting techniques described?*

Chop Cut food into small, irregular pieces, as in chopping carrots or green peppers.

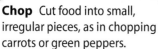

Mince Chop food into pieces that are as small as possible, as in mincing an onion.

Cube Cut into evenly shaped pieces about ½ inch on each side, as in cubing bread.

Dice Cut into evenly shaped pieces about ¼ inch on each side, as in dicing ingredients for a salad.

Pare Cut off the outside covering of a fruit or vegetable, as in paring an apple or a potato.

Grate and Shred Rub food over a grater to make fine particles or shredded food, as in grating or shredding cheese. New photo-etched graters easily grate and shred food.

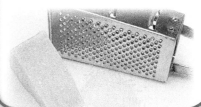

Figure 20.5

Mixing Terms

Stir Use a spoon to make circular or figure eight motions, as in stirring soup when it warms or making a sauce.

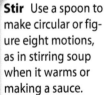

Blend, Mix, or Combine Use a spoon to stir two or more ingredients together thoroughly.

Beat Use this technique to add air to foods, as in beating eggs. When beating cake batter, you can use a quick, over-and-under motion with a spoon, wire whisk, rotary beater, or electric mixer.

Whip Use a wire whisk, rotary beater, or electric mixer to whip ingredients. This rapid movement adds air and makes food fluffy.

Cream Use a spoon, beater, or mixer to combine ingredients until soft and creamy, as in creaming fat and sugar for a cake.

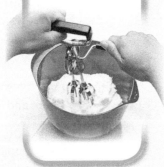

Cut in Use a pastry blender or two knives and a cutting motion to mix solid fat with dry ingredients, as in cutting fat into flour for a pie crust.

Fold Use a rubber scraper to gently combine ingredients in a delicate mixture, such as adding a lighter ingredient to a heavier one. Folding keeps air in the mixture.

Figure 20.6

Other Cooking Terms

Taking Action When following a recipe, pay close attention to verbs that are used. Each term has very different meanings. *What meals do you make that require basting or coating food?*

Baste Moisten foods, such as meat, while cooking. Basting adds flavor and helps keep food from drying out.

Brush Use a brush to lightly cover the surface of one food with another, as in brushing butter sauce on fish.

Coat Cover the surface of a food with a dry ingredient, such as flour, cornmeal, dry bread crumbs, or sugar. Coatings can also include liquid ingredients.

Garnish Decorate a food dish with a small decorative food item, such as parsley sprigs, vegetable confetti, carrot curls, or an edible flower.

Grease Rub lightly with fat, such as butter, margarine, oil, or shortening, as in greasing a baking sheet or muffin tins.

Season Add seasonings, such as salt, pepper, herbs, or spices, to flavor a food.

Drain Remove excess liquid by placing food in a colander or strainer, as in draining pasta.

Collect and Organize Recipes

If you do not have a recipe collection yet, now is the perfect time to start! Now that you understand common recipe terms, you can determine which recipes will best suit your interests, needs, and skills.

Like an organized kitchen, an organized recipe collection makes cooking easier and more enjoyable. Many cooks write or paste the recipes they collect on index cards and store them in a card file box. Others insert the recipe cards in the clear plastic pockets of photo albums. Some cooks write recipes in a divided notebook or binder, attaching a photo to each. If your recipes are mostly online or in an electronic format, you can save them to a folder on your computer. Whichever organization method you choose, you will want to create special tabs or sections to organize your recipes. These sections can be based on food types or special interests, such as appetizers, main dishes, vegetarian dishes, or low-fat recipes.

You can also use a database to save recipes on a computer. This allows you to search for recipes by food group, course, or occasion. When you use the computer, you can easily print recipes to share with friends, or put together your very own cookbook!

Section 20.1

After You Read

Review Key Concepts

1. **Identify** how recipes are developed and shared.
2. **Explain** the term equivalent and why equivalents are helpful when preparing a recipe.
3. **Describe** the difference between mincing and chopping and the difference between garnishing and seasoning.

Check Your Answers Go to connectED. mcgraw-hill.com to check your answers.

Practice Academic Skills

English Language Arts

4. Look up new recipes in print cookbooks or on cooking Web sites. As you read, identify cooking terms that are new to you. Research the meaning of the terms, and create a short list of those terms with their definitions.

Social Studies

5. Is there a recipe that has been passed down in your family that you find comforting? Describe a comforting recipe that your family has made for generations. What is it about the recipe that is comforting?

Altering Recipes

Reading Guide

Before You Read
Study with a Buddy It can be difficult to review your notes and quiz yourself on what you have just read. According to research, studying with a partner for just twelve minutes can help you study better.

Read to Learn
Key Concepts
- **Explain** how to change the yield of a recipe.
- **List** examples of ingredient substitutions that work.
- **Identify** four things you can do to make a recipe more healthful.

Main Idea
Simple tips and techniques will allow you to change a recipe's yield, substitute ingredients, or make a recipe more healthful.

Content Vocabulary
◇ yield

Academic Vocabulary
You will find these words in your reading and on your tests. Use the glossary to look up their definitions if necessary.
- alter
- flexible

Graphic Organizer
As you read, record substitutions that work. Use a graphic organizer like the one below to organize your information.

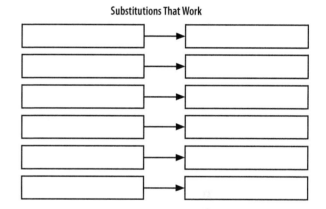

Substitutions That Work

 Graphic Organizer Go to connectED.mcgraw-hill.com to download this graphic organizer.

Change the Yield of a Recipe

As You Read

Connect As you read this section, think about why you might want to change the number of servings, or the yield, of a recipe.

◆ **Vocabulary**

You can find definitions in the glossary at the back of this book.

You do not always have to follow a recipe exactly as it is written. Sometimes you can alter, or change, a recipe to increase or decrease the number of servings. You can also alter a recipe by substituting one ingredient for another or adding various spices and herbs. Knowing how to alter recipes allows you more creativity in your food preparation.

The **yield** is the amount of food or the number of servings a recipe makes. If you want more or fewer servings, you will need to alter the recipe. Not all recipes can be altered successfully, but many can. To do this, put your math skills and knowledge of equivalent measurements to work. For example, if you are preparing a recipe that yields eight servings but you want only four, follow these steps:

1. **Divide the number of servings you want by the original yield.** The answer is the number you will use to calculate the new amount of each ingredient. In this example, $4 \div 8 = \frac{1}{2}$.

HOW TO...   Make Salsa

Salsa, a favorite in Mexican cooking, outsells ketchup in the United States. It is healthful, flavorful, easy to make, and has a variety of uses. Traditional salsas are based on tomatoes, onions, and chili peppers. Zucchini, carrots, corn, and beans are other popular additions. Sweet-hot fruit salsa contains fruits like mangos, apricots, and pineapples. Traditional seasoning choices include lime juice, an herb called cilantro, and a spice called cumin. Depending on your tastes and ingredients, you might try flavored vinegar, garlic, chili powder, honey, or sugar. Once you have settled on your ingredients and seasonings, it is time to assemble the salsa.

Peel Tomatoes To loosen the skin, place the tomatoes one at a time into boiling water for about 40 seconds and then into a bowl of ice water until cool enough to handle. The skin should slip off.

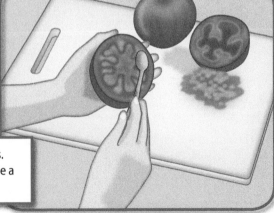

Seed Tomatoes Halve the tomatoes and scoop out the seeds. Chop the tomatoes into small chunks, about ½ inch. You can use a knife or a food processor. Place the tomatoes in a large bowl.

2. **Multiply the amount of each ingredient by the answer in step 1.** If the recipe calls for 2 pounds of ground beef, you should use 1 pound (2 x ½ = 1).

3. **Convert measurements as needed.** If a recipe calls for ¼ cup grated cheese, the new amount would be ⅛ cup (¼ x ½ = ⅛). If you do not have a ⅛ cup utensil, use the chart on page 492 to help you figure out an equivalent measure.

4. **Calculate the new amount for each ingredient in the recipe.** Afterward, write the amounts down so that you do not forget them.

To double a recipe, simply multiply the amount of each ingredient by 2. To triple it, multiply by 3, and so on. Remember that increasing the number of servings requires larger pans. The baking or cooking time may also need to be increased for a larger number of servings.

✓ Reading Check **Clarify** What does it mean to alter a recipe?

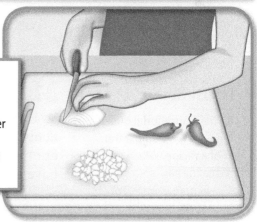

Chop Other Foods into Smaller Pieces Other foods should be chopped into ¼-inch pieces. Add them to the bowl with the tomatoes. Handle hot chilies with care. The heat-producing substance, called capsaicin (cap-SAY-ih-sin), can burn your eyes and nose. Always wear rubber or latex surgical gloves and keep your hands away from your face. Most of the capsaicin is in the seeds and membranes of the peppers. Remove these parts before cooking.

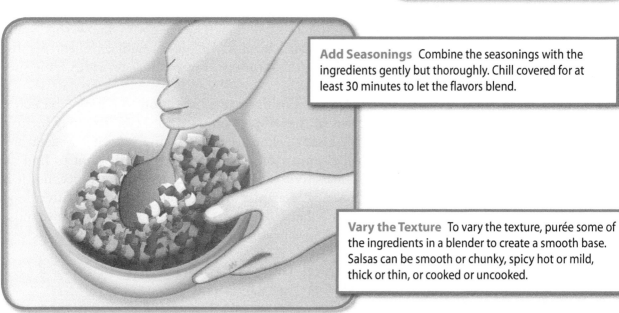

Add Seasonings Combine the seasonings with the ingredients gently but thoroughly. Chill covered for at least 30 minutes to let the flavors blend.

Vary the Texture To vary the texture, purée some of the ingredients in a blender to create a smooth base. Salsas can be smooth or chunky, spicy hot or mild, thick or thin, or cooked or uncooked.

▲ **Adjust the Yield**

If you have additional guests, you may have to adjust the yield of a recipe. *Which foods would be the easiest to adjust for last-minute guests? Why?*

SUCCEED IN SCHOOL

Your Expectations

Determine what your own idea of success is. Success in school may not always mean getting straight As. The progress you make in a subject is another type of academic success.

Making Substitutions

Have you ever been in the middle of preparing a recipe and suddenly discovered you are missing an ingredient? To avoid this situation, read through the recipe ingredients list and make sure you have all necessary items on hand before you start to prepare food.

However, if you are missing an ingredient, you may be able to make a substitution. For example, if you are making oatmeal cookies and you do not have raisins, you can substitute nuts or dried cranberries for the raisins. Experienced cooks know that some ingredients can be used in place of others with excellent results. Some cookbooks list substitutions. **Figure 20.7** provides some substitution suggestions.

You may also need to make a substitution to a recipe based on special concerns of the people you need to serve. You may invite a friend over for lasagna, knowing that your friend is a vegetarian. Instead of using your usual meat sauce, you will want to find an alternative choice. Tofu is often used in place of meat because it is high in protein. You may also need to serve someone with a food allergy. Research what ingredients you can use to substitute those that the person cannot or does not eat.

✓ **Reading Check** **Describe** When is it necessary to use a substitution when preparing a recipe?

Figure 20.7 Ingredient Substitutions That Work

Replacing Ingredients Sometimes you will need to make substitutions for ingredients in a recipe. *Why do you make ingredient substitutions in recipes?*

Ingredient	Substitutions
2 Tbsp. (30 mL) flour (for thickening)	1 Tbsp. (15 mL) cornstarch
1 c. (250 mL) sifted cake flour	1 c. + 2 Tbsp. (260 mL) sifted all-purpose flour
1 c. (250 mL) whole milk	½ c. (125 mL) evaporated milk + ½ c. (125 mL) water
1 c. (250 mL) sour milk or buttermilk	1 c. (250 mL) fresh milk + 1 Tbsp. (15 mL) vinegar or lemon juice
1 square (1 oz. or 28 g) unsweetened chocolate	3 Tbsp. (45 mL) unsweetened cocoa powder + 1 Tbsp. (15 mL) butter or margarine
1 c. (250 mL) granulated sugar	1 c. (250 mL) packed brown sugar or 2 c. (500 mL) sifted powdered, or confectioner's sugar

Creative and Healthy Changes

You may be a new cook or about to try a new dish or style of cooking. When you first try a recipe, follow the instructions closely. After you have used the recipe, you may want to try something new and explore your creativity.

You can begin by changing the seasonings and a few ingredients. If you are making pasta, you can add extra herbs for taste, or onion or garlic to the sauce for more "punch." You can also add diced bell pepper or diced carrots to change the texture and taste and boost the nutrition. If you like meat in your sauce, you can add lean ground beef or ground turkey. Venison and buffalo meat are also lean and tasty additions to sauce.

Casserole, stew, soup, pasta, and salad recipes are extremely flexible, or open to adaptation, when it comes to making changes. These dishes allow you to experiment with different amounts and ingredients to help you develop your range. Most baked goods such as breads, cakes, and cookies depend on exact amounts of their main ingredients, such as flour, baking soda, and eggs, to turn out right. But you can still experiment with additional ingredients. You can add a raspberry swirl to your favorite cheesecake, for example. Pieces of dates or dried fruit are also great additions to baked recipes.

Math You Can Use

Change Yield

Lamar needs to change the yield of the following chocolate chip cookie recipe from 40 cookies to 20 cookies. Use the ingredient list below to figure out the new amounts for each.

2 eggs

½ cup sugar

1 cup brown sugar

1 teaspoon baking soda

1 tablespoon vanilla extract

1 cup butter

2 ½ cups flour

2 cups chocolate chips

Math Concept **Multiplying Fractions** To multiply a fraction by a fraction, multiply the numerators of the fractions and the denominators of the fractions. Then, place the product of the denominators under the product of the numerators. Simplify the fraction.

Starting Hint Divide 20 by 40 to figure out what number to multiply the ingredients by. That number is 0.5. You can convert it to the fraction ½.

 For math help, go to the Math Appendix at the back of the book.

Chapter 20 Recipes and Measuring **503**

Health & Wellness

TIPS

Healthful Substitutions

For health reasons, some people avoid using wheat flour, eggs, or salt. There are tasty, healthful alternatives. You might try these ingredient substitutions:

▶ **Replace** wheat flour with oat or buckwheat flour.

▶ **Substitute** applesauce for eggs in some cake recipes.

▶ **Replace** salt with herbs in many recipes.

To cut back on fat for a more healthful dish, you can substitute vegetable oil or olive oil for butter or margarine. Olive oil with herbs is delicious drizzled over vegetables. Balsalmic vinegar makes a tasty and low-calorie salad dressing. Plain, low-fat yogurt is a great replacement for sour cream in dips. Some varieties are thicker and more creamy than others. Try yogurts from different companies and cultures to find your favorite. What other things can you do to decrease the amount of fat in the foods you eat?

Chefs and test kitchen experts alter recipes all the time. They are always developing new recipes and new approaches to eating. You can do the same thing in your own "test kitchen." You can use your understanding of measuring, combining, and cooking terms to create dishes that will bring a new adventure in eating to your family dinner table. Try new dishes made with similar methods to the ones you already know. As you become more comfortable in the kitchen, do not be afraid to branch out. Try new styles of cooking from different cultures. Sample different herbs and spices from the ones you usually use. Find a cultural dish and learn how other people eat!

Section 20.2

After You Read

Review Key Concepts

1. **Clarify** what it means to alter a recipe in order to change its yield.
2. **List** ingredients that you could substitute for raisins in a recipe for oatmeal cookies.
3. **Describe** how you might create recipes in your own "test kitchen" to add adventure to your family's meals.

Check Your Answers
Go to **connectED. mcgraw-hill.com** to check your answers.

Practice Academic Skills

English Language Arts

4. Choose a recipe. Prepare the recipe. Then, write a short evaluation of your experience, noting what was successful and what you could do to improve. How would you alter the recipe, and how would doing so improve it?

Social Studies

5. Use reliable print or Internet sources to research a recipe specific to a certain culture. How do people from other cultures view this recipe? Are there any recipes from your own culture that people from other places might find strange?

CHAPTER SUMMARY

Section 20.1
Reading Recipes and Measuring Ingredients

Recipes can come from many different places. You can make a recipe from scratch, or you can use a store-bought mix. To re-create recipes accurately, you need to carefully measure all ingredients. Different tools are used to measure dry ingredients, liquid ingredients, and fats. Many recipe terms have meanings unique to specific food preparations. Good knife skills and the right equipment can help you cut food properly and safely.

Section 20.2
Altering Recipes

Recipes can be successfully altered to change the yield and to allow creativity. You can change the yield of a recipe by using a simple formula. You can substitute certain ingredients for others with little change to the outcome of a recipe. Ingredient substitutions can also change the taste of a dish, and even make it more healthful. Some recipes are easier to modify than others. Even slight changes to a recipe can make a huge difference in taste. Be adventurous and try new styles and tastes.

Vocabulary Review

1. Use each of these content and academic vocabulary terms to create a crossword puzzle. Use their definitions as clues.

Content Vocabulary
◇ recipe (p. 489)
◇ abbreviation (p. 492)
◇ customary measurement system (p. 492)
◇ metric system (p. 492)
◇ equivalent (p. 492)
◇ yield (p. 500)

Academic Vocabulary
▢ acquire (p. 490)
▢ adequate (p. 493)
▢ alter (p. 500)
▢ flexible (p. 503)

Review Key Concepts

2. **Identify** the questions you should ask to evaluate a recipe.
3. **Explain** how to measure dry ingredients, liquid ingredients, and solid fats accurately.
4. **Define** commonly used recipe terms.
5. **Explain** how to change the yield of a recipe.
6. **List** examples of ingredient substitutions that work.
7. **Identify** four things you can do to make a recipe more healthful.

Critical Thinking

8. **Conclude** Select two recipes, one for a family dinner during the week and one for a holiday meal. What should you consider in your selection?
9. **Analyze** Ask family members, neighbors, or friends for some favorite recipes. Read each recipe carefully. Choose two that you could make, and share them with your class.
10. **Apply** If you were to make a vegetable or fruit tray as an appetizer for your family, which cutting terms might you practice as you prepare it?
11. **Predict** You have no measuring utensils but would like to make cookies. What kind of recipe should you use, and how will you measure your ingredients?

ACTIVE LEARNING

12. Alter a Recipe You can alter a recipe if you want to try to improve it, or just to try something new. You might also want to alter a recipe in order to increase or decrease the number of servings or to make it with more healthful ingredients. Express your creativity by changing a recipe to create your own version of a dish. Substitute some ingredients with others or use less or more of some ingredients in order to change the taste of the dish. Prepare the dish, and share it with your class. Have copies of your recipe and the original on hand to share with classmates. Explain how you changed the recipe to reflect your creativity or to change the recipe yield.

Family & Community Connections

13. Customary and Metric Measurements Many recipes are written using customary measurements, such as cups, teaspoons, and tablespoons. Other recipes, however, are written using metric measurements, such as milliliters and kilograms. Knowing how to convert units of one type of measurement to units of the other type can be helpful. That way, you will be able to prepare recipes that use measurements for which you do not have measuring tools. Follow your teacher's instructions to form into small groups. Choose a recipe from a cookbook or cooking Web site. Then, work together to convert all measurements from customary to metric, or vice versa. After you have converted all measurements, make the recipe using the newly converted measurements.

Real-World Skills and Applications

Leadership Skills

14. Cooking Class Choose a favorite recipe and show the class how to follow it. Bring the ingredients to class and demonstrate how to properly measure and combine them. If you do not have all the necessary appliances in the classroom, simply explain the steps you need to follow to complete the recipe in a kitchen.

Financial Literacy

15. Calculate the Cost In order to bake a batch of bran muffins to feed 12 people, you need 2 cups of flour, 2 cups of bran, and $\frac{1}{5}$ cup of milk. Flour costs \$2.50 for a 5-cup bag, bran costs \$12.75 for a 10 cup bag, and milk costs 75¢ for 2 cups. How much will you spend on ingredients to make enough muffins for 60 people?

Cooperative Learning

16. Healthful Alterations Follow your teacher's instructions to form into groups. Choose two recipes you like that you could alter to make more healthful. For each recipe, you and your group or partner should each replace one ingredient with a more healthful alternative. After you are finished, try making both of the recipes. Do they taste the same? Do they taste better or worse?

Academic Skills

 English Language Arts

17. Create a Recipe There are flavors and textures that you enjoy. In the food lab or at home, develop a simple, original recipe. Try to use ingredients that are healthful and also widely available. Write the recipe instructions, and ask people to critique the organization and clarity.

 Social Studies

18. Food Associations Food may remind you of tastes, smells, and sounds from your past. Think of a common dish that reminds you of something. For example, mashed potatoes and cranberries may remind you of Thanksgiving, or there may be a dish that you eat every year on your birthday. Describe the dish and the connection you have to it. Write the recipe down, and share it with your class.

 Mathematics

19. Pizza Percent After a student council meeting, Sanjay, Katherine, and Michael were hungry. They decided to go to Guilia's Pizza Kitchen for dinner. They shared a pizza with 8 slices. Sanjay ate 3 slices, Katherine ate 1, and Michael ate 4. What percent of the pizza did each person eat?

Math Concept **Percent** To convert a decimal to a percent, you can either multiply the decimal by 100 or simply move the decimal 2 places to the right. To convert a percent to a decimal, you can either divide the decimal by 100 or simply move the decimal 2 places to the left.

Starting Hint Divide the number of slices each person ate by the number of overall slices to figure the percent that person ate in decimal form.

 For math help, go to the Math Appendix at the back of the book.

 Standardized Test Practice

MULTIPLE CHOICE
Directions Read the question. Then, choose the correct answer.

Test-Taking Tip When you are working on a multiple choice question, it is a good idea to first eliminate the answers you know are not correct. You will be more likely to guess correctly from the remaining choices.

20. Which of the following is the equivalent of 1 teaspoon?
a) 1 milliliter
b) 5 milliliters
c) 10 milliliters
d) 12 milliliters

Design Your Dream Kitchen

In this project you will research different kitchen layouts and design a kitchen that meets your basic needs and preferences.

 My Journal

If you completed the journal entry from page 436, refer to it to see if your thoughts have changed after reading the unit.

Project Assignment

In this project you will:

- Conduct research on kitchen equipment and appliances.
- Write a descriptive essay about your dream kitchen.
- Interview someone in your community who is knowledgeable about kitchen equipment and kitchen design.
- Create a blueprint, model, or other visual representation of your dream kitchen.
- Present your final project to the class.

The Skills Behind the Project

Life Skills

Key personal and relationship skills you will use in this project include:
- Making wise choices.
- Interacting with adults.
- Speaking with a large group.
- Creative thinking

STEP 1 Research Kitchen Equipment

Research various kitchen equipment and supplies, including large and small appliances. Identify those items that you would want to include in your ideal kitchen. As you conduct your research, save electronic files of photos of the various types of equipment and supplies you would want to include in your ideal kitchen. You may use these images later when you create your presentation about your kitchen design. Also, research different layouts for kitchens and choose one to use for the kitchen you will design. When you are done conducting your research, visualize your dream kitchen and write a descriptive essay about it. The purpose of a descriptive essay is to describe a person, place, or thing in such vivid detail that the reader can easily form a precise mental picture of what is being written about.

Writing Skills

- Use imaginative language.
- Make interesting comparisons.
- Describe images that appeal to the senses.

STEP 2 Write Interview Questions

Identify an adult in your community who you can interview about kitchen equipment and design. This person can be a homemaker

Life Skills Project Checklist

Plan	☑ Research kitchen supplies and equipment, including large and small appliances.
	☑ Write a descriptive essay about your dream kitchen.
	☑ Write a list of interview questions.
	☑ Conduct an interview.
	☑ Create a blueprint, model, or other visual representation of a kitchen that will suit your needs and personal preferences.
Present	☑ Present your kitchen design to your class.
	☑ Invite the students in your class to ask you any questions they may have. Answer these questions.
	☑ When students ask you questions, demonstrate in your answers that you respect their perspectives.
	☑ Turn in your descriptive essay, the notes from your interview and your kitchen design to your teacher.
Academic Skills	☑ Adapt and modify language to suit different purposes.
	☑ Speak clearly and concisely.

or a restaurant chef, cook, manager, or owner. Prepare a list of questions about kitchen equipment and design. Here are some examples.

- How many meals per day do you prepare in this kitchen?
- What safety precautions must you take?
- What are the most important appliances, tools, and other pieces of equipment?
- What would you change about the design of your kitchen if you could?
- What is the biggest challenge of working in a kitchen like this one?

STEP 3 Connect to Your Community

Arrange to interview the adult you identified in Step 2. Arrange to take a tour of the kitchen. Bring your list of questions and take notes of the answers. When you are finished, transcribe your notes in complete sentences.

Interpersonal Skills

- Be polite and confident when you contact the adult.
- Ask questions to gain a better understanding.

- Wait until the adult is finished answering the question before you move on to the next question.

STEP 4 Design a Kitchen

Use the Life Skills Project Checklist to plan and create your presentation to share what you have learned with your classmates.

STEP 5 Evaluate Your Life Skills and Academic Skills

Your project will be evaluated based on:
- Content and organization of your information.
- Quality of your research.
- Mechanics—presentation and neatness.
- Speaking and listening skills.

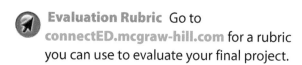

Evaluation Rubric Go to **connectED.mcgraw-hill.com** for a rubric you can use to evaluate your final project.

UNIT 8

From Kitchen to Table

Chapter 21   Basic Cooking Techniques
Chapter 22   Preparing Grains, Fruits, and Vegetables
Chapter 23   Preparing Protein Foods
Chapter 24   Eating Together

Unit Life Skills Project Preview

Plan a Meal

In this unit you will learn about what happens to food as it goes from the kitchen to your table. In your life skills project you will plan a meal for six people.

 My Journal

Experiencing Flavor Write a journal entry about one of these topics. This will help you prepare for the unit project at the end of this unit.

- Describe what your favorite meal tastes like.
- Explain how a food you love stimulates your five senses: taste, smell, touch, sight, and hearing.
- List three of your favorite foods and use similes or metaphors in a paragraph that describes how they make you feel.

Explore the Photo

Cooking gives you the opportunity to try new things. *What are some of the benefits of learning to cook different foods?*

511

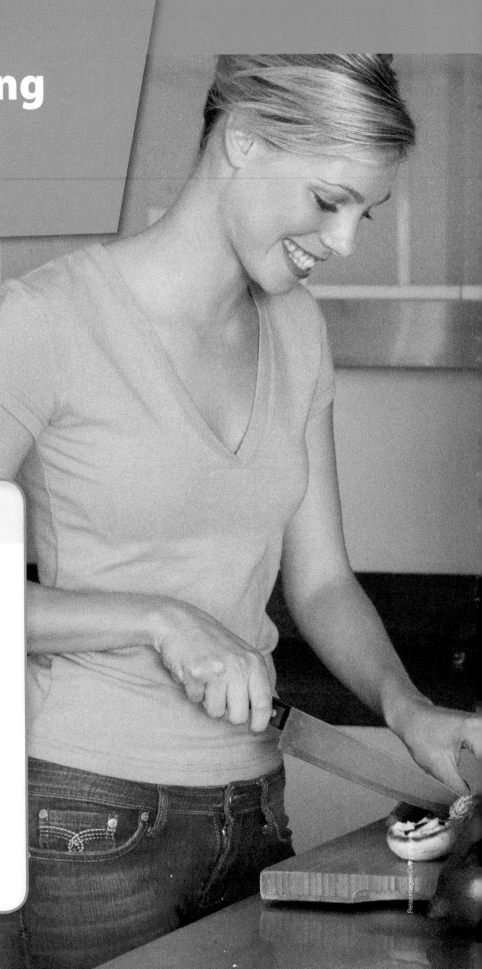

Chapter 21

Basic Cooking Techniques

Section 21.1
Choosing Cooking Techniques

Section 21.2
Healthful Cooking Methods

Chapter Objectives

Section 21.1
- **Explain** conduction, convection, and radiation.
- **Describe** the four different dry-heat cooking methods.
- **Describe** the six different moist-heat cooking methods.
- **Compare** different methods for cooking with fat.
- **Summarize** microwave cooking techniques.

Section 21.2
- **Identify** five ways to tell if a food you are cooking is done.
- **Give** guidelines for conserving nutrients while cooking.

Writing Activity

Describe an Event

Birthday Celebrations Special events often revolve around special meals. Many individuals indulge in their favorite foods on their birthdays. Think about how you might describe your ideal birthday meal to someone. Describing an event requires that you visualize and portray the event accurately. Write a short paragraph describing an event that includes a meal you would like to have on your birthday.

Writing Tips Use these tips to describe an event:
- Decide what mood you want to create in the paragraph.
- Use sensory details to draw your reader in.
- Present details in a logical order.

Explore the Photo

Different cooking methods require different steps and techniques. *What kinds of cooking methods have you tried?*

Section 21.1

Choosing Cooking Techniques

Before You Read

Understanding It is normal to have questions as you read. Write down questions while reading. Many will be answered as you continue. If they are not, you will have a list ready for your teacher when you finish.

Read to Learn
Key Concepts
- **Explain** conduction, convection, and radiation.
- **Describe** the four different dry-heat cooking methods.
- **Describe** the six different moist-heat cooking methods.
- **Compare** different methods for cooking with fat.
- **Summarize** microwave cooking techniques.

Main Idea
Mastering the use of different cooking methods and equipment will allow you to cook a variety of foods.

Content Vocabulary
◇ conduction
◇ convection
◇ radiation
◇ dry-heat cooking
◇ roast
◇ broil
◇ moist-heat cooking
◇ boil
◇ steam
◇ poach
◇ simmer
◇ braise
◇ stew
◇ deep-fat fry
◇ panfry
◇ stir-fry

Academic Vocabulary
You will find these words in your reading and on your tests. Use the glossary to look up their definitions if necessary.
▢ transfer
▢ circulation

Graphic Organizer
As you read, list four dry-heat cooking methods, six moist-heat cooking methods, and three methods for cooking with fat. Use a graphic organizer like the one below to organize your information.

Dry-Heat Methods	Moist-Heat Methods	Cooking with Fat

 Graphic Organizer Go to **connectED.mcgraw-hill.com** to download this graphic organizer.

Cooking Defined

Put simply, cooking is the transfer, or movement, of heat from a heat source, to food. Heat is a form of energy. When this energy comes into contact with food, it causes molecules in the food to vibrate. These vibrations cause chemical changes in the food which make the food look, smell, and taste different. In other words, they cook the food.

Heat affects the appearance and flavor of food. It softens some foods, and makes others crispy. Because heat tenderizes some foods, such as meat and oatmeal, they are easier to chew and digest. Though heat can cause some nutrient loss, it also helps our bodies more easily process some nutrients that would otherwise be lost. Heat also destroys harmful bacteria in the foods we eat. The more surface area a food has, the faster heat transfers to it. The transfer of heat to food happens in three different ways:

- **Conduction** is the transfer of heat energy through direct contact between a hot surface and food. Panfrying is a common form of conduction. The heat energy transfers from the stove top to the pan, causing molecules in the pan to vibrate. The heated molecules in the pan then bump into the molecules in the food, causing the food molecules to vibrate. This cooks the food in the pan.

- **Convection** cooking is the transfer of heat through the flow of hot air or hot liquid. Boiling and baking are both examples of convection cooking. When you boil water or soup, heat first transfers to the pot through conduction. As the soup at the bottom of the pot warms up, it starts to rise. This is because heated liquid weighs less than cold liquid. As the heated liquid rises to the top of the pot, cooler liquid sinks to the bottom, where it begins to heat up. This circulation, or flow, continues until all the liquid is the same temperature. When you bake in a convection oven, heating elements heat the air in the oven. A fan in the oven moves the hot air around the food, which heats and cooks the food.

- **Radiation** is energy that is transmitted through air waves. The heat you feel rising from the coals of an outdoor grill comes from radiation. When this heat energy reaches food, it causes the molecules in the food to vibrate, which heats the food. Radiation cooking is different from convection cooking because the air does not circulate. When you put a roast in a convection oven, the circulating air cooks it on all sides. When you put a steak on a grill, the radiating heat only cooks it on one side. You need to flip the steak to cook both sides.

✓ **Reading Check** **Compare** How do conduction, convection, and radiation differ in terms of transferring heat?

As You Read

Connect Think about cooking terms you already know, such as bake, boil, or fry. Which of these cooking methods does your family use the most often?

◇ Vocabulary

You can find definitions in the glossary at the back of this book.

V Combination Methods

Some cooking methods involve a combination of conduction, convection, or radiation. *How do conduction, convection, and radiation all play a role in baking?*

Figure 21.1   **Cooking with Dry Heat**

Dry-Heat Techniques   Cooking with dry heat works best with foods that are naturally tender. For dishes that require more than 45 minutes of cooking time, cover the dish for the first half of the cooking time to keep the food from drying out. *What kinds of foods do you cook using dry heat?*

Broiling and Grilling   Popular broiled and grilled foods include steak, hamburgers, chicken, and some vegetables (especially if cheese is involved).

Roasting and Baking   Foods often baked or roasted include meat, poultry, fish, breads, and vegetables.

Dry-Heat Cooking

When you bake dinner rolls in the oven, you are using a dry-heat method. **Dry-heat cooking** is cooking food uncovered without adding liquid or fat. Dry-heat methods include roasting, baking, broiling, and grilling. Naturally tender foods are best cooked with dry-heat methods. The dry heat gives food a crisp brown crust with a distinctive flavor, while the inside remains moist and tender. See **Figure 21.1**.

- **Roasting and Baking**   To **roast** most often refers to cooking large pieces of meat or poultry in a shallow pan. Sometimes the food is placed on a metal rack inside the pan to drain the fat from the food. Baking can be used to cook cookies and cakes, as well as meat and vegetables. In both roasting and baking, air in the oven circulates around the food being cooked. Always preheat the oven for 10 to 15 minutes before you bake or roast food, unless the recipe says otherwise.

- **Broiling and Grilling**   To **broil** means to cook food directly under a heat source, also called the heating element. You can broil food in the oven by placing the food on the broiler pan. Broiling pans have two parts: the grill rack or grid, and a lower pan that sometimes can be attached to the grill rack. This lower pan is also called the drip pan, because it catches the fat drippings from the cooking meat. Grilling is the opposite of broiling. With grilling, the heat source is below, not above.

(l)©Tierra Images/Alamy; (r)©VStock/Alamy

Convection Oven Cooking

Convection ovens have both upper and lower heating elements and a fan on the back wall, which circulates the hot air from these elements. Some convection ovens have a third heating element in the back of the oven, near the fan. The rapidly circulating air cooks food faster and regulates the oven temperature, preventing hot spots in the oven.

The main advantage of convection oven cooking is reduced cooking time. Quick cooking not only saves time, it helps foods retain their nutrients and stay moist. For example, when cooked in a convection oven, meat, poultry, fish, and seafood develop brown crusts on the outside while remaining juicy on the inside.

Cooking may vary from convection oven to convection oven. You will need to experiment to find the cooking speed of your oven. When experimenting with cooking times, you can do one of the following:

- Bake food at the temperature recommended for the standard oven, and reduce the time.
- Bake food for the time recommended for the standard oven, and reduce the temperature by 25°F (-4°C).

The cookware you choose is a factor when cooking with a convection oven. Casserole lids and high-sided roasting pans block the circulating air and prevent convection ovens from cooking efficiently. For better air circulation, the cookware should be open and not much higher than its contents. Cookie sheets and shallow pans with 1-inch sides are good choices for a convection oven. Covered dishes, roasting bags, and deep pans are best in a standard oven.

✓ **Reading Check** **Contrast** How are the methods of roasting and broiling different?

Community Connections

Environmentally-Friendly Cooking

We can all help the environment in small ways, even while cooking dinner. Convection ovens are more energy-efficient than regular ovens. Because of their circulating air cooking method, they use up to 20 percent less energy to roast a meal.

TAKE CHARGE!

Use a Convection Oven

For best results, follow these guidelines when using a convection oven:

- **Prepare** Always preheat the oven unless your recipe tells you otherwise.
- **Retain the Heat** Keep the oven door closed so that the heat is not lost.
- **Choose the Right Cookware** Dark and dull pans absorb heat, resulting in darker browning and a crisp crust. Shiny, bright pans reflect heat, resulting in light browning.
- **Consider Food Shape** Long or thin cuts of meat, which have more surface area, cook faster than bulky cuts of the same weight.
- **Monitor Food** Check on the food about 10 minutes before you expect it to be finished. The more food you have in the oven at one time, the longer the cooking time will be.

Real-World Skills

Bake or Roast The next time you want to bake cookies or roast a chicken, use the tips outlined above for using a convection oven. When you finish baking or roasting, identify how the tips helped you successfully use a convection oven.

Figure 21.2   **Cooking with Moist Heat**

Moist-Heat Techniques   Cooking with moist heat tenderizes foods. It is especially effective when cooking less-expensive, tougher cuts of meat. *In what type of cooking vessel should you cook with moist heat?*

Boiling Foods that you would typically boil include potatoes, pasta, rice, and eggs.

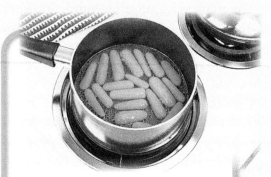

Simmering Vegetables, meat, poultry, dry fruits, and fish can be cooked in simmering liquid.

Steaming Steaming vegetables, such as broccoli, is considered a healthful way to cook because more of the food's nutrients are conserved.

Poaching A gentle cooking process, poaching helps food keep its shape. You can poach poultry, fish, eggs, and dry fruit.

Braising Less tender cuts of meat, such as pork chops, are frequently braised in a covered pan to keep the moisture in the pan.

Stewing Poultry, less tender cuts of meat, and vegetables are often stewed.

Moist-Heat Cooking

Moist-heat cooking methods use added liquid or steam to cook and tenderize foods. Moist-heat methods generally require a longer cooking time than dry-heat methods. Water, broth, and even vegetable or fruit juices can be used in moist-heat cooking. The amount of liquid you need to use varies with the recipes and the type of food you are cooking. Foods cooked using this method can be prepared in a casserole dish, with or without a tight-fitting cover.

Which of the following moist-heat cooking methods have you used? See **Figure 21.2**.

- **Boiling** To **boil** food involves heating liquid to a high temperature so that bubbles rise and break on the liquid surface. When you boil food, you bring food to a boiling point (212°F or 100°C). Boiling can rob foods of their nutrients. You can counteract the nutrient loss by adding your remaining cooking liquid to sauces and soups or using it to cook rice or beans.
- **Steaming** To **steam** means to cook food over boiling water, rather than in it. When you steam food, you put it in a metal steam basket and place the basket over the boiling water. You can also use an electric steamer. When you steam foods, make sure there is water left in the pot. Keeping some liquid in the pot prevents the pot from boiling dry and burning.
- **Poaching** To **poach** refers to cooking whole or large pieces of food in a small amount of liquid. When poaching, the cooking temperature should be just below simmering (185°F or 85°C). Any liquid can be used for poaching, including water, milk, or broth. The liquid can be seasoned to add flavor to the food.
- **Simmering** To **simmer** is to heat liquid to a temperature just below the boiling point until bubbles barely break on the liquid surface. Fewer nutrients are lost when you simmer food than when you boil it.
- **Braising** To **braise** is to simmer and steam food in a small amount of liquid. Braising can be done on a cooktop, in an oven, or in a slow cooker. Braising works extremely well for less tender cuts of meat. Generally, meat is first browned before it is braised.
- **Stewing** To **stew** something is to cook it slowly in liquid for a long period of time. This cooking method is similar to braising, but stewed food is generally cut into smaller pieces, and more liquid is used.

You can use several different types of appliances for moist-heat cooking. In a conventional oven, you can cook food in a covered dish, a foil package, or a special plastic cooking bag. In a microwave oven, you can cook or steam food in a vented covered dish. On a cooktop, you can boil, steam, or simmer in cookware on the top of the range. You can also use a small appliance like a slow cooker or a covered electric skillet to cook foods in liquid.

✓ Reading Check **Identify** What are the methods of moist-heat cooking?

How I See It

Hannah, 16

French fries have always been one of my favorite foods. But after my stepdad started having heart problems, my mom decided we all needed to start eating more healthfully. She found a recipe for making crispy potatoes in the oven. It's a lot healthier and even easier to make than french fries. We tried the recipe last night, and I was surprised because I liked them a lot! The potatoes are just as crunchy and tasty as french fries, but they're a lot healthier because they are lower in fat. Now we can eat baked fries without my mom worrying about our health!

Critical Thinking
How can you change a favorite recipe to be more healthful and nutritious?

Cooking with Fat

What do onion rings, omelets, and stir-fried vegetables have in common? They are all fried. Frying food involves cooking with fat. You can use melted fat, such as butter or shortening, or you can use liquid fat, such as vegetable oil or olive oil. When using vegetable oil sprays, so little is used that it is not considered cooking with fat.

To **deep-fat fry** means to cook food by completely covering it in fat. French fries, fried chicken, fried okra, and onion rings are deep-fat fried. Foods that are deep-fat fried are usually very high in saturated and trans fats, so you should only eat them occasionally.

To **panfry** means to fry tender cuts of meat, fish, and eggs in smaller amounts of fat in a skillet. Cooking thinly sliced vegetables in a small amount of fat over low to medium heat is called sautéing.

To **stir-fry** means cooking small pieces of food quickly at high heat in a very small amount of fat, stirring the entire time. Vegetables, meat, fish, and poultry can be stir-fried. Because it uses so little fat, stir-frying is suggested for those trying to reduce fat in their diet. Stir-frying is often done in a bowl-shaped pan called a wok, although a skillet works just as well. A small amount of seasoned liquid can be added to flavor stir-fried food.

To safely fry foods, follow these guidelines:
- Dry the food before putting it in fat or oil. Any moisture can cause hot fat to spatter and burn you.
- Put food into fat slowly and carefully so that it will not spatter. Use tongs, not your fingers.
- If a grease fire starts, smother the flame with the pan cover, a larger pan, or salt. Do not throw water on the fire. Putting water on a grease fire causes the flames to spread.

✓ **Reading Check** **Clarify** What types of fat are used to fry foods?

Microwave Cooking

In microwave cooking, electricity is converted into microwaves. The microwaves pass through glass, ceramic, paper, and plastic to cook food by causing water molecules in the food to vibrate. A microwave oven can cook food two to four times faster than other methods. It is ideal for frozen and canned foods, convenience foods, and leftovers. Microwaving does not work as well for baked foods or foods that you want to crisp or brown.

Microwaves bounce off of metal, which is why the metal pans that you use in conventional ovens should never be used in microwave ovens. You should also avoid using brown paper bags and towels made of recycled paper in the microwave because they can burn when heated. Polystyrene foam containers, often used for restaurant leftovers, take-out boxes, and disposable coffee cups, melt and release toxic chemicals when heated. Do not use foam containers in a microwave. Instead, transfer your leftovers to a microwave-safe container. Plastic containers that are safe for microwave cooking will be labeled microwave safe.

Microwaving food is easy and fast, and it preserves the nutrients in foods. To ensure successful and safe microwave cooking, follow these guidelines:

- **Choose a rounded container.** Choose a round or oval microwave-safe container that fits your microwave. Round containers allow the microwaves to hit the food from all angles, cooking it evenly. Food in the corners of rectangular or square containers tends to overcook.
- **Use a large container.** When you heat foods with liquids, use a container two or three times larger than the amount of food to help prevent contents from boiling over.
- **Pierce skins.** Pierce foods with skins, such as potatoes, with a fork before cooking to allow steam to escape.
- **Ensure even cooking.** Cut pieces of food into uniform sizes to help food cook evenly. Arrange foods as indicated in your instruction manual to ensure even cooking.
- **Read instructions.** Follow package instructions on microwavable convenience foods carefully.

Safety Check

Avoid Scalds

Microwaves are simple to use, and they can make meals ready to eat in minutes. However, you can easily get a steam burn, or scald, when uncovering a container of food or biting into a microwaved snack.

Write About It

How would you avoid scalds when using the microwave? Research microwave safety. Then, write a paragraph about how you can avoid burns and scalds when using a microwave and when eating microwaved foods.

> ### Proper Microwave Use
> Microwaving allows you to cook food nutritiously and quickly without creating a big mess. *What safety procedure do you think this teen is following for microwave cooking?*

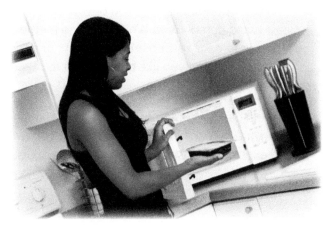

Ingram Publishing

- **Allow for standing time.** When a microwave oven shuts off, the water molecules in the food still vibrate. Standing time is a period of time when food continues to cook after the microwave has stopped. If instructions say to let food stand, cover it and let it stand for the time specified.
- **Rotate food for even cooking.** Most microwave ovens rotate automatically, but it may be necessary to pause the cooking about half way through to rotate, stir, rearrange, or turn food over.
- **Use a cover.** Cover foods to prevent them from drying out and spattering the inside walls and ceiling of the microwave. Use a microwave-safe lid rather than plastic wrap. Recent health studies have discouraged the use of plastic wrap to cover food while microwaving.
- **Use a potholder.** Use an oven mitt or a potholder to remove containers from the microwave. Plastic and glass containers can become extremely hot in a very short period of time when microwaved.
- **Open covers carefully.** When removing any covering, open it away from you to avoid a steam burn.

Section 21.1

After You Read

Review Key Concepts

1. **Describe** how cooking affects the appearance and flavor of food.
2. **Explain** how convection ovens work.
3. **Compare** boiling and simmering. Which is the healthier method?
4. **List** the guidelines you should follow to fry foods safely.
5. **Identify** the benefits of microwave cooking.

Check Your Answers Go to connectED. mcgraw-hill.com to check your answers.

Practice Academic Skills

English Language Arts

6. Think of a food or dish that you or your parents have cooked in at least two different ways. Which cooking method do you prefer? Write a half-page response explaining your preferred cooking method and what you like better about it.

Social Studies

7. Use reliable print or Internet sources to research different types of cookware used in convection ovens. Choose two types of cookware and explain their uses, benefits, and drawbacks.

Section 21.2

Healthful Cooking Methods

Before You Read

Preview Scan the bold words, headings, and photos. Write one or two sentences predicting what you think the section will be about.

Read to Learn

Key Concepts
- **Identify** five ways to tell if a food you are cooking is done.
- **Give** guidelines for conserving nutrients while cooking.

Main Idea

To be successful in the kitchen, you should know how to determine when food is cooked properly and understand ways to conserve nutrients while cooking.

Content Vocabulary

◇ texture
◇ aroma

Academic Vocabulary

You will find these words in your reading and on your tests. Use the glossary to look up their definitions if necessary.

▪ translucent
▪ fragrant

Graphic Organizer

As you read, record how to use appearance to identify when food is done. Use a graphic organizer like the one below to organize your information.

Appearance: When Is Food Done?

	Cake	Pancakes	Beef	Poultry
Undercooked				
Cooked				

Graphic Organizer Go to connectED.mcgraw-hill.com to download this graphic organizer.

Checking Food for Doneness

As You Read

Connect Think about the ways your senses tell you when a food has cooked enough. Which of your five senses do you think is the most important when cooking? Why?

Some people use their senses to decide whether food has cooked long enough. Sight, touch, and smell can be excellent guides if you know how to use them. More is at stake than eating enjoyment, wasted food, or wasted money. As you have learned, some foods can be unsafe if not thoroughly cooked.

Recognizing signs of doneness is important throughout a recipe, not just when testing the final product. For example, when you cook garlic to flavor a dish, it should be sautéed until soft and translucent, or see-through. When garlic turns brown, it is burned and will spread its bitterness through the food.

Apply these guidelines to help determine doneness in different foods:

- **Appearance** Recipe directions and your own experience can help you judge when a food is ready by its appearance. A coffee cake may be golden brown and start to pull away from the edges of the pan. Pancakes should be flipped when the edges start to solidify and bubbles appear on the surface. Ground beef is browned when no pink remains. Clear juices indicate a cooked piece of poultry. No pink should remain in the center. Check the temperature to be sure! Checking the internal temperature is the only way to be absolutely sure a food is fully cooked.

- **Texture** The **texture** of a food is the way it feels. The texture of a food can help you determine whether it is thoroughly cooked or not. When fully cooked, a food might feel springy, like muffins and cookies, or fluffy, like rice. Pasta is done when it is tender but firm. The texture of meat will vary depending on the method of preparation and the cut of the meat. When fish is done, it should separate into flakes with the touch of a fork, but not turn into mush. Many people prefer their vegetables tender but still crisp and not mushy.

Vocabulary

You can find definitions in the glossary at the back of this book.

Food Safety

Using a thermometer is one way to check for food safety.

How do you or your family check for the safety of food when cooking?

Ingram Publishing/SuperStock

- **Consistency** The moisture left in a food can be a gauge of doneness. Gravy is simmered to a certain consistency, pudding to another. Inner consistency of baked foods, from cake to custard, can be tested by inserting a knife or toothpick. When you insert a wooden toothpick into cakes, breads, or muffins, it should come out cleanly. If it has moisture on it or sticky crumbs, the food has not finished baking.

- **Aroma** A pleasant or savory smell is an **aroma**. Properly cooked foods smell pleasant but not potent. Toasted seeds and nuts are fragrant, or sweet-smelling, while burned nuts smell sharp or bitter. Vegetables that already give off a strong odor when cooked, such as cauliflower and cabbage, smell even stronger when overcooked. A harsh odor from a spicy food can mean the seasonings have burned.

- **Temperature** Although a food's observable qualities are helpful, remember that internal temperature is the "gold standard" of safety, especially for protein foods. Cooking meat, poultry, fish, and egg dishes to the temperatures specified in Chapter 23 helps ensure that these foods will be safe and enjoyable to eat.

✓ Reading Check **Give Examples** How can you use appearance and texture to determine doneness when cooking?

Math You Can Use

Cooking Time

Genevieve is cooking a 5-pound, 10-ounce rib roast with the bone in. She wants the roast to be well done. So, the roast has to be cooked for 33 minutes for every pound of meat. What is the total time the roast has to be cooked?

Math Concept **Unit Conversion** There are 16 ounces in one pound.

Starting Hint First, figure out how many total pounds the roast weighs. You need to convert the 10 ounces to pounds. To do this, divide 10 by 16. Then, add this number to the pound weight of the roast. Finally, multiply by 33.

For math help, go to the Math Appendix at the back of the book.

Food Readiness

Different foods have different measures of readiness. *When you make pancakes, how do you tell if they are done?*

McGraw-Hill Education/Eclipse Studios

Tuna Melt Stuffed Tomatoes

Yield
4 servings

Nutrition Analysis
Per serving: 260 calories, 12 g total fat, 6 g saturated fat, 0 g trans fat, 30 mg cholesterol, 910 mg sodium, 25 g total carbohydrate, 3 g dietary fiber, 10 g sugars, 13 g protein

Ingredients

2 cans (6 oz. ea) tuna, drained (packed in spring water)
1 small onion
1 stalk celery
2 Tbsp. sweet pickle relish
3 Tbsp. light salad dressing
1 tsp. lemon juice
¼ tsp. celery salt
¼ tsp. salt
¼ tsp. pepper
4 large tomatoes
¾ cup crumbled feta cheese or shredded part-skim mozzarella
Freshly chopped parsley, optional

Directions

1. Drain tuna well; place in a medium-sized bowl.
2. In the food processor, using the chopping blade, finely chop onion and celery. Add to tuna.
3. Combine relish, salad dressing, lemon juice, celery salt, salt, and pepper. Mix with tuna.
4. Wash tomatoes; pat dry with a paper towel. Cut a thin slice off tops of tomatoes and a small slice off the bottom to stabilize them. Using a melon baller or teaspoon, remove seeds and tomato pulp. Leave a ½-inch shell wall. Place upside down on paper towels to drain off excess liquid.
5. Fill each tomato with tuna salad, divided evenly among the tomatoes; sprinkle with cheese; place on glass plate.
6. Put tomatoes in microwave on high for about 15 seconds just to melt the cheese. Do not overcook.
7. If desired, sprinkle each tomato with freshly chopped parsley just before serving.

I. Rozenbaum/PhotoAlto

Conserve Nutrients

During the cooking process, foods can lose some of their nutrients. You can help preserve as many nutrients as possible by following these guidelines:

- **Choose methods wisely.** When choosing cooking methods, consider nutrition. Cooking with dry heat or in a small amount of water generally conserves more nutrients than boiling.
- **Avoid overcooking food.** Carefully follow directions for cooking temperature and time. The longer food cooks, the more nutrients it loses.
- **Leave the skins on.** The skins of fruits and vegetables contain vitamins, minerals, and fiber. Leave them on whenever possible.
- **Save the liquid.** If possible, use the liquid in which food is cooked. It contains valuable nutrients. If you cannot use it for that meal, save it to make soup.
- **Use large pieces.** Keep food whole or in large pieces when possible.

Now that you are familiar with some basic cooking methods and the most healthful cooking techniques, you will be able to explore recipes with confidence, and your family and friends will enjoy the results!

SUCCEED IN SCHOOL

Your Teacher

Your teacher is most likely the best source for giving you feedback on your schoolwork. He or she knows what you do best and what you are struggling with. He or she may offer additional assistance or have helpful suggestions for you.

Section 21.2

After You Read

Review Key Concepts

1. **Identify** which senses help you decide when food is done.
2. **Recall** the reason it is important to leave skins on fruits and vegetables whenever possible.

Practice Academic Skills

English Language Arts

3. Read a variety of healthy-cooking magazines or Web sites. Analyze the recipes and techniques described in the magazines. Do the recipes share any general healthy-cooking methods? Briefly describe methods shared by the recipes.

Social Studies

4. The skins of fruits and vegetables contain vitamins, minerals, and fiber. Did your parents use techniques when you were younger to convince you to eat the skins of fruits or vegetables? Describe one of them, or think up your own.

Check Your Answers Go to connectED. mcgraw-hill.com to check your answers.

What Does a Dietitian Do?

Registered dietitians use up-to-date scientific information to promote healthful eating habits. Dietitians plan food and nutrition programs, supervise meal preparation, and oversee the serving of meals. They help individuals improve their health by recommending dietary modifications that suit their specific needs.

Skills To become a dietitian, you must have strong interpersonal and communication skills. This is because most dietitians need to listen to other people and teach them new ways of eating. Dietitians should also have strong math and science skills, and effective time-management skills.

Education and Training Becoming a dietitian requires a bachelor's degree in dietetics, foods and nutrition, food service systems management, or related areas. High school students should take courses in biology, chemistry, mathematics, health, and communications. College students take courses in foods, nutrition, and a variety of science and math classes.

Job Outlook The employment of dietitians is expected to increase significantly during the next decade. Job growth will result from an increasing emphasis on disease prevention through improved dietary habits. A growing and aging population will boost demand for nutritional counseling and treatment.

Critical Thinking Review the job duties and needed skills of a dietitian. Write a paragraph explaining why you would want to be a dietitian. Discuss what motivates you and why. Make sure to discuss whether or not you feel the job would be personally rewarding.

Career Cluster

Hospitality and Tourism

Dietitians work in the Hospitality and Tourism career cluster. Here are some of the other jobs in this career cluster:

- Food Service Manager
- Health Educator
- Dietetic Technician
- Registered Nurse
- Institutional Food Preparation and Service Manager
- Food Technologist
- Institutional Food Service Worker
- Facility Manager
- Club Manager
- Casino Manager
- Food Safety and Sanitation Inspector and Instructor
- Pantry Person
- Cook
- Baker
- Pastry Chef
- Food, Beverage, and Banquet Manager

Explore Further Research this career cluster. Choose a career in this cluster that appeals to you and write a career profile.

HallLight Fotografie – StockFood Munich/StockFood

CHAPTER SUMMARY

Section 21.1
Choosing Cooking Techniques

Cooking is the transfer of heat from a heat source to food. Cooking involves conduction, convection, radiation, or a combination of these methods. Naturally tender foods are best cooked by dry-heat methods. Convection ovens speed cooking times and help conserve nutrients. Moist-heat cooking methods generally require a longer cooking time than dry-heat methods. Cooking with fat includes deep-fat frying, panfrying, and stir-frying. Microwaving is an easy and effective method for cooking many foods.

Section 21.2
Healthful Cooking Methods

Using your senses can help you to tell when a food has finished cooking. Recognizing signs of doneness is important throughout a recipe, not just when testing the final product. Some foods are dangerous when undercooked. Check the temperature to make sure meat is cooked through. When foods are overcooked they are not dangerous, but they do not taste very good. During the cooking process, foods can lose some of their nutrients. Some cooking methods are better than others for conserving nutrients.

Vocabulary Review

1. Create multiple-choice test questions for each content and academic vocabulary term.

Content Vocabulary
◇ conduction (p. 515)
◇ convection (p. 515)
◇ radiation (p. 515)
◇ dry-heat cooking (p. 516)
◇ roast (p. 516)
◇ broil (p. 516)
◇ moist-heat cooking (p. 519)
◇ boil (p. 519)
◇ steam (p. 519)
◇ poach (p. 519)
◇ simmer (p. 519)
◇ braise (p. 519)
◇ stew (p. 519)
◇ deep-fat fry (p. 520)
◇ panfry (p. 520)
◇ stir-fry (p. 520)
◇ texture (p. 524)
◇ aroma (p. 525)

Academic Vocabulary
▢ transfer (p. 515)
▢ circulation (p. 515)
▢ translucent (p. 524)
▢ fragrant (p. 525)

Review Key Concepts

2. **Explain** conduction, convection, and radiation.
3. **Describe** the four different dry-heat cooking methods.
4. **Describe** the six different moist-heat cooking methods.
5. **Compare** different methods for cooking with fat.
6. **Summarize** microwave cooking techniques.
7. **Identify** five ways to tell if a food you are cooking is done.
8. **Give** guidelines for conserving nutrients while cooking.

Critical Thinking

9. **Predict** In the future, do you think standard ovens will be replaced with convection ovens? Explain your answer.
10. **Conclude** Stir-frying and vegetable oil sprays have become increasingly popular. Explain why you think this is happening.
11. **Analyze** You are cooking dinner and want to conserve nutrients wherever possible. What steps can you take to prepare your meal successfully?

ACTIVE LEARNING

12. Check for Doneness Follow your teacher's instructions to form into groups of five students and choose a food you all like. How do you prepare this food? As a group, agree on a cooking method for the food. Then, have each group member write a few sentences or a paragraph about how to tell when the food is done cooking. One person should write about appearance, one should write about texture, one should write about consistency, one should write about aroma, and one should write about temperature. When your group is finished, present your information to the class. Is it necessary to check the doneness of the food in all the manners you describe? What is the most important thing to do when checking the doneness of the food?

Family & Community Connections

13. Talk to Your Local Grocer Many grocery stores have a meat counter, seafood counter, and produce section. Did you realize that there are very knowledgeable people in each of these departments? Butchers, produce managers, and other fresh food section managers need special training for their jobs. Not only can they help you select items, they often know excellent ways to prepare these foods. Go to your favorite fresh foods section at your local grocery store, and ask to speak with one of these experts. Select a specific cut of meat, seafood, or vegetable with which you are unfamiliar, and ask the butcher or area manager for cooking ideas. Also ask if he or she can suggest any cost-saving tips when selecting ingredients. See if you can get as many as three different recipes or cooking techniques for the same item. Make sure to take notes. If possible, prepare one of these recipes at home. Present your findings to the class.

Real-World Skills and Applications

Leadership Skills

14. Cooking Tips Imagine a friend prepared a hamburger in the microwave oven. Your friend was unhappy with the results because the hamburger was "leathery" and lacked flavor. What advice would you offer? Be sure to note the benefits and drawbacks of each cooking method in terms of taste, convenience, time required, supplies required, and necessary clean-up.

Financial Literacy

15. Steamed Broccoli You want to serve steamed broccoli as a side dish for a meal you are preparing for a dinner party. Including yourself, there will be 8 people at the dinner party. Each bag of broccoli costs $3.75 and will serve 3 people. How much money will you spend on broccoli in order to have enough to feed all 8 people?

Information Literacy

16. Discover New Methods Using reliable print or Internet sources, research different vegetable recipes. What techniques have you used before? What techniques are the most unusual? Write a one-page essay explaining the most unusual technique you come across for cooking vegetables.

Academic Skills

 English Language Arts

17. Healthful Alternatives When frying foods, you can use melted fat, such as butter or shortening, or liquid fat, such as vegetable oil or olive oil. Research the health benefits of olive oil. Write an essay explaining the benefits of olive oil and why people should consider more healthful oils for cooking.

 Science

18. Oil Temperatures Heating an oil too hot can cause it to smoke as well as destroy its health benefits. Research and record the recommended temperatures of cooking oils.

Procedure Choose 5 cooking oils to research. Then, find the recommended average and maximum temperatures at which they should be used for cooking.

Analysis Make a chart listing the five oils, their ideal temperatures, and their maximum temperatures.

 Mathematics

19. Meet in the Middle Eric and Kiko are still best friends, even though Kiko moved 120 miles away last year. To celebrate Kiko's upcoming birthday, Eric and Kiko have decided to meet at a restaurant that is between their homes. Eric is traveling toward Kiko at a speed of 45 miles per hour. Kiko is traveling toward Eric at a speed of 35 miles per hour. If they both leave at noon and reach the restaurant at the same time, what time will they meet?

Math Concept **Distance** The distance formula states that distance is equal to the rate one is traveling multiplied by the time one travels ($d = r \times t$). In this case, the total distance traveled should equal the traveling speed in miles per hour multiplied by the total time measured in hours.

Starting Hint You can use relative speed to solve this problem. To find the relative speed, simply add the speed of you and your friend, as you are traveling toward one another.

Math For math help, go to the Math Appendix at the back of the book.

Standardized Test Practice

SHORT ANSWER
Directions Read the question. Then provide a response.

Test-Taking Tip Be sure to answer all parts of the question and to ignore information in the question that is not necessary. Outlining your answer quickly before writing it on the test may help you to make sure you cover all parts of the question asked.

20. You can cook with fat in many different ways. Briefly explain the process of deep-fat frying, and distinguish it from panfrying.

Preparing Grains, Fruits, and Vegetables

Section 22.1
Grains in Your Diet

Section 22.2
Fruits and Vegetables in Your Diet

Chapter Objectives

Section 22.1
- **Identify** the parts of a grain kernel and the nutritional benefits of each.
- **Summarize** preparation techniques for pasta, rice, bread, and cereals.
- **Describe** what to look for when choosing grain products.

Section 22.2
- **Explain** why it is important to eat a variety of fruits and vegetables.
- **Demonstrate** ways to conserve nutrients when preparing fresh produce.
- **Identify** ways to incorporate more fruits and vegetables into your daily eating plan.

Tanya Constantine/Blend Images/Getty Images

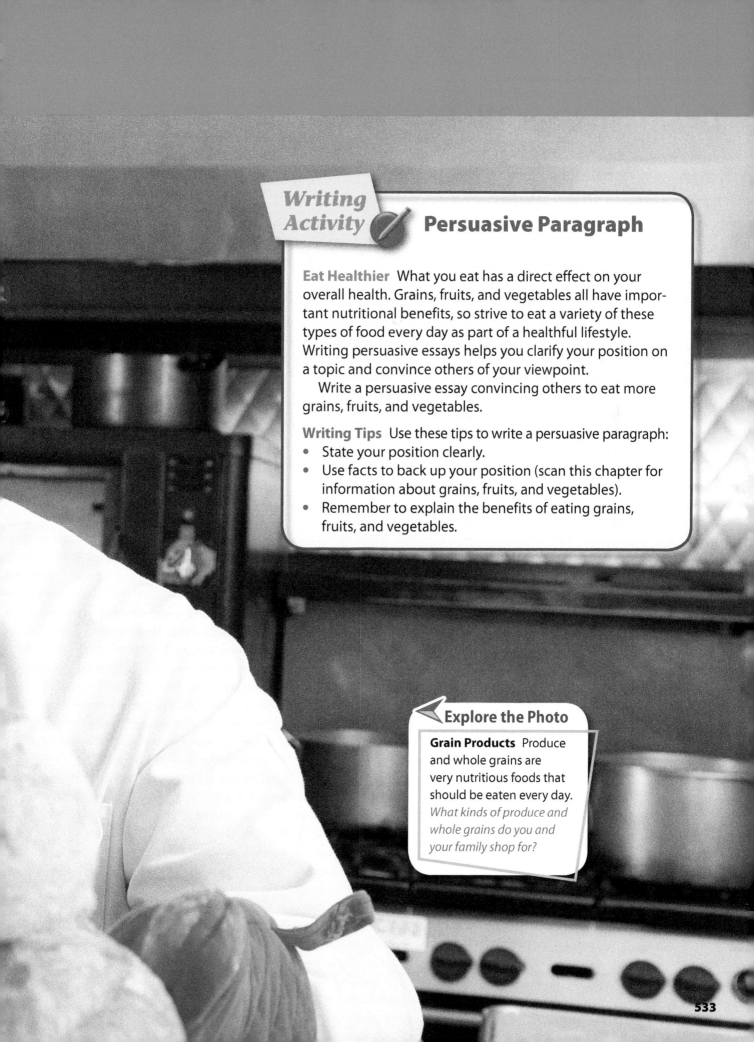

Writing Activity

Persuasive Paragraph

Eat Healthier What you eat has a direct effect on your overall health. Grains, fruits, and vegetables all have important nutritional benefits, so strive to eat a variety of these types of food every day as part of a healthful lifestyle. Writing persuasive essays helps you clarify your position on a topic and convince others of your viewpoint.

Write a persuasive essay convincing others to eat more grains, fruits, and vegetables.

Writing Tips Use these tips to write a persuasive paragraph:
- State your position clearly.
- Use facts to back up your position (scan this chapter for information about grains, fruits, and vegetables).
- Remember to explain the benefits of eating grains, fruits, and vegetables.

◄ Explore the Photo

Grain Products Produce and whole grains are very nutritious foods that should be eaten every day. *What kinds of produce and whole grains do you and your family shop for?*

Section 22.1

Grains in Your Diet

Before You Read

Preview Read the main headings and boldface words. Write one or two sentences predicting what you think the section will be about.

Read to Learn

Key Concepts

- **Identify** the parts of a grain kernel and the nutritional benefits of each.
- **Summarize** preparation techniques for pasta, rice, bread, and cereals.
- **Describe** what to look for when choosing grain products.

Main Idea

Knowing how to prepare grains makes it easier for you to incorporate this nutritious type of food into your diet.

Content Vocabulary

- ◇ whole grain
- ◇ endosperm
- ◇ germ
- ◇ bran
- ◇ refined grain
- ◇ enriched
- ◇ al dente
- ◇ cereal grain
- ◇ leavening agent

Academic Vocabulary

You will find these words in your reading and on your tests. Use the glossary to look up their definitions if necessary.

- ▢ consist
- ▢ coarse

Graphic Organizer

As you read, use a table like the one below to write notes about the two main types of grains. Include examples of types of foods for each.

Whole Grains	Refined Grains

 Graphic Organizer Go to **connectED.mcgraw-hill.com** to download this graphic organizer.

Nutrients in Whole Grains

When you make a sandwich or toast, what kind of bread do you use? If you have only eaten white bread and have never tried whole-grain varieties, you are missing out! Whole grains have been a popular food throughout history. In fact, if you had lived a century ago when white bread was not available, whole grains would have been the basis of your diet.

Whole Grains

Grains are the small dried fruits of cereal grasses, often called kernels. They pack a strong nutritional punch. **Figure 22.1** shows the three main parts of a grain kernel. A **whole grain** is a grain that has the entire grain kernel. A grain kernel consists, or is made up of, three parts. The **endosperm** is the inner section and is mostly carbohydrate and some protein. The **germ** is the small base of the seed. It contains protein, B vitamins, vitamin E, minerals, and some fat.

As You Read

Connect As you read, think about the different grain products you usually eat. Do you eat more whole grains or refined grains?

Vocabulary

You can find definitions in the glossary at the back of this book.

Figure 22.1 Anatomy of a Grain Kernel

Whole grains are loaded with fiber, which has many nutritional benefits. *Which whole-grain foods do you eat regularly?*

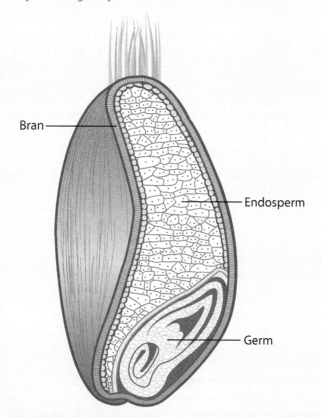

Bran

Endosperm

Germ

BRAN	ENDOSPERM	GERM
Bran The bran is the kernel's edible outer covering.	**Endosperm** The endosperm is the largest part of the grain kernel, and is made of starch and protein.	**Germ** The germ is the seed of the kernel that grows into another plant.

The **bran** is the coarse, or rough, outer layer of the grain. It provides B vitamins, minerals, and most of the fiber. Some grains also have an inedible covering called the hull.

Oats, brown rice, barley, buckwheat, bulgur, corn, kamut, millet, and quinoa (kēn-wä) are just some of the whole grains you can add to your diet. They are excellent sources of complex carbohydrates, fiber, B vitamins, iron, and zinc. Most important, because they are plant foods, they do not contain saturated fat or cholesterol.

Refined Grains

A **refined grain** is a grain that is milled to remove the bran and the germ. Refined grains have a finer texture and longer shelf-life than unrefined grains. Unfortunately, removing the bran and germ also removes much of the fiber, vitamins, and minerals. Many nutrients are lost in refining, so the government requires that refined grains be **enriched**, or have nutrients added back after processing. Food labels indicate which grains are enriched.

White flour, white bread, cornflakes, and white rice are some examples of refined grain products.

✔ **Reading Check** **Compare** What is the difference between a whole grain and a refined grain?

HOW TO... Buy Great Grains

Food trends come and go, but grains remain the most plentiful and popular foods in the world. Supermarkets, specialty bakeries, and online vendors offer an array of products, from "ancient" grains like amaranth to microwavable bowls of macaroni and cheese. Here are some tips to follow when buying grains:

Avoid Being Misled A brown color may suggest "wholeness," but it may simply come from molasses. Multigrain breads, such as seven- or nine-grain bread, contain different types of grain but may not use the entire grain. Always read labels carefully.

Breads Remember that whole grains are most healthful. They contain most of the grain's nutrients, including phytonutrients and fiber. Whole-grain flour, either wheat or some other grain, is key when comparing bread choices. It should be the first ingredient listed. Rye and oats are particularly healthful.

Cereals Today, many cereals are made with whole grains. For maximum grain nutrition, however, plain oatmeal is hard to beat. "Old-fashioned" and some quick-cooking varieties use the whole grain. However, flavored instant oatmeal has added sugar and sodium. If plain oats do not interest you, add fruit, cinnamon, vanilla extract, a sprinkle of sugar, or a drizzle of maple syrup.

Preparing Grains

You probably enjoy a lot of ready-to-eat grain products already, such as dry cereal, granola bars, and packaged breads. Other grains require at least some preparation.

Different grain products require different preparation techniques and cooking times. Many grain products, such as pasta, rice, and oatmeal are cooked in water. As they cook, they absorb water and double or triple in size. Grain products should be tender when cooked. Undercooked grains are hard or chewy. Overcooked grains become sticky and mushy.

Cooking Pasta

To cook pasta, you need a large pot that will allow the food to expand. Additional space is also needed for the water to boil. You need quite a bit of water, usually 1 gallon of water for 1 pound of pasta.

Bring the water to a boil before you add the pasta, and keep it boiling while you cook. Stir the pasta occasionally to prevent it from sticking to itself. Do not cover the pot. Most pasta packages give estimated cooking times which can guide you, but you should sample the pasta near the end of the cooking period to make sure it does not overcook. Experienced pasta makers cook pasta until it is tender but not too soft. This is called **al dente**.

Community Connections

Preferred Pasta

Many recipes worldwide feature pasta, or noodles. Historians debate whether the Italians, Chinese, or Arabic tribes invented pasta. Determine how your school rates various pastas by conducting a school-wide survey. Do students favor Italian spaghetti, Chinese chop suey, or another noodle dish?

Rice Many varieties of rice have brown alternatives. Brown rice includes the whole grain, except the inedible hull. Overall, it is the most nutritious type. Enriched white rice, which contains the endosperm only, can also contribute to a healthful diet. Instant rice, which is precooked and then dried, has the least nutrients.

Pasta Whole-grain pasta is available in most grocery stores. Online sellers and health food shops carry pasta made from buckwheat, spelt, brown rice, quinoa, and other less common grains.

(r) Stepan Popov/Getty Images; (l) Author's Image/Glow Images

Fiber and Oats

Americans should consume between 25 and 30 grams of fiber per day. Oats are an excellent way to increase your daily intake of fiber. Use these tips to add more oats to your diet:

► Avoid instant oatmeal with added sugar.

► Add oats to meatloaf recipes.

► Bread chicken with oats instead of flour.

Effects of Yeast

Yeast is used as a leavening agent in most breads. Like baking powder or baking soda, it helps the bread rise.

Procedure Follow your teacher's instructions to form into small groups. Discuss the use of yeast in breads. Use reliable print or Internet sources to research information on how yeast causes bread to rise.

Analysis Write a one- to two-paragraph report explaining what happens in bread as a result of the yeast. Make sure to include details from your research.

Use a colander to drain the cooking water from the pasta. Avoid rinsing the pasta after you drain it, because rinsing washes away the pasta's nutrients. Pasta is best when served right away. If this is not possible, stir a teaspoon of oil into the pasta to prevent it from sticking together.

Cooking Rice

Rice is a common staple for many people of different cultures around the world. Rice not only tastes good, it is easy to prepare. When you cook rice in water, the starch absorbs water, becomes soft, and expands in size. Rice increases up to three times its original volume when cooked!

When cooking pasta, you can estimate the amount of water. When you cook rice, however, you need to use the exact amount of water called for in the recipe or the package instructions. To cook rice, boil the water first then add the rice. Do not stir rice while cooking. The rice should absorb all or almost all of the cooking water. If some cooking water remains in the rice at the end of the time specified on the package, drain the rice but do not rinse it. For additional flavor and nutrients, you can cook rice in chicken or vegetable broth instead of water.

Cooking Cereals

A **cereal grain** is a seed from a grass such as wheat, rice, oats, corn, rye, or barley. The grain is processed, perhaps ground for flour, and is then cooked to become edible.

Cooking oatmeal in water creates a chemical change in its starch. Some bonds between the atoms of the carbohydrate molecules break. They form new bonds with atoms of different molecules. As starch granules, or clusters, absorb water molecules, they swell and soften. Eventually, they break apart, releasing the nutrients inside. The oatmeal gets softer and easier to digest.

Oatmeal that starts cooking in cold water is creamier than oatmeal that starts cooking in boiling water. Because it takes time to heat the water, the oatmeal has more time to absorb liquid.

Cooking Breads

There are many different varieties of bread, but all fall into one of three categories: quick breads, yeast breads, or flat breads. Yeast breads and quick breads are both made with leavening agents. A **leavening agent** is a substance that causes baked products to rise.

Yeast, baking powder, and baking soda are all leavening agents. These substances react to certain bread ingredients and heat, producing carbon dioxide gas. This gas causes bread to rise and expand. It causes the air pockets you see in muffins, sandwich bread, cakes and many other baked products.

Pita bread, tortillas, and naan are called flat breads because they are made without, or with very little, leavening agent. These breads do not rise much, if at all.

Muffins and biscuits are called quick breads because they take less time to mix and rise than yeast breads do. These breads use baking powder or baking soda instead of yeast. You can find delicious recipes and box mixes for whole-grain muffins, such as bran muffins, and for popular flavors, such as blueberry and banana nut muffins.

Muffins

When making muffins, you generally do the following:
1. Measure the ingredients accurately.
2. Mix together the dry ingredients. These usually include flour, sugar, salt, and baking powder.
3. Mix together the wet ingredients. Quick breads are usually made with milk, eggs, and oil.
4. Make a well in the dry ingredients. When you make a well, you push the dry ingredients to the sides of the bowl to make a hole for the wet ingredients. Fold or mix the wet and dry ingredients together. Do not overmix the batter. It should be somewhat lumpy, not smooth.

Biscuits

To make biscuits, follow these steps:
1. Measure all ingredients accurately.
2. Sift dry ingredients together.
3. Cut fat into the dry ingredients. "Cutting in" means breaking the solid fat, usually shortening, into pea-size pieces. This makes the biscuits flaky.
4. Make a well in the middle of the dry ingredient mixture. Pour the wet ingredients into the well, then mix into the dry ingredients. Do not overmix the batter.
5. If you roll out the dough and cut the biscuits with a cutter, they are called rolled biscuits. If you spoon them out, they are called drop biscuits. When baking either rolled or drop biscuits, expect them to enlarge with baking.

Seal containers and packages of grains tightly to retain freshness and keep them free of insects. Bread can be stored at room temperature. In hot and humid weather, you should refrigerate or freeze it.

✓ **Reading Check** **Explain** How is preparing rice similar to preparing hot cereal?

SUCCEED IN SCHOOL

Reach Out

Talk to your teacher or guidance counselor if you have questions about how to set or maintain realistic goals. He or she can give you tips on how to stay on track with your goal-setting.

Incorporate Whole Grains Into Your Diet

The amount of grains you should eat each day depends on your age, gender, and activity level. Consult MyPlate to determine how many servings you should eat every day. For a healthful diet, make sure at least half of the grains you eat each day are whole grains. This can be hard to do unless you know what to look for.

Products labeled multi-grain, stone-ground, 100% wheat, cracked wheat, seven-grain, and bran do not mean whole grain. Do not judge a bread by its color. Dark-colored bread does not always contain whole-grain flour. It may be enriched bread with color added. Though white breads are usually refined, some whole-grain breads are white. They are made with flour from a white-wheat grain.

To be sure you are choosing wisely, always check the label when selecting grain products. Whole grains are indicated by the word "whole" on the label. Check the list of ingredients. Whole-grain ingredients such as brown rice, bulgur, oatmeal, whole-grain corn, oats, whole rye, whole wheat, and wild rice should appear at the top of the list. Finally, check the Nutrition Facts label. A bread with a higher percent Daily Value for fiber contains more whole grain or bran.

Section 22.1

Grains in Your Diet

Review Key Concepts

1. **Describe** what is an enriched grain and identify why many grain products are enriched.
2. **Identify** the three types of bread and what makes them different from one another.
3. **Explain** why you should not judge a bread by its color.

Check Your Answers Go to connectED.mcgraw-hill.com to check your answers.

Practice Academic Skills

English Language Arts

4. Visit your local supermarket and find an unusual grain you have not heard of. Research the health benefits and uses of the grain. When you are finished, present your information to the class.

Social Studies

5. Use reliable print or Internet resources to research the history of grains. When were grains first used in people's diets? How were they prepared? Write a short, one-page essay briefly describing the early history of grains in people's diets.

Section 22.2

Fruits and Vegetables in Your Diet

Before You Read

Preview Scan the photos and photo titles. Write one or two sentences predicting what you think the section will be about.

Read to Learn

Key Concepts
- **Explain** why it is important to eat a variety of fruits and vegetables.
- **Demonstrate** ways to conserve nutrients when preparing fresh produce.
- **Identify** ways to incorporate more fruits and vegetables into your daily eating plan.

Main Idea

Knowing how to handle and prepare fruits and vegetables makes it easier for you to incorporate this nutritious type of food into your diet.

Content Vocabulary
◇ wilt
◇ core

Academic Vocabulary

You will find these words in your reading and on your tests. Use the glossary to look up their definitions if necessary.
☐ conserve
☐ dissolve

Graphic Organizer

As you read, name four techniques you can use to make your produce look more appealing. Write down an example for each technique.

Technique	Example
1.	
2.	
3.	
4.	

 Graphic Organizer Go to **connectED.mcgraw-hill.com** to download this graphic organizer.

As You Read

Connect As you read the section, think about the fruits and vegetables you usually eat. Do you often choose salad but refuse eggplant without ever trying it?

Nutrients in Fruits and Vegetables

Fruits and vegetables are generally low in calories but packed with generous amounts of vitamins, minerals, and phytonutrients. Although nutrient amounts may differ, fruits and vegetables are good sources of carbohydrates, vitamin A, vitamin C, and minerals, such as calcium and potassium. Scientific evidence shows that fruits and vegetables protect against heart disease, stroke, cancer, and other serious health problems.

Everyone benefits from eating a variety of fruits and vegetables. When you are choosing vegetables, remember that variety is as important as quantity. No single fruit or vegetable has all of the nutrients you need to be healthy. Also, eating the same foods over and over gets boring, no matter how good the food tastes. Eating a variety of fruits and vegetables makes meals interesting.

Think Color

One characteristic that indicates the amount of nutrients in fruits and vegetables is color. Deeper yellow or dark green vegetables are better sources of vitamin A than those with a paler color. Look for yams, apricots, cantaloupe, carrots, broccoli, spinach, kale, and green peppers for vitamin A. Citrus fruits, such as oranges and grapefruit, are outstanding sources of vitamin C. Other good sources include tomatoes, strawberries, red sweet peppers, and white potatoes.

 Reading Check **Describe** What nutritional value do fruits and vegetables have?

Orange Is Not the Only Juice

Tired of orange juice every morning? Look for carrot, pineapple, and tomato juice at the store or try making your own juice blend at home. *What kinds of juices have you tried? Which juices do you like best?*

When preparing fruits and vegetables, there are different things you can do to make them look more appealing before serving. The next time you have to prepare fruits and vegetables, try the following:

- **Create Interesting Shapes** Cut red and yellow peppers in long strips or rings. Run a fork down the sides of a cucumber before slicing. This gives the edges a lacy look. Instead of cutting melon in cubes for a fruit salad, use a melon baller. Use a vegetable peeler to make wide, paper-thin strips of carrot for a salad topping.
- **Use Citrus Juice** Before serving fruit slices, toss them in a tablespoon of lemon juice or another citrus juice to keep them from turning brown. For cut vegetables, rub the cut edge with lemon juice to prevent discoloring in the vegetable ends.
- **Always Al Dente** When cooking vegetables, cook them al dente. This means they are tender but firm. The color will be bright and appealing instead of washed out and boring.
- **Try a Variety** Use purple grapes, orange melon, red strawberries, cream-colored banana, and bright green kiwi together in a salad to make it more festive and appealing.

Preparing Fruits and Vegetables

Depending on personal preferences and the season, your family may use fresh, frozen, canned, or dried fruits and vegetables. You will need to cook most fresh and frozen vegetables and only warm canned vegetables to the desired temperature.

Preparing Fresh Produce

Be sure to rinse fresh fruits and vegetables thoroughly under cold running water. Use a stiff brush to clean firmer vegetables, such as potatoes and carrots. Proper washing of produce helps prevent foodborne illness. Avoid soaking vegetables in water, however. This causes the loss of water-soluble nutrients. Some fruits and vegetables, such as apples and cucumbers, have a wax coating. This protective coating, which is safe to eat, keeps the produce moist and protects against bruising.

Cut vegetables just before you use them to conserve, or save, nutrients destroyed by air. Also cut fresh fruits, such as bananas, apples, peaches, and pears, just before serving. Their flesh darkens when cut open and exposed to the air. To prevent browning, you can squeeze lemon or another citrus juice on fruits.

Health & Wellness

TIPS

Tasty Tomatoes

Tomatoes are an especially healthful food. Tomatoes contain the antioxidant lycopene, which can lower risks for some cancers and heart disease. Your body absorbs lycopene better from cooked rather than raw tomatoes, so try these tips:

- ► Eat tomato paste and sauce products often.
- ► Cook raw tomatoes before eating.
- ► Choose vine-ripened tomatoes, which contain more lycopene.

◤◇ Vocabulary

You can find definitions in the glossary at the back of this book.

Making Salads

When you think of salad, what do you imagine? Many people think of salad as lettuce with a few tomato slices on top. But salads can be so much more than that. Try using different kinds of lettuce for a variety of textures and colors. Add bell pepper, tomatoes, carrots, sprouts, red onion, avocado, or mandarin orange slices. Main-dish salads can be made from a number of ingredients, including vegetables, fruits, pasta, grains, legumes, eggs, meat, fish, poultry, and cheese.

Salad greens taste best when they are crisp, so keep them in the refrigerator until you are ready to use them. Remove any discolored leaves, and rinse the greens thoroughly in cold water. Be especially careful of the dirt clinging to some greens, such as spinach and escarole. Put them in cold water, move them around, and lift them out of the water. The dirt usually settles to the bottom. You should rinse these greens more than once.

To keep salad dressing from diluting or clinging to wet leaves, dry greens in a salad spinner, or dab with a clean towel before adding them to a salad. If you make a tossed salad, tear the greens into small pieces. When you add other vegetables or fruits to a salad, be sure they are clean as well. Drizzle salad dressing on just before serving to keep the greens from wilting. When plants **wilt**, they become less crisp.

Cooking Fruits and Vegetables

Fruits and vegetables change dramatically when they are cooked. They become less crisp because their starch and fiber soften. Some water-soluble nutrients dissolve, or break apart, in water, and others are destroyed by heat. However, careful cooking can save nutrients. To conserve nutrients in cooked fruits and vegetables, follow these guidelines:

- **Save the skin.** Whenever you can, leave edible skins on your fruits and vegetables. The skin contains a lot of nutrients and fiber.
- **Think big.** When fruits and vegetables are cooked whole or in large chunks, fewer nutrients are lost.
- **Keep them crisp.** Cook fruits and vegetables until just tender. Slightly crisp is even better. Keep in mind that larger pieces take longer to cook than smaller pieces.
- **Limit the water.** Use as little water as possible to cook vegetables. Steaming, stirfrying, or microwaving vegetables in very little water conserves nutrients. Starchy vegetables, such as potatoes, are an exception and need to be cooked in more water.
- **Cover up.** Cover vegetables when you simmer, steam, or microwave them. This speeds cooking time, which preserves nutrients.
- **Bake or roast.** Prevent nutrient loss by baking potatoes, yams, and squash in their skins.
- **Try the grill.** You can also grill vegetables and fruits on an indoor or outdoor grill. Grilling adds flavor yet retains the food's crispness and nutrients.

Crunchy Melon Bowl

Yield
6–8 servings (1 cup each)

Nutritional Analysis
Per Serving: 255 calories, 2.5 g total fat, 1.6 g saturated fat, 0 g trans fat, 0 mg cholesterol, 17.8 mg sodium, 59.1 g total carbohydrates, 5.5 g dietary fiber, 33 g sugars, 4 g protein

Ingredients

1 cantaloupe
1 fresh pineapple, cored
2 bananas
2 Granny Smith apples
1 cup halved seedless grapes, red or green
½ cup raisins
½ cup apple cider or juice
1 cup granola
Non-dairy, fat free or light whipped topping, for garnish (optional)
Maraschino cherries, for garnish, (optional)

Directions

1. Wash the melon carefully. Create melon bowls by cutting across the center of the cantaloupe making two halves. Remove a small slice from the bottom of each half to stabilize the melon. Remove seeds.
2. With a melon baller, make cantaloupe melon balls from flesh of the fruit leaving a ½ inch wall of melon next to the skin.
3. Slice off top of pineapple. Cut off skin and core. Cut into slices; then into bite-sized pieces. Place in a large bowl.
4. Slice bananas; toss with pineapple immediately to prevent bananas from turning brown.
5. Wash apples; pat dry with a paper towel. Slice in half and core. Do not remove skins. Cut into bite-sized pieces; add to bowl; toss immediately to prevent browning.
6. Wash grapes; pat dry with a paper towel. Cut grapes in half; add to bowl of fruit.
7. Add raisins and apple juice to bowl; toss all ingredients together.
8. Place ingredients in melon bowl.
9. Top each half with ½ cup of the granola.
10. If desired, add a dollop of whipped topping and a maraschino cherry, for garnish.

Koki Iino/Getty Images

How I See It

John, 15

I know we are supposed to eat lots of fruits and vegetables, and now everyone's talking about whole grains. When I got sick several times during the last school year, my parents got concerned. They made sure all of our meals included fresh vegetables, fruits, and whole grains. After just a few weeks, I realized that eating healthy like that made me feel better, and even more energetic. Now, I eat whole grains and both fresh vegetables and fruits every day. I rarely get sick now, and when I do, I'm not sick for as long a time as I used to be. I used to think it was a hassle to try to eat all that stuff, but I learned a lot thanks to my parents. Not only are those foods important to your health, but they actually taste really good!

> **Critical Thinking**
> John suggests that eating fresh vegetables and fruits and whole grains can help improve your health. How do you or someone you know benefit from eating those foods?

- **Follow the directions.** Follow package directions when you cook frozen vegetables. The flavor and nutrition will be better if you put the food in boiling water when it is still frozen. Separate frozen pieces with a fork after cooking begins so that the pieces cook evenly.
- **Do not overcook canned varieties.** Remember that canned vegetables are already cooked and only need to be heated.

✓ **Reading Check** **Identify** When might you prepare frozen produce instead of fresh produce?

Incorporate More Produce into Your Diet

Have you ever looked carefully at the selection of fruits and vegetables in a supermarket? More fresh produce is available today than ever before. New agricultural developments, increasing international trade, and the influence of different ethnic groups have introduced an array of fruits and vegetables throughout the year.

How many different fruits and vegetables have you tried? Jicama ('hē-kə-mə), mango, tomatillo (,tō-mə-'tē-(,)yō), bok choy ('bäk-'choi), taro ('ter-(,)ō), plantain, papaya (pə-'pī-ə), and more are available in many stores. Add carrots, celery, apples, lettuce, broccoli, oranges, green beans, strawberries, watermelon, potatoes, peppers, raisins, and corn to this growing list and you might have a difficult time saying you do not like fruits or vegetables.

Health & Wellness

TIPS

Frozen for Convenience

Many people prefer fresh fruits and vegetables to frozen. However, frozen produce is very nutritious because fruits and vegetables are preserved at their nutritional peaks. Choose frozen over fresh when a fruit or vegetable is no longer in its peak growing season. For the best use of canned fruits and vegetables:

- Read labels to avoid excess sugar or salt.
- Avoid packages with a lot of ice on them. The contents may have freezer burn.
- Use clean, sealable storage containers for any leftovers.

Everyone needs different amounts of fruits and vegetables each day depending on their age, gender, and level of physical activity. Consult MyPlate to determine how much of each kind of food you should eat every day. Be sure to eat fruits and vegetables of different colors. Each vegetable offers different nutritional benefits. For adequate fiber and nutrients, eat more dark green and orange vegetables than other varieties. Limit the amount of starchy vegetables you eat, such as potatoes. Make sure to eat a variety of vegetables. When you are choosing fruit, think "fresh." The fresh fruit you choose should be ripe and free of bruises. Canned and dried fruits are also good choices. Make sure to buy fruit that is canned in juice instead of heavy syrup. Dried fruit is also a good source if you buy dried fruit without added sugar. Also, limit the amount of fruit juices you drink to less than half of your fruit intake. When you do choose fruit juice, make sure it is 100% juice. Limit the amount of fruit drinks that you consume. These have added sugar and are not a good source of nutrients.

How can you increase the amount of fruits and vegetables you eat each day? Be creative! Add avocado, tomato, red pepper, spinach, and carrot shavings to sandwiches. Make a parfait with your favorite berries and low-fat yogurt. You can add vegetables to casseroles and experiment with various fruits and vegetables in salads.

You can also incorporate vegetables into your day's food choices in other ways. Salsa and guacamole are tasty ways to eat avocados and tomatoes. Pico de gallo (pīkō də gī-yō) is a kind of fresh salsa made with tomatoes, onions, and cilantro.

> ### Creative Cooking

Use your creativity when preparing fruits. Smoothies are an easy way to enjoy a healthful, sweet, and refreshing snack without adding unnecessary sugar. *Describe the different ways you have prepared and enjoyed fruits.*

i love images/Alamy

For more ideas, find a country that interests you and find out how they prepare fruits and vegetables. Gazpacho (gəz-pä-chō) is a Spanish soup dish made of chopped tomatoes, cucumbers, onion, garlic, oil and vinegar. It is served cold, and makes a nice summertime dish.

Here are a few more creative and tasty ways to incorporate more produce into your diet.

- Stuff bell peppers with a mixture of cooked ground beef, spices and tomatoes, then bake them in the oven.
- Skewer zucchini and other types of squash and grill them on the barbeque. You can also grill onions, bell peppers, tomatoes, and any other vegetable that you enjoy.
- Stir-fry carrots, bean sprouts, green beans, and broccoli with some ginger root and sesame oil for a light, Asian taste.
- **Core** apples by removing the seeds and stem, then bake them in the oven with cinnamon until they are soft for dessert. Fruit of any kind can be a great choice for a dessert.

Section 22.2

After You Read

Review Key Concepts

1. **Identify** the characteristic that makes it quick and easy to choose nutrient-rich produce.
2. **Describe** why it is necessary to thoroughly wash produce before serving.
3. **Explain** why there is more fresh produce available today than ever before.

Check Your Answers Go to connectED. mcgraw-hill.com to check your answers.

Practice Academic Skills

English Language Arts

4. Locate several unusual fruits or vegetables in the market. Where were they grown and how are they served? Prepare a few and present the information you learned about the fruits or vegetables while serving them to your class.

Social Studies

5. Choose three different countries and research the fruit or vegetable grown most in each country. Why do the countries grow these crops? Is it because of history, trade agreements, or natural resources, such as soil, elevation, and average temperature?

Chapter 22   Review and Applications

CHAPTER SUMMARY

Section 22.1
Grains in Your Diet

Grains are the small fruits of cereal grasses. Grains are excellent sources of complex carbohydrates, fiber, B vitamins, and iron. When a whole grain is milled to remove the bran and the germ, it becomes a refined grain. Pasta, rice, and cereals absorb water when cooked and increase in volume. There are three types of breads. Quick breads include muffins and biscuits and can be easily prepared. There are certain things you should look for when choosing healthful grain products.

Section 22.2
Fruits and Vegetables in Your Diet

Fruits and vegetables contribute many essential nutrients to the diet. You should eat a wide variety of fruits and vegetables. Proper handling of fresh produce helps conserve nutrients and prevents foodborne illness. Following certain guidelines when cooking fruits and vegetables can help conserve nutrients. Agricultural developments and international trade have made many fruits and vegetables available year-round. These developments have also introduced many new fruits and vegetables.

Vocabulary Review

1. Create multiple-choice test questions for each content and academic vocabulary term.

Content Vocabulary
- ◇ whole grain (p. 535)
- ◇ endosperm (p. 535)
- ◇ germ (p. 535)
- ◇ bran (p. 536)
- ◇ refined grain (p. 536)
- ◇ enriched (p. 536)

- ◇ al dente (p. 537)
- ◇ cereal grain (p. 538)
- ◇ leavening agent (p. 538)
- ◇ wilt (p. 544)
- ◇ core (p. 548)

Academic Vocabulary
- ▢ consist (p. 535)
- ▢ coarse (p. 536)
- ▢ conserve (p. 543)
- ▢ dissolve (p. 544)

Review Key Concepts

2. Identify the parts of a grain kernel and the nutritional benefits of each.
3. Summarize preparation techniques for pasta, rice, bread, and cereals.
4. Describe what to look for when choosing grain products.
5. Explain why it is important to eat a variety of fruits and vegetables.
6. Demonstrate ways to conserve nutrients when preparing fresh produce.
7. Identify ways to incorporate more fruits and vegetables into your daily eating plan.

Critical Thinking

8. Conclude You are sent to buy bread at the grocery store. How will you decide which breads might be the healthiest choice for your family?
9. Examine Why do you think pasta is such a popular grain? List ways you could prepare a healthful pasta dish.
10. Analyze Some people consider salads to be "rabbit food." What factors do you think contribute to this viewpoint? Why is this viewpoint a limited one?
11. Identify How has international trade and the presence of different ethnic groups influenced the types of produce you eat on a daily basis?

 **ACTIVE LEARNING**

 **Family & Community Connections**

12. Produce Descriptions Imagine you work in the marketing department of a large supermarket chain. Your job is to write brief descriptions of produce to publish on the company's Web site. Select six fruits and vegetables and write a brief, appealing description of each. Include information about the history of the fruits and vegetables you have chosen. Where did they originate? Use the information from this chapter as well as other information from cookbooks or cooking Web sites to write your descriptions. When you are finished, present your descriptions to the rest of the class.

13. Take a Survey Survey your classmates about what their favorite fruits and vegetables are. Ask them each to choose one favorite fruit and one favorite vegetable. When you are finished, create a chart showing the five most popular fruits and the five most popular vegetables. Be sure to label the number of students who chose each as their favorite. Also, note any fruits or vegetables for which there is only one vote. Are these foods that you have never heard of before? Are they grown in your region, or somewhere else in the world? Then, using cookbooks, cooking Web sites, or family recipes, describe one way to prepare, serve, and eat the favorite fruit and vegetable of the class. Create a graph that describes the results of your survey. Present your findings to the class.

Real-World Skills and Applications

Leadership Skills

14. Healthy Grains Prepare a presentation on the health benefits of grains. Use information from this chapter, plus other information from print or online resources. Be sure to include descriptions of various foods containing grains. As part of your presentation, bring a food containing whole or processed grains for your classmates to try.

Financial Literacy

15. Green Beans Imagine that you are making dinner for your family, and you want to prepare a side of green beans to go with the main dish. Fresh green beans are $1.29 per pound. A ½-pound package of frozen green beans costs $0.59. If you are going to buy 1 ½ pounds of green beans, which is the less expensive option—fresh or frozen?

Technology Skills

16. Modern Food Tools Think of a fruit or vegetable for which a specific tool has been developed. How does this tool make preparation of the fruit or vegetable easier or less time-consuming? What are the safety benefits of the tool? Explain the tool and its use, and compare the method of preparation the tool makes possible with the method of preparation required without the tool.

Tanya Constantine/Blend Images/Getty Images

Academic Skills

English Language Arts

17. Explain the Benefits Children and adults of all ages experience health benefits from fruits and vegetables. Write two one-page essays on the benefits of eating a variety of fruits and vegetables. Include the nutrients that they contain. One essay should be directed at an audience comprised of elementary school students. The other essay should be directed at an audience comprised of adults. Adjust your writing in each essay accordingly.

Social Studies

18. Various Grains Different regions of the world produce different types of grains. Research two traditional grain dishes from different regions of the world. Try to find two dishes that use the same grain. Do the dishes have anything in common? How do they differ? Compare the two dishes and present your analysis to the class.

Mathematics

19. Smoothie Fractions Desiree has recently decided to include more fruits and vegetables in her diet. She does not generally like to eat plain fruit, but she wants the health benefits that come from eating a variety of fruits. She decides to make a berry smoothie every day. About $\frac{1}{8}$ of her smoothie is low-fat milk, $\frac{3}{8}$ is frozen blueberries, and $\frac{1}{2}$ is frozen raspberries. Desiree uses 6 ounces of frozen raspberries. How many ounces of frozen blueberries does she include?

Math Concept **Multiplying Fractions** To multiply a whole number by a fraction, first change the whole number to a fraction by giving it a denominator of 1.

Starting Hint First, find the size of the smoothie. You know it contains 6 ounces of frozen raspberries and that frozen raspberries make up $\frac{1}{2}$ of the smoothie. Thus, you know that the smoothie is 12 ounces (6 ounces × 2).

 For math help, go to the Math Appendix at the back of the book.

Standardized Test Practice

MULTIPLE CHOICE
Directions: Read the problem. Then, choose the correct answer.

Test-Taking Tip When taking a multiple-choice test, you may want to avoid spending too much time on a question you are having difficulty with. You may have time at the end of the test to revisit the difficult questions you skipped.

20. Select the item below that is not a part of a grain kernel.
a) the bran
b) the endosperm
c) the germ
d) the cochlea

Chapter 23

Preparing Protein Foods

Section 23.1
Meat, Poultry, and Fish

Section 23.2
Eggs, Legumes, Milk, and Milk Products

Chapter Objectives

Section 23.1

- **Describe** the nutritional benefits of meat, fish, and poultry.
- **Outline** safe handling and preparation guidelines for meat, poultry, and fish.

Section 23.2

- **Identify** safe methods for handling and cooking eggs.
- **Describe** methods for handling and cooking milk products.
- **Explain** how to safely prepare and store legumes.

Writing Activity

Write an Explanation

Balance Is Important When you make healthful food choices, it is important to have balance among your food groups. Write a paragraph that explains how to balance protein foods with fruits, vegetables, and grains. Use complete, descriptive sentences.

Writing Tips Use these tips to write an explanation:
- **Explain** how food choices affect your overall health.
- **State** your opinion clearly, and support it with facts.
- **Use** descriptive words.

▲ Your Portion of Protein

Meat, poultry, fish, eggs, legumes, and milk products all offer tasty ways to get many of the nutrients you need to get through the day. *What are some ways you like to eat protein-rich foods?*

Section 23.1

Meat, Poultry, and Fish

Before You Read

Helpful Memory Tools Successful readers use tricks to help them remember. Scan the headings in the chapter and think about memory tools you can use to help you to remember the information.

Read to Learn

Key Concepts

- **Describe** the nutritional benefits of meat, fish, and poultry.
- **Outline** safe handling and preparation guidelines for meat, poultry, and fish.

Main Idea

Meat, poultry, and fish contain nutrients you need and can be prepared in many ways.

Content Vocabulary

◇ marbling
◇ perishable

Academic Vocabulary

You will find these words in your reading and on your tests. Use the glossary to look up their definitions if necessary.

▪ accurate
▪ exposed

Graphic Organizer

As you read, use a graphic organizer like the one below to list the nutrients found in meat, poultry, and fish.

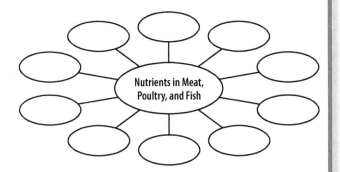

Nutrients in Meat, Poultry, and Fish

 Graphic Organizer Go to
connectED.mcgraw-hill.com
to download this graphic organizer.

Nutrients in Meat, Poultry, and Fish

Meat, poultry, and fish are all excellent sources of the complete proteins that your body needs. Protein helps your body build and repair tissues. It also promotes growth in your teen years.

Meat, poultry, and fish also provide important vitamins and minerals. They supply B vitamins including niacin, thiamin, and vitamins B_6 and B_{12} to help keep your nervous system healthy. These foods also provide iron for red blood cells, and vitamin E and potassium for a healthy heart. Zinc in these foods helps your immune system. Fish supplies iodine and omega-3 fatty acid. Some smaller fish with edible bones, like sardines, can also provide calcium. Poultry contains phosphorus, which is necessary for the growth and repair of cells. Phosphorus also promotes skeletal growth and tooth development, and is essential for the kidneys to function properly.

Fat and Cholesterol

Meat, poultry, and fish also contain fat and cholesterol. Fat is a nutrient just like vitamins, protein, and minerals. Your body needs some fat and cholesterol to maintain a healthy weight and stay healthy, but you do not need much. Be careful about how much you eat. Too much saturated fat, which comes from fat in animals, is not heart healthy.

Choose lean meat from beef, pork, and lamb. Processed meats, such as sausage, hot dogs, and bacon, are high in saturated fat. Organ meat, which includes heart, liver, kidney, and tongue, is high in cholesterol.

Poultry contains less total fat, cholesterol, and saturated fat than many meats. Most of its fat is in the skin or just under it. To prepare poultry dishes with less fat, remove the skin before it is cooked.

Fish is usually low in fat. Some of the fat on fish is also unsaturated. Unsaturated fat is good for heart health.

As You Read

Connect Think about the meals you have eaten this week. How many included meat? How many included chicken or fish?

Nutrients in Meat, Poultry, and Fish

Meals are often planned around meat, poultry, and fish. *What are some important nutrients that they provide?*

Pixtal/AGE Fotostock

Tolerance Sylvia and Lyle invited Manisha for lunch at the cafeteria. Manisha had brought her lunch from home, and as she prepared to eat it, Lyle commented that her food looked weird. She explained that she is a vegetarian, and her lunch was a traditional vegetarian dish from her culture. Lyle made a disgusted face and said that he could never live a life without hamburgers and steaks. Sylvia thought Lyle's comments were out of line.

You Make the Call
Should Sylvia keep her thoughts to herself? Or, should she explain to Lyle that Manisha should expect to eat her lunch without being judged for her food choices? What could Lyle learn from this experience?

◆ Vocabulary
You can find definitions in the glossary at the back of this book.

How Much Protein Do You Need?

Depending on your age, weight, and gender, you need five to seven ounces of protein foods a day. Three ounces of cooked meat, poultry, or fish is about the size of a deck of playing cards. This equals one medium pork chop, one half of a small chicken breast, one small hamburger patty, or a bun-sized fish fillet. Two ounces of meat, poultry or fish is equal to one half cup of canned tuna or ground beef, one small chicken leg or thigh, or two slices of thinly-sliced sandwich meat.

Meat, poultry, and fish provide different nutrients, so it is important to vary your protein choices. Most of your protein probably comes from meat. Try to replace some of your meat-based meals with chicken or fish, which are lower in cholesterol and saturated fat. For optimal health, you should eat fish once or twice a week.

✓ Reading Check **List** What twelve nutrients can you find in meat, poultry, and fish?

Shop, Prepare, and Clean Up

It is important to remember food safety when you prepare and store meat, poultry, and fish. Consider how much it costs and how you are going to cook it. Choose lean cuts. Meat, poultry, and fish can be bought fresh, frozen, or canned. Broil, grill, roast, braise, or stew meat, poultry, and fish. Frying adds fat and calories. Remember to store your meat, poultry, and fish properly after your meal.

Compare Cost and Check for Freshness

When you buy food, especially meat, poultry, and fish, consider how much you want to buy. How many people do you need to feed? Do you want leftovers? The cost of meat, poultry, and fish depends on the fat content and cut of the meat. A cut of meat tells you what part of the animal the meat is from.

When you shop for meat, poultry, and fish, think about the cost per serving, and whether the amount of meat, without the bones, is enough or too much for what you are planning to cook. Look for bargains. Sometimes, a whole chicken costs less than cut-up parts.

The cost may also be affected by marbling within the meat. **Marbling** is flecks of fat throughout the meat that add flavor and tenderness. Often, cuts of meat with more marbling are more expensive than leaner meat cuts because of these factors.

Every package of fresh meat, poultry, and fish you will find in the store should be labeled with a freshness date. Make sure to check the packages to confirm that the sell-by date has not expired.

Check for signs that the meat was defrosted, and then frozen again. This should be avoided. Condensation or ice build-up is a sign that it may have thawed. When you shop for canned meat, poultry, and fish, make sure that there are no dents or bulges in the can. Harmful bacteria that lead to foodborne illness may be present.

TAKE CHARGE!

Cut the Fat

Meat, poultry, and fish contain many nutrients, but can be high in saturated fat. To reduce the fat in protein foods, follow these tips:

- **Choose Meat Wisely** Choose lean meats, which can be flavorful and juicy if cooked properly.
- **Trim Fat** Remove any visible fat found on meat before cooking.
- **Remove the Skin** The fat in poultry is concentrated in its skin. Remove it to reduce fat.
- **Select Low-Fat Options** Instead of red meat, choose fish, light-meat poultry, and legumes, which are lower in fat.
- **Use a Healthful Cooking Method** Baking, grilling, and broiling help limit fat.

Real-World Skills

Rewrite a Recipe Review some of your favorite protein-rich meals. Do you use most of the guidelines to prepare them? Choose a recipe that is high in fat and use these guidelines to modify it. Test your more healthful recipe if possible.

Defrost Safely

Meat, poultry, and fish are **perishable**, which means they are likely to spoil easily. Spoiled food does not just taste terrible. It can also cause foodborne illness. Always check the labels of frozen meat, poultry, and fish. Some must be defrosted before they are cooked. Others should be cooked while frozen. Do not rinse frozen meat or poultry. This causes the spread of harmful bacteria.

The safest way to defrost meat, poultry, and fish is in the refrigerator. Place the frozen meat in the refrigerator in a pan or on a plate. While the refrigerator keeps the meat at a safe temperature, it is also warm enough to allow the meat to thaw, or defrost. Smaller pieces usually defrost within a day. Larger pieces, such as roasts or whole chickens, may take two days. Never thaw meat on the countertop at room temperatures or in a sink filled with water. Bacteria begin to multiply, or grow, at temperatures above 40°F (4°C). Room-temperature defrosting can be dangerous, since most homes are about 70°F (21°C).

You can also carefully thaw meat in the microwave at a reduced power level. Check your microwave owner's manual for defrosting procedures. You must be cautious when defrosting in a microwave, as the food can begin to cook. The result is unevenly cooked food. Never keep thawed food in a microwave while you wait to cook. The inside of the microwave is room temperature, a suitable temperature for bacteria to multiply. After defrosting meat, poultry, and fish, cook them within a couple days. Do not freeze them again until after they are cooked.

Shop wisely. You can save money and satisfy even the pickiest eaters by making a casserole with ground beef at $2.30 per pound, instead of top sirloin steak at $9.99 per pound. Compare the difference in cost of each in one-pound and two-pound portions.

Cook Meat, Poultry, and Fish

Braising, roasting, broiling, stir-frying, and stewing are just some of the many ways to cook meat, poultry, and fish. No matter which method you choose, food safety should be your first concern. When you cook protein foods, you must make sure that the internal temperature reaches a certain point. This is the only way you can ensure that harmful bacteria have been killed.

Cook Meat

Use cuts of meat within three to five days, and ground meat within one or two days of purchase. Meat should be cooked immediately after thawing. You do not need to rinse meat before cooking it. Doing so only spreads bacteria. Also remember that once you start cooking, you should not stop. Partially cooked foods can harbor bacteria. Cook all meat thoroughly.

Try to use low to moderate cooking temperatures. Lower temperatures help keep meat tender, while higher temperatures make it tougher. Broiling and grilling are exceptions because with these methods, the higher temperatures seal in the juices.

Tender cuts of meat are usually cooked using dry-heat methods, such as grilling, roasting, broiling, sautéing, or frying. Less tender cuts of meats are generally cooked using a moist-heat method, such as braising or stewing. These methods can be used to make less expensive, tougher cuts of meat more tender and flavorful.

You can find suggested cooking times based on the size and weight of the meat you are preparing in cookbooks and other resources. Remember that these are guidelines. Brownness on the outside of hamburgers does not mean they are done and safe to eat. Meat can be cooked to different levels of doneness. Cooking times vary depending on the type of meat, the cut, and the desired doneness. The only **accurate**, or error-free, method of determining whether meat is done is to check for safe temperatures using a meat thermometer. Insert the thermometer into the center of the meat. Ground meat dishes, such as hamburgers and meatloaf, should be cooked to 160°F (71°C). Other cuts of meat, such as venison and beef steaks, should be cooked to at least 145°F (63°C). Pork should be cooked to at least 160°F (71°C).

Cook Poultry

Poultry can be cooked with dry heat or moist heat. Turkey, duck, and goose are best roasted, but if chicken is cooked with dry heat, it should first be marinated or basted while cooking to prevent it from drying out.

Poultry must be cooked until no pink remains and the juices run clear. When roasting whole poultry, check the temperature using a rapid-read meat thermometer. Insert the thermometer deep into the inner thigh of the poultry, near the breast. Whole poultry should be cooked to at least 180°F (82°C). Poultry pieces and ground turkey or chicken should be cooked to at least 170°F (77°C).

Stuffing should be loosely packed in the bird's cavity just before roasting to prevent bacterial growth. Brush on barbeque sauce or any other sweet marinade about two minutes before the chicken is done. This prevents the sauce from burning.

Cook Fish and Shellfish

Fish and shellfish should be cooked within two days of purchase or immediately after thawing. Dry-heat cooking methods are best for deep-colored fatty fish such as salmon, tuna, and trout, and moist-heat cooking methods are best for pale, lower-fat fish such as cod, perch, halibut, and red snapper. If you want to use a dry-heat method to cook lower-fat fish, make sure to baste the fish with oil, melted butter, or a marinade to prevent it from drying out. Shellfish are often boiled or steamed. Some shellfish, such as shrimp, can be cooked with dry heat, as long as they are first marinated or basted as they cook.

Cookbooks provide suggested cooking times for fish products based on weight and size. The general rule of thumb is to allow 10 minutes of cooking time for every inch of thickness. Some moist-heat recipes may call for longer cooking times to allow flavors to blend, however. Cook fish and shellfish just until the meat turns opaque and flakes easily. Overcooking fish in dry heat turns it tough and rubbery. Overcooking fish in moist heat causes it to fall apart. Shellfish is done when the flesh is opaque and their shells turn bright red, orange, or pink. Mollusks, such as clams, are done when their shells open.

Check the Internal Temperature

Cook meat thoroughly to help prevent foodborne illness. *What should the internal temperature of a beef steak be?*

Store Leftovers

Even after meat, poultry, and fish are cooked, they are still perishable, and can spoil quickly if not stored properly. Refrigerate or freeze leftovers within two hours after cooking. This includes the time you spend serving and eating. If it is 90°F (32°C) or warmer, do not keep food out for longer than one hour. If it has been sitting out for longer than that, throw it away. It is a good rule of thumb to refrigerate food as soon as the meal is done.

If you want the leftovers to keep for more than a few days, you should freeze them within two hours of cooking. Wrap the leftovers tightly in airtight plastic bags, containers, or freezer paper. If the meat is **exposed** to, or not shielded from, the cold air of your freezer, it can lead to freezer burn. Meat with freezer burn is still edible, but does not taste as good. Keep leftover meat, poultry, and fish dishes frozen until you are ready to use them.

Eat refrigerated leftovers within three to four days. Frozen leftovers can be stored for a long time, but are usually best if eaten within a month. Reheat leftover solid foods to 165°F (74°C). Boil leftover soups, stews, sauces, and gravies before eating.

Section 23.1

After You Read

Review Key Concepts

1. **Identify** four ways you can limit the amount of saturated fat and cholesterol you consume when you eat meat, poultry, and fish.
2. **Explain** how to determine when poultry is completely cooked.

Practice Academic Skills

**English Language Arts**

3. Write a summary of a recent and local incident of foodborne illness. Identify the cause of the illness, learn where the incident occurred, and determine how it could have been avoided. List your resources.

Social Studies

4. The lack of adequate nutrition is a problem for individuals and whole populations throughout the world. Poverty, famine, floods, and overpopulation are causes in some countries. Research a country where many people suffer from malnutrition. Write a paragraph about the causes of malnutrition in that country and possible solutions.

Check Your Answers Go to connectED. mcgraw-hill.com to check your answers.

Section 23.2

Eggs, Legumes, Milk, and Milk Products

As You Read

Connect Look at the labels on the foods you eat every day. How many of these foods contain eggs?

Eggs

The egg is one of the most inexpensive, convenient, and multipurpose foods there is. Eggs come in a variety of sizes and colors. A carton of eggs usually contains a dozen eggs, but you can also find half cartons and cartons of eighteen. Egg size reflects weight per dozen.

Eggs are usually white or brown. The outside color of the egg is determined by the breed of hen that laid it. Color does not affect the taste or nutrition. When you shop for eggs, buy only refrigerated, uncracked eggs, and check the sell-by date for freshness. See **Figure 23.1** on page 563 to learn about the basic parts of an egg.

Nutrients in Eggs

Eggs are excellent sources of complete protein. They supply many important vitamins and minerals, including vitamin A, which is essential for skin cells, growth, and vision in dim light. Eggs are also rich in folate and other B vitamins, which are necessary for the proper formation of blood cells and nerve cells. Minerals such as iron, phosphorus, and small amounts of calcium are found in eggs. These minerals contribute to the production of bone and red blood cells.

Egg yolks contain cholesterol, and some fat, which you should pay attention to for heart health. If you want to reduce the amount of fat and cholesterol in your eating plan, look for egg substitutes near the eggs in the refrigerated section. These substitutes include only the egg white. This means they do not have cholesterol and fat.

Eggs are a part of a healthful diet, but always be sure to eat the amount that is right for you. Depending on your age, gender, and level of physical activity, you should eat between five and seven ounces of protein foods a day. One egg is usually about one ounce.

Prepare and Cook Eggs

How do you like your eggs? Poached, fried, or boiled? Do you like eggs in omelets, salads, or sandwiches? Eggs can be used in a variety of ways, for breakfast, lunch, dinner, or as an added ingredient. Most recipes are made using large eggs.

Eggs are as perishable as raw meat, poultry, and fish, so they need to be handled and cooked with care. If not handled properly, you may not destroy harmful bacteria. Follow these handling guidelines to enjoy eggs safely:

- **Do not eat raw eggs.** This includes any products made with uncooked eggs, such as raw-egg drinks and uncooked cake batter.
- **Handle eggs safely.** Wash your hands and utensils with warm soapy water before and after cooking with eggs.

The Incredible Egg

You can find eggs in literally hundreds of dishes, from breakfast to dessert. *What are some healthful choices you can make when you cook eggs?*

John A. Rizzo/Getty Images

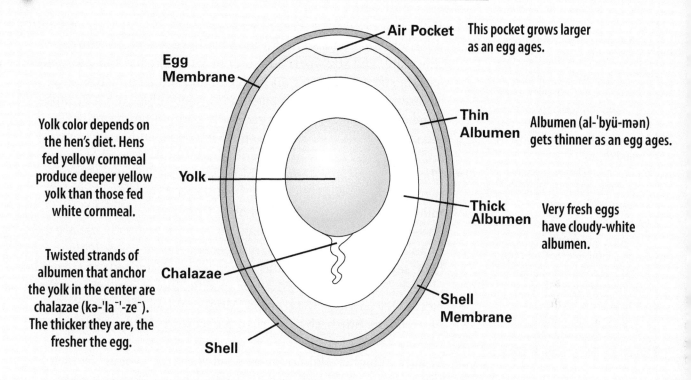

Figure 23.1 Parts of an Egg

Egg Basics These are the basic parts of an egg. *What determines the color of the yolk? What is the purpose of the chalazae?*

Air Pocket This pocket grows larger as an egg ages.

Egg Membrane

Thin Albumen Albumen (al-ˈbyü-mən) gets thinner as an egg ages.

Yolk color depends on the hen's diet. Hens fed yellow cornmeal produce deeper yellow yolk than those fed white cornmeal.

Yolk

Thick Albumen Very fresh eggs have cloudy-white albumen.

Twisted strands of albumen that anchor the yolk in the center are chalazae (kə-ˈlaˉ-zeˉ). The thicker they are, the fresher the egg.

Chalazae

Shell Membrane

Shell

- **Use an egg separator.** When a recipe calls for egg yolks or egg whites only, use an egg separator. Using the shell to separate an egg can allow bacteria on the egg shell to contaminate the egg's contents.
- **Cook eggs thoroughly.** Whether you poach, boil, or fry them, eggs must be cooked until the yolks are firm. Scrambled eggs should not be runny. Egg dishes should be 160°F (71°C) in the center.

Store Eggs

Eggs must always be refrigerated. They are animal products and may carry dangerous bacteria that can cause foodborne illnesses such as **salmonella**. Eggs can be stored for two to five weeks. Do not wash eggs before you store them.

Egg substitutes come in containers or cartons that have a sell-by date. You can keep unopened pasteurized eggs and egg substitutes frozen for up to one year. If the container is unopened, it can remain in your refrigerator for up to 10 days. Once you open it, use the rest within three days.

✓ **Reading Check** **Identify** Why are eggs healthful choices in your eating plan?

Community Connections

Farmers' Market

A farmers' market is a place for local farmers to sell the foods that they grow, including produce like legumes. Fresh eggs are also sold. Visit a farmers' market and talk to the farmers to learn about the foods that are locally grown, and how you can support your community.

▷ **Vocabulary**

You can find definitions in the glossary at the back of this book.

Milk and Milk Products

If you are like most people, milk was the staple of your diet when you were a very young child. Today, you probably have milk in your cereal or drink it with lunch. Other popular dairy foods include cheeses and yogurt.

- **Milk** This creamy beverage comes in whole, low-fat, and nonfat varieties. You can also find it in many flavors such as vanilla, chocolate, and strawberry. If you have a sensitivity to lactose, the natural sugar found in milk, you can find reduced-lactose and lactose-free milk. You can also find canned milk, such as evaporated and sweetened condensed milk, and nonfat dry milk. To increase milk in your diet, use milk in cocoa, and make oatmeal and condensed cream soups with low-fat milk instead of water.

- **Cheese** A concentrated form of milk, cheese is grouped into two categories: fresh and aged, or ripened. Fresh cheese has a mild flavor and is highly perishable. Cottage cheese, a bland cheese made with large or small curds, and cream cheese are two popular fresh cheeses. Aged, or ripened, cheese is available in firm, semisoft, soft, and blue-veined forms. Hundreds of ripened cheeses, each with a **distinct**, or specific, flavor, can be found in stores. Try cheddar, mozzarella, Monterey Jack, feta ('fe-tə), or blue cheese. Stir herbs into ricotta cheese or cottage cheese to make a vegetable dip.

- **Yogurt** Whether plain or sweetened with fruit, yogurt is one of the most healthful milk products you can buy. Yogurt is naturally low in fat, but you can find reduced-fat and fat-free versions in your grocer's dairy case. Many people use yogurt to make smoothies or in recipes in place of sour cream. Try adding fruit yogurt to crunchy cereal for a healthful breakfast or snack.

Nutrients in Milk and Milk Products

Milk and milk products contain many nutrients that your body needs to stay healthy. Milk contains complete protein. This helps your body build, repair, and maintain your body's tissues. Milk and other milk products also contain bone-building nutrients like calcium. Milk and some yogurt have added vitamin D, which helps your body absorb the calcium in milk. For an additional calcium boost, try calcium-enriched milk, which contains 500 milligrams of calcium per cup.

Milk and other milk products also contain B vitamins, vitamin A, potassium, carbohydrates, water, and some fat. The fat content in milk products varies. Whole milk and products that are made from it are high in saturated fat. Other milk and milk products can be bought as reduced fat or fat free.

In addition to calcium, potassium, and other important nutrients, yogurt with live, active cultures provides other health benefits. These friendly bacteria used to make yogurt aid in digestion and also support your immune system. Studies show that eating yogurt regularly can lead to fewer illnesses.

Dairy Substitutions

Tara has a milk allergy, and Dan eats a vegan diet, which means he eats no animal products. How do they get the nutrients milk and milk products provide without eating dairy products? They eat dairy substitutes such as rice milk, a processed drink usually made with brown rice. Other substitutions include soymilk, which is made from soybeans and provides complete proteins.

Prepare and Cook Milk and Milk Products

A lot of dairy products you eat are convenience foods that do not require cooking. You can pour milk into a glass, eat yogurt from the container, or snack on a cube of cheese. However, you may decide to make a melted cheese sandwich, a quesadilla (ˌkā-sə-ˈdē-ə), macaroni and cheese, or a cup of cocoa, all of which need to be cooked or heated.

To successfully prepare milk and milk products, keep the following tips in mind:

- **Avoid high heat.** Use low to moderate heat when cooking milk and milk products. High heat will **scorch** heat-sensitive proteins in these foods, which means they will burn. Cheese should be cooked just until it melts. If overcooked, it becomes tough and rubbery.

- **Add cold milk carefully.** When you add cold milk to hot foods or acidic foods such as tomato soup, the milk can **curdle**, which means it separates into curds and whey. To prevent this, first pour a small amount of the hot or acidic mixture into the cold milk you plan to add. Stir constantly while doing this. This raises the temperature or acidity of the milk. Then, very slowly add your milk mixture to the acidic or hot mixture.

- **Cover or stir.** When heating milk, use a cover to prevent a film from forming on top. If you do not use a cover, stir it often.

- **Keep frozen.** When making ice cream, do not allow the mixture to stand on the counter for long once it is finished. Eat it right away, or put in the freezer immediately to prevent foodborne illness. This is especially important if the recipe you use includes eggs.

▼ **Yogurt and Cheese**

Yogurt and cheese are packed with calcium. Yogurt provides bacteria that aids digestion. Try plain yogurt or one of the many flavored varieties, either regular, low-fat, or nonfat. *What are some ways you can integrate yogurt or cheese into your favorite snacks and dishes?*

SUCCEED IN SCHOOL

Update Your Daily Schedule

Review your schedule every morning. Add to your daily schedule any work that you did not complete the day before.

Store Dairy Foods

Almost all dairy foods are highly perishable, so you will need to store them properly to avoid spoilage. Keep all dairy foods in their original containers. Refrigerate milk, and use it by the date indicated on the package, usually within two to seven days. To store cheese, be sure it is wrapped tightly before refrigerating. Fresh cheese should be used within two weeks. Throw out any fresh cheese that contains mold. Aged cheeses and cheese products with preservatives usually last several weeks in the refrigerator. You can also freeze cheese for later use, though you should slice or cube it beforehand if that is how you plan to serve it when thawed. This is because many cheeses crumble more easily after they have been frozen.

✓ **Reading Check** **Identify** What health benefits do milk products provide?

Legumes and Nuts

Legumes and nuts are an important part of a balanced diet. A **legume** is an edible seed grown in a pod. As legumes such as beans and peas mature, they dry out. How many types of dry beans and peas can you name? You may have heard of black beans, kidney beans, navy beans, pinto beans, black-eyed peas, split green or yellow peas, pink and green lentils, garbanzo beans, and soybeans. Though commonly considered to be nuts, peanuts are actually legumes as well. Walnuts, hazelnuts, and pecans are some of the more common nuts. Though they contain many of the same nutrients as nuts, cashews are not nuts, but seeds.

Nutrients in Legumes and Nuts

Legumes, nuts, and other seeds have many nutritional benefits. Legumes are naturally low in fat and rich in fiber and complex carbohydrates. They are easy to prepare, and they do not harbor, or contain, dangerous bacteria. They can also be easily substituted for one another and substituted for meat. Legumes are rich in carbohydrates, fiber, calcium, phosphorus, B vitamins, and vitamin E. Nuts and seeds provide fiber, vitamin E, and essential minerals such as magnesium and potassium.

Prepare and Cook Legumes

To prepare dry beans, sift through them and remove any debris or stones. Then wash them thoroughly and remove the discolored ones. Presoaking beans helps them cook more thoroughly and in less time. It also dissolves gas-causing substances and allows for better digestion. Most presoaked beans cook within 60 to 90 minutes. Lentils and split peas will be tender sooner than whole beans.

You can soak dry beans overnight using three cups of water for every cup of dry beans. Remember to always discard the soaking water. If you forget to soak them overnight, you can cover the beans with water and simmer them until they swell. Avoid boiling the beans, which breaks the skin and makes them mushy. Then, take the pan off the heat, cover it, and let the beans stand for one hour. Drain and rinse the beans, and follow your recipe's directions. Many recipes for legumes are available in cookbooks and online. Various ingredients, along with spices and herbs, can bring out the flavor of beans and peas.

Beans are great in soup, salads, dips, and baked dishes. The flavors and textures of beans, peas, and lentils blend well with other foods. If you do not have time to prepare dry beans, you can try these quick dishes using canned beans:

- Add canned garbanzo, kidney, or white beans to tossed salads, soups, stews, or pasta sauce.
- Mash canned beans for spreads or dips.
- Wrap refried beans, scrambled eggs, and cheese in a flour tortilla for a breakfast burrito.
- Combine lima beans and corn for a complete protein.

Nuts for Flavor and Texture

Nuts taste great just as they are. They also add flavor and texture to mixed dishes such as salads and baked goods. Since nuts are high in fat, use small amounts. Chop them so they go further. Toast them to enhance their flavor.

Health & Wellness
TIPS

Nutrition Challenges

Vegetarians can be healthy if they get enough food variety, nutrients, and food energy. Here are some ways to include essential nutrients in a vegetarian meal plan:

- Avoid high-calorie, high-fat, sugary foods.
- Eat plenty of fruits, vegetables, and whole grains.
- Eat high-fiber foods, dry fruit, and nuts for energy.
- Calcium can come from broccoli, dry beans, fortified tofu, and soymilk.
- Get iron from enriched whole-grain cereals and breads.

◀ Vegetarian Protein

A vegetarian is a person who does not eat meat, poultry, or fish, and often avoids dairy products and eggs as well. *How can vegetarians make sure they get essential proteins?*

Light and Healthy Recipe

Mediterranean Hummus and Vegetable Dip

Yield
8-10 servings (⅓ cup each)

Nutrition Analysis
Per Serving: 215 calories, 12 g total fat, 3.5 g saturated fat, 0 g trans fat, 20 mg cholesterol, 400 mg sodium, 18 g total carbohydrate, 4 g dietary fiber, 5 g sugars, 9 g protein

Hummus Directions

Hummus Ingredients
1 can (15 oz.) garbanzo beans/chickpeas
3 Tbsp. minced garlic
3 Tbsp. freshly chopped parsley
2 Tbsp. olive oil
2 ½ tsp. lemon juice
¼ tsp. red pepper flakes

1. Drain garbanzo beans well.
2. Put garbanzo beans in a food processor with garlic, parsley, olive oil, lemon juice, and red pepper flakes. Combine until smooth.
3. If hummus is too thick, add 1 tablespoon water at a time until desired consistency is achieved.

Vegetable Dip Directions

Vegetable Dip Ingredients
1 med. cucumber, finely chopped
2 scallions, thinly sliced
⅓ cup low-fat sour cream
⅓ cup low-fat yogurt, plain
¼ cup finely chopped onion
½ tsp. fresh basil, chopped
2 med. tomatoes
½ cup fresh spinach
¾ cup sun dried tomato and basil feta cheese
2 tsp. freshly chopped parsley (optional)

1. To prepare vegetable mixture: Reserve 2 tablespoons each of cucumber and scallions for garnish. In a small bowl, combine sour cream, yogurt, cucumber, scallions, onion, and basil.
2. Wash tomatoes; gently pat dry; slice tomatoes in half. Remove seeds and chop into small diced pieces; reserve 2 tablespoons for garnish.
3. Wash spinach and pat dry with a paper towel. Stack spinach leaves and roll up tightly. Thinly slice into strands. This process is called chiffonade.
4. Add tomatoes, spinach, and crumbled feta cheese to sour cream/yogurt mixture. Gently fold to combine.
5. Spread mixture evenly in the bottom of a 10-inch round serving dish or glass pie plate; set aside.
6. Cover vegetable mixture with hummus.
7. Garnish with reserved vegetables and parsley if desired.
8. Serve with pita wedges.

There are many delicious ways to include legumes, nuts, and seeds at mealtime or as a snack. Look for these recipes in a cookbook and try a few:

- Black beans and rice
- Vegetarian chili (with tofu)
- Refried beans
- Mixed bean salad
- Lentil soup
- Falafel
- Hummus
- Peanut butter soup

Storing Legumes

Legumes can be bought canned, dried, fresh, or frozen. Each type should be stored differently.

- Keep uncooked dry beans in an airtight container in a cool place.
- Store canned beans and legumes in a cool dry place.
- Refrigerate cooked beans promptly. The same rules that apply to meat food safety and foodborne illness apply to legumes.
- Keep frozen legumes frozen until you are ready to use them.

Section 23.2

After You Read

Review Key Concepts

1. **Identify** one way you can lower the amount of cholesterol you consume when you eat eggs.
2. **Explain** how someone with a milk allergy can receive the nutrients milk products provide.
3. **Identify** at least five types of legumes and the nutrients legumes provide.

Practice Academic Skills

 **English Language Arts**

4. Write a dialogue between two teens. One teen is misinformed about milk. In the dialogue, disprove at least one misconception, and provide at least three facts about milk.

Social Studies

5. Many food companies pay for their products or logos to appear on popular television shows. This is called product placement. With the permission of a parent or teacher, watch a television show, and note the products you see in the show and during commercial breaks. Write a paragraph to describe what these product placements tell you about the audience.

Check Your Answers Go to connectED. mcgraw-hill.com to check your answers.

Environmental Scientist

What Does an Environmental Scientist Do?

Environmental scientists study environmental hazards that affect the Earth. They measure the air, food, water, and soil to determine how to clean and preserve the environment. They must also understand concepts like conservation and recycling to design and monitor waste disposal, preserve water supplies, and reclaim contaminated land and water.

Skills Environmental scientists need computer skills to use modeling programs, data analysis, and other systems used to monitor environmental systems. They must also know how to use Global Positioning Systems (GPS). Good interpersonal and communication skills are important because environmental scientists usually work in teams, and will need to write reports.

Education and Training A few entry-level positions require a bachelor's degree in an earth science, but environmental scientists usually need a master's degree. Most environmental scientists have a degree in life science, chemistry, geology, geophysics, or a related subject, and they apply their education to the environment.

Job Outlook Many environmental scientists hold faculty positions in colleges and universities. They are also employed in government positions, management, scientific and technical consulting services, architecture, and engineering.

Critical Thinking Look for information about careers in environmental science. You may find it on a university Web site, a brochure, or another resource. Is it appealing and informative? Explain your answer in a paragraph.

Career Cluster

Science, Technology, Engineering, and Mathematics

Environmental scientists work in the Science, Technology, Engineering, and Mathematics career cluster. Here are some of the other jobs in this cluster:

- Physicist
- Biologist
- Mechanical Engineer
- Statistician
- Electrical Engineer
- Hazardous Materials Technician
- Nuclear Technician
- Astronomer
- Mathematician
- Environmental Geologist
- Archeologist
- Laboratory Technician
- Agricultural Engineer
- Endocrinologist
- Mammalogist
- Systems Engineer
- Environmental Risk Analyst
- Anthropologist

Explore Further Research this career cluster. Choose a career in this cluster that appeals to you, and write a career profile.

Chapter 23   Review and Applications

CHAPTER SUMMARY

Section 23.1
Meat, Poultry, and Fish

Meat, poultry, and fish provide protein and many other important nutrients. Small amounts of fat and cholesterol are necessary for proper body functioning, but should be limited. Meat, poultry, and fish are perishable and should be handled and cooked carefully to avoid foodborne illness. There are safe ways and unsafe ways to defrost frozen meat, poultry, and fish. Moist-heat and dry-heat cooking methods can be used on a variety of cuts of meat, fish, and poultry, though dry-heat methods are better for protein foods with higher fat contents. Leftovers can last for a few days if refrigerated, or for a few months if frozen.

Section 23.2
Eggs, Legumes, Milk, and Milk Products

Eggs are excellent sources of protein and many other important vitamins and minerals, including B vitamins. Eggs are used in a variety of main dishes and baked goods. Milk and milk products contain protein and bone-building nutrients like calcium. Almost all milk products are highly-perishable and should be stored properly to prevent spoiling. People who are vegan or allergic to milk can use dairy substitutes such as soymilk to get many of the same nutrients. Legumes are an excellent source of fiber and protein. They can be used in vegetarian dishes in place of meat.

Vocabulary Review

1. Write your own definition for each content and academic vocabulary term.

Content Vocabulary
◇ marbling (p. 556)
◇ perishable (p. 557)
◇ salmonella (p. 563)
◇ scorch (p. 565)
◇ curdle (p. 565)
◇ legume (p. 566)

Academic Vocabulary
▪ accurate (p. 558)
▪ exposed (p. 560)
▪ distinct (p. 564)
▪ harbor (p. 566)

Review Key Concepts

2. Describe the nutritional benefits of meat, fish, and poultry.
3. Outline safe handling and preparation guidelines for meat, poultry, and fish.
4. Identify safe methods for handling and cooking eggs.
5. Describe methods for handling and cooking milk products.
6. Explain how to safely prepare and store legumes.

Critical Thinking

7. Conclude Based on what you know about the ideal preparation techniques for meat, poultry, fish, eggs, legumes, milk, and milk products, which requires the most amount of preparation time and effort? Which requires the least amount of time and effort? Explain your answers.
8. Design Plan a meal that uses two or more of the protein-rich foods mentioned in this chapter to maximize nutrition and minimize fat content.
9. Evaluate Consider the possible effects of not eating enough protein-rich foods.
10. Analyze Why is eating a variety of protein foods more healthful than eating only one type?
11. Critique "The best way to lose weight is to eat a lot of protein." Is this statement true? Explain why or why not.

ACTIVE LEARNING

12. Ethnic Menus Using ethnic cookbooks or other resources, find a menu for a traditional meal from another culture. This meal should contain at least one of the protein foods discussed in this chapter: meat, poultry, fish, eggs, legumes, milk, or a milk product. Create a visual representation, and outline how it fits within a healthful eating plan. Explain how the meal is prepared and any special tools a person might need to prepare it. How are protein foods represented in the meal?

How does this differ from your usual eating habits? Does it include any foods you rarely eat, or have never tried? What might explain the differences?

Family & Community Connections

13. Beef, Pork, Poultry, or Fish? What sources of animal protein do you think people most prefer: beef, pork, poultry, or fish? Using online or print resources, find out the number of pounds of beef, pork, poultry, and fish that were sold in the United States in the last year. Create a pie chart illustrating this information. Then, with the help of your parents or guardians, estimate how much beef, pork, poultry, and fish your family consumes in an average week. If your family practices vegetarianism, ask a friend or someone you know who includes meat in his or her eating plan to help you make estimates. Create a pie chart illustrating this information. How do the charts compare? Are the percentages of each protein similar or very different? Why do you think this is? Consider your culture and location. Share your findings with your class.

Real-World Skills and Applications

Leadership Skills

14. Keep Poultry Safe With your teacher's permission, break into small groups. Imagine that you all belong to a service club that helps support a homeless shelter. You decide to sponsor a chicken lasagna dinner for 100 people to raise funds. Identify food and safety issues for purchasing, storing, preparing, cooking, and serving a large chicken lasagna.

Financial Literacy

15. Pre-Cooked vs. Home-Cooked You can buy a roasted 3-pound chicken at the supermarket for $7.99. You can also buy a 3-pound uncooked chicken for $1.79 per pound, then roast it yourself. How much will you save by making it yourself?

Information Literacy

16. Milk Products Around the World With your teacher's permission, use the library's resources including the Internet to research milk and milk products in a culture other than yours. Learn about the animal source of the milk and how it is collected. Describe the common milk products of this culture and their use in the culture's meals and snacks. Present your findings to the class.

Academic Skills

English Language Arts

17. Research Agriculture Use the library or the Internet to research the journey that a specific food takes from where it is grown or raised to your table. Write two or three paragraphs describing this process, and the factors that influence food prices in the market.

Science

18. The Science of Cheese Cheese cannot release much heat in the form of steam, as foods with water do. Every food has a different heat capacity that determines how long it takes to reach a certain temperature.

Procedure Research recipes with cheese in cookbooks and online. How do they prevent the cheese from burning?

Analysis Draw conclusions about the methods these recipes use and write a one-page report on your findings.

Mathematics

19. Dry Beans Tien invited several of his good friends over for dinner on Sunday evening.

Because he does not know how many people will be coming, he is going to make bean soup, which can easily be doubled. Tien must figure out how many pounds of dry beans he needs to purchase to make the bean soup. One pound, or 16 ounces, of dry beans makes 12 servings. How many ounces of beans will Tien need to serve a group of three, four, or six people?

Math Concept Estimate It is important to check your work by considering how reasonable the answer is. You can use front-end estimation, or you can round and estimate a reasonable answer.

Starting Hint One pound of beans will make too much soup for a group of three, four, or even six people, so divide three, four, and six into 12 to find out how much of a pound is needed.

 For math help, go to the Math Appendix at the back of the book.

Standardized Test Practice

MULTIPLE CHOICE
Directions Read the paragraph. Then choose the correct answer.

Test-Taking Tip When answering multiple-choice questions, ask yourself if each option is true or false. This may help you find the best answer.

Food labels can be confusing. MSG (monosodium glutamate) makes people crave more food. MSG contains no healthful nutrients. However, the government allows food manufacturers to list MSG on labels as a spice.

20. Based on the above paragraph, which of the following statements is true?
   a) Unknown nutrients get into food.
   b) Knowledge of nutrition helps to understand food labels.
   c) All food labels hide the truth about ingredients.
   d) Reading labels is difficult.

Chapter 24

Eating Together

Section 24.1
Enjoying Family Meals

Section 24.2
Special Occasions

Chapter Objectives

Section 24.1

- **Explain** the importance of family mealtime.
- **Explain** how and why place settings are arranged in a certain pattern.
- **Identify** three different serving styles.
- **Outline** basic table manners.

Section 24.2

- **Describe** appropriate restaurant behavior.
- **Recall** how to safely serve a meal outdoors.

Asia Images Group/Getty Images

Write a Personal Narrative

Family Meals Write a short story about a special family meal you have had. Describe the reason for the meal. Was it someone's birthday? Describe the food, how the meal was served, and anything else that you remember about the event. Be descriptive and use details.

Writing Tips Use these tips to write a personal narrative:

1. Test your ideas by talking them through or by freewriting.
2. Ask yourself questions to fill out details of the narrative.
3. Construct a timeline or other graphic organizer as a visual map for your narrative.

▲ Explore the Photo

Sharing a meal with friends and family is a custom in every culture on earth. *At what common occasions might people meet for a meal?*

Section 24.1

Enjoying Family Meals

Before You Read

How Can You Improve? Before starting the section, think about the last exam you took on material you had to read. Make a list of ways to improve your reading strategy in order to succeed on your next exam.

Read to Learn

Key Concepts

- **Explain** the importance of family mealtime.
- **Explain** how and why place settings are arranged in a certain pattern.
- **Identify** three different serving styles.
- **Outline** basic table manners.

Main Idea

Meal service, table setting, and table manners are customs that make mealtime and entertaining enjoyable.

Content Vocabulary

◇ etiquette
◇ place setting
◇ tableware
◇ flatware

Academic Vocabulary

You will find these words in your reading and on your tests. Use the glossary to look up their definitions if necessary.

▢ reduce　　　　　　▢ encourage

Graphic Organizer

As you read, write down ways to demonstrate basic table manners. Use a graphic organizer like the one below to organize your information.

Basic Table Manners

When You Sit Down	When You Start Eating
1.	1.
2.	2.
3.	3.
4.	4.

 Graphic Organizer Go to connectED.mcgraw-hill.com to download this graphic organizer.

Mealtime Etiquette

Mealtime can come with its own special set of rules. How should you set a table? Where should you place your napkin during meals? When do you use all of the different utensils? Mealtime requires accepted rules of behavior called **etiquette**. It might seem overwhelming at first, but it can actually bring you and your family a sense of fun and togetherness. It can also prepare you socially for adult life.

Every family works out its own approach to handling meals. Sometimes meals have to be hurried because of conflicts in family schedules. Other times, family members can take more time to enjoy the food and each other's company. Some families welcome unexpected guests, perhaps friends who drop by, and do not mind a loud dinner table. Others prefer a quiet meal. Many families follow the same routine at mealtime, but change that routine when company is present.

Mealtime should provide families with a chance to relax and spend time together. During meals, families can listen to each others' news and enjoy each others' feedback. Mealtime communication is so important that many families turn off their television, tablet, and computer. They also do not answer the phone or text messages during meals. This focus on mealtime helps strengthen family relationships.

✓ **Reading Check**) **Explain** What are the advantages of eating as a family?

Setting the Table

Have you ever been confused about the arrangement of plates, glasses, and utensils on a restaurant table? If so, you are not alone in your confusion, but table settings are not as complicated as they first seem.

Except at picnics and buffets, most tables are set with individual place settings. A **place setting** is the arrangement of tableware and flatware for each person. **Tableware** includes dishes, glasses, and flatware. **Flatware** includes eating utensils, such as spoons, knives, and forks.

As You Read

Connect Think about how food is served in different situations.

Vocabulary

You can find definitions in the glossary at the back of this book.

Family Meals

Meals are one time when families with hectic schedules can meet to reconnect with each other. *How can teens help make mealtimes enjoyable?*

The tableware at each person's place has a logical organization. See **Figure 24.1** on page 579. Each place setting usually has at least one plate, glass, fork, knife, spoon, and napkin. Depending on what food is being served, other tableware may be used, such as a salad plate, a cup and saucer, a salad fork, or a soup spoon. Flatware is positioned by order of use, from the outside in. A salad fork is placed farther from the plate than a dinner fork because the salad is usually eaten before the main meal. Sometimes the dessert fork and spoon are placed above the plate.

Table Coverings

Think about attractive tables you have seen in restaurants, store displays, or events you may have attended, such as weddings. Besides the place setting, what makes the dining area attractive? One way to make an ordinary table more eye-catching is to use a table covering. When setting a table, you can choose to use a tablecloth or placemats or both. You may also choose a table runner, which goes down the center of the table. Tablecloths are sold in sizes to fit different table dimensions and shapes, such as oval, rectangular, and round.

Added Touches

At times you may want to use your creativity and add something special to the dinner table to make it more attractive. If your family has a flower garden, you could cut a few flowers to make an arrangement and place it in a vase at the center of the table. Fruits and vegetables also make nice centerpieces. Another edible centerpiece is a basket holding a variety of breads and breadsticks.

Candles add elegance to a dinner table. You can use large candlesticks or put small floating candles in a shallow bowl of water. Remember to blow out the candles when you leave the table, and remove any candle wax that has dripped onto the table.

✓ **Reading Check** **Identify** What are the six components of the average place setting?

Serving Style

Meals are the time when people all around the world share food and company with friends, family, and colleagues. There are many customs for serving and eating a meal. Every region in the world has a different set of rules about how food should be served and what is considered polite.

Math You Can Use

Choose the Right Table

You have been asked to shop for a dining room table for your family that is big enough to fit eight people comfortably. Each person should have at least 20 inches of space for his or her own place setting. You have found three tables with these dimensions: 48″ × 36″, 78″ × 40″, and 60″ × 36″. Which table would be the best choice?

Math Concept **Perimeter** The perimeter of rectangles can be found by adding the lengths of each side.

Starting Hint Solving problems can be made simpler by using strategies such as drawing a picture or diagram. Sketch a diagram to help you see how people would sit around each table.

For math help, go to the math appendix at the back of the book.

Figure 24.1 Set the Table

What Goes Where? Place settings are arranged to be convenient. *If you do not eat soup during a meal, do you need to set a soup spoon?*

These steps will help you set an attractive table.

STEP 1 Place the fork to be used first farthest from the plate.

STEP 2 Place the dinner knife so that the blade faces the plate.

STEP 3 Place spoons to the right of the knife. If soup is the first course, the soup spoon should be placed at the far right.

STEP 4 Line up the bottom of the flatware with the lower edge of the plate.

STEP 5 Only put out the tableware you need to eat a meal.

STEP 6 Make sure your placemats and tablecloths are clean and free of wrinkles.

Meals in the United States are usually served in one of three ways:

- **Family Service** In this style of eating, food is placed in serving dishes on the table. People serve their own food, and pass serving dishes to one another. It is polite to pass food to your right.
- **Plate Service** In this style of serving food, every person is given a plate with food already served to them. Food is placed on a plate, then brought to each individual. Formal meals with more than one course are often served this way.
- **Buffet Service** In this popular style of serving, serving dishes are arranged on a table or counter. People line up and serve themselves. Then they carry their own food to their place. Buffet service is common for large gatherings where plate service and family service would be impractical.

✓ **Reading Check** **Identify** What purpose does each type of serving style serve?

Ingram Publishing/SuperStock

Caitlin, Age 15

Introducing my friends to my family can be uncomfortable. My friend, Chelsea, came over to my house for my birthday, and I was worried my family would say something embarrassing. And they did. My brothers talked about their model jets. My sister insisted on telling Chelsea about every person in my sister's fourth-grade class. When she left, I apologized for my siblings.

Chelsea told me not to worry, because she had felt welcome and accepted by my family. I realized that there was a reason my siblings acted the way they did. It is nice that they wanted to include my friend in the family.

Critical Thinking
Caitlin suggests that one way to deal with embarrassing situations is to look for the reasons people act the way they do. Do you agree? Why or why not?

Basic Table Manners

There is an etiquette that should be followed at each meal. These basic gestures of hospitality and politeness allow the host and his or her guests to enjoy the meal. Remember these rules as you eat and you will reduce, or lessen, the chance of something awkward ruining everyone's enjoyment. If awkward or embarrassing moments do happen, apologize for the disturbance, and move on. Accidents can happen to anyone, so try not to dwell on them.

What to Do Once Seated

Knowing basic mealtime etiquette, or table manners, will give you confidence in different social situations and help you make a positive impression on others. Although it seems like a lot to remember, once you start to follow these tips they will become automatic.

- **Wait before eating.** If you have been invited to eat at someone's house, do not begin eating until everyone has been served. You may also wait for your host to encourage, or invite, you to start. At a buffet, everyone does not have to be seated for you to begin eating, but wait until a few people are seated.
- **Ask for food to be passed to you.** If an item is not placed in front of you, ask for the item to be passed to you. Do not reach across the table.
- **Put your napkin in the correct place.** Your napkin should lie across your lap while you are eating. At the end of the meal, place it to the left of the plate. Do not blow or wipe your nose with a napkin. If you need to do this, excuse yourself from the table and use tissues in the restroom.

Community Connections

Serving Your Community

Food pantries and homeless shelters provide some of the most basic necessities for people unable to provide for themselves. These people deserve your respect and compassion. Research a shelter or pantry in your area and find a way to help.

Proper Use of Flatware

- **Use the correct flatware.** If you are not sure which piece of flatware to use, observe what the person at the head of the table uses.
- **Use fingers for finger foods only.** Eat with a fork unless you are eating actual finger foods, such as corn on the cob, sandwiches, or raw carrot and celery sticks. Never use your fingers to push food onto your fork. Instead, use your knife to place food on your fork or spoon.
- **Keep your flatware in the right place.** During a meal, do not set your fork, knife, or spoon in such a way that part of it is on the table and the other part is on the plate. Instead, place it across the edge of your plate. After eating, put your knife and fork across the center of your plate.
- **Cut food correctly.** Cut one small bite of food at a time and eat it. When eating a dinner roll, break off and butter one piece at a time.

Courteous Dining

- **Eat slowly.** Eating quickly is not only considered bad table manners, but it is also bad for digestion. Avoid stuffing your mouth with food. It looks unpleasant and can cause you to choke.
- **Eat quietly.** Always chew with your mouth closed, and refrain from making noises while you eat. Finish eating your mouthful of food before talking.
- **Do not clean your teeth at the table.** Do not pick anything out of your teeth while seated at the dining table. If something seems caught in your teeth, excuse yourself and go to the restroom to deal with the problem. This also applies to combing your hair!
- **Calmly correct mistakes.** Do not let a mistake ruin your dinner. If you do something incorrectly, calmly correct the behavior. More than likely, no one will have noticed.
- **Always offer to help.** As a guest, it is appropriate for you to ask if you can help serve or clean up. The hostess or host will let you know what to do.
- **Show appreciation.** If invited to someone's home for a meal, it is thoughtful to bring a small gift. If you do not like what is being served, take a small portion anyway. Whether you are a guest at someone's home or at a restaurant, always thank the host or hostess.

SUCCEED IN SCHOOL

Reading Assignments

It is important to finish any reading before you come to class. That way, you will understand what your teacher is talking about and can take notes only on the most important points.

Prevent Accidents

Using the correct flatware can help prevent unnecessary spills. *What utensil would you use for the first course of a meal if it is soup?*

Stockbyte/Getty Images

Light and Healthy Recipe

Potato-Tomato Soup in a Bread Bowl

Yield
4–6 servings

Nutrition Analysis
Per serving: 530 calories, 11 g total fat, 4.5 g saturated fat, 0 g trans fat, 45 mg cholesterol, 1,070 mg sodium, 85 g total carbohydrate, 7 g dietary fiber, 11 g total sugars, 26 g protein

Ingredients

2 carrots, diced
1 yellow onion, thinly sliced
2 ribs celery, diced
2 Tbsp. butter
1 can (16 oz.) tomato sauce
2 cans (10 oz. ea.) low-sodium chicken or beef broth
4 cups water
4 large russet potatoes, peeled and quartered
½ tsp. salt
¼ tsp. pepper
½ lb. lean beef or chicken, pre-cooked and diced, optional
½ cup milk
2 Tbsp. fine gravy flour (such as Wondra®)
⅓ cup shredded mozzarella cheese
Large rolls or small round loaf of bread

Directions

1. Cut vegetables as indicated in ingredient list.
2. Place vegetables in a 3- or 4-quart pot with butter. Sauté vegetables until onions are caramelized.
3. Add tomato sauce, broth and water. On a two-burner hot plate or stove top, bring liquids just to boiling point.
4. Add potatoes, salt and pepper. Reduce heat and simmer about 30 minutes until potatoes are fork tender. Remove from heat.
5. With a fork or potato masher, mash most of the potatoes, leaving some chunks of potato in the soup.
6. Add meat, if using in recipe.
7. Return to low heat and add milk. Simmer on low heat until meat is thoroughly heated, about 5 minutes.
8. Slowly sprinkle in fine gravy flour to thicken broth to desired consistency. If necessary, add salt and/or pepper to taste.
9. While soup is cooking, prepare bread bowls by slicing off the top of each roll or the loaf of bread. Remove inside bread, leaving a ½-inch-thick wall. Place on serving plate.
10. Ladle soup directly into each bread bowl.
11. Garnish with shredded cheese. Divide equally.
12. Serve immediately.

Tetra Images/Getty Images

Clearing the Table

Think about how family meals end at your home. In many families, each person is responsible for clearing his or her own place setting from the table. However, if you are serving guests in your home, it is impolite to expect them to remove their own dishes from the table. Clearing the table is part of entertaining guests, and is the host's responsibility. Here are some suggestions:

- Stand to the side of someone who is seated as you clear the tableware from each setting.
- Clear one or two plates at a time between courses, placing the flatware across each plate.
- Scrape the plates when you reach the kitchen.
- Stack the scraped plates quietly in or near the sink or dishwasher.
- Clear all plates from the table before serving dessert.
- Wait until your guests have gone home before washing the dishes or loading them into the dishwasher.

Section 24.1

After You Read

Review Key Concepts

1. **Describe** mealtime etiquette and why it is important.
2. **Describe** how you can make your table look appealing for guests.
3. **List** serving styles from least formal to most formal.
4. **Explain** how to clear a table quietly and efficiently.

Check Your Answers Go to connectED. mcgraw-hill.com to check your answers.

Practice Academic Skills

English Language Arts

5. Pick a recipe that you enjoy. Create two workplans to prepare the recipe: one by yourself, and the other with two other people using teamwork. Make the recipe using both plans. Which plan was more efficient? Which plan was more enjoyable? Explain your answers in a brief essay.

Social Studies

6. Conduct research to learn about the way a culture other than your own uses utensils for serving, eating, and drinking. Look for a contemporary or historical culture that uses a utensil other than a fork, knife, or spoon. How is this utensil used? What rules of etiquette are users expected to follow? Is the utensil used for anything other than eating or serving food and beverages? How, if at all, is it decorated? Write a short essay to describe how and why the culture you selected uses its utensils.

Special Occasions

Before You Read

Understanding It is normal to have questions when you read. Write down questions while reading. Many of them will be answered as you continue. If they are not, you will have a list ready for your teacher when you finish.

Read to Learn

Key Concepts
- **Describe** appropriate restaurant behavior.
- **Recall** how to safely serve a meal outdoors.

Main Idea
Eating in restaurants and in the outdoors present unique etiquette challenges.

Content Vocabulary
◇ course
◇ appetizer
◇ entrée
◇ à la carte

Academic Vocabulary
You will find these words in your reading and on your tests. Use the glossary to find their definitions if necessary.
- requirements
- norm

Graphic Organizer
As you read, list the places where you can use proper etiquette. Use a graphic organizer like the one below to organize your information.

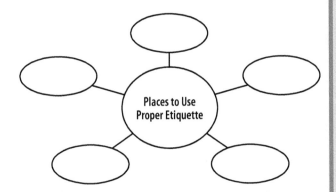

 Graphic Organizer Go to connectED.mcgraw-hill.com to download this graphic organizer.

Dining Out

When you think about dining out, what pictures flash through your mind? Do you see a fast-food restaurant or a restaurant at which food is served to you? At fast-food restaurants, you order your food at the counter or drive-through window. At many casual restaurants, you wait for a table to become available. Someone may seat you or you may seat yourself, and a server takes your order after you are seated at the table.

At more formal restaurants, you may need to reserve a table. In this case, you must phone the restaurant ahead of time and make a reservation. You will be asked what time you plan to dine and how many people will be in your group, or party. Many fine-dining restaurants have dress requirements, or rules. If you are not sure what the restaurant requires, ask when you make the reservation.

Once you make a reservation, the restaurant depends on you to arrive on time. If you cannot get there on time, call. You can either cancel the reservation or reserve a table for a later time.

Ordering from the Menu

Casual and formal restaurants have menus categorized by type of food. A **course** is a part of a meal. For example, the menu might include appetizers, soups, salads, entrées, desserts, and beverages. An **appetizer** is an optional first course, and generally a small portion. The **entrée** is the main course, and a larger portion than the appetizer.

Some menus list and price food separately, or **à la carte**, which means each item has an individual, or separate, price. Other menus list a complete meal for one certain price.

As You Read

Connect Think about behavior that you have seen in a restaurant that you recognize as inappropriate.

**Vocabulary**

You can find definitions in the glossary at the back of this book.

Restaurant Etiquette

When greeted by a restaurant employee, you can request a preference for a table location. *What is the most polite way to get the attention of your server?*

Ethical Behavior Jenna and her friends were at a restaurant for dinner. They were served promptly, and the server visited the table a few times. However, some of the food had to be sent back. It took 20 minutes to replace it, so some of the group decided not to leave a tip. Jenna did not think this was fair.

You make the call

Should Jenna tell her friends that the food problem was not the server's fault? Or should she go along and not leave a tip?

Restaurant Behavior

Have you ever been seated next to a loud, disruptive group of people at a restaurant? You probably know how annoying that kind of behavior can be to others. Most people go out to eat to enjoy their meal and each others' company, not to be around rude people.

To keep from being a diner no one wants to sit next to, avoid talking loudly with others at your table. If you see someone you know at another table, do not shout across the restaurant to get their attention. Quietly wave, and if you must talk to the person, excuse yourself and walk over to the table. Other diners do not want to hear your conversation, so keep your voice low. If you need something during the meal, go to the counter where you ordered your food or ask your server when he or she comes to your table. If you want to get a server's attention, catch the server's eye or say, "Excuse me" in an ordinary voice as the server passes your table. If there is something wrong with your meal, politely tell the server. Thank him or her, especially when the problem is corrected and if you made any special requests.

Put your cell phone on silent so if it rings, it will not disturb other diners. Put tablets and phones away so you can give your server and those at your table your full attention.

HOW TO . . . Plan a Celebration

From the everyday to the once-in-a-lifetime, some events call for celebrating. Any celebration, even an informal gathering, can benefit from some preplanning. Follow these guidelines to make your next event a memorable one.

Extend Invitations Send written invitations for casual events at least two weeks in advance. Allow for four weeks for a major event. If you want to save on printing costs, and the occasion is not too formal, electronic invites are acceptable. Include the date, time, address, and reason for the occasion. Add "RSVP," meaning "response if you please." Guests should tell you whether they can attend in a reply using a phone number or e-mail address you have included on the invitation.

Set the Menu Foods should fit the occasion. An elaborate meal might be right for a holiday. New neighbors may feel more comfortable sharing favorite family recipes. A selection of snacks or pizza would probably be better at a teen party. Learn beforehand whether any guests have a food allergy or follow a restricted diet.

Marko Lazarevic/Getty Images

Paying the Bill

Unlike counter-service restaurants, which require you to pay before you eat, sit-down restaurants bill you after you eat. Before paying, check the bill to be sure it is accurate. You may notice a sales tax, which some states require restaurants to add to customer bills. If a server brought food to your table, you should leave the server a tip. Tip amounts are generally 15 to 20 percent of the bill before tax. No matter what you thought of the food, if the service was good, leave a tip. If something went wrong, and therefore an item is deducted from your bill, it is still appropriate to tip on the original amount.

If your check says to pay the cashier, leave a tip on the table and pay the cashier on the way out. Sometimes the server takes your money and pays the cashier for you. If you are paying by credit card, write the tip and the total on the charge receipt.

When dining out with friends, agree on who will pay before you go to the restaurant. If you are invited out and are not sure about who is paying, bring enough money to cover your own bill, just in case.

✓ **Reading Check** **List** What behavior guidelines should you follow when dining out?

Consider Space Needs Space can be a limitation but also an asset if it is creatively used. If you have little space but a big crowd, think in terms of cozy, rather than cramped. Serve simple finger foods on unbreakable plates, and encourage guests to mingle on the porch or patio, in the backyard, or on the balcony.

Choose Decorations Decorations are fun for creating a theme. These are not essential, but they do add a festive touch. Look for things you can borrow or buy at little cost. Create multi-leveled flower vases with jars left over from jam, pickles, olives, or other foods. Take off the labels and clean the jars before filling them with water.

Plan Your Time You may need to be creative to fit tasks into your schedule. You can prepare some dishes in advance, or choose convenience foods to save time. You can also turn the preparation of food into a party activity. If your friends enjoy making their own pizzas, the food can double as entertainment, saving you time and effort.

(l)©Floresco Productions/age fotostock; (r)Design Pics Inc./Alamy

Grilling Fire Hazards

A person who follows the rules of safety can avoid accidents, including burns and fires that result from unsafe outdoor cooking. Outdoor picnic and camping areas post rules about fire hazards and using grills, fire pits, and camp stoves to cook. These rules are created to protect you and the environment.

Write About It

Create a poster that advertises fire safety rules, the reasons they exist, and what can happen if they are not followed. Illustrate your poster to help relate your message.

Serve Meals Outdoors

Eating outdoors offers a change of pace from the norm, or usual patterns, of eating. There are unique challenges and rules that apply to events such as picnics and barbeques. Eating a meal outside often requires preparation in advance. When you take a meal on the road, to a park, to the beach, or other places, you need to be aware of safety.

Picnics

Picnics are a fun way to eat outdoors. Whether you are on a road trip and find a place to eat, or are enjoying the neighborhood park, there are a few things you should remember to keep your experience as enjoyable as possible:

- **Use an insulated cooler.** A cooler and frozen packs keep your food safe as you transport perishable foods.
- **Take only what you need.** Take only the amount of food you think you will need. Leftovers may not keep.
- **Keep hot foods hot.** Hot foods should only be brought if you think you will eat them within two hours.
- **Separate raw foods.** If you are planning to cook your meat when you reach your picnic site, pack raw meat separately from other foods to prevent contaminating other picnic foods.
- **Bring a meat thermometer.** Grilling is fun but less controllable than cooking on a stove top or in an oven. Take a meat thermometer to make sure foods are cooked thoroughly.

Section 24.2

After You Read

Review Key Concepts

1. **Recall** how much you should tip your server when dining out.
2. **Identify** the five things you need to remember when you plan to eat outdoors.

Practice Academic Skills

English Language Arts

3. Imagine you are organizing a get-together for a group of friends that includes a meal outside of your home. What would you do? Where would you go? Write a paragraph explaining your plan and how you would prepare for the outing. Include information from this chapter in your plan.

Social Studies

4. Choose a country from another part of the world that interests you. Then use online and other resources to find out about the etiquette customs in that country. Compare your own culture to the one that you research. Present your findings in an oral presentation.

Check Your Answers Go to connectED.mcgraw-hill.com to check your answers.

CHAPTER SUMMARY

Section 24.1
Enjoying Family Meals

Enjoying family meals requires respect for the people around you. Families use mealtime to strengthen their relationships, and to share news about their lives. When setting a table, place settings are arranged in a logical order for convenience. People observe generally accepted rules of behavior when eating to show consideration to others.

Section 24.2
Special Occasions

When you know how to behave when dining out, you can increase your level of enjoyment, as well as the enjoyment of those around you. Consider your companions, the servers, and other diners. Pay your bill and leave an appropriate tip. Follow the rules of etiquette for restaurants and outdoor dining to be sure that everyone remains safe and comfortable.

Vocabulary Review

1. Create a fill-in-the-blank sentence for each of these vocabulary terms. The sentence should contain enough information to help determine the missing word.

Content Vocabulary
- etiquette (p. 577)
- place setting (p. 577)
- tableware (p. 577)
- flatware (p. 577)
- course (p. 585)
- appetizer (p. 585)
- entrée (p. 585)
- à la carte (p. 585)

Academic Vocabulary
- reduce (p. 580)
- encourage (p. 580)
- requirements (p. 585)
- norm (p. 588)

Review Key Concepts

2. **Explain** the importance of family mealtime.
3. **Explain** how and why place settings are arranged in a certain pattern.
4. **Identify** three different serving styles.
5. **Outline** basic table manners.
6. **Describe** appropriate restaurant behavior.
7. **Recall** how to safely serve a meal outdoors.

Critical Thinking

8. **Analyze** How would you politely correct a friend's rude behavior toward a restaurant server?
9. **Create** Plan for a meal held outdoors. What will you bring? How will you keep the food safe to eat?
10. **Analyze** What would you do if you planned a party for 10 people, but two of those people brought unexpected guests? Imagine that you have 10 potatoes, five steaks that you had planned to cut in half, just enough ingredients for 10 appetizer salads, and a cake that serves 8-10 people. You do not have time to shop for the two additional guests. What are your options?
11. **Compare** Explain your idea of formal and casual dining. How can you transform a casual meal to a more formal meal?

ACTIVE LEARNING

Family & Community Connections

12. Choosing Tableware Imagine that you work at a department store where couples about to be married get to choose their tableware. Your job is to help couples make appropriate selections. Visit a store that sells a variety of tableware, or look through catalogs or magazines that sell tableware. Look for different types, designs, costs, and materials. Help your imaginary couple choose flatware, dishes, glasses, and linens for casual home dining and for formal meals. What questions would you ask them? What suggestions would you make? Write a short essay to describe and explain what items you would likely recommend to a newly married couple. Include pictures if possible.

13. Dinner Guests A vegetarian is a person who chooses not to include meat in his or her eating plan. Some vegetarians eat some animal products, such as eggs, cheese, and milk. Others, called vegans, eat foods that come exclusively from plant sources. Some people choose vegetarianism for health reasons, and others are vegetarians because it is part of their culture. Using this information, plan a dinner party to which you will invite a group that includes vegetarians, vegans, and non-vegetarians. To gather information about appropriate menu items, interview at least one vegetarian or vegan, and one or two people who include meat and animal products in their meals. Find out what foods, desserts, and beverages they would enjoy at a party. Do they have any preferred foods or drinks in common? Compile your information from both sources, and then create a menu for your party that would satisfy the tastes of all of your guests.

Real-World Skills and Applications

Leadership Skills

14. Lead by Example A leader models good behavior for others. Write an essay in which you explain how you can lead by example when dining with others. This may include eating with family at home, at someone else's house, or in a restaurant. It may also include outdoor dining. Explain a situation that may realistically arise, and how to sensitively and politely lead others to better behavior through your good example.

Financial Literacy

15. Menu Costs Use a calculator to plan a nourishing dinner for your family with three different budget levels. Plan each menu. Determine the cost for each ingredient. Figure the cost of the total menu, then figure the cost per person.

Technology Skills

16. Electronic Shopping List Use a spreadsheet to create a checklist of staples and specialty items for your family's grocery shopping. List everything that is bought often. Categorize the list by their store location. Use the list while shopping. Report any changes you make and why.

Asia Images Group/Getty Images

Academic Skills

English Language Arts

17. Salad as a Meal Salads can be much more than just lettuce and dressing. Many countries, including the United States, have salads listed on menus as main courses. Choose three international salads. Using a large index card for each salad, name the country of origin, and create a glossary that includes definitions and pronunciations of the ingredients. Briefly describe how each salad is prepared, and include a picture if possible.

Social Studies

18. Shopping Frequency In many parts of the world, kitchens may have small refrigerators. In other places, electricity is not readily available. Research how these factors might affect food shopping habits. Present your results in a report to your class.

Mathematics

19. Delivery Tipping How often do you or your family order pizza to be delivered to your home? How much money do you think you should give the delivery person as a tip? Servers and deliverers count on tips to add to their wages. If you order a pizza delivered to your home, figure a reasonable tip by estimating 15% of the cost of pizza before any delivery fee. What would you tip a person who delivers a pizza that costs $15.99, including a $1.00 delivery fee?

Math Concept **Percent** A percent (%) is a ratio that compares a number to 100. Convert a fraction to a decimal by dividing the numerator by the denominator.

Starting Hint First find how much the pizza costs before the delivery fee. Then, find 15% of the pizza's cost for a tip. Round up to the nearest tenth.

 For math help, go to the Math Appendix at the back of the book.

Standardized Test Practice

TIMED WRITING
Directions Read the prompt. Then write a one-page essay using details and examples to illustrate your points.

Test-Taking Tip Plan out your essay before you begin writing. Jot down the main points or details you want to focus on in the margins of your test. Refer to these points frequently as you write. This will help you remain focused.

Tim thinks he has perfect manners. He chews with his mouth closed and he speaks politely to other people at the table. When he is at a restaurant, he demands things from the server and flags him down by snapping his fingers.

20. Do you agree that he has perfect manners? Explain your answer.

Plan a Meal

In this project you will plan a meal for at least six people and interview someone who plans meals regularly or as a profession. You will then present your plan to the class in a presentation.

 My Journal

If you completed the journal entry from page 510, refer to it to see if your thoughts have changed after reading the unit.

Project Assignment

In this project you will:

- Design a meal that you would like to prepare for six people.
- Create a plan for shopping, preparing, and serving the meal.
- Interview an adult in your community and discuss your plan.
- Make a presentation to your class to discuss your meal plan.

The Skills Behind the Project

Life Skills

Key personal and relationship skills you will use in this project include:

- Taking initiative.
- Writing creatively.
- Understanding directions.

STEP 1 Plan Your Meal

Plan a meal for six people. Decide on a theme for the meal and research dishes that you think would complement each other. Find recipes for each dish you will serve. Include an appetizer, a salad, a main course, and a dessert. Collect your research in a portfolio to keep everything organized. Then write a descriptive essay about your meal that explains:

- The theme of the meal.
- The dishes you would like to prepare.
- The ingredients needed.
- The tools and equipment needed to prepare the meal.
- The time involved in preparing the meal.

Writing Skills

- Use imaginative language.
- Make interesting comparisons.
- Describe images that appeal to the senses.

STEP 2 Write Interview Questions

Identify an adult in your community who plans and prepares meals professionally. This person may be a chef, banquet manager, party planner, restaurant manager, or another professional familiar with planning meals. Write questions you would like to ask this person about meal planning. Here are some examples:

Life Skills Project Checklist

Plan	☑ Design a meal that you would like to prepare for six people.
	☑ Write a descriptive essay about your meal plan.
	☑ Create a plan for shopping, preparing, and serving the meal.
	☑ Interview an adult in your community and discuss your plan.
	☑ Create a presentation to describe your meal and your plan for preparing it.
Present	☑ Make a presentation to your class.
	☑ Invite the students in your class to ask you any questions they may have. Answer these questions.
	☑ When students ask you questions, demonstrate in your answers that you respect their perspectives.
	☑ Turn in your descriptive essay, your interview questions and answers, and your presentation to your teacher.
Academic Skills	☑ Communicate effectively.
	☑ Speak clearly and concisely.

- What are the most important things to remember when planning a meal?
- What is the hardest thing about planning a meal?
- What advice would you give me about planning the meal I designed?

STEP 3 Connect to Your Community

Arrange to interview an adult in your community who plans and prepares meals professionally. Bring the meal plan you designed and share it with him or her. Bring the list of questions you wrote in Step 2 and take notes of the answers. After your interview, transcribe your notes in full sentences and write a paragraph summarizing your experience.

Interpersonal Skills
- Be polite and confident when you contact the adult.
- Follow directions.
- Respond appropriately to information, advice, and humor.

STEP 4 Create and Present Your Meal Plan

Use the Life Skills Project Checklist to create your presentation and share what you have learned with your classmates.

STEP 5 Evaluate Your Life Skills and Academic Skills

Your project will be evaluated based on:
- Content and organization of your information.
- Speaking skills.
- Mechanics—presentation and neatness.
- Descriptive language.

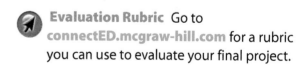

Evaluation Rubric Go to **connectED.mcgraw-hill.com** for a rubric you can use to evaluate your final project.

UNIT 9

Clothing

Chapter 25 Clothing that Suits You

Chapter 26 Fabric Selection and Care

Chapter 27 Preparing to Sew

Chapter 28 Sewing Skills

Unit Life Skills Project Preview

Your Personal Style

In this unit you will learn about how to choose and care for clothing. In your life skills project you will analyze personal styles and reflect on your own personal style.

 My Journal

Personal Style Write a journal entry about one of these topics. This will help you prepare for the project at the end of this unit.

- Describe the outfit that makes you feel the most confident and explain why.
- List the colors that you believe are flattering to you and explain why.
- Imagine you could create the perfect outfit for a special occasion (graduation, school dance, sports event) and describe what it would look like.

Chapter 25

Clothing that Suits You

Section 25.1
Your Clothing Style

Section 25.2
Your Working Wardrobe

Chapter Objectives

Section 25.1

- **Explain** the benefits of well-chosen clothing.
- **List** the five elements of clothing design.
- **Identify** the five principles of clothing design.
- **Understand** how to use the elements and principles of design to express your individuality.

Section 25.2

- **Outline** the process of wardrobe assessment.
- **Summarize** clothes-shopping strategies.

Pixland/Corbis

Writing Activity

Objective Description

Personal Style Observing someone's personal style, whether it is the way they enter a room or where they sit in a movie theater, tells you a lot about that person. It also helps to make your writing more accurate and entertaining.

Observe someone with a distinct style of dressing. Write a detailed, descriptive paragraph about that person and their clothes. Being objective means that you do not criticize or praise. Simply describe what you see.

Writing Tips Use these tips to write your objective description:

1. Start with a sentence that gives an overall description of what you see.
2. Give details that help paint a picture in your reader's mind.
3. Sum up your description with a conclusion that supports your opening sentence.

Explore the Photo

The way you feel about yourself is often reflected in the clothes you choose. *How do you think clothes can affect how you feel?*

Your Clothing Style

Reading Guide

Before You Read

Preview Read the Key Concepts, photo captions, and headings in this section. Write one or two sentences predicting what you think the section will be about.

Read to Learn

Key Concepts

- **Explain** the benefits of well-chosen clothing.
- **List** the five elements of clothing design.
- **Identify** the five principles of clothing design.
- **Understand** how to use the elements and principles of design to express your individuality.

Main Idea

Clothing offers a wide variety of ways to express yourself, and can have an influence on how others view you as a person.

Content Vocabulary

◇ fashion
◇ illusion
◇ element of design
◇ silhouette
◇ principle of design

Academic Vocabulary

You will find these words in your reading and on your tests. Use the glossary to look up their definitions if necessary.

☐ convey
☐ influence

Graphic Organizer

As you read, list three qualities of color and describe the effects of each. Use a graphic organizer like the one shown to organize your information.

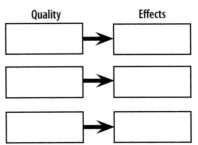

 Graphic Organizer Go to **connectED.mcgraw-hill.com** to download this graphic organizer.

How Clothing Speaks for You

What is the first thing people notice about you? Is it your personality, your sense of humor, your intelligence? Yes, these are important traits, but chances are what people notice first is your clothing. Clothes can convey, or communicate, many messages. People with positive self-esteem display a sense of pride in their appearance. For some teens, wearing designer labels and trendy fashions is important. A **fashion** is a style of something that is currently popular. Labels and fashions may influence, or have an effect on, people's clothing choices and how they care for their clothing.

To make sure your clothing is suited to you and communicates who you are, you need to consider several factors. These include your needs, wants, and budget, as well as the ways in which you want others to perceive you. Good planning and resource management can help you develop a wardrobe, or collection of clothes, that makes you feel good about the way you look.

Every person is different, with a specific body shape, a different texture and color of hair, and a unique skin complexion. Your clothing can help you enhance and personalize your individual style. Before you shop for or make your own clothes, consider how you can make garments work to improve your appearance.

One way to enhance how you look in your clothing is to create an illusion. An **illusion** is something that can influence or lead the eye to see something that does not exist. A short person who wears vertical stripes creates the illusion of height. On the other hand, a tall person can appear shorter by wearing horizontal stripes. Black and other dark colors can create an illusion of a sleek appearance. You can use illusion to draw attention to your best features. You create illusions by using the elements and principles of design.

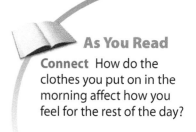

As You Read

Connect How do the clothes you put on in the morning affect how you feel for the rest of the day?

◇ Vocabulary

You can find definitions in the glossary at the back of this book.

JUPITERIMAGES/Creatas/Alamy

✓ Reading Check

Explain How can you use illusion in clothing to change your look?

➤ Express Yourself

Clothes provide a way for people to show individuality through color, pattern, and style choices. *What do you include in your wardrobe to show off your unique style?*

(tl) Blend Images/Alamy; (tr) Blend Images/Alamy

> **Optical Illusion**

Even slight changes to clothing can change your appearance. *What do you notice about these teens' outfits and appearance?*

Elements of Design

Line, shape, space, texture, and color are each an **element of design**. Understanding how these elements work will help you choose styles that look good on you. There are even some computer programs that can show you how various garments will look on you without having to try them on.

- **Line** Line guides your eye movement up, down, and across an area. Lines can be straight or curved and can flow vertically, horizontally, or diagonally.
- **Shape** Sometimes called a **silhouette**, shape is the form created when lines are combined. Types of shapes include natural (following the body's line), tubular (forming a rectangular shape with no waistline), bell (combining diagonal and horizontal lines to create a bell outline), and full (combining horizontal and curved lines).
- **Space** The area inside the silhouette is the space. Space can be divided by accessories, decorative trim, and seams.
- **Texture** Texture is the surface characteristic that you see or feel in a fabric. Textures can be soft or crisp, bulky or smooth, and dull or shiny.
- **Color** Color is one of the most important design elements. Your best colors are the ones that flatter the color of your hair, skin, and eyes.

Using Color

Of all design elements, color is the one most people notice first. Many people choose their clothes based on their favorite color, whether the color flatters them or not. If you understand color and know how to use it, you can choose clothing in colors that suit you. See **Figure 25.1** on page 602.

The Effects of Color

Sharon wears one-color outfits because they make her look taller. Jake wears darker colors for a slimming effect. You, too, can create illusions with color. If you can control the following qualities, you can enhance your appearance.

- **Value** is the lightness or darkness of a color. For example, the lightest value of red is pink, and its darkest value is maroon. Light values are called tints and make things look larger. Dark values are called shades and make things look smaller.
- **Intensity** describes how bright or dull a color appears. A color at full intensity, such as bright red, tends to stand out. Colors with lower intensity, such as dusty rose, are less obvious. In general, low-intensity colors are used for larger pieces, such as jackets. Bright colors are better for smaller pieces, such as tops.
- **Warm and cool** describe how colors can make you feel. Yellow, orange, and red are associated with warmth. Warm colors make areas appear larger and closer to you. Green, violet, and blue may remind you of cool water, trees, and sky. Cool colors tend to make areas look smaller and farther away.

✓ **Reading Check**) **Explain** How do warm and cool colors affect a person's appearance?

How I See It

SHOPPING BUDDIES

Kim, 15

I am my sister's favorite shopping buddy. Mindy is older than I am, but she needs extra help when it comes to shopping because she has multiple sclerosis (MS). Mindy is able to walk, but she uses a cane to keep her balance. MS affects Mindy's hands the most. They shake a lot, so it's hard for her to do certain simple things, like get dressed.

I always go with Mindy to help her buy new clothes. I have learned by heart which types of clothing are best for her disability. I help her look for pants that aren't too long and baggy so they won't get tangled in her cane. Clothing fasteners can be a problem, so we look for things with very few fasteners. If there are buttons, zippers, hooks, or belts, we find ones that are large and easy to handle. If Mindy really loves something but the fasteners are too small, she buys it anyway. Our mom replaces the fasteners with larger, easier-to-use ones.

In the store dressing room, I help Mindy practice putting on and taking off the clothes until she's satisfied. I don't think Mindy takes any longer to find new clothes than anyone else. It's just a matter of choosing what works for her.

Critical Thinking
Do you believe that the right clothing is easily available to everyone, regardless of their needs? Or are there exceptions? Explain.

Figure 25.1

Using the Elements of Design

Flatter Yourself When you understand how to use the elements of design, you can choose styles that look good on you. *What kinds of garments should you wear if you want to appear taller and slimmer? What look would help you if you want the illusion of increased size?*

Bulky textures, such as the fluffy yarn in this sweater and the corduroy in the pants, add apparent size. Smoother textures produce the opposite effect.

Vertical lines run lengthwise and can make the body seem taller than it is.

Horizontal lines run from side to side and can lead the eyes across the body, making it seem broader.

Bold patterns can draw attention and give the illusion of increased size.

Shiny textures, as in the fabric of this shirt, tend to give the illusion of increased size.

Subtle patterns can blend to give the illusion of a solid color.

Round or square shapes can give the illusion of increased size.

Tubular shapes have an elongating effect, which can make the body appear taller and slimmer.

Cool colors tend to pull back and give the illusion of reduced size.

Warm colors tend to draw attention and can give the illusion of increased size.

Principles of Design

Sandra examined the garments laid out on her bed. She had tried on all of them and still was not sure which combination worked best. Does this ever happen to you? If so, the principles of design can help. Each **principle of design** is an artistic guideline that helps you combine the elements of design.

- **Proportion** involves the relationship of one part to another and to the whole. If you make one section of your body look long, wide, or large, the other section will appear shorter, narrower, or smaller. For example, if you tuck a shirt into your slacks, your legs will appear longer. Wearing an untucked, long shirt will make your legs look shorter.
- **Emphasis** is the point of interest that the eyes see first. It can be used to draw attention to your best features. A colorful belt emphasizes the waist. A bright tie or scarf draws attention to the face.
- **Balance** gives a feeling of equal weight among all parts of a design. Balance is either symmetrical or asymmetrical. When one side of a garment or outfit is exactly the same as the other side, it is called symmetrical balance. Asymmetrical balance occurs when the two sides of the garment or outfit are different in size, form, texture, or color. An example is a trendy top with only one sleeve or a skirt that is long in the back and short in the front.
- **Rhythm** is the feeling of movement, leading the eye around a garment or outfit. For example, when you repeat the color of an outfit in a scarf or you choose square patch pockets to repeat a jacket's boxy shape, you create rhythm.
- **Harmony** occurs when the design elements work together. That does not mean all items have to match. Variety is interesting if the design details grouped together have something in common, such as shape, style, color, or size. See **Figure 25.2** on pages 605 and 606.

✓ **Reading Check** **Suggest** How can someone use emphasis to draw attention to his or her best features?

Individuality and Design

All you need to do is look around at fashions to see that designers do not follow the rules all of the time. The elements and principles of design are flexible. Once you know how the elements and principles work and why, you can choose how flexible you want to be.

Math You Can Use

Price vs. Cost

Ari bought a sports jacket for $75, which he felt was a good price, especially for the camel-hair fabric. It was less pricy than the plain wool jacket, which was $120. However, Ari soon found that he needed to wear a jacket to work twice a week. He realized that he would have to dry-clean the jacket twice a month in order to keep it wearable. Because of the fragile fabric, the cost for cleaning the camel-hair jacket would be $15, whereas the wool jacket would only cost $10 per cleaning. Five months later, did Ari still make the less expensive choice? What is the difference in the overall cost after five months?

Math Concept **Order of Operations** Do all operations within grouping symbols first. Multiply and divide in order from left to right, then add and subtract in order from left to right.

Starting Hint Calculate the relative costs of the dry-cleaning fees. Add each fee to the price of the jackets, before subtracting the lower figure from the higher figure. This will give you the difference in overall cost.

 For more math practice, go to the Math Appendix at the back of the book.

Figure 25.2

Using the Principles of Design

Sharp Design The principles of design can help you decide which design elements will work well together. *How might you use emphasis and rhythm together to create a look?*

Proportion refers to how separate parts of an outfit relate to each other and to the whole outfit. Clothing looks best when it is in proportion to your own size. When an outfit does not relate well to your body size, or the parts of the outfit do not relate well to each other, the outfit is said to be out of proportion.

Emphasis is the focal point of a garment. Emphasis can be used to make an outfit more interesting or to draw attention to your best features. You can create emphasis with a bright belt, a colorful scarf, a bright tie, or an interesting necklace, among other items.

Harmony occurs when the elements of design complement each other. When an outfit is harmonious, each part looks like it belongs. To achieve harmony, plan your accessories along with your outfit so that together they create a unified theme.

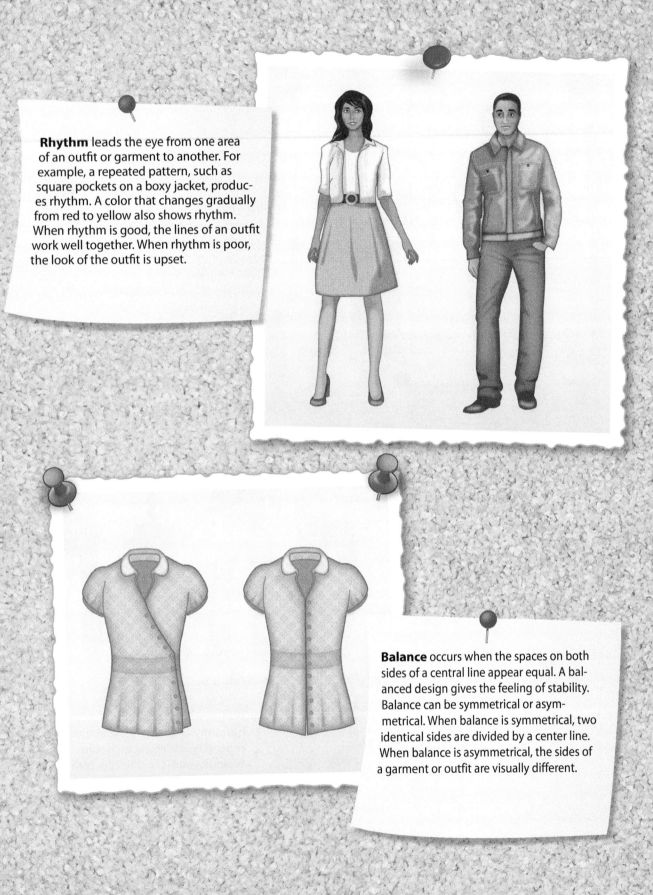

Rhythm leads the eye from one area of an outfit or garment to another. For example, a repeated pattern, such as square pockets on a boxy jacket, produces rhythm. A color that changes gradually from red to yellow also shows rhythm. When rhythm is good, the lines of an outfit work well together. When rhythm is poor, the look of the outfit is upset.

Balance occurs when the spaces on both sides of a central line appear equal. A balanced design gives the feeling of stability. Balance can be symmetrical or asymmetrical. When balance is symmetrical, two identical sides are divided by a center line. When balance is asymmetrical, the sides of a garment or outfit are visually different.

As you add more garments to your wardrobe and create new looks with clothes and accessories you already own, the elements and principles of design can help you look your best. You can create subtle, or understated, illusions that you may not have thought possible. You can have confidence that your design choices will make a good impression on others. For example, a carefully chosen outfit can help you look capable and professional at a job interview.

Designers often get attention by taking unconventional approaches to design. Imagine military boots with a skirt, a plaid shirt with floral-print sleeves, or a floor-length jacket over pants. Knowing the elements and principles of design allows designers to use them selectively to create unexpected and dramatic combinations. By appearing to bend or ignore the rules, designers can offer up new and interesting looks every season.

The outfits you put together may not follow every element or principle of design. Like some designers, you may choose to bend or break some design rules and allow your individuality to come through. You might decide to mix colors or fabrics that are not likely combinations, or add accessories that stand out because they are unexpected. Experimenting with your creativity can be fun, but remember the elements and principles of design when planning for an important occasion. They are the keys to looking your best and making a good impression.

Section 25.1

After You Read

Review Key Concepts

1. **Recall** the factors people should take into account before buying an item of clothing.
2. **Describe** what is meant by the silhouette of an outfit.
3. **Explain** how an outfit can be balanced.
4. **Determine** when it is acceptable and when it is not acceptable to be flexible with the elements and principles of design.

Practice Academic Skills

English Language Arts

5. Write down the thinking process you use when choosing a pair of shoes at the store. Prioritize the factors you take into account. Give examples of occasions when you were happy with your purchase and when you were not. Explain why.

Social Studies

6. How do you think a person's upbringing or cultural background might influence his or her clothing choices? How might these choices be affected if he or she moved to an area where another culture was dominant?

 Check Your Answers Go to connectED. mcgraw-hill.com to check your answers.

Section 25.2

Your Working Wardrobe

Reading Guide

Before You Read

Helpful Memory Tools Successful readers use tricks to help them remember. For example, the acronym HOMES is a memory aid where each letter stands for one of the five Great Lakes. Some students may try to create a song using the information. As you read the section, look for opportunities to make up your own memory aids.

Read to Learn

Key Concepts
- **Outline** the process of wardrobe assessment.
- **Summarize** clothes-shopping strategies.

Main Idea

Creating a wardrobe that works for you requires understanding what you need and do not need, what is appropriate for you, and shopping effectively for these items.

Content Vocabulary

◇ accessory
◇ fad

Academic Vocabulary

You will find these words in your reading and on your tests. Use the glossary to look up their definitions if necessary.

☐ inventory   ☐ prioritize

Graphic Organizer

Pretend you are dividing your wardrobe into three categories so you can decide what to keep and what to give away. Prioritize your clothing items from left to right by writing in the names of categories you will find as you read. Use a graphic organizer like the one below to organize your information.

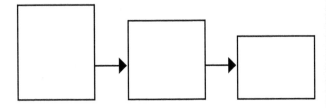

 Graphic Organizer Go to **connectED.mcgraw-hill.com** to download this graphic organizer.

Wardrobe Assessment

You know the look you want, and you understand the elements and principles of design. So how can you use this information to create a wardrobe that showcases your style? Begin by taking a look at what you already have. Take an inventory, or make an organized list detailing what you have. Sort your clothing into the following groups:

- Clothes you like or wear regularly and want to keep.
- Clothes you do not want.
- Clothes about which you are not sure.

Jot down all garments in your Keep group. Then look again at the clothes in your Not Sure group. Would updating or repairing any of these clothes make them work in your wardrobe? Would you wear any of these clothes during messy activities, such as painting, house cleaning, or working out? If so, add these garments to your Keep list. Now consider the clothes in the Do Not Want group. If they are in good condition, you could donate them to a charitable organization or give them to a sibling, friend, or relative. You could also sell them at a yard sale.

Find Gaps in Your Wardrobe

Do you see any gaps in your wardrobe? If so, you will need to expand your clothing options by making, restyling, or purchasing clothes. Before expanding your wardrobe, think about the following:

- **Consider your needs and wants.** Which items do you really need? Which do you want but could do without? Needs are usually more important than wants.
- **Try accessories.** An **accessory** is a small item of clothing that completes an outfit. Scarves, shoes, necklaces, and belts are just some examples. Accessories add interest to or dress up an outfit and are usually less expensive than new clothes.
- **Plan for core clothing pieces.** A clothing **fad** is a fashion that is extremely popular but soon goes out of style. Fads are not ideal additions to your wardrobe. Core pieces, or garments that are considered classic and can be used in a variety of situations, last much longer. Males might choose a pair of well-fitting jeans, a pair of khaki pants, and a few solid-color knit shirts with collars. Females might select a solid-color skirt, a few solid-color shirts or shirts with a simple design, and a pair of well-fitting jeans.
- **Keep your budget in mind.** How much money do you have to spend on garments or fabric to make them wearable? Be sure to consider the cost per wearing of each garment. Consider the garment's purchase price, the cleaning costs over time, and the number of times you expect to wear it. Some garments, such as jeans, are worn often and have a lower cost per wearing. Some clothing items are fads that come and go, and their cost per wearing is usually high.

 **As You Read**

Connect Size is not the only way in which you can outgrow your clothing. Does your current wardrobe reflect who you are today?

 **Vocabulary**

You can find definitions in the glossary at the back of this book.

 **Community Connections**

Shades of Uniformity

Schools whose policy is for their students to wear uniforms have adopted the view that wearing the same clothing helps students avoid competition, comparing, and judging with regard to clothing. Other schools do not view this as necessary, or believe it is too difficult for all students to buy and wear uniforms. Although there are strong feelings on both sides, there is no one answer on this issue.

✓ Reading Check **Identify** What is core clothing?

SUCCEED IN SCHOOL

Achieve Your Goals

After you determine what success means to you, set goals to achieve that success. Break these goals into steps that will help you gauge your progress.

Shopping for Clothes

After you complete your clothing inventory, look over the clothes you decided to keep. Make sure you have clothes for daily wear and clothes you wear for special activities. You should have a few items for special occasions, such as weddings, special celebrations, or funerals. Clothing for different seasons is also needed, such as swimwear and shorts for summer, and sweaters and heavy socks for winter.

You have learned about the elements and principles of design and have taken a clothing inventory. Now you need to shop for new clothes. Are you prepared? To be a savvy shopper, use a plan. If you shop with a plan, you are more likely to be pleased with your purchases.

To create your plan, prioritize, or rate in order of priority, your clothing needs. You need to buy your highest-priority items first. If you start at the bottom of your list, you may run out of money before you reach the top. Use catalogs, sales flyers, and the Internet to find clothing prices and create your priority list.

HOW TO . . . . Select Quality Clothing

When buying clothing, you want to make sure you do not have any regrets later. Fortunately, there are strategies you can use to make sure that the clothes you select are of good quality and will have a place in your wardrobe for a long time to come. To improve your chances for a long and happy relationship with a garment, check these features.

Wrinkling Crush the material in your hand, then release it. Any wrinkles should smooth or shake out easily. Otherwise, the garment will take on a slept-in look soon after you put it on. Remember, however, that some fabrics, such as linen, wrinkle no matter what.

Wear Hold the garment to the light to check that the weave is tight and even throughout. Loose weaves tend to lose their shape. An uneven weave means uneven wear. Check for a lining. Clothes with linings are typically higher quality.

Pattern A plaid or print should run in the same direction throughout the garment. It should match at the seams, including pockets and collars.

Picturenet/drr.net

Shopping Options

Once you have your needs prioritized, you are ready to shop. What shopping options do you have? If you live in a large city, you may have many shopping options, including specialty stores or boutiques, discount stores, resale shops, outlet stores, and department stores. If you live in a rural area, your choices are probably limited. However, online shopping allows people in rural areas to shop extensively without making a trip to a city or store. If you shop online, you will probably need a credit card. Also, remember to add the shipping costs to the price of the item. Some companies offer free shipping if you spend a certain amount.

Consignment shops and thrift stores often carry items that are like new without the new-clothing price tag. For special-occasion clothes, such as a tuxedo or formal gown, you can rent an outfit from a rental shop.

Seams Garment sections should meet smoothly at the seams, without pulling or puckering. Check for tight stitches on the underside. About 8 to 12 stitches per inch indicate sturdy construction.

Hems Hems should be straight and flat, not wrinkled or rumpled. Stitches should be invisible from the outside. Turn over the hemmed area to check for secure stitching on the underside.

Corners Points on collars, lapels, and pocket flaps should be clean and symmetrical. They should lie flat and smooth, with no lumps, bumps, or puckers.

Trims Decorations such as patches, braids, and ribbons should be neatly and securely attached. The thread should blend into the fabric, unless it is meant as part of the decoration.

Fastenings Fastenings should open easily, close smoothly, and stay closed during wearing. Look for evenly spaced buttons and buttonholes that are well defined with tight, even stitching. Zippers should lie flat. Metal zippers are more durable than plastic ones. All fastenings, such as hooks, eyes, and snaps, should be securely sewn.

Care Read the garment labels. Some clothes require more care, such as dry-cleaning or hand washing, than others. Decide whether the garment is worth the upkeep.

(tr) Maria Teijeiro/Getty Images; (b) Hill Street Studios/Getty Images

Shopping Strategies

When you shop, remember your priority list. If you are not able to locate the exact item you want, look for a good substitute at a comparable cost. Here are some other tips to keep in mind as you shop:

- **Check the care label.** Be sure you can give the garment proper care. A dry-clean-only garment means continuing costs not only for the garment but also for the trips to and from the dry cleaner.
- **Check the fit.** Buy only what fits comfortably. Try on the garment to be sure it does not pull, wrinkle, or feel uncomfortable when you sit or bend. Sizes can vary by manufacturer, so do not assume that size 12 from Brand X is the same as size 12 from Brand Y. Try on everything, and buy clothes that fit you right now.
- **Check the quality.** Choose the best quality you can afford to buy. The garment will have to stand up to repeated laundering and wear.
- **Check the price tag.** If clothing items in a store seem too expensive to fit your budget, shop around. Try a resale shop, a discount store, or a sale for better value. On the other hand, do not buy items simply because they are on sale. You might end up with good deals on clothes that you never wear.

TAKE CHARGE!

Shop Responsibly

Shopping involves handling merchandise that does not belong to you. It is the property of the store until you pay for it. If you choose not to buy an item you have handled, the item should be left in good condition for other potential buyers. Use these guidelines on all of your clothes-shopping trips. Note any additional tips that may come up.

- **Remove Jewelry** Take off jewelry that could easily snag or catch on clothing.
- **Prevent Pulls and Tears** When taking clothes off hangers, carefully unbutton buttons and unzip zippers.
- **Watch Out for Dirt and Makeup** Make sure you have clean hands before handling clothes. If you are wearing makeup, be careful not to get it on the clothes as you put them on and take them off.
- **Speak Up** If a garment is damaged or missing buttons, report it to a salesperson.
- **Help Restock** If you decide not to purchase a garment, return it to the correct rack or give it back to the salesperson.
- **Do Not Shoplift** Pay for the clothes you can afford, and create a budget to purchase the others later.

Real-World Skills

Be a Shopping Role Model
The next time you are clothes shopping, be aware of how you interact with other shoppers. Focus on being courteous by sharing aisle and display space, and waiting patiently in lines for the dressing room and checkout line. See if your behavior influences the behavior of other shoppers.

Deciding to Buy

After taking a clothing inventory and checking the care instructions, fit, quality, and price of a garment, you should have a good idea of whether it is the right one for you. If you have any doubts about a garment, do not buy it. Sometimes a purchase is not a wise idea. Perhaps you found the outfit you wanted because it looked so good on the mannequin or in the catalog, but after trying it on it just did not suit you. Listen to your sense of reason and logic to help keep you from buying something that is too costly or is not right for you.

When you cannot find exactly what you want, consider compromises and trade-offs. Could you purchase a lower-quality item and improve it with nicer buttons or accessories? Perhaps you could buy one well-made, more expensive jacket that can be worn with many garments instead of buying different jackets for every outfit. Keep sewing in mind as an option for getting exactly what you want, possibly for less money.

If you do decide to buy an item, check the exchange or return policies of the store before you pay. If the store has a policy of exchanges only, no returns, you know you will not get your money back. You will only be able to exchange an item for one of equal value. Keep the sales receipt, and keep the tags on the clothing until you are sure you are keeping the item.

Section 25.2

After You Read

Review Key Concepts

1. **Give** examples of things you can do with clothes you no longer want.
2. **Explain** how the care needs of a garment might affect your decision to purchase it.

Practice Academic Skills

English Language Arts

3. Conduct a survey asking 10 people five multiple-choice questions about their clothes-shopping habits. Ask what makes them decide to buy a garment, where they do their clothes shopping, and how often. Give them four choices per question. Compile their responses and see if the responses reveal a pattern of behavior.

Social Studies

4. Many of the clothing looks that were considered in style 10 years ago are not considered fashionable today. However, the most up-to-date looks from 20 or 30 years ago are coming back into style. Find old and new pictures of clothing items that have come in, gone out, and come back into style. Write a description of the look and why you think it is popular again.

 Check Your Answers Go to connectED. mcgraw-hill.com to check your answers.

Information Designer

What Does an Information Designer Do?

Information designers are communicators who use words, numbers, images, sounds, and videos to create effective messages. They transform complex information into communications that are quick and easy to understand. An information designer might design something as simple as a bus schedule or as complex as a Web site for a large company. Information designers are sometimes called graphic designers.

Skills To be an information designer, you will need visual and verbal communication skills. Because designers use software applications to create their work, you will need strong computer skills as well. Creativity, adaptability, and problem-solving skills are also key.

Education and Training You can study information design at two-year colleges, four-year colleges, technical schools, and art schools. You can get the skills you need for information design through classes in the fine arts, graphic design, creative writing, art history, and Web design.

Job Outlook Many new jobs open up every year in information design. Gaining experience in advanced computer applications like motion graphics can lead to higher pay. Many information designers are self-employed.

Critical Thinking Find an example of information design, such as a Web site, brochure, sign, instruction manual, or magazine. Is the information presented effectively? Is it appealing and easy to use? Write a paragraph about your observations.

Career Cluster
Arts, Audio/Video Technology, and Communications

Information designers work in the Arts, Audio/Video Technology, and Communications career cluster. Here are some of the other jobs in this career cluster:

- Musician
- Dancer
- Fashion Designer
- Sculptor
- Museum Curator
- Photographer
- Animator
- Actor
- Make up Artist
- Film Director
- Cinematographer
- Playwright
- Book Author
- Journalist
- Editor
- Web Designer
- Broadcast Engineer
- Textile Designer

Explore Further Research this career cluster. Choose a career in this cluster that appeals to you and write a career profile.

Ingram Publishing

Chapter 25   Review and Applications

CHAPTER SUMMARY

Section 25.1
Your Clothing Style

Clothing is one of the first things people notice about you. When choosing your clothes, think about your needs and wants, your budget, and how you want to be perceived by others. You can use the elements and principles of design to create outfits that help you look your best. Color is generally the most noticeable design element. It is important to understand and learn how to properly use the elements and principles of design before attempting more unconventional approaches to creating your wardrobe.

Section 25.2
Your Working Wardrobe

Taking a clothing inventory is a good first step in putting together a wardrobe. Fill in your wardrobe gaps by making, restyling, or purchasing clothes and accessories. Create a prioritized shopping plan before heading to clothing stores. Shopping options vary by region and include specialty, department, outlet, discount, and resale stores, as well as online and catalog shopping. Evaluate care requirements, fit, quality, and price before buying. If you cannot find exactly what you want, keep your mind open to other options.

Vocabulary Review

1. Use these content and academic vocabulary terms to create a crossword puzzle on graph paper. Use the definitions as clues.

Content Vocabulary
◇ fashion (p. 599)
◇ illusion (p. 599)
◇ element of design (p. 600)
◇ silhouette (p. 600)
◇ principle of design (p. 604)
◇ accessory (p. 609)
◇ fad (p. 609)

Academic Vocabulary
■ convey (p. 599)
■ influence (p. 599)
■ inventory (p. 609)
■ prioritize (p. 610)

Review Key Concepts

2. **Explain** the benefits of well-chosen clothing.
3. **List** the five elements of clothing design.
4. **Identify** the five principles of clothing design.
5. **Understand** how to use the elements and principles of design to express your creativity.
6. **Outline** the process of wardrobe assessment.
7. **Summarize** clothes-shopping strategies.

Critical Thinking

8. **Reflect** Have you ever made an incorrect assumption about someone because of the way he or she dresses?
9. **Critique** Stand in front of a full-length mirror and evaluate your current outfit. What do you think it says about you? Does it say what you want it to say?
10. **Imagine** Picture yourself at an important job interview. What are you wearing?
11. **Create** If you were to create your own line of clothing for teens, what would you call it? What would be some of your signature pieces?

ACTIVE LEARNING

12. Tune in to Color Visit a fabric store. Using what you learned in this chapter about color, walk the aisles and take notes about the fabric colors. Are they warm or cold? Do they have a low or high intensity? What is their value level? Notice how the colors make you feel. Some people feel happier surrounded by warm colors, while others prefer the calming effect of cooler shades. Hold your arm against the various fabrics and observe the effect of the colors against your skin. Note which colors seem to be in harmony with your skin tone and which are not as flattering. After your visit, write what you learned about which colors work best for you.

Family & Community Connections

13. Community Service Many charities, hospitals, and shelters accept clothing donations for those in need. With your class, organize a school-wide clothes drive to benefit one of these organizations. Group one will create posters to advertise the clothing drive. Posters should describe the charity, and provide a collection goal and goal date. Group two will write pamphlets that provide donation guidelines. They should explain what types of clothes are needed and the condition clothes should be in. Group three will talk to local business owners about the project. This group will ask businesses for gift certificates or other donations they can use to award the individual or class that donates the most clothing. Group four will track the items each individual and classroom donates. With your teacher, make arrangements to deliver the clothing to the charity.

Real-World Skills and Applications

Leadership Skills

14. Forming Policy A policy is a rule or set of rules and procedures established by the leadership of a group. Imagine that you are establishing a dress code policy for your school. Talk to classmates, teachers, and parents to get their opinions about what should be included. Consider your own ideas. Then prepare an outline of your dress code policy and show it to your teacher. Be prepared to support your policy with reasons for each decision.

Financial Literacy

15. Buying Smart You have decided to add to your core clothing by buying three high-quality T-shirts in classic colors. When you get to the store, you see that a shirt you like is on sale, one for $12 or two for $15. Further into the store, you spot a display of other shirts you like just as well. They are priced at one for $20 or three for $34. Both shirt styles offer the same quality and color selection. Which shirts should you buy to spend the least amount of money?

Information Literacy

16. Analyze Media The wardrobe for television characters is chosen carefully to make sure it communicates the desired message. Analyze a popular television program geared to teens. How are the characters dressed? Are there differences between the way they dress? Why or why not? Summarize your findings.

Academic Skills

 English Language Arts

17. **Test Your Vocabulary** Create a word search puzzle using as many clothing and design terms from the chapter as possible. Make the puzzle run 15 letters horizontally by 15 letters vertically. Make a list of the words as you use them. Then present the puzzle to a friend to see how long it takes him or her to find every word.

 Science

18. **Environmental Awareness** Every decision you make can have an impact on the environment.

Procedure Research green-friendly strategies for buying, wearing, and caring for your clothes. Create a checklist of 20 environmentally-friendly things clothes shoppers can do. Put a check by the ones you already use.

Analysis If everyone followed all of these guidelines, what would the outcome be? Share your predictions with the class.

 Mathematics

19. **Calculate a Budget** Jen recently accepted a job as a fashion consultant, and she needs to create a budget for her growing expenses. She will be bringing home $200 a week. She figures that 10% of that money will pay her cell phone bill, 25% will go into her savings account, and 30% will go toward movies, lunches, and gifts. Now, Jen needs to include money to spend on new clothes for the job. How much money per week will Jen be able to spend for a new wardrobe? What if she was earning $100 a week? Or $300 a week?

Math Concept **Calculate Percentages** A percent is a ratio that compares a number to 100.

Starting Hint First calculate the percentage that is left over each week for Jen's clothing budget. Convert the percentage to a dollar amount. Use the same function for alternative amounts of income.

 For math help, go to the Math Appendix at the back of the book.

Standardized Test Practice

TRUE/FALSE
Directions Read each statement. On a separate sheet of paper, write T if the statement is true, and write F if the statement is false.

Test-Taking Tip Make sure you understand the full statement. All parts of a statement must be correct for the statement to be true. Statements that contain extreme words, such as all, none, never, or always, or that have unsupported opinions, are often false.

20. Decide if each statement is true or false.

a) _____ Plastic zippers are less durable than metal ones.

b) _____ Red, yellow, and blue are considered warm colors.

c) _____ If a store has an exchanges only, no returns policy, you cannot get your money back for returning an item.

Chapter 26

Selection and Care of Fibers and Fabrics

Section 26.1
Fibers and Fabrics

Section 26.2
Caring for Clothing

Chapter Objectives

Section 26.1

- **Identify** natural and manufactured fibers.
- **Summarize** the concepts of fabric construction and performance finishing.
- **List** the six traits of fabric that can help you choose a fabric that meets your needs.

Section 26.2

- **Give** guidelines for routine clothing care and storage.
- **Explain** clothes cleaning and drying procedures.
- **Describe** options for simple clothing repairs.

Explore the Photo

There are hundreds of thousands of fabrics you can choose from. *What should you consider when choosing fabric for a project?*

Writing Activity

Letter to the Editor

Support Your Opinion Communicating your opinion on an issue is an important part of being a confident participant in society. Respectfully expressing opinions and listening to others' opinions increases overall understanding between people.

Pretend you are writing a letter to the editor of a newspaper to offer your opinion about a new shopping center in your town. Support your views with valid reasons and facts.

Writing Tips Use these tips to write a letter to the editor:

- Make sure you write the letter in letter format.
- Write a topic sentence that clearly expresses your opinion on the given subject. Then provide reasons supporting this opinion.
- Conclude your letter by restating your opinion in light of the reasons you have presented.

Fibers and Fabrics

Before You Read

Preview Choose a content or academic vocabulary word that is new to you. When you find it in the text, write down the definition and an example.

Read to Learn

Key Concepts
- **Identify** natural and manufactured fibers.
- **Summarize** the concepts of fabric construction and performance finishing.
- **List** the six traits of fabric that can help you choose a fabric that meets your needs.

Main Idea
There are many varieties of fibers, and methods of fabric construction and finishes, that account for the wide choice of garments available to us today.

Content Vocabulary
◇ fiber
◇ yarn
◇ natural fibers
◇ manufactured fibers
◇ generic name
◇ trade name
◇ microfiber
◇ finish

Academic Vocabulary
You will find these words in your reading and on your tests. Use the glossary to look up their definitions if necessary.
☐ durable   ☐ drape

Graphic Organizer
As you read, look for listings of natural and manufactured fibers. Use a graphic organizer like the one shown to make your information organized and complete.

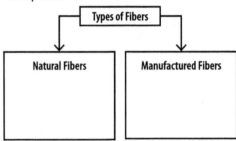

Graphic Organizer Go to **connectED.mcgraw-hill.com** to download this graphic organizer.

Fibers

Every fabric starts with fiber. A **fiber** is a hair-like strand of material. Twisting these hair-like strands together forms a slightly thicker, continuous strand called a **yarn**. Weaving or kitting different yarns together is what makes fabric.

Like people, fibers have unique characteristics. Some fibers are strong, some are soft, and others are very stretchable. When selecting fibers, manufacturers consider the fibers' qualities that will affect the appearance and performance of the fabric they want to make.

- **Strength** Different fibers have different tensile strengths. Tensile strength is the ability to withstand pulling or tension. The higher the tensile strength of a fiber, the more durable the finished garment will be.
- **Durability** A fiber's durability refers to its ability to resist wear and decay. The greater the durability, the longer a garment will last before wearing out.
- **Resiliency** A resilient fiber is able to spring back to shape after it has been crushed or wrinkled.
- **Elasticity** Some fibers immediately return to their original lengths after they have been stretched out. This is an especially important characteristic for athletic clothing such as swimwear and bike shorts.
- **Abrasion Resistance** Abrasion is a worn spot that develops when fibers rub against each other or something else. A sweater might develop worn elbows from contact with your desk. Or it could develop balls, or pills, of fiber where your arm brushes against your side.
- **Wrinkle Resistance** Some fibers resist wrinkling, while others wrinkle very easily.
- **Shape Retention** Fibers that retain, or hold, their shape well look the same after they have been washed or worn. Some fibers stretch out after they have been worn, or shrink once they have been washed.
- **Luster** The more light a fiber reflects, the more luster, or shine, it has. Luster only affects a fabric's appearance.
- **Absorbency** Fibers that are absorbent are able to take in moisture.
- **Wicking** Some fibers are able to pull moisture away from the body, without absorbing the moisture. This means both the person and the clothing will stay dry. This is especially important for athletic clothing.
- **Washability** Some fibers can be washed, while others do not react well to water. They may shrink, lose shape, or fall apart.

As You Read

Connect Consider the clothes you are wearing right now. Without looking at the tags, see if you can identify what type of fiber was used in the fabric.

Vocabulary

You can find definitions in the glossary at the back of this book.

Naturally Soft

Cotton fiber, which grows on shrubs, is the most commonly used natural fiber. *What common item of clothing is made from cotton?*

Get Technical

The science of textiles has contributed many advances to help people maintain quality of life. From the stain-resistance of your bedroom floor carpet to the warmth and protection of your ski jacket, textiles have become a high-tech field of discovery.

Procedure Research a scientific development in textiles. Tell how it began and what happened to make it a reality.

Analysis Present your findings to the class in a step-by-step format.

Fibers are grouped into two categories: natural and manufactured.

Natural Fibers

Natural fibers are produced from plant and animal sources, and have been used for thousands of years. The jeans you wear today are manufactured from the same type of cotton fiber from which people made their clothes centuries ago. Of course, today's jeans may have more stretch or be softer than the cotton garments of long ago. The following are some of the more common natural fibers:

- **Cotton** comes from the seed pod of the cotton plant. It is the most widely used natural fiber. It is soft to the touch, absorbs moisture, and is easy to launder. Cotton can wrinkle and shrink. These problems can be prevented with special finishes.
- **Flax** comes from the stalk of the flax plant. Linen is made from flax. Linen is stronger than cotton, though it also feels rougher to the touch. Linen does not yellow with age as many other fibers do, but it wrinkles very easily.
- **Ramie** is a durable, or strong and long-lasting, fiber that comes from the stalk of China grass, grown mainly in Southeast Asia. It has natural stain-resisting ability, and is also resistant to bacteria, mildew, and light. Ramie is not very elastic, and is often blended with other fibers, such as cotton or flax, for softness.
- **Wool** is made from the fleece of sheep and is valued for its warmth. Because wool contains moisture in each fiber, it also naturally resists flame. It shrinks when washed in hot water, so it is best to dry-clean or wash wool clothing in cold water. Wool resists wrinkling and stains, but can be damaged by insects, such as moths.
- **Silk** comes from the cocoons spun by silkworms. It is extremely light, yet extremely strong and flexible. Silk resists moth damage, wrinkles, and has a luxurious feeling. It is often cleaned professionally. Always check labels on silk clothing for safe cleaning techniques.

Manufactured Fibers

Manufactured fibers are produced in laboratories through chemical processes and are made from substances such as wood pulp, petroleum, and other chemicals. Chemical engineers have designed these fibers to have special, desirable characteristics. They are generally wrinkle-free, strong, and spring back easily to their original shape, so they are easy to maintain. Manufactured fibers are less likely to absorb water. As a result, they dry quickly and shrink slightly, if they shrink at all.

- **Rayon** was the first manufactured fiber. Rayon is comfortable to wear and is often combined with other fibers. Some rayon fabrics can be washed, but most need to be dry-cleaned. Rayon clothing can shrink easily and should not be put in clothes dryers.
- **Polyester** is combined with other fibers or alone. Most often it is mixed with cotton to make shirts, pants, and table and bed linens. When enough polyester is blended with other fibers that require dry-cleaning, such as wool, the fabric becomes washable.
- **Spandex** is an elastic fiber that has replaced rubber in most clothing uses. It can be stretched repeatedly, and will still retain its original length and shape. Spandex is often combined with other fibers to make undergarments, sportswear, and swimwear.
- **Elastoester** is a stretchable fiber that can be used instead of spandex. You can find it in sportswear, swimwear, sweaters, hosiery, and socks.
- **Acetate** has a silky appearance and an ability to drape, or hang in loose folds when placed over something, nicely. Most acetate fabrics must be dry-cleaned, but some can be washed. Acetate is often used in special-occasion dresses, blouses, and home fashions.
- **Triacetate** is similar to acetate, but stronger. It resists shrinking, and can be easily laundered. Triacetate is used in skirts, dresses, and sportswear.
- **Acrylic** is a soft fiber that provides warmth without heaviness. It resembles wool, but is easier to care for. Acrylic is machine washable, and resistant to moths.
- **Lyocell** is similar to rayon in appearance, but unlike most rayon fabrics, lyocell can be machine washed and dried. It is a strong fiber, absorbent, and generally comfortable to wear. Any wrinkles in lyocell can be removed with light ironing.
- **Nylon** is a strong, lightweight, resilient fabric used in pantyhose, swimwear, and jackets. It is easy to wash, quick-drying, and needs no pressing. However, nylon does not absorb moisture well and can be uncomfortable to wear in hot weather.
- **PLA fiber**, whose letters stand for polylactic acid, is similar to cotton in appearance. It can be used alone or blended with cotton or polyester. Developed in recent years, PLA fiber is a corn-based polymer that is biodegradable. It is found in swimwear, sportswear, and undergarments.
- **Polyolefin** is strong, fast drying, and able to float. Traditionally used in clothing for backpacking and canoeing, it is now being used in swimwear. It is also blended with cotton to make jeans.

Fashionable Function

Many garments contain manufactured fibers, such as spandex. *Why might this be so?*

Look to Friends

If you feel down about your grades in a subject, ask your close friends for support. They can help you remember your strong subjects so you keep a positive attitude, and help you study to improve your grades.

Generic and Trade Names

Every manufactured fiber carries two names, a generic name and a trade name. A **generic name** is the common name for a group of similar fibers. Cotton, wool, acrylic, and spandex are examples of generic names. All members of a generic group have similar characteristics and need the same type of care. Labels on garments must list the generic name.

A **trade name** is a company's name for a specific fiber that it manufactures. For example, Cresloft® and Duraspun® are both trade names for acrylic. Trade names are protected by law, which means that only the company that owns and registers the name can use it. Labels on garments may or may not list the company's trade name.

Microfibers

Imagine a fiber twice as fine as the finest silk and 100 times finer than human hair! This superfine manufactured fiber is known as **microfiber**. Microfibers are made from polyester, nylon, rayon, and acrylic. They can be used alone or can be blended with natural fibers.

Microfiber yarns are much denser and stronger than other yarns of similar weight, which is why they make such durable fabrics. Microfiber fabrics repel water, yet they are very lightweight and comfortable to wear. Air passes through microfiber fabrics, and body moisture is taken from the skin's surface to the outside of the fabric. This makes microfiber perfect for undergarments and outerwear. Nylon microfiber fabrics are used mostly in active wear. Polyester microfibers are popular for luxurious blouses, skiwear, and rainwear. Polyester microfibers have the look and feel of fine silk, but they wear better, are less expensive, and can be washed like other polyesters.

Elemental Items

Clothing often has to serve a purpose, and fabric helps clothing accomplish its purpose. *What is the purpose of this teen's clothing? What fibers or fabrics are best suited for this purpose?*

Creatas/SuperStock

Trent, 14

When my brother Aaron told me I should get a blazer for his college graduation ceremony, I was hoping that a "blazer" was some kind of cool bike. But he was talking about a jacket. Fortunately, Aaron agreed to take me shopping. At the clothing store, the saleswoman pulled out a navy blue blazer in my size. I put it on. The fabric felt smooth, and I had to admit, I looked pretty good. The price was in my budget, so I was ready to buy it, but Aaron told me I should find out what it was made of first. Luckily, the jacket's tag said it was a blend of Dacron polyester and worsted wool. The saleswoman explained that the wool made the jacket look and feel good, but the polyester made it less expensive and easier to keep in good condition.

Critical Thinking
Imagine that you need to buy clothing for a special event, such as a graduation or a wedding. Which fibers would you consider? How would these fibers fill your needs?

Fiber Blends

Every fiber has favorable qualities, but no fiber is perfect. As a result, manufacturers produce fabric blends, or fabrics containing two or more fibers. Blends combine the best qualities of each fiber. Fibers are usually blended to improve fabric performance. Have you noticed how cotton is often combined with polyester? The cotton provides softness, comfort, and absorbency. The polyester makes the fabric stronger, wrinkle-resistant, shrink-resistant, mildew-resistant, and quick-drying.

Some fibers are also blended for appearance. Angora, a natural fiber from the coat of the angora rabbit, can be blended with wool to give a sweater more texture. Silk can be added to increase a fabric's luster and improve the way it drapes.

✓ **Reading Check** **List** What fiber qualities do manufacturers consider before selecting a fiber to make a fabric?

Fabric Construction and Finishes

People have been making fabric for thousands of years. Through technology and people's creativity, more fabric choices are available today than ever before.

Fabric is an important factor to consider when you buy or sew clothes. In addition to the comforts and conveniences that come with various types of fibers, there are construction methods and finishes that can be done to add desired features to clothing. You may want your clothes to be wrinkle free, or able to wick (take away) perspiration from your body. Some of these qualities are a natural part of the fabric.

Fabric Construction

As you have already learned, fibers are twisted together to make yarns. What you may not know is that yarns are usually about the thickness of sewing thread. They are then put together to form fabric. The way the yarns are arranged affects the appearance and the wear of the fabric. It also affects the type of care it will need.

Woven Fabrics

To weave fabric, lengthwise and crosswise yarns are laced together at right angles. The tightness of the weave determines the firmness of the fabric and affects how it will wear. Tightly woven fabrics usually wear better than loosely woven fabrics. See **Figure 26.1**.

Four types of weaves are used to make fabric:

- **Plain Weave** This is the simplest of all weaves. In a plain weave, each crosswise yarn passes over and under each lengthwise yarn. Broadcloth, chambray, and canvas are examples of plain weave fabrics.
- **Twill Weave** In a twill weave, the lengthwise yarns pass over two, and then under two, crosswise yarns. You can see the diagonal ridges made by yarns on the surface of the fabric. The twill weave produces a stronger fabric than that of other weaves. Denim and fleece are both made with twill weaves.
- **Satin Weave** The lengthwise yarns in a satin weave pass over four or more crosswise yarns and generally under one crosswise yarn. This produces a shiny surface. The satin weave is not as strong as the twill and plain weaves. Satin fabrics are used for blouses and evening wear.
- **Pile Weave** Three sets of yarn are used to make the pile weave. Pile fabrics are first woven in a plain, twill, or satin weave. Then an extra set of yarns is woven in so that loops or cut ends are produced on the fabric surface. The loops are cut to make corduroy and velvet. If left uncut, the fabric is terrycloth.

Figure 26.1 Fabric Weaves

An Effective Arrangement Almost all woven fabrics are based on plain, twill, and satin weaves. *Which of these weaves is used to make blue jeans?*

PLAIN

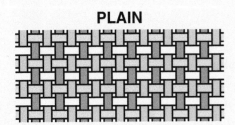

TWILL

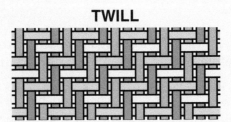

SATIN

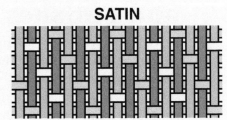

Knit Fabrics

Fabrics can also be made by knitting, either by hand or machine. Knitting is created by repeating rows of interlocking loops of yarn. Different yarn fibers, weights, and textures are used to create distinctive designs. Knitted fabrics are stretchy and comfortable, and they generally hold their shape well. However, knits can snag more easily than woven fabric. When making knitted clothes, measurement is important.

- **Single Knits** T-shirts and simple dresses are most often made with single knits. Single knits, sometimes called jersey knits, have a flat, smooth appearance on the front side and horizontal loops on the back side. Single knits have a tendency to curl at the edges.

- **Rib Knits** Rib knits have a lot of stretch, making them ideal for close-fitting tops and neck, wrist, and bottom bands on sweaters and jackets.

- **Interlock Knits** This variation of the rib knit has an identical smooth surface on both sides. Interlock knits have less stretch than rib knits, so they are used for soft, casual garments.

- **Double Knits** These knits are made with two interlocking layers on the front and back that cannot be separated. Double knits are durable and wrinkle resistant.

- **Tricot Knits** Tricot (trē-kō) knits have narrow vertical ribs on the front and crosswise ribs on the back. They have plenty of stretch, are snag-resistant, and will not run or unravel. Tricot knits are used for undergarments, nightgowns, and uniforms.

Other Fabric Constructions

Other fabrics can be made using methods other than knitting or weaving. Nonwovens are created by bonding fibers with heat, moisture, pressure, or adhesives. Felt, sew-in and fusible interfacings, and disposable surgical gowns are made from nonwoven fabric. Quilted fabrics consist of two fabric layers with a batting, or stuffing, between them.

Woven for Wear

The construction of the fabric affects its appearance. *What characteristics does this teen's dress have?*

Federal law requires use of flame-retardant fabrics for children's pajamas. *Why do you think this is so?*

Fabric Finishes

A **finish** is a special treatment that makes a fiber or fabric more useful and appealing. It is one of the final touches added to yarns and fabrics. Clothing can have different types of finishes, including performance finishes and color.

Performance Finishes

Some finishes help the fabric perform better. For example, a shirt might have a finish that prevents wrinkling or creasing. Which of the following finishes would you like your clothing to have?

- **Antibacterial or Antiseptic** This finish checks the growth of bacteria, mold and mildew. It also reduces the germs that cause odor and disease.
- **Antistatic** Static electricity causes some fabrics to stick together. When treated with an antistatic finish, a fabric will absorb small amounts of moisture from the air, which reduces static electricity.
- **Crease-Resistant** These finishes are applied to fabrics made from cotton, rayon, linen, and other fibers that wrinkle easily when worn.
- **Durable Press** Durable press fabrics resist wrinkling due to wear, and maintain their shape, pleats, and creases even when washed and dried by machine. Wrinkles simply disappear when these fabrics are hung for a few hours.
- **Shrinkage Control** These finishes limit shrinking, though some shrinking might occur. If a fabric is labeled "preshrunk," a shrinkage finish has been applied.
- **Soil-Release** These finishes allow dirt and stains to be removed more easily.
- **Water- and Stain-Repellent** These finishes help fabric repel water and oil-based stains. The water or staining liquid stays on the surface of the fabric in small beads. The fabric remains porous so air and body moisture can pass through.
- **Waterproof** These finishes prevent fabric from absorbing water, which keeps the wearer completely dry.
- **Flame-Retardant and Flame-Resistant** These finishes reduce flaming and burning in fabrics that have been exposed to flame or high heat.

Color

Some fabric dyes come from nature, and others are developed in a laboratory. Dyes can be applied in various ways. Sometimes dye is applied to yarn before it is woven into fabric. In the most common method of dyeing, called piece dyeing, dye is applied after the yarn has been made into fabric. A printing process can also be used to apply color.

✔ **Reading Check**) **Explain** How do fabric finishes improve a garment's performance?

Darren Baker/Alamy

Choose the Right Fabric

Not every fabric is equally suited for every need. Knowing about the following fabric traits can help you decide whether a fabric will meet your specific needs.

- **Hand** Hand is the term for how a fabric behaves when handled. For example, silk falls in soft folds. Hand affects a garment's wear and appearance.
- **Care Needs** Weigh the care needs of a fabric against the use you expect from the garment. Is a dry-clean-only garment worth the cost? Also, compare its needs with those of other fabrics. Does it require extra energy for a separate wash?
- **Strength** A fabric should meet the wear needs of its intended use. For example, work shirts should be made of a rugged fabric to protect your arms and prevent rips and tears.
- **Texture** A fabric's feel and appearance affect the "mood" of the finished garment. For example, a silk scarf adds elegance to an outfit.
- **Breathing** Air circulation helps moisture evaporate, so breathable fabrics (those that let air flow freely) are more comfortable in warm weather than in cold.
- **Weight** A fabric's lightness or heaviness affects how it feels on your body.

Section 26.1

After You Read

Review Key Concepts

1. **Explain** the advantage of blending different fibers into one fabric to make a garment.
2. **Name** the strongest type of weave.
3. **Give** an example of a texture affecting a fabric's mood.

Practice Academic Skills

English Language Arts

4. In sales, a pitch is the speech the salesperson uses to convince a customer that his or her product is worthwhile. Imagine you are selling a line of active wear made from microfiber. Write a persuasive sales pitch about the benefits of your clothing line.

Social Studies

5. One of the factors that affect how we dress is climate. Because climates vary all over the world, so do choices in clothing. Which types of fabrics would be most valuable in a cold and wet climate?

 Check Your Answers Go to connectED. mcgraw-hill.com to check your answers.

Caring for Clothing

Reading Guide

Before You Read

Study Strategy Before starting this section, think about the last test you took on material you had to read. What reading strategies helped you on the test? Make a list of ways you can improve your strategies so that you will succeed on your next exam.

Read to Learn

Key Concepts

- **Give** guidelines for routine clothing care and storage.
- **Explain** clothes cleaning and drying procedures.
- **Describe** options for simple clothing repairs.

Main Idea

Laundering, storing, pressing and repairing your clothing saves you time, money and trouble in the long run.

Content Vocabulary

◇ pretreatment
◇ press
◇ iron
◇ dry-cleaning

Academic Vocabulary

You will find these words in your reading and on your tests. Use the glossary to look up their definitions if necessary.

▢ mend   ▢ establish

Graphic Organizer

Identify three main laundering products and their functions. Use a graphic organizer like the one below to organize your information.

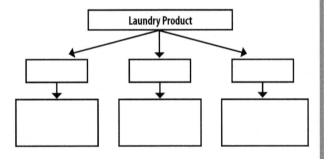

 Graphic Organizer Go to **connectED.mcgraw-hill.com** to download this graphic organizer.

Routine Clothing Care and Storage

Michael picked up his pants from the heap of clothes on the floor. "Great," he thought. "My only dress pants are a wrinkled mess." He pulled a white button-down shirt from a hanger and noticed a tear in the sleeve. "I can't believe I have to accept my sports award in clothes like this. The varsity coach is not going to be very impressed."

Have you ever been in a situation like Michael's? If so, you might need to take better routine care of your clothing. A routine is something you do regularly. Taking a little extra time each day to wash, mend, or repair, and properly store clothes can prevent you from having embarassing clothing problems later. Make the following suggestions part of your daily clothing care routine.

- **Dress and undress carefully.** Use all of your clothing fasteners, such as buttons, zippers, and snaps, to prevent clothing tears. Remove your shoes before getting in and out of shorts and pants.

- **Treat stains.** Look for any stains on your clothes and try to remove them right away. The longer a stain remains, the harder it is to take out. You can usually get a fresh stain out of washable fabric if you rinse it or soak it in cold water. More stubborn stains may need to be treated with a paste of water and detergent or a special stain remover shortly before washing. It is important to treat stains before laundering a garment. Hot water and heat can set a stain, making it extremely difficult to remove later.

- **Remove lint and pills.** Use a lint roller, a lint brush, or a battery-operated or electric lint and pill remover on your clothes. Rubbing fabric softener sheets across clothes also removes lint.

- **Repair clothes regularly.** Check for repairs you need to make, such as replacing buttons or sewing up a seam, and make the repairs as soon as possible. The longer you wait, the more likely you are to forget a garment is damaged. This can lead to frustration when you want to wear that garment.

- **Store clothes properly.** Put dirty clothes in a laundry basket or hamper. Fold or hang up clean clothes. This way your clothes are neat and easy to find.

PIXTAL/AGE Fotostock

As You Read

Connect Think about how you care for your clothes. Is there anything you would change?

Vocabulary

You can find definitions in the glossary at the back of this book.

Make Room

There are numerous ways to organize a closet. *Which organizational strategies in this photo can you try in your own closet?*

Clothing Storage

Do you have a small closet or dresser? Organizing your clothing can increase your storage space. Proper storage can keep your clothes from wrinkling or stretching out of shape. Here are some tips to help you properly store your clothes.

- **Fold clothing for drawer storage.** Folded storage is good for garments such as sweaters and knitwear. Avoid stacking too many folded items into a drawer. Stuffing drawers will cause clothing to crease. Also, fold garments a different way each time to prevent permanent creasing. You can also put tissue paper between garment folds to keep items from wrinkling. Roll up items that will not wrinkle, such as undergarments and socks, to save space. Always place the heaviest folded garments on the bottom of a drawer. Smaller items can be placed in boxes or in drawer dividers to keep them in place.

HOW TO . . .   Pack a Bag

Packing a bag, or suitcase, is an exercise in engineering as well as clothing care. The goal is to fit as many items as you can into a space about the size of a school locker, and find them still looking good when you take them out. To achieve this feat, remember these packing pointers.

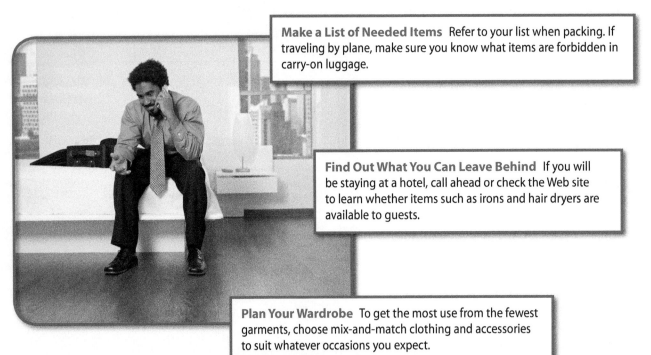

Make a List of Needed Items Refer to your list when packing. If traveling by plane, make sure you know what items are forbidden in carry-on luggage.

Find Out What You Can Leave Behind If you will be staying at a hotel, call ahead or check the Web site to learn whether items such as irons and hair dryers are available to guests.

Plan Your Wardrobe To get the most use from the fewest garments, choose mix-and-match clothing and accessories to suit whatever occasions you expect.

- **Hang clothing properly.** Avoid all-wire hangers, unless they are covered in paper or foam sheeting. They can become rusty, and the metal edges can snag the fabric. Plastic hangers provide good support for tightly woven, lightweight shirts and blouses. Padded fabric hangers are good for sheer-fabric blouses, jackets, and dresses. Garment fasteners at the neckline of shirts and blouses and at the waistline of pants and skirts keep them positioned on the hanger. Provide enough space between hanging garments to allow the air to circulate around the clothes.
- **Store clothing that is out of season.** Make sure you store clean clothes in a storage area that is clean. Attic and basement areas are often too damp, hot, or cold. Garment bags or storage boxes can protect clothes from dust, dirt, and insects. Cedar, herbal bags, or just loose bay leaves work well to deter insects.

✓ **Reading Check** **List** What tasks should be a part of your daily clothing care routine?

Prepare Your Clothing Iron clothes just before packing. Close buttons and zippers.

Pack Heavy Items First To make the most of space, fill the suitcase in layers. Fill the bottom first with shoes, guidebooks, and other heavy objects. Stuff shoes with socks or pantyhose, and place them sole to sole and heel to toe in plastic bags to keep clothes clean. Then lay clothes on top.

Minimize Wrinkling If your clothes are in dry-cleaner bags, pack them in the bags. Roll up jeans, T-shirts, and other wrinkle-resistant clothes tightly. Rolling two or more items together "fattens" the rolls, making fewer wrinkles. To reduce wrinkling, layer clothes with white tissue paper. If you are staying at a hotel or motel, use the tissue paper to line the dresser drawers.

Pack the Small Items Fill corners and small spaces with nonbreakable belongings such as a travel clock and boxed jewelry. Place travel-size liquid toiletries in a zippered plastic bag. Add another plastic bag for dirty laundry.

Take Action Use the suggestions to pack a suitcase with items you would need for a trip you plan to, or would like to, take. Leave the bag packed for at least six hours, if possible. Remove the clothes and assess the results.

Corbis

Laundering Clothes

Leigh's mother had been out of town for a week, and Leigh's dirty clothes were spilling out of her hamper and onto the floor. "I'll just toss all of these clothes into the washer and surprise Mom when she gets home. I've seen her do laundry a ton of times. How hard can it be?"

In a way, Leigh was right. Doing laundry is not difficult. However, carelessness can create some clothing disasters, such as shrunken or stained garments. By taking the time to read clothing labels, sort garments, pretreat clothes when needed, and wash and dry them properly, you can keep clothes in good condition for a long time.

Care Labels

Clothing labels are your guide to keeping your clothes looking fresh and clean. Clothing manufacturers are required to attach or stamp care labels onto garments. The labels explain, using either words or symbols, how to properly wash the clothes. Common fabric symbols are shown in **Figure 26.1**. You can also use labels to sort your clothes. Always read the care instructions on a garment before you begin a wash!

Sort Clothes

Some of the worst laundry disasters occur when clothes are not properly sorted before being tossed into the washing machine or dryer. The classic example is the bright red T-shirt sharing a wash with a collection of white socks. The red dye from the shirt runs, or transfers some color to the socks. The result? A brand-new collection of pink socks!

To avoid such accidents, you need to separate your white and light-colored clothing from your dark and deeply colored items. This is just the beginning of sorting. You also need to think about which items need special attention. Establish, or set up, a system of laundry sorting that makes sense to you and stick to it. That way, your only pair of pink socks will be the ones you chose on purpose.

Wash Clothes

Keeping your clothes clean keeps them free of dirt, stains, and odors. When done correctly, washing clothes keeps their colors brighter and helps them last longer.

 Read the Label

Reading a care label before washing can help you to properly sort laundry. *What type of care do you think this shirt would need?*

©Hero/Corbis/Glow Images

Figure 26.1

Fabric Care Symbols

Handle with Care Checking fabric care symbols before doing laundry will help you prevent laundry mishaps. *Which of these symbols appear on the tags of the clothes you are currently wearing?*

FABRIC CARE SYMBOLS

WASH	Cool/Cold Temperature	Warm Temperature	Hot Temperature		Do Not Wring
	Normal Cycle	Permanent Press Cycle	Delicate/ Gentle Cycle	Hand Wash	Do Not Wash
BLEACH	Bleach As Needed	Nonchlorine Bleach As Needed			Do Not Bleach
TUMBLE	No Heat/ Air	Low	Medium Heat	High Heat	Do Not Tumble Dry
	Any Heat/ Normal Cycle	Permanent Press Cycle	Delicate/ Gentle Cycle		
DRY	Line Dry	Drip Dry	Dry Flat	Dry in the Shade	Do Not Dry (Used With Do Not Wash)
IRON	Heat	Medium Heat	High Heat	Do Not Iron with Steam	Do Not Iron
DRY-CLEAN	Dry-Clean				Do Not Dry-Clean

JUPITERIMAGES/Comstock Images/Alamy

TAKE CHARGE!

Sort Your Laundry

Now that you are older, you may be responsible for washing your own clothes. The process will go smoothly if you follow this routine.

- **Get Organized** Gather four different-colored laundry bags, pillowcases, or laundry baskets. Bag A will be for light-colored clothes, bag B for dark-colored clothes, bag C for heavily soiled clothes, and bag D for clothing that requires special care.
- **Sort as You Go** Laundry will be an easy task if you take a few moments at the end of each day to place your used clothing in the appropriate bag.
- **Check the Labels** Check the care labels on each garment for proper washing and drying instructions before placing in the appropriate bag.
- **Pretreat Stains** Be sure to scan clothes for stains so you can pretreat them, following package instructions.

Pretreat Clothes

Pretreatment refers to any special attention you give a garment before laundering. Pretreatment helps remove heavy soil and stains that washing alone may not remove. Necklines and shirt cuffs often need pretreatment. You can use a soil-and-stain remover or an enzyme presoak. Whichever you choose, you should always read the package directions.

Use the following tips to remove some common problem stains:

- **Oil and Grease** Scrape off excess grease or blot with paper towels. Use a prewash stain remover following label directions.
- **Ink** Spray the stain with hair spray or sponge with rubbing alcohol. Blot with paper towels after a few minutes. Repeat if necessary. Rub detergent paste into stain, and wash.
- **Blood** As soon as possible, soak the fabric in cold water for 30 minutes to loosen the stain. Pretreat any remaining stain, then wash. Wash in cool water only.
- **Perspiration** Use a prewash stain remover on fresh sweat stains. Sponge old stains with white vinegar and rinse. Rub a paste of detergent and water into the stain and wash in the hottest water safe for fabric.

When removing stains, place a clean cloth behind the stained fabric layer to keep the stain and the remover from bleeding through to another layer of fabric. If the stain is not entirely removed after washing, pretreat and wash the item again before drying. The heat from a clothes dryer can set a stain, making it impossible to remove.

Machine Washing

You have probably seen the television commercials for laundry products, such as detergents, bleaches, and fabric softeners, each with a different job. The primary job of detergents is to remove dirt from clothes. Bleaches are used to remove stains and to whiten and brighten 100-percent cotton fabrics. New color-safe bleach options can be used for some clothes. Before using a bleach, read the label carefully. If it contains chlorine, the bleach should only be used for white clothing. If the label says it is color-safe, make sure to read the directions on the bottle. Test a small amount of bleach on an inside seam. Fabric softeners reduce static cling, make fabrics softer, and reduce wrinkling. In addition to products, you need to consider the washing machine's water temperature and wash cycle. Different fabrics and types of clothing require different temperatures and cycles. Place clothes loosely in the washer tub, and do not overload the washer.

If a bag does not contain a full load, wait until next time or ask family members if they would like to combine their clothes with yours to make a full load. Depending on how many full loads you have, you may need to do four loads of laundry or more.

Hand Washing

Some clothing is made from delicate fabric, and requires hand washing. To hand wash a garment, follow these steps.

1. Select a detergent suitable for delicate garments and follow the package directions.
2. Run water into a clean sink or pour water into a container large enough for the clothes to move freely.
3. Add the detergent and mix.
4. Add the clothes and soak for 5 to 30 minutes to release the dirt.
5. Gently squeeze the sudsy water through the garment. Do not wring, or twist, the clothing.
6. Drain the sink and add fresh water. Rinse at least twice in fresh water to remove both suds and soil.
7. Gently squeeze water from the garment and either lay it flat on a dry towel or hang it to dry, according to care label directions.

> **Pretreat Before Washing**
>
> Many hand-wash-only clothes can be pretreated for stains. *How can you tell if a fabric can be pretreated for stains?*

Andrew Olney/Getty Images

Are some chemicals used to clean clothes at the dry-cleaners better or safer than others? Contact several dry-cleaning businesses and ask what chemicals are used to clean their customers' garments. Do some research on these chemicals to see how they work, how long they have been used and whether they are proven safe for dry-cleaning professionals and the public. Are there alternatives to these chemicals that some people prefer? Report your findings.

Dry Clothes

Generally, articles that can be washed together can be dried together. However, some garments need to be dried in a particular way. The care label will provide the information. It might indicate that an item needs to line-dry (dry hanging up) or dry flat on a surface. If the label says an item is "tumble dry," it can go into the dryer. Check temperatures and cycles, and do not overload the machine.

Remove the clothes from the dryer as soon as they are dry. Leaving the clothes in the machine for too long increases the risk of wrinkles. Hang or fold the garments as needed and put them away.

Pressing and Ironing

After washing and drying, some clothes wrinkle and need to be pressed, or ironed. To **press** is to lift and lower an iron onto areas of the fabric. To **iron** is to move the iron back and forth over the fabric to press out wrinkles. Most fabrics can be ironed, though more delicate items that stretch and lose shape easily should be pressed. Use the iron temperature setting shown on the care label. Leaving a hot iron for too long in one spot can burn or otherwise damage the garment.

Steamers can also be used to remove wrinkles. Fabric steamers use heat to turn water into steam. The combination of heat and steam releases the wrinkles. Though some irons can steam clothes, steamers work faster than irons and do not scorch, or burn, fabrics. They come in large sizes for home use and smaller travel sizes.

To press and iron your clothes safely, follow these guidelines:
- Keep your hands and face away from the steam.
- Position the cord to keep it from snagging and pulling the iron off of the ironing board.
- Keep the iron upright when it is not in use.
- Turn off and unplug the iron after using it.
- Never leave an iron plugged in and unattended!

Dry-Cleaning

Some clothing care labels say to dry-clean garments. **Dry-cleaning** is cleaning with chemicals rather than water and detergent. The cleaned garment is then steamed to remove wrinkles.

You will find two types of dry-cleaning services. Professional dry-cleaners, although more expensive, can remove most spots and stains. Professional pressing is part of this service. Coin-operated dry-cleaning machines cost less but are limited in their ability to clean. They do not always perform special spot and stain treatment, and leave you to do the pressing. You can buy products to do your own dry-cleaning at home, but you will need a dryer to do so. Be sure to follow product directions carefully.

✓ **Reading Check** **Explain** What is the difference between pressing and ironing clothes?

Repair Clothing

Your clothes look better when they are kept in good repair. Simple repairs are not difficult to make, but you must do some planning. Before you plunge into repair work, ask yourself a few questions. Do you have the skills to make the repair? If the garment is too severely damaged and not wearable, you may want to pass up the repair. If you can make the repair, do you have the right supplies and equipment? If not, you will need to ask someone to help you. Make sure you have all of the supplies and equipment you need before you start.

Rips and Tears

Rips and tears can ruin clothing, especially when the openings are left alone to get bigger. If you act promptly to repair ripped clothing, it will most likely be wearable. Ripped seams are generally easy to repair. You can sew up the tear by hand or use a sewing machine. Just stitch a new line, beginning and ending the stitching just beyond the ripped section. Secure each end of stitching. If handstitching, backstitch to strengthen the seam.

Iron-on mending tape can help you repair other types of tears. Iron the tape to the inside of the garment. Be sure to follow the package directions. Tears can also be repaired with patches on the right side of the garment. Use hand stitching or machine stitching to attach the patch. You can also use fusible patches or iron-on patches to repair tears. Each of these is pressed onto the garment with an iron.

Buttons

There are two types of buttons, sew-through and shank. Sew-through buttons allow the sewing thread to come up through the button, showing on the top side. Shank buttons have a shank, or stem, underneath to hold the thread. The shank gives you room to work the button through the buttonhole. Because sew-through buttons do not have shanks, you should make a thread shank as you sew them on.

Follow the steps in **Figure 26.2** on page 640 when replacing a sew-through button.

Follow the steps in **Figure 26.2** on page 640 when replacing a sew-through button.

> **Keep Supplies Handy**
>
> Gathering your supplies before making a clothing repair will save you time and frustration. *What basic supplies might you include in a quick-repair kit?*

SUCCEED IN SCHOOL

Follow Up

When you get a test or quiz back, review any questions you got wrong. Try to spot your errors, and work through these problems again until you understand them and get them right. If you need help, refer to your textbook or ask your teacher for help.

Figure 26.2

Sew a Button onto Clothing

Button Up You can sew a button in a few easy steps. *Where can you find spare buttons?*

1. Place a pin where the missing button was located. Select a matching thread color.

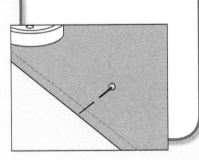

2. Double the thread in the needle and knot both ends together. Bring the needle up from the wrong side to the right side of the garment.

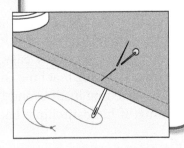

3. Take a small stitch to secure the thread knot. Remove the pin you used to mark the button replacement.

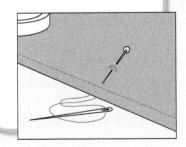

4. Bring the needle through the button. Place a tooth-pick or needle across the top of the button to allow a thread shank.

5. Make several stitches through the fabric, the button, and over the toothpick or needle.

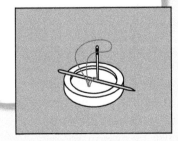

6. Remove the toothpick or needle. Bring the sewing needle and thread between the button and the fabric. Wrap the thread around the threads under the button several times to make a thread shank.

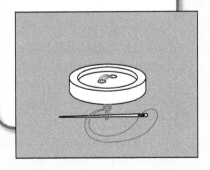

7. Bring the needle back to the wrong side of the fabric and fasten the thread securely to the fabric. Clip the thread. Your button is now securely attached.

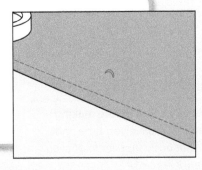

Figure 26.3 Snaps

Snap to It To sew a snap, first sew the ball section, then sew the socket section.
When would you want to use a snap closure?

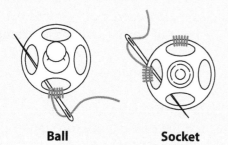

Ball   **Socket**

Snaps

An opening that does not cause much strain against the fabric is often fastened with a snap. To sew snaps, follow these steps:

1. Place the ball section of the snap about ⅛ inch (3 mm) from the underside of the overlap. Make several small stitches through each hole of the snap using a single thread. Make sure to sew through only one layer of fabric so that the stitches do not show on the right side.

2. Pin the closing together and mark the socket location, for the flat part of the snap. Mark the position of the socket by placing a pin through the center hole of the ball section. Sew the socket in place as you did the ball section. Carry the thread under the snap and secure. See **Figure 26.3**.

Figure 26.4 Hooks and Eyes

Get Hooked To sew a hook and eye, first sew the hook, then sew the eye.
When would you use a hook-and-eye attachment?

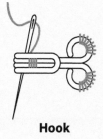

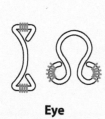

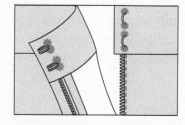

Hook   **Eye**

Hooks and Eyes

Hooks and eyes are often used to fasten openings that cause strain against the fabric. To properly sew hooks and eyes, follow these three steps:

1. Place the hook on the underside of the overlap at least $\frac{1}{8}$ inch (3 mm) from the edge. Stitch through each loop, around the curve. Sew through only one layer of fabric so that the stitches will not show on the right side.
2. Take three to four stitches around the shank of the hook so that it is held down firmly.
3. Overlap the edge and mark the position of the straight eye on the left-hand side with a pin. Stitch the eye in place through both loops. Fasten the thread. See **Figure 26.4** on p. 641.

Section 26.2

After You Read

Review Key Concepts

1. **Explain** why it is a good idea to treat a clothing stain as soon as possible after it occurs.
2. **Describe** what can happen if you do the laundry without sorting the clothing by color first.
3. **Identify** the difference between a sew-through button and a shank button.

Check Your Answers Go to connectED. mcgraw-hill.com to check your answers.

Practice Academic Skills

English Language Arts

4. Imagine that your younger sister has offered to do your laundry in exchange for a favor you did for her. When she tells you she is finished, you go to your bedroom only to find a big pile of recently washed but wrinkled clothes on your bed. Write a page of dialogue between you and your sister in which you discuss the situation.

Social Studies

5. What is considered proper or fashionable clothing for one culture may be looked upon differently by another. Choose a garment or style of dress popular in the United States. Research a culture that would not consider it proper or fashionable. Give reasons for the differing viewpoints.

CHAPTER SUMMARY

Section 26.1
Fibers and Fabrics

Natural and manufactured fibers offer characteristics that affect how they wear. An especially fine fiber called microfiber has many benefits and is often blended with natural fibers to offer the best of each. The appearance, wear and care of fabric depend partly on the way the yarns are woven and what finishes are applied. Color can be added before or after weaving takes place.

Section 26.2
Caring for Clothing

Routine care helps keep clothes in good condition. Such care includes organizing your clothing, which increases your storage space and keeps clothes from wrinkling and stretching. It is also important to practice good laundering habits. Always read clothing labels to help care for clothes. Many clothing repairs are simple, take little time, and allow people to maintain their clothing's appearance and length of wear.

Vocabulary Review

1. Use each of these content and academic vocabulary terms in a sentence.

Content Vocabulary
◇ fiber (p. 621)
◇ yarn (p. 621)
◇ natural fibers (p. 622)
◇ manufactured fibers (p. 622)
◇ generic name (p. 624)
◇ trade name (p. 624)
◇ microfiber (p. 624)
◇ finish (p. 628)
◇ pretreatment (p. 636)
◇ press (p. 638)
◇ iron (p. 638)
◇ dry-cleaning (p. 638)

Academic Vocabulary
▪ durable (p. 622)
▪ drape (p. 623)
▪ mend (p. 631)
▪ establish (p. 634)

Review Key Concepts

2. Identify natural and manufactured fibers.
3. Summarize the concepts of fabric construction and performance finishing.
4. List the six traits of fabric that can help you choose a fabric that meets your needs.
5. Give guidelines for routine clothing care and storage.
6. Explain clothes cleaning and drying procedures.
7. Describe options for simple clothing repairs.

Critical Thinking

8. Evaluate Which type of fiber do you think is better for the environment: natural, manufactured, or blends? Why?
9. Predict What do you think would happen if more people were forced to weave or knit their own clothing? How would it affect people's lives, the economy, and the environment?
10. Analyze Do you think it is harder to take time to care for clothing properly in this day and age than it was years ago? Why or why not?
11. Critique Think about the last time you had to pack a suitcase. Did you bring too much or too little? Did the clothes look good when you arrived at your destination? What would you do differently next time?

ACTIVE LEARNING

12. Be an Active Consumer The next time you go shopping for clothes, practice being an aware consumer. Consider everything about the pants or skirts you pick up. What are they made of? Will they wear well? Will they retain their shape after a long day? Will they need a lot of care? Will they stay in style for more than a few months? Considering all of these questions, are they worth the price? Take notes before shopping to decide whether to purchase a garment based on all of these questions.

Write a report on your process and what you eventually decided to do.

Family & Community Connections

13. Wardrobe Problem? Interview several of your friends and family members and ask them to describe an occasion in which they felt they were dressed inappropriately. What was the nature of the problem? Were they over dressed or under dressed? Were their clothes overly wrinkled, stained, or damaged in some way? Was it a job interview, wedding, or religious ceremony? At what point during the occasion did they realize the situation? Did they acknowledge it to someone? Did they remain in public or did they leave? How did they feel? What did they learn from the experience? Present your findings to the class. Share any similar experiences you may have had and invite your classmates to do the same. Work together on a list of guidelines that will help a person prevent such awkward clothing issues.

Real-World Skills and Applications

Leadership Skills

14. Clothing Clinic Create a plan for a "clothing clinic," in which people with garments in need of attention can learn how to repair the damage. What supplies would be needed and from where would they come? Where could the clinic be located? Who could supply the expertise? Talk to others to get feedback on your proposal. If possible, carry out your ideas.

Financial Literacy

15. Should You Sweat It? You are moving across the country to a cold, snowy climate. You would like to buy a new scarf and hat set that you saw when shopping, but it costs $70.00. You have knitting needles and the pattern seems simple, so you decide to try to make the set. The cashmere yarn you need costs $28 per skein, and you will need two skeins. To make the tassels, you will need a crochet hook that costs $7.95 and a tapestry needle that costs $2.50. You will also have to pay 8 percent sales tax on all of these items. Is it worth it to make the set?

Information Literacy

16. Read the Fine Print Whenever you bring a garment to the dry-cleaners, you should be aware of their customer policies. Most dry-cleaners will post signs and include information on the claim checks they give customers about what is their responsibility and what is yours. Get a claim check, and read this information. Summarize that dry-cleaner's policies.

Academic Skills

 English Language Arts

17. Expanded Research Check out any book from the library on the subject of clothing. Locate a statement that relates to this chapter and that you found interesting. Expand on this statement with additional research from another source. Present the result in writing.

 Science

18. Environmental Action Laundry products are necessary for clean clothing. However, they can have a negative effect on the environment.

Procedure Visit the Environmental Protection Agency (EPA) Web site to find out how you can use laundry products in the most environmentally responsible way.

Analysis Detail your findings in a one-paragraph summary.

 Mathematics

19. Generic Advice You need 15 matching wristbands for your soccer team. At the store, you see a display of white wristbands with tags bearing a popular trade name. The bands cost $6.95 each, or two for $9.99. You see another display of blue wristbands made of the same fabric but they are generic. The price is $5.01 each. Every penny counts. What should you do?

Math Concept Multiplying Decimals When multiplying numbers with decimals, remember to count the number of decimal places. If the numbers you are multiplying have a total of 3 decimal places, place the decimal in your answer after the third number from the right.

Starting Hint Remember that the 15th brand-name wristband will be full-price.

Math For math help, go to the Math Appendix at the back of the book.

 ## Standardized Test Practice

ESSAY
Directions Use a separate sheet of paper to write a one-page response to the following writing prompt.

Test-Taking Tip Before answering an essay question, think about what you want to say. Write down a few notes to help you organize your thoughts. Number your thoughts in the order you will write about them.

20. Suppose you have a part-time job helping neighbors do repairs on their homes. You are in demand, and could work as much as 25 hours a week, but your parents will not let you work more than 12 hours a week because of your other responsibilities. You believe you could work extra hours and still get your homework and household chores done. Besides, you need the money for some new clothes that your parents cannot afford to buy for you. You decide to have a talk with your parents about this. Describe how you would go about expressing your argument.

Chapter 27

Preparing to Sew

Section 27.1
Sewing Equipment

Section 27.2
Patterns, Fabric Preparation, and Notions

Chapter Objectives

Section 27.1

- **Identify** four small sewing equipment categories and their functions.
- **Explain** how to use a sewing machine.
- **Describe** the difference between a sewing machine and a serger.

Section 27.2

- **Explain** how to select patterns, fabric and notions.
- **Recall** how to prepare fabric for a pattern.
- **Outline** the five major steps you follow when using a pattern.

Vico Collective / Alamy

Writing Activity

Write a Glossary

Sewing Terms A glossary is a listing of words and short phrases, all pertaining to a chosen topic, with their definitions included alongside. Write your own glossary that consists only of sewing-related terms. You can include all parts of speech, as long as the words pertain to the subject. Include at least 20 terms.

Writing Tips Use these tips to compile a glossary:
- List glossary terms in alphabetical order.
- Write each definition next to the word it defines and on the same line.
- Definitions do not need to be written in complete sentences.

Explore the Photo

Sewing allows you to repair favorite pieces of clothing and create new, one-of-a-kind garments. *What are the other benefits of sewing?*

Sewing Equipment

Before You Read

Stay Engaged One way to stay engaged when reading is to turn each of the headings into a question, then find the answers to these questions. For example, Pressing Equipment might become "What is the purpose of pressing equipment?"

Read to Learn

Key Concepts

- **Identify** four small sewing equipment categories and their functions.
- **Explain** how to use a sewing machine.
- **Describe** the difference between a sewing machine and a serger.

Main Idea

Sewing is an enjoyable and productive activity when you learn to use the proper equipment, tools, materials and techniques.

Content Vocabulary

◇ embroider
◇ tension

Academic Vocabulary

You will find these words in your reading and on your tests. Use the glossary to look up their definitions if necessary.

☐ gauge
☐ versatile

Graphic Organizer

Name the most common sewing tools used in cutting and in measuring. Use a graphic organizer like the one below to organize your information.

Cutting Tools	Measuring Tools

 Graphic Organizer Go to **connectED.mcgraw-hill.com** to download this graphic organizer.

Small Sewing Equipment

When you have the right tools, sewing projects are more fun and your work goes faster and easier. Small sewing equipment includes cutting and measuring equipment, marking equipment, and pressing equipment, as well as a few other assorted items.

Measuring and Cutting Equipment

You will use cutting equipment to cut fabric and thread. Keep all cutting equipment sharp by using it only for sewing. You will use measuring equipment to measure patterns, fabric, and garment pieces accurately as you sew. See **Figure 27.1**. Here are the basics:

- **Small Scissors** Use small scissors to clip threads and trim, or cut fabric.
- **Shears** Cut fabric with shears. Shears have long blades with one handle for the thumb and one handle for two or more fingers. Bent-handled shears improve your accuracy because they allow the fabric to lie flat and hardly lift from the table as you cut.
- **Seam Ripper** The seam ripper has a hooklike point. It is used to cut and remove stitches, mostly in seams.
- **Tape Measure** This is a flexible, narrow strip of durable plastic or cloth used to take body measurements and measure fabric.
- **Yardstick** This ruler, which is 36 inches (91.5 cm) or one yard long, is useful for measuring patterns and fabrics on a flat surface and for checking hemlines.
- **Sewing or Seam Gauge** This small, metal ruler has a slide marker that can be set to gauge, or measure, specific lengths, such as the width of a seam or hem.

As You Read

Connect Think about what types of small sewing equipment you would use to take in the seam of a pair of pants. Would you be prepared?

Vocabulary

You can find definitions in the glossary at the back of this book.

Figure 27.1 **Measuring and Cutting Equipment**

Measure Twice, Cut Once Cutting and measuring tools are essential for sewing. *Why is it important to double-check your measurements before cutting fabric?*

Small Scissors

Shears

Seam Ripper

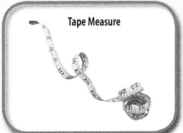
Tape Measure

Yardstick

Seam Gauge

McGraw-Hill Education

Health & Wellness

TIPS

Back Basics

Activities like sewing can take an unexpected toll on the back, especially if you have been leaning over a cutting table. Keep the following tips in mind while working on your project:

▶ Do not lock your knees. Keep them slightly bent to distribute your weight.

▶ Move around every 15 minutes to prevent muscles from getting stiff.

▶ Stand on a mat or wear padded shoes. Hard floors, flat soles, and long periods of standing don't mix!

Marking Equipment

Marking equipment helps you transfer construction markings, such as buttonhole and pocket positions, from your pattern pieces to the fabric. The more accurate your marks are, the easier clothing construction will be.

The marking equipment you need depends on the fabric. See **Figure 27.2** for examples of the most commonly used marking tools:

- **Tracing Wheel** You can use a tracing wheel and a special, colored waxed paper called dressmaker's tracing paper to transfer pattern markings to fabric. A saw-toothed tracing wheel should be used on most fabrics. Choose a smooth-edged tracing wheel when working with delicate fabrics. These tracing marks will disappear once the garment is washed or dry-cleaned.

- **Fabric Marker** Fabric markers are also called fabric pens. These special pens are used to put temporary marks on the right side of fabric or the wrong side. Some fabric pen marks can be removed with water. Others fade by themselves after a short period, usually 48 hours. Test fabric markers on a fabric scrap before using them.

- **Tailor's Chalk** Pencils, small squares, or small wheels of chalk are also used to mark fabrics. Most chalk markings can be brushed away with your hand when you no longer need them. Any remaining chalk marks will disappear when pressed with an iron.

- **Ordinary Thread** You can also make simple hand-sewn stitches to mark construction lines on fabric. These stitches can easily be cut out when they are no longer needed.

| Figure 27.2 | **Marking Equipment** |

Mark It Up Pens and markers are not just for paper. There are several special marking tools you can use on your sewing projects. *Why would you want to use a fabric pen instead of a regular ballpoint pen on fabric?*

Tracing Wheel

Tailor's Chalk

Fabric Marker

Other Small Sewing Equipment

Some other small sewing aids can help you as you work on your sewing project. Your sewing kit will not be complete without these helpful tools:

- **Straight Pins** These are used to anchor the pattern to the fabric and to hold layers of fabric together for sewing.
- **Pincushion** Use a pincushion to keep needles and pins handy while you work. Many pincushions come with an attached emery bag. Push rusty or sticky needles and pins into this bag a few times and it will clean them.
- **Thimble** A thimble can be used to push the needle through fabric while hand sewing. Thimbles come in different sizes and are made of metal or plastic, with small dimples to help hold the end of the needle. A thimble should fit snugly on the third finger of the hand that holds the needle.
- **Hand Sewing Needles** Needles are numbered from 1 (very thick) to 12 (very fine). A sharp point and medium length make "sharps" best for general hand sewing, so try a size 7 or 8.
- **Machine Needles** Machine needles range from 60 (very fine for delicate fabrics) to 110 (very thick for coarse, heavy fabrics). Select the size best suited for your fabric. Use ballpoint needles for knit fabric. A needle that is dull, bent, or rough needs to be replaced.
- **Needle Threader** This small tool has a very thin and flexible metal wire that helps thread a needle.
- **Basting Tape** Use this narrow, double-faced tape to hold two layers of fabric together or a zipper in place for stitching.
- **Glue Stick** A glue stick is a fast, easy way to hold two layers of fabric together. Make sure the glue is completely dry before stitching through it.

Small Sewing Aids

Sewing aids help make sewing jobs easier. *Where can you find these and other sewing aids?*

Pressing Equipment

Pressing your project as you sew helps your work stay neat and gives it a finished and professional look. Basic pressing equipment includes an iron and ironing board. Choose a steam iron with a wide temperature range and a well-padded ironing board with a tight-fitting cover. You also need a press cloth when pressing certain fabrics to keep them from scorching or developing a shine or glossy marking. You can buy ready-made press cloths at your local fabric store. Or you can use a clean handkerchief or large, lightweight cloth.

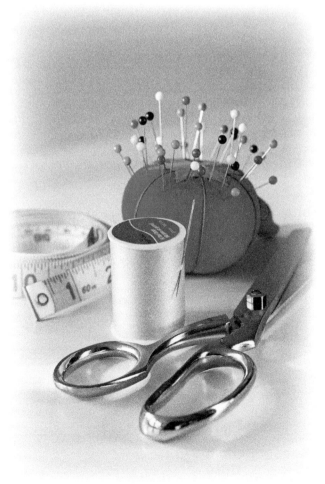

✓ Reading Check **Compare** What is the difference between a fabric marker and tailor's chalk?

Learn from Mistakes

Do not get upset with yourself if you make a mistake. Making mistakes is part of the learning process. The next time you have to solve a similar problem, you will know what will not work, which can help point you to the right solution.

Sewing Machines

Sewing projects at home is much faster and easier when you have a sewing machine to help you. A sewing machine is a versatile, or multipurpose, piece of equipment that requires considerable investment. Machines range from basic models to computerized machines that allow you to **embroider**, or add needlework details, with the touch of a button. However, you do not need a fancy machine to handle most sewing projects.

Here are some things to check when buying a sewing machine:

- The machine starts and stops smoothly.
- The bobbin is easy to wind and insert.
- The foot pedal is comfortable and easy to use.
- The needle area is well lit.
- Machine stitching is even and attractive, no matter what direction the machine is sewing.
- You know whom to contact if you have a problem with the machine.

Before you purchase a sewing machine, review the features carefully to make sure it will fit your needs. After you get the sewing machine home, read the operating manual. Take some time to learn about the parts of the sewing machine and how to use it safely. You might also ask an experienced person to show you how to operate and care for the machine.

Figure 27.3   Basic Parts of a Sewing Machine

Know Your Machine   All sewing machines share the same basic parts. *How many of these parts can you identify without looking at the labels?*

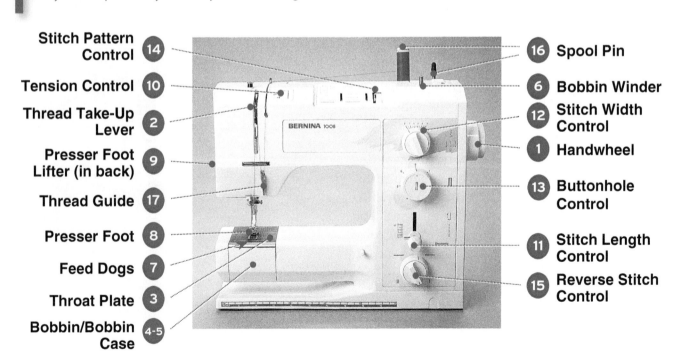

Stitch Pattern Control 14

Tension Control 10

Thread Take-Up Lever 2

Presser Foot Lifter (in back) 9

Thread Guide 17

Presser Foot 8

Feed Dogs 7

Throat Plate 3

Bobbin/Bobbin Case 4-5

16 Spool Pin

6 Bobbin Winder

12 Stitch Width Control

1 Handwheel

13 Buttonhole Control

11 Stitch Length Control

15 Reverse Stitch Control

Parts of the Machine

All sewing machines operate in a similar manner. Knowing a machine's major parts helps you operate it successfully and safely. The parts shown in **Figure 27.3** on page 652 are found on most machines. Check your manual to find them on your machine. Machines that embroider and monogram have additional parts or components.

1. **Hand Wheel** This large wheel on the right side of the machine controls the up-and-down movement of the needle and thread take-up lever.
2. **Thread Take-up Lever** This lever feeds thread from the spool to the needle.
3. **Throat Plate** This is the metal plate under the machine needle. On most machines, the throat plate is also etched with seam allowance markings for accurate sewing.
4. **Bobbin** This small, flat, spool holds the bottom thread.
5. **Bobbin Case** This holds the bobbin and is found beneath the throat plate.
6. **Bobbin Winder** This spindle holds the bobbin while thread is wound from the thread spool to the bobbin. The location of this spindle varies with each machine.
7. **Feed Dogs** The feed dogs are a set of metal "teeth" that move the fabric during stitching.
8. **Presser Foot** This holds the fabric firmly in place against the feed dogs for sewing.
9. **Presser Foot Lifter** This lever raises and lowers the presser foot.
10. **Tension Control** This dial adjusts the tightness or looseness of the needle thread.
11. **Stitch Length Control** This is used to adjust the length of stitches from short to long.
12. **Stitch Width Control** This control is used to adjust the width of other stitches, such as the zigzag stitch.
13. **Buttonhole Control** The built-in buttonhole maker creates perfect buttonholes.
14. **Stitch Pattern Control** The stitch pattern control can be adjusted to make different stitching patterns.
15. **Reverse Stitch Control** This button or lever allows backward stitching.
16. **Spool Pin** This pin holds the spool of thread.
17. **Thread Guides** These guide the thread as it travels from the spool to the needle.
18. **Foot or Knee Control** This control regulates the starting, running, and stopping of the machine (not shown).

Guiding Fabric

When guiding fabric through the machine, keep one hand in front and one hand in back of the presser foot. *Why is this technique effective?*

Care for Your Sewing Machine

Routine care will keep your sewing machine in good working order. To care for your machine, follow these steps once a month:

- **Pull the Plug** Unplug the machine before cleaning or doing other machine maintenance.
- **Remove Lint** Use a soft cloth to remove lint from the needle bar and the base of the machine.
- **Clean the Bobbin** Use a soft brush to clean the bobbin case and bobbin. Follow the manual's directions to remove the entire bobbin case for further cleaning.
- **Add Oil** Follow the manufacturer's directions to oil the machine. Use only high-grade sewing machine oil. Wipe away any drips after oiling. Plug in the machine and stitch on a scrap of fabric to remove excess oil.

Real-World Skills

Sewing for Profit Equipment care is only part of what you need to take into consideration when starting your own clothing line. Do some research to find out what it takes to start a new clothing business, including equipment, design, and marketing. Present your findings to the class.

Threading the Machine

Before you can start sewing with a machine, you need to wind the bobbin and thread the machine.

Some sewing machines have a bobbin winder built right into the bobbin case. But most bobbins must be removed from the bobbin case in order to be wound. Your machine's manual will provide instructions for winding the bobbin. Make sure the bobbin winds evenly.

Threading a machine is not as difficult as it looks. The general procedure for threading a machine is the same for all machines. Refer to **Figure 27.3** on page 652 if you need help visualizing these instructions:

1. Raise the presser foot and turn the hand wheel toward you to raise the needle and take-up lever to the highest position.
2. Place the spool of thread on the spool pin.
3. Lead thread through all threading points.
4. Thread tension discs. The thread should be placed between two of the discs and then brought up and caught on a spring or a hook on the tension discs.
5. Run the thread through the take-up lever from right to left.
6. Thread needle. If the last thread guide is on the right, thread the needle from the right. If the last guide is on the left, thread the needle from the left. If the guide is on the front of the needle bar, thread the needle from front to back.

After threading the machine and putting the filled bobbin into the bobbin case, bring the bobbin thread up through the hole in the throat plate. To do this, hold the end of the needle thread while turning the hand wheel toward you one full turn. The needle thread will pull up a loop of bobbin thread. Pull up on this loop until the thread end is out of the throat plate.

Machine Stitching

All machines do straight stitching the same way. If you have not sewn before or will be using a different machine, practice stitching. Here are the general directions.

1. Raise the take-up lever and needle to the highest point. Do the same when you finish stitching. This keeps the thread from pulling out of the needle or tangling in the bobbin.
2. Pull the needle thread and bobbin thread to the right side of the presser foot. The threads should also be underneath the presser foot.
3. Place the fabric under the presser foot. First lower the needle into the fabric at the beginning of the stitching line and then lower the presser foot. The bulk of the fabric should be to the left of the machine.
4. Start the machine slowly. A smooth, steady speed allows better control.
5. Use the throat plate markings to guide your fabric through the machine. This helps you keep an even seam width.
6. Slow the machine speed for the last few stitches. This helps prevent stitching beyond the edge of the fabric.
7. Secure stitching at both ends of a seam. There are several ways that you can do this. Backstitching, or retracing your stitches about ½ inch (1.3 cm), is done by using the reverse stitch control on the machine. Another way to secure stitching is to tie the threads at the end of the seam. See **Fig. 27.4** below.

Figure 27.4 **Secure Stitching**

A Stitch In Time Saves Nine There are several ways you can secure stitching. Backstitching and tying off threads are the most common methods. *Can you suggest a third way to make sure your stitches stay put?*

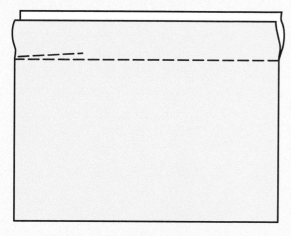

Reverse Stitching or Backstitching

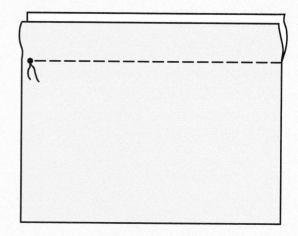

Tied Threads

Adjusting Stitch Length and Tension

The correct stitch length and tension make a seam attractive and strong. A medium-length stitch (2 to 2.5 mm or 10 to 12 stitches per inch) is used for most fabrics. Check the machine stitching on a two-layer scrap of your fabric before beginning to sew. Change the stitch length by adjusting the stitch length control.

Tension refers to the tightness or looseness of the thread. The tension is balanced when the stitching looks the same on both sides. It is not in balance if thread loops form on either side of the fabric. Newer machines seldom require adjustments when regular sewing thread is used in the needle and the bobbin. If tension problems occur, check the machine and bobbin threading before adjusting the tension dial. If the tension needs adjusting, your machine manual will tell you how to correct it. If the thread has become tangled in the bobbin area, the thread must be removed. Turn off the machine and check the manual or ask your teacher for further directions. See **Figure 27.5** below.

✓ **Reading Check** **Identify** What should you look for when purchasing a sewing machine?

Figure 27.5 **Checking Tension**

Properly Balanced Stitches A properly balanced stitch has two threads that lock in the center between the two layers of fabric. If there are loops on one side of the fabric, the tension will need to be adjusted. Most new machines rarely require tension adjustments. *What should you do if tension problems occur?*

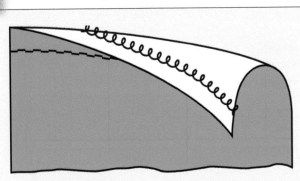

Upper Tension too Tight

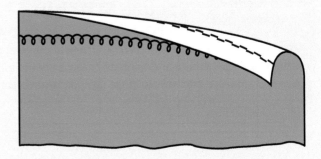

Lower Tension too Tight

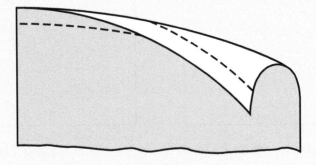

Balanced Tension

Serger Sewing

Why do the seams in ready-to-wear clothes appear so smooth and neat? You can make garments that look as good as ready-to-wear clothing by using a serger. A serger, or overlock machine, stitches, trims, and finishes a seam in one step, and it is twice as fast as a sewing machine. Some garments, such as sweatshirts, can be sewn entirely on the serger. However, many projects also require a sewing machine. This is because a serger cannot make buttonholes, insert a zipper, or do embroidery.

Comparing Sergers and Sewing Machines

Unlike sewing machines, sergers have cutters that trim the seam before it is stitched, and they may also use two needles, depending on the model. Sergers use more thread than sewing machines. Most serger thread comes on cones that hold 1,000 or more yards. Some sergers use two or more cones of thread for stitching. Sergers also have no bobbin. Two loopers take the place of bobbins.

Figure 27.6   Basic Parts of a Serger

A Professional Touch   Using a serger can make a homemade garment appear professionally made. As the detailed illustration shows, the serger loopers and knives shown in the diagram are found under the looper cover. When the looper cover is open on most sergers, the machine will not sew. *In what ways do sergers differ from conventional sewing machines?*

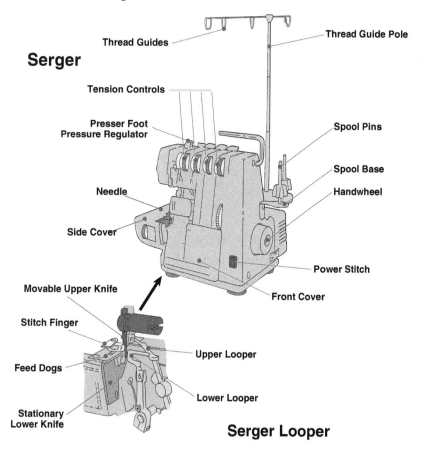

When sewing with a serger, it is not necessary to lift the presser foot when starting to sew, unless the fabric is thick. The serger feed dogs grip the fabric as you begin to sew. Also, you should never sew over pins with a serger because the pins will damage the serger's cutting knives and the pins could fly out and hurt you. Always follow proper safety precautions when you use a serger.

Using a Serger

All brands of sergers sew basically the same way. When you feed the fabric into the machine, the feed dogs grip the fabric and pull it toward the cutters. The cutters trim the fabric edges before the fabric reaches the loopers and needles for stitching. Rather than backstitching, you simply run the fabric off the serger behind the needles. Securing the ends of stitching is not necessary for most projects. See **Figure 27.6** on page 657.

Section 27.1

After You Read

Review Key Concepts

1. **Recall** why machine needles come in so many different sizes.
2. **Explain** how to thread a sewing machine.
3. **Give** two examples of what can happen if you sew over a straight pin with a serger.

Check Your Answers Go to connectED. mcgraw-hill.com to check your answers.

Practice Academic Skills

English Language Arts

4. Making a garment from scratch requires knowledge, skill and practice. Not everyone, however, can become an expert at the craft. Describe what traits you think a person needs to learn how to sew major projects. How would those traits come in handy during the learning and working process? Conclude your writing by telling whether you think you can develop the necessary skills to become successful at sewing.

Social Studies

5. Learning how to sew can bring awareness in several ways. Once you learn how to make your own shirt or dress, you may find yourself looking at ready-made clothes in a different light. When you go clothes shopping, do you examine garments a bit more carefully? Describe how learning about clothing design and construction has affected your clothes-buying habits. If you have not been affected, explain why.

Patterns, Fabric Preparation, and Notions

Reading Guide

Before You Read

Adjust Reading Speed Improve your comprehension by adjusting your reading speed to match the difficulty of the text. Slow down, and reread difficult paragraphs. Reading this way may take longer, but you will understand and remember more.

Read to Learn

Key Concepts

- **Explain** how to select patterns, fabric, and notions.
- **Recall** how to prepare fabric for a pattern.
- **Outline** the five major steps you follow when using a pattern.

Main Idea

Sewing your own garment begins with knowing how to select and use a pattern, choose and prepare fabric, and gather and use the appropriate sewing notions.

Content Vocabulary

◇ interfacing
◇ notions
◇ ease
◇ selvage
◇ bias

Academic Vocabulary

You will find these words in your reading and on your tests. Use the glossary to look up their definitions if necessary.

☐ proportions   ☐ excess

Graphic Organizer

As you read, take note of the different types of sewing notions that can be used to enhance a garment. Use a graphic organizer like the one below to organize your information.

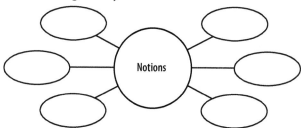

Graphic Organizer Go to **connectED.mcgraw-hill.com** to download this graphic organizer.

Select Project Materials

In sewing, you can use a pattern from which to make an item or clothing. Constructed out of paper or cardboard, the pattern is a set of templates that represent the different parts of the garment. By tracing and cutting out fabric around the templates, you create a collection of pieces needed for your final product.

Choose a Pattern

You can find hundreds of sewing projects by looking through a pattern catalog, either in the fabric store or online. Catalogs are organized into different sections, such as easy-to-sew styles, sportswear, and dresses, and show different views of a garment. Patterns in catalogs have assigned numbers. When you find the pattern you want, write the number down. You can find the pattern in the numbered cabinet drawers at the fabric store.

Pattern Envelopes

The front and back of the pattern envelope contain important information that you can use to select a project. They also provide a list of the supplies you need for a project.

- **Special Information** Helpful information such as "easy to sew" is called out on the envelope front.
- **Pictures** Colorful views, or garment styles, that can be made from the pattern are shown on the front of the package.
- **Garment Description** The explanation of the garment provides details that may not be obvious from the illustration.
- **Views** This shows design lines and details not easily seen on the envelope front.
- **Suggested Fabrics** Most envelopes have a guide to selecting the fabric that will give you the best results.
- **Notions** This section identifies the extra items, such as buttons, zippers, and trims, needed to make the garment.
- **Yardage Chart** The yardage chart lists the amount of fabric needed for each view, size, and fabric width.
- **Body Measurements** These guidelines help you to determine your correct pattern size.

Body Measurements

When you construct garments, you must take body measurements. Take the measurements over close-fitting clothes. Remove bulky sweaters, jackets, and belts. **Figure 27.7** gives guidelines for measuring specific body parts.

As You Read

Connect Think about the wide variety of clothes available at stores. Can you picture them well enough to choose a clothing pattern suited to your tastes?

▼ Pattern Envelope

The front of a pattern envelope shows the item. The back of the envelope is your guide for selecting the proper fabric and any additional items you will need. *Why is it important to review the back of an envelope before leaving the fabric store?*

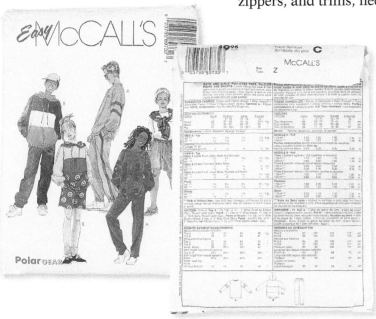

Figure 27.7 **Taking Measurements**

Just Your Size Use these measuring methods to determine your pattern size.
Why should you be careful when taking measurements?

FOR MALES	
Neck	Measure around the base of the neck and add ½ inch (1.3 cm) or buy a pattern based on the shirt size you regularly purchase.
Chest	Measure around the fullest part of the chest.
Waist	Tie a string around the waist to identify where the measurement should be taken.
Hip/Seat	Measure around the fullest part of the hip or seat, about 8 inches (20.5 cm) below the waist.
Outseam	Measure along the outside of the leg from the waist to the desired length of the pants, usually where the pants bottom breaks slightly on the shoe.
Inseam	Place pants that are the correct length on a flat surface. Measure along the inner seam from the bottom of one leg to where the two legs meet.

FOR FEMALES	
Back Waist Length	Measure from the base of the neck to the waistline.
Bust	Measure around the fullest part of the bust and under the arms.
Waist	Tie a string around the waist to identify the narrowest point. Measure around the body exactly where the string settles.
Hip	Measure around the fullest part of the hips, 7 to 9 inches (18 to 23 cm) below the waist.
Outseam	Measure along the outside of the leg from the waist, over the hips, to the desired length of the skirt or pants.
Inseam	Place pants that are the correct length on a flat surface. Measure along the inner seam from the bottom of one leg to where the two legs meet.

When you take measurements, hold the tape measure, with two fingers beneath the tape, so that it fits snugly. Be sure it is not too tight or too loose. It is easier to work with a partner so you can measure each other. Write each measurement down as you take it. You will use your body measurements to determine your figure type and the pattern size.

- **Figure types** are size categories, such as juniors and misses, based on height and body proportions, or relative size. Girls also need to know back waist length to identify figure type. Compare this information with the body measurement charts in the back of the pattern catalog to determine your figure type.

- **Pattern size** is determined by comparing your chest or bust, waist, and hip measurements with those listed on the pattern envelope. You will choose your pattern size for most garments according to your chest or bust measurement. When making pants or a skirt, use your waist measurement. However, if your hips are large compared with your waist, use the hip measurement for the best fit. When your measurements fall between two sizes, pick the smaller size unless the design is close fitting.

◆ Vocabulary

You can find definitions in the glossary at the back of this book.

Community Connections

On the Job

Observe an employee waiting on a customer at a fabric store. Does the employee seem to be helping the customer find or get what they need? Can you tell by watching the customer whether he or she is satisfied? How might you handle this customer differently if you were the fabric store employee?

Choose Fabric

Before purchasing garment fabric, ask yourself several questions: How appropriate is the fabric for your pattern and your sewing skills? How will the fabric look on you? What kind of care will the fabric need?

Buy fabric you like and with which you will enjoy working. If you are making an active sportswear garment, concentrate on fabrics that are durable. On the other hand, if you are making something for a special occasion, you may want a dressier fabric. When you purchase your fabric, remember to ask for the fabric care label and attach this to your garment.

Interfacing is a special fabric that gives support and body to a garment or project. It is placed between the facing and the outer fabric and is not visible. It can be found in hats, belts, bags, and around necklines to keep them from stretching. You can buy sew-in or fusible interfacing. Sew-in interfacing is stitched to the garment. Fusible interfacing is pressed on with a hot iron.

HOW TO... Select Notions

The name sounds fanciful, but notions are a practical part of a garment. Choose notions for your sewing project with as much care as you choose fabric. In fact, choose them when you choose your fabric because notions and fabric should complement each other. In particular, make sure they have the same care needs. Using your pattern as a guide, look at these basic notions.

Thread Polyester or polyester-cotton thread works for most fabrics because it combines strength, flexibility, stretch, and shrink resistance. Mercerized cotton thread works on natural fiber woven fabrics, such as 100 percent cotton. Silk thread is for silk or woolen fabrics, heavy-duty thread for heavy fabrics and buttonhole twist thread for decorative top stitching. Always use a quality brand. Inferior thread may break or tangle in machines.

Buttons Besides usefulness, buttons offer a chance to enhance the look of a garment. Designs run from plain discs to bow ties. Materials range from mother-of-pearl to plastic. You can even find wooden buttons "designed" by termites. They were shaped by the patterns created as the termites ate through the wood.

Zippers A look through your closet will likely show a variety of zippers that meet a number of applications. Conventional zippers are used in pants and dresses. A jacket shell needs a separating zipper. Invisible zippers blend into the seam. Decorative zippers are meant to stand out.

Choose an interfacing that has similar weight, body, and care requirements as your fabric. If you are unsure about a fabric, talk to a salesperson or your teacher.

Choose Notions

Notions are the small items, such as thread, zippers, buttons, trim, seam binding, hooks and eyes, and snaps, needed to complete a garment. The back of the pattern envelope lists the notions you will need.

Select thread just slightly darker than the fabric. If you have a print, match the thread with the main color in the print. Zippers come in a variety of colors, lengths, and styles. Check the pattern envelope for the zipper length and type suggested. Match the color of the zipper to the fabric as closely as possible. If the fabric has several colors, match the zipper to the background color.

✓ **Reading Check** **Explain** What guidelines should you follow when taking measurements?

Other Fasteners Depending on the garment, you may need buckles or two-piece fasteners such as snaps or hooks and eyes. Check the pattern for the recommended size and style.

Elastic Width is the main difference in elastics used in garments. Both woven and knitted elastic maintain their width when stretched and can be sewn directly onto fabric. Read labels to learn other qualities, such as shrink or roll resistance.

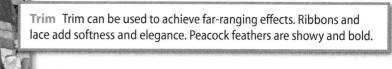

Trim Trim can be used to achieve far-ranging effects. Ribbons and lace add softness and elegance. Peacock feathers are showy and bold.

Take Action Choose a garment that you own. Think of three ways you could change or improve the look or fit by changing or adding notions. Sketch your ideas or implement the changes.

Prepare Fabric

All woven fabric is made up of two sets of yarn, or grain, lengthwise and crosswise. The lengthwise grain, running the length of the fabric, has little or no stretch. The **selvage** is the finished lengthwise edge of the fabric. It will not ravel. The crosswise grain, running from selvage to selvage, has more stretch than the lengthwise grain. The true bias has the most stretch. **Bias** is the diagonal line formed when the fabric is folded with the crosswise grain parallel to the selvage. See **Figure 27.8**.

A fabric's crosswise and lengthwise grains must be square (at right angles to each other) when you cut out your pattern; otherwise, the finished garment may not hang properly.

Straighten Fabric Ends

It is difficult to check whether the fabric grain is straight if the crosswise edges are uneven. To straighten the fabric ends, clip into the selvage and pull one crosswise thread (yarn) with one hand while pushing the fabric back with the other hand. Cut along this pulled-thread line. If the thread breaks before you reach the other selvage, pick up the end of the broken thread and continue pulling and cutting as necessary. See **Figure 27.9** on the next page.

Figure 27.8 **Selvage and Bias**

Go With the Grain Most garments are cut with the lengthwise grain running vertically, or up and down, for more strength and durability during wear. *What can happen if you cut your fabric on the bias instead?*

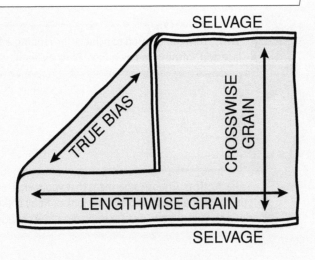

SELVAGE

TRUE BIAS

CROSSWISE GRAIN

LENGTHWISE GRAIN

SELVAGE

Preshrink Fabric

Have you ever noticed the word "preshrunk" on the care label of one of your tee shirts? This means the fabric was washed or dry-cleaned before the shirt was made, in order to prevent later shrinking.

Before you start any sewing project, you need to launder any fabric you will be using. Otherwise, you may spend hours working on a garment that fits you perfectly, only to have it shrink to a size too small for you to wear the first time you wash it! Preshrinking also removes fabric finishes that could cause stitching problems. Preshrink washable fabrics in the same manner you plan to launder the finished garment.

Follow the care label you received when you purchased your fabric. For fabrics that ravel easily, zigzag stitch or serge the cut edges before washing the fabric. All woven interfacings, zippers, and trims should also be preshrunk.

✓ **Reading Check** **Explain** Why is it important to prepare fabric before working with it?

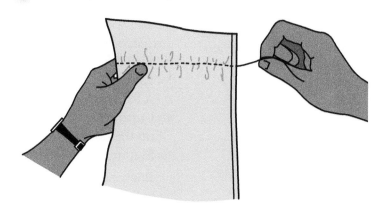

Figure 27.9 Straightening Fabric Ends

No Marking Tool Necessary The pulled thread leaves a mark you can use as a cutting line. *How can you make sure this line stays secure when you start to cut?*

How I See It

HANDLE WITH CARE
Alexis, 14

I have been sewing ever since I was seven years old. My grandmother used to sew and would give me her remnants of material so I could make outfits for my dolls. I got better and better at it, and by the time I was 12, all I could think of was having my own sewing machine for big projects. I began saving my allowance, birthday checks and babysitting money. By my 14th birthday last month, I was finally able to pick out my own machine.

Because I had to wait so long and work so hard for it, I take really good care of my sewing machine. I have a special table for it and I always keep it covered when I'm not using it. I guess I'm a sewing nerd but I don't feel embarrassed about it. I get a lot of compliments on my original creations. Plus, just about everyone has something they are nerdy about.

Critical Thinking Alexis talks about being a nerd when it comes to sewing. Does being passionate about something make someone too different from everyone else, especially other teens? What has your own experience taught you?

Use the Pattern

Once you have chosen a pattern, taken measurements, and prepared the fabric you will use, you are ready to put everything together!

Read the Pattern

You will find the guide sheet and pattern pieces inside the pattern envelope. The guide sheet contains the following:

- Sketches of different styles or views that can be made from the pattern.
- A list and diagram of pattern pieces.
- Cutting layouts, or diagrams, that show how to lay pattern pieces on the fabric for different sizes, fabric widths, and types of fabric.
- Step-by-step instructions for sewing the garment or project.

Each pattern piece has pattern symbols or markings that serve as guides for laying out, cutting, and sewing your project. See **Figure 27.10**. These are common symbols you will see.

1. **Cutting Line** This is the heavy line you follow on the outside of the pattern to cut out the fabric.
2. **Grainline** The grainline is a straight line with arrows on each end to be placed in the direction of the lengthwise grain, crosswise grain, or bias. See **Figure 27.8** on page 664.
3. **Place on Fold** A bracketed grainline indicates the pattern edge to be placed exactly on the fold of the fabric.
4. **Darts** Folded and stitched triangular or diamond shapes indicated by dots and broken lines show where darts belong.
5. **Placement Line** Not to be confused with the cutting line, this solid line shows where to locate pockets, trims, and other features.
6. **Seamline or Stitching Line** This broken line, usually $5/8$ inch (1.5 cm) inside the cutting line, shows where to stitch the seams.
7. **Adjustment Line** This line is actually two parallel lines that indicate where to cut or fold a pattern for lengthening or shortening.
8. **Notches** Diamond-shaped symbols along the cutting line show where to join the pattern pieces together.
9. **Dots, Squares, and Triangles** These symbols help you match and join project sections together.

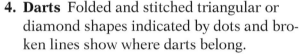

Follow the Lines

Before you choose a cutting line, remember that pattern pieces are generally larger than your exact body measurements. *What should you do when you are between two sizes?*

Figure 27.10 **Pattern Symbols**

Look Carefully Some pattern pieces have many markings, so it can be hard to tell which is which. *What could happen if you mistake the seamline for the cutting line?*

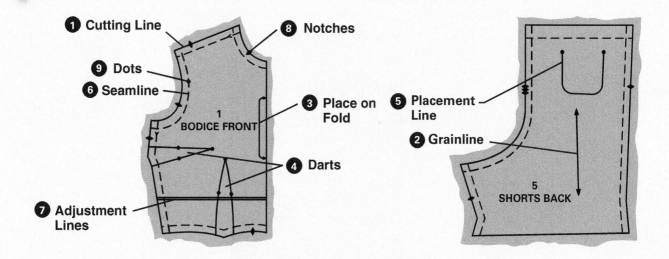

- **1** Cutting Line
- **8** Notches
- **9** Dots
- **6** Seamline
- **3** Place on Fold
- **5** Placement Line
- **2** Grainline
- **4** Darts
- **7** Adjustment Lines

1 BODICE FRONT

5 SHORTS BACK

Fit the Pattern

When you make a garment, you need to check to see how well the pattern fits you. You can do this by comparing your measurements with those of the pattern. Follow these three steps:

1. Smooth out the pattern with your hands or press the pattern pieces with a warm, dry iron.
2. Measure the pattern between stitching lines at the same places where the body measurements were taken and write them down.
3. Do not include seam allowances (the fabric between the cutting line and the stitching line) or darts when measuring the pattern pieces.

In most cases, you can expect the pattern pieces to be larger than your exact body measurements. Do not worry! Your pattern should be larger to account for wearing and design ease. **Ease** refers to the extra room needed for movement and comfort. Some garments have plenty of ease. However, if the garment is close-fitting and the pattern measurements are much larger or smaller than your body measurements, you need to make some adjustment in the pattern.

Lay Out the Pattern

The pattern guide sheet lists the pattern pieces needed for each view. Before you lay out the pattern, cut apart the pattern pieces you need. Leave some excess, or extra paper outside of the cutting lines on all pieces. On the guide sheet, check off the pattern pieces needed as you find them, and put the extra ones back into the envelope. Press the pattern pieces with a warm, dry iron if they are wrinkled. If you are working in the clothing lab, write your name on the pattern pieces so that you do not lose them.

Figure 27.11 **Positioning Pattern Pieces**

Line Up Place a pin at the end of each grain-line arrow. Measure carefully from the point of each arrow to the edge of the fabric. *What is the easiest way to correct a slight difference in measurement?*

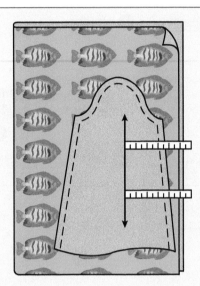

Position Pattern Pieces

It is important to place pattern pieces on the fabric correctly. Once fabric has been cut, it is difficult to correct layout mistakes. Follow these four steps.

1. **Circle the layout you are using on the pattern guide sheet.** The layout shows how to place the pattern pieces for the view, fabric width, and size you are making.
2. **Check the layout instructions carefully.** Note the markings indicating the right and wrong sides of the fabric, the right and wrong sides of the pattern, the pattern pieces to be cut a second time, and any pattern pieces to be cut from a single layer of fabric.
3. **Fold the fabric as shown in the layout diagram.** Generally, fabric is folded in half on the lengthwise grain with right sides together.
4. **Position any large pattern pieces that go on the fold first.** Then position the remaining pattern pieces so that their grain-line symbols are straight on the fabric grain. See **Figure 27.11**. Pin the pieces securely, inserting the pins perpendicular to, but not on, the cutting line.

Cut Out the Pattern

Use sharp shears to cut out the fabric. Follow the outside cutting lines carefully. Do not cut on the fold line. Try to hold the pattern and fabric flat with one hand as you cut with the other to prevent the fabric from moving under the pattern. Do not pick up the fabric to cut it. Move around the table as you work instead of moving the fabric.

Cut the notches outward, not inward. When you cut inward, you can weaken the seam. You can also accidentally cut into the garment. If two or three notches are together, cut them across the top as one long notch.

Keep pattern pieces pinned to the fabric for marking and identification. If you are using interfacing, cut out the interfacing when you finish cutting the fabric.

Mark Fabric

The lines and symbols on your pattern are your guides for sewing accurately. Transfer these markings to the wrong side of your fabric before the pattern is unpinned. They must be visible as you sew but should not show on the outside of the finished project.

You can transfer markings to the fabric in one of several ways. You can make temporary markings on fabric using fabric markers. Test the markers on a fabric scrap first to be sure the markings can be removed. You can also use chalk and pins. Put a pin through the pattern and fabric at the place to be marked. Make a chalk mark on the wrong side of both fabric layers at the pin marking. Another option is to use tracing paper and a tracing wheel. Select a color of tracing paper that will be easily seen yet is close enough to the color of your fabric. Slide the tracing paper under the pattern with the waxy, colored side against the wrong side of the fabric. If you need to mark two layers of fabric, use two sheets of tracing paper, each facing the wrong side of the fabric. Roll the tracing wheel along the marking lines. Using a ruler will help keep the lines straight. Mark dots with an X.

Section 27.2

After You Read

Review Key Concepts

1. **Identify** what you should consider when choosing fabric?

2. **Explain** why you should you cut a pattern so that the fabric's lengthwise and crosswise grains are square.

3. **Recall** the steps you should follow when positioning pattern pieces.

Practice Academic Skills

English Language Arts

4. Skim the chapter and find at least five sewing terms that have other, non-sewing-related meanings. Give both definitions.

Social Studies

5. Research the sewing tools and equipment and the garment construction techniques of settlers in colonial America. Write an essay comparing their tools and techniques with those used today.

Check Your Answers Go to connectED. mcgraw-hill.com to check your answers.

Exploring Careers   Pilot

What Does a Pilot Do?

Pilots fly airplanes, jets, and helicopters. Most pilots fly people and cargo from place to place. Some pilots test new flight technology, fight fires, do police work, or rescue people. Pilots are responsible for the safety of passengers, so they must make sure their planes are working properly before takeoff.

Skills To be a pilot, you will need to be able to stay calm under pressure. You will need to have an eye for detail and be quick to respond to emergencies. Adaptability, communication, and problem-solving skills are also key.

Education and Training Many pilots learn how to fly while in the military. Others go to flight school. Before you can get paid to fly, you must first get a license from the federal government. To do this, you must be at least 18 years old and have 250 hours of flight experience. You must also pass a written test. Airline pilots must be at least 23 years old, and have at least 1,500 hours of flight experience or go to a special flight school. Most companies want pilots with some college education.

Job Outlook Competition for jobs will be strong through the year 2016. This is because technology has made it easier to fly a plane. Planes have gotten larger, but do not need more pilots to fly them. Also, few pilots quit because they love their jobs and the pay is very high. Opportunities will be better with fast-growing regional and low-fare airlines. Military pilots may have an advantage over other job seekers because they have spent more time flying, and have used more advanced equipment than other pilots.

Critical Thinking What do you think would be the most challenging aspect of being a pilot? Consider physical and mental requirements and scheduling demands.

Career Cluster   Transportation, Distribution, and Logistics

Pilots work in the transportation, distribution, and logistics career cluster. Here are some of the other jobs in this career cluster.

- Aircraft Mechanic
- Airline Pilot
- Air Traffic Controller
- Airfield Operations Specialist
- Bus Driver
- Civil Engineer
- Dredge Operator
- Flight Engineer
- Freight Agent
- Locomotive Engineer
- Ship Captain
- Shipping Clerk
- Transportation Inspector
- Truck Driver

Explore Further Research this career cluster. Choose a career in this cluster that appeals to you and write a career profile.

CHAPTER SUMMARY

Section 27.1
Sewing Equipment

Knowing how to use sewing tools and equipment safely and correctly is important in the success of any sewing project. Sewing equipment includes measuring, cutting, and marking tools, and other small items such as straight pins, thimbles, and needles. As you sew, be sure you are working in a well-lit and comfortable place. Using a serger or machine to sew will help you keep a neat stitch that is also strong. Be sure you understand your machine before you use it.

Section 27.2
Patterns, Fabric Preparation, and Notions

Work with a partner and wear close-fitting clothes to take accurate body measurements. Refer to the back of the pattern envelope when selecting fabric and notions. It is important to prepare fabric and pattern pieces correctly when working on a sewing project. Follow the pattern guide sheet carefully when working on a sewing project. Review the symbols and markings on a pattern piece before you begin cutting.

Vocabulary Review

1. Find a visual example of each of these content and academic vocabulary words in the textbook, or bring an example in from home.

   Content Vocabulary
   ◇ embroider (p. 652)
   ◇ tension (p. 656)
   ◇ interfacing (p. 662)
   ◇ notions (p. 663)
   ◇ selvage (p. 664)
   ◇ bias (p. 664)
   ◇ ease (p. 667)

   Academic Vocabulary
   ▢ gauge (p. 649)
   ▢ versatile (p. 652)
   ▢ proportions (p. 661)
   ▢ excess (p. 667)

Review Key Concepts

2. **Identify** four small sewing equipment categories and their functions.
3. **Explain** how to use a sewing machine.
4. **Describe** the difference between a sewing machine and a serger.
5. **Explain** how to select patterns, fabric, and notions.
6. **Recall** how to prepare fabric for a pattern.
7. **Outline** the five major steps you follow when using a pattern.

Critical Thinking

8. **Analyze** What are the pros and cons of making your own clothes?
9. **Examine** Do you think Americans are encouraged to sew their own clothing? Explain your answer.
10. **Create** Imagine that you are putting together a very basic sewing kit, and can only choose five different pieces of sewing equipment. Which items would you choose? Explain your answer.
11. **Judge** Do you think it is important for a skill like sewing to be passed down from one generation to another? Explain your answer.

ACTIVE
LEARNING

 **Family & Community Connections**

12. Eye for Design Find a fashion you like, either in a store or from someone's wardrobe, and imagine how you would create that garment yourself. Visit a fabric store and look through patterns to find something as close to it as possible. Walk through the fabric store and find the fabric and notions you would like to use. Imagine the garment with your own twist, perhaps with a higher collar or different type of buttons. Once you have all of the details, sketch the garment. If possible, act on your ideas and make the garment.

13. Take a Survey Although some people still sew their own clothes, the majority of people buy them off-the-rack. Why do you think this is? How do people feel about sewing education? Take a survey that includes people of different ages to find out what their own sewing education experience has been. Has it been enough? Has it been helpful? What do they wish had been different? Do they believe that everyone should be taught sewing in school, or should it be a choice? Do they think that sewing skills can lead to career opportunities? Include fellow students, family members and teachers. Make sure to ask each person the same questions. Summarize your findings and share them with your class.

Real-World Skills and Applications

Leadership Skills

14. Organize a Drive Not everyone who wants to sew has the use of a sewing machine. Sometimes people are willing to donate items they no longer use. Write up plans to organize a Sewing Machine Drive for students who aspire to work in the clothing and fashion industries. Think about tasks you can delegate. Perhaps there is someone who can fix old or broken machines. You might contact sewing machine companies and ask for donations of used machines. Present your plan to your teacher and see if you can put it into action.

Financial Literacy

15. Calculate Interest Interest is the amount of money that a business or lender charges you for paying off an item in installments over time. Jolene bought new furniture for her sewing room that was priced at $1,500. She paid the store 10 percent of the price and agreed to pay the rest of the price in 16 monthly installments of $100 each. How much total interest will she pay?

Information Literacy

16. Consumer Research Pretend you are planning to buy a new sewing machine. Find out where you can look to get reliable information about the latest sewing machine models and how they are being reviewed by experts and other consumers. Draw a comparison chart to help you decide which machine to buy. Include such factors as reliability, versatility, usability, looks, price, weight, and service agreement. Write the sources you used underneath the chart.

Academic Skills

 English Language Arts

17. Write a Biographical Sketch Research someone who has made a career in the clothing industry. Find out why this person chose the career, how he or she got started, and what he or she is responsible for at work. Add any additional information about this person that you think might be interesting. Write a one-page biographical sketch of the person.

 Science

18. Parts of a Whole Understanding the parts of a sewing machine helps you operate and maintain it successfully.
Procedure While looking at a sewing machine, identify the following parts:
Handwheel
Thread take-up lever
Throat plate
Feed dogs
Presser foot
Analysis Next to each part's name, write the function it performs.

 Mathematics

19. Communicate Income Jerry makes and sells men's ties. Jerry's profits from January through June are listed below. Use this data to create a line graph to show his income over these six months. What is the outlook for his business?

Month	Income
January	$256
February	$345
March	$445
April	$400
May	$567
June	$595

Math Concept **Line Graphs** Line graphs are useful for displaying information about quantities that change over time.

Starting Hint Put the months along the horizontal axis and the dollar amounts in $50 increments along the vertical axis. Then plot the actual dollar amounts and connect the plotted data.

 For math help, go to the Math Appendix at the back of the book.

Standardized Test Practice

TRUE/FALSE
Directions Read each statement. On a separate sheet of paper, write T if the statement is true, or write F if the statement is false.

Test-Taking Tip Make sure you understand the full statement. All parts of a statement must be correct for the statement to be true. Statements that contain extreme words, such as *all, none, never,* or *always,* or that are unsupported opinions, are often false.

20. Decide if each statement is true or false.
a) If you have a serger, you will never need a sewing machine.
b) It is best to buy your sewing notions at the same time as your fabric.
c) The cutting line is the heavy line you follow on the outside of the pattern to cut out the fabric.

Chapter 28

Sewing Basics

Section 28.1

Basic Sewing Techniques

Section 28.2

Hems, Alterations, and Special Touches

Chapter Objectives

Section 28.1

- **Explain** why sewing is an important life skill.
- **Define** the role of basting.
- **Identify** the purpose of different stitching techniques.

Section 28.2

- **Give** instructions on how to hem a garment.
- **Describe** simple alterations.
- **Identify** ways you can personalize sewing work.

©Hardcape fotostock

Explore the Photo

You can create lasting memories and a one-of-a-kind garment when you work with a parent or grandparent on a major sewing project. *Why would a parent or grandparent be a good sewing mentor?*

Writing Activity — Journal Writing

Your First Sewing Project Writing down your thoughts and experiences in a diary or journal helps develop your writing skills and keep a record of your life at the same time. Think about one of the first times you had to sit down and sew something. For some people, it was years ago and for others, just recently. Write a journal entry about the experience, including what you set about to do, what went right or wrong, how you thought and felt about it then, and how you think and feel about it now.

Writing Tips Use these tips to write a journal entry:
- Include the date of your journal entry at the top of the page.
- Write your entry in the first person, as if you were telling the story to a friend.
- Do not edit or censor yourself as you go. Let the words flow freely.

Basic Sewing Techniques

Before You Read

Create Visual Aids Some people understand concepts better when they can see them. Many of the concepts in this chapter have visual aids, but others do not. Try drawing pictures of the concepts that are not pictured. Review the drawings with your teacher to make sure you fully understand each concept.

Read to Learn

Key Concepts
- **Explain** why sewing is an important life skill.
- **Define** the role of basting.
- **Identify** the purpose of different stitching techniques.

Main Idea

There is a place for sewing in everyone's life. Learning these basic sewing skills can prepare you for a wide range of sewing projects.

Content Vocabulary

◇ basting
◇ stay-stitching
◇ directional stitching
◇ seam allowance
◇ interfacing

◇ facing
◇ grading
◇ notching
◇ clipping
◇ understitching

Academic Vocabulary

You will find these words in your reading and on your tests. Use the glossary to find their definitions if necessary.

☐ grasp
☐ dictate

Graphic Organizer

As you read, find the three types of seam finishes that can be used. Use a chart like the one below to organize your information.

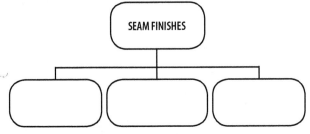

 Graphic Organizer Go to **connectED.mcgraw-hill.com** to download this graphic organizer.

Sewing Is a Common Thread

Everyone in Jamie's family sews. Her mom owns a tailoring shop and makes custom clothing for clients. Her older sister makes her own clothes and recently made an original wedding dress for a friend. Even Jamie's little brother can sew buttons onto clothes. As for Jamie herself, she sews mainly to repair her clothes.

As Jamie's family shows, sewing can be useful in everyone's life, whether the activity involves only themselves or hundreds of people. Jamie's mom earns a living from her sewing knowledge. Her sister is demonstrating an ability to turn her skills into a future career, perhaps in fashion design. Her brother's beginner skills will hopefully give him a jumpstart in caring for his own clothes as he gets older. And, although Jamie does not plan to become a fashion designer or professional tailor like her mother, she knows she will use her sewing skills throughout her life. Just being able to repair her garments now makes them last longer, and that helps Jamie stick to a clothing budget.

In addition to the practical side, there is an expressive and artistic side to sewing. Sewing skills allow you to stylize and personalize your clothing. You can even personalize certain items in your home, such as curtains, pillows, and bedspreads once you have a grasp, or understanding, of some basic sewing techniques.

Perhaps you want to pursue a career that involves sewing, such as fashion design or interior design. Or maybe the everyday advantages of knowing how to sew appeal to you. Whatever your reasons may be, the techniques in this chapter will help you develop your sewing know-how.

✓ **Reading Check** **Explain** Why is sewing described as a skill that is meaningful to everyone?

As You Read

Connect Think about the ways you currently use, or would like to use, sewing skills to improve your life. What would be some of the advantages?

Vocabulary

You can find definitions in the glossary at the back of this book.

Be an Original

Whether you alter pre-made clothing, or start from scratch with a pattern, sewing gives you the opportunity to make one-of-a-kind creations. *How can learning to sew benefit you?*

Basting

To be certain about the way a project will look or fit, you may want to baste parts of a garment together and try it on. **Basting** means holding two or more pieces of fabric together temporarily until they are permanently stitched. There are several types of basting. See **Figure 28.1**.

- **Hand Basting** You use a needle and thread to baste by hand. Hand-basted stitches should be long. Make stitches ¼-inch (6 mm) long, and even on both sides of the fabric.

- **Machine Basting** Most machines include stitch length adjustment. Set the machine's stitch length at its longest. Slightly loosen the upper tension on the machine, so that the stitches will be easier to remove later. Or use disappearing basting thread, which dissolves when washed or ironed with a damp press cloth.

- **Pin Basting** Pin basting is quick and effective when you have very little extra fabric to work with. Choose very sharp and thin pins so that they do not damage the fabric. Push pins through both pieces of fabric two to three inches apart. You can also use basting tape, which is a sticky, double-sided tape.

When basting, make sure the stitches or pins are next to the seam line, but not directly on it. Remember, basting work is meant to be temporary. Your basting stitches should be easy to remove after the permanent seam is sewn.

✓ Reading Check **Explain** What is the purpose of basting?

Figure 28.1 Basting Techniques

Temporary Attachment Basting should be strong enough to hold fabric together until it is properly sewn, but loose enough so that it is easily removed. *Why might you choose thread instead of pins for basting?*

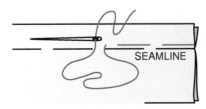

Hand Basting

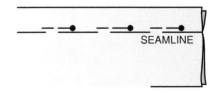

Pin Basting

Machine Stitching Techniques

When working on a sewing project, you will likely use a number of different machine stitches. This is because each type of stitching has a specific purpose. Pattern instructions will dictate, or tell, the sewing techniques you will need to use to complete a garment. Some basic techniques you will probably see in pattern instructions are explained in this section.

Though pattern instructions often prescribe a stitch length setting as well, you may need to adjust this recommendation, depending on the fabric you have chosen. In general, you will use a stitch length setting of 2.5 mm for most fabrics. Finer fabrics require a shorter stitch of 1.5 to 2 mm in length. Heavier fabrics may need a longer stitch of 3 mm in length.

Stay-Stitching

Before you begin to put a garment or project together, it should be stay-stitched. **Stay-stitching** is a row of stitching on one layer of fabric that prevents the edges from stretching as you handle the fabric. Follow these guidelines for stay-stitching fabric:

- Stay-stitch after you mark the fabric but before pinning or basting.
- Stay-stitch in the direction of the grain.
- Use the same thread tension and stitch length you will use for the project seams.
- Stay-stitch ½ inch (1.3 cm) from the raw edge. This is one-eighth inch (3 mm) inside the seamline. Stay-stitching should not show on the outside of a project.
- Stay-stitch all edges that are curved, on the bias, or cut off-grain, such as shoulder seams, necklines, and armholes. See **Figure 28.2**.

Figure 28.2 **Stay-Stitching**

Prevent Pulling Stay-stitching is done on curved areas to prevent the fabric from stretching. *At what point in the sewing process should you stay-stitch a piece of fabric?*

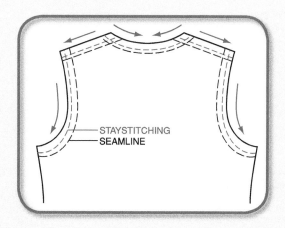

STAYSTITCHING
SEAMLINE

Sewing Equipment

Whether sewing at home or in your school's sewing lab, you need to be aware of potential hazards. When using a machine, keep your fingers away from the path of the needle, and do not sew over pins. Do not attempt to use the machine if it is jammed or making an unusual noise. Use a pin cushion to hold pins and needles – not your mouth!

Write About It

Create a list of tips to prevent injuries and equipment damage in the sewing lab.

Directional Stitching

Fabric can easily become distorted or misshapen just from stitching. To avoid this potential problem, all stitching on a garment should be sewn with the grain of the fabric. When you sew with the fabric grain, or in the same direction as the fabric grain, you are less likely to stretch and warp the fabric. Stitching in the direction of the grain is called **directional stitching**.

How do you identify the grain direction? Move your finger along the raw edge of the fabric. The direction that smooths the yarns against the fabric is going with the grain. You can also look at the pattern tissues, which have arrows pointing to the grain direction.

As a rule, you should stitch from the wide to the narrow part of the garment. For example, sew from the hem to the waist of a skirt. See **Figure 28.3**. Whether scoop or V-neck, the necklines on garments should be sewn from the upper edge toward the center on each side. Seams that are on a straight grain can be stitched in either direction.

Seams

A seam is a line of stitching that holds two pieces of fabric together. There are several types of seams, but the plain seam is used for most sewing. Plain seams are also called standard seams, and are 5/8 inch (1.5 cm) wide. The fabric between the seam line and the cut edge is called the **seam allowance**.

Before you begin to sew, make a sample seam on a scrap of your fabric. Examine the seam to check the tension, stitch length, and general appearance.

| Figure 28.3 | Directional Stitching |

Keep Seams Straight Directional stitching prevents seams from stretching or changing shape. *How can you identify a fabric's grain direction?*

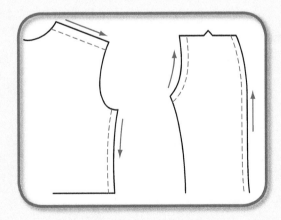

Follow these steps to make a plain seam:

1. Place the right sides of the fabric together. Match notches, cut edges, and both ends of the fabric. Place pins at right angles to the seamline at the ends and notches. Pin the rest of the seam. Place pins 2 to 3 inches (5 to 7.5 cm) apart with the pin heads outward.
2. Place the fabric under the sewing machine's presser foot, with the cut edges of the seam allowance lined up with the proper seam guide numbers on the machine's throat plate. Turn the hand wheel to lower the needle into the fabric ½ inch (1.3 cm) from the top of the seam. Lower the presser foot.
3. Backstitch to secure the top end of the seam. You do this by retracing your stitches about ½ inch (1.3 cm). Use the reverse button or lever on your sewing machine.
4. Using a medium speed and an even pace, stitch to the other end of the seam. Remove pins as you stitch.
5. Backstitch to secure the bottom end of the seam.
6. Remove fabric by turning the hand wheel to raise the take-up lever and needle. Lift the presser foot and slide the fabric toward the back of the machine.
7. Finish the seam edges if necessary.
8. Press the seam open.

Figure 28.4 Seam Finishes

Prevent Raveling When choosing a seam finish, consider the type and weight of the fabric you are using. *Which seam finish would you use for a fabric that frays easily?*

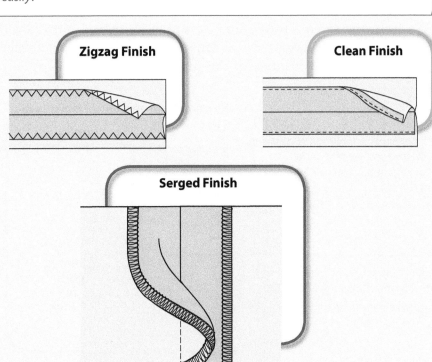

Zigzag Finish

Clean Finish

Serged Finish

Seam Finishes

Seam finishes are used to prevent raveling on the cut edges of seams and facings. The seam finish to use depends on the type of fabric and the potential degree of raveling. Loosely woven fabrics are likely to fray, so they require more sewing in the seam finish than tightly woven fabrics which do not fray easily. If you are not sure which finish will work best with your fabric, you should experiment with different finishes on your fabric scraps. See **Figure 28.4** on page 681.

- **Zigzag Finish** For fabrics that ravel, zigzagging is a very quick, yet practical seam finish. Use a medium-width machine zigzag stitch and sew along the edge of each seam allowance.
- **Clean Finish** Also called a turned-and-stitched, or hemmed finish, a clean finish is a turned and stitched finish used on light-weight and medium-weight fabrics. Turn the edges under ¼ inch (6 mm) and press. Machine-stitch close to the folded edge.
- **Serged Finish** This may be used on any fabric. Serge along the cut edge of the seam, just skimming the edge as you sew. A serged finish is especially helpful on heavy or bulky fabric and fabric that ravels very easily.

HOW TO ...   Serge Seams

In a world where everyone from a doctor to a chef may be considered a specialist, the serger is right at home. A serger specializes in sewing seams. Using a serger requires basic sewing skills. You will need to distinguish the seamline, where the needle enters the fabric, from the serger cutting line, generally ¼ inch (6 mm) beyond the seamline. Once you have gained some serging savvy, these steps can help you take advantage of this machine's expertise.

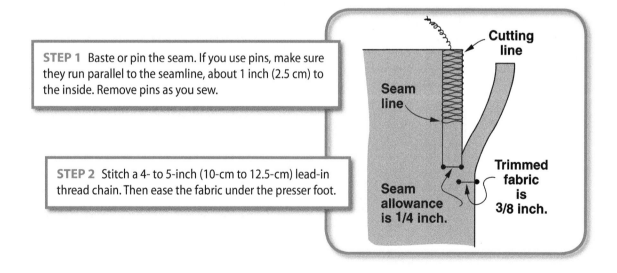

STEP 1 Baste or pin the seam. If you use pins, make sure they run parallel to the seamline, about 1 inch (2.5 cm) to the inside. Remove pins as you sew.

STEP 2 Stitch a 4- to 5-inch (10-cm to 12.5-cm) lead-in thread chain. Then ease the fabric under the presser foot.

Cutting line

Seam line

Seam allowance is 1/4 inch.

Trimmed fabric is 3/8 inch.

- **Hand-Overcast Finish** Though finishing a seam by hand is very time consuming, it is sometimes used for very delicate or sheer fabrics. A person using this finish simply makes diagonal stitches by hand over the edge of the seam allowances. Overcast stitches should be spaced evenly, and as close together as necessary to prevent raveling.

- **Pinked Finish** Most tightly woven fabrics can be trimmed with pinking shears, which leave a zigzagged cut edge. Pinking does not require a machine. It reduces raveling, but does not prevent it. Pinking works best for items that will be dry-cleaned, as seams are more likely to fray in the wash.

Interfacing

Interfacing is material used on the unseen or "wrong" side of fabrics to make an area of a garment more rigid. Interfacing is placed between the outer fabric and the facing. It stiffens shirt collars, strengthens the area around buttonholes and keeps knit fabrics from stretching out of shape. Interfacing is applied before the facing is attached to the garment. **Figure 28.5** on page 685 shows two ways to apply interfacing.

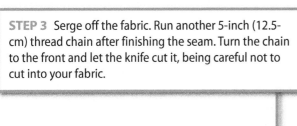

STEP 3 Serge off the fabric. Run another 5-inch (12.5-cm) thread chain after finishing the seam. Turn the chain to the front and let the knife cut it, being careful not to cut into your fabric.

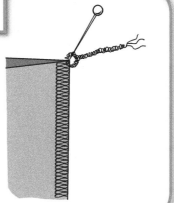

STEP 4 Secure the thread ends. Serged ends are fairly ravel-proof, especially if stitched over by another seam, such as at the cuffs and sleeves of a sweatshirt. As a safeguard, you can pull the thread chain back through the seam stitches using a small crochet hook or a large-eyed needle. Alternately, knot the threads using this technique: make a slip knot in the thread close to the fabric; slip the knot around a pin; holding the pin tip next to the fabric edge, pull the thread to tighten it around the pin tip; and remove the pin.

Facings

A **facing** is fabric that finishes a raw edge, such as a neckline, front opening, armhole, or collar. The facing piece may be separate or cut in one with the garment. There are several different types of facings. A shaped facing is used most often. It is cut in the same shape as the edge onto which it is sewn. See **Figure 28.6** on page 685.

Before sewing a facing to a garment, you need to understand several cutting and stitching techniques:

- **Grading** After facings are joined to a garment, the seams may be thick and bulky. **Grading**, or trimming the seam allowances in layers, is done to reduce the bulk.

- **Notching or Clipping** Outward-curved edges, as on collars, and inward-curved edges, as on necklines, need special treatment to lie flat. Outward curves need **notching**, which means clipping V-shaped notches from the seam allowance. Inward curves need **clipping**, or small, straight cuts in the seam allowance.

- **Understitching** This row of stitching gives facings a smooth, flat edge. **Understitching**, or stitching the facing to the seam allowances, also keeps seams and facings from rolling to the outside of the garment.

Follow these steps to attach a facing:

1. Staystitch curved facing edges that are to be attached to the garment. Sew facing pieces together as directed in the pattern. Trim the seams to ¼ inch (6 mm) and press open.
2. Finish the unnotched outer edges of the facing to prevent raveling. Use one of the seam finishing methods. Press.
3. Place the right side of the facing against the right side of the garment. Match notches and seams and pin together.
4. Stitch the facing to the garment at ⅝ inch (1.5 cm), sewing as evenly as possible.
5. Grade and clip the seams to reduce bulk.
6. Press the facing and seam allowance away from the garment and toward the facing.
7. Understitch the seam allowance to the facing. Turn the facing to the inside and press.
8. Hand-sew the facing to the inside of the garment at the seam allowances only. Do not hand-sew the facing to the garment.

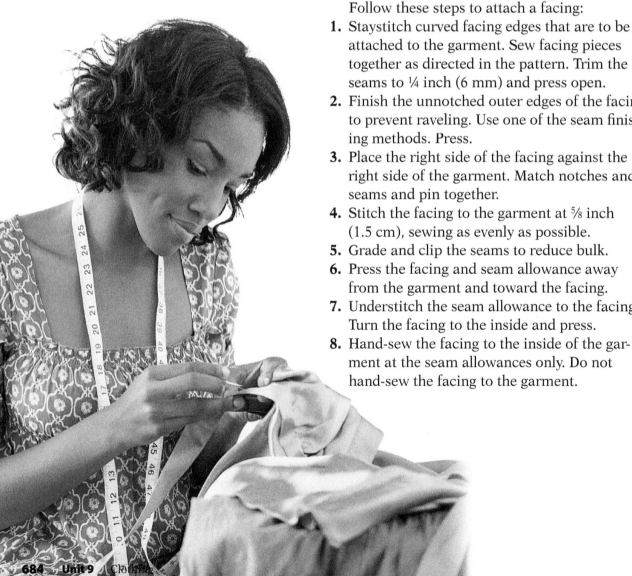

Sewing by Hand

Though machines make most sewing jobs faster and easier, some sewing jobs are best done by hand. *Which sewing tasks should be done by hand?*

Figure 28.5

Applying Interfacing

Added Strength Sew-in interfacing needs to be stitched into place, while fusible interfacing bonds to fabric when pressed with a hot iron. *Why might you choose to use sew-in interfacing instead of fusible interfacing?*

Fusible Interfacing Place the coated side of the interfacing on the wrong side of the fabric. Trim away any interfacing that extends beyond the fabric edge. Follow the fusing instructions that come with the interfacing.

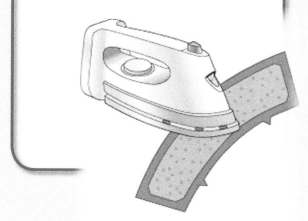

Sew-in Interfacing Trim the pointed corners off the interfacing about ¼ inch (3 mm) Inside the seamline. Pin the interfacing to the fabric ½ inch (1.3 cm) from the outer edges. Stitch with the direction of the grain. Finally, trim the interfacing as close to the stitching line as possible.

Figure 28.6 # Sewing Facing

Smooth Finish It takes a number of steps to sew a facing, but the result is well worth the effort. *What can happen if you do not sew facing into the collar or sleeves of a sleeveless shirt?*

Step 1

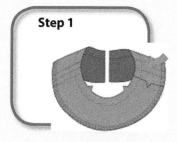

Step 4

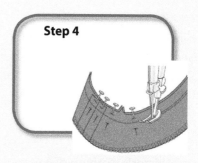

Step 6

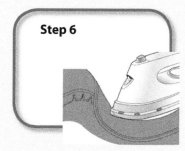

Step 7

Understitching

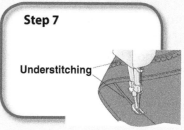

Press as You Sew

Good pressing techniques are as necessary as good sewing skills. At the beginning of a project, pressing ensures that both your pattern and fabric are wrinkle-free for exact cutting. Pressing each seam as it is completed increases neatness and sewing accuracy, expecially at points where seams intersect.

Here are some additional pressing pointers:

- Check for the correct temperature setting on the fabric care label.
- Press rather than iron. Raise and lower the iron on to the cloth, and let the steam do the work. An iron sliding back and forth can stretch out the fabric.
- Press with the grain of the fabric. This too, prevents stretching.
- Press on the wrong side of the fabric, or use a press cloth in order to prevent shine.
- Press each seam as you sew.
- Use the point of the iron to press seams open.
- Avoid pressing over pins. They can scratch the bottom of the iron and mark the fabric.
- Do not over press. Let the steam do the work.

Section 28.1

After You Read

Review Key Concepts

1. **Explain** why sewing is useful to both amateurs and professionals.
2. **Identify** three different basting techniques.
3. **Describe** how you can identify the grain direction in a fabric.

Practice Academic Skills

English Language Arts

4. Go to at least three different sources to gather information on "the basic black dress." Use the information to write a properly structured, five-paragraph essay on the subject. Make sure your essay has a title, introduction, and conclusion. Write your list of sources at the end.

Social Studies

5. Research the traditional historic clothing of your own cultural or national background. Find a garment that you would probably be wearing if you lived in that other time and place. Would you be glad to wear it? Why or why not? How does it compare to the clothing you wear today?

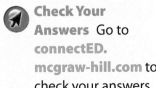
Check Your Answers Go to connectED. mcgraw-hill.com to check your answers.

Hems, Alterations, and Special Touches

Reading Guide

Before You Read

Pace Yourself Short blocks of concentrated reading are more effective than one long, uninterrupted session. Focus on reading for 10 minutes. Take a short break. Then read for another 10 minutes. Continue until you have finished this section.

Read to Learn

Key Concepts

- **Give** instructions on how to hem a garment.
- **Describe** simple alterations.
- **Identify** ways you can personalize sewing work.

Main Idea

Learning to hem clothes, make simple alterations, and add special touches to clothes will add value to your sewing skills and your wardrobe.

Content Vocabulary

◇ gathers
◇ casing

Academic Vocabulary

You will find these words in your reading and on your tests. Use the glossary to find these definitions if necessary.

▢ configuration
▢ subtle

Graphic Organizer

As you read, note in order the steps for altering a garment to make it smaller. Use a graphic organizer like the one below to organize your information.

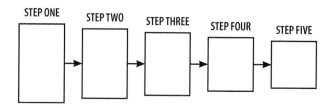

 Graphic Organizer Go to **connectED.mcgraw-hill.com** to download this graphic organizer.

Hems

The bottom edges of pants, skirts, sleeves, jackets, and window treatments are finished with hems. The type of hem you will use depends on the type of fabric and the design of the project.

Marking the Hem

To mark the length of the hemline, put on shoes of the heel height you expect to wear with the finished garment. Have another person measure the correct length up from the floor using a yardstick. Place pins or chalk marks at the same distance all the way around the garment. Check to be sure that the markings form an even line. See **Figure 28.7**.

Using the marked line as a guide, turn the hem to the wrong side of the garment. Insert pins at right angles along the fold line. The depth of the hem varies depending on the fullness of the garment. Pants usually have a hem of 1.5 to 2 inches (3.8 to 5 cm). Skirt hems vary from 1 to 3 inches (2.5 to 7.5 cm), depending on the fullness. Use a narrower hem depth for a fuller skirt.

Measure the hem depth needed plus ¼ inch (6 mm) for finishing. Cut off the extra fabric from the edge of the hem. Machine stitch or hand sew ½ inch (1.3 cm) from the cut edge. Stitch only through the hem, not the outside of the garment.

Finishing the Hem

When a garment has extra fullness, the hem must be eased in so that it fits flat against the garment. Otherwise, it will be bulky and lumpy. This will make the garment uncomfortable. There are several ways to finish raw edges of hems, such as zigzagging, clean finishing, and serging. Revisit **Figure 28.4** on page 681.

Choose the method that best suits your fabric. Next, attach the hem to the garment. Two methods include slip stitching (a method of hand stitching) and machine stitching. See **Figure 28.8**.

As You Read

Connect Think about how you might completely change one of your outfits using the sewing skills described. Is it worth it to work on a garment instead of buying a new one?

Figure 28.7 **Marking Hems**

Determine the Hemline It is best to mark a hem while the garment and shoes are being worn. *Why do you think this is?*

Marking with Chalk

Marking with Pins

Figure 28.8 **Sewing Hems**

A Clean Finish You may need to hand stitch and machine stitch to sew a hem. *Why might you choose to hand stitch in some stages?*

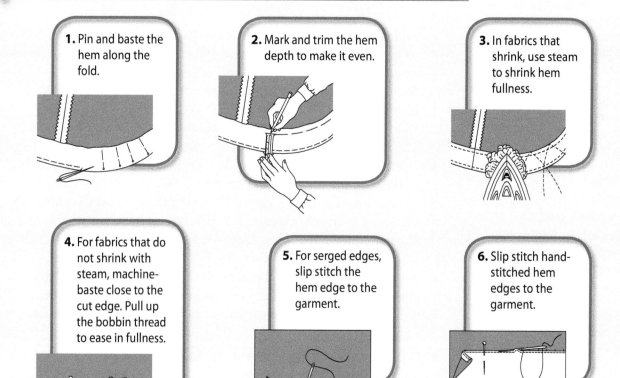

1. Pin and baste the hem along the fold.

2. Mark and trim the hem depth to make it even.

3. In fabrics that shrink, use steam to shrink hem fullness.

4. For fabrics that do not shrink with steam, machine-baste close to the cut edge. Pull up the bobbin thread to ease in fullness.

5. For serged edges, slip stitch the hem edge to the garment.

6. Slip stitch hand-stitched hem edges to the garment.

- **Slip stitching** To slip stitch a hem, use a single strand of thread in the needle. Make sure the stitches do not show on the outside of the garment. Keep the stitches somewhat loose so that the fabric does not pull. Start by attaching the thread to a seam. Pick up only one or two threads on the outer layer of the garment or fabric. Then insert the needle into the fold of the hem edge. Space the stitches about ¼ inch (6 mm) to ½ inch (1.3 cm) apart.
- **Machine Stitching** Blindstitching or topstitching can also be used to attach a hem to a garment. If your machine has a built-in blind stitch, fold the garment back ¼ inch (6 mm) below the hem edge. Machine stitch so the straight stitches fall on the hem allowance, and the peak of the single zigzag stitches catch the garment just past the fold line. Blindstitched hems are nearly invisible. If you want a more decorative hem, try topstitching. For topstitching, fold the hem to the width you want and press. Stitch on the right side of the fabric close to the inside edge of the hem.

✓ **Reading Check** **Summarize** What are the stitching methods for making a hem?

Health & Wellness TIPS

Healthy Identity

As you grow older and enter adulthood, you gain more control over the person you are becoming. As you continue to mature, follow these tips to build a healthy identity:

▶ List your skills and strengths to keep you inspired.

▶ Surround yourself with supportive people.

▶ Find something you love to do, and do it often.

▶ Look for opportunities to help others.

Generosity Gina has a job interview this afternoon at a sportswear store. She needs to look her best, but her nicest outfit is stained with tomato juice. She does not have time to buy anything new, so she asks her sister, Linda, if she can borrow something. Linda has a nice outfit that would fit Gina. However, it is brand new and Linda does not want her clumsy sister to spill anything on it!

You Make the Call

Should Linda let Gina wear her new outfit? Since Gina already ruined one outfit, would it be acceptable for Linda to say no? Is there a way for both sisters to be happy? Explain what you think the sisters should do.

Simple Alterations

Garments do not always fit perfectly. But with a little planning and skill, simple alterations can extend the usefulness of a garment.

Lengthen or Shorten a Garment

Whether you purchase a garment that does not fit you perfectly, or receive a hand-me-down from a taller sibling, it is easy to adjust a garment so it suits your height and fashion sense.

To shorten or add length to a garment, follow these steps:
1. Remove the old hem stitching.
2. Put the garment on and have someone mark the new hemline.
3. Turn the hem under along the new hemline and pin in place.
4. Baste the hem close to the folded edge. Try on the garment to make sure the hem length is correct.
5. Measure and mark the desired hem depth. Trim off the extra fabric when shortening a garment. When lengthening a garment, if the hem allowance is too narrow, sew hem tape to the hem edge to create a new hem allowance.
6. Finish the raw edge of the hem. Pin the top of the hem edge to the garment. Ease the hem fullness to the garment as needed.
7. Stitch the hem to the garment. Remove the basting and press.

Adjust the Width of a Garment

Most people cannot afford to buy a whole new wardrobe when they gain or lose weight. Thankfully you can adjust the width of most of the clothes in your current wardrobe.

To make a garment larger, follow these steps:
1. Check the seam allowances to be sure there is enough fabric for new seams.
2. Remove the old stitching from the section of the seam to which the width will be added.
3. Try on the garment inside out and have someone pin the new seams.
4. Machine baste the new seams, removing pins as you sew.
5. Try the garment on to check the fit.
6. Stitch the new seams with a regular stitch length, carefully tapering the stitching into the old seam. Backstitch at each seam end.
7. Remove the basting. Press the seams open.

To make a garment smaller, follow these steps:
1. Put the garment on inside out. Have someone pin the new seams on each side.
2. Machine baste on the pin line, removing the pins as you sew.
3. Try the garment on to check the fit.
4. Stitch the new seams using a regular machine stitch, carefully tapering the new stitching into the old.
5. Remove the basting and old seam. Press the new seams open.

✓ **Reading Check** **Identify** Give four examples of alterations.

Personalizing a Garment

Clothing is one of the ways in which we express our individuality. When you can sew, your options for creating a one-of-a-kind garment are limitless. Imagine giving a simple black T-shirt and a sewing kit to a dozen different people. There is no doubt that the result would be a dozen very unique T-shirts.

Fabric Arrangements

You can make a garment dramatically different by rearranging or manipulating the fabric to change the garment's contour or silhouette. Think of the various ways you might fold, turn, pull, roll, or twist a piece of fabric. For just about every configuration, or arrangement, there is a sewing technique.

Gathers

Gathers are soft folds of fabric. They are formed by pulling up basting stitches to make a larger piece of fabric fit onto a smaller space. Fullness on shirts, skirts, and sometimes window curtains is often created by gathers. See **Figure 28.9**. Follow these steps to make gathers.

1. Sew two parallel rows of machine basting on the right side of the fabric, with a stitch length of at least 4 mm. Leave a 2-inch (5 cm) tail of thread at the beginning and the end of each row. Do not backstitch because you will be pulling the thread tails. Stitch the first row on the seamline. Stitch the second row about ¼ inch (6 mm) from the seamline inside the seam allowance.
2. Place the edge of the piece to be gathered against the fabric piece it is to be sewn to (such as skirt to waistband or ruffle to curtain edge). Put right sides together and make edges even. Match all markings, notches, and seams, and pin only at these locations.
3. Tie a knot in each pair of bobbin-thread tails (now facing you). Gently pull these bobbin-thread tails at each end to gather the fabric. Slide the fabric along with your fingers until the gathered fabric fits the shorter fabric piece. At both ends, wrap the excess bobbin thread around the pins in figure eights.
4. Adjust the gathers evenly. Pin about every ½ inch (1.3 cm).
5. Stitch the seam with standard stitching. Sew with the gathered edge on top. This way, stitching is more accurate and the gathers will not be caught in the stitching. For safe sewing, remove the pins as you sew.

◇ **Vocabulary**

You can find definitions in the glossary at the back of this book.

Figure 28.9 **Sewing Gathers**

The Ruffle Effect Gathering creates soft folds of fabric. *Why should you rethink your fabric measurements if you decide to make gathered curtains instead of straight curtains?*

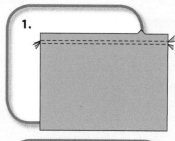
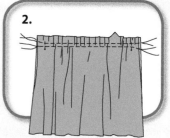
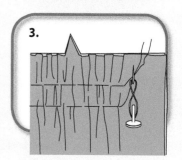
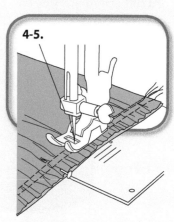

Figure 28.10

Shirring

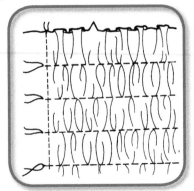

Shirring

Shirring is formed by several rows of gathering. Shirring is often used to add texture to dresses, skirts, and the sleeves of shirts. It is also used to define the waist of tops and dresses that would otherwise be rather shapeless or overly boxy. Shirring works best on soft or lightweight fabrics.

To create shirring, stitch as many evenly-spaced rows of gathering as you want, and secure each row with a knot. Then stitch over the knots in the seam allowance to permanently secure the gathers. You can wind the bobbin with elastic thread if you want elasticized shirring. Stitches should be long, about 3 to 4 mm in length, and on the right side of the fabric. Stretch previously stitched rows as you sew each new row to prevent the gathered rows from growing more and more narrow.

Casings

A **casing** is a closed tunnel or space of fabric that can hold a piece of elastic or a drawstring in a waistband. Casings are also used as curtain rod pockets for simple curtains or valances. A casing is made like a hem. You generally fold over the edge of the waistband or the top of the curtain and sew it in place. The width of the casing will vary depending on the size opening needed. For example, waistband casings are usually 1 inch (2.5 cm) wide. See **Figure 28.11**. To sew a self-casing, follow these directions:

1. Finish the raw edge of fabric by turning it under ¼ inch (6 mm) and press. Otherwise, zigzag or serge the raw edge.
2. Turn the casing to the inside on the fold line with wrong sides together. Pin in place. Press the outer edge of the casing.
3. Stitch close to the inner pinned edge of the casing. If you are inserting elastic or a drawstring, you need to leave a small opening.

Figure 28.11

Sewing Casings

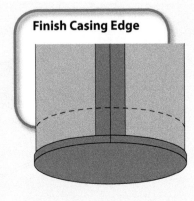

Finish Casing Edge

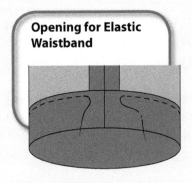

Opening for Elastic Waistband

Elastic Waistbands

An elastic waistband has saved many a loose pair of pants and a shapeless dress from the back of a clothes closet. Adding this feature first requires making a casing, as explained on page 692. Then it is time to add the elastic. The elastic needs to be about ¼ inch (6 mm) narrower than the finished casing so you can pull it through the casing. If the casing is too wide, the elastic will twist inside the casing when the garment is worn. See **Figure 28.12**. Follow these steps to sew an elastic waistband.

1. Leave a 1½-inch (3.8 cm) opening when stitching the inner edge of the casing to insert elastic. Backstitch at each end of the seam.
2. Cut a piece of elastic to fit snugly around your waist. Remember, it must be able to slide over your hips. Add 2 inches (5 cm) to overlap.
3. Put a safety pin in one end of the elastic. Insert the pin and elastic into the casing opening. Pull the pin and elastic through the casing, using the pin to guide the elastic. Hold on to the loose end of the elastic.
4. Overlap the elastic ends 1 inch (2.5 cm). Machine stitch the overlap securely in a square pattern.
5. Stitch the opening of the casing closed. Backstitch at each end of the opening.

Figure 28.12 **Sewing Elastic Waistbands**

Fantastic Elastic Elastic allows a secure fit that will not hamper movement. From tracksuits to swimsuits, most athletic clothing contains at least some elastic. *How would you replace a worn-out elastic waistband in your favorite workout pants?*

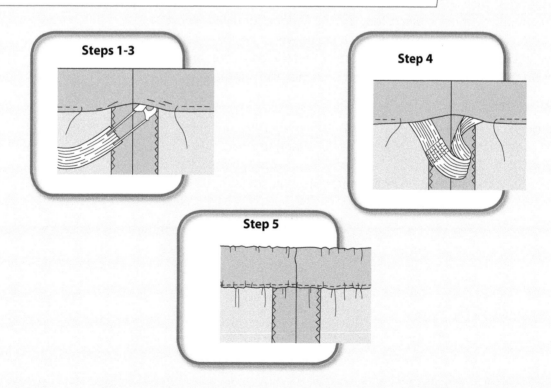

Steps 1-3

Step 4

Step 5

Trim and Piping

Trim or piping can make a garment more interesting to look at, and a little tends to go a long way. Trim and pipe are used as accents to a garment. This means that they are a small part of the garment that attracts the eye in a pleasant and subtle, or not obvious way. Trim is often applied to the ends of a garment at the collar, cuffs, or hem. Piping can be used anywhere on a garment. Piping can be inserted into a seam while it is stitched. Either addition can become the essential design element of an item of clothing.

If you decide to use trim or piping in your garment, prepare to use them before you begin to sew. Often, these accents can be sewn into the seams for a secure and neat finish. These elements can help you be more creative with the design of your clothes, and express yourself.

Section 28.2

After You Read

Review Key Concepts

1. **Explain** why you need a second person to help you make a hem.
2. **Recall** why it is helpful to know how to alter a garment.
3. **Describe** what can happen if a casing is much wider than the elastic waistband it contains.

Check Your Answers Go to connectED. mcgraw-hill.com to check your answers.

Practice Academic Skills

English Language Arts

4. Pretend you are a fashion magazine journalist attending a seasonal fashion runway show in Milan, Italy. Write a fictional, detailed report on several of the clothing pieces you imagine would be presented. Review a leading fashion magazine article and try to use the same writing style. Make sure to use correct grammer and puntuation.

Social Studies

5. Although clothing is often used to express individuality, uniforms are used to help identify individuals as belonging to a particular group. Think about examples of uniforms in our society. When and where do you think they are important? Write your ideas.

CHAPTER SUMMARY

Section 28.1
Basic Sewing Techniques

There are basic sewing skills used frequently in clothing projects. These include basting, sewing seams and facings, and performing basic machine stitching. Basting allows you to check a garment's fit before sewing it permanently. Seams hold a garment together and facings help finish off raw edges. Directional stitching and staystitching are frequently used when using a sewing machine.

Section 28.2
Hems, Alterations, and Special Touches

Being able to make hems, alterations, and additional enhancements on a garment helps to expand your wardrobe. The type of hem you will use depends on the type of fabric and the design of the project. Simple alterations such as lengthening, shortening, widening, and taking in can extend the usefulness of a garment. Fabric manipulations and added materials add interest and uniqueness to garments.

Vocabulary Review

1. Some words, such as *grasp* and *dictate*, have many meanings. Choose one of these words and write three sentences, each one using a different meaning of the word.

Content Vocabulary
◇ basting (p. 678)
◇ stay-stitching (p. 679)
◇ directional stitching (p. 680)
◇ seam allowance (p. 680)
◇ interfacing (p. 683)
◇ facing (p. 684)
◇ grading (p. 684)
◇ notching (p. 684)
◇ clipping (p. 684)
◇ understitching (p. 684)
◇ gathers (p. 691)
◇ casing (p. 692)

Academic Vocabulary
■ grasp (p. 677)
■ dictate (p. 679)
■ configuration (p. 691)
■ subtle (p. 694)

Review Key Concepts

2. **Explain** why sewing is an important life skill.
3. **Define** the role of basting.
4. **Identify** the purpose of different stitching techniques.
5. **Give** instructions on how to hem a garment.
6. **Describe** simple alterations.
7. **Identify** ways you can personalize sewing work.

Critical Thinking

8. **Examine** What special skills do you think it takes to be successful at sewing?
9. **Critique** Observe a fellow sewing student at work. How can he or she improve? What can you learn from his or her technique?
10. **Judge** Do you think you need to be good at math to sew your own clothes? Explain why or why not.
11. **Analyze** What inspires you to be creative with your clothing?

ACTIVE LEARNING

12. Practice Sewing Follow your teacher's instructions to form into pairs. You and your partner should each work on your own sewing project. After a while, switch projects. What is it like to take over someone else's work? Do you have any concerns handing over your work to someone else? Does each of you understand what the other has done and what still needs to be done? Ask each other any necessary questions. You can also try the activity with a small group, with each person handing over their project to the person on their left or right. Examine the finished projects. Can you tell by looking at them at which points someone else took over? Discuss your findings with the class.

Family & Community Connections

13. Teach a Skill Think of a simple sewing project that a second- or third-grader could learn. Imagine the type and amount of materials you would need if you were teaching this project to a small group of children. How would you explain the activity? Would you demonstrate it yourself? How long do you think it would take for the children to complete the project? What types of questions do you think they would ask you during the project? How would you answer these questions? Plan your lesson down to the last possible detail. You can ask a teacher for advice. If possible, present your idea to a local elementary school teacher, community or recreational center leader, or camp director. See if you can participate in presenting your project to a group of children. Is this something you would enjoy?

Real-World Skills and Applications

Leadership Skills

14. Organize a Fundraiser Plan a fundraising event in which people will sponsor sewing students in a day-long event. Figure out how many sewing participants and sponsors you would need, what kinds of sewing services will be offered, and how much money each participant would need to collect in donations to raise a total of $500. Write out your plan and present it to a teacher.

Financial Literacy

15. Personal Finances Before starting any sewing project, you should make sure you can afford all of the necessary fabric and notions. Make a two-column list of items that relate to your finances. The first column will include savings and income. The second column will include monthly expenses. Is your income higher or lower than your average monthly expenses? Can you afford the sewing materials you need? If not, what options do you have?

Information Literacy

16. Read a Sewing Pattern Read a sewing pattern you have never seen before from beginning to end. Analyze all instructions and markings. Can you envision the finished project just by reading the pattern? Are the instructions clear? How can they be improved? Think how the pattern was constructed. Summarize your findings.

Academic Skills

English Language Arts

17. Downsize an Article Choose a magazine or Internet article about clothing. Create a version of the article that is about one-fourth the length of the article itself. Read your finished product aloud. Does it flow as smoothly as the original-length article?

Science

18. Environmental Action From Plastic to Parkas Many clothing items are now made with recycled plastic bottles.

Procedure Find at least three samples of clothing or cloth swatches at a fabric store that have EcoSpun® or Eco-fi® on the label. At least one item should be 100% EcoSpun®. Compare each sample to a similar product made of natural or non-recycled fibers.

Analysis Using a scale of 1-10, rate each sample according to softness, strength, wrinkle-resistance, hand, and care needs. Show your results in a bar graph.

Mathematics

19. Stitch Count Suppose you are making yourself a new shirt. You still need to stitch a 14-inch side seam. The pattern tells you to use a stitch length of 2.5 mm. How many total stitches will you do to complete the side seam?

Math Concept **Multistep Problems** When solving problems with more than one step, think through each step first.

Starting Hint First convert both numbers to the same units of measurement, using the conversion formula: 1 inch = 25.4 mm. Then divide the total length of the seam by the length of a single stitch. Round your answer to the nearest whole number.

 For math help, go to the Math Appendix at the back of the book.

Standardized Test Practice

READING COMPREHENSION
Directions Read the question and select the best answer from the choices.

Test-Taking Tip Tip Summarize a reading passage in your head before reading the questions that follow. This can help you weed out wrong answers that would otherwise sound logical.

20. When people think something you have made is a professionally-made garment, you know you have serious sewing skills! Tell-tale signs that a garment was homemade include puckers, visible stitches, uneven areas, and poor fit. Based on this information, which question is not a question to consider when determining whether or not your hand-made garment looks professional?

a) Do the sleeves hang straight?

b) Are the collar points identical?

c) Is this garment currently in style?

d) Can I stand, sit, bend and stretch comfortably?

Life Skills Project

Your Personal Style

In this project you will analyze personal styles, reflect on your own personal style, and interview an adult in your community who has a personal style you admire or find interesting. These observations will help you understand the influences people may share when forming their personal style.

My Journal

If you completed the journal entry from page 594, refer to it to see if your thoughts have changed after reading the unit.

Project Assignment

In this project you will:
- Reflect on your personal style and clothing preferences.
- Identify and interview an adult in your community whose style you admire or find interesting.
- Create a presentation that describes your own personal style and the influences on it.

The Skills Behind the Project

Life Skills

Key personal and relationship skills you will use in this project include:
- Personal reflection.
- Making well-informed choices.
- Using creative skills.

STEP 1 Analyze Your Personal Style

Use the information from the Unit as well as personal reflection to analyze your own personal style. In what types of clothing are you most comfortable? What are the styles that you are drawn to when shopping or reading fashion magazines? As you conduct your research, save electronic files of images of clothing and accessories that reflect your personal style. You will use these images when you create your presentation. Write a summary of your research to:
- Identify the styles that are the most flattering to your body type.
- Describe the clothing that you like the most.
- List the color palettes that look best on you.
- Explain why you choose to dress the way you do.

Writing Skills
- Use complete sentences
- Use correct spelling and grammar.
- Organize your interview questions in the order you want to ask them.

Vico Collective/Alamy

Life Skills Project Checklist

Plan	☑ Analyze your own personal style and write a summary about it.
	☑ Write your interview questions.
	☑ Interview an adult in your community and write a summary of what you learned.
	☑ Create a presentation for your class that uses words and images to describe your personal style and explain what you learned from the person you interviewed.
Present	☑ Make a presentation to your class.
	☑ Invite the students in your class to ask you any questions they may have. Answer these questions.
	☑ When students ask you questions, demonstrate in your answers that you respect their perspectives.
	☑ Turn in the summary of your research, your interview questions and notes, and your presentation to your teacher.
Academic Skills	☑ Speak clearly and concisely.
	☑ Thoughtfully express your ideas.

STEP 2 Plan Your Interview

Use the results of your research to write a list of interview questions to ask someone in your community about his or her personal style. Your questions might include:

- What do you think of today's fashions?
- Is there anyone whose style you respect that influences your own clothing choices?
- How has your style helped express your identity?
- Do you think it is important for someone to develop a personal style? Why or why not?

STEP 3 Connect to Your Community

Identify an adult in your community whose personal style you admire or find interesting. Ask the questions you wrote in Step 2. Take notes during the interview and write a summary of the interview.

Interviewing Skills
- Record interview responses and take notes.
- Listen attentively.

- Write in complete sentences and use correct spelling and grammar when you transcribe your notes.

STEP 4 Share What You Have Learned

Use the Life Skills Project Checklist to plan and create your presentation to share what you have learned with your classmates.

STEP 5 Evaluate Your Life Skills and Academic Skills

Your project will be evaluated based on:
- Content and organization of your information.
- Presentation skills.
- Thoughtfulness of your design.

Evaluation Rubric Go to connectED.mcgraw-hill.com for a rubric you can use to evaluate your final project.

UNIT 10

Housing and the Environment

Chapter 29   Your Home
Chapter 30   Clean and Safe Environments

Unit Life Skills Project Preview

Design Your Ideal Room

In this unit you will learn about your home, both the one you sleep in and the planet you live on. In your unit life skills project you will design your ideal room, incorporating elements of "green" design.

 My Journal

Living Spaces Write a journal entry about one of these topics. This will help you prepare for the unit project at the end of the unit.
- Describe the room in your house where you feel most comfortable.
- List design elements in your home that can be swapped for more environmentally conscious choices.
- Imagine and describe your ideal living space.

Explore the Photo

Frequently people who recycle and work hard at keeping the environment green in their daily life have a hard time being "green" in their own homes. *What are some changes you can make in your home that can save energy and decrease pollution?*

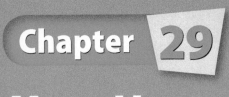

Chapter 29

Your Home

Section 29.1
Housing and Human Needs

Section 29.2
Decorating Living Space

Chapter Objectives

Section 29.1
- **Identify** seven factors that contribute to housing decisions.
- **Compare** single-family housing and multiple-family housing.
- **Describe** the advantages and disadvantages of renting and home ownership.

Section 29.2
- **Identify** four factors to consider before redecorating.
- **List** the elements of design.
- **Outline** the principles of design.
- **Describe** four elements of background.

©Ariel Skelley/Blend Images LLC

▲ Family Living Arrangements

Owning and renting a home are possible choices for living arrangements. *What are some reasons people may prefer one to the other?*

Writing Activity — Business Letter

Zoning Laws Land is divided into zones that regulate the kinds of buildings that can be built in any area. Write a letter to your local government or zoning commission and ask about the zoning laws in your neighborhood. Ask what types of homes can be built in the area. Inquire about the kinds of animals you can have in the neighborhood and the height of the buildings.

Writing Tips Use these tips to write a business letter:
- Be clear about the purpose of your letter.
- Be brief and considerate. Arrange your questions in an organized, logical way.
- Proofread to correct errors in grammar, usage, spelling, and punctuation.

703

Section 29.1

Housing and Human Needs

Reading Guide

Before You Read

Use Color As you read this section, try using different colored pens to take notes. This can help you learn new material and study for tests. For instance, you might use red for vocabulary words, blue for explanations, and green for examples.

Read to Learn

Key Concepts

- **Identify** seven factors that contribute to housing decisions.
- **Compare** single-family housing and multiple-family housing.
- **Describe** the advantages and disadvantages of renting and home ownership.

Main Idea

There are many factors that help people decide where they want to live.

Content Vocabulary

- ◇ utility
- ◇ duplex
- ◇ multiplex
- ◇ townhouse
- ◇ apartment
- ◇ landlord
- ◇ lease
- ◇ mortgage
- ◇ condominium
- ◇ cooperative

Academic Vocabulary

You will find these words in your reading and on your tests. Use the glossary to find these definitions if necessary.

- ☐ contrast
- ☐ suit

Graphic Organizer

Use a graphic organizer like the one below to organize the information in section 29.1. Complete the chart by filling in facts that you learn.

Physical Needs	Emotional Needs	Social Needs

Graphic Organizer Go to connectED.mcgraw-hill.com to download this graphic organizer.

Housing Decisions

What does an apartment in the city have in common with a house in the suburbs? Or a houseboat with a cabin in the woods? Each living unit is someone's home. Whether large or small, each structure fulfills its residents' basic needs:

- **Physical Needs** Housing provides people with shelter. It allows them to create an environment that meets their particular needs.
- **Emotional Needs** Housing meets people's emotional needs by allowing them to relax and pursue their own interests in privacy and comfort. Decorating a home to reflect personal tastes also fulfills emotional needs.
- **Social Needs** A home promotes family strength by giving family members a place to live, share their lives, work, play, entertain guests, and relax.

Although people share the same basic human needs, they also have individual needs and wants. When a person chooses a place to live, he or she first needs to consider his or her specific needs and wants. Then he or she has to find a way to balance those needs and wants with available resources.

Consider Needs, Wants, and Priorities

People's needs, wants, and priorities differ. What one family sees as a necessity might be seen as a drawback or as unimportant to another family. When considering housing, people need to think about the following factors:

- **Family Size** How much room does the family need? Suppose your friend lives with foster parents and five other children. His family's need for space is quite different from that of another friend's family, which only includes herself, her brother, and her father.

As You Read

Connect Think about your family's home. How do you think your home meets your physical, emotional, and social needs?

Home Sweet Home

A home provides a space for families to spend time together. *How do your family members spend time with one another at home?*

Digital Vision/Alamy

TAKE CHARGE!

Keep Your Family Strong

A family's home can affect the strength of the family. Good relationships are dependent upon patience, courtesy, and compromise. Here are some tips for keeping your family strong:

- **Respect Privacy** If space is limited, make sure everyone can enjoy privacy. Even if you share a bedroom, respect your roommate and give him or her some privacy, when possible.
- **Enjoy Each Other's Company** Make time to spend together as a family. Even if space is limited, you can gather around the table for game night.
- **Help Maintain the Budget** Every family member can help look for ways to cut expenses. Maybe you could offer to take your lunch to school instead of buying it in the cafeteria.

Real-World Skills

Take Responsibility Think about the time that your family spends together. What are some things that you could suggest to help your family enjoy more time together?

◧◇ Vocabulary

You can find definitions in the glossary at the back of this book.

- **Family Changes** Changes that families experience can affect housing needs. A young couple expecting a baby may need a larger place with an outdoor play area. An older adult's preferences might contrast, or differ. If a couple lives alone, they may prefer a smaller space that requires little upkeep. For many older couples, they may decide to move from a larger home to a smaller one after their children are grown and have moved out.
- **Special Needs of Family Members** A person who uses a wheelchair or walker needs an accessible home and environment. Someone with limited vision or mobility may prefer or require a single-level home. Accessible homes have wide doorways and hallways, which allow wheelchairs and walkers to easily move from room to room.
- **Location** It may be important for a family member to be close to his or her job. The family may prefer a quiet location, a busy neighborhood, or an area with access to stores and public transportation. The family may want to stay close to friends or other family members.
- **Environmental Concerns** Many people are concerned about the environment. They want housing with features that conserve resources, such as extra insulation or plastic lumber.
- **Technology** Is the home wired for high-speed Internet access? Is wiring available in multiple rooms or just one? Is there a security system? What other technology might be available?
- **Lifestyle** Consider the interests of the people in the household. This may mean a large backyard for an active family, or a home with a large living area for watching movies. Some families need a home office.

Consider Family Resources

After considering needs, wants, and priorities, a family will have a good idea of the location and type of housing that would suit, or please, everyone in the family. If the family members cannot find what they are looking for, they may have to rethink their housing needs and wants, or design exactly what they want. This would require that they have adequate resources.

Families need to choose affordable housing. When calculating the cost of housing, take all expenses into account. In addition to monthly payments for the housing unit, consider other possible costs, such as insurance, taxes, repairs, outdoor maintenance, and utilities. A **utility** is a basic service, such as electricity, cable, gas or oil, phone, water, and sewer service. Some homes have wells that provide water and septic tanks that take care of waste.

Most people must make some compromises to find housing that fits their budget. One family hoped to find a home where two sisters could have their own bedrooms. The family also had a need for an office space. The best value the family could find met all of the family members' needs, except for separate bedrooms for the girls. The family members had to compromise.

Human resources, such as construction and decorating skills, time, energy, and creativity can save families a considerable amount of money. For instance, one family bought a large older house that needed a lot of repairs. Without skills and willingness to make improvements, the family would have had to settle for a much smaller house.

✓ **Reading Check** **Recall** What basic human needs does housing fulfill?

▼ How-To Can-Do

Making your own home improvements can save money and help you personalize your living space. *What are some basic tools that every person should have around the house?*

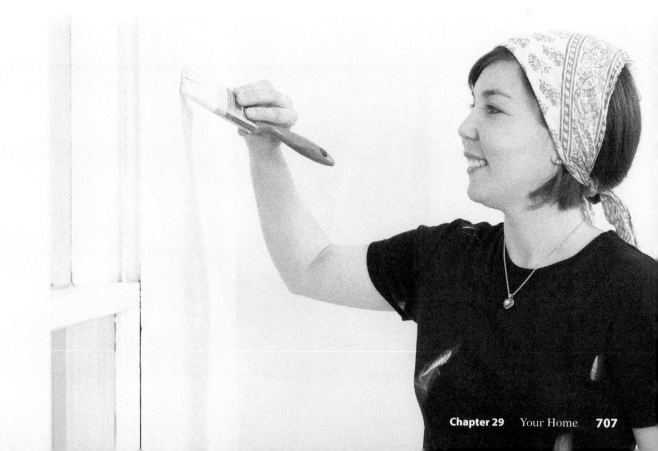

Masterfile

HOW TO... Meet Special Family Needs

People come in all shapes and sizes, with widely ranging abilities. All of them need and want to live as independently as possible. Think of how satisfying it feels when you are self-reliant. Would that feeling disappear if a condition limited your ability to get around your home? Increasingly, architects and home planners are incorporating elements of universal design, creating living and working spaces that are accessible to as many people as possible. Using these ideas, families can make simple changes to make a home user-friendly for members and guests who have physical limitations.

Limited Mobility People who use wheelchairs or walkers need safe, clear, wide pathways. Outside the home, sidewalks can be widened and ramps can be built over steps.

Decorating Adjustments Inside, furniture can be rearranged or put on casters or carts. Deep carpeting, throw rugs, and thresholds between rooms should be removed.

Limited Motor Skills Installing a lazy Susan or storing frequently used items at lower levels can accommodate a limited reach. "Grabbers" or tongs are handy devices for extending a reach. Comfortably rounded handrails and grab bars help people maneuver on their own.

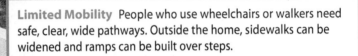

Visual Impairment Good lighting is a good idea for everyone. Large digital clocks are easy to read. Bright colors or colored tape can highlight edges of counters and changes in surface levels. Label items in large fonts when proper use is essential to health and safety, as with medicines and household chemicals.

Textural Cues Use textural cues to help visually impaired people identify items by feel. Put salt in a round salt shaker and pepper in a square one. Rearrange furniture and objects as little as possible.

Limited Strength People with weakness in arms and hands may find it helpful to exchange doorknobs with levers or easy-to-grip, D-shaped handles. Some spray attachments on sinks eliminate the need to turn faucets. In the kitchen, clear counters of small appliances to allow sliding, rather than carrying, of heavy objects.

Hearing Impairment Furniture and lighting should be arranged to help hearing-impaired family members see and focus on speakers. Families can buy plug-in signalers that trigger lamps to flash when a baby cries, an oven timer goes off, or a doorbell rings.

Using the Phone Amplified phones make incoming calls louder and clearer. A TTY (teletypewriter) lets users carry on phone conversations by typing their words on a keyboard.

Building Character ?!

Compromise Sally's family just moved into a new home. Sally must share a bedroom with her younger sister, Megan. Each wants to decorate the room in her own style. Sally wants to paint the walls and hang up some of her favorite landscape photography. Megan wants to cover the walls with posters of her favorite bands. They have been fighting for days over it, but their mother has told the girls they must work this out for themselves. How can Sally and Megan decorate a room that they can both live in and be happy with?

You Make the Call

Should Sally decorate the room the way she wants? Or should she set a good example and let her younger sister have her way? What other options are there?

Housing Options

When looking for a place to live, you may be presented with many housing options. There are many factors that can influence whether or not you decide to move. Types of housing, cost, utilities, and location are all important aspects of living on your own that you must keep in mind when loking for a place to live.

Types of Housing

Two basic categories of housing are single-family homes and multiple-family homes. Single-family housing is built to house one family. Multiple-family housing contains several single-family housing units in one structure. Learning about the types of single-family and multiple-family housing, and understanding the advantages and disadvantages of each, can help you make good housing decisions in the future.

Single-Family Housing

Single-family homes are freestanding homes built for one family. They do not share any walls with another housing unit. They may be small or large, with one story or several stories.

Single-family homes offer more privacy than other types of housing. They are also usually more expensive because they require more land and building materials. There are many types of single-family homes. Some single-family homes are tract homes, or mass-produced homes with similar floor plans. Some are custom-built homes. Others are spec homes, which are built on speculation; subdivisions developed by builders; or historic structures. Single-family homes can also be prefabricated homes, which are system-built homes with parts made in a factory and assembled on-site.

Manufactured, or mobile, homes are also considered to be single-family homes. Manufactured homes are built in a factory and are moved to a specific site. Some communities restrict where manufactured homes can be placed. Most manufactured homes are less expensive than a traditional single-family home. They also may come completely furnished.

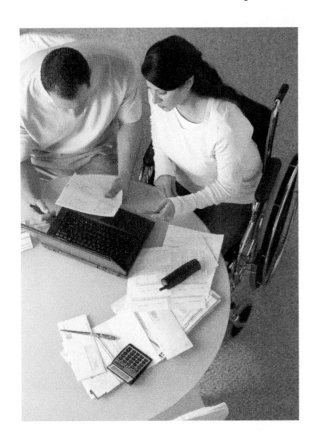

◄ **Financial Responsibilities**

Living on your own includes paying for rent or mortgage as well as utilities like water, power, and your phone. *Why do you think that larger homes tend to have larger utility bills?*

©Terry Vine/Blend Images LLC

How I See It

LIVING SPACES

Junichi, 14

My family recently moved from a house in a small town into an apartment downtown. This has required some adjustments, to say the least! Instead of having a backyard, I go to the park across the street. My dad buys fresh vegetables at a green grocer, rather than growing them in his own garden. Instead of riding my bicycle to school, now I ride the bus. It is interesting living in a highrise building with lots of other people. Not only do we share walls with our neighbors, but the building has elevators, stairwells, and fire sprinklers. What a change!

Critical Thinking
Sharing a building is one of the many ways people share living space. What do you think people may learn from sharing space? How can they use these lessons in the future?

Multiple-Family Housing

Multiple-family dwellings are connected to one another and may be more affordable. Cost, however, varies with location, size, and features. Individual units may be small or large. Residents may or may not share the use of a laundry room, swimming pool, workout room, or other special features.

Multiple-family dwellings require much less land per person than single-family houses, which means less or no yard maintenance. However, these dwellings tend to be noisier and less private than single-family homes, depending on the structure and the insulation. Storage space may be limited, and pets may not be allowed. The following dwellings are considered multiple-family houses:

A **duplex** is a single structure that contains two separate units. The units may be side by side and share one wall, or they may be on separate floors.

A **multiplex** is similar to a duplex, but three or more units share one building.

A **townhouse** is a house built in a row of other townhouses. It is attached to another townhouse at a side wall.

An **apartment** is a rental unit in a building, or a structure that houses units for more than two families. Some apartments are not just one building. Some are an actual complex, or a community of apartments.

✓ **Reading Check** **Identify** Give examples of multiple-family housing and single-family housing.

Community Connections

Housing in Your Community

Many communities have programs that offer affordable housing for those who may not be able to buy it on their own. Look into ways you can help people in your community meet their housing needs with the dignity they deserve.

Ways to Obtain Housing

Some people own the housing unit in which they live. Others rent their home from the person or company who owns the property. Renting and buying both have advantages and disadvantages.

Renting a Home

Renting means paying money to live in a housing unit owned by someone else. An owner of rental housing is sometimes called a **landlord**. Many different types of housing units are available for rent. People can rent apartments, duplexes, houses, and even individual rooms in houses. Some rental units come furnished, usually for an extra fee. Typically, the larger the housing unit, the higher the cost of rent.

When you rent a housing unit, you may have to fill out an application and sign a **lease**, a written rental agreement. The lease states that you agree to pay rent for a certain period of time. It specifies the monthly fee and what is or is not included, such as utilities and maintenance. It also includes any rules you must follow. Always read a lease carefully before you sign it. If you do not understand the lease, ask a qualified person to explain it. Even if you understand it, having a lawyer look over a lease is a wise decision, since a lease is a legal document. Many landlords require a security deposit, often equal to one month's rent or the first and last months' rent. This is returned when you move out if the unit is clean and has not been damaged. If damage has occurred, you may receive a partial refund of your security deposit. Make sure there is an agreement to the condition of the rental when you move in and when you move out.

Many people enjoy the following advantages of renting:
* **Convenience** The landlord, rather than the tenant, usually handles painting, maintenance, and any household repairs.
* **Flexibility** Renters do not have to sell their home when it is time to move. Selling a home can be a long and costly process.
* **Financial Advantages** People who rent homes do not have to pay for general repairs. If something breaks, the owner is obligated to fix it. This also usually applies to property taxes and any upkeep of the facility. Homeowner's insurance is the responsibility of the homeowner. Renters should have renter's insurance for their personal items.

Owning a Home

Many people choose to buy a home because they value a feeling of permanence. Owning a home also offers freedom. Homeowners can redecorate or remodel their home to meet their personal needs and tastes. One major reason for owning a home is to develop an investment that can provide a sense of financial security.

Science You Can Use

Fire Safety

Fire requires three ingredients: heat, fuel, and oxygen. When you add a source of ignition, fire is created. The ignition is the mechanism that lights the fuel. To ignite is to start burning.

Procedure Choose one type of fire to research. Types of fire include grease, electrical, wood, and chemical. Find out how to safely put out the type of fire you choose.

Analysis Write a report on your findings. In your report, describe the type of fire, typical causes, and safe ways to put out that type of fire.

Purchasing a place to live is not a decision to be made lightly. A home is usually the most expensive purchase families will ever make. To buy a home, most people take out a long-term loan called a **mortgage**. The mortgage is typically for 15 to 30 years. The interest paid on the mortgage can be deducted on the homeowner's income tax return. This is an incentive for many people to buy instead of rent a home.

The part of the purchase price paid up front is called a down payment. The down payment can be quite large, often at least 10 percent of the total house cost. Other costs must also be considered. A homeowner usually must pay property taxes and insurance, along with utilities and repair fees.

Many people want to invest in a home but do not want the responsibilities of yardwork and maintenance outside of the main living space. Two special kinds of housing, which combine some advantages of home ownership and apartment living, offer a solution. A **condominium** is an individually owned unit in a multiple-family dwelling. Some are physically connected, and some are freestanding. The owner of each unit pays a fee to help cover the cost of maintaining hallways, landscaping, parking lots, and other common areas. A less common form of ownership is a **cooperative**, or co-op. In a co-op, residents of a multiple-family dwelling form a corporation that owns the building. Instead of buying or renting a housing unit, owners buy shares in the co-op and contribute to its monthly costs. In return, each member receives use of one of the units.

Condominium and co-op owners often have less freedom to make decisions about their homes compared with single-family housing owners. For example, the exterior color of the home and the landscaping, such as flowers, trees, and lawn ornaments, may be restricted.

Roommates

When two people share a home, they usually share the expenses and the household chores. *How can you avoid conflicts with roommates?*

SUCCEED IN SCHOOL

Find Space

It is important to have a quiet space where you can focus on your studies. Let your family members know when you are doing your homework so you can work undisturbed.

Yellow Dog Productions/Getty Images

Sharing a Home

Many people choose to share a home. When they share a home, individuals combine their finances to meet their housing needs yet stay within their spending plans. Classmates may share an apartment to save money. Adult children sometimes return to live with a parent for a time. Older adults may move in with their adult child for care and companionship. Siblings will sometimes live together. Sharing a home works best when people are thoughtful of one another. Every member of the household should have a degree of privacy.

Making the Decision

Most people live in several types of housing and in many locations during their lifetime. People often change housing as their needs and resources change. For example, people may move from an apartment in the city to a home in a suburban area.

The decision to move should be made carefully. Moving can be expensive. You may need to hire movers or rent a truck to move on your own. Having the phone or electric service hooked up involves additional fees. The more information you have with which to make a housing decision, the happier you are likely to be with your choice.

Section 29.1

After You Read

Review Key Concepts

1. **Explain** how housing provides for a person's emotional needs.
2. **List** the four types of multiple-family dwellings.
3. **Identify** reasons for sharing a home.

Practice Academic Skills

English Language Arts

4. Many people believe that young adults expect too much, too soon. Compared to previous generations, young adults want more money, better housing and clothing, and expensive cars. Do you agree? If so, is the trend a negative one? Explain your answers in a brief essay.

Social Studies

5. Find out what your local and state laws are regarding renters' rights and responsibilities. What are renters' options if they have a disagreement with their landlord? What are the landlord's rights if a tenant does not meet the lease agreement? Present your findings in a table that separates the tenant's rights and responsibilities from the landlord's rights and responsibilities.

 **Check Your Answers** Go to connectED. mcgraw-hill.com to check your answers.

Decorating Living Space

Reading Guide

Before You Read

Buddy Up for Success One advantage to sharing your notes with a buddy is that you can fill in gaps in each other's information. You can also compare notes before you start quizzing each other.

Read to Learn
Key Concepts
- **Identify** four factors to consider before redecorating.
- **List** the elements of design.
- **Outline** the principles of design.
- **Describe** four elements of background.

Main Idea
Interior design helps you decorate your home to match your personality and lifestyle.

Content Vocabulary

◇ symmetrical balance
◇ asymmetrical balance
◇ background
◇ functional furniture
◇ traffic pattern

Academic Vocabulary
You will find these words in your reading and on your tests. Use the glossary to find these definitions if necessary.

☐ delineate   ☐ emphasis

Graphic Organizer
As you read, note the three types of lighting and the purpose for each. Use a chart like the one below to organize your information.

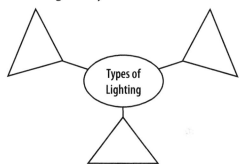

Graphic Organizer Go to connectED.mcgraw-hill.com to download this graphic organizer.

Using Design

As You Read

Connect Think about the decor in your bedroom. Is there anything you would like to change? Why?

Some people seem to have a natural talent for decorating a room. However, in most cases, good design does not just happen. Effective interior design requires careful planning. Whether your project is as simple as painting your bedroom walls a new color, or as complicated as a complete remodel, think about the project before you begin. If you do a little planning, you are more likely to be pleased with the results. When planning a decorating project, do the following:

- **Identify What You Need** What is your major goal? How will the space be used? What type of storage is needed?
- **Evaluate Your Current Space** What parts of the present design work well? What needs improvement? What specifically would you like to keep or change?
- **Keep Your Resources in Mind** How much can you afford to spend? There is no point in planning expensive changes if they are beyond your budget. Remember that skills are resources, too. Changing a room's look can mean adding a few new touches to what you already have.
- **Identify Your Preferences** What look do you want? What styles do you like?

✓ **Reading Check** **Explain** How can you make sure your design is effective?

Signature Style

The elements of design add to the comfort and beauty of your space. *What are some ways you can express yourself through design?*

Radius Images/Corbis

Elements of Design

Many people attempt to design a living space with little success. No matter what accessory they add, or how they arrange the furniture, they are never pleased. To achieve a satisfying look, people should use the five elements of design. These elements include space, line, form, texture, and color. See **Figure 29.1**.

Space The three-dimensional area to be designed, such as a room, as well as the area around or between objects within that expanse, is the space. You have two basic choices: fill the space or leave much of it empty. Your choice can make a room seem quite different. For example, a room with a lot of furniture may give some people a cozy feeling, but others may feel cramped. Too much empty space creates the feeling that something is missing.

Line Often considered the most basic design element, line refers to the outline of an object or to the obvious lines within it. All lines are either straight or curved and are placed in a direction—vertical, horizontal, or diagonal. Lines can be combined to make zigzags or other variations, and can cause your eyes to move up and down or across an object. Lines delineate, or define, space when they intersect, such as at the edges of a wall, floor, or ceiling. You can combine and place lines to create certain effects and feelings. For example, tall bookcases give the illusion of height.

Form The shape and structure of solid objects created when lines are combined is called form. Form may be two-dimensional or three-dimensional. Examples of two-dimensional forms are walls and rugs. They have length and width, but little or no depth. A piece of furniture is a three-dimensional form. It has depth in addition to length and width. An object's form can make it seem heavy or light. A large, heavy sofa gives a feeling of stability to a room.

Texture The way an object's surfaces look and feel is texture. People respond to texture in different ways. For example, plush rugs and furniture covered with soft fabric provide a sense of warmth and luxury. Glass, metal, and stone tend to give a feeling of coolness. Texture can also affect color. Smooth textures appear lighter in color than rough textures.

Color Often called the most important of all decorating elements, color influences how people feel and can be used to create a certain mood. For these reasons, color should be chosen carefully. For example, red often conveys strength and excitement. Many greens and blues have a calming effect. Yellow can give a feeling of cheerfulness, but large expanses of gray may do the opposite. Colors associated with the sun, such as red, orange, and yellow, are called warm colors. Blues and greens, like the colors of the sea, are considered cool colors. For more information on using color, see **Figure 29.2** on page 718.

✓ **Reading Check** **Identify** What do the elements of design do?

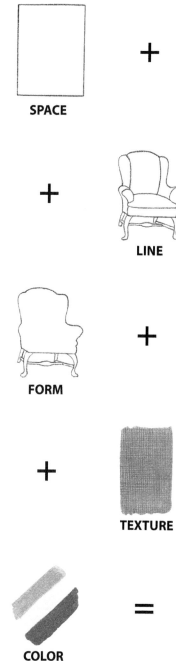

Figure 29.1 **Basic Elements**

Put It Together To achieve the best design, you need to use all five elements together. *How might this chair be effected if the shape were different?*

SPACE

+

LINE

+

FORM

+

TEXTURE

=

COLOR

DESIGN

Figure 29.2 ## Using Color

Spin the Wheel The color wheel is a helpful tool for understanding and using color. *What might you use this for in your home?*

 Color Wheel The wheel is divided into 12 pie-shaped sections that display three types of colors: primary, secondary, and intermediate.

 Secondary Colors When two primary colors are mixed, the result is a secondary color. The three secondary colors are violet, green, and orange. To make violet, red and blue are mixed together. Green is a mixture of yellow and blue, and orange is made from red and yellow. On the color wheel, the secondary colors are halfway between the primary colors from which they are made.

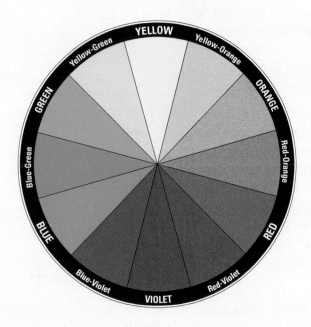

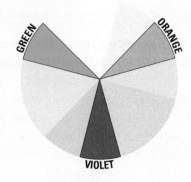

 Primary Colors Red, yellow, and blue are primary colors and are placed an equal distance apart on the wheel. The other colors on the wheel can be made from them.

 Intermediate Colors When a primary and a neighboring secondary color are mixed, an intermediate color is made. The six intermediate colors are yellow-green, blue-green, blue-violet, red-violet, red-orange, and yellow-orange. (Note that the primary color comes first in the name of the intermediate color.) The intermediate colors fill the remaining spaces on the wheel.

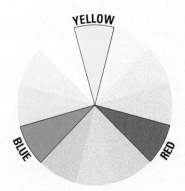

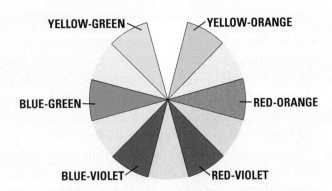

Color Schemes You may have noticed that neutral colors—black, white, and gray—are not on the color wheel. However, neutral colors can be used to change the lightness or darkness of a color. Color schemes, or combinations of color, are also important in the study of color. Color schemes are pleasing to the eye and are based on the color wheel.

 Complementary schemes are made up of two colors directly opposite each other on the color wheel, such as red and green.

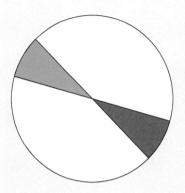

 Monochromatic schemes use variations of only one color. For example, you could combine light and dark or dull and bright greens.

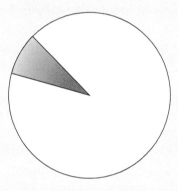

 Split-complementary schemes result when a color is combined with colors on each side of its complement. Yellow, blue-violet, and red-violet are examples of a split-complementary scheme.

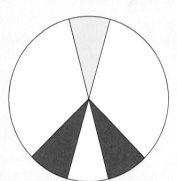

 Analogous schemes are made up of two or more colors next to one another on the color wheel. For example, blue-green, green, and blue form an analogous color scheme.

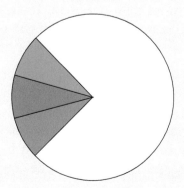

 Triadic schemes use three colors the same distance from one another on the color wheel. For example, green, orange, and violet form a triadic scheme.

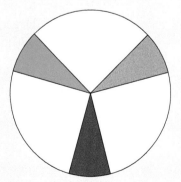

Principles of Design

All good designs follow certain principles that have evolved over time. By applying the following six principles to the elements of design, you can achieve appealing decorating results that fit your personality.

Proportion Proportion is the way one part of a design relates in size to another part and to the whole design. For example, wooden chairs with thick legs and backs would be in proportion to a bulky oak table. Small, spindly chairs would not. When considering proportion, think of shape, as well as size. Designers know that certain shapes are more pleasing than others because of their proportions. For example, rectangles are often more desirable than squares. Consider how often you see rectangular rugs, windows, and picture frames compared with square ones. However, a rectangle that is too long and narrow may not work visually.

Scale Scale refers to the overall size of an object compared with other objects. Scale is not the same as proportion. A lamp may be well proportioned, with a pleasing ratio of shade to base. To be in scale with a room, however, it must also be an appropriate size in relation to the other furnishings. A small lamp might be the right scale for a medium-sized nightstand. If would be out of scale if placed on a large coffee table, though.

Balance Balance gives a feeling of equal weight to objects on both sides of a design's center point. **Symmetrical balance** is achieved when objects on one side of an imaginary center line are the mirror image of those on the other side. Symmetrical balance is also known as formal balance. **Asymmetrical balance** means that something is not symmetrical. Asymmetrical objects on each side are unmatched but appear balanced. Asymmetrical balance is also called informal balance.

Emphasis Every room has an emphasis, or focal point. This is a place in the room where your eye is drawn. This usually means that it is the point of greatest interest in a room or a living area. Examples of emphasis include a brightly painted headboard, a large poster or painting, a large couch, or a bookshelf. The focal point does not have to be expensive, and it can be more than one item. Instead of one large framed painting, you can create a center of interest on a wall with a collection of smaller items, such as photographs or drawings.

Unity The feeling that all parts of a design belong together is unity. However, everything does not have to match for unity to be achieved. A design should also have variety, or the combination of different but compatible styles. Without some variety, rooms can be dull and monotonous. Too much variety, on the other hand, can be visually distracting. To be effective, unity and variety need to be combined to create a harmonious effect.

The Center of Attention

When people enter a room, they are drawn first to its focal point. *What is the focal point of this room?*

Vocabulary

You can find definitions in the glossary at the back of this book.

Rhythm A feeling of movement, leading the eye from one point to another, is called rhythm. A specific color repeated at various points in a room creates a sense of rhythm. Different sizes of candles arranged from tall to short, or chairs arranged around a circular table also create rhythm. Draperies with flowing swags and a sofa with a back curving into the arms are other examples.

✓ **Reading Check** **Contrast** What is the difference between proportion and scale?

Backgrounds, Furniture, and Accessories

Now that you are familiar with the elements of design and the principles of design, you are ready to see what design theory looks like in practice. A room's background, furniture, and accessories all play important roles in creating a pleasant environment.

Background

The background of your room is the artist's canvas for the elements of design. The **background** can be the walls, windows, floors, and ceiling of a room. Sometimes, a room's background may be the center of interest. At other times, a background may go almost unnoticed, only helping to display furniture and other possessions to their best advantage.

Walls Walls define areas, provide privacy, and help absorb noise. Although walls serve as boundaries, the number of ways you can decorate walls is limited only by your imagination. The two most popular ways to decorate walls are painting and wallpapering. If you paint, you can choose from many colors and techniques. You can paint a mural or stencil on all or part of a wall. Wallpaper adds interesting patterns and textures to all or a portion of a wall.

Windows Sometimes windows are left bare to expose a beautiful view. Usually, however, they are covered in some way for privacy. Window treatments, or window coverings, can provide both privacy and decoration. Window treatment choices include curtains, drapes, shutters, blinds, and shades in a variety of colors and materials. Some people like to combine treatments. For example, you might use shutters and curtains on the same window.

Floors Flooring materials are a permanent part of the floor. They can include concrete, wood, ceramic, or stone, such as granite, marble, slate, and brick. Floor coverings, which are temporary, may be installed over permanent flooring. They can add comfort, warmth, and beauty to a room. Vinyl, for example, is easy to clean. It is warmer and quieter to walk on than ceramic tile and other hard materials, but vinyl is more easily damaged. Carpets and rugs provide extra warmth and comfort, muffle noise, and add color. Wood laminate is durable, attractive, and usually more affordable than hardwood floors.

SUCCEED IN SCHOOL

Avoid Distraction

It is easy to get distracted when trying to focus on homework. Try to eliminate any background noise, like the television and cell phone notifications, before you begin studying.

Health & Wellness

TIPS

Health and Safety in the Home

There are a few health issues you should be aware of when looking for a place to live:

▶ Standing water or water damage

▶ Mold in the walls, ceiling, and floor

▶ Cracks in the structure due to age or earthquakes

Ceilings The ceiling is an important feature of a room that is often forgotten. Higher ceilings, common in older homes, give a feeling of dignity and elegance. Lower ceilings can create a warm, informal feeling. Wallpaper, paint, and window treatments can be used to create the illusion of ceiling height.

Furniture

Furniture provides a place for various activities. Most furniture is **functional furniture**; it meets specific needs. Chests, for example, are used to store things. Tables provide space for eating, doing homework, or playing cards. Functional furniture is also decorative.

Furniture Styles There are two basic styles of furniture: traditional and contemporary. Traditional styles are based on designs used for hundreds of years. This furniture can be formal or informal, fancy or plain. Contemporary furniture is simple and reflects today's lifestyles. It has straight or gently curved lines with little or no decoration.

Furniture Choice and Arrangment Before selecting furniture, think about what you need and what you have. If your budget is limited, put your creativity to work. Garage sales, flea markets, and consignment stores often have used furniture bargains. With a fresh coat of paint or a new cushion, these pieces can be good as new.

When choosing furniture for a specific room, look for styles that have a similar feeling, such as different wood furniture pieces with similar simple lines. Every piece of furniture in a room does not have to match exactly. Even if the pieces are from different time periods, they still can be interesting and can complement one another.

The smart way to arrange furniture is to use graph paper or a computer program before using your muscles. Think about your arrangement. Check to see whether the **traffic pattern**, or the path people use to get from one area or room to another, is uncluttered and fairly direct. Avoid blocking traffic patterns with furniture or other obstacles.

Accessories

What is the easiest and least expensive way to change a room? Accessories, such as lamps, plants, posters, books, baskets, pictures, and mirrors, can change a room dramatically. When selecting accessories, keep in mind the elements and principles of design and use them to create the effect you want.

Dress Up or Down

Furniture comes in a variety of formal and informal styles. *How would you decorate a room for everyday use?*

Safety Check

Light the Way

Lighting is especially important in the homes of people with visual impairments. Be sure that walkways and steps are well lit. This can be accomplished with both overhead lights and area lamps.

Write About It

Write a paragraph that explains other ways you can keep the home safe for people with visual impairments.

When you consider accessories, let your imagination soar. You might choose to accessorize a room by displaying your collection of sports memorabilia, CDs, old record album covers, baseball caps, art, jewelry, or other items that express your personality and interests.

Lighting Lighting is part of interior design and should be considered when you are planning a project. Each of the three main types of lighting has a unique purpose.

- **General Lighting** This provides enough light that you can move around a room safely and comfortably. In most cases, general lighting is not good light for reading or studying.
- **Task Lighting** This focuses light where it is needed. You use task lighting to prevent eyestrain when reading or working on hobbies. It should be free of glare and shadows. If you use a lamp for reading, the bottom of the shade should be slightly below eye level when you are seated. If the lighting is above your eye level, the lamp should be about 10 inches (4 cm) behind your shoulder.
- **Accent Lighting** This intense beam of light aimed at a painting, sculpture, or other object creates a dramatic or directed effect. It can be installed in the ceiling or can be freestanding.

Section 29.2

After You Read

Review Key Concepts

1. **Describe** resources to consider when planning a decorating project.
2. **Explain** why color should be chosen carefully.
3. **Compare** symmetrical and asymmetrical balance.
4. **Describe** the use and appeal of window treatments.

Practice Academic Skills

English Language Arts

5. One important aspect of looking for a place to live and designing the interior is self-discipline. You must remember your budget and not make purchases that can end up as debt. Create a checklist of items you should consider when you create a budget for setting up a new home.

Social Studies

6. Imagine you are looking for a place to live. You can spend $550 a month on rent, including utilities. Use the newspaper, magazines, and the Internet to look for housing in your area. Then research housing prices in a region that is different from the one in which you live. Remember to research the area you choose for statistics such as crime rate as well as rental prices.

Check Your Answers Go to connectED.mcgraw-hill.com to check your answers.

Veterinarian

What Does a Veterinarian Do?

Veterinarians care for the health of pets, livestock, and animals in zoos, racetracks, and laboratories. Some veterinarians use their skills to protect humans against diseases carried by animals and conduct clinical research on human and animal health problems. Others work in basic research, broadening our knowledge of animals and medical science, and in applied research, developing new ways to use this knowledge.

Ariel Skelley/Blend Images LLC

Skills Experience working with veterinarians or scientists in clinics will help you to pursue a career as a veterinarian. Other experience, like working with animals at a farm, ranch, or animal shelter, can also be helpful. You should enjoy working with animals and their owners.

Education and Training People who want to study veterinary medicine should emphasize the sciences including chemistry and biology. Veterinarians must graduate with a Doctor of Veterinary Medicine degree from a four-year program at a college of veterinary medicine.

Job Outlook Employment of veterinarians is expected to grow through 2016. Veterinarians usually practice in animal hospitals or clinics. Understanding the most popular pets, dogs and cats, will be important for success in a private practice.

Critical Thinking Some veterinarians focus on family pets and know cats and dogs best. Others work with horses, cows, and other large animals. Why would it be an advantage to specialize in a certain kind of animal? Write a paragraph explaining your reasons.

Career Cluster

Agriculture and Natural Resources

Veterinarians work in the Agriculture and Natural Resources career cluster. Here are some of the other jobs in this career cluster:

- Fish and Game Warden
- Forest Harvesting and Production
- Meat Cutter and Butcher
- Agricultural Product Inspector
- Soil and Land Preservation
- Mining Engineer
- Geologist
- Gardener and Groundskeeper
- Petroleum Technician
- Sprayer and Irrigation Worker
- Landscape Architect
- Feed, Fertilizer, and Pest Control Service Worker
- Nursery and Greenhouse Manager, or Worker

Explore Further Research this career cluster. Choose a career in this cluster that appeals to you and write a career profile.

Section 29.1
Housing and Human Needs

Housing fulfills people's basic needs. People's needs, wants, priorities, and resources influence their housing decisions. Single-family and multiple-family housing options have advantages and disadvantages. Buying a home is a major decision that should be considered carefully. Most people live in several types of housing and several locations over the course of their lifetimes.

Section 29.2
Decorating Living Space

You will be more pleased with a decorating project if you do a little planning. Use the elements and principles of design to create living spaces that you and your family will enjoy. Backgrounds are the walls, windows, floors, and ceiling of a room. Before moving furniture, take time to plan your arrangement. Respect and consideration can help make sharing space easier.

Vocabulary Review

1. Use at least seven of these content and academic vocabulary terms in a short essay about where you would like to live in five years.

Content Vocabulary
◇ utility (p. 707)
◇ duplex (p. 711)
◇ multiplex (p. 711)
◇ townhouse (p. 711)
◇ apartment (p. 711)
◇ landlord (p. 712)
◇ lease (p. 712)
◇ mortgage (p. 713)

◇ condominium (p. 713)
◇ cooperative (p. 713)
◇ symmetrical balance (p. 720)
◇ asymmetrical balance (p. 720)
◇ background (p. 721)
◇ functional furniture (p. 722)
◇ traffic pattern (p. 722)

Academic Vocabulary
■ contrast (p. 706)
■ suit (p. 707)
■ delineate (p. 717)
■ emphasis (p. 720)

Review Key Concepts

2. Identify seven factors that contribute to housing decisions.
3. Compare single-family housing and multiple-family housing.
4. Describe the advantages and disadvantages of renting and home ownership.
5. Identify four factors to consider before redecorating.
6. List the elements of design.
7. Outline the principles of design.
8. Describe four elements of background.

Critical Thinking

9. Analyze your neighborhood. What advice would you offer a friend whose family is considering buying a home in your community?
10. Hypothesize the challenges that may face two friends who become roommates.
11. Design a display of photos from decorating magazines that show the elements and principles of design. Label and discuss each example.

 ACTIVE LEARNING

12. Organization Skills Anya's mom loved to cook. She was always looking for new recipes to try. She also loved to look for new ways to cook. She would often buy new kitchen appliances and tools. After a while, Anya noticed that her mom was having trouble finding a place to store all of her kitchen appliances and gadgets. Unfortunately, she also had trouble finding what she needed to use. Anya began to think of ways she could help her mom rearrange  the kitchen. Look in magazines and catalogs to find ways Anya might use the space in her kitchen to its best potential.

13. Life Simulation Each member of a family has a unique personality. This can often cause tension when family members have to share a space. Work with a partner to create a brief skit you can perform for the class. You should enact a scene in which two family members are in conflict over a shared space. This space might be a bedroom shared by siblings. It might also be a kitchen, living room, or game room that all family members can use. In your role play, explain why each of the family members wants to use the space, or how they want to use it differently. After your performance, brainstorm with the audience to think of ground rules that will help the family members share the space successfully.

Real-World Skills and Applications

Leadership Skills

14. Creative Teams When you are faced with a task such as moving to a new home or decorating a room, you may want to have a team of people who can assist you with moving furniture, choosing colors, or helping you make decisions about design. Create a plan of action for a team of which you will be a leader. What tasks do you need done? How many people will help you? How can you divide the tasks?

Financial Literacy

15. Paying Interest Imagine you have just received $100 for your birthday. You can use the money to buy a pair of bindings for your snowboard. You go snowboarding four times every year, and have to pay $6 to rent them every time. On the other hand, you can put the $100 against your credit card that helped pay for the couch. This would help you avoid paying the 27 percent annual interest charge, which amounts to $2.25 per month. How much money would you save in one year if you bought the bindings? How much interest would you pay in a year if you did not pay what you owe on the credit card?

Information Literacy

16. Write a Résumé A well-written résumé can help you get the job you want. Use print or online resources to learn how to write a résumé. Then use a word processing program to write your résumé. Limit it to a single page.

Academic Skills

English Language Arts

17. **The World of Design** Many design terms have foreign origins. For example, *appliqué*, meaning cutout decorations, is from the French word *appliquer*, meaning "to put on." Create a list of at least five terms used in design and research their language origins. Then compile these words and their origins into a short glossary that defines each word

Social Studies

18. **Credit Laws** In addition to federal laws that govern the use of credit, most states also have credit laws. Investigate the laws that control the use of credit in your state. What is the highest interest rate that can be legally charged? Are there any limits on the fees that can be assessed? What happens when people cannot or do not pay their bills? Write a report of your findings.

Mathematics

19. **Area Rugs** Raj just moved into a new apartment. His living room measures 15 ft. × 16 ft. and has hardwood floors. He wants to buy an area rug to soften the look of the wood and add warmth to the room. He finally finds one with a pattern and colors that he likes. It measures 11 ft. × 8 ft. How much of his hardwood floor will still be visible when he lays out the rug?

 Area The area of geometric objects can be found using simple equations. The equation for rectangular objects is: area = length × width.

Starting Hint If a rectangle is inside a square, find the area of each and then subtract. Use the formula for area to find the area for Raj's floor and for his rug. Then subtract the two answers.

 For math help, go to the Math Appendix at the back of the book.

Standardized Test Practice

TRUE/FALSE
Directions: Read each statement. On a separate sheet of paper, write T if the statement is true, and write F if the statement is false.

Test-Taking Tip When answering true/false questions, pay close attention to the wording as you read the questions. Look for words such as not, nor, any, or all. These words are important in determining the correct answer.

20. Read these statements and determine if they are true or false.
   a) Families always live in single-family homes.
   b) It is not always important to ask your landlord questions before you sign a lease.
   c) The way you design a room is a great way to express yourself.

Chapter 30

Clean and Safe Environments

Michelle Pedone/Getty Images

Section 30.1
Establishing a Safe and Clean Home Environment

Section 30.2
The Earth—Your Home

Chapter Objectives

Section 30.1
- **Create** a home maintenance plan.
- **Identify** home safety procedures.
- **List** the things you need to know when you make an emergency call.

Section 30.2
- **Contrast** renewable and nonrenewable resources.
- **List** five ways you can conserve the Earth's resources.
- **Give** guidelines for making wise consumer decisions.

Explore the Photo

Whether at home or exploring the great outdoors, it is important to take care of your environment. *What do you think the consequences would be for treating your home and outdoor environments poorly?*

Writing Activity

Write a Persuasive Essay

Safety First When you take precautions against accidents and break-ins, you feel more secure about the safety of your home. Write a persuasive essay that explains a few simple measures people should take to ensure the safety of their homes. This may include something as simple as locking the door before leaving. Be descriptive in your essay, and support your ideas and opinions in an organized and logical way.

Writing Tips Use these tips to write a persuasive essay:
- State your position clearly.
- Use facts to back up your position.
- Remember to explain the benefits of thinking ahead.

Section 30.1

Establishing a Safe and Clean Home Environment

Reading Guide

Before You Read

Two-Column Notes Two-column notes are a useful way to study and organize what you have read. Divide a piece of paper into two columns. In the left column, write down main ideas. In the right column, list supporting details.

Read to Learn

Key Concepts

- **Create** a home maintenance plan.
- **Identify** home safety procedures.
- **List** the things you need to know when you make an emergency call.

Main Idea

Maintain a safe living environment through proper cleaning and attention to physical safety.

Content Vocabulary

◇ home maintenance
◇ hazard

Academic Vocabulary

You will find these words in your reading and on your tests. Use the glossary to look up their definitions if necessary.

▫ entail
▫ survey

Graphic Organizer

Use a graphic organizer like the one below to list some tips for keeping your home safe.

How to Keep the House Safe
1.
2.
3.
4.
5.
6.
7.
8.
9.

 Graphic Organizer Go to **connectED.mcgraw-hill.com** to download this graphic organizer.

Keeping Your Home Clean

A comfortable and clean home environment does not just happen on its own. Maintaining a home so that it benefits everyone who lives there takes careful planning. **Home maintentance** includes eliminating clutter, organizing household and personal items, cleaning, making minor repairs or changes, and keeping household equipment in good working order.

Home Maintenance Planning

A home maintenance plan can catch small problems before they develop into large and costly ones. The most successful home maintenance plans are those that family members develop together. To develop a plan, list maintenance tasks for each room of your home. Then, decide if each task should be done daily, weekly, monthly, or annually. Consider how much time each job will take and whether tasks need to be done in a certain order. Then, decide who will be responsible for each job and whether jobs can be rotated. Even young children can be given simple tasks.

Daily and Weekly Tasks

Everybody needs to agree on daily and weekly household tasks that are important for health and safety. These tasks do not take long to accomplish and can quickly turn into habits.

Daily tasks entail, or involve, putting away clothes and other belongings, making beds, disposing of trash, caring for pets, and washing dishes with hot, soapy water. Also, wiping up spills as they occur and keeping traffic patterns, stairs, and doorways free of clutter are important for safety.

Many families do overall cleaning once a week. Individual families can determine how often to vacuum, dust, change bed linens, clean bathrooms, wash floors, do laundry, and perform other cleaning tasks that must be done. If you have pets, you may have some extra cleaning to do. Pets need a clean environment as well.

Occasional Tasks

Some maintenance tasks only need to be taken care of occasionally, whether that is once a month, every few months, or once a year. These tasks include cleaning the oven and refrigerator, shampooing carpets, washing walls and windows, cleaning blinds and curtains, and cleaning closets and drawers.

As You Read

Connect Think about the chores you do on a daily basis. What would happen if they were left undone?

Vocabulary

You can find definitions in the glossary at the back of this book.

Cleaning Up

Washing dishes is a small task that should be done daily. *What might happen if dishes are left unwashed?*

©Hero/Corbis/Glow Images

TAKE CHARGE!

Clean Outdoors

Maintaining the area outside your home will help its curbside appeal and keep it safe. Follow these guidelines for cleaning outdoors:

- **Prevent Porch Clutter** Keep the porch, patio, and deck areas swept and free of clutter and debris. Check the condition of outside gas or charcoal grills.
- **Clear a Path** Remove fallen tree limbs and branches from walkways. In the winter, keep snow and ice off pathways where someone might walk.
- **Wash Windows and Walls** Use a broom to sweep away cobwebs and dirt from the outside walls. Wash windows and screens once a year.
- **Mind the Overgrowth** Mow the lawn, rake fallen leaves, and prune overgrown trees and shrubs.
- **Put Toys Away** Put bikes and other sports equipment away immediately after use to prevent theft and accidents.

Keep and file instruction booklets that come with furnishings and equipment, and check to find out what special care is required. Add these jobs to the list. Also, you may need to add outdoor jobs, such as raking leaves and cutting grass, to your home maintenance task list. Even if you live in an environment where outdoor maintenance is done by others, do your part to keep the area clean.

Cleaning Products and Equipment

Part of becoming organized includes selecting products and equipment for cleaning jobs. Products that clean more than one type of surface often are a good buy. Some jobs, however, may require a specific product. As you shop, compare labels on various brands to get the best quality for your money.

Using the proper equipment also makes cleaning easier. Every home should have a broom, mop, bucket, and vacuum cleaner, if there is carpeting. Scrub brushes, discarded toothbrushes, sponges, and dusting cloths, are other basic cleaning tools.

To stay safe as you use cleaning products:

- Keep cleaning products in their original containers so that you will know what they are and how they should be used.
- Store cleaning products away from food and out of the reach of small children. Keep chemicals in a locked cabinet.
- When using products with powerful fumes, make sure there is adequate ventilation. Use a fan and open windows to bring in fresh air.
- Never mix products. The results could be poisonous, explosive, or fatal.

Home Maintenance Tasks

Keeping your home free of dirt and bacteria that can lead to illness is extremely important. By removing dust and dirt, disposing of garbage, and controlling pests, you help make your home a healthy place to live. Quick cleaning takes a little planning. Keep needed supplies handy, and add the needed time to your schedule. Then, with practice, the following tasks can easily become part of your routine.

Clutter

The best way to control clutter is to pick up and put away your belongings immediately after you use them. How you organize your storage depends on what you have to store and the kind and size of storage space you have available. If possible, it is best to store items near the area where they are used and to store frequently used items where they can be easily reached.

Dust and Dirt

Dust and dirt can be removed by sweeping, dusting, vacuuming, washing, and mopping. Sweeping with a broom removes dirt from hard floors. You can also use brooms for seasonal jobs, such as cleaning window screens and dusting cobwebs from walls and ceilings.

Vacuum or wipe windowsills and baseboards. Then dust all furnishings except upholstered pieces. Do not forget areas such as chair legs and lampshades. Wood furniture needs occasional polishing to keep it in good condition. Make sure that the cleaning products you use on wood furniture are compatible with the furniture you have.

A vacuum cleaner can remove dust and dirt from carpeting, hard floors, upholstered furniture, and draperies. Its suction draws soil particles into the machine, where it is trapped inside a bag or container. For proper operation, change vacuum bags, filters, and containers frequently.

Washable hard floors need regular washing to remove stubborn dirt. Use a mop, water, and a cleaner that is safe for the type of floors you have. Be sure to purchase replacement mop heads if you own a mop that requires replacements.

Cleaning is usually most efficient if certain tasks are performed in a particular order. For example, as you dust, work from the top to the bottom to keep dust from ending up on already dusted areas. Some people prefer cleaning the outside edges of a room first. Then they clean the center and finish with the floor. This sequence helps make sure no areas are skipped.

SUCCEED IN SCHOOL

Study Location

When studying, do not sit or lie on your bed. Because a bed is extremely comfortable, it will be difficult for you to stay alert and focus on your studies. Choose a good table and chair instead.

Science You Can Use

Water Safety

Polluted water is a problem. Human activity can pollute bodies of water with sewage, fertilizers, pesticides, and herbicides. The chemicals we use to clean our houses may end up in our water supply. Can dissolved chemicals be filtered out of the water they have mixed with?

Procedure Test 50 mL of water with litmus paper. Then add 50 mL of vinegar to the water. Test the mixture with litmus. Pour the water and vinegar solution through filter paper, and retest the solution with litmus paper.

Analysis Study the litmus paper and the filter you used for any residue. Did the filter remove the acid from the water?

Garbage

An overflowing garbage can and dirty dishes in the sink can make an otherwise clean house look dirty. Because standing garbage may contain millions of germs, it is also a safety hazard. Garbage also gives off a bad odor. Make sure to secure garbage can covers. To keep garbage under control, dispose of garbage often.

Pests

Roaches, ants, flies, and mice are household pests that carry germs that can cause illness. With regular home maintenance, you can usually keep pests under control. If you use pest control products, read and follow directions carefully. Always store the products out of the reach of children, and wear rubber gloves when using them. If a pest problem becomes severe, call a professional to get rid of the pests.

✓ **Reading Check** **Identify** What sorts of tasks should be done on a daily or weekly basis, and which tasks only need to be taken care of occasionally?

HOW TO . . . Clean as you go

By following the motto "clean as you go," you can avoid being overwhelmed by dust, dirty dishes, and piles of clothes. Taking a few minutes or less for small cleanups makes the tasks less burdensome. That not only saves your personal energy supply but also reduces the need for harsh cleaners that can be toxic.

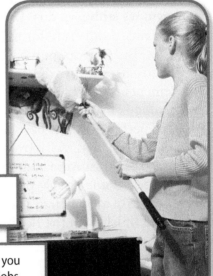

Prevent Residue Build-Up Wipe down sinks, the bathtub, and the shower after using them. Keep spray cleaner on the side of the tub for ease in cleanup.

Keep Clothes Off the Floor Put clothes away in a clothes hamper, closet, or drawer, immediately after wearing them. That way you will not have to guess if an item is clean or dirty.

Organize Clutter Straighten magazines, CDs, and DVDs while passing through a room.

Clean as You Go Pick up crumbs or small bits of dirt as you notice them. Keep a dust pan and brush handy for small jobs.

Keeping Your Home Safe

Proper home maintenance can prevent illness and reduce allergy symptoms, but alone, it can not guarantee your family's safety. To keep your home safe, you also need to survey, or examine, your house for potential hazards. A **hazard**, is a source of danger. Avoid falls, electric shocks, fires, and poisoning by eliminating hazards.

Falls

Falls are one of the most common accidents to occur in homes. Fortunately, most falls are preventable. You can avoid falls by putting a nonskid backing on throw rugs and keeping traffic patterns, stairs, and doorways free of clutter and furniture. Use a sturdy ladder or stepstool to reach high items. If the item is used often, think about not keeping it in a hard-to-reach place so that you use ladders and stepstools less often. When climbing stairs, always use the handrail and keep the stairs illuminated.

Separate Mail Have a box or container specifically for daily mail.

Recycle Junk Mail Recycle or throw out unwanted mail as soon as it comes in. Shred unwanted mail and fliers. It makes great packing material for outgoing packages.

Never Leave Litter Pick up litter in your yard on your way to school, and place it in the trash. Never throw trash out of a car window.

Recycle or Reuse Unless you plan to reuse them, dispose of containers as soon as they are empty, either in a recycling bin or trash can.

Electrical Hazards

Electricity can be dangerous or even fatal. To avoid electrical hazards, keep electrical appliances away from water. Never touch them with wet hands or use them while standing on a wet floor. Do not overload an outlet with too many cords, and never run cords under rugs or carpeting. Keep all appliances and cords in good repair, and cover outlets that small children can reach.

Fires

Most fires in the home are caused by matches, candles, cigarettes, grease, incense, and electrical appliances. Garbage cans, kitchen ranges, mattresses, and upholstered furniture are common places for fires to start.

Every home should have fire extinguishers and an exit plan. All two-story homes should have a rope ladder for escape. Make sure family members know where the rope ladder is kept and how to use it properly. Keep a chemical extinguisher near, but not above, the kitchen range for grease and electrical fires. Be sure you know how to use it. Keep matches out of children's reach, and always monitor candles after you light them. Store flammable products away from all heat sources. If you smell gas in your home, leave the home immediately, and call the gas company from a cell phone or a neighbor's home.

Smoke detectors can provide early warning in case of fire and smoke. Make sure your home has smoke detectors near bedroom areas and on each floor. Check all detectors once a month to see that they function properly, and replace batteries twice a year.

Schedule fire drills so that everyone in the family knows the emergency plan and the quickest way to exit your home in case of fire or another emergency. Remember that saving your home is not as important as saving your life.

▼ **Prevent Fire Hazards**

Taking time to inspect your home can reveal electrical hazards. *What hazards do you see in the photo on the right?*

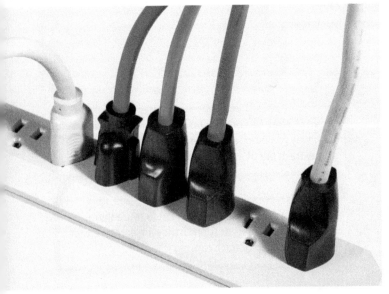

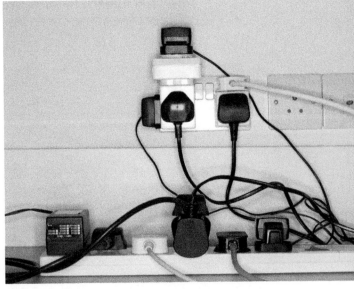

Poisons

Poisons can be found in nearly every room of your home. Prescription drugs, pest control products, and some cleaning products are just a few poisonous items you may have in your home. Make sure that poisonous products are stored out of children's reach, preferably in a locked cabinet. Never store poisons in another container, such as a soda bottle, because they can be mistaken for something else. Also, never encourage children to take medicine by telling them medicine is candy. They may go back for more.

Carbon monoxide, an odorless and poisonous gas, is produced by defective gas appliances. If you have gas appliances, install a carbon monoxide detector that alerts you to the presence of carbon monoxide.

✓ **Reading Check** **Identify** Give four examples of common household hazards.

Take Emergency Action

Taking basic precautions like those shown in **Figure 30.1** on page 738 can help keep you and your home safe and secure. However, not every emergency is predictable or preventable. Despite even the best efforts to create a safe environment, emergencies happen. Because there is usually little to no warning before an emergency occurs, you and your family should be prepared for a variety of emergency situations.

Call for Help

Post the following emergency phone numbers near the telephone so that everyone can see them:
- Police, fire, and ambulance (911 or dial 0).
- A poison control center.
- A doctor or clinic.
- Parents' or guardians' work numbers.
- Nearest relative.
- Friend or neighbor.

If you must make an emergency telephone call, you need to stay calm, above all else. Wait for the dial tone, then dial 911 or 0 for an operator. Speak clearly and state the emergency. Give the dispatcher your name, address, and phone number. If you are not at home, describe your exact location. Do not hang up the phone until someone tells you to do so. It may be important to stay on the line to receive additional instructions. Follow all directions the dispatcher gives you. You may want to repeat the instructions to be sure that you understand them.

Figure 30.1 **Safety at Home**

Basic Home Safety Precautions You and your family want to feel safe at home. Some neighborhoods are safer than others, but even in the safest areas, law enforcement authorities suggest that you and your family follow some basic safety precautions. *Which of these safety precautions do you follow?*

Keep Contact Information Private Never give your phone number or address to anyone you do not know, and do not share information about your family or their schedules. Never give out personal information over the Internet or the phone.

Do Not Allow Strangers In If a stranger asks to come inside your home, have an adult come to the door. If you are alone, do not open the door. Tell the person to come back at another time. Always check the identification of repair workers and community employees.

Secure Sliding Glass Doors Prevent sliding glass doors from being opened from the outside by placing a piece of thick wood, such as a dowel, in the door track. You can purchase rods that are made just for that purpose.

Keep Doors and Windows Locked Deadbolt locks are the most secure locks for doors. When you turn the key from inside or outside the door, a strong metal bar slides into the door frame. Use ventilation locks on windows. These locks, which you can find at hardware stores, are inexpensive metal stops you can adjust to any level for air to enter.

Be Prepared Have your house key ready when you enter or leave your home. If you witness suspicious activity near your home, do not go into the house. Go to a neighbor's home, and contact the police. Be prepared to explain why you are concerned. Accurate descriptions of people, cars, and license plates are helpful.

Keep Alert Form a neighborhood volunteer patrol system. Many neighbors make it a point to look out for one another and report any suspicious activity.

Light Entryways Make sure that the areas around outside doors are well lit. This is especially important in an area with large bushes in which someone could hide.

Enter Your Home Safely If someone drops you off at home, ask the driver to wait until you are safely inside. Flash a light when you are inside to show you entered safely.

(tl) Ingram Publishing/SuperStock; (cl) ©Adam Gault/age footstock; (cr) Bloomimage/CORBIS; (bl) Purestock/SuperStock

Give First Aid

Every emergency situation is different, and it is critical to know when and how to act. Become familiar with the basic principles of first aid. The American Red Cross and other organizations offer classes and information on first aid. You should know the basics in these areas:

Choking Timing and action are important in the case of choking. Food lodged in the throat or airway can cause a person to choke. When you see someone choking, use abdominal thrusts. Alternate between back blows and chest thrusts for a choking baby. See **Figure 30.2**.

CPR Giving first aid to an injured or ill person may include performing cardiopulmonary resuscitation (CPR). This technique is used to keep a person's heart and lungs functioning until medical care arrives. The rescuer breathes into the person's mouth and applies pressure to the chest to force the heart to pump. You should be trained in CPR before performing it. The American Heart Association and the American Red Cross have information about this technique and about classes you can take to learn it.

Burns Burns can result from exposure to heat, electricity, and certain chemicals such as bleach. Burns caused by heat are the most common type.

Figure 30.2 Treatment for Choking

Knowing How to Respond Abdominal thrusts can be performed on a person who is standing or sitting. *How can you assist a choking infant?*

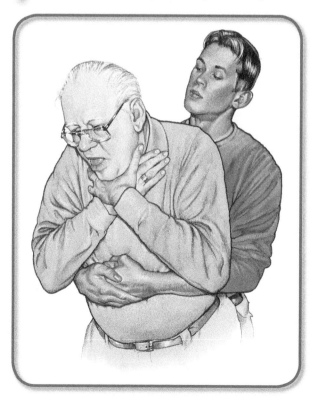

STEP 1 If the person can speak, cough, or breathe, do not interfere. Often, the person will be able to cough out the food or blockage.

STEP 2 If the person cannot speak, cough, or breathe, ask someone to call for help or call 911 immediately for medical assistance.

STEP 3 Stand behind the person, and wrap your arms around his or her waist. Make a fist with one hand and wrap your other hand around the fist. Make a sharp inward and upward thrust just above the person's waist. Repeat six to ten times until the blockage is dislodged.

- **First-degree burns** are considered minor burns. The skin becomes red and may become slightly swollen and painful.
- **Second-degree burns** involve several layers of skin. The skin becomes deep red and blisters. There is severe pain and swelling. A second-degree burn no larger than three inches in diameter can be treated as a minor burn.
- **Third-degree burns** are the most serious. These damage all skin layers and may also damage the tissues underneath. The skin may appear black, or white and dry. You may see muscle fibers. These burns destroy nerve endings, so victims may not be in pain.

To treat first-degree burns and small second-degree burns:

1. Hold the burned area under cold running water or wrap it in cold, wet cloths for at least five minutes. Do not use ice.
2. Cover the burn loosely with a sterile gauze bandage.
3. Minor burns usually heal without further treatment. If signs of infection occur, such as increased pain, fever, swelling, or oozing, seek medical help.

All third-degree burns and large second-degree burns require immediate medical care. Do not remove burned clothing unless it is still smoldering. Call 911, and cover the burned area with a clean, moist cloth until help arrives.

Section 30.1

After You Read

Review Key Concepts

1. **Explain** the proper use and storage of household cleaning supplies.
2. **Describe** the precautions you must take when handling electrical cords and appliances.
3. **Identify** the things you need to remember when calling for help.

Check Your Answers Go to connectED.mcgraw-hill.com to check your answers.

Practice Academic Skills

English Language Arts

4. Procedures allow people to perform tasks in a consistent manner. Checklists can be used to organize a procedure into steps. Imagine you will be leaving your home for two weeks on vacation. Before you leave, you want to make sure you leave the house clean and safe. Write a procedure to prepare the house for your absence.

Social Studies

5. All the waste you produce every day has to go somewhere. Use print and online resources to find out how most solid waste is processed and stored. What is done with land when it is no longer used to store waste? Which methods of waste storage and land use do you feel best reflect the values and ideals of people today?

The Earth—Your Home

Before You Read

Pace Yourself Short blocks of concentrated reading repeated frequently are more effective than one long session. Focus on reading for 10 minutes. Take a short break. Then read for another 10 minutes.

Read to Learn

Key Concepts

- **Contrast** renewable and nonrenewable resources.
- **List** five ways you can conserve the Earth's resources.
- **Give** guidelines for making wise consumer decisions.

Main Idea

The earth has many renewable and nonrenewable natural resources that can be preserved or prolonged with careful management and conservation.

Content Vocabulary

◇ global environment
◇ natural resource
◇ renewable resource
◇ nonrenewable resource
◇ conservation
◇ global warming

Academic Vocabulary

You will find these words in your reading and on your tests. Use the glossary to look up their definitions if necessary.

▢ indefinitely
▢ erosion

Graphic Organizer

Use a graphic organizer like the one below to remember ways to make Earth-friendly choices as a consumer.

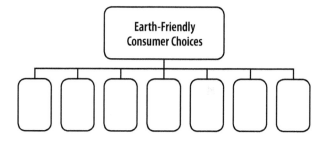

 Graphic Organizer Go to **connectED.mcgraw-hill.com** to download this graphic organizer.

Pollution in a small part of the world can soon become a global problem. This is because air and water currents can carry pollution for thousands and thousands of miles. Remember, what you do to help the environment locally, helps your city, your state, your country, and other countries around the world.

The Earth's Natural Resources

One major issue that the Earth faces is pollution. Pollution is the presence of harmful substances on land, in water, and in the air. This problem affects our global environment. The **global environment** consists of all living and nonliving elements on Earth. Fortunately, there is some good news. Many people are becoming aware of environmental problems and are making positive changes. Are you among those making a difference?

Air, water, and trees are some of the Earth's natural resources. A **natural resource** is a resource that occurs in nature. Think about what life would be like without forests, rivers, lakes, and blue skies. The air you breathe and the water you drink help keep you alive and healthy. Other natural resources include coal and natural gas. These fuels are used to provide heat, light, and energy to run machines. Natural resources are broken into two categories:

- **Renewable Resources** A **renewable resource** replaces or renews itself over time. Plants renew themselves by producing seeds, which in turn produce new plants. Air, water, and soil are also renewed through natural cycles, unless something interferes with them.

- **Nonrenewable Resources** A **nonrenewable resource** does not replace itself, and its supply is limited. For example, once current world supplies of oil, copper, iron, and other minerals are used up, no more will be available. Supplies of nonrenewable resources could last indefinitely, or without end, but only if people use them wisely.

✓ **Reading Check**) **Explain** How do some natural resources renew themselves?

Making a Difference

Many teens are taking responsible action against pollution. *What can you do to help fight pollution?*

Fancy Collection/SuperStock

Conserving Earth's Resources

Everyone has the responsibility to help manage the Earth's natural resources. You can do your part by practicing **conservation**, which is the protection of resources against waste and harm.

Water

What if you turned on the faucet one morning and no water came out of the tap? Severe water shortages exist in many parts of the world. In other areas, water supplies are polluted and unusable. No matter where you live, clean, fresh water is a precious resource that should not be wasted. Here are some simple ways you and your family can conserve water:

- **Avoid wasting water.** Take quick showers instead of long baths. Turn faucets completely off while brushing your teeth or washing dishes. Wait until you have a full load before running the dishwasher or washing machine. Also, do not overwater your lawn or garden. Talk to your parents about buying low-flow showerheads, low-flow toilets, and aerators for your faucets. These devices use less water while supplying the same water pressure.
- **Make a compost pile.** Instead of putting fruit and vegetable scraps in the garbage disposal, which requires water, put them in a compost pile. In time, this waste will become fertile organic matter that can be used to grow plants. You might even see interesting new plants come out of your compost pile.
- **Make needed repairs.** Leaky faucets can waste gallons of water each day. Repair plumbing leaks promptly.
- **Keep water supplies clean.** Improperly disposing of household chemicals, such as detergents and pesticides, can pollute local streams, rivers, and lakes. Always follow package instructions when disposing of household chemicals.

Trees

Trees are one of our greatest natural resources. In addition to making the world a more beautiful place, trees provide foods we eat and the wood we use for building materials, furniture, decorations, and pencils. They provide paper products for printing, packaging, and sanitation. Trees prevent the erosion, or wearing away, of soil. They support thousands of different animal and insect species, which would otherwise not be able to live.

Trees also absorb carbon dioxide and produce fresh oxygen, cleaning our air and reducing the amount of greenhouse gasses that contribute to global warming. **Global warming** is the gradual increase in the Earth's surface temperature. Research has shown that human activity and industry is partly to blame for recent increases in temperature.

SUCCEED IN SCHOOL

Presentation Preparation

Before you give a presentation, it is important to prepare what you will say. Write down the main points of your speech in the order you want to present them. Also, write an introduction and conclusion to your speech.

The average American consumes the equivalent of seven trees each year through the use of paper, wood, and other products made from trees. Though trees are a renewable resource, it takes 50 to 70 years for a tree to reach maturity after it is planted. For this reason, it is important to take measures to conserve this valuable resource. Here are some things you and your family can do to help:

- **Use paperless bills.** Some bills can be more than ten pages long. After a while this paper really adds up. Ask your parents if they can receive their bills online when given a choice. It saves time, money, and trees.
- **Choose recycled paper products.** Nowadays, there are many paper products that are partially or completely made from recycled materials. Look for the recycling symbol on the paper products that you buy.
- **Do not print unless necessary.** How many times have you gone to print directions or a Web site page, only to print out 20 pages of information you did not even need? Before you print, make sure you are only printing the information you want.

▲ Smart Gardening

Natural compost provides much needed nutrients to gardens while saving consumers money. *How does composting save water?*

Gas and Oil

Most vehicles are powered by either gasoline or diesel fuel. These fuels are made from crude oil, or petroleum, which is a nonrenewable resource.

There are many ways you can conserve gas and oil:

- **Drive a hybrid vehicle.** Some of today's vehicles, known as hybrid vehicles, are powered by a combination of gasoline and electric power.
- **Bike or walk.** Use transportation that does not require fuel, such as biking and walking.
- **Carpool.** Family members and friends can form carpools to share rides.
- **Combine errands into one trip.** Combining errands into one trip also conserves fuel. Try to plan the most efficient route possible instead of driving back and forth past some of your destinations. When in line at a bank or fast-food restaurant, avoid wasting fuel by idling the car. Instead, go inside.
- **Maintain your vehicle.** Vehicle maintenance also affects a vehicle's energy efficiency. Change the family vehicle's oil at recommended intervals (every 3,000 miles), check tire pressure monthly, have tires rotated regularly, and schedule tune-ups to keep the vehicle running properly.

©Jetta Productions/Blend Images LLC

Heating and Cooling Energy

It takes natural resources to heat and cool a home. Some heating requires nonrenewable fuels, such as oil. Other kinds of heating and air conditioning depend on electricity, which is often produced by burning a nonrenewable fuel. For fuel supplies to last, it is important to use less electricity. Home improvements, such as installing weather stripping around doors and windows, plastic film over windows, and insulation in the attic, can help conserve fuel. Here are some other ideas to help you and your family conserve heating and cooling resources:

- **Heating Resources** These can be conserved by setting the heater no higher than 68°F (20°C) during the day and turning the thermostat down at bedtime. Close shades and draperies at night in cold weather to keep in the heat and keep out the cold. On sunny days, open shades and draperies to let the sun's energy heat your home. Also, layer clothing by wearing sweaters and turtleneck shirts under clothes and wear additional heavy socks in cooler months.

- **Cooling Resources** These can be conserved by setting the air conditioner thermostat no lower than 78°F (26°C) during summer months. Be sure to clean or replace the air conditioning filter when it is dirty. Choose fans over air conditioners whenever possible. Fans use less electricity. Install solar screens to keep the sun's heat from entering through windows, and close draperies during the day to keep heat out. Also, dress in lightweight clothing to keep cool in warm weather.

Energy for Lighting and Appliances

Lighting and appliances use electricity, which is generated through the use of oil and other nonrenewable fuels. The following tips can help you and your family stretch electric resources:

- **Lighting** Replace light bulbs with compact fluorescent lights, which use less electricity. Use only the number of lights you need in a room. For example, if you can get a job done with one lamp, turn off all others. Also, always turn off lights when you leave a room.

- **Appliances** Keep oven doors closed when cooking, and avoid opening the refrigerator door unnecessarily. Try air drying dishes and clothes. If using a clothes dryer, remove clothes as soon as they are dry, and clean the dryer's lint filter after each use. Also, use an appliance that requires the smallest amount of energy for the specific task. For example, hand chop a small onion instead of using a food processor. Save appliances for bigger jobs.

✓ Reading Check **Examine** Give examples of ways you can conserve water.

Health & Wellness TIPS

Mood and Natural Light
Studies show that natural light stimulates the brain to produce serotonin, a brain chemical involved in mood. To battle depression and stress, many doctors recommend at least half an hour of natural light every day. Use these tips to get more natural light:

▶ Open your curtains. Allow natural light into your room, or study in a sunny place in the library.

▶ Exercise outside. Even a brief walk out in natural light is a double-mood booster. This is because exercise also boosts serotonin.

Figure 30.3 **PRECYCLE, RECYCLE, REUSE**

Take Action Against Pollution Not only is trash unpleasant to look at, it can also be harmful to people, animals, and the planet. The good news is you can take action against trash by precycling, reusing, and recycling. *In what ways can you precycle, recycle and reuse?*

PRECYCLE
When you precycle, you reduce the amount of trash you produce. There are many ways to become a precycler:
Buy in bulk. Buy bulk snacks, and store them in reusable containers. Avoid disposable items. Razors, cameras, and cups are a few disposable goods that increase the load on landfills.
Use environmentally friendly cleaning products.
Manual pump spray products are better for the environment then aerosols, and the bottles can be refilled and reused.
Buy fewer fast foods. Each part of a fast-food meal is individually wrapped. Skip the fast-food lines, and bring your meal in a reusable lunch bag.
Choose products with little or no packaging. You can also buy products that come in recyclable packaging.
Bring your own shopping bag. Either use a cloth bag or reuse a sturdy paper or plastic bag from the store. If you are buying just one item, skip the bag.

REUSE
Many things you throw away can be reused. If you use your imagination, you will find there are ways to use almost everything at least twice. Here are some ideas to get you started:
Plastic containers. Use these items to organize your belongings. They can also be donated to a child or adult care facility where they can be used for art projects.
Old, ripped towels and sheets. Cut these items into small pieces for housecleaning chores, such as cleaning and dusting. Unlike paper towels, they can be washed and used over and over.
Books and magazines. School and local libraries, community centers, and homeless shelters will often gladly accept these donated items.
Old clothing and toys. You can donate these to charity or sell them in a yard sale or on the Internet.
Wrapping paper, plastic bags, and boxes. All of these items can be reused if they are in good condition.

RECYCLE

Recycling is the treatment of trash so that it can be reused rather than buried in landfills. Many communities have recycling programs. Check for your local recycling facilities. You and your family can recycle the following items:

- Paper and cardboard
- Glass bottles and jars
- Aluminum cans and containers
- Certain plastics
- Motor oil and tires
- Batteries

TAKE ACTION

Incorporate wise environmental practices. Many companies, as well as various state and local agencies, have chosen to incorporate wise environmental practices in the workplace. Employees are encouraged to precycle, recycle, and reuse items. Interview family members or friends about the recycling practices they follow in the workplace. Summarize your interviews in a short report.

ENJOY

Get outdoors. Make a point to get outside at least once a week to enjoy the fruits of your labor. Go hiking, spend time at the beach, or play a quick game of catch in the park. The more you appreciate the environment, the better care you will take to protect it.

Earth-Friendly Choices

Although government regulations restrict pollution, you, the consumer, also play an important role. Think before you buy. You can help conserve natural resources and reduce pollution by taking the following steps:

- **Recycle as many products as possible.** Plastic containers with specified numbers and bottles and cans are reused or recycled in many communities. Some stores give customers incentives to recycle printer cartridges and film containers.
- **Buy products that feature the recycling symbol.** This symbol is on packages that can be recycled and packages made from recycled materials.
- **Choose items that are long-lasting.** Examples include rechargeable batteries and long-lasting lightbulbs.
- **Select items with little or no packaging.** It takes resources to make wrappers and boxes that are quickly discarded. If you buy something with packaging material, see if you can reuse or recycle it.
- **Reuse plastic, sturdy paper, and cloth shopping bags.** Keep them handy so that you will remember to use them each time.
- **Buy energy-efficient appliances.** EnergyGuide and EnergyStar labels will help you choose appliances that make good use of fuels.

See **Figure 30.3** on pages 746 and 747 for other tips.

Section 30.2

After You Read

Review Key Concepts

1. **Explain** the difference between a renewable and nonrenewable resource.
2. **Identify** eight ways trees benefit people and the environment.
3. **List** four ways you can do your part to help lower pollution.

Practice Academic Skills

English Language Arts

4. Write a letter to the editor of your school newspaper about the local recycling program. Are there ways you can improve it? How can you expand the program?

Social Studies

5. Use the library and Internet to research international environmental initiatives. Focus on a country that interests you, and discuss the policies of that country concerning the environment and pollution. These may include lowering pollution levels, fostering wildlife populations, or protecting land from overuse.

Check Your Answers Go to connectED. mcgraw-hill.com to check your answers.

CHAPTER SUMMARY

Section 30.1
Establishing a Safe and Clean Home Environment

Establishing and maintaining a clean home environment is essential to the health of those who live there. This includes regular cleaning and clearing away of clutter. Keeping up with cleaning on a regular basis prevents small tasks from turning into big chores. Keeping a home healthy and safe also includes safeguarding it against hazards and preparing for emergencies.

Section 30.2
The Earth—Your Home

Natural resources are either renewable or nonrenewable. Unless something interferes with natural cycles, renewable resources, such as trees, replace themselves over time. Nonrenewable resources do not replace themselves. You can protect natural resources by doing your part to conserve water, paper products, fuel, and electricity. Tomorrow's trash often comes from what you buy today, so make wise consumer decisions. Precycle, reuse, and recycle whenever possible.

Vocabulary Review

1. Use each of these content and academic vocabulary terms to create a word-search puzzle on graph paper. Provide an example of each word or its definition for clues.

Content Vocabulary
◇ home maintenance (p. 731)
◇ hazard (p. 735)
◇ global environment (p. 742)
◇ natural resource (p. 742)
◇ renewable resource (p. 742)
◇ nonrenewable resource (p. 742)
◇ conservation (p. 743)
◇ global warming (p. 743)

Academic Vocabulary
▪ entail (p. 731)
▪ survey (p. 735)
▪ indefinitely (p. 742)
▪ erosion (p. 743)

Review Key Concepts

2. **Create** a home maintenance plan.
3. **Identify** home safety procedures.
4. **List** the things you need to know when you make an emergency call.
5. **Contrast** renewable and nonrenewable resources.
6. **List** five ways you can conserve the Earth's resources.
7. **Give** guidelines for making wise consumer decisions.

Critical Thinking

8. **Analyze** Consider various methods of pest control. Explain the advantages and disadvantages of each.
9. **Create** Generate a plan of action to prepare for emergencies.
10. **Hypothesize** What would happen if people used the last bit of Earth's oil this month? Would we be prepared? Why or why not?
11. **Design** Outline a detailed plan to make your school's campus as paperless as possible.

ACTIVE LEARNING

12. Market Research Fire safety is an important consideration in the home and in the workplace. Use product brochures and Internet sources to research the various types of fire extinguishers. Compare information about them, and prepare a two-minute presentation about consumer ratings and features that you have found. Are there different types of fire extinguishers or ones with different uses? What would be the best fit for your needs? Consider cost and where the fire extinguisher will be used. Rehearse your presentation before giving it to the class.

Family & Community Connections

13. Neighborhood Watch Neighborhood Watch programs are made up of members of a neighborhood who look out for people causing trouble. People involved in Neighborhood Watch programs have helped the police solve crimes they witnessed. They can also stop a crime from happening by keeping officials aware of issues in the neighborhood. Investigate starting a Neighborhood Watch program in your community. Report on the steps that must be taken to put this program in place. Invite a police officer or a Neighborhood Watch organizer to your classroom to offer information about Neighborhood Watch programs and answer questions that you might have. Consider how using social media sites can be beneficial for Neighborhood Watch groups.

Real-World Skills and Applications

Leadership Skills

14. Fire Safety Plan If you have a plan in place, you will be ready to act during an emergency. Develop a fire safety plan for your home. Take into account routes each family member should take to exit your home. Show the plan to a parent or guardian for approval. Once the plan is approved, encourage your family members to hold regular fire drills.

Financial Literacy

15. Find Costs Babies and small children need to live in a safe environment. They often pick things up and put them in their mouths. This can present several safety concerns. They may swallow something poisonous or choke on a small toy. It is important to keep a house safe for younger children. This means securing cupboards, blocking off stairways, and keeping small items that they may choke on out of reach. Write a report about the products available to make your house safer. Present your findings to your class, including the costs of the various safety products.

Information Literacy

16. Create a Presentation Natural resources are found in nature and help us create products such as paper, computer parts, gasoline, and clothing. Use presentation software to prepare a presentation on conservation and natural resources. Use information found in the library or on the Internet about geology, ecology, and the Earth's resources. Look for information from reliable sources, such as the Environmental Protection Agency (EPA).

Academic Skills

English Language Arts

17. Stewards of the Earth There are many ways to do your part to keep the environment as clean as possible. Write a paragraph describing how your behaviors affect the local ecosystem and the global environment. What daily behaviors can you change to reduce the waste and pollution you produce? What behaviors can you develop to reduce the waste and pollution of others?

Science

18. Chlorine in Your Water Chlorine is used in the supply of drinking water to help keep it free of harmful bacteria. Can you detect chlorine in your drinking water?

Procedure In three separate test tubes, obtain 2 mL of chloride standard solution, distilled water, and drinking water. Carefully add five drops of silver nitrate solution to each and stir. Avoid contact with the silver nitrate solution.

Analysis Observe the reaction the silver nitrate has in each test tube. Record which solution shows the most in common with the reaction to chloride. Which result most resembles your drinking water?

Mathematics

19. Working to Scale After years of saving, Desiree's parents are finally able to build their dream house. If they design a model that has a scale of 5 in: 8ft, and their model is 25 inches wide, how wide do they plan their dream house to be? If they want their house to be 600 square feet, how many feet long will it be?

Math Concept **Multiplying Ratios** Ratios can be written as fractions and can be cross-multiplied just like fractions.

Starting Hint First, find the full-scale width of the house. Write the ratios as fractions (5 in: 8ft becomes $\frac{5}{8}$), and cross-multiply to find the width in feet. Make sure that like measurements align. (In this case, both measurements in inches should be numerators.)

 For math help, go to the Math Appendix at the back of the book.

Standardized Test Practice

MULTIPLE CHOICE
Directions Read the directive and then choose the correct answer from the list.

Test-Taking Tip In a multiple-choice test, the answers should be specific and precise. Read the question first. Then, read all the answer choices. Eliminate answers you know are not correct.

20. Select the item that is not a true statement.
   a) Hybrid vehicles are energy efficient and do not need to be re-fueled often.
   b) Plastic cannot always be recycled.
   c) Some stores offer incentives, such as free grocery trips, to customers who return their plastic bags.
   d) We do not need to conserve renewable resources because they are replaced by nature.

Design Your Ideal Room

In this project you will research the decorating styles that appeal to you, interview an adult in your community who works in an aspect of interior design, and design an ideal room for yourself using environmentally responsible materials.

My Journal

If you completed the journal entry from page 700, refer to it to see if your thoughts have changed after reading the unit.

Project Assignment

In this project you will:

- Research interior design concepts that appeal to you.
- Identify and interview an adult in your community who works in an aspect of interior design.
- Create a design for your ideal room and share it with your class.

The Skills Behind the Project

Life Skills

Key personal and relationship skills you will use in this project include:
- Making responsible choices.
- Gaining perspective.
- Communicating respectfully.

STEP 1 Research Design Styles

Use the material in this textbook and independent research to find design styles that appeal to you. You may cut out pictures from magazines or print web pages with appealing designs so that you may reference them later. Write a summary of your research to:
- Describe the type of design that appeals to you.
- Identify different elements in the design that appeal to you.

Writing Skills
- Write in complete sentences.
- Use examples that illustrate your points.
- Write concisely (briefly but completely).

STEP 2 Plan Your Interview

Use the results of your research to write a list of interview questions that you will ask an adult in your community about interior design. Your questions might include:
- What type of design appeals to you?
- How do you communicate with your clients?
- What are the current trends in interior design?

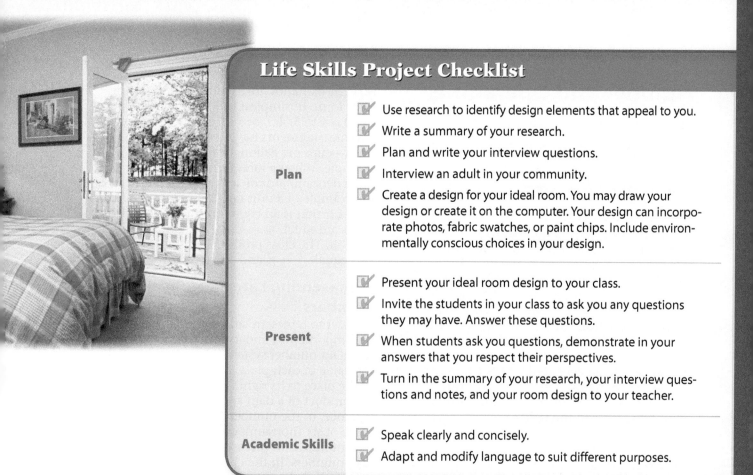

Life Skills Project Checklist

Plan	☑ Use research to identify design elements that appeal to you. ☑ Write a summary of your research. ☑ Plan and write your interview questions. ☑ Interview an adult in your community. ☑ Create a design for your ideal room. You may draw your design or create it on the computer. Your design can incorporate photos, fabric swatches, or paint chips. Include environmentally conscious choices in your design.
Present	☑ Present your ideal room design to your class. ☑ Invite the students in your class to ask you any questions they may have. Answer these questions. ☑ When students ask you questions, demonstrate in your answers that you respect their perspectives. ☑ Turn in the summary of your research, your interview questions and notes, and your room design to your teacher.
Academic Skills	☑ Speak clearly and concisely. ☑ Adapt and modify language to suit different purposes.

- What do you do if you think a client is making poor design choices?
- How has your design taste changed over the years?
- Do you incorporate "green" aspects into your designs? Do you think this is important to do?

STEP 3 Connect to Your Community

Identify an adult in your community who works in an aspect of interior design. This person can be a designer, a contractor, an employee at a home goods store, or anyone else who works in the industry. Arrange to interview the person using the questions you wrote in Step 2. Take notes during the interview and write a summary of the interview.

Interviewing Skills

- Record interview responses and take notes.
- Listen attentively.
- Write in complete sentences and use correct spelling and grammar when you transcribe your notes.

STEP 4 Create a Presentation and Share What You Learned

Use the Life Skills Project Checklist to plan and create your room design and share what you have learned with your classmates.

STEP 5 Evaluate Your Life Skills and Academic Skills

Your project will be evaluated based on:
- Clarity and cohesiveness of your design.
- Incorporation of "green" elements in your design.
- Mechanics – presentation and neatness.
- Speaking and listening skills.

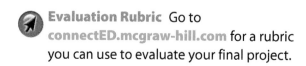

Evaluation Rubric Go to connectED.mcgraw-hill.com for a rubric you can use to evaluate your final project.

Number and Operations

▶ *Understand numbers, ways of representing numbers, relationships among numbers, and number systems*

Fraction, Decimal, and Percent

A percent is a ratio of a number to 100. To write a percent as a fraction, drop the percent sign, and use the number as the numerator in a fraction with a denominator of 100. Simplify, if possible. For example, $76\% = \frac{76}{100}$, or $\frac{19}{25}$. To write a fraction as a percent, convert it to an equivalent fraction with a denominator of 100. For example, $\frac{3}{4} = \frac{75}{100}$, or 75%. A fraction can be expressed as a percent by first converting the fraction to a decimal (divide the numerator by the denominator) and then converting the decimal to a percent by moving the decimal point two places to the right.

Comparing Numbers on a Number Line

In order to compare and understand the relationship between real numbers in various forms, it is helpful to use a number line. The zero point on a number line is called the origin. The points to the left of the origin are negative, and those to the right are positive. The number line below shows how numbers in fraction, decimal, percent, and integer form can be compared.

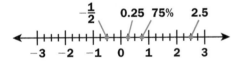

Percents Greater Than 100 and Less Than 1

Percents greater than 100% represent values greater than 1. For example, if the weight of an object is 250% of another, it is 2.5, or $2\frac{1}{2}$, times the weight.

Percents less than 1 represent values less than $\frac{1}{100}$. In other words, 0.1% is one tenth of one percent, which can also be represented in decimal form as 0.001, or in fraction form as $\frac{1}{1,000}$. Similarly, 0.01% is one hundredth of one percent or 0.0001 or $\frac{1}{10,000}$.

Ratio, Rate, and Proportion

A ratio is a comparison of two numbers using division. If a basketball player makes 8 out of 10 free throws, the ratio is written as 8 to 10,

8:10, or $\frac{8}{10}$. Ratios are usually written in simplest form. In simplest form, the ratio 8 out of 10 is 4 to 5, 4:5, or $\frac{4}{5}$. A rate is a ratio of two measurements having different kinds of units—cups per gallon, or miles per hour, for example. When a rate is simplified so that it has a denominator of 1, it is called a unit rate. An example of a unit rate is 9 miles per hour. A proportion is an equation stating that two ratios are equal. $\frac{3}{18} = \frac{13}{78}$ is an example of a proportion. The cross products of a proportion are also equal. $\frac{3}{18} = \frac{13}{78}$ and $3 \times 78 = 18 \times 13$.

Representing Large and Small Numbers

In order to represent large and small numbers, it is important to understand the number system. Our number system is based on 10, and the value of each place is 10 times the value of the place to its right. The value of a digit is the product of a digit and its place value. For instance, in the number 6,400, the 6 has a value of six thousands and the 4 has a value of four hundreds. A place value chart can help you read numbers. In the chart, each group of three digits is called a period. Commas separate the periods: the ones period, the thousands period, the millions period, and so on. Values to the right of the ones period are decimals. By understanding place value you can write very large numbers like 5 billion and more, and very small numbers that are less than 1, like one-tenth.

Scientific Notation

When dealing with very large numbers like 1,500,000, or very small numbers like 0.000015, it is helpful to keep track of their value by writing the numbers in scientific notation. Powers of 10 with positive exponents are used with a decimal between 1 and 10 to express large numbers. The exponent represents the number of places the decimal point is moved to the right. So, 528,000 is written in scientific notation as 5.28×10^5. Powers of 10 with negative exponents are used with a decimal between 1 and 10 to express small numbers. The exponent represents the number of places the decimal point is moved to the left. The number 0.00047 is expressed as 4.7×10^{-4}.

Factor, Multiple, and Prime Factorization

Two or more numbers that are multiplied to form a product are called factors. Divisibility rules can be used to determine whether 2, 3, 4, 5, 6, 8, 9, or 10 are factors of a given number.

Multiples are the products of a given number and various integers.

For example, 8 is a multiple of 4 because $4 \times 2 = 8$. A prime number is a whole number that has exactly two factors: 1 and itself. A composite number is a whole number that has more than two factors. Zero and 1 are neither prime nor composite. A composite number can be expressed as the product of its prime factors. The prime factorization of 40 is $2 \times 2 \times 2 \times 5$, or $2^3 \times 5$. The numbers 2 and 5 are prime numbers.

Integers

A negative number is a number less than zero. Negative numbers like -8, positive numbers like $+6$, and zero are members of the set of integers. Integers can be represented as points on a number line. A set of integers can be written $\{..., -3, -2, -1, 0, 1, 2, 3, ...\}$ where ... means continues indefinitely.

Real, Rational, and Irrational Numbers

The real number system is made up of the sets of rational and irrational numbers. Rational numbers are numbers that can be written in the form $\frac{a}{b}$ where a and b are integers and $b \neq 0$. Examples are 0.45, $\frac{1}{2}$, and $\sqrt{36}$. Irrational numbers are non-repeating, non-terminating decimals. Examples are $\sqrt{71}$, π, and 0.020020002....

Complex and Imaginary Numbers

A complex number is a mathematical expression with a real number element and an imaginary number element. Imaginary numbers are multiples of i, the imaginary square root of -1. Complex numbers are represented by $a + bi$, where a and b are real numbers and i represents the imaginary element. When a quadratic equation does not have a real number solution, the solution can be represented by a complex number. Like real numbers, complex numbers can be added, subtracted, multiplied, and divided.

Vectors and Matrices

A matrix is a set of numbers or elements arranged in rows and columns to form a rectangle. The number of rows is represented by m and the number of columns is represented by n. To describe the number of rows and columns in a matrix, list the number of rows first using the format $m \times n$. Matrix A is a 3×3 matrix because it has 3 rows and 3 columns. To name an element of a matrix, the letter i is used to denote the row and j is used to denote the column, and the element is labeled in the form $a_{i,j}$. In matrix A below, $a_{3,2}$ is 4.

$$\text{Matrix A} = \begin{pmatrix} 1 & 3 & 5 \\ 0 & 6 & 8 \\ 3 & 4 & 5 \end{pmatrix}$$

A vector is a matrix with only one column or row of elements. A transposed column vector, or a column vector turned on its side, is a row vector. In the example below, row vector b' is the transpose of column vector b.

$$b = \begin{pmatrix} 1 \\ 2 \\ 3 \\ 4 \end{pmatrix}$$

$$b' = \begin{pmatrix} 1 & 2 & 3 & 4 \end{pmatrix}$$

▶ Understand meanings of operations and how they relate to one another

Properties of Addition and Multiplication

Properties are statements that are true for any numbers. For example, $3 + 8$ is the same as $8 + 3$ because each expression equals 11. This illustrates the Commutative Property of Addition. Likewise, $3 \times 8 = 8 \times 3$ illustrates the Commutative Property of Multiplication.

When evaluating expressions, it is often helpful to group or associate the numbers. The Associative Property says that the way in which numbers are grouped when added or multiplied does not change the sum or product. The following properties are also true:

- **Additive Identity Property:** When 0 is added to any number, the sum is the number.

- **Multiplicative Identity Property:** When any number is multiplied by 1, the product is the number.

- **Multiplicative Property of Zero:** When any number is multiplied by 0, the product is 0.

Rational Numbers

A number that can be written as a fraction is called a rational number. Terminating and repeating decimals are rational numbers because both can be written as fractions. Decimals that are neither terminating nor repeating are called irrational numbers because they cannot be written as fractions.

Terminating decimals can be converted to fractions by placing the number (without the decimal point) in the numerator. Count the number of places to the right of the decimal point, and in the denominator, place a 1 followed by a number of zeros equal to the number of places that you counted. The fraction can then be reduced to its simplest form.

Writing a Fraction as a Decimal

Any fraction $\frac{a}{b}$, where $b \neq 0$, can be written as a decimal by dividing the numerator by the denominator. So, $\frac{a}{b} = a \div b$. If the division ends, or terminates, when the remainder is zero, the decimal is a terminating decimal. Not all fractions can be written as terminating decimals. Some have a repeating decimal. A bar indicates that the decimal repeats forever. For example, the fraction $\frac{4}{9}$ can be converted to a repeating decimal, $0.\overline{4}$

Adding and Subtracting Like Fractions

Fractions with the same denominator are called like fractions. To add like fractions, add the numerators and write the sum over the denominator. To add mixed numbers with like fractions, add the whole numbers and fractions separately, adding the numerators of the fractions, then simplifying if necessary. The rule for subtracting fractions with like denominators is similar to the rule for adding. The numerators can be subtracted and the difference written over the denominator. Mixed numbers are written as improper fractions before subtracting. These same rules apply to adding or subtracting like algebraic fractions. An algebraic fraction is a fraction that contains one or more variables in the numerator or denominator.

Adding and Subtracting Unlike Fractions

Fractions with different denominators are called unlike fractions. The least common multiple of the denominators is used to rename the fractions with a common denominator. After a common denominator is found, the numerators can then be added or subtracted. To add mixed numbers with unlike fractions, rename the mixed numbers as improper fractions. Then find a common denominator, add the numerators, and simplify the answer.

Multiplying Rational Numbers

To multiply fractions, multiply the numerators and multiply the denominators. If the numerators and denominators have common factors, they can be simplified before multiplication.

If the fractions have different signs, then the product will be negative. Mixed numbers can be multiplied in the same manner, after first renaming them as improper fractions. Algebraic fractions may be multiplied using the same method described above. Dividing Rational Numbers. To divide a number by a rational number (a fraction, for example), multiply the first number by the multiplicative inverse of the second. Two numbers whose product is 1 are called multiplicative inverses, or reciprocals. $\frac{7}{4} \times \frac{4}{7} = 1$. When dividing by a mixed number, first rename it as an improper fraction, and then multiply by its multiplicative inverse. This process of multiplying by a number's reciprocal can also be used when dividing algebraic fractions.

Adding Integers

To add integers with the same sign, add their absolute values. The sum takes the same sign as the addends. An addend is a number that is added to another number (the augend). The equation $-5 + (-2) = -7$ is an example of adding two integers with the same sign. To add integers with different signs, subtract their absolute values. The sum takes the same sign as the addend with the greater absolute value.

Subtracting Integers

The rules for adding integers are extended to the subtraction of integers. To subtract an integer, add its additive inverse. For example, to find the difference $2 - 5$, add the additive inverse of 5 to 2: $2 + (-5) = -3$. The rule for subtracting integers can be used to solve real-world problems and to evaluate algebraic expressions.

Additive Inverse Property

Two numbers with the same absolute value but different signs are called opposites. For example, -4 and 4 are opposites. An integer and its opposite are also called additive inverses. The Additive Inverse Property says that the sum of any number and its additive inverse is zero. The Commutative, Associative, and Identity Properties also apply to integers. These properties help when adding more than two integers.

Absolute Value

In mathematics, when two integers on a number line are on opposite sides of zero, and they are the same distance from zero, they have the same absolute value. The symbol for absolute value is two vertical bars on either side of the number. For example, $|-5| = 5$.

Multiplying Integers

Since multiplication is repeated addition, $3(-7)$ means that -7 is used as an addend 3 times. By the Commutative Property of Multiplication, $3(-7) = -7(3)$. The product of two integers with different signs is always negative. The product of two integers with the same sign is always positive.

Dividing Integers

The quotient of two integers can be found by dividing the numbers using their absolute values. The quotient of two integers with the same sign is positive, and the quotient of two integers with a different sign is negative. $-12 \div (-4) = 3$ and $12 \div (-4) = -3$. The division of integers is used in statistics to find the average, or mean, of a set of data. When finding the mean of a set of numbers, find the sum of the numbers, and then divide by the number in the set.

Adding and Multiplying Vectors and Matrices

In order to add two matrices together, they must have the same number of rows and columns. In matrix addition, the corresponding elements are added to each other. In other words $(a + b)_{ij} = a_{ij} + b_{ij}$. For example,

$$\begin{pmatrix} 1 & 2 \\ 2 & 1 \end{pmatrix} + \begin{pmatrix} 3 & 6 \\ 0 & 1 \end{pmatrix} = \begin{pmatrix} 1+3 & 2+6 \\ 2+0 & 1+1 \end{pmatrix} = \begin{pmatrix} 4 & 8 \\ 2 & 2 \end{pmatrix}$$

Matrix multiplication requires that the number of elements in each row in the first matrix is equal to the number of elements in each column in the second. The elements of the first row of the first matrix are multiplied by the corresponding elements of the first column of the second matrix and then added together to get the first element of the product matrix. To get the second element, the elements in the first row of the first matrix are multiplied by the corresponding elements in the second column of the second matrix then added, and so on, until every row of the first matrix is multiplied by every column of the second. See the example below.

$$\begin{pmatrix} 1 & 2 \\ 3 & 4 \end{pmatrix} \times \begin{pmatrix} 3 & 6 \\ 0 & 1 \end{pmatrix} = \begin{pmatrix} (1\times3)+(2\times0) & (1\times6)+(2\times1) \\ (3\times3)+(4\times0) & (3\times6)+(4\times1) \end{pmatrix} = \begin{pmatrix} 3 & 8 \\ 9 & 22 \end{pmatrix}$$

Vector addition and multiplication are performed in the same way, but there is only one column and one row.

Permutations and Combinations

Permutations and combinations are used to determine the number of possible outcomes in different situations. An arrangement, listing, or pattern in which order is important is called a permutation. The symbol P(6, 3) represents the number of permutations of 6 things taken 3 at a time. For P(6, 3), there are $6 \times 5 \times 4$ or 120 possible outcomes. An arrangement or listing where order is not important is called a combination. The symbol C(10, 5) represents the number of combinations of 10 things taken 5 at a time. For C(10, 5), there are $(10 \times 9 \times 8 \times 7 \times 6) \div (5 \times 4 \times 3 \times 2 \times 1)$ or 252 possible outcomes.

Powers and Exponents

An expression such as $3 \times 3 \times 3 \times 3$ can be written as a power. A power has two parts, a base and an exponent. $3 \times 3 \times 3 \times 3 = 3^4$. The base is the number that is multiplied (3). The exponent tells how many times the base is used as a factor (4 times). Numbers and variables can be written using exponents. For example, $8 \times 8 \times 8 \times m \times m \times m \times m \times m$ can be expressed $8^3 m^5$. Exponents also can be used with place value to express numbers in expanded form. Using this method, 1,462 can be written as $(1 \times 10^3) + (4 \times 10^2) + (6 \times 10^1) + (2 \times 10^0)$.

Squares and Square Roots

The square root of a number is one of two equal factors of a number. Every positive number has both a positive and a negative square root. For example, since $8 \times 8 = 64$, 8 is a square root of 64. Since $(-8) \times (-8) = 64$, -8 is also a square root of 64. The notation $\sqrt{\ }$ indicates the positive square root, $-\sqrt{\ }$ indicates the negative square root, and $\pm\sqrt{\ }$ indicates both square roots. For example, $\sqrt{81} = 9$, $-\sqrt{49} = -7$, and $\pm\sqrt{4} = \pm2$. The square root of a negative number is an imaginary number because any two factors of a negative number must have different signs, and are therefore not equivalent.

Logarithm

A logarithm is the inverse of exponentiation. The logarithm of a number x in base b is equal to the number n. Therefore, $b^n = x$ and $\log_b x = n$. For example, $\log_4(64) = 3$ because $4^3 = 64$. The most commonly used bases for logarithms are 10, the common logarithm; 2, the binary logarithm; and the constant e, the natural logarithm (also called $ln(x)$ instead of $\log_e(x)$). Below is a list of some of the rules of logarithms that are important to understand if you are going to use them.

$$\log_b(xy) = \log_b(x) + \log_b(y)$$
$$\log_b \tfrac{x}{y} = \log_b(x) - \log_b(y)$$
$$\log_b \tfrac{1}{x} = -\log_b(x)$$
$$\log_b(x)y = y\log_b(x)$$

▶ Compute fluently and make reasonable estimates

Estimation by Rounding
When rounding numbers, look at the digit to the right of the place to which you are rounding. If the digit is 5 or greater, round up. If it is less than 5, round down. For example, to round 65,137 to the nearest hundred, look at the number in the tens place. Since 3 is less than 5, round down to 65,100. To round the same number to the nearest ten thousandth, look at the number in the thousandths place. Since it is 5, round up to 70,000.

Finding Equivalent Ratios
Equivalent ratios have the same meaning. Just like finding equivalent fractions, to find an equivalent ratio, multiply or divide both sides by the same number. For example, you can multiply 7 by both sides of the ratio 6:8 to get 42:56. Instead, you can also divide both sides of the same ratio by 2 to get 3:4. Find the simplest form of a ratio by dividing to find equivalent ratios until you can't go any further without going into decimals. So, 160:240 in simplest form is 2:3. To write a ratio in the form *1:n,* divide both sides by the left-hand number. In other words, to change 8:20 to *1:n,* divide both sides by 8 to get 1:2.5.

Front-End Estimation
Front-end estimation can be used to quickly estimate sums and differences before adding or subtracting. To use this technique, add or subtract just the digits of the two highest place values, and replace the other place values with zero. This will give you an estimation of the solution of a problem. For example, 93,471 − 22,825 can be changed to 93,000 − 22,000 or 71,000. This estimate can be compared to your final answer to judge its correctness.

Judging Reasonableness
When solving an equation, it is important to check your work by considering how reasonable your answer is. For example, consider the equation $9\tfrac{3}{4} \times 4\tfrac{1}{3}$. Since $9\tfrac{3}{4}$ is between 9 and 10 and $4\tfrac{1}{3}$ is between 4 and 5, only values that are between 9×4 or 36 and 10×5 or 50 will be reasonable. You can also use front-end estimation, or you can round and estimate a reason-

able answer. In the equation 73×25, you can round and solve to estimate a reasonable answer to be near 70×30 or 2,100.

Algebra

▶ Understand patterns, relations, and functions

Relation
A relation is a generalization comparing sets of ordered pairs for an equation or inequality such as $x = y + 1$ or $x > y$. The first element in each pair, the *x* values, forms the domain. The second element in each pair, the *y* values, forms the range.

Function
A function is a special relation in which each member of the domain is paired with exactly one member in the range. Functions may be represented using ordered pairs, tables, or graphs. One way to determine whether a relation is a function is to use the vertical line test. Using an object to represent a vertical line, move the object from left to right across the graph. If, for each value of *x* in the domain, the object passes through no more than one point on the graph, then the graph represents a function.

Linear and Nonlinear Functions
Linear functions have graphs that are straight lines. These graphs represent constant rates of change. In other words, the slope between any two pairs of points on the graph is the same. Nonlinear functions do not have constant rates of change. The slope changes along these graphs. Therefore, the graphs of nonlinear functions are *not* straight lines. Graphs of curves represent nonlinear functions. The equation for a linear function can be written in the form $y = mx + b$, where *m* represents the constant rate of change, or the slope. Therefore, you can determine whether a function is linear by looking at the equation. For example, the equation $y = \tfrac{3}{x}$ is nonlinear because *x* is in the denominator and the equation cannot be written in the form $y = mx + b$. A nonlinear function does not increase or decrease at a constant rate. You can check this by using a table and finding the increase or decrease in *y* for each regular increase in *x*. For example, if for each increase in *x* by 2, *y* does not increase or decrease the same amount each time, the function is nonlinear.

Linear Equations in Two Variables

In a linear equation with two variables, such as $y = x - 3$, the variables appear in separate terms and neither variable contains an exponent other than 1. The graphs of all linear equations are straight lines. All points on a line are solutions of the equation that is graphed.

Quadratic and Cubic Functions

A quadratic function is a polynomial equation of the second degree, generally expressed as $ax^2 + bx + c = 0$, where a, b, and c are real numbers and a is not equal to zero. Similarly, a cubic function is a polynomial equation of the third degree, usually expressed as $ax^3 + bx^2 + cx + d = 0$. Quadratic functions can be graphed using an equation or a table of values. For example, to graph $y = 3x^2 + 1$, substitute the values −1, −0.5, 0, 0.5, and 1 for x to yield the point coordinates (−1, 4), (−0.5, 1.75), (0, 1), (0.5, 1.75), and (1, 4). Plot these points on a coordinate grid and connect the points in the form of a parabola. Cubic functions also can be graphed by making a table of values. The points of a cubic function from a curve. There is one point at which the curve changes from opening upward to opening downward, or vice versa, called the point of inflection.

Slope

Slope is the ratio of the rise, or vertical change, to the run, or horizontal change of a line: slope = rise/run. Slope (m) is the same for any two points on a straight line and can be found by using the coordinates of any two points on the line:

$$m = \frac{y_2 - y_1}{x_2 - x_1}, \text{ where } x_2 \neq x_1$$

Asymptotes

An asymptote is a straight line that a curve approaches but never actually meets or crosses. Theoretically, the asymptote meets the curve at infinity. For example, in the function $f(x) = \frac{1}{x}$, two asymptotes are being approached: the line $y = 0$ and $x = 0$. See the graph of the function below.

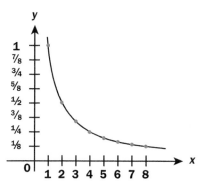

Represent and analyze mathematical situations and structures using algebraic symbols

Variables and Expressions

Algebra is a language of symbols. A variable is a placeholder for a changing value. Any letter, such as x, can be used as a variable. Expressions such as $x + 2$ and $4x$ are algebraic expressions because they represent sums and/or products of variables and numbers. Usually, mathematicians avoid the use of i and e for variables because they have other mathematical meanings ($i = \sqrt{-1}$ and e is used with natural logarithms). To evaluate an algebraic expression, replace the variable or variables with known values, and then solve using order of operations. Translate verbal phrases into algebraic expressions by first defining a variable: Choose a variable and a quantity for the variable to represent. In this way, algebraic expressions can be used to represent real-world situations.

Constant and Coefficient

A constant is a fixed value unlike a variable, which can change. Constants are usually represented by numbers, but they can also be represented by symbols. For example, π is a symbolic representation of the value 3.1415…. A coefficient is a constant by which a variable or other object is multiplied. For example, in the expression $7x^2 + 5x + 9$, the coefficient of x^2 is 7 and the coefficient of x is 5. The number 9 is a constant and not a coefficient.

Monomial and Polynomial

A monomial is a number, a variable, or a product of numbers and/or variables such as 3×4. An algebraic expression that contains one or more monomials is called a polynomial. In a polynomial, there are no terms with variables in the denominator and no terms with variables under a radical sign. Polynomials can be classified by the number of terms contained in the expression. Therefore, a polynomial with two terms is called a binomial ($z^2 - 1$), and a polynomial with three terms is called a trinomial ($2y^3 + 4y^2 - y$). Polynomials also can be classified by their degrees. The degree of a monomial is the sum of the exponents of its variables. The degree of a nonzero constant such as 6 or 10 is 0. The constant 0 has no degree. For example, the monomial $4b^5c^2$ had a degree of 7. The degree of a polynomial is the same as that of the term with the greatest degree. For example, the polynomial $3x^4 - 2y^3 + 4y^2 - y$ has a degree of 4.

Equation

An equation is a mathematical sentence that states that two expressions are equal. The two expressions in an equation are always separated by an equal sign. When solving for a variable in an equation, you must perform the same operations on both sides of the equation in order for the mathematical sentence to remain true.

Solving Equations with Variables

To solve equations with variables on both sides, use the Addition or Subtraction Property of Equality to write an equivalent equation with the variables on the same side. For example, to solve $5x - 8 = 3x$, subtract $3x$ from each side to get $2x - 8 = 0$. Then add 8 to each side to get $2x = 8$. Finally, divide each side by 2 to find that $x = 4$.

Solving Equations with Grouping Symbols

Equations often contain grouping symbols such as parentheses or brackets. The first step in solving these equations is to use the Distributive Property to remove the grouping symbols. For example $5(x + 2) = 25$ can be changed to $5x + 10 = 25$, and then solved to find that $x = 3$.

Some equations have no solution. That is, there is no value of the variable that results in a true sentence. For such an equation, the solution set is called the null or empty set, and is represented by the symbol $\varnothing$ or $\{\}$. Other equations may have every number as the solution. An equation that is true for every value of the variable is called the identity.

Inequality

A mathematical sentence that contains the symbols $<$ (less than), $>$ (greater than), $\leq$ (less than or equal to), or $\geq$ (greater than or equal to) is called an inequality. For example, the statement that it is legal to drive 55 miles per hour or slower on a stretch of the highway can be shown by the sentence $s \leq 55$. Inequalities with variables are called open sentences. When a variable is replaced with a number, the inequality may be true or false.

Solving Inequalities

Solving an inequality means finding values for the variable that make the inequality true. Just as with equations, when you add or subtract

the same number from each side of an inequality, the inequality remains true. For example, if you add 5 to each side of the inequality $3x < 6$, the resulting inequality $3x + 5 < 11$ is also true. Adding or subtracting the same number from each side of an inequality does not affect the inequality sign. When multiplying or dividing each side of an inequality by the same positive number, the inequality remains true. In such cases, the inequality symbol does not change. When multiplying or dividing each side of an inequality by a negative number, the inequality symbol must be reversed. For example, when dividing each side of the inequality $-4x \geq -8$ by -2, the inequality sign must be changed to $\leq$ for the resulting inequality, $2x \leq 4$, to be true. Since the solutions to an inequality include all rational numbers satisfying it, inequalities have an infinite number of solutions.

Representing Inequalities on a Number Line

The solutions of inequalities can be graphed on a number line. For example, if the solution of an inequality is $x < 5$, start an arrow at 5 on the number line, and continue the arrow to the left to show all values less than 5 as the solution. Put an open circle at 5 to show that the point 5 is *not* included in the graph. Use a closed circle when graphing solutions that are greater than or equal to, or less than or equal to, a number.

Order of Operations

Solving a problem may involve using more than one operation. The answer can depend on the order in which you do the operations. To make sure that there is just one answer to a series of computations, mathematicians have agreed upon an order in which to do the operations. First simplify within the parentheses, often called graphing symbols, and then evaluate any exponents. Then multiply and divide from left to right, and finally add and subtract from left to right.

Parametric Equations

Given an equation with more than one unknown, a statistician can draw conclusions about those unknown quantities through the use of parameters, independent variables that the statistician already knows something about. For example, you can find the velocity of an object if you make some assumptions about distance and time parameters.

Recursive Equations

In recursive equations, every value is determined by the previous value. You must first plug an initial value into the equation to get the first value, and then you can use the first value to determine the next one, and so on. For example, in order to determine what the population of pigeons will be in New York City in three years, you can use an equation with the birth, death, immigration, and emigration rates of the birds. Input the current population size into the equation to determine next year's population size, then repeat until you have calculated the value for which you are looking.

▶ *Use mathematical models to represent and understand quantitative relationships*

Solving Systems of Equations

Two or more equations together are called a system of equations. A system of equations can have one solution, no solution, or infinitely many solutions. One method for solving a system of equations is to graph the equations on the same coordinate plane. The coordinates of the point where the graphs intersect is the solution. In other words, the solution of a system is the ordered pair that is a solution of all equations. A more accurate way to solve a system of two equations is by using a method called substitution. Write both equations in terms of y. Replace y in the first equation with the right side of the second equation. Check the solution by graphing. You can solve a system of three equations using matrix algebra.

Graphing Inequalities

To graph an inequality, first graph the related equation, which is the boundary. All points in the shaded region are solutions of the inequality. If an inequality contains the symbol $\leq$ or $\geq$, then use a solid line to indicate that the boundary is included in the graph. If an inequality contains the symbol $<$ or $>$, then use a dashed line to indicate that the boundary is not included in the graph.

▶ *Analyze change in various contexts*

Rate of Change

A change in one quantity with respect to another quantity is called the rate of change. Rates of change can be described using slope:

$$\text{slope} = \frac{change\ in\ y}{change\ in\ x}$$

You can find rates of change from an equation, a table, or a graph. A special type of linear equation that describes rate of change is called a direct variation. The graph of a direct variation always passes through the origin and represents a proportional situation. In the equation $y = kx$, k is called the constant of variation. It is the slope, or rate of change. As x increases in value, y increases or decreases at a constant rate k, or y varies directly with x. Another way to say this is that y is directly proportional to x. The direct variation $y = kx$ also can be written as $k = \frac{y}{x}$. In this form, you can see that the ratio of y to x is the same for any corresponding values of y and x.

Slope-Intercept Form

Equations written as $y = mx + b$, where m is the slope and b is the y-intercept, are linear equations in slope-intercept form. For example, the graph of $y = 5x - 6$ is a line that has a slope of 5 and crosses the y-axis at $(0, -6)$. Sometimes you must first write an equation in slope-intercept form before finding the slope and y-intercept. For example, the equation $2x + 3y = 15$ can be expressed in slope-intercept form by subtracting $2x$ from each side and then dividing by 3: $y = -\frac{2}{3}x + 5$, revealing a slope of $-\frac{2}{3}$ and a y-intercept of 5. You can use the slope-intercept form of an equation to graph a line easily. Graph the y-intercept and use the slope to find another point on the line, then connect the two points with a line. Analyze characteristics and properties of two- and three-dimensional geometric shapes and develop mathematical arguments about geometric relationships

Geometry

▶ *Analyze characteristics and properties of two- and three-dimensional geometric shapes and develop mathematical arguments about geometric relationships*

Angles

Two rays that have the same endpoint form an angle. The common endpoint is called the vertex, and the two rays that make up the angle are called the sides of the angle. The most common unit of measure for angles is the degree. Protractors can be used to measure angles or to draw an angle of a given measure. Angles can be classified by their degree measure. Acute angles have measures less than 90° but greater than 0°. Obtuse angles have measures greater than 90° but less than 180°. Right angles have measures of 90°.

Triangles

A triangle is a figure formed by three line segments that intersect only at their endpoints. The sum of the measures of the angles of a triangle is 180°. Triangles can be classified by their angles. An acute triangle contains all acute angles. An obtuse triangle has one obtuse angle. A right triangle has one right angle. Triangles can also be classified by their sides. A scalene triangle has no congruent sides. An isosceles triangle has at least two congruent sides. In an equilateral triangle all sides are congruent.

Quadrilaterals

A quadrilateral is a closed figure with four sides and four vertices. The segments of a quadrilateral intersect only at their endpoints. Quadrilaterals can be separated into two triangles. Since the sum of the interior angles of all triangles totals 180°, the measures of the interior angles of a quadrilateral equal 360°. Quadrilaterals are classified according to their characteristics, and include trapezoids, parallelograms, rectangles, squares, and rhombuses.

Two-Dimensional Figures

A two-dimensional figure exists within a plane and has only the dimensions of length and width. Examples of two-dimensional figures include circles and polygons. Polygons are figures that have three or more angles, including triangles, quadrilaterals, pentagons, hexagons, and many more. The sum of the angles of any polygon totals at least 180° (triangle), and each additional side adds 180° to the measure of the first three angles. The sum of the angles of a quadrilateral, for example, is 360°. The sum of the angles of a pentagon is 540°.

Three-Dimensional Figures

A plane is a two-dimensional flat surface that extends in all directions. Intersecting planes can form the edges and vertices of three-dimensional figures or solids. A polyhedron is a solid with flat surfaces that are polygons. Polyhedrons are composed of faces, edges, and vertices and are differentiated by their shape and by their number of bases. Skew lines are lines that lie in different planes. They are neither intersecting nor parallel.

Congruence

Figures that have the same size and shape are congruent. The parts of congruent triangles that match are called corresponding parts. Congruence statements are used to identify corresponding parts of congruent triangles. When writing a congruence statement, the letters must be written so that corresponding vertices appear in the same order. Corresponding parts can be used to find the measures of angles and sides in a figure that is congruent to a figure with known measures.

Similarity

If two figures have the same shape but not the same size they are called similar figures. For example, the triangles below are similar, so angles A, B, and C have the same measurements as angles D, E, and F, respectively. However, segments AB, BC, and CA do not have the same measurements as segments DE, EF, and FD, but the measures of the sides are proportional.

For example, $\dfrac{\overline{AB}}{\overline{DE}} = \dfrac{\overline{BC}}{\overline{EF}} = \dfrac{\overline{CA}}{\overline{FD}}$.

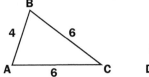

Solid figures are considered to be similar if they have the same shape and their corresponding linear measures are proportional. As with two-dimensional figures, they can be tested for similarity by comparing corresponding measures. If the compared ratios are proportional, then the figures are similar solids. Missing measures of similar solids can also be determined by using proportions.

The Pythagorean Theorem

The sides that are adjacent to a right angle are called legs. The side opposite the right angle is the hypotenuse.

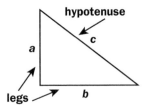

The Pythagorean Theorem describes the relationship between the lengths of the legs a and b and the hypotenuse c. It states that if a triangle is a right triangle, then the square of the length of the hypotenuse is equal to the sum of the squares of the lengths of the legs. In symbols, $c^2 = a^2 + b^2$.

Sine, Cosine, and Tangent Ratios

Trigonometry is the study of the properties of triangles. A trigonometric ratio is a ratio of the lengths of two sides of a right triangle. The most common trigonometric ratios are the sine, cosine, and tangent ratios. These ratios are abbreviated as *sin*, *cos*, and *tan*, respectively.

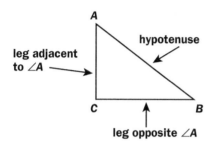

If $\angle A$ is an acute angle of a right triangle, then

$$sin \angle A = \frac{\text{measure of leg opposite } \angle A}{\text{measure of hypotenuse}},$$

$$cos \angle A = \frac{\text{measure of leg adjacent to } \angle A}{\text{measure of hypotenuse}}, \text{ and}$$

$$tan \angle A = \frac{\text{measure of leg opposite } \angle A}{\text{measure of leg adjacent to } \angle A}.$$

▶ Specify locations and describe spatial relationships using coordinate geometry and other representational systems

Polygons

A polygon is a simple, closed figure formed by three or more line segments. The line segments meet only at their endpoints. The points of intersection are called vertices, and the line segments are called sides. Polygons are classified by the number if sides they have. The diagonals of a polygon divide the polygon into triangles. The number of triangles formed is two less than the number of sides. To find the sum of the measures of the interior angles of any polygon, multiply the number of triangles within the polygon by 180. That is, if n equals the number of sides, then $(n - 2)\,180$ gives the sum of the measures of the polygon's interior angles.

Cartesian Coordinates

In the Cartesian coordinate system, the y-axis extends above and below the origin and the x-axis extends to the right and left of the origin, which is the point at which the x- and y-axes intersect. Numbers below and to the left of the origin are negative. A point graphed on the coordinate grid is said to have an x-coordinate and a y-coordinate. For example, the point $(1,-2)$ has as its x-coordinate the number 1, and has as its y-coordinate the number -2. This point is graphed by locating the position on the grid that is 1 unit to the right of the origin and 2 units below the origin.

The x-axis and the y-axis separate the coordinate plane into four regions, called quadrants. The axes and points located on the axes themselves are not located in any of the quadrants. The quadrants are labeled I to IV, starting in the upper right and proceeding counterclockwise. In quadrant I, both coordinates are positive. In quadrant II, the x-coordinate is negative and the y-coordinate is positive. In quadrant III, both coordinates are negative. In quadrant IV, the x-coordinate is positive and the y-coordinate is negative. A coordinate graph can be used to show algebraic relationships among numbers.

▶ Apply transformations and use symmetry to analyze mathematical situations

Similar Triangles and Indirect Measurement

Triangles that have the same shape but not necessarily the same dimensions are called similar triangles. Similar triangles have corresponding angles and corresponding sides. Arcs are used to show congruent angles. If two triangles are similar, then the corresponding angles have the same measure, and the corresponding sides are proportional. Therefore, to determine the measures of the sides of similar triangles when some measures are known, proportions can be used.

Transformations

A transformation is a movement of a geometric figure. There are several types of transformations. In a translation, also called a slide, a figure is slid from one position to another without turning it. Every point of the original figure is moved the same distance and in the same direction. In a reflection, also called a flip, a figure is flipped over a line to form a mirror image. Every point of the original figure has a corresponding point on the other side of the line of symmetry. In a rotation, also called a turn, a figure is turned around a fixed point. A figure can be rotated 0°–360° clockwise or counterclockwise. A dilation transforms each line to a parallel line whose length is a fixed multiple of the length of the original line to create a similar figure that will be either larger or smaller.

▶ *Use visualizations, spatial reasoning, and geometric modeling to solve problems*

Two-Dimensional Representations of Three-Dimensional Objects

Three-dimensional objects can be represented in a two-dimensional drawing in order to more easily determine properties such as surface area and volume. When you look at the triangular prism, you can see the orientation of its three dimensions, length, width, and height. Using the drawing and the formulas for surface area and volume, you can easily calculate these properties.

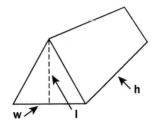

Another way to represent a three-dimensional object in a two-dimensional plane is by using a net, which is the unfolded representation. Imagine cutting the vertices of a box until it is flat then drawing an outline of it. That's a net. Most objects have more than one net, but any one can be measured to determine surface area. Below is a cube and one of its nets.

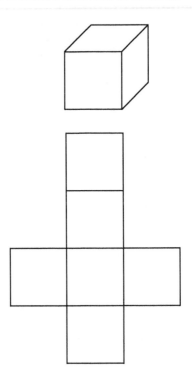

Measurement

▶ *Understand measurable attributes of objects and the units, systems, and processes of measurement*

Customary System

The customary system is the system of weights and measures used in the United States. The main units of weight are ounces, pounds (1 equal to 16 ounces), and tons (1 equal to 2,000 pounds). Length is typically measured in inches, feet (1 equal to 12 inches), yards (1 equal to 3 feet), and miles (1 equal to 5,280 feet), while area is measured in square feet and acres (1 equal to 43,560 square feet). Liquid is measured in cups, pints (1 equal to 2 cups), quarts (1 equal to 2 pints), and gallons (1 equal to 4 quarts). Finally, temperature is measured in degrees Fahrenheit.

Metric System

The metric system is a decimal system of weights and measurements in which the prefixes of the words for the units of measure indicate the relationships between the different measurements. In this system, the main units of weight, or mass, are grams and kilograms. Length is measured in millimeters, centimeters, meters, and kilometers, and the units of area are square millimeters, centimeters, meters, and kilometers. Liquid is typically measured in milliliters and liters, while temperature is in degrees Celsius.

Selecting Units of Measure

When measuring something, it is important to select the appropriate type and size of unit. For example, in the United States it would be appropriate when describing someone's height to use feet and inches. These units of height or length are good to use because they are in the customary system, and they are of appropriate size. In the customary system, use inches, feet, and miles for lengths and perimeters; square inches, feet, and miles for area and surface area; and cups, pints, quarts, gallons or cubic inches and feet (and less commonly miles) for volume. In the metric system use millimeters, centimeters, meters, and kilometers for lengths and perimeters; square units millimeters, centimeters, meters, and kilometers for area and surface area; and milliliters and liters for volume. Finally, always use degrees to measure angles.

▶ *Apply appropriate techniques, tools, and formulas to determine measurements*

Precision and Significant Digits

The precision of measurement is the exactness to which a measurement is made. Precision depends on the smallest unit of measure being used, or the precision unit. One way to record a measure is to estimate to the nearest precision unit. A more precise method is to include all of the digits that are actually measured, plus one estimated digit. The digits recorded, called significant digits, indicate the precision of the measurement. There are special rules for determining significant digits. If a number contains a decimal point, the number of significant digits is found by counting from left to right, starting with the first nonzero digit. If the number does not contain a decimal point, the number of significant digits is found by counting the digits from left to right, starting with the first digit and ending with the last nonzero digit.

Surface Area

The amount of material needed to cover the surface of a figure is called the surface area. It can be calculated by finding the area of each face and adding them together. To find the surface area of a rectangular prism, for example, the formula $S = 2lw + 2lh + 2wh$ applies. A cylinder, on the other hand, may be unrolled to reveal two circles and a rectangle. Its surface area can be determined by finding the area of the two circles, $2\pi r^2$, and adding it to the area of the rectangle, $2\pi rh$ (the length of the rectangle is the circumference of one of the circles), or $S = 2\pi r^2 + 2\pi rh$. The surface area of a pyramid is measured in a slightly different way because the sides of a pyramid are triangles that intersect at the vertex. These sides are called lateral faces and the height of each is called the slant height. The sum of their areas is the lateral area of a pyramid. The surface area of a square pyramid is the lateral area $\frac{1}{2}bh$ (area of a lateral face) times 4 (number of lateral faces), plus the area of the base. The surface area of a cone is the area of its circular base (πr^2) plus its lateral area (πrl, where l is the slant height).

Volume

Volume is the measure of space occupied by a solid region. To find the volume of a prism, the area of the base is multiplied by the measure of the height, $V = Bh$. A solid containing several prisms can be broken down into its component prisms. Then the volume of each component can be found and the volumes added. The volume of a cylinder can be determined by finding the area of its circular base, πr^2, and then multiplying by the height of the cylinder. A pyramid has one-third the volume of a prism with the same base and height. To find the volume of a pyramid, multiply the area of the base by the pyramid's height, and then divide by 3. Simply stated, the formula for the volume of a pyramid is $V = \frac{1}{3}bh$. A cone is a three-dimensional figure with one circular base and a curved surface connecting the base and the vertex. The volume of a cone is one-third the volume of a cylinder with the same base area and height. Like a pyramid, the formula for the volume of a cone is $V = \frac{1}{3}bh$. More specifically, the formula is $V = \frac{1}{3}\pi r^2 h$.

Upper and Lower Bounds

Upper and lower bounds have to do with the accuracy of a measurement. When a measurement is given, the degree of accuracy is also stated to tell you what the upper and lower bounds of the measurement are. The upper bound is the largest possible value that a measurement could have had before being rounded down, and the lower bound is the lowest possible value it could have had before being rounded up.

Data Analysis and Probablity

▶ *Formulate questions that can be addressed with data and collect, organize, and display relevant data to answer them*

Histograms

A histogram displays numerical data that have been organized into equal intervals using bars that have the same width and no space between them. While a histogram does not give exact data points, its shape shows the distribution of the data. Histograms also can be used to compare data.

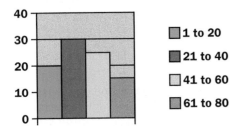

- ■ 1 to 20
- ■ 21 to 40
- □ 41 to 60
- ■ 61 to 80

Box-and-Whisker Plot

A box-and-whisker plot displays the measures of central tendency and variation. A box is drawn around the quartile values, and whiskers extend from each quartile to the extreme data points. To make a box plot for a set of data, draw a number line that covers the range of data. Find the median, the extremes, and the upper and lower quartiles. Mark these points on the number line with bullets, then draw a box and the whiskers. The length of a whisker or box shows whether the values of the data in that part are concentrated or spread out.

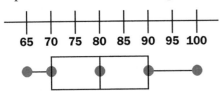

Scatter Plots

A scatter plot is a graph that shows the relationship between two sets of data. In a scatter plot, two sets of data are graphed as ordered pairs on a coordinate system. Two sets of data can have a positive correlation (as *x* increases, *y* increases), a negative correlation (as *x* increases, *y* decreases), or no correlation (no obvious pattern is shown). Scatter plots can be used to spot trends, draw conclusions, and make predictions about data.

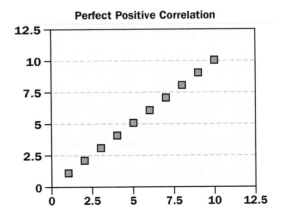

Perfect Positive Correlation

Randomization

The idea of randomization is a very important principle of statistics and the design of experiments. Data must be selected randomly to prevent bias from influencing the results. For example, you want to know the average income of people in your town but you can only use a sample of 100 individuals to make determinations about everyone. If you select 100 individuals who are all doctors, you will have a biased sample. However, if you chose a random sample of 100 people out of the phone book, you are much more likely to accurately represent average income in the town.

Statistics and Parameters

Statistics is a science that involves collecting, analyzing, and presenting data. The data can be collected in various ways—for example through a census or by making physical measurements. The data can then be analyzed by creating summary statistics, which have to do with the distribution of the data sample, including the mean, range, and standard error. They can also be illustrated in tables and graphs, like box-plots, scatter plots, and histograms. The presentation of the data typically involves describing the strength or validity of the data and what they show. For example, an analysis of ancestry of people in a city might tell you something about immigration patterns, unless the data set is very small or biased in some way, in which case it is not likely to be very accurate or useful.

Categorical and Measurement Data

When analyzing data, it is important to understand if the data is qualitative or quantitative. Categorical data is qualitative and measurement, or numerical, data is quantitative. Categorical data describes a quality of something and can be placed into different categories. For example, if you are analyzing the number of students in different grades in a school, each grade is a category. On the other hand, measurement data is continuous, like height, weight, or any other measurable variable. Measurement data can be converted into categorical data if you decide to group the data. Using height as an example, you can group the continuous data set into categories like under 5 feet, 5 feet to 5 feet 5 inches, over 5 feet five inches to 6 feet, and so on.

Univariate and Bivariate Data

In data analysis, a researcher can analyze one variable at a time or look at how multiple variables behave together. Univariate data involves only one variable, for example height in humans. You can measure the height in a population of people then plot the results in a histogram to look at how height is distributed in humans. To summarize univariate data, you can use statistics like the mean, mode, median, range, and standard deviation, which is a measure of variation. When looking at more than one variable at once, you use multivariate data. Bivariate data involves two variables. For example, you can look at height and age in humans together by gathering information on both variables from individuals in a population. You can then plot both variables in a scatter plot, look at how the variables behave in relation to each other, and create an equation that represents the relationship, also called a regression. These equations could help answer questions such as, for example, does height increase with age in humans?

▶ Select and use appropriate statistical methods to analyze data

Measures of Central Tendency

When you have a list of numerical data, it is often helpful to use one or more numbers to represent the whole set. These numbers are called measures of central tendency. Three measures of central tendency are mean, median, and mode. The mean is the sum of the data divided by the number of items in the data set. The median is the middle number of the ordered data (or the mean of the two middle numbers).

The mode is the number or numbers that occur most often. These measures of central tendency allow data to be analyzed and better understood.

Measures of Spread

In statistics, measures of spread or variation are used to describe how data are distributed. The range of a set of data is the difference between the greatest and the least values of the data set. The quartiles are the values that divide the data into four equal parts. The median of data separates the set in half. Similarly, the median of the lower half of a set of data is the lower quartile. The median of the upper half of a set of data is the upper quartile. The interquartile range is the difference between the upper quartile and the lower quartile.

Line of Best Fit

When real-life data are collected, the points graphed usually do not form a straight line, but they may approximate a linear relationship. A line of best fit is a line that lies very close to most of the data points. It can be used to predict data. You also can use the equation of the best-fit line to make predictions.

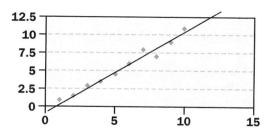

Stem and Leaf Plots

In a stem and leaf plot, numerical data are listed in ascending or descending order. The greatest place value of the data is used for the stems. The next greatest place value forms the leaves. For example, if the least number in a set of data is 8 and the greatest number is 95, draw a vertical line and write the stems from 0 to 9 to the left of the line. Write the leaves from to the right of the line, with the corresponding stem. Next, rearrange the leaves so they are ordered from least to greatest. Then include a key or explanation, such as 1|3 = 13. Notice that the stem-and-leaf plot below is like a histogram turned on its side.

```
0|8
1|3 6
2|5 6 9
3|0 2 7 8
4|0 1 4 7 9
5|1 4 5 8
6|1 3 7
7|5 8
8|2 6
9|5
```
Key: **1**|3 = **13**

▶ Develop and evaluate inferences and predictions that are based on data

Sampling Distribution

The sampling distribution of a population is the distribution that would result if you could take an infinite number of samples from the population, average each, and then average the averages. The more normal the distribution of the population, that is, how closely the distribution follows a bell curve, the more likely the sampling distribution will also follow a normal distribution. Furthermore, the larger the sample, the more likely it will accurately represent the entire population. For instance, you are more likely to gain more representative results from a population of 1,000 with a sample of 100 than with a sample of 2.

Validity

In statistics, validity refers to acquiring results that accurately reflect that which is being measured. In other words, it is important when performing statistical analyses, to ensure that the data are valid in that the sample being analyzed represents the population to the best extent possible. Randomization of data and using appropriate sample sizes are two important aspects of making valid inferences about a population.

▶ Understand and apply basic concepts of probability

Complementary, Mutually Exclusive Events

To understand probability theory, it is important to know if two events are mutually exclusive, or complementary: the occurrence of one event automatically implies the non-occurrence of the other. That is, two complementary events cannot both occur. If you roll a pair of dice,

the event of rolling 6 and rolling doubles have an outcome in common (3, 3), so they are not mutually exclusive. If you roll (3, 3), you also roll doubles. However, the events of rolling a 9 and rolling doubles are mutually exclusive because they have no outcomes in common. If you roll a 9, you will not also roll doubles.

Independent and Dependent Events

Determining the probability of a series of events requires that you know whether the events are independent or dependent. An independent event has no influence on the occurrence of subsequent events, whereas, a dependent event does influence subsequent events. The chances that a woman's first child will be a girl are $\frac{1}{2}$, and the chances that her second child will be a girl are also $\frac{1}{2}$ because the two events are independent of each other. However, if there are 7 red marbles in a bag of 15 marbles, the chances that the first marble you pick will be red are $\frac{7}{15}$ and if you indeed pick a red marble and remove it, you have reduced the chances of picking another red marble to $\frac{6}{14}$.

Sample Space

The sample space is the group of all possible outcomes for an event. For example, if you are tossing a single six-sided die, the sample space is {1, 2, 3, 4, 5, 6}. Similarly, you can determine the sample space for the possible outcomes of two events. If you are going to toss a coin twice, the sample space is {(heads, heads), (heads, tails), (tails, heads), (tails, tails)}.

Computing the Probability of a Compound Event

If two events are independent, the outcome of one event does not influence the outcome of the second. For example, if a bag contains 2 blue and 3 red marbles, then the probability of selecting a blue marble, replacing it, and then selecting a red marble is $P(A) \times P(B) = \frac{2}{5} \times \frac{3}{5}$ or $\frac{6}{25}$.

If two events are dependent, the outcome of one event affects the outcome of the second. For example, if a bag contains 2 blue and 3 red marbles, then the probability of selecting a blue and then a red marble without replacing the first marble is $P(A) \times P(B \text{ following } A) = \frac{2}{5} \times \frac{3}{4}$ or $\frac{3}{10}$. Two events that cannot happen at the same time are mutually exclusive. For example, when you roll two number cubes, you cannot roll a sum that is both 5 and even. So, $P(A \text{ or } B) = \frac{4}{36} + \frac{18}{36}$ or $\frac{11}{18}$.

MAKING CAREER CHOICES

A career differs from a job in that it is a series of progressively more responsible jobs in one field or a related field. You will need to learn some special skills to choose a career and to help you in your job search. Choosing a career and identifying career opportunities require careful thought and preparation. To aid you in making important career choices, follow these steps:

STEPS TO MAKING A CAREER DECISION

1. Conduct a self-assessment to determine your:
   - values
   - lifestyle goals
   - interests
   - skills and aptitudes
   - personality
   - work environment preferences
   - relationship preferences
2. Identify possible career choices based on your self-assessment.
3. Gather information on each choice, including future trends.
4. Evaluate your choices based on your self-assessment.
5. Make your decision.

After you make your decision, plan how you will reach your goal. It is best to have short-term, medium-term, and long-term goals. In making your choices, explore the future opportunities in this field or fields over the next several years. What impact will new technology and automation have on job opportunities in the next few years? Remember, if you plan, you make your own career opportunities.

PERSONAL CAREER PORTFOLIO

You will want to create and maintain a personal career portfolio. In it you will keep all the documents you create and receive in your job search:

- Contact list
- Résumé
- Letters of recommendation
- Employer evaluations
- Awards
- Evidence of participation in school, community, and volunteer activities
- Notes about your job search
- Notes made after your interviews

CAREER RESEARCH RESOURCES

In order to gather information on various career opportunities, there are a variety of sources to research:

- **Libraries.** Your school or public library offers good career information resources. Here you will find books, magazines, pamphlets, films, videos, and special reference materials on careers. In particular, the U.S. Department of Labor publishes three reference books that are especially helpful: the *Dictionary of Occupational Titles (DOT)*, which describes about 20,000 jobs and their relationships with data, people, and things; the *Occupational Outlook Handbook (OOH)*, with information on more than 200 occupations; and the *Guide for Occupational Exploration (GOE)*, a reference that organizes the world of work into 12 interest areas that are subdivided into work groups and subgroups.
- **The Internet.** The Internet is becoming a primary source of research on any topic. It is especially helpful in researching careers.
- **Career Consultations.** Career consultation, an informational interview with a professional who works in a career that interests you, provides an opportunity to learn about the day-to-day realities of a career.
- **On-the-Job Experience.** On-the-job experience can be valuable in learning firsthand about a job or career. You can find out if your school has a work-experience program, or look into a company or organization's internship opportunities. Interning gives you direct work experience and often allows you to make valuable contacts for future full-time employment.

THE JOB SEARCH

To aid you in your actual job search, there are various sources to explore. You should contact and research all the sources that might produce a job lead, or information about a job. Keep a contact list as you proceed with your search. Some of these resources include:

- **Networking with family, friends, and acquaintances.** This means contacting people you know personally, including school counselors, former employers, and professional people.

- **Cooperative education and work-experience programs.** Many schools have such programs in which students work part-time on a job related to one of their classes. Many also offer work-experience programs that are not limited to just one career area, such as marketing.

- **Newspaper ads.** Reading the Help Wanted advertisements in your local papers will provide a source of job leads, as well as teach you about the local job market.

- **Employment agencies.** Most cities have two types of employment agencies, public and private. These employment agencies match workers with jobs. Some private agencies may charge a fee, so be sure to know who is expected to pay the fee and what the fee is.

- **Company personnel offices.** Large and medium-sized companies have personnel offices to handle employment matters, including the hiring of new workers. You can check on job openings by contacting the office by telephone or by scheduling a personal visit.

- **Searching the Internet.** Cyberspace offers multiple opportunities for your job search. Web sites, such as Hotjobs.com or Monster.com, provide lists of companies offering employment. There are tens of thousands of career-related Web sites, so the challenge is finding those that have jobs that interest you and that are up-to-date in their listings. Companies that interest you may have a Web site, which will provide valuable information on their benefits and opportunities for employment.

APPLYING FOR A JOB

When you have contacted the sources of job leads and found some jobs that interest you, the next step is to apply for them. You will need to complete application forms, write letters of application, and prepare your own résumé.

Before you apply for a job, you will need to have a work permit if you are under the age of 18 in most states. Some state and federal labor laws designate certain jobs as too dangerous for young workers. Laws also limit the number of hours of work allowed during a day, a week, or the school year. You will also need to have proper documentation, such as a green card if you are not a U.S. citizen.

JOB APPLICATION

You can obtain the job application form directly at the place of business, by requesting it in writing, or over the Internet. It is best if you can fill the form out at home, but some businesses require that you fill it out at the place of work.

Fill out the job application forms neatly and accurately, using standard English, the formal style of speaking and writing you learned in school. You must be truthful and pay attention to detail in filling out the form.

PERSONAL FACT SHEET

To be sure that the answers you write on a job application form are accurate, make a personal fact sheet before filling out the application:

- Your name, home address, and phone number
- Your Social Security number
- The job you are applying for
- The date you can begin work
- The days and hours you can work
- The pay you want
- Whether or not you have been convicted of a crime
- Your education
- Your previous work experience
- Your birth date
- Your driver's license number if you have one
- Your interests and hobbies, and awards you have won
- Your previous work experience, including dates
- Schools you have attended
- Places you have lived

- Accommodations you may need from the employer
- A list of references—people who will tell an employer that you will do a good job, such as relatives, students, former employers, and the like

LETTERS OF RECOMMENDATION

Letters of recommendation are helpful. You can request teachers, counselors, relatives, and other acquaintances who know you well to write these letters. They should be short, to the point, and give a brief overview of your assets. A brief description of any of your important accomplishments or projects should follow. The letter should end with a brief description of your character and work ethic.

LETTER OF APPLICATION

Some employees prefer a letter of application, rather than an application form. This letter is like writing a sales pitch about yourself. You need to tell why you are the best person for the job, what special qualifications you have, and include all the information usually found on an application form. Write the letter in standard English, making certain that it is neat, accurate, and correct.

RÉSUMÉ

The purpose of a résumé is to make an employer want to interview you. A résumé tells prospective employers what you are like and what you can do for them. A good résumé summarizes you at your best in a one- or two-page outline. It should include the following information:

1. **Identification.** Include your name, address, telephone number, and e-mail address.
2. **Objective.** Indicate the type of job you are looking for.
3. **Experience.** List experience related to the specific job for which you are applying. List other work if you have not worked in a related field.
4. **Education.** Include schools attended from high school on, the dates of attendance, and diplomas or degrees earned. You may also include courses

related to the job you are applying for.

5. **References.** Include up to three references or indicate that they are available. Always ask people ahead of time if they are willing to be listed as references for you.

A résumé that you put online or send by e-mail is called an electronic résumé. Some Web sites allow you to post them on their sites without charge. Employers access these sites to find new employees. Your electronic résumé should follow the guidelines for a regular one. It needs to be accurate. Stress your skills and sell yourself to prospective employers.

COVER LETTER

If you are going to get the job you want, you need to write a great cover letter to accompany your résumé. Think of a cover letter as an introduction: a piece of paper that conveys a smile, a confident hello, and a nice, firm handshake. The cover letter is the first thing a potential employer sees, and it can make a powerful impression. The following are some tips for creating a cover letter that is professional and gets the attention you want:

- **Keep it short.** Your cover letter should be one page, no more.
- **Make it look professional.** These days, you need to type your letter on a computer and print it on a laser printer. Do not use an inkjet printer unless it produces extremely crisp type. Use white or buff-colored paper; anything else will draw the wrong kind of attention. Type your name, address, phone number, and e-mail address at the top of the page.
- **Explain why you are writing.** Start your letter with one sentence describing where you heard of the opening. "Joan Wright suggested I contact you regarding a position in your marketing department," or "I am writing to apply for the position you advertised in the Sun City Journal."
- **Introduce yourself.** Give a short description of your professional abilities and background. Refer to your attached résumé: "As you will see in the attached résumé, I am an experienced editor with a background in newspapers, magazines, and textbooks." Then highlight one or two

specific accomplishments.

- **Sell yourself.** Your cover letter should leave the reader thinking, "This person is exactly what we are looking for." Focus on what you can do for the company. Relate your skills to the skills and responsibilities mentioned in the job listing. If the ad mentions solving problems, relate a problem you solved at school or work. If the ad mentions specific skills or knowledge required, mention your mastery of these in your letter. (Also be sure these skills are included on your résumé.)

- **Provide all requested information.** If the Help Wanted ad asked for "salary requirements" or "salary history," include this information in your cover letter. However, you do not have to give specific numbers. It is okay to say, "My wage is in the range of $10 to $15 per hour." If the employer does not ask for salary information, do not offer any.

- **Ask for an interview.** You have sold yourself, now wrap it up. Be confident, but not pushy. "If you agree that I would be an asset to your company, please call me at [insert your phone number]. I am available for an interview at your convenience." Finally, thank the person. "Thank you for your consideration. I look forward to hearing from you soon." Always close with a "Sincerely," followed by your full name and signature.

- **Check for errors.** Read and re-read your letter to make sure each sentence is correctly worded and there are no errors in spelling, punctuation, or grammar. Do not rely on your computer's spell checker or grammar checker. A spell check will not detect if you typed "tot he" instead of "to the." It is a good idea to have someone else read your letter, too. He or she might notice an error you overlooked.

INTERVIEW

Understanding how to best prepare for and follow up on interviews is critical to your career success. At different times in your life, you may interview with a teacher or professor, a prospective employer, a supervisor, or a promotion or tenure committee. Just as having an excellent résumé is vital for opening the door, interview skills are critical for putting your best foot forward and seizing the opportunity to clearly articulate why you are the best person for the job.

RESEARCH THE COMPANY

Your ability to convince an employer that you understand and are interested in the field you are interviewing to enter is important. Show that you have knowledge about the company and the industry. What products or services does the company offer? How is it doing? What is the competition? Use your research to demonstrate your understanding of the company.

PREPARE QUESTIONS FOR THE INTERVIEWER

Prepare interview questions to ask the interviewer. Some examples include:

- "What would my responsibilities be?"
- "Could you describe my work environment?"
- "What are the chances to move up in the company?"
- "Do you offer training?"
- "What can you tell me about the people who work here?"

DRESS APPROPRIATELY

You will never get a second chance to make a good first impression. Nonverbal communication is 90 percent of communication, so dressing appropriately is of the utmost importance. Every job is different, and you should wear clothing that is appropriate for the job for which you are applying. In most situations, you will be safe if you wear clean, pressed, conservative business clothes in neutral colors. Pay special attention to grooming. Keep makeup light and wear very little jewelry. Make certain your nails and hair are clean, trimmed, and neat. Do not carry a large purse, backpack, books, or coat. Simply carry a pad of paper, a pen, and extra copies of your résumé and letters of reference in a small folder.

EXHIBIT GOOD BEHAVIOR

Conduct yourself properly during an interview. Go alone; be courteous and polite to everyone you meet. Relax and focus on your purpose: to make the best possible impression.

CAREER APPENDIX

- Be on time.
- Be poised and relaxed.
- Avoid nervous habits.
- Avoid littering your speech with verbal clutter such as "you know," "um," and "like."
- Look your interviewer in the eye and speak with confidence.
- Use nonverbal techniques to reinforce your confidence, such as a firm handshake and poised demeanor.
- Convey maturity by exhibiting the ability to tolerate differences of opinion.
- Never call anyone by a first name unless you are asked to do so.
- Know the name, title, and the pronunciation of the interviewer's name.
- Do not sit down until the interviewer does.
- Do not talk too much about your personal life.
- Never bad-mouth your former employers.

BE PREPARED FOR COMMON INTERVIEW QUESTIONS

You can never be sure exactly what will happen at an interview, but you can be prepared for common interview questions. There are some interview questions that are illegal. Interviewers should not ask you about your age, gender, color, race, or religion. Employers should not ask whether you are married or pregnant, or question your health or disabilities.

Take time to think about your answers now. You might even write them down to clarify your thinking. The key to all interview questions is to be honest, and to be positive. Focus your answers on skills and abilities that apply to the job you are seeking. Practice answering the following questions with a friend:

- "Tell me about yourself."
- "Why do you want to work at this company?"
- "What did you like/dislike about your last job?"
- "What is your biggest accomplishment?"
- "What is your greatest strength?"
- "What is your greatest weakness?"
- "Do you prefer to work with others or on your own?"
- "What are your career goals?" or "Where do you see yourself in five years?"
- "Tell me about a time that you had a lot of work to do in a short time. How did you manage the situation?"
- "Have you ever had to work closely with a person you didn't get along with? How did you handle the situation?"

AFTER THE INTERVIEW

Be sure to thank the interviewer after the interview for his or her time and effort. Do not forget to follow up after the interview. Ask, "What is the next step?" If you are told to call in a few days, wait two or three days before calling back.

If the interview went well, the employer may call you to offer you the job. Find out the terms of the job offer, including job title and pay. Decide whether you want the job. If you decide not to accept the job, write a letter of rejection. Be courteous and thank the person for the opportunity and the offer. You may wish to give a brief general reason for not accepting the job. Leave the door open for possible employment in the future.

FOLLOW UP WITH A LETTER

Write a thank-you letter as soon as the interview is over. This shows your good manners, interest, and enthusiasm for the job. It also shows that you are organized. Make the letter neat and courteous. Thank the interviewer. Sell yourself again.

ACCEPTING A NEW JOB

If you decide to take the job, write a letter of acceptance. The letter should include some words of appreciation for the opportunity, written acceptance of the job offer, the terms of employment (salary, hours, benefits), and the starting date. Make sure the letter is neat and correct.

STARTING A NEW JOB

Your first day of work will be busy. Determine what the dress code is and dress appropriately. Learn to do each task assigned properly. Ask for help when you need it. Learn the rules and regulations of the workplace.

You will do some paperwork on your first day. Bring your personal fact sheet with you. You will need to fill out some forms. Form W-4 tells your employer how much money to withhold for taxes. You may also need to fill out Form I-9. This shows that you are allowed to work in the United States. You will need your Social Security number and proof that you are allowed to work in the United States. You can bring your U.S. passport, your Certificate of Naturalization, or your Certificate of U.S. Citizenship. If you are not a permanent resident of the United States, bring your green card. If you are a resident of the United States, you will need to bring your work permit on your first day. If you are under the age of 16 in some states, you need a different kind of work permit.

You might be requested to take a drug test as a requirement for employment in some states. This could be for the safety of you and your coworkers, especially when working with machinery or other equipment.

IMPORTANT SKILLS AND QUALITIES

You will not work alone on a job. You will need to learn skills for getting along and being a team player. There are many good qualities necessary to get along in the workplace. They include being positive, showing sympathy, taking an interest in others, tolerating differences, laughing a little, and showing respect. Your employer may promote you or give you a raise if you show good employability skills.

There are several qualities necessary to be a good employee and get ahead in your job.

- Be cooperative.
- Possess good character.
- Be responsible.
- Finish what you start.
- Work fast but do a good job.
- Have a strong work ethic.
- Work well without supervision.
- Work well with others.

- Possess initiative.
- Show enthusiasm for what you do.
- Be on time.
- Make the best of your time.
- Obey company laws and rules.
- Be honest.
- Be loyal.
- Exhibit good health habits.

LEAVING A JOB

If you are considering leaving your job or are being laid off, you are facing one of the most difficult aspects in your career. The first step in resigning is to prepare a short resignation letter to offer your supervisor at the conclusion of the meeting you set up with him or her. Keep the letter short and to the point. Express your appreciation for the opportunity you had with the company. Do not try to list all that was wrong with the job.

You want to leave on good terms. Do not forget to ask for a reference. Do not talk about your employer or any of your coworkers. Do not talk negatively about your employer when you apply for a new job.

If you are being laid off or face downsizing, it can make you feel angry or depressed. Try to view it as a career-change opportunity. If possible, negotiate a good severance package. Find out about any benefits you may be entitled to. Perhaps the company will offer job-search services or consultation for finding new employment.

🌑 TAKE ACTION!

It is time for action. Remember the networking and contact lists you created when you searched for this job. Reach out for support from friends, family, and other acquaintances. Consider joining a job-search club. Assess your skills. Upgrade them if necessary. Examine your attitude and your vocational choices. Decide the direction you wish to take and move on!

CAREER APPENDIX

Glossary

How to Use This Glossary

- Content vocabulary terms in this glossary are words that relate to this book's content. They are **highlighted yellow** in your text.

- Words in this glossary that have an asterisk (*) are academic vocabulary terms. They help you understand your school subjects and are used on tests. They are boldfaced blue in your text.

- Some of the vocabulary words in this book include pronunciation symbols to help you sound out the words. Use the pronunciation key to help you pronounce the words.

Pronunciation Key		
a . . . . at	ô . . . . fork, all	th . . . thin
ā . . . . ape	oo . . . wood, put	th . . . this
ä . . . . father	o͞o . . . fool	zh . . . treasure
e . . . . end	oi . . . oil	ə . . . . ago, taken, pencil, lemon, circus
ē . . . . me	ou . . . out	
i . . . . it	u . . . . up	' . . . . indicates primary stress (symbol in front of and *above* letter)
ī . . . . ice	ū . . . . use	
o . . . . hot	ü . . . . rule	ˌ . . . . indicates secondary stress (symbol in front of and *below* letter)
ō . . . . hope	u̇ . . . . pull	
ȯ . . . . saw	ŋ . . . . sing	

à la carte Each item has a separate price. (p. 585)

abbreviation A short form of a word. (p. 492)

abstinence A deliberate decision to avoid high-risk behaviors, including sexual activity and the use of tobacco, alcohol, and other drugs. (p. 353)

*abstract** Vague. (p. 179)

academic skill Competencies in reading, writing, mathematics, or science. (p. 88)

accessory A small item of clothing that completes an outfit. (p. 609)

*accommodate** Fit. (p. 281)

*accumulate** Slowly gain. (p. 125)

*accurate** Free from error. (p. 425, 558)

acne A skin problem that develops when pores in the skin becomes blocked with oil, dead skin cells, and bacteria. (p. 259, 333)

acquaintance A person you may know but who is not a personal friend. (p. 185)

*acquire** Develop. (p. 490)

acquired immunodeficiency syndrome (AIDS) A life-threatening STI that interferes with the body's natural ability to fight infection. (p. 356)

active listening Listening and responding with full attention to what another person says. (p. 141)

*acuity** Sharpness. (p. 348)

addiction A dependence upon a particular substance or action. (p. 238, 348)

*address** Deal with. (p. 98)

*adequate** Enough. (p. 493)

adolescence The stage of growth between childhood and adulthood. (p. 7)

adoptive family A family with a child who was made part of the family through legal action. (p. 207)

*adverse Harmful. (p. 350)

age span The number of years between siblings. (p. 216)

al dente Tender but firm to the tooth. (p. 537)

alcoholic Someone who is addicted to alcohol. (p. 238)

alcoholism Physical and mental dependence on alcohol. (p. 238)

*alter Change. (p. 500)

amino acid A molecule that combines with other amino acid molecules to make up proteins. (p. 369)

anabolic steroid A manufactured substance that alters body characteristics. (p. 351)

anorexia nervosa Characterized by self-starvation. (p. 346)

*anticipate Predict. (p. 478)

apartment A rental unit in a building, or a structure that houses units for more than two families. (p. 711)

appetizer An optional first course, and generally a small portion. (p. 585)

*appropriate Suitable. (p. 138)

aptitude Natural tendency or talent that makes it easy for each of us to learn certain skills. (p. 71)

aroma A pleasant or savory smell. (p. 525)

assertiveness Standing up for yourself and your beliefs in a firm but positive way. (p. 146)

asymmetrical balance Something is not symmetrical. (p. 720)

*attentive Pay special attention. (p. 343)

B

background The walls, floors, windows, and ceiling of a living area. (p. 721)

bacteria One-celled living organisms so small that they can be seen only with a microscope. (p. 451)

basal metabolic rate (BMR) The rate at which your body uses energy when you are inactive. (p. 345)

basting A sewing technique that is used at the beginning of a project or project step to help you prevent later mistakes in clothing fit or appearance. (p. 678)

*beneficial Producing results that are to your advantage. (p. 176)

benefit A reward for employment besides salary, may include health insurance, personal financial savings plans or retirement plans, and paid vacations. (p. 125)

bias The diagonal line formed when the fabric is folded with the crosswise grain parallel to the selvage. (p. 664)

blended family A husband and wife, at least one of whom has children from a former relationship. (p. 207)

body language The use of gestures and other body movements to communicate. (p. 139)

boil Involves heating liquid at a high temperature so that bubbles rise and break on the liquid surface. (p. 519)

braise To simmer and steam food in a small amount of liquid. (p. 519)

bran The coarse outer layer of the grain. (p. 536)

broil To cook food directly under a heat source. (p. 516)

budget A plan for spending and saving the money you have available. (p. 308)

bulimia nervosa A disorder in which people eat large quantities of food in a short period of time and then purge. (p. 346)

C

calorie A unit for measuring energy. (p. 377)

carbohydrate A nutrient that provides your body with most of its energy. (p. 368)

cardiopulmonary resuscitation (CPR) A rescue technique used to keep a person's heart and lungs functioning until medical care arrives. (p. 270)

career A series of related jobs or occupations in a particular field over a lifetime. (p. 63)

career cluster A large grouping of occupations that have certain characteristics in common. (p. 71)

casing A closed tunnel or space of fabric that can hold a piece of elastic or a drawstring in a waistband. (p. 692)

cereal grain A seed from a grass. (p. 538)

character A combination of traits that show strong ethical principles and maturity. (p. 37)

childproof Take steps to identify possible hazards and remove them, to help ensure children's safety. (p. 268)

cholesterol A fat-like substance found in the bloodstream and body cells that is needed for many body processes. (p. 371)

chronological résumé Lists your work experience and employment history in chronological order, that is, by date. (p. 110)

*circulation Flow. (p. 515)

citizen A member of a community, such as a school, city or town, or country. (p. 41)

citizenship Responsibilities of a citizen. (p. 41)

clipping Making small, straight cuts in the seam allowance. (p. 684)

clique A group that excludes others from its circle of friendship. (p. 183)

closure Finality, which helps people deal with a reality of a loss. (p. 235)

*coarse Rough. (p. 536)

communication The process of sending and receiving messages. (p. 137)

comparison shopping Comparing products, prices, and services to get the most value for the money. (p. 302, 444)

complete protein A food that contains all nine of the essential amino acids. (p.369)

*component Part. (p. 454)

*compress Squeeze together. (p. 124)

compromise Giving in on some points of disagreement and getting your way on others. (p. 164)

concussion A type of head injury, usually a jarring injury of the brain. (p. 270)

condominium An individually owned unit in a multiple-family dwelling. (p. 713)

conduction The transfer of heat energy through direct contact between a hot surface and food. (P. 515)

*configuration Arrangement. (p. 691)

conflict A disagreement or fight between people with opposing points of view. (p. 155)

conflict resolution The process of settling a conflict through cooperation and problem solving. (p. 163)

conscience An inner sense of right or wrong. (p. 255)

*conscious Deliberate. (p. 219)

*consensus A decision agreeable to everyone. (p. 213)

conservation The protection of resources against waste and harm. (p. 743)

*conserve Save. (p. 543)

*consideration Continued and careful thought. (p. 45)

*consist Is made up of. (p. 535)

*consistent Free from variation of contradiction. (p. 387)

*constructive Positive and useful ways. (p. 155)

consumer Someone who buys and uses goods and services produced by others. (p. 301)

*contrast Differ. (p. 706)

convection The transfer of heat through the use of hot air or hot liquid. (p. 515)

convenience foods Prepared or partially prepared foods. (p. 418)

*convey Communicate. (p. 599)

cookware Pots, pans, and other containers for use on top of the range, in the oven, or in the microwave. (p. 471)

cooperative A less common form of ownership where residents of a multiple-family dwelling form a corporation that owns the building. Also called a co-op. (p. 713)

cooperative play Children play with other children and learn to share, take turns, solve problems, and control their emotions. (p. 256)

cooperative program An arrangement in which schools partner with local businesses. (p. 78)

core To remove the center. (p. 548)

*correspond Relate. (p. 254)

cost-effective Less expensive for the benefits produced. (p. 315)

*counteract Neutralize. (p. 391)

course Part of a meal. (p. 585)

cover letter A document that tells the employer that you are applying for a position in the company. (p. 112)

credit rating A record that shows your ability and willingness to pay your debts. (p. 229)

creditor A person or company to whom you owe money. (p. 229)

crisis (ˈkrī-səs) A situation that has reached a critical phase. (p. 239)

cross-contamination When harmful bacteria are transferred from one food or surface to another. (p. 455)

culture Everything that defines the identity of a specific group of people, including their common traits and customs. (p. 208)

curdle Separate into curds and whey. (p. 565)

*current Up-to-date. (p. 67)

customary measurement system The measurement system used in the United States. (p. 492)

dandruff Scales and flakes on the scalp. (p. 334)

*deadlock A situation in which no further progress is possible in a dispute. (p. 165)

decision making The act of making a choice. (p. 45)

*decline Refuse. (p. 319)

deep-fat fry To cook food by completely covering it in fat. (p. 520)

deficiency Shortage. (p. 381)

*deliberate Done on purpose. (p. 288)

*delineate Define. (p. 717)

*demographics Changes in the characteristics of the population. (p. 47)

dependable Able to be counted on. (p. 185)

depressant Reduces blood pressure and slows heart and breathing rates. (p. 351)

*designate Select. (p. 27)

GLOSSARY

developmental milestone A skill achieved at a particular stage of life. (p. 254)

diabetes A condition in which the body cannot control blood sugar properly. (p. 402)

*dictate To give specific direction. (p. 679)

Dietary Guidelines for Americans Scientifically based advice for making smart food choices, balancing food choices and physical activity, and getting the most nutrition out of your calories. (p. 389)

dietary supplements Pills, capsules, and powders that are taken in addition to, or to supplement, a person's diet. (p. 408)

directional stitching Stitching in the direction of the grain. (p. 680)

discipline The process of helping children learn to behave in acceptable ways. (p. 286)

discrimination Unequal treatment based on factors such as race, religion, nationality, gender (male or female), age, or physical appearance.(p. 99)

*disintegrate Break down into small parts. (p. 443)

*dissolve Break apart. (p. 544)

*distinct Specific. (p. 564)

domestic violence When physical force is used to harm a family member. (p. 242)

dovetail Skillfully fitting tasks together to make the best use of time. (p. 429)

downsizing When a company eliminates jobs to save money. (p. 101)

*drape Hang in loose folds when placed over something. (p. 623)

dry-cleaning Cleaning with chemicals rather than water and detergent. (p. 638)

dry-heat cooking Cooking food uncovered without adding liquid or fat. (p. 516)

duplex One structure that contains two separate units. (p. 711)

*durable Strong and long-lasting. (p. 622)

E

ease The extra room needed for movement and comfort. (p. 667)

element of design Line, shape, space, texture, and color. (p. 600)

embroider Add needlework details. (p. 652)

emotional abuse The wrong or harmful treatment of someone's emotional health. (p. 242)

*empathy The ability to understand what someone else is experiencing. (p. 146, 185)

*emphasis Focal point. (p. 720)

empty nest A home where children have left to be on their own, allowing couples more time to enjoy hobbies, community activities, and volunteer work. (p. 209)

*encourage Persuade or urge. (p. 580)

endorse Sign your name on the back. (p. 309)

endosperm The inner part of the grain that is mostly carbohydrate or some protein. (p. 535)

*enhance Improve. (p. 8)

enriched Nutrients added back after processing. (p. 536)

*entail Involve. (p. 731)

entrée The main course. (p. 585)

entrepreneur Someone who sets up and operates a business. (p. 65)

enunciate (ē-'nen(t)-sē-ˌ'at) To speak each sound clearly and distinctly. (p. 138)

environment Everything around you, including people, places, things, and events. (p. 9)

equivalent An amount that is equal to another amount. (p. 492)

*erosion Wearing away of soil. (p. 743)

escalate Grow. (p. 163)

*establish Set up. (p. 146, 634)

ethical principle A standard for right and wrong behavior. (p. 37)

etiquette Accepted rules of behavior. (p. 577)

*excess More than the needed amount. (p. 406, 667)

expense A good or service you purchase.(p. 308)

*exploit Use others for selfish purposes. (p. 322)

exploratory interview A short, informal talk with someone who works in a career that appeals to you. (p. 73)

*exposed Not shielded. (p. 560)

extended family A family that includes relatives other than parents and their children. (p. 207)

external conflict A disagreement between family members, friends, or community members. (p. 155)

F

facing A fabric that finishes a raw edge, such as a front opening, armhole, or collar. (p.684)

fad Fashion that is extremely popular but soon goes out of style. (p. 609)

family life cycle Certain predictable stages from couplehood to final years. (p. 209)

fashion A style of something that is currently popular. (p. 599)

*fatigue Extreme exhaustion. (p. 381)

fiber Plant material that does not break down during digestion. (p. 368)

fiber A hair-like substance twisted together with other hair-like strands to make yarns and fabric. (p. 621)

GLOSSARY

financial Money-related. (p. 228)

***fine** Thin. (p. 468)

finish A special treatment that makes a fiber or fabric more useful and appealing. (p. 628)

flatware Eating utensils. (p. 577)

***flexible** Open to adaptation. (p. 503)

flextime Workers adjust their daily work schedules to meet family needs as long as the workers put in the required number of hours on the job. (p. 124)

food additive A substance added to foods during processing to make them safer, more appealing or more nutritious. (p. 407)

food allergy A reaction of the body's immune system to ingested food. (p. 402)

food product dating The process of dating food to indicate product freshness. (p. 446)

foodborne illness Food poisoning caused by eating unsafe food. (p. 451)

foster family A family that takes care of children on a short-term basis. (p. 207)

***fragrant** Sweet-smelling. (p. 525)

fraud Telling lies to steal money or valuables. (p. 319)

fringe benefit A service or product you receive for little or at no cost to you. (p. 74)

***function** Work. (p. 205)

functional food A food that provides benefits beyond basic nutrition. (p. 407)

functional furniture Furniture that meets specific needs. (p. 722)

G

gathers Soft folds of fabric. (p. 691)

***gauge** Measure. (p. 649)

gene The basic unit of heredity. (p. 253)

generic name The common name for a group of similar fibers. (p. 624)

germ The small base of the seed. (p. 535)

global environment All living and nonliving elements on Earth. (p. 742)

global warming The gradual increase in the Earth's surface temperature. (p. 743)

goal Something you plan to do, be, or obtain. (p. 15)

grading Trimming the seam allowances in layers to reduce the bulk. (p. 684)

***grasp** Understanding. (p. 677)

graze Eating several small meals throughout the day. (p. 415)

grief Emotions and physical feelings that can be very painful. (p. 235)

grooming The personal care routine you follow to keep yourself clean and well-groomed. (p. 332)

H

hallucinogen A street drug that distorts the user's thoughts, moods, and senses. (p. 351)

hand-eye coordination The ability of the eyes and the hand and arm muscles to work together to make complex movements. (p. 251)

harassment Behavior that is unwelcome and disturbing to others. (p. 100)

***harbor** Contain. (p. 566)

hazard A source of danger. (p. 735)

heredity The characteristics passed from parents to children, also influences your personality. (p. 9)

high-density lipoprotein A type of protein that removes cholesterol from blood and artery walls to the liver. (p. 371)

home maintenance Eliminating clutter, organizing household and personal items, cleaning, making minor repairs or changes, and keeping household equipment in good working order. (p. 731)

homogenize (hō-ˌmä-jə-ˌnīz) To break up the fat particles and distribute them throughout the milk. (p. 448)

hormone A chemical substance in the body that helps stimulate body changes and the development of the reproductive system. (p. 7)

hybrid A vehicle that uses a combination of electricity and fuel. (p. 315)

I

identity theft The illegal use of someone else's personal information. (p. 318)

illusion Something can influence or lead the eye to see something that does not exist. (p. 599)

***immerse** Plunge into something completely. (p. 29)

immersible The entire appliance can be put safely into water to be washed. (p. 473)

***implement** Carry out. (p. 89)

impulse purchase An unnecessary item that is bought without much thought. (p. 302, 441)

income The amount of money that you receive. (p. 301)

incomplete protein A food that lacks one or more of the nine essential amino acids. (p. 369)

***incorporate** Blend or combine. (p.417)

***incur** Become subject to. (p. 228)

***indefinitely** Without end. (p. 742)

***indicate** Point out. (p. 116, 268)

infatuation Intense attraction to another person that may or may not be one-sided. (p. 191) *influence Have an effect on. (p. 599)

*insight The power to understand the inner nature of things. (p. 8)

*instill Inspire. (p. 167)

insulin A chemical that helps blood sugar move into body cells. (p. 402)

interest Money a financial institution pays customers at regular intervals. (p. 309)

interfacing Special fabric used between the facing and the outside of a garment for stiffening and shape retention. (p. 662, 663)

internal conflict A struggle inside your heart or your head. (p. 155)

internship A short-term job or work project that usually requires formal commitment. (p. 77)

interview A meeting between a job applicant and an employer. (p. 115)

*invaluable Extremely useful and important. (p. 160)

*inventory An organized list detailing what you have. (p. 609)

iron To move the iron back and forth over the fabric to press out wrinkles. (p. 638)

irradiated food Food that has gone through a process that destroys bacteria, mold, and insects by passing it through a field of radiant energy similar to X-rays. (p. 407)

J

job Work that you do for pay. (p. 63)

job shadowing Following a worker for a few days on the job. (p. 76)

job sharing Two part-time workers share one full-time job, splitting the hours and the pay. (p. 124)

L

landlord An owner of rental housing. (p. 712)

large motor skill Movement and control of the back, legs, shoulders, and arms. (p. 251)

leader A person who has influence over and guides a group. (p. 50)

leadership The ability to lead, not just hold an office. (p. 50)

lease A written rental agreement. (p. 712)

leavening agent A substance that causes baked products to rise. (p. 538)

legume A plant in which seeds grow in pods. (p. 448, 566)

lifelong learning Keeping skills and knowledge up-to-date throughout your life. (p. 67)

low-density lipoprotein A type of protein that deposits cholesterol on artery walls, causing them to harden. (p. 371)

M

*major Most important. (p. 425)

manipulation A dishonest way to control or influence someone. (p. 177)

manufactured fibers Produced in laboratories through chemical processes and are made from substances such as wood pulp, petroleum, and other chemicals. (p. 622)

marbling Flecks of fat throughout the meat that add flavor and tenderness. (p. 556)

marinade A sauce used to flavor food. (p. 457)

meal pattern A way of grouping daily food choices into meals and snacks. (p. 415)

mediation A neutral third party is used to help reach a solution that is agreeable to everyone. (p. 165)

*mend Repair. (p. 631)

mentor An informal teacher or guide who demonstrates correct work behavior and shares knowledge. (p. 75)

metric system A system of weights and measures based on multiples of 10. (p. 492)

microfiber Superfine manufactured fiber. (p. 624)

microwaves Energy waves. (p. 477)

*mind Pay attention to. (p. 476)

*minimize Greatly reduce. (p. 141)

*minute Very small. (p. 372)

*model Imitate. (p. 286)

moist-heat cooking Method of cooking that uses added liquid or steam to cook and tenderize foods. (p. 519)

mortgage A long-term loan used to buy a home. (p. 713)

motor skill An ability that depends on the use and control of muscles. (p. 251)

multiplex Similar to a duplex, but three or more units share one building. (p. 711)

MyPlate An easy-to-use food guidance system developed by the U.S. Department of Agriculture (USDA). (p. 395)

N

natural fibers Fibers produced from plant and animal sources. (p. 622)

natural resource A resource that occur in nature. (p. 742)

need Something essential to your survival and well-being. (p. 47)

*neglect (v) Give little attention to. (p. 239)

neglect (n) A form of abuse that occurs when people fail to meet the needs of their children or the disabled adults in their care. (p. 242)

negotiate To deal or bargain with another person. (p. 160)

networking Making use of personal connections to achieve your goals. (p. 109)

night terror A type of sleep disorder that is more intense than a nightmare. (p. 267)

nightmare A bad dream. (p. 267)

nonrenewable resource Does not replace itself, and its supply is limited. (p. 742)

nonverbal communication Communication without words. (p. 137)

***norm** Usual. (p. 588)

notching Clipping V-shaped notches from the seam allowance. (p. 684)

notions The small items, such as thread, zippers, buttons, trim, seam binding, hooks and eyes, and snaps, needed to complete a garment. (p. 663)

nuclear family A mother, a father, and their children. (p. 206)

nurturing Giving of love, affection, attention, and encouragement. (p. 285)

nutrient A chemical substance that your body needs to function, grow, repair itself, and create energy. (p. 367)

nutrient density The amount of nutrients in a food item in relation to the number of calories. (p. 379)

nutrient-dense food A food that provides high amounts of vitamins and minerals for relatively few calories. (p. 390)

O

obesity Serious overweight as a result of excess body fat. (p. 390)

obligation Something you must do, such as a homework assignment, household chore, or after-school activity. (p. 23)

obsolete Out of date and no longer useful. (p. 318)

***obtain** Gain by planned action. (p. 90, 377)

occupation The type of work you do. (p. 63)

***occur** To take place. (p. 144)

P

panfry To fry tender cuts of meat, fish, and eggs in smaller amounts of fats in a skillet. (p. 520)

parallel play Children play alongside other children but not with them. (p. 255)

***pare** Peel. (p. 466)

parenting The process of caring for children and guiding their growth and development. (p. 279)

pasteurize ('pas-che-ˌrīz) To heat milk to destroy harmful bacteria. (p. 448)

peer A person of the same age group. (p. 175)

peer mediator A young person who listens to both parties in conflict and helps them find a solution. (p. 166)

peer pressure The pressure you feel to do what others your age are doing. (p. 175)

***perishable** Something that is likely to spoil easily. (p. 448, 557)

personality The combination of feelings, traits, attitudes, and habits that you show others. (p. 9)

***perspective** A particular evaluation of a situation or facts. (p. 184)

***philanthropy** Goodwill toward fellow humans, or an active effort to promote human welfare. (p. 64)

phytochemicals Substances that plants produce naturally to protect themselves from harm. (p. 374)

place setting The arrangement of tableware and flatware for each person. (p. 577)

plaque A sticky film that clings to your teeth, is formed by the food, bacteria, and air in your mouth. (p. 335)

poach Cooking whole or large pieces of food in a small amount of liquid. (p. 519)

poison control center A place that gives advice on treatment for poisoning. (p. 268)

portfolio A collection of work samples demonstrating your skills. (p. 114)

potential The possibility of becoming more than you are right now. (p. 11)

***praise** Expressions of approval. (p. 252)

prejudice An unfair opinion made without knowledge of the facts. (p. 148)

press To lift and lower an iron onto areas of the fabric. (p. 638)

pretreatment Any special attention you give a garment before laundering. (p. 636)

***primary** Main. (p. 417)

principle of design An artistic guideline that helps you combine the elements of design. (p. 604)

***prioritize** Rate in order of priority. (p. 610)

priority Something that is important to you. (p. 12)

problem solving Using thinking skills to suggest a solution to a problem. (p. 91)

produce Fruits and vegetables. (p. 447)

***proficient** Well advanced. (p. 71)

***proportions** Relative size with respect to another size. (p. 661)

protein A nutrient used to build, maintain, and repair body tissues. (p. 369)

puberty The set of changes that result in a physically mature body that is able to reproduce. (p. 7, 259)

R

radiation Energy that is transmitted through air waves. (p. 515)

rapport (ra-ˈpȯr) Harmony or understanding among people. (p. 146)

recipe A list of ingredients and instructions for preparing a dish. (p. 489)

redress The right to have a wrong corrected quickly and fairly. (p. 305)

*reduce Lessen. (p. 580)

refined grain A grain that is milled to remove the bran and the germ. (p. 536)

*reflect Think quietly and calmly. (p. 280)

*refrain Keep yourself from. (p. 453)

refusal skill A basic communication skill you can use to say no effectively. (p. 180)

*reinforce Strengthen. (p. 38)

*relevant Related. (p. 112)

renewable resource Replaces or renews itself over time. (p. 742)

repetitive stress injury A joint injury caused by repeated motions. (p. 320)

requirement Something needed. (p. 585)

*resolve Find a solution to a problem. (p. 99)

resource Anything you use to help accomplish something. (p. 13)

respect Belief in the equal worth of others. (p. 144)

responsibility Accountability for choices you make and things you do. (p. 39)

résumé (ˈre-zə-ˌmā) A brief history of your work experience and education. (p. 110)

roast Refers to cooking large pieces of meat or poultry in a shallow pan. (p. 516)

role An expected pattern of behavior. (p. 212)

role model A person who sets a positive example for others. (p. 37)

*route A course of action. (p. 70)

S

salmonella A dangerous bacteria that causes foodborne illness. (p. 563)

sanitize Thoroughly clean. (p. 451)

scorch Burn. (p. 565)

seam allowance The fabric between the seam line and the cut edge. (p. 680)

sedentary Inactive. (p. 392)

self-esteem The confidence you feel about yourself. (p. 10)

self-respect A belief in your own worth. (p. 144)

selvage The finished lengthwise edge of the fabric. (p. 664)

sensory Related to one or more of the five senses. (p. 264)

serrated Saw-toothed. (p. 466)

sexually transmitted infection (STI) An illness passed from one person to another through sexual contact. (p. 353)

shock A physical condition characterized by inadequate blood flow which can be very serious. (p. 270)

sibling A brother or sister. (p. 213)

sibling rivalry Competition for the love and attention of parents. (p. 217)

silhouette The form created when lines are combined. (p. 600)

simmer To heat liquid to a temperature just below the boiling point until bubbles barely break on the liquid surface. (p. 519)

single-parent family One parent raises the children. (p. 206)

skill The ability to do a certain task well. (p. 70)

skills résumé Experience organized according to specific skills or functions. (p. 110)

*slight Small. (p. 304)

small motor skill Movement and control of smaller body parts, such as the hands and fingers. (p. 251)

social skills Ways of relating to other people. (p. 205)

society A group of people who have developed patterns of relationships from being around one another. (p. 205)

*sole Only. (p. 303)

staple A food you are likely to use often, such as milk, eggs, pasta, rice, or bread. (p. 441)

stay-stitching A row of stitching on one layer of fabric that prevents the edges from stretching as you handle the fabric. (p. 679)

steam To cook food over boiling water, rather than in it. (p. 519)

stereotype The belief that an entire group of people are alike in certain ways. (p. 148)

stew To cook it slowly in liquid for a long period of time. (p. 519)

stimulant Increases a person's heart rate, speeds up the central nervous system, increases breathing rate, and raises blood pressure. (p. 351)

stir-fry Cooking small pieces of food quickly at high heat in a very small amount of fat, stirring the entire time. (p. 520)

*strenuous Demanding. (p. 405)

stress Mental, emotional, or physical strain. (p. 27, 124, 341)

*subtle Not obvious. (p. 698)

*suit Please. (p. 707)

*survey Examine. (p. 735)

symmetrical balance When objects on one side of an imaginary center line are the mirror image of those on the other side. (p. 720)

tableware Includes dishes, glasses, and flatware. (p. 577)

tact The ability to communicate something difficult without hurting another person's feelings. (p. 146)

teamwork Members of a group work together to reach a common goal. (p. 91)

technology The application of science to help people meet needs and wants. (p. 314)

telecommute Work at home and communicate with customers and coworkers by phone, fax, and computer. (p. 124)

telemarketing Selling over the telephone. (p. 319)

tension The tightness or looseness of the thread. (p. 656)

texture The way something feels. (p. 524)

thinking skill Mental skills you use to learn, make decisions, analyze, and solve problems. (p. 91)

*thrive Gain in size, wealth, or possessions. (p. 41)

tolerance The ability to accept and respect other people's customs and beliefs. (p. 158)

townhouse A house built in a row of other townhouses. (p. 711)

*trace A barely detectable amount. (p. 373)

trade name A company's name for a specific fiber that it manufactures. (p. 624)

tradition A custom passed from one generation to another. (p. 206)

traffic pattern The path people use to get from one area or room to another. (p. 722)

*transfer Movement. (p. 515)

transferable skill A skill that can be used in many different situations. (p. 87)

*translucent See-through. (p. 524)

U

understitching Stitching the facing to the seam allowances. (p. 684)

*unique (yü'nēk) One of a kind. (p. 206)

unit price The price per ounce, pound, or other unit of measure. (p. 445)

universal values Values that are generally accepted and shared worldwide. (p. 38)

*upset Turned upside down. (p. 232)

utensil A small cooking tool. (p. 466)

utility A basic service, such as electricity, cable, gas, or oil, phone, water, and sewer service. (p. 707)

vaccine A small amount of dead germs introduced to the body so that the body can recognize danger and build resistance to a disease. (p. 285)

value A belief or idea about what is important. (p. 37)

vegan Someone who does not eat any animal products, including dairy products or eggs. (p. 403)

vegetarian Someone who does not eat meat, poultry, or fish. (p. 403)

verbal communication Communication using words, both spoken and written. (p. 137)

*versatile Having many uses or functions. (p. 652).

video teleconferencing Enables people in different locations to see and hear each other at the same time. (p. 315)

*view Observe. (p. 238)

*vigorous Forceful and energetic. (p. 338)

W

want Something you desire, even though it is not essential. (p. 47)

warranty A guarantee that a product will work properly for a specific length of time unless misused or mishandled by the consumer. (p. 306)

wellness A positive approach to life based on healthy attitudes and actions. (p. 331)

whole grain A grain that has the entire grain kernel. (p. 535)

wilt Become less firm. (p. 544)

work ethic Working hard, being honest, and staying committed to your work responsibilities. (p. 92)

work simplification The easiest and quickest way to do a job well. (p. 26)

yarn Hair like strands of materials. (p. 621)

yield The amount of food or the number of servings a recipe makes. (p. 500)

GLOSSARY

Index

A

À la carte, 585
Abbreviations, recipe, 492
Abstinence, 353
Abuse. *See also* Violence in the home
    breaking the silence of, 240–241
    responding to, 243
Academic skills, 88–89
Accent lighting, 723
Accessibility, 706, 708–709
Accessory, 609
Accidents
    preparing for, 270
    preventing, 581
Accusations, 147
Acetate, 622
Acne, 259, 333
Acquaintance, 185
Acquired immunodeficiency syndrome (AIDS), 354
Acrylic, 623
Acting responsibly, 215
Active listening, 141–142
Activities
    aerobic, 336
    prioritizing, 343
    and reaching your potential, 12
Addiction, 238–241
    alcoholism, 238
    and crime, 240
    defined, 238, 348
    drug, 239
    effects of, on family and society, 239
    solutions to, 241
Addition, with decimal places, 65
Additives, food, 405
Adjustment line, 666
Adolescence
    changes during, 7–8
    defined, 7
    development during, 259
    intellectual changes during, 8
    physical changes during, 7
    social and emotional changes during, 8
Adoptive family, 207
Advertisement (writing assignment), 299
Advertising, and purchases, 301
Aerobic activity, 336, 337
After-school programs, 112
Age span, 216
Aggressive response, 180
Agreeing to disagree, 166
AIDS (acquired immunodeficiency syndrome), 354

Al dente, 537, 543
Alcohol use
    avoiding, 392
    and drugs, 352
    fun without, 348
    as health risk, 349
Alcoholism, 238, 349
Allergies
    fabric, 634
    food, 400–401, 564
    science of, 401
Alterations, sewing, 690, 691
Alternative basting, 678
Amino acids, 369
Anabolic steroids, 351
Analogous colors, 719
Anemia, 381
Anger
    hot, 160
    pent-up, 159
Anger management, 159–160
Anorexia nervosa, 346
Anti-smoking campaigns, 348
Anxiety, controlling, 28
Apartment, 711
Apartment living, 732
Apologies, accepting, 166
Appeal
    meal, 416, 543
Appearance
    and food doneness, 524
    for job, 122
    as nonverbal communication, 140
Appetite, 404
Appetizers, 421, 585
Appliances
    carbon monoxide and gas, 737
    cost of, 475
    energy for, 745
    energy-efficient, 748
    major kitchen, 475–479
    small kitchen, 473–475
Applying for jobs, 109–120
    cover letters, 113–114
    following up after, 119–120
    interviewing, 115–120
    networking, 109
    portfolios, 114
    résumés, 110–112
Appreciation
    for meal, 581
    showing, 215
Aptitude, 71
Aroma, food, 525
Asian Pasta Salad (recipe), 480
Asking questions, 604
Assertive response, 180
Assertiveness, 146, 179
Asymmetrical balance, 720
Athletes, food choices for, 403
ATM (automatic teller machine), 310, 317

ATM cards, 310
Attendance, 179
Attention, paying, 370
Attitude
    know-it-all, 147
    poor-me, 147
    positive, 96, 119, 331
Audience, of message, 486
Autobiographical paragraphs, 153
Automatic teller machine. (ATM), 310, 317

B

Babysitting skills, 267
Backgrounds, 721–722
    ceilings, 722
    floors, 721
    walls, 721
    windows, 721
Backstitching, 655
Bacteria, 451
Bakeware, 470
Baking
    as dry-heat cooking, 516
    of fruits and vegetables, 544
    reducing fat in, 393
Baking sheets, 470
Balance (design principle), 604, 606, 720
Balancing your life, 21–29
    energy management for, 25, 26
    importance of, 21
    management plan for, 22
    organizing possessions for, 26–27
    and stress, 341
    stress management for, 27–29
    time management for, 23–25
    and work, 124–126
Banana Cream Trifle (recipe), 456
Bank deposits, 309
Bank statements, 310
Banking, 317
Basal metabolic rate (BMR), 345
Basters, 469
Basting (cooking), 497
Basting (sewing), 678
Bath time, 266
Bean Salad (recipe), 402
Beans. *See* Legumes
Beaters, 468
Beating, 496
Bedtime, 267
Beef steak, 558
Behavior
    observing, 636
    restaurant, 586
Behavior management
    in child care, 262–263
    in parenting, 286–289
Belong, desire to, 177
Benefits, employer, 74, 126

Best-if-used-by date, 446
Bias, fabric, 664
Biking, 744
Bills
    paperless, 744
    paying restaurant, 587
Binge eating disorders, 346
Biscuits, 539
Bleach, 635, 636
Blended family, 206
Blenders, 474
Blending (cooking term), 497
Blends, fabric, 625
BMR (basal metabolic rate), 345
Bobbin, 653–654
Bobbin case, 653–654
Bobbin winder, 653–654
Body composition, 345
Body language, 139
Body weight. *See* Weight, body
Boiling, 518, 519
Bones, 338
Bonuses, 678
Bookkeeping clerk, 458
Bowls, mixing, 468
Brainstorm, 164
Braising, 518
Bran, 536
Brand names, generic vs., 444–445
Bread knife, 466
Breads, 538–539
Break, taking a, 165, 190, 354
Breakfast
    eating, 118
    importance of, 415
    planning, 416
Breathing
    deep, 160
    and presentation skills, 138
Breathing (fabric term), 629
Broil, 516
Bruised produce, 447
Brushing (cooking term), 497
Buddy list, 139
Buddy system, 190
Budget
    clothing, 609
    creating a, 308
    food, 417, 442, 558
Buffet service, 579
Bulimia nervosa, 346
Bulk buying, 442, 746
Bulk food, storing, 454
Bullying
    cyberbullying, 164, 165,
        167, 178
    dealing with, 164–165, 178
    understanding, 167
Buttonhole knob, 652, 653
Buttons
    choosing, 662
    sewing on, 639–640
Buyer, retail, 102

Buyer beware, 303
Buying. *See* Shopping

C

Caffeine, 342
Cake pans, 470
Calories
    and energy, 377–378
    and nutrient-dense food, 390
    sources of, 378, 379
Canned goods
    buying, 447
    wiping lids of, 452
Carbohydrate intake, 404
Carbohydrates, 368
Carbon monoxide, 737
Cardiopulmonary resuscitation
    (CPR), 270, 739
Care, clothing, 611
Care label, 612, 634, 635
Care needs (fabric term), 629
Career cluster, 71–72
Career pathways, 63–79
    firsthand experience with,
        75–78
    and future job market, 78–79
    personal inventory for, 70–71
    preparing for, 67–68
    researching, 71–75
    and work, 63-68
Careers *See also* Job; Work
    bookkeeping clerk, 458
    computer programmer, 220
    correctional officer, 168
    defined, 63
    dietitian, 528
    early childhood teacher, 272
    EMT/paramedic, 382
    environmental scientist, 570
    information designer, 614
    investment advisor, 324
    landscape architect, 80
    legislator, 430
    life coach, 30
    parenthood changes in, 281
    pilot, 670
    power plant dispatcher, 482
    retail buyer, 102
    veterinarian, 724
Caring, 38, 185. *See also* Child care
Carpooling, 744
Cash loans, 311
Casings, 692–693
Casseroles, 470, 557
Cause and effect essay, 387
Ceilings, 722
Celebrations, planning, 586–587
Cell phones, 25, 125, 144, 339,
    441, 577, 586, 721
Cereals, 538
Character
    defined, 37
    demonstrating, 147

Character development, 37–43
    with citizenship, 41–43
    leadership skills, 50–52
    with personal responsibility,
        40, 41
    problem-solving skills, 50
    recognizing character in
        others, 37
    responsible decision making,
        45–49
    and values, 37–39
Check register, 310
Checkbooks, 310
Checking accounts, 309
Checks, 310
Cheese, 564
Chef's knife, 466
Chemicals, 268
Chicken, 558
Chicken Salad Extraordinaire
    (recipe), 419
Child care, 262–272
    accidents and emergencies,
        270–271
    bath time, 266
    becoming an expert, 267
    bedtime, 267
    behavior management,
        262–263
    clothing, 264–265
    early childhood teacher, 272
    entertaining children, 264
    fire emergencies, 271
    home safety, 270
    mealtime and snacks, 265–266
    outdoor safety, 269–270
    safety, 268–270
    toy safety, 269
Child development, 251–260
    adolescents, 259
    emotional, 252
    importance of play in, 258
    influences on, 253
    intellectual, 252
    language, 252
    moral, 252
    older infants, 255
    older toddlers, 255
    physical, 251
    and play, 258
    preschoolers, 256
    school-age children, 257
    social, 252
    and special needs, 259–260
    stages of, 254–259
    young infants, 254
    young toddlers, 255
Childproof, 268
Children. *See also* Infants; Toddlers
    entertaining, 264
    kitchen safety for, 481
    school-age, 257, 263
    supervision of, 268–269, 481

Choking, first aid for, 739
Cholesterol
    defined, 371
    in meat, poultry, and fish, 555
Choose, right to, 305
Chopping, 495
Chopping utensils, 466
Chronological résumé, 110
Circulation, 515
Circumstances, changes in, 227–231
    financial problems, 228–229
    health problems, 231
    homelessness, 231
    moving, 227–228
    natural disasters, 230
    unemployment, 229–230
Citizen, 41
Citizenship, 41–43
    defined, 41
    involvement in community, 42
    volunteering, 43
Citrus juice, 543
Clarity, 141
Clean finish, 681
Cleaning
    of clothes. *See* Laundering
    of home. *See* Home
    maintenance of kitchen
        equipment, 479
    outdoor, 732
Cleaning pads, 479
Cleaning products and equipment,
    732, 746
Cleaning up, in foods lab, 428
Clearing table, 583
Cleavers, 466
Clipping, 682
Cliques, 183
Closet organization, 631
Closure, 235
Clothing
    adjusting width of, 690
    for children, 264–265
    for cooking, 476
    for job interview, 115
    lengthening or shortening, 691
    optical illusions with, 664
    putting away, 734
    selecting quality, 610–611
    shopping for, 610–613
    as skin protection, 335
    and wardrobe assessment, 609
Clothing care, 631–642
    laundering, 634–638
    packing, 632–633
    repairing clothing, 638–642
    storage, 632–633
Clothing care labels, 634, 635
Clothing style, 599–607. *See also*
    Working wardrobe
    design elements, 600–603
    design principles, 604–607

Clutter, 733, 734
Coating, 497
Colanders, 469
Cold foods, 454
Color(s)
    analogous, 719
    in clothing design, 600–
        601, 603
    complementary, 719
    effects of, 601
    of fabric, 628
    of fruits and vegetables, 542
    in home decorating, 717–719
    intermediate, 718
    in meals, 416
    of meat, poultry and fish, 448
    monochromatic, 719
    primary, 718
    secondary, 718
    split-complementary, 719
    triadic, 719
Color-safe bleach, 636
Combine, 497
Communication, 137–148
    active listening, 141–142
    defined, 137
    mistakes in, 157
    nonverbal, 139–140
    overcoming roadblocks to,
        147–148
    positive, 137
    respectful, 144–147
    technology for, 315
    verbal, 137–138
    written, 140–141
Communication skills, 51, 94
Communications technology, 315
Community, responsibility to
    the, 188
Community Connections
    antismoking campaign, 348
    community pride, 176
    community resources, 46
    consumer research, 638
    converting measurements, 491
    cultural knowledge, 157
    environmentally-friendly
        cooking, 517
    farmers' market, 563
    food banks, 369
    give back, 184
    global interaction, 148
    health fair, 270
    hometown foods, 402
    housing for your
        community, 712
    international flavor, 416
    kitchen stores, 478
    on the job, 662
    pollution, 742
    preferred pasta survey, 537
    promoting school safety, 241

    recycled treasures, 309
    serving your community, 580
    sewing for a cause, 679
    sharing your cultural
        traditions, 210
    surplus food, 442
    uniforms, 609
    volunteering, 75
Community housing, 712
Community organizations and
    agencies, 244
Community pride, 176
Community resources, 13, 46
Community safety technology, 316
Compare and contrast essay, 329
Comparison shopping, 302,
    444–445
Compensation, 74
Complementary colors, 719
Complete protein, 369
Compost pile, 743
Compromise, 164
Computer programmer, 220
Computer virus, 319
Concentration, 141
Concussion, 270
Condiments, 393
Condominium, 713
Conduction, 515
Confidence, 11, 181
Conflict, 155–167
    avoiding, 158–160, 163
    with bullies, 164–165, 167
    causes of, 156–157
    defined, 155
    and friendship, 192
    negotiating, 160–161
    resolving, 163–166
    responding to, 163
    types of, 155
    understanding, 155
    in workplace, 98–99
Conflict resolution, 163–166
    agreeing to disagree, 166
    defined, 163
    mediation, 165, 166
    process of, 164
Conscience, 255
Conserving resources, 14, 742–748
    choices for, 748
    gas and oil, 744
    for heating and cooling, 745
    for lighting and
        appliances, 745
    natural resources, 742
    with precycle, reuse, and
        recycle, 746–747
    trees, 743–744
    water, 743
Consistency, and food
    doneness, 525
Consistent, being, 286

INDEX

Consumer credit counseling, 229
Consumer education, right to, 305
Consumer research, 638
Consumers, 301–312
    and credit, 311–312
    defined, 301
    factors affecting, 301
    and financial services, 308–311
    and money management,
        307–308
    and planning, 302–304
    resolving consumer
        problems, 306
    rights and responsibilities of,
        304–306
Contact information, 738
Convection, 515
Convection oven cooking, 517
Convection ovens, 477
Convenience foods, 418
Converting measurements, 490
Cooking, 515–527
    checking food for doneness,
        524–525
    combining methods of, 515
    conserving nutrients, 527
    convection-oven, 517
    creative, 547
    defined, 515
    dry-heat, 516–517
    eggs, 563
    environmentally-friendly, 517
    with fat, 520–521
    fruits and vegetables, 544, 546
    legumes, 566–567, 569
    meat, poultry, and fish, 558–559
    microwave, 521–522
    milk and milk products,
        565–566
    with moist heat, 518–519
    outdoor, 588
Cooking terms, 393
Cooking time, 525
Cookware
    defined, 471
    for dry-heat cooking, 517
    types of, 470
Cool colors, 601, 603
Cool down, 339
Coolers, 588
Cooling energy, 745
Cooling racks, 469
Cooperative education, 78
Cooperative play, 256
Cooperative program, 78
Cooperatives (co-ops), 713
Core (cooking term), 548
Corners, clothing, 611
Corporations, 65
Correctional officer, 168
Corruption, 242
Cost, price vs., 604
Cost-effective, 315

Cotton, 621
Countertops, washing, 452
Counting to ten, 160
Couples, 206
Coupons, 442
Courage, 177, 178
Course (meal term), 585
Cover letters, 107, 113–114
CPR. Cardiopulmonary resuscita-
    tion, 270, 739
Creaming, 496
Crease-resistant, 628
Creativity
    with cooking, 503–504, 547
    with sewing, 677
Credit, 311–312
    calculating cost of, 230
    controlling use of, 312
    costs of, 311
    types of, 311
Credit card finance charges, 230
Credit card statements, 318
Credit cards, 311
Credit rating, 229
Creditor, 229
Crime, and substance abuse, 240
Crisis, 239
Crisp food, 544
Criticism
    understanding, 516
    in workplace, 98
Cross-contamination, 455
Crunchy Melon Bowl (recipe), 545
Cubing, 495
Cultural differences, 157
Cultural knowledge, 157
Culture
    defined, 208
    ethnic foods, 416
    family, 208
    and food choices, 399
    influence of, 253
    and pasta survey, 537
    research your, 10
    sharing your, 210
Curdle, 565
Custard cups, 470
Customary measurement
    system, 492
Cutting, 495
Cutting boards
    cross-contamination with, 455
    as kitchen utensil, 469
    with knives, 494
    washing, 452
Cutting equipment (for sewing),
    649
Cutting in, 496
Cutting line, 666
Cutting out patterns, 668–669
Cutting up foods, at table, 581
Cutting utensils, 466
Cycles of abuse, 242–243

D

Daily tasks, 731
Dairy. *See* Milk and milk products
Dairy substitutions, 565
Dandruff, 334
Darts, 666
Dating, 191
Day care costs, 281
Death, 235–236
Debit cards, 310
Debt-to-income ratio, 160
Decimals
    addition with, 65
    rounding, 475
Decision making
    about having children, 279–280
    considering consequences
        of, 48
    defined, 45
    influences on, 45–47
    learning from decisions, 49
    making responsible, 45–49
    process of, 48–49
Decorating
    home. *See* Home decorating
    for mealtime, 587
Decorations, 587
Deep-fat frying, 520
Deficiencies, in nutrition, 381
Defrosting, 557
Dehydration, 374
Demographics, 47
Denominator, 281
Dented cans, 447
Dentists, 335
Department stores, 304
Dependability, 19, 185
Deposits, bank, 309
Depressants, 351
Depression
    and health, 342
    and suicide prevention, 343
Design
    in clothing, 600–607
    in home decorating, 716–721
Design elements, 600–603
    in clothing, 600–603
    color, 600–601, 603, 717–719
    form, 717
    in home decorating, 717–719
    line, 600, 602, 717
    shape, 600
    space, 600, 717
    texture, 600, 717
Design principles, 604–606
    balance, 604, 606, 720
    in clothing, 604–607
    emphasis, 604, 606, 720
    harmony, 604, 605
    in home decorating, 720–721
    proportion, 604–605, 720
    rhythm, 604–606, 721

scale, 720
unity, 720
Developmental milestone, 254
Diabetes, 400
Dialogue essay, 277
Dicing, 495
Diet. *See also* Nutrition
    fad diets, 391
    fruits and vegetables in your,
      546–548
    grains in your, 540
    meat, poultry, and fish in
      your, 556
    well-balanced, 367
Dietary Guidelines, 389–393
    alcohol, 392
    calories, 390
    fats, 393
    and food choices, 391
    and food safety, 393
    MyPyramid, 394–397
    nutrition planning, 395
    physical activity, 390
    potassium, 391
    recommended daily amounts,
      395–398
    sodium, 391
    sugar, 391
    and weight management, 390
Dietary Guidelines for
  Americans, 389
Dietary supplements, 406
Dietitian, 528
Digestive process, 377–381
    deficiencies in nutrition, 381
    energy and calories, 377–378
    nutrient density, 379
Digestive system, 377
Dining out, 585–587
    and nutrition, 418
    ordering from the menu, 585
    paying the bill, 587
    restaurant behavior, 586
Dining room table, 578
Directional stitching, 685
Dirt, 733
Disabilities
    and accessibility, 706, 708–709
    children with, 259–260
    learning, 260
    physical, 260
Discipline, 286
Discount stores, 304
Discrimination, 99
Discussion groups, 322
Dishtowels and dishcloths, 452, 479
Disrespect, 157
Distractions, avoiding, 455
Diversity
    of friends, 184
    promoting, 40
Divorce, 234–235

Doctors, 339–340
Documents, disposal of, 318
Domestic violence, 242
Doors, 268, 738
Double knits, 627
Dovetail, 429
Downsizing, 101
Draining, 497
Drape (fabric term), 622
Drawer storage, 632
Drug abuse, detecting, 352
Drug addiction
    and crime, 240
    effects of, on family and
      society, 239
    solutions to, 241
Drug use
    alcohol, 349
    and conflict, 157
    as health risk, 347
    illegal drugs, 350–351
    inhalants, 350
    prescription and over-the-
      counter, 351–352
    tobacco, 348
Dry cleaning, 635, 638
Dry food, storing, 454
Dry ingredients, measuring, 491
Dry measuring cups, 467
Dry-heat cooking, 516–517
Drying clothes, 635, 637
Duck, 558
Duplex, 711
Durable, 621
Dust, 733

E

Early childhood teacher, 272
Ease (sewing term), 667
Eating. *See also* Food
    away from home, 418, 420–422
    breakfast, 118
    and emotional changes, 8
    healthy. *See* Dietary guidelines
Eating disorders, 346–347
Eating patterns, 415
Education
    completing your, 279
    cooperative, 78
    parenting, 285
    technology for, 317
Educational requirements, 74
Egg separator, 563
Eggs
    checking for cracks on, 448
    nutrients in, 562
    preparing and cooking, 563
    storing, 563
Elastic, 663
Elastic waistbands, 693–694
Elastoester, 622
Electric grill, 474

Electric skillet, 474
Electrical hazards, 736
Electronic shopping, 304
Element of design, 600. *See also*
  Design elements
Emergencies, 737–740
    and accidents, 270
    calling for help, 737
    fire, 271, 740
    first aid, 739
    and home safety, 738
Emergency medical technician
  (EMT), 382
Emotional abuse, 242
Emotional control, 18
Emotional development, 252
Emotional health, 47, 340–343
Emotional needs, 705
Emotional problems, 260
Emotional support, 205
Emotions
    and conflict, 156
    science of, 192
Empathetic, 185
Empathy, 146, 185
Emphasis (design principle), 604,
  605, 720
Employee discrimination, 99
Employees, positive characteristics
  for, 96–97
Employer benefits, 74, 126
Employment options, 65
Empty nest, 209
EMT (emergency medical
  technician), 382
Ending a friendship, 193
Endorse, 309
Endosperm, 535
Endurance, muscular, 336
Energy
    and calories, 377–378
    from gas and oil, 744
    for heating and cooling, 745
    for lighting and appliances, 745
    managing your, 25–26
Energy needs
    calculating, 346
    and weight, 345
Energy-efficient appliances, 748
Enriched food, 536
Entertaining children, 264
Entertainment technology, 317
Entrée, 585
Entrepreneur, 65
Entrepreneurship, 65
Entryways, 738
Enunciate, 138
Environment. *See also* Conserving
  resources
    appreciating, 747
    defined, 9
    and development, 253

and personality, 9
and purchases, 301
for safe child care, 268–270
Environmental scientist, 570
Environmentally-friendly
cooking, 517
EPA (U.S. Environmental Protec-
tion Agency), 123
Equivalents, for ingredients,
492
Ergonomics, 88
Escalate, 163
Escape plans, 205
Essential elements, 372–375
minerals, 373, 374
phytochemicals, 373
vitamins, 372–373
water, 373–375
Estimating amounts, 493
Ethical principle, 37
Ethnic background, 10
Etiquette. *See also* Manners
for family meals, 577
restaurant, 585, 586
Evaluating your work, in
foods lab, 428
Event description essay, 249, 512
Example
being a positive, 288–289
learning by, 287
setting an, 38, 40 *See also*
Exercise, 336–339. *See also*
Physical activity
and anger, 159
and appetite, 404
and emotional changes, 8
family, 213
fitness log of, 338
and nutrition, 337
program for, 336, 337
regular, 342
and safety, 338–339
Exercise program, 336, 337
Exit plans, 736
Expectations, for success, 502
Expense, 308
Expiration date, 446
Explanation essay, 365, 552
Explanations
asking for, 445
giving simple, 287
Exploratory interviews, 73
Extended family
defined, 207
support from, 244
Extended stays, 234
External conflict, 155
Eye contact
with interviewer, 116
as nonverbal
communication, 139
in presentations, 138
Eye protection, 338

F

Fabric
choosing, 629, 662–663
marking, 669
preparing, 664–665
preshrinking, 665
straightening ends of, 664
Fabric allergies, 627
Fabric care symbols, 635
Fabric construction, 625–627
knitting, 627
nonwoven, 627
weaving, 626
Fabric finishes, 628
and color, 628
performance, 628
Fabric marker, 650
Fabric softeners, 636
Facial expressions, 139
Facing, 681–684
Factory outlets, 304
Fad diets, 391
Fad, clothing, 609
Fairness, 38, 305
Falls, preventing, 481, 735
Familial responsibility, 41
Familiarity, 116
Family, 205–219
building strengths within,
218–219
cultural background of, 208
effects of addiction on, 239
emotional support of, 205
and food choices, 401
getting along with, 214–217
importance of, 205
learning social skills and
moral values from, 205
life cycle of, 209–210
personality of, 208
physical needs of, 205
responsibility to, 189
roles and responsibilities
within, 212–213
types of, 206–207
Family, Career and Community
Leaders of America (FCCLA),
51–52
Family bonds, 209
Family challenges, 227–244
addiction, 238–241
alcoholism, 238
changes in circumstances,
227–231
changes in family structure,
232–235
cycles of abuse, 242, 243
death, 235–236
drug addiction, 239–241
emotional abuse, 242
financial problems, 228–229
health problems, 231

homelessness, 231
moving, 227, 228
natural disasters, 230
new family members, 232–234
physical abuse, 242
separation and divorce, 234–235
sources of support for, 243–244
suicide, 236
unemployment, 229–230
violence in the home, 242–243
Family exercise, 213
Family life cycle, 209–210
Family meals, 577–581, 583
etiquette for, 577
manners for, 580–581, 583
serving of, 578, 579
setting the table, 577–579
Family meetings, 213
Family members, interviewing, 10
Family recipes, 421
Family scrapbook, 10
Family service (meal service
style), 579
Family structure, 206–207
Family structure, changes in,
232–235
extended stays, 234
grandparents, 232
new family members, 232–234
new siblings, 232
separation and divorce, 234–235
stepparents, 232–233
teenage pregnancy, 234
Family support, 88, 208
Farmers' market, 563
Fashion, 599
Fast food, 746
Fasteners, clothing, 611,
639–642, 662–663
Fat and fats, 370–371, 393
avoiding added, 519
and cholesterol, 371
cooking with, 520–521
food labeling of, 449
lowering dietary, 392–393
measuring, 491
in meat, poultry, and fish, 555
reducing, 557
saturated, 370
trans fats, 371
unsaturated, 370
Fat-soluble vitamins, 371
FCCLA. *See* Family, Career and
Community Leaders of America
Feed dogs (sewing machine), 652,
653
Feedback
giving, 142
from teachers, 527
Fiber (in diet), 368, 538
Fibers, 621–629
defined, 621

and fabric construction, 625–627
and fabric finishes, 627–628
fabric selection, 629
manufactured, 622–625
natural, 622
Fig cookies, 368
Figure types, 661
Finances, 281
Financial Literacy
bike repair conflict, 160
bonus calculation, 678
child care costs, 281
cost of appliances, 475
credit card finance charges, 230
food budget, 417, 558
percent discount calculation, 39
summer business, 65
Financial problems, 228–229
Financial services, 308–311
checkbooks, 310
checking accounts, 309
debit and ATM cards, 310
reading bank statements, 310
reconciling bank
statements, 310
savings accounts, 309
Finger foods, 581
Finishes
fabric, 628
hem, 688–690
Fire
kitchen, 476
and outdoor cooking, 588
preventing, 736
responding to, 271, 740
safety, 712
Fire drills, 736
Fire emergencies, 271
Fire extinguishers, 736
First aid, 270, 739, 740
First impressions, 116
Fish. See Meat, poultry, and fish
Fit, of clothing, 612
Fitness log, 338
Fitting patterns, 667
Flame-resistant, 628
Flame-retardant, 628
Flammable items, 476, 736
Flattery, 177
Flatware, 577, 581
Flavor, of food, 416
Flax, 621
Flexibility, 97, 336
Flexible, 503
Flextime, 124
Floors, 721, 733
Flossing, 335
Flour, 491
Focal point, 720
Fold, place pattern on, 666
Folding (cooking term), 495
Folding clothing, 632

Following up
after job interviews, 119–120
on mistakes, 639
Food
cooking. See Cooking
equipment for cooking, 465
frozen, 544
functional, 405
refrigerated, 475
surplus, 442
Food additive, 407
Food allergies
and food choices, 400–401
and safety, 565
Food banks, 369
Food budget, 417, 558
Food choices, 401–408
for athletes, 405
and food allergies, 402–408
and food sensitivities, 402
for healthy eating, 391
for medical conditions, 402
for special nutritional needs,
402–405
for vegetarians, 403
Food claims, 406
Food facts, 406–408
additives, 407
carbohydrate intake and
weight, 406
dietary supplements, 408
exercise and appetite, 406
frozen vs. fresh foods, 406
irradiated foods, 407
organic foods, 407
Food intake, and weight, 346
Food labels
on grain products, 449
reading, 443–444
Food preparation and service
in the foods lab, 425–428
in home kitchen, 429
and safety, 454–455
Food processors, 474
Food product dating, 446
Food quality, 445–449
and food product dating, 446
of fruit and vegetables, 447
of grain products, 449
of legumes, 448
of meat, poultry, and
seafood, 448
of milk and milk products, 448
Food readiness, 524
Food safety and sanitation, 451–457
food preparation and service,
454–455
food storage, 454–455, 457
foodborne illness, 451
guidelines for, 393
kitchen sanitation, 452
personal cleanliness, 453
Food sensitivities, 400

Food shopping, 441–449
budgeting for, 442
and bulk buying, 442, 746
for canned goods, 447
comparison shopping, 444–445
and food product dating, 446
for fruit and vegetables, 447
for grain products, 449, 536–537
and hunger, 442
for legumes, 448
for meat, poultry, and seafood,
448, 556
for milk and milk products, 448
and quality of food, 445–449
reading labels, 443–444
shopping lists for, 441
Food storage, 454–455, 457
Foodborne illness, 451
Foods lab, 425–428
cleaning up, 428
evaluating your work in, 428
planning, 425–427
Foot control (sewing machine), 653
Forgetting mistakes, 166
Forgiving, 166, 185
Form (design element), 717
Foster family, 207
Fractions
multiplying, 503
numerator and denominator
of, 281
Fraud, 319
Freewriting, 5
Freezers, 455
Frequent-customer cards, 442
Fresh foods
frozen vs., 404, 544
preparing, 543
Freshness, checking for, 447
Friends
choosing, 183
and dating, 191
diverse, 184
and emotional changes, 8
hanging out with, 188–190
making new, 186–187, 228
older, 184
qualities of true, 185, 193
responsibility to, 189
support of, 208, 244, 624
younger, 184
Friendships, 183–194
between age groups, 184
cliques, 183
diverse, 184
end of, 192–194
peer, 183
strengthening, 187
supportive, 12
Fringe benefit, 74
Frozen foods
fresh vs., 406, 546
storing, 454, 455

Fruit parfait, 368
Fruit smoothies, 368, 422
Fruits, 542–546
    buying, 447
    and color, 542
    cooking, 544, 546
    fresh produce, 543
    nutrients in, 542
    preparing, 543–544, 546
    recommended amount of,
        395, 396
    salads, 544
    as sweet substitute, 368
    in your diet, 546–548
Frying foods, 476
Fuel conservation, 744
Fun, having
    with friends, 189
    importance of, 158, 266
    without alcohol, 348
Functional foods, 407
Functional furniture, 722
Furniture, 722
    choosing and arranging, 722
    dusting and polishing, 733
    styles of, 722
Fusible interfacing, 681
Future job market, 78–79

G

Games with rules, 258
Gangs, 178
Garbage, 734
Garbage disposal, 452
Gardening, 744
Garnish, 497
Gas appliances, 737
Gas conservation, 744
Gathers
    manipulating fabric with,
        690, 692
    sewing, 684
Gene, 253
General lighting, 723
Generic name, 624
Generic products, brand names
    vs., 444–445
Genetic makeup, and weight, 345
Geographic area, and food
    choices, 401
Germ (of seed), 535
Getting along with family, 214–217
    acting responsibly, 215
    parents, 214, 215
    showing appreciation, 215
    showing respect, 215
    siblings, 215–217
Giving back, to the community, 184
Global environment, 742
Global warming, 743
Glossary assignment, 647
Goals, 15–17

achieving your, 610
asking for help with your, 539
defined, 15
group, 16–17
importance of, 15
personal, 15–16
setting, 16–17
Goose, 558
Gossip, 147, 194
Grading (sewing term), 682
Grainline, 666
Grains and grain products, 449,
    535–540
    breads, 538–539
    buying, 449, 536–537
    cereals, 538
    nutrients in, 535–536
    pasta, 537, 538
    preparing, 537–539
    recommended amount of,
        395, 396
    refined, 536
    rice, 538
    whole, 535–536
    in your diet, 540
Grandparents, 232
Grater, 469
Grating, 495
Grazing, 415
Greasing, 497
Green Bean Salad (recipe), 402
Grief, 235
Grilling
    as dry-heat cooking, 516
    of fruits and vegetables, 544
    safety with, 478–479, 587
Grills, 474
Grocery list, 441
Grooming, 332
Gross profit, 147
Ground meat, 556, 557
Group work, 282
Guilt, appeal to your, 177

H

Hallucinogens, 351
Hand (fabric term), 629
Hand basting, 678
Hand sewing needles, 651
Hand washing (clothing), 637
Hand-eye coordination, 251
Handwheel (sewing machine), 653
Handheld mixers, 474
Hanging clothing, 633
Hanging out with friends, 188–190
    places and activities for, 188
    responsibilities when, 188–189
    and safety, 190
Harassment, 100
Harmony (design principle),
    604, 605

Hazardous objects and
    furniture, 268
Hazards
    defined, 735
    electrical, 736
    and foods, 455
Health and wellness, 331–343
    avoiding added fat, 519
    avoiding fad diets, 391
    avoiding office injuries, 124
    controlling anxiety, 28
    and depression, 342–343
    dining out, 418
    and doctors, 340
    eating breakfast, 118
    emotional, 47
    and exercise, 213, 286, 336–
        339
    fabric allergies, 634
    fiber and oats, 538
    and friendships, 193
    frozen foods, 544
    functional foods, 407
    grilling safety, 587
    healthful substitutions, 504
    healthy identity, 689
    housing issues, 721
    limiting TV viewing, 255
    and medical checkups, 339–340
    mental and emotional, 340–343
    and nutrition, 339, 567
    nutrition appeal, 471
    nutrition appeal, 471
    and personal hygiene, 332–
        335, 453
    physical, 331–340
    positive attitudes, 96
    preventing anemia, 381
    preventing dehydration, 374
    prioritizing, 67,
    and refrigerated foods, 475
    resources for, 355
    saving leftovers, 446
    self-worth, 242
    and sleep, 332
    with social interaction, 320
    soda, 428
    and stress, 140, 159, 341–342
    taking care of yourself, 231
    teeth, 335
    tasty tomatoes, 543
    and tobacco, 348
    safe weight loss, 339
    using colors, 601
    your back, 650
Health care technology, 316
Health fairs, 270
Health problems, changes in cir-
    cumstances due to, 231
Health risks, 345–354
    AIDS and HIV, 354
    alcohol use, 349
    avoiding, 356

detecting drug abuse, 352
drugs, 347–352
eating disorders, 346–347
help for drug abuse, 352
illegal drug use, 350–351
inhalant use, 350
prescription and over-the-
counter drugs, 351–352
sex-related, 353–354
sexually transmitted
diseases, 353
with technology, 320
teenage pregnancy, 354
tobacco use, 348
weight, 345–347
Health-smart, 12
Healthy eating. *See* Dietary
Guidelines
Heard, right to be, 305
Hearing impairment, 709
Heart, 336
Heating energy, 745
Heimlich maneuver, 739
Helmet, 338
Help
for alcohol abuse, 238
asking for, 341, 418
calling for help in
emergencies, 270, 737
for drug abuse, 352
finding, 227
offer to, 581
seeking, 165
from teachers, 494
with your goals, 539
Helping, with meal planning,
420–421
Helping others, 19
Hems, 688–690
clothing, 611
finishing, 688–690
marking, 688
Herbal supplements, 352
Herbs, 494
Heredity
and development, 253
and personality, 9
Heritage, exploring your, 10
HHS (U.S. Department of Health
and Human Services), 389
HIV (human immunodeficiency
virus), 354
Hobbies, 70
Home decorating, 716–723
with backgrounds, 721–722
and color, 718–719
and design, 716–721
design elements in, 717–719
and design principles, 720–721
with furniture, 722
with lighting, 723
Home kitchen, preparing food
in, 429

Home maintenance, 731–735
cleaning products and
equipment, 732
clutter, 733
daily and weekly tasks, 731
defined, 731
dust and dirt, 733
electrical hazards, 736
and emergencies, 737–740
and fire, 736
garbage, 734
occasional tasks, 731, 732
outdoors, 732
pests, 734
planning, 731–732
and poison, 737
preventing falls, 735
Home management technology, 316
Home safety. *See also* Safety
precautions for, 738
technology for, 315
Homelessness, 231
Hometown foods, 400
Homework, keeping up with, 24
Homogenize, 448
Honesty
employee, 96
in interviews, 118
in purchasing, 305
as universal value, 38
Hook and eye, 641–642
Hormone, 7
Hot anger, 160
Housing, 705–714
health issues with, 721
and location choices, 714
multiple-family, 711
owning, 712–713
renting, 712
sharing, 714
single-family, 710
types of, 710, 711
Housing decisions, 705–709
and family resources, 707
and needs, wants, and
priorities, 705–706
for special family needs,
708–709
Human immunodeficiency virus
(HIV), 354
Human resources, 13, 707
Hummus and Vegetable Dip
(recipe), 568
Humor, sense of, 123
Hunger, and shopping, 442
Hybrid, 316
Hybrid vehicles, 744
Hydrate, 338

I

Identity theft, 190, 318–321
Illegal drugs, 350–351

anabolic steroids, 351
depressants, 351
hallucinogens, 351
marijuana, 351
stimulants, 351
Illusion
defined, 599
optical, 600, 664
Images, Internet, 322
Immersible, 473
Impulse purchase, 302, 441
Income, 301
Incomplete protein, 369
Independence, 18
Individual proprietorship, 65
Individual responsibilities, 212–213
Infants
behavior management of, 262
development in, 254–255
mealtime and snacks for, 265
Infatuation, 191
Information designer, 614
Information skills, 90
Informed, right to be, 305
Ingenuity, 89
Inhalant use, 350
Initiative, 96
Injuries, avoiding office, 124
Inseam, 661
Insecurity, 157
Inspiring others, 175
Instill, 167
Instinct, 190
Insulated coolers, 588
Insulin, 400
Insults, 147
Integrity, 38
Intellectual development, 252
Intensity, color, 601
Interest (money)
calculating, 208
on savings, 309
Interests
changing, 192
personal, 12
personal inventory of, 70
and purchases, 301
Interfacing, 681–684
defined, 662
fusible, 681
sew-on, 681
Interlock knits, 627
Intermediate colors, 718
Internal conflict, 155
International flavor, 416
Internet safety, 322–323
Internships, 77
Interpersonal skills, 91
Interviewing
of family members, 10
for jobs, 115–120
Interviews
defined, 115

exploratory, 73
practice, 119
Investment advisor, 324
Invitations, 586
Ironing clothes, 635, 638
Irradiated foods, 405
Isolation, and emotional abuse, 242

J

Jealousy, 157, 192
Job, 122–123. *See also* Careers;
Work
appearance for, 122
applying for. *See* Applying
for jobs
and decision making, 123
defined, 63
and safety, 122–123
skills for. *See* Workplace skills
Job fairs, 74
Job outlook, 75
Job shadowing, 76
Job sharing, 124
Joints, 338
Journal entry, 85
Journal writing, 675
Juice, 543

K

Kitchen
child safety in, 481
fire safety, 476
size of, 465
Kitchen appliances
major, 475–479
small, 473–475
Kitchen equipment, 465–481
cleaning, 479
cookware, 470, 471
major kitchen appliances,
475–479
selecting, 465
small kitchen appliances,
473–475
utensils, 466–469
Kitchen sanitation, 452
Kitchen shears, 469
Knee control (sewing machine), 653
Knitting, 627
Knives
safety with, 494
types of, 466
washing, 452
Knowing when to leave, 180
Know-it-all attitude, 147

L

Labels, food, 443–444, 449
Ladle, 469
Landlord, 712
Landscape architect, 80

Language development, 252
Large motor skills, 251
Launching stage, of family life
cycle, 209
Laundering, 634–638
and care labels, 634, 635
dry-cleaning, 638
drying, 637
pressing and ironing, 638
safety, 637
sorting, 634, 636
washing, 634–637
Law enforcement agencies, 244
Lay out patterns, 667
Leader, 50
Leadership
opportunities for, 51–52
responsible, 50–52
skills for, 51
Leadership skills, 92, 93
Learning
by example, 287
focus on, 23
lifelong, 67
and sleep, 373
Learning disabilities, 260
Learning styles, 252
Lease, 712
Leave, knowing when to, 180
Leavening agent, 538
Leftovers
heating, 457
as meals, 417
saving, 446
serving, 418
storing, 560
Legislator, 430
Legumes, 448, 566–569
buying, 448
defined, 448, 566
nutrients in, 566–567
preparing and cooking, 566,
567, 569
recommended amount of,
395, 396
storing, 569
Lengthening garments, 691
Letters
to the editor, 619
personal, 173
Library, school, 73, 146
Lies, 147
Life coach, 30
Life cycle, family, 209–210
Lifelong learning, 67
Lifestyle
parenthood changes in, 281
personal inventory of, 71
Lighting
energy for, 745
for entryways, 738
safety, 722
types of, 723

Limits, setting, 286
Line (design element), 600,
602, 717
Lint, 631
Liquid ingredients, measuring, 491
Liquid measuring cups, 467
Listening, active, 141–142
Listening skills, 89
Litter, 735
Loaf pans, 470
Loans, 311
Long-distance relationships, 10
Lost, getting, 190
Love, mature, 192
Loyalty, 185
Lungs, 336
Lyocell, 623

M

Machine basting, 678
Machine needles, 651
Machine stitching, 679–686, 689
Machine washing (clothing), 636
Mail, separating, 735
Mail security, 318
Mail-order companies, 304
Maintenance. *See also* Home
maintenance
sewing machine, 654
vehicle, 744
Major appliances, 475–479
microwave ovens, 477–478
ranges, 476
refrigerators, 475
standard and convection ovens,
477
Management plan, 22
Management skills, 51
Manipulated fabric
casings, 692
elastic waistband, 693
gathers, 691, 692
shirring, 692
trim and piping, 694
Manipulation, 176, 177
Manners, 580–581, 583. *See
also* Etiquette
Manufactured fibers, 622–625
blends, 624
defined, 622
generic and trade names, 624
microfibers, 625
Manufactured homes, 710
Marbling, 556
Marijuana, 351
Marinade, 457
Marinated Vegetables (recipe), 380
Marking
of fabric, 669
of hems, 688
Marking equipment (for sewing),
650

Matches, 268, 736
Material resources, 13
Math Concepts
    addition with decimal
        places, 65
    credit, 230
    debt-to-income ratio, 160
    division, 14
    fractions, 281
    interest, 208
    multiplication, 417
    multiplying fractions, 503
    multi-step problems, 678
    order of operations, 147, 604
    percentage, 379
    percents, 114
    perimeter, 578
    rounding decimals, 475
    statistics, 558
    unit conversions, 265, 525
Math skills, 88
Math You Can Use
    calculating gross profit, 147
    calculating interest, 208
    calculating table size, 578
    changing recipe yield, 503
    cooking time, 525
    healthy weight range, 346
    price vs. cost, 604
    saving your money, 14
    sources of calories, 379
    take-home pay, 114
    unit conversion, 265
Mature love, 192
Maturity
    conveying, 116
    signs of, 18–19
Meal appeal, 416
Meal pattern, 415
Meal planning, 415–418, 420–423
    appeal of meals, 416
    away from home, 418, 420–422
    breakfast, 416
    budget, 417
    helping with, 420–421
    nutrition, 417
    patterns of eating, 415
    snacks, 422–423
    timesavers, 418
Mealtime
    for children, 265–266
    dining out, 585–587
    family, 577–581, 583
Measurement(s)
    converting, 490
    customary system of, 492
    fabric, 668
    pattern, 660–661
Measuring equipment (for sew-
    ing), 649
Measuring ingredients, 490–494
    abbreviations and equivalents
        for, 492, 493

dry ingredients, 490
by estimating, 493
fats, 491
liquid ingredients, 491
and units of measure, 492
Measuring spoons, 467
Measuring utensils, 467
Meat, poultry, and fish, 555–560
    buying, 448
    cooking, 558–559
    cutting fat from, 392
    daily requirements, 556
    defrosting frozen, 557
    fat and cholesterol in, 555
    nutrients in, 555
    recommended amount of,
        395–399
    shopping for, 556
    storing leftovers, 560
Meat thermometers, 588
Media, 146
Media, and food choices, 401
Mediation, 165, 166
Medical checkups, 339–340
Medical conditions, food choices
    for, 400
Meditation, 159
Mediterranean Hummus and
    Vegetable Dip (recipe), 568
Melon Bowl (recipe), 545
Mental health, 340–343
Mentor, 75
Menu
    for celebration, 586
    ordering from the, 585
Menu terms, 393
Merchandise returns, 305
Metal spatulas, 469
Metric system, 492
Microfiber, 625
Microwave cooking, 521–522
Microwave ovens, 477–478
Microwaves, 477
Milk and milk products
    buying, 448
    and dairy substitutions, 565
    nutrients in, 564-565
    preparing and cooking, 565–566
    recommended amount of,
        395, 396
    reducing fat in, 392
    storing, 566
Mincing, 495
Minerals, 373, 374
Mistakes
    following up on, 639
    forgiving and forgetting, 166
    learning from, 98
    at mealtime, 581
Mixers, 474
Mixing, 496
Mixing bowls, 468
Mixing spoons, 468

Mixing utensils, 467–468
Mobility, limited, 708
Moist-heat cooking, 518–519
Money management, 307–308
    budgeting, 308
    and paychecks, 307
Monochromatic colors, 719
Mops, 733
Moral development, 8, 252
Moral values, learning, 205
Mortgage, 713
Motivational skills, 51
Motor skills
    defined, 251
    limited, 708
Mouth guard, 338
Moving, 227–228
Muffin pans, 470
Muffins, 539
Multiplex, 711
Multiplication, 417
Multiplying fractions, 503
Multi-step math problems, 678
Muscular endurance, 336
Muscular strength, 336
MyPlate, 394–397

N

Nagging, 147
Napkins, 580
Natural disasters
    coping with, 231
    effects on families from, 230
Natural fibers, 622
Natural resources, 13, 742
Needles, 651
Needs
    children's, 285–286
    defined, 47
    housing, 705
    physical, 205
Negative peer pressure, 176–178
    from bullies, 178
    from gangs, 178
    manipulation, 176, 177
    responding to, 179–181
Neglect, 242
Negotiation, of conflict, 160–161
Networking, 109
Neutral colors, 719
New family members, 232–234
Night terror, 267
Nightmare, 267
911, 737
No, saying, 180, 349
Nonrenewable resource, 742
Nonverbal communication, 137,
    139–140
Notches, 666
Notching, 682
Note taking, 23, 24
Notions, sewing, 663

Nuclear family, 206
Numerator, 281
Nurturing, 285
Nutrient density, 379
Nutrient-dense food, 390
Nutrients, 367–375. *See also*
    Digestive process
      carbohydrates, 368
      conserving nutrients in
        cooking, 527
      defined, 367
      in eggs, 562
      essential elements, 372–375
      fats, 370-371
      in fruits and vegetables, 542
      in grains, 535–536
      in legumes, 566–567
      in meat, poultry, and fish, 555
      in milk and milk products, 564
      minerals, 373, 374
      phytochemicals, 373
      proteins, 369
      vitamins, 372–373
      water, 373–375
Nutrition. *See also* Diet
    deficiencies in, 381
    and exercise, 337
    and health, 339
    and meal planning, 417
Nutrition planning, 395
Nutrition plans, 395
Nuts, 566
Nylon, 623

O

Oatmeal, 538
Oats, 538
Obesity, 390
Objective description essay, 597
Obligation, 23
Observing behavior, 636
Obsolete, 318
Occasional tasks, 731, 732
Occupation, 63
Occupational Safety and Health
    Administration (OSHA), 122–123
Odor, 448
Oil
    conserving, 744
    for sewing machines, 654
Older friends, 184
Older infants, development in, 255
Older toddlers, development in, 255
Online career research, 73
Open mind, keeping an, 142, 161
Optical illusion, 600, 664
Order of operations (in math),
    147, 604
Ordering from the menu, 585
Organic foods, 407
Organizing
    your closet, 631

your possessions, 26–27
your schedule, 429
your thoughts, 141
OSHA. *See* Occupational Safety
    and Health Administration
OTC drugs. *See* Over-the-counter
    drugs
Outdoor cooking, 588
Outdoor maintenance, 732
Outdoor meals, 588
Outdoor safety, 269–270
Outseam, 661
Ovens, 477–478
Overcooking, 527, 546
Over-the-counter (OTC) drugs,
    351–352
Owning a home, 712–713

P

Packaging, 449, 746, 748
Packed-on date, 446
Packing clothing, 632–633
Pajamas, children's, 628
Panfrying, 520
Paper products, recycled, 744
Paperless bills, 744
Paragraph development, 135
Parallel play, 255
Paramedic, 382
Parent test, 280
Parental resources, 285
Parenting, 279–290
    behavior management, 286–289
    career changes, 281
    decision to have children,
      279–280
    defined, 279
    family-life-cycle stage of, 209
    financial changes, 281
    lifestyle changes, 281
    responsibilities with, 285–286
    sources of help, 289–290
    teen parenthood, 282–283
Parenting education, 285
Paring, 495
Paring knife, 466
Partnership, 65
Passing food, 580
Passive response, 179
Passwords, 319, 322
Pasta, cooking, 537, 538
Pasta Salad, Asian (recipe), 480
Pasta survey, 537
Pasteurize, 448
Pastry blenders, 468
Paths, 732
Pattern (design element), 602
Pattern envelope, 660
Pattern size, 661
Patterns
    choosing, 660–661
    clothing, 610

cutting out, 668–669
fitting, 667
information on envelope,
    660
laying out, 667
and marking fabric, 669
measuring for, 660–661
positioning pieces of, 668
reading, 666
Pay, take-home, 114, 208
Paychecks, 307
Paying the restaurant bill, 587
Peelers, 469
Peer friendships, 183
Peer mediator, 166
Peer pressure, 175–181
    defined, 175
    on Internet, 323
    negative, 176–178
    positive, 175–176
    and purchases, 301
    responding to negative, 179–181
    of role models, 175, 176
Peer relationships, 175–194. *See
    also* Friendships
Peers, 175
Pent-up anger, 159
Percent discount, 39
Percentages, 114, 379
Performance finishes, 627–628
Performance tests, 109
Perimeter, 578
Perishable, 557
Perishable foods, 455
Personal cleanliness, 453
Personal hygiene, 332–335
    skin, 332–334
    teeth, 335
Personal information, 319, 322
Personal inventory, 70–71
    of interests, 70
    of lifestyle, 71
    of skills, 71
Personal letters, 173
Personal narrative, 574
Personal responsibility, 40–41, 189
Personal time, finding, 124
Personality
    conflict and differences in, 156
    defined, 9
    of family, 208
    your, 9
Personalizing a garment, 690
Persuasive essay, 729
Persuasive paragraph, 225, 533
Pests, 734
Phones, 709. *See also* Cell phones
Physical abuse, 242
Physical activity. *See also* Exercise
    healthy eating, 390
    and weight, 346
Physical development, 251
Physical disabilities, 260

Physical distance, 140
Physical health, 331–340
    exercise, 336–339
    medical checkups, 339–340
    nutrition, 339
    personal hygiene, 332–335
    physical, 331–340
    sleep, 332
Physical needs, 205, 705
Phytochemicals, 373
Picnics, 588
Picture something calming, 160
Pie pans, 470
Pile weave, 626
Pills, removing fabric, 631
Pilot, 670
Pincushion, 651
Pins, 651
Piping, 694
PLA fiber, 623
Place setting, 577
Placemats, 481
Placement line, 666
Plain weave, 626
Planning
    for celebrations, 586–587
    for foods lab work, 425–427
    for shopping, 302–304
Plant safety, 268
Plaque, 335
Plastic scrapers, 468
Plate service, 579
Play
    cooperative, 256
    importance of, 258
Play areas, 269
Poaching, 518, 519
Poem, 203
Poison control center, 268
Poisoning, preventing, 453
Poisons, 737
Polishing, 733
Polyester, 622
Polyolefin, 623
Poor-me attitude, 147
Porches, 732
Portfolios, 114
Portions, meal, 420
Positive attitude, 96, 119, 331
Positive communication, 137
Positive example, being a, 288–289
Positive influence, being a, 262
Positive self-talk, 11
Possessions
    organizing your, 26–27
    and theft, 190
Posture, 139
Potassium, 391
Potato-Tomato Soup in a Bread
    Bowl (recipe), 588
Potential, your, 11–14
    defined, 11

discovering, 11
    reaching, 12–13
    resources for achieving, 13, 14
Potholders, 476
Poultry. See Meat, poultry, and fish
Power issues, 157
Power plant dispatcher, 482
Praise, giving, 286
Preaching, 147
Precycle, 746
Pregnancy, teenage, 234
Prejudice, 148
Preschoolers
    behavior management of, 263
    development in, 256
    mealtime and snacks for, 266
Prescription drugs, 351–352
Presentations
    with first impressions, 116
    making effective, 138
    preparation, 743
Preshrinking, of fabric, 665
Presser foot (sewing machine), 653
Presser foot lifter (sewing
    machine), 653
Pressing clothes, 638
Pressing equipment, 651
Pretend play, 258
Pretreating clothing, 634, 636, 637
Price, cost vs., 604
Price tag, 612
Primary colors, 718
Principle of design, 604. See also
    Design principles
Printing, avoiding unnecessary, 744
Prioritizing activities, 343
Priority, 12
Privacy issues, 318–319
Private sector businesses, 65
Problem, defining the, 164
Problem solving
    defined, 91
    with a stepparent, 207
    at work, 100
Problem-solving skills, 51
Produce (food)
    appealing, 543
    buying, 447
    defined, 447
    washing, 453, 454
Product information, 306
Professionalism, 97, 112, 116
Proportion (design principle), 604,
    605, 720
Protein, 369
Protein foods, 555–569
    eggs, 562–563
    legumes and nuts, 566–569
    meat, poultry, and fish, 555–560
    milk and milk products,
        564–566
    vegetarian, 567

Puberty, 7, 259
Purchase, impulse, 302
Purpose, of message, 487

Q

Qualities, of true friends, 185, 193
Quality
    of clothing, 610–612
    of cooking equipment, 465
Quality of food. See Food quality
Question-and-answer essay, 439

R

Racks, cooling, 469
Radiation, 515
Ramie, 621
Ranges, 476
Rapport, 146
Raw foods, 588
Rayon, 623
Reaching out, 40
Reading aloud, 287
Reading assignments, 581
Reading bank statements, 310
Reading food labels, 443–444
Reading patterns, 666
Reading skills, 88
Realistic, being, 343
Recipe alteration, 500–504
    creative and healthy changes,
        503–504
    number of servings, 500–501
    substituting ingredients,
        502–503
Recipe terms, 495–497
    baste, 497
    beat, 496
    blend, mix, or combine, 496
    brush, 497
    chop, 495
    coat, 497
    cream, 496
    cube, 495
    cut in, 495
    cutting, 494
    dice, 495
    drain, 497
    fold, 496
    garnish, 497
    grate and shred, 495
    grease, 497
    mince, 495
    mixing, 494–496
    pare, 495
    season, 497
    stir, 496
    whip, 496
Recipes, 489–504
    Asian Pasta Salad, 480
    Banana Cream Trifle, 456
    changing yield of, 503

INDEX

Chicken Salad Extraordinaire, 419
Crunchy Melon Bowl, 545
defined, 489
Green Bean Salad, 404
knife safety, 494–495
Marinated Vegetables, 380
measuring ingredients for, 490–494
Mediterranean Hummus and Vegetable Dip, 568
Potato-Tomato Soup in a Bread Bowl, 588
Salsa, 500–501
selecting, 489–490
Tuna Melt Stuffed Tomatoes, 526
Recommended daily amounts, of foods, 395, 396
Reconciling bank statements, 310
Recycle, 735, 747, 748
Recycled paper products, 744
Recycled treasures, 304
Redirecting your energy, 160
Redress, 305
Reference books, 73
References, job, 113
Refined grains, 536
Refrigerators, 475
Refusal skills, developing, 180–181
Rejection
    and emotional abuse, 242
    handling, 193–194
Religious beliefs, 401
Renewable resource, 742
Renting, 712
Repairing clothing, 631, 638–642
    buttons, 639–640
    hook and eye, 641–642
    rips and tears, 639
    snaps, 641
Repetitive stress injury, 320
Research
    about company, 117
    your ethnic background and culture, 10
Resource, 13
Respect, 39
    avoiding conflict with, 158
    defined, 144
    showing, 147, 191
    in workplace, 123
Respectful, 185
Respectful communication, 144–147
    building rapport, 146
    kindness and openness, 144
    showing interest in others, 144
Respecting others' values, 40
Responsibilities, 45–52
    to community, 189
    of consumers, 305–306
    in decision making, 45–49
    family, 212–213

to family, 189
to friends, 189
individual, 212–213
in leadership, 50–52
of parenting, 285–286
personal, 40–41, 189
Responsibility
    defined, 39
    demonstrating, 188
    employee, 97
    for role in conflict, 164
Responsible action, 215
Restaurant behavior, 586
Restaurant etiquette, 585
Résumés, 110–112
    contents of, 112
    defined, 110
    preparing, 110
    sample, 111
Retail buyer, 102
Retirement stage, of family life cycle, 210
Returning merchandise, 305
Reuse, 735, 746, 748
Reverse stitch control, 653
Reverse stitching, 655
Revising, 141
Rewriting, 141
Rhythm (design principle), 604, 606, 721
Rib knits, 627
Rice, 537, 538
Rights of consumers, 304–305
Rips and tears, 639
Rituals, 208
Road rage, 156
Roasting
    defined, 516
    of fruits and vegetables, 544
Role models
    defined, 37
    peer pressure from, 175, 176
Roles, family, 212–213
Roommates, 713
Root vegetables, 447
Rope ladders, 736
Rotary beaters, 468
Rounding decimals, 475
Rubber scrapers, 468
Rules of sport, 338
Rumors, 194
Running away, dangers of, 243, 319
Rusted cans, 447

S

Safe foods, purchasing, 449
Safety
    and adjusting to change, 8
    at ATMs, 317
    with cell phones, 144
    and children in the kitchen, 481
    and children's pajamas, 628
    cooking, 521

electrical, 736
and escape planning, 205
and exercise, 338–339
fire, 476, 736
and food allergies, 564, 565
with food preparation and service, 454–455
grilling, 478–479, 587
at home, 268–269, 738
and home maintenance, 735–737
on Internet, 322–323
job, 122, 123
kitchen fire safety, 476
laundry, 637
and lighting, 722
with microwave cooking, 477–478
outdoor, 269–270
outdoor cooking, 588
plant, 268
in play areas, 269
and preventing falls, 735
and preventing road rage, 156
promoting school, 241
in purchasing food, 449
with range cooking, 476
right to, 305
science of fire safety, 712
serger, 657
and shaken baby syndrome, 289
shopping, 302
with small appliances, 473, 475
and street smarts, 190
and technology, 315, 316
toy, 269
water, 733
with weight loss, 351
workout, 339
Safety guidelines, 473
Salad recipes
    Asian Pasta Salad, 480
    Chicken Salad Extraordinaire, 419
    Green Bean Salad, 402
Salads, 544
Sales credit, 311
Salmonella, 451, 563
Salsa (recipe), 500–501
Sanitation, kitchen, 452
Sanitize, 451
Sarcasm, 147
Satin weave, 626
Saturated fats, 370
Saucepans, 470
Saving money, 14
Savings accounts, 309
Saying no, 180, 349
Scalds, 521
Scale (design principle), 720
Scams, 319
Schedule

organizing your, 429
    updating your daily, 566
School library, 73
School safety, promoting, 241
School uniforms, 609
School-age children
    behavior management of, 263
    development in, 257
School-work connection, 66–68
Science skills, 88–89
Science You Can Use
    allergies, 403
    brand names vs. generic, 444
    clothing optical illusions, 664
    designing communications
        technology, 315
    emotions, 192
    fire safety, 712
    inventing new vaccines, 286
    textiles, 622
    water safety, 733
    workplace ergonomics, 88
    yeast effects, 538
Scissors, 649
Scorch, 565
Scrapbook, family, 10
Scrapers, 468
Seafood, 448
Seam finishes, 679–681
Seam gauge, 649
Seam ripper, 649
Seamline, 666
Seams
    clothing, 611
    serging, 682–683
    sewing, 679, 680
Seasonal clothing, 633
Seasonal produce, 447
Seasonal specials, 442
Seasoning, 497
Secondary colors, 718
Secondhand smoke, 348
Sedentary, 390
Self-concept, 10–11
Self-discipline, 39
Self-esteem, 10
Self-image, 347
Self-respect, 144
Self-talk
    anger management with, 160
    positive, 11
Self-understanding, 7–19
    appreciating who you are,
        9–11
    changes during adolescence,
        7–8
    discovering your potential,
        11–14
    exploring your heritage, 10
    goals, 15–17
    maturing process, 18–19
    moral development, 8
Self-worth, 241

Sell-by date, 446
Selvage, 664
Sense of humor, 123
Sensorimotor play, 258
Separation, 234–235
Serged finish, 681
Sergers, 657–658
    safety with, 657
    sewing machines vs., 657, 658
Serging seams, 682–683
Serrated, 466
Service, right to, 305
Serving meals, 578, 579
Servings, altering number of,
    500–501
Setting an example, 40, 286
Setting limits, 286
Setting the table, 578–579
Sewing aids, 651
Sewing equipment, 649–658
    for marking, 650
    for measuring and cutting,
        649
    miscellaneous aids, 651
    for pressing, 651
    serging machines, 657–658
    sewing machines, 652–656
Sewing gauge, 649
Sewing machines, 653–658
    adjusting stitch length and
        tension, 656
    caring for your, 654
    parts of machine, 653
    sergers vs., 657
    stitching with, 655
    threading, 654
Sewing preparation, 660–669
    fabric preparation, 663–664
    fabric selection, 661, 662
    notions selection, 662–665
    pattern selection, 660–662
    pattern usage, 666–669
Sewing techniques, 678–694
    alterations, 690, 691
    basting, 678
    buttons, 639–640
    casings, 692–693
    directional stitching, 685
    elastic waistbands, 693–694
    facing and interfacing, 681–684
    gathers, 684, 690, 692
    hems, 688–690
    hook and eyes, 641–642
    personalizing a garment, 690
    seam finishes, 679–681
    seams, 679, 680
    serging seams, 682–683
    snaps, 641
    staystitching, 686
    trim and piping, 694
Sew-on interfacing, 681
Sex-related risks, 353–354
    AIDS and HIV, 354

early pregnancy, 354
    sexually transmitted
        diseases, 353
Sexually transmitted infections
    (STIs), 353
Shaken baby syndrome, 288
Shape
    and design, 600, 603
    food, 416, 543
Sharing
    home, 714
Shears
    fabric, 649
    kitchen, 469
Shellfish, 559
Shock, 270
Shopping
    for clothing, 610–613
    for food. See Food shopping
    and returning merchandise, 305
    technology for, 317
Shopping bags, 746, 748
Shopping lists, 441
Shopping safety, 302
Shortening garments, 691
Shredding, 495
Shrinkage control, 628
Sibling rivalry, 214, 217
Siblings
    defined, 213
    getting along with, 218
    new, 232
Sifter, 468
Sifting, 491
Silhouette, 600
Silk, 622
Simmering, 518, 519
Single knits, 627
Single-parent family, 206
Situations, conflict in specific, 156
Skillet, 470, 474
Skills
    defined, 71
    personal inventory of, 71
Skills résumé, 110
Skin, 332–334
    acne, 333
    protecting your, 334–335
Skins, food, 527, 544
Sleep
    and health, 342
    importance of, 125
    improving your, 332
    and learning, 373
Sleep safety, 628
Sliding glass doors, 738
Slipstitching, 689
Slotted spoons, 469
Slow cookers, 474
Small appliances, 473–475
    safe use of, 473, 475
Small motor skills, 251
Smoke detectors, 736

INDEX

Smoke, secondhand, 348
Smoothies, fruit, 422
Snacks
    for children, 265–266
    choosing nutritious, 392
    healthy, 422–423
Snaps, 641
Social development, 252
Social interaction, 320
Social media, 25, 42, 47, 109, 112, 114, 125, 128, 165, 167, 194, 442, 750
Social needs, 705
Social skills, 205
Society
    defined, 205
    effects of addiction on, 239
    effects of drug addiction on, 239
    influence of, 47
Soda, 428
Sodium, 391, 449
Soil-release, 628
Sole proprietorship, 65
Solutions, suggesting, 164
Sorting clothes, 634, 636
Soup in a Bread Bowl, Potato-Tomato (recipe), 588
Space
    in clothing design, 600
    in home decorating, 717
Spandex, 623
Spatulas, 469
Speaking skills, 89
Speaking up, 40
Special family housing needs, 708–709
Special needs, children with, 259–260
Special nutritional needs, food choices for, 400–403
Specialty stores, 304
Speeches, 743
Spices, 393, 494
Split-complementary colors, 719
Sponges, 452
Spool pin, 653
Spoons
    measuring, 467
    mixing, 468
    slotted, 469
Sports, playing, 390
Stain-repellent, 628
Stains, treating, 631
Stairways, 268
Stand mixers, 474
Standard ovens, 477
Standing up for yourself, 179
Staples, 441
Statistics, 558
Staystitching, 685–686
Steamers, 638
Steaming, 518, 519

Step-by-step guide (writing activity), 413
Stepparents, 207, 232–233
Stereotypes, 148
Stewing, 518, 519
Stimulants, 351
Stir-frying, 520
Stirring, 496
STIs (sexually transmitted infections), 353
Stitch length, 656
Stitch length control, 653
Stitch pattern control, 653
Stitch width control, 653
Stitching
    directional, 685
    hems, 688–690
    staystitching, 685–686
    types of, 683
Stitching line, 666
Stockpots, 470
Storage
    cleaning, 455
    clothing, 632–633
Store brands, 445
Storing
    eggs, 563
    leftovers, 560
    legumes, 569
    milk and milk products, 566
Storing food, 454–455, 457
Straight pins, 651
Straightening ends, of fabric, 664
Strainers, 469
Strangers, 190, 738
Strength(s)
    building, 337
    fabric, 629
    focusing on your, 11
    limited, 709
    muscular, 336
Stress
    coping with, 341–342
    defined, 27, 124, 341
    and health, 341
    and tobacco, 348
    working off, 159
Stress management, 27–29
Stretching, 337
Study buddy list, 139
Studying
    every day, 547
    location for, 733
    management plan for, 22
    time for, 465
Stuffed Tomatoes (recipe), 526
Stuffing, poultry, 559
Substitute resources, 14
Substituting ingredients, 502–503
Substitutions, healthful, 504
Succeed in School
    achieving your goals, 610
    after-school programs, 112

asking for explanations, 445
asking for help, 341, 418, 539
asking questions, 604
asking your teacher, 494
attendance, 179
avoiding comparisons, 11
avoiding distractions, 455
communities for success, 74
create a study buddy list, 139
defining success, 24
family support, 88, 208
following up on mistakes, 639
getting ahead, 547
getting enough sleep, 125
giving full attention, 370
group work, 282
having fun, 158, 266
learning styles, 252
making mistakes, 98
media center tour, 146
online research, 585
organizing your schedule, 429
preparing a speech, 167
presentation preparation, 743
reading assignments, 581
school library, 73
sibling rivalry, 214
study location, 733
study time, 467
support of friends, 208, 624
taking a break, 190, 354
three-ring binders, 477
time for tasks, 560
understanding criticism, 516
updating your daily schedule, 566
your expectations, 502
your teacher, 527
Success
    defining, 24
    expectations for, 502
Sugar, 391, 449, 491
Suicide
    as family challenge, 236
    preventing, 343
Summary, writing a, 61
Sun exposure, 334
Sunscreen, 335
Supermarket specials, 442
Supervision, of children, 268–269, 481
Supplements
    dietary, 408
    herbal, 352
Support
    from family, 205
    from friends, 624
    seek, 11
    sources of, 243–244
Support groups, 244
Surplus food, 442
Sweeping, 733
Sweet tooth, 368

Swollen cans, 447
Symbolic play, 258
Symmetrical balance, 720

T

Table
    clearing the, 583
    setting the, 577–579
    size of dining room, 578
Table coverings, 578
Table settings, 577–579
Tablets, 314, 441, 577, 586
Tableware, 577
Tact, 146
Tailor's chalk, 650
Take-home pay, 114, 208
Taking measurements, 661
Talents, 71
Talking it out, 159, 343
Tantrums, temper, 256–257
Tape measure, 649
Task lighting, 723
Tasks
    estimating time for, 560
    home maintenance, 731, 732
Teacher
    asking for help from your, 494
    asking questions of your, 604
    communicating with your, 74
    early childhood, 272
    feedback from your, 527
Teamwork
    defined, 91
    in food lab, 425
    skills needed for, 91–93
    successful, 282
Technology, 314–323
    banking and shopping, 317
    benefits of, 314
    communication, 315
    defined, 314
    drawbacks of, 317–320
    education, 317
    entertainment, 317
    flaws in new, 320
    and food choices, 399
    and free time, 317
    future, 315
    health care, 316
    health risks with, 320
    home and community
        safety, 315
    home management, 316
    identity theft with, 318–320
    and Internet safety, 322–323
    managing, 25, 48, 125,
        320–323, 721
    privacy issues with, 109, 318–
        319, 321
    rapid change of, 318
    and safety, 316
    scams with, 319

transportation, 316
Technology skills, 90, 314
Teen parenthood, 282–283
Teenage pregnancy, 234, 354
Teeth, 335, 581
Telecommuting, 125
Teleconferencing, video, 315
Telemarketing, 318
Telephones, 709
Teletypewriter (TTY), 709
Temper tantrums, 256–257
Temperature
    checking food's internal, 559
    and food doneness, 525
    of meal, 416
Tension, sewing machine, 656
Tension control (sewing
    machine), 653
Text messages, 125, 167, 577
Textile science, 627
Textural cues, 709
Texture
    in clothing design, 600, 602
    fabric, 629
    and food doneness, 524
    in home decorating, 717
    meal, 416
Thawing food, 455
Theft, identity, 190, 318–320
Thermometers
    for checking food doneness,
        524–525
    as kitchen utensils, 469
    and picnic food, 588
Thimble, 651
Thinking skills, 91
Thread, 662
Thread guides, 653
Thread take-up lever, 653
Threading your sewing
    machine, 654
Threats
    and emotional abuse, 242
    as negative
        communication, 147
    as negative peer pressure, 177
Three-ring binders, 477
Throat plate (sewing machine), 653
Tied threads, 655
Time management, 23–25
    for family, friends, and
        activities, 24–25
    for learning, 23, 24
Timesavers, for meal planning, 418
Toaster ovens, 474
Toasters, 474
Tobacco use, 348
Toddlers
    behavior management of, 263
    development in, 255
    mealtime and snacks for, 266
Tolerance, 158
Tomatoes

health benefits of eating, 544
    in salsa, 500–501
    tuna melt stuffed, 526
Tone of voice, 140
Tongs, 469
Toothbrush, 335
Topic sentence, 107
Townhouse, 711
Toys
    putting away, 732
    safety with, 269
Tracing wheel, 650
Trade name, 624
Tradition, 208
Traffic pattern, 722
Trans fats, 371
Transferable skills, 87
Transportation technology, 316
Trees, 743–744
Triacetate, 623
Triadic colors, 719
Tricot knits, 627
Trifle, Banana Cream (recipe), 456
Trim
    clothing, 611
    selecting, 663
    sewing on, 694
Trusted adults, 244
Trustworthiness, 39
TTY (teletypewriter), 709
Tumble dry, 635
Tuna Melt Stuffed Tomatoes
    (recipe), 526
Turkey, 558
Turners, 469
TV viewing, limiting, 125,
    255, 577
Twill weave, 626

U

Understitching, 684
Unemployment, 229–230
Uniforms, school, 609
Unit conversion, 265
Unit conversions, 525
Unit price, 445
Units of measure, 492
Unity (design principle), 720
Universal values, 38
Unsaturated fats, 370
U.S. Department of Agriculture
    (USDA), 389
U.S. Department of Health and
    Human Services (HHS), 389
U.S. Environmental Protection
    Agency (EPA), 123
USDA (U.S. Department of Agri-
    culture), 389
Usernames, 322
Utensils, kitchen, 466–469
    for cutting and chopping, 466
    defined, 466

INDEX

for measuring and mixing, 467–468
miscellaneous, 469
washing, 452
Utilities
bills for, 318
defined, 707
paying for, 710
Utility knife, 466
UV index, 334

V

Vaccines
defined, 285
inventing new, 286
Vacuum cleaners, 733
Vacuuming, 733
Value, color, 601
Values
and character, 37–39
and culture, 208
defined, 37
learned, 38
and purchases, 301
shared, 38–39
Vegan, 401
Vegetable Dip (recipe), 568
Vegetable peeler, 469
Vegetables
buying, 447
and color, 542
cooking, 544, 546
fresh produce, 543
marinated, 380
nutrients in, 542
preparing, 543–544, 546
recommended amount of, 395, 396
salads, 544
in your diet, 546–548
Vegetarian protein, 567
Vegetarians, 401
Vehicle maintenance, 744
Vending machine selections, 423
Venison, 558
Verbal communication, 137–138
Veterinarian, 724
Video teleconferencing, 315
Video games, 48, 125
Viewpoint essay, 463
Violence in the home, 242–243
cycles of abuse, 242–243
emotional abuse, 242
physical abuse, 242
solutions to, 243
Viruses, computer, 319
Visual impairment, 709
Vitamin supplements, 371
Vitamins, 372–373
fat-soluble, 371
water-soluble, 371, 372
Voice, tone of, 140
Volunteering
and emotional changes, 8
opportunities for, 42–43

W

Waistbands, 693–694
Walking, 744
Walls, 721, 732
Wants, 47
Wardrobe assessment, 609
Warehouse clubs, 304
Warm colors, 601, 603
Warmup, exercise, 338
Warranty, 306
Washing clothing, 634–637
by hand, 637
by machine, 636
pretreating, 634, 636
Washing dishes, 731
Water
conserving, 743
as essential nutrient, 373–375
and pollution, 733
and tooth health, 335
and vegetable cooking, 544
Waterproof, 628
Water-repellent, 628
Water-soluble vitamins, 371, 372
Weaknesses, address, 11
Weaving, 626
Weekly tasks, 731
Weight, body, 345–347
and carbohydrate intake, 404
and eating disorders, 346–347
factors affecting, 345–346
maintaining a healthy, 378–379
Weight (fabric term), 629
Weight loss, 351
Weight management, 390
Well-balanced diet, 367
Wellness, 331. See also Health and wellness
Whipping, 496
Whisk, 468
Whole grains, 535–536
Whole-grain products, 449
Width of garment, adjusting, 691
Willingness to work hard, 19
Wilt, 544
Wilted produce, 447
Windows
and child safety, 268
decorating, 721
locking, 738
washing, 732
Win-win solution, 161
Wire whisks, 468
Wireless connections, 319
Wool, 621
Work, 63–68. See also Job
balancing personal life with, 124–126
positive employee characteristics for, 96–97
preparing for, 122
reasons for working, 63–64
school-work connection, 66–68
skills for. See Workplace skills
world of, 64–66
Work ethic, 92, 97
Work simplification, 26
Working conditions, 75
Working wardrobe, 609–613
assessing your, 609
shopping for your, 610–613
Working with people
inclusive environment for, 40
from other cultures, 99
Workouts, safe, 339
Workplace
avoiding injuries in the, 124
dangers in the, 123
ergonomics in the, 88
harmony in the, 123
Workplace issues, 97–100
conflict, 98–99
criticism, 98
discrimination, 99
harassment, 100
Workplace skills, 87–94
academic skills, 33
communication, 94
information, 90
interpersonal, 91
and job changes, 101
leadership, 92
listening, 89
math, 88
reading, 88
science, 88–89
speaking, 89
teamwork, 91–93
technology, 90
thinking, 91
transferable, 87
writing, 88
Wrinkling, 610, 633
Writing effectively, 140–141
Writing skills, 88

Y

Yardstick, 649
Yeast, 538
Yield
changing recipe, 503
defined, 500
Yogurt, 368, 564, 567
Young infants, development in, 254
Young toddlers, development in, 255
Younger friends, 184

Z

Zigzag finish, 681
Zippers, 662–663